NADIA LIM

Vegful

PHOTOGRAPHY BY
VANESSA & MICHAEL LEWIS

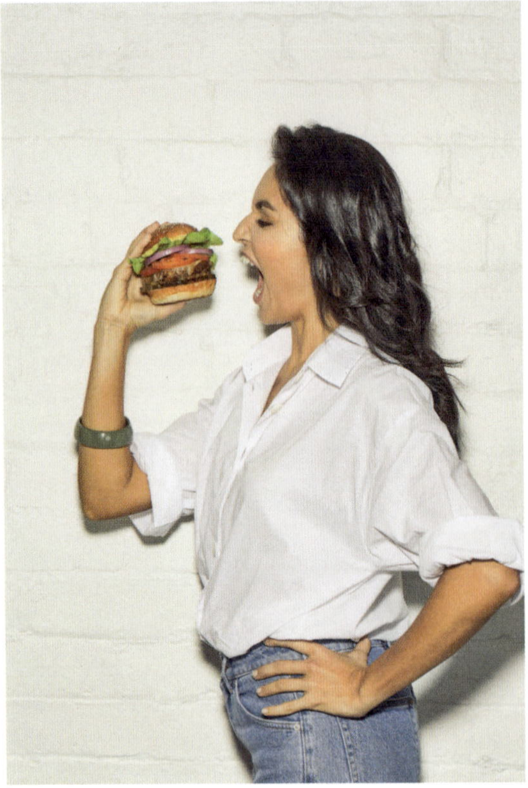
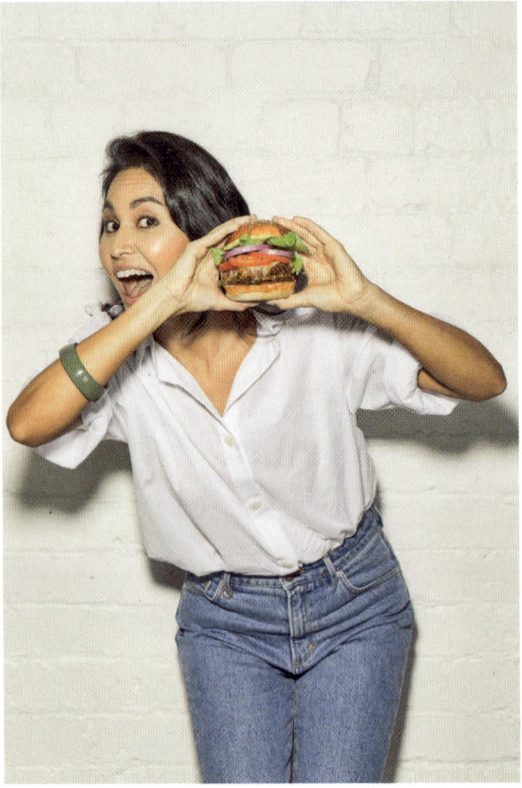
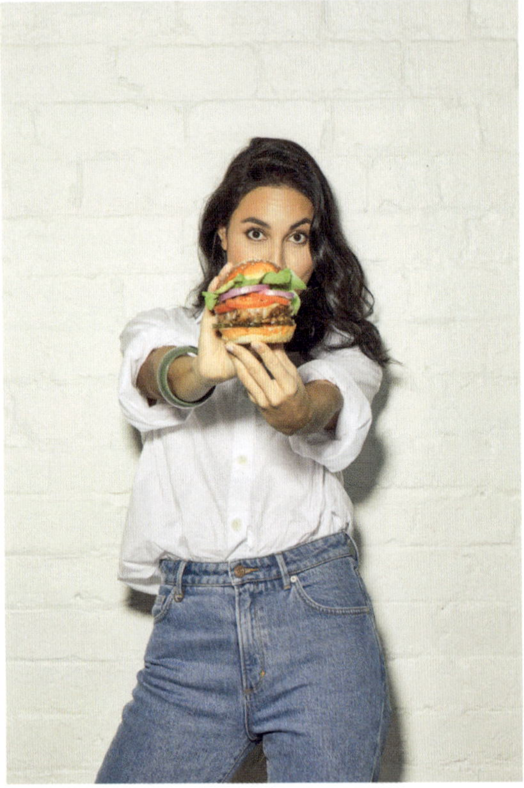
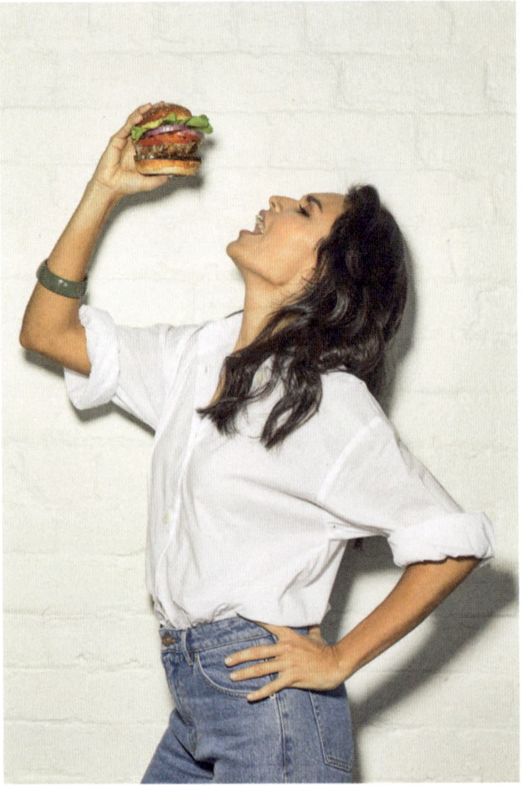

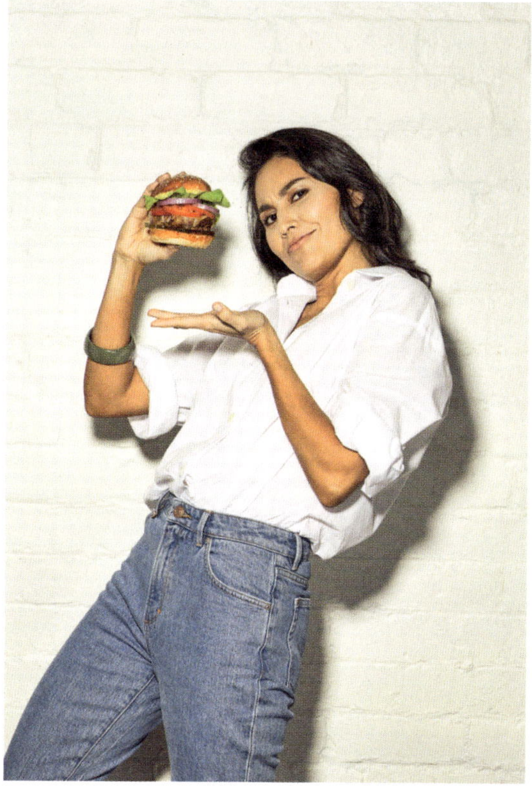
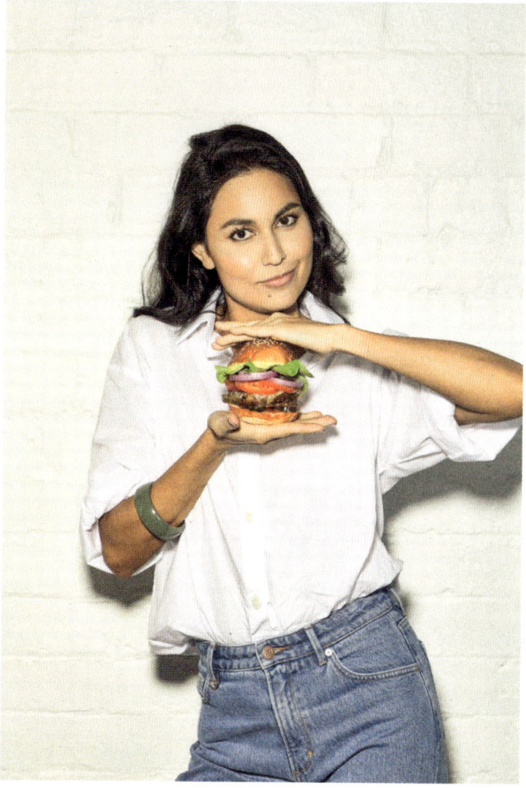
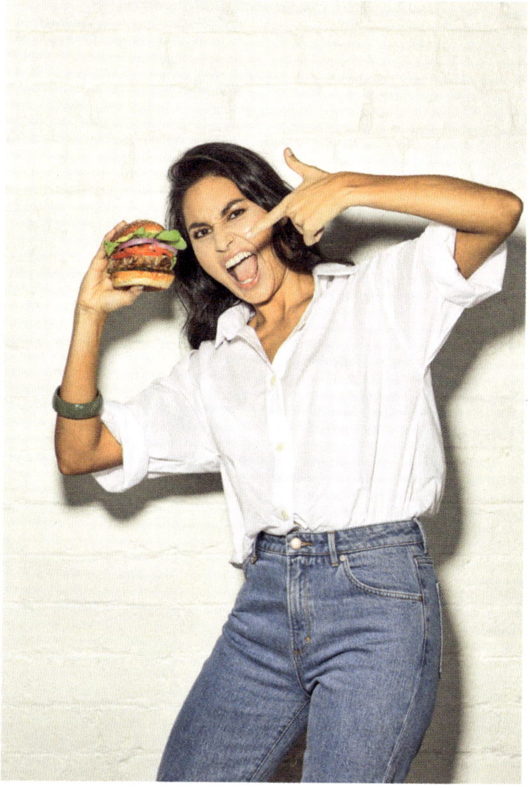
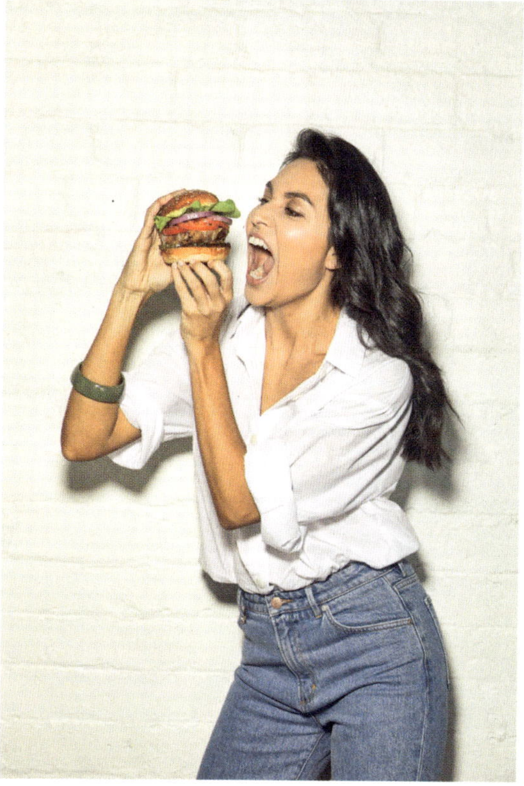

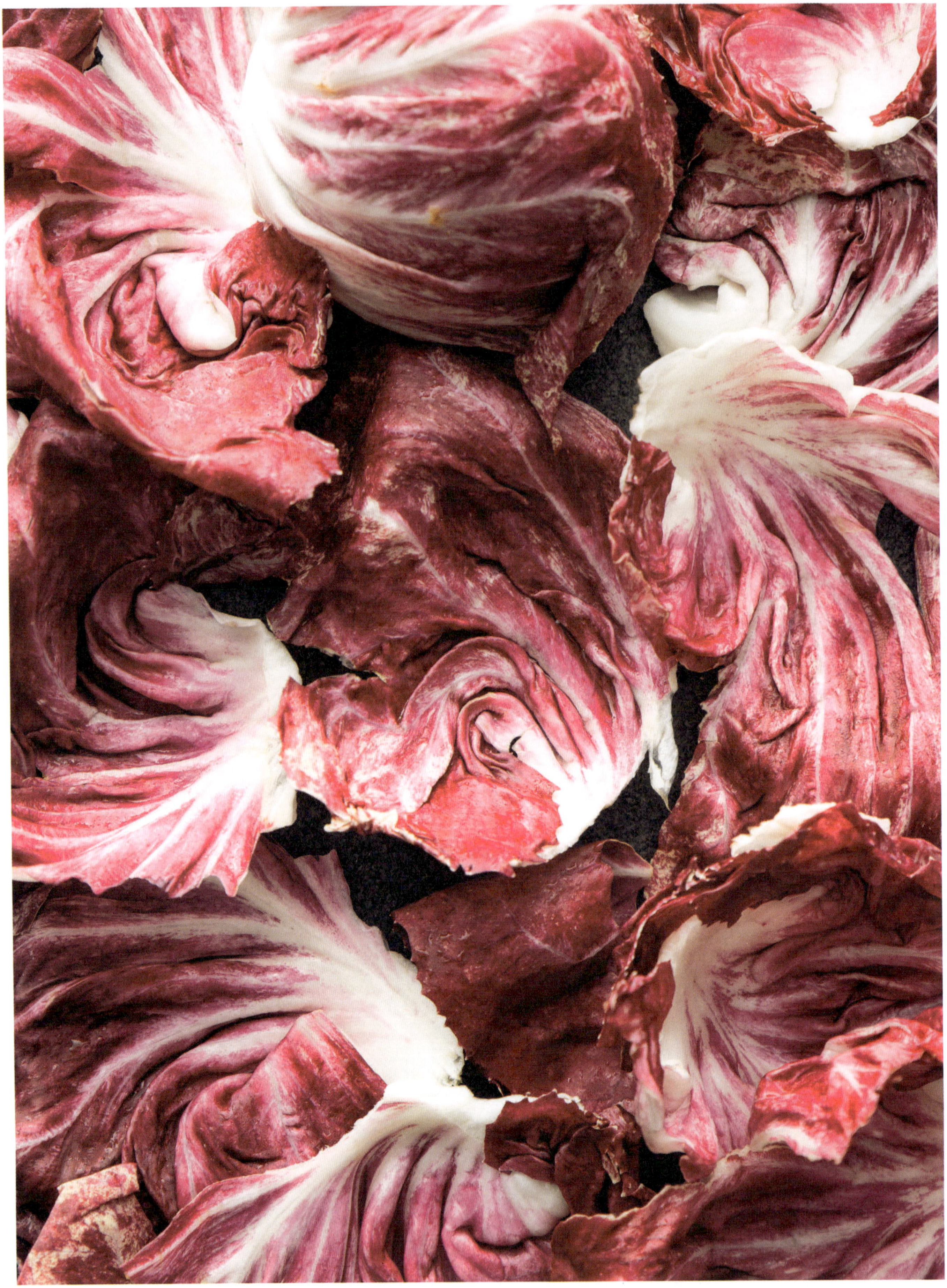

P. 06
INTRODUCTION

P. 15
A SEASONAL GUIDE

•

CHAPTER ONE — P. 33
FEASTS & SHARING

CHAPTER TWO — P. 79
HEARTY SALADS & SOUPS

CHAPTER THREE — P. 111
LUNCH & DINNER

CHAPTER FOUR — P. 161
QUICK, EASY & LEFTOVERS

CHAPTER FIVE — P. 197
SPICY & EXOTIC

CHAPTER SIX — P. 221
SMALL SALADS & SIDES

CHAPTER SEVEN — P. 257
SWEET & BAKING

•

P. 324
THANK YOU

P. 327
NUTRITION INFORMATION

P. 332
INDEX

INTRODUCTION

I'm stoked that you have picked up this book. Perhaps, like so many others, you are curious to explore a more plant-based way of eating, or perhaps you've already discovered the incredibly satisfying and delicious world of vegetable-centric eating and simply want more to add to your repertoire.

Is this a vegetarian cookbook? Well, yes, in the sense that it only contains vegetarian and vegan recipes, and not a scrap of meat or fish. So it's perfect for vegetarians and vegans who don't mind making some small adaptations. But this book is just as much for omnivores and carnivores too. I'm not vegetarian myself (if I had to call myself anything, I'd say I'm a selective omnivore) but, rather, just a huge fan of vegetables. So I would more accurately describe this as a vegetable cookbook. Or, a very 'vegful' cookbook! One to celebrate beautiful, colourful, bountiful vegetables.

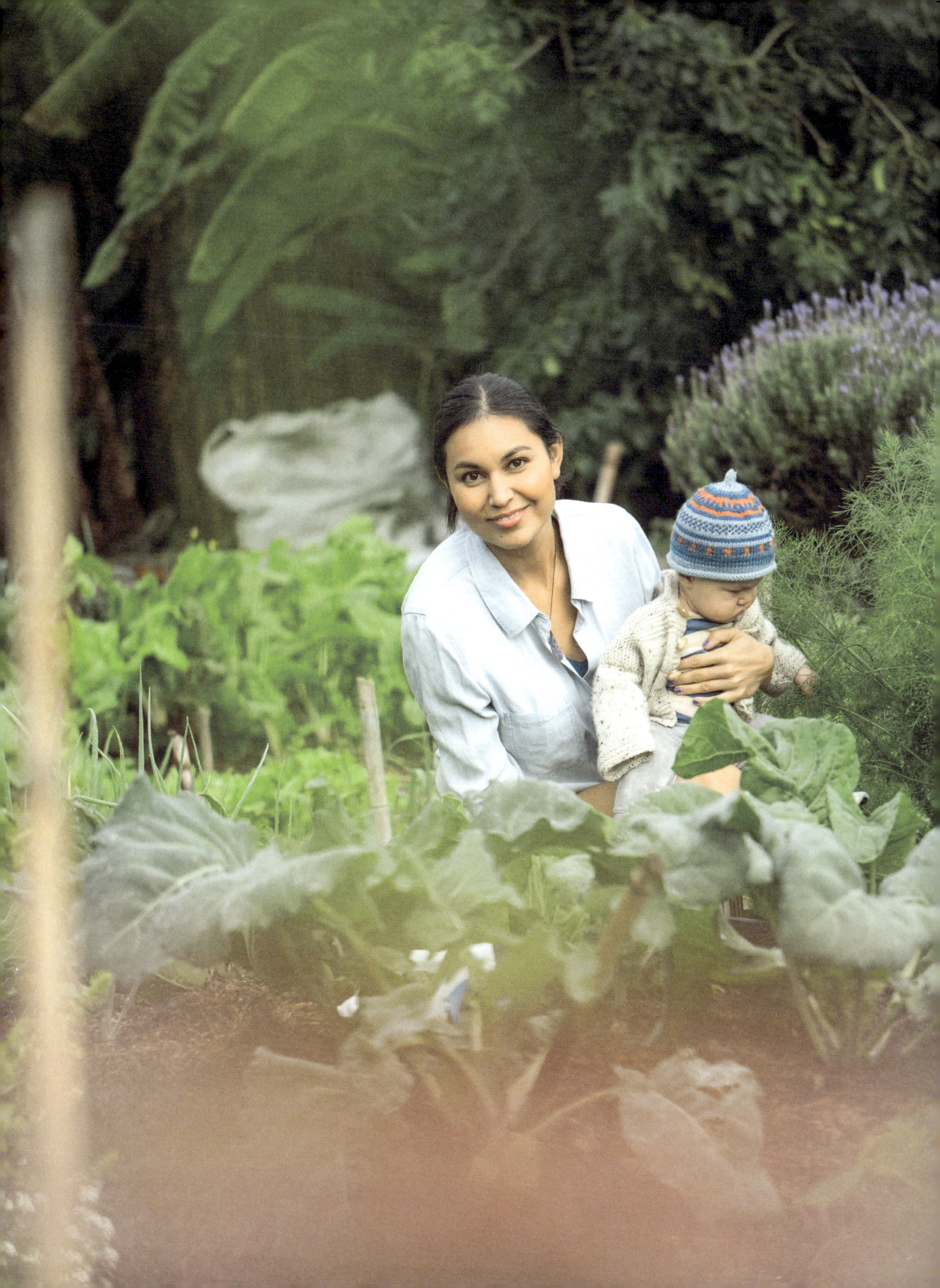

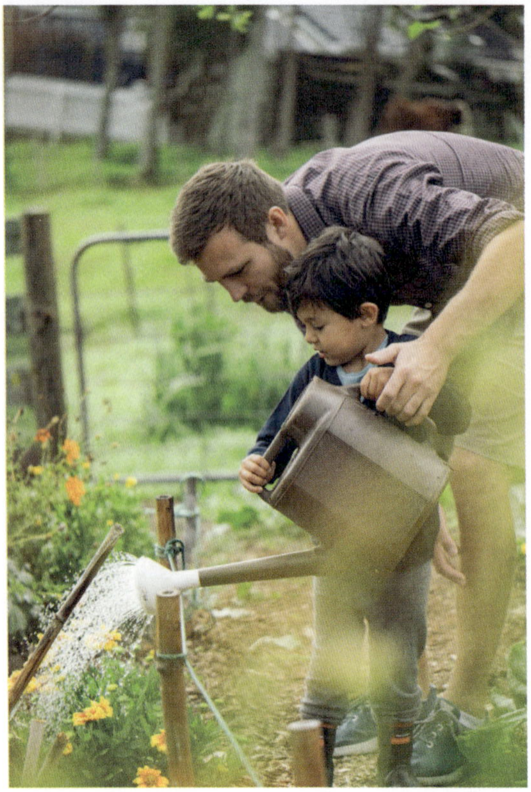
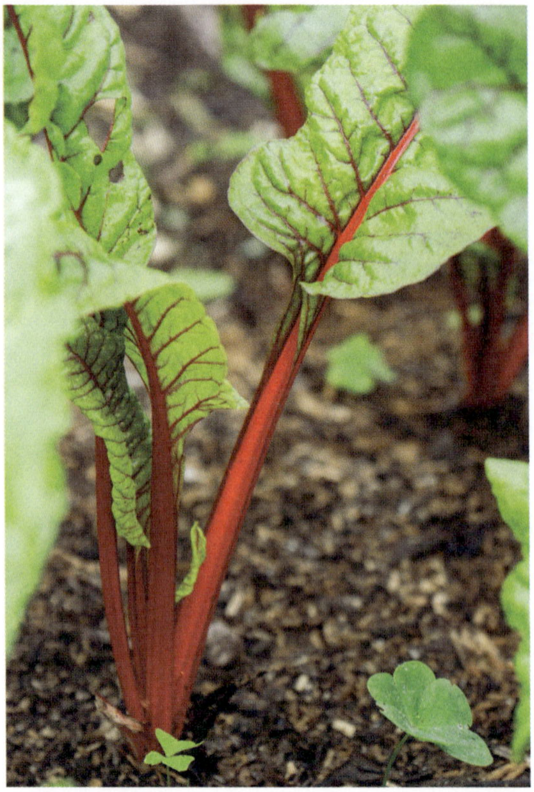
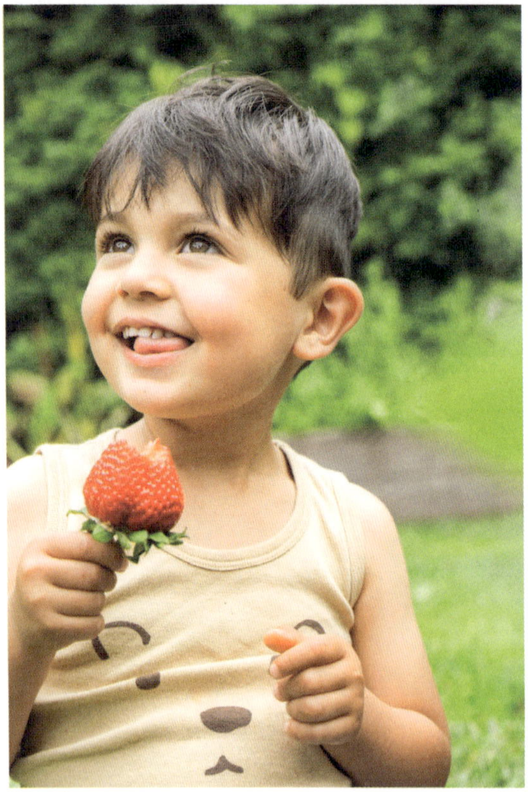
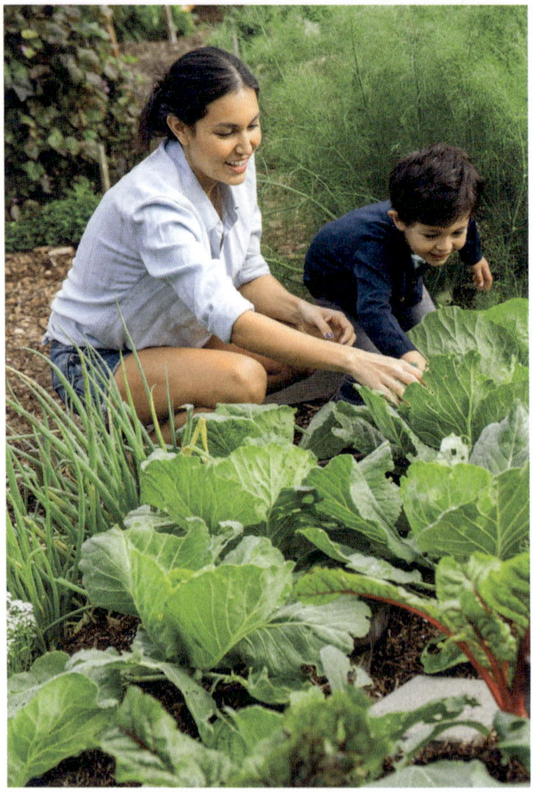

There is no other food source quite like vegetables, one that beats boredom by continually changing through the seasons, that's so unreservedly good for us, that works in every course you serve, and that's so wickedly versatile — crisp and raw, roasted, sweet and caramelised, braised and meltingly tender, blended and velvety smooth, stir-fried, grilled, barbecued, steamed, blanched, mashed, baked, you name it. There are so many possibilities in the vegetable world that we will forever be discovering new varieties and ways with them.

And there is no doubt about it that eating more vegetables would do *all* of us lots of good. No one can argue with that. As Michael Pollan, author of *In Defense of Food*, says: 'In all my interviews with nutrition experts, the benefits of a plant-based diet provided the only universal consensus'. It's the one food source of which we simply can't eat too much. And of course, by default, when you eat more of one thing, it leaves less room for eating other (not as good for you) things. So really, it's a win-win.

Whilst we are aware of all the great reasons to eat lots more vegetables, and less processed foods and meat, many of us find it a difficult change to tackle. Our cooking culture has largely been based around meat — most of the time it's the starting point of a meal ('should we have chicken or steak tonight?'), so there are often concerns that vegetarian food might be somehow 'lacking' ... in flavour, satiety, ease. I can promise you that whilst, at first, it might require a bit of a shift in mindset and culinary focus, you'll find that it's an easy adjustment to make. Once you get used to thinking of vegetables as your starting point, and exploring new varieties, ways and techniques, you'll wonder why vegetables weren't the star of your main meals all along. I'd go as far as saying that, for many cooks, it will feel liberating because there is just so much more to choose from in the vegetable world, and it is far more creative, colourful and exciting.

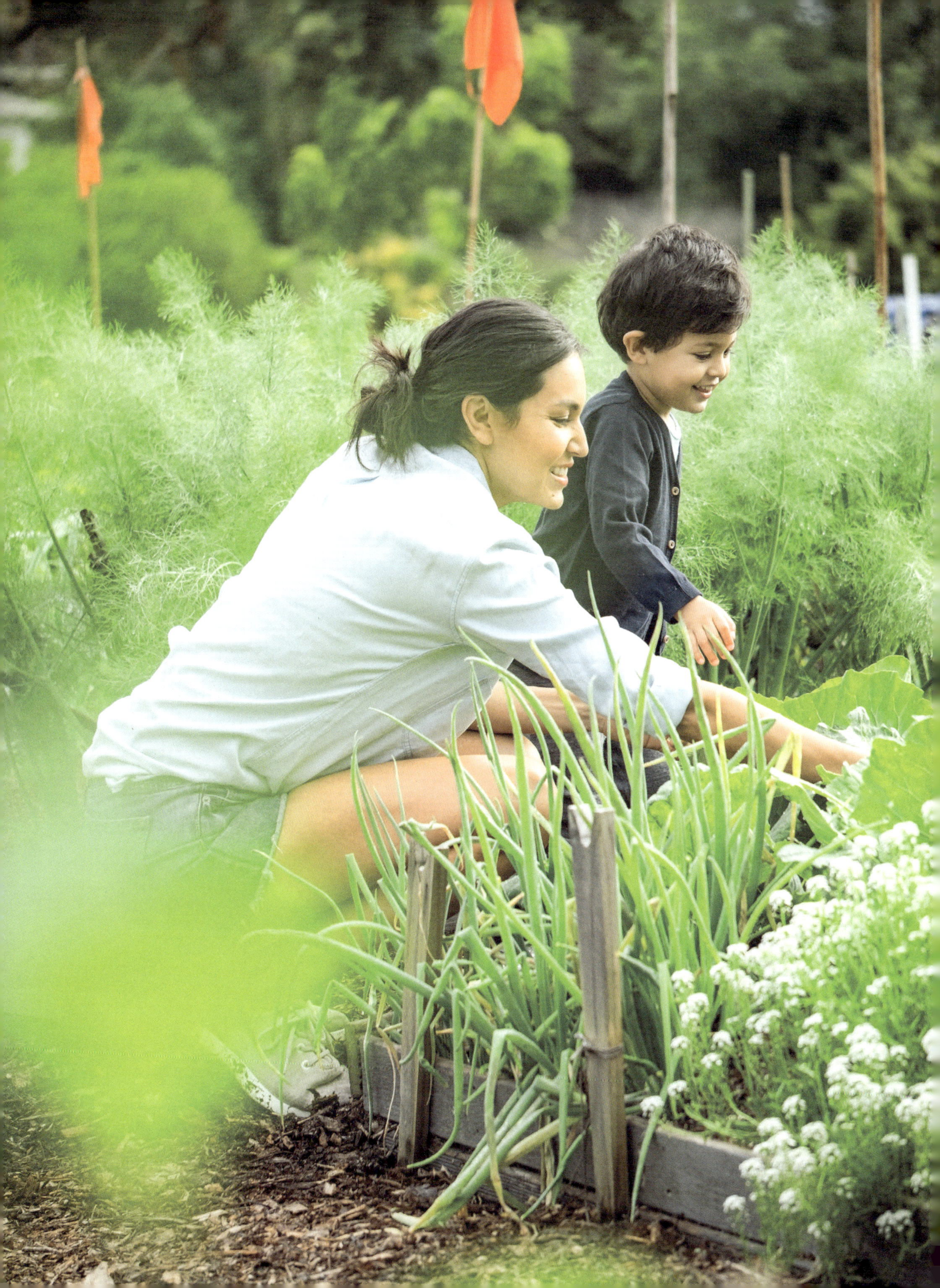

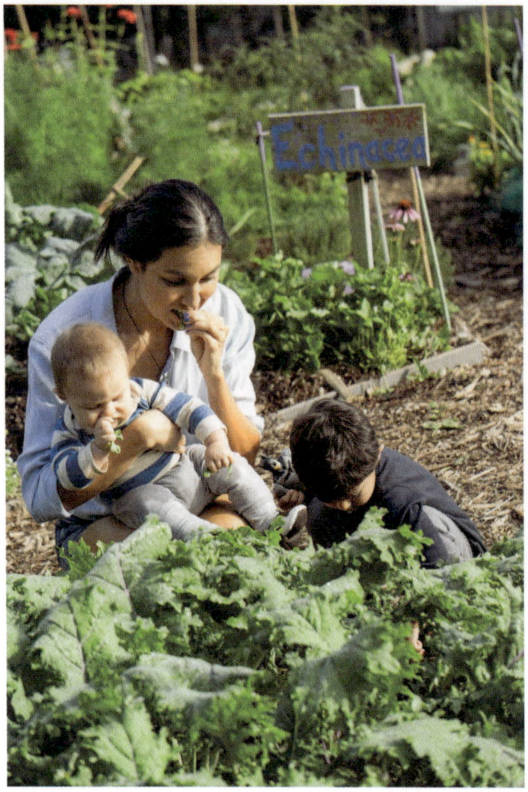

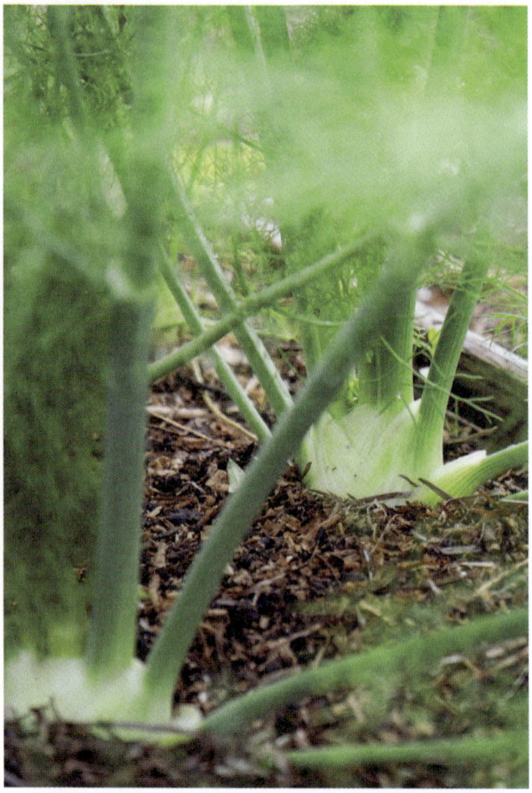

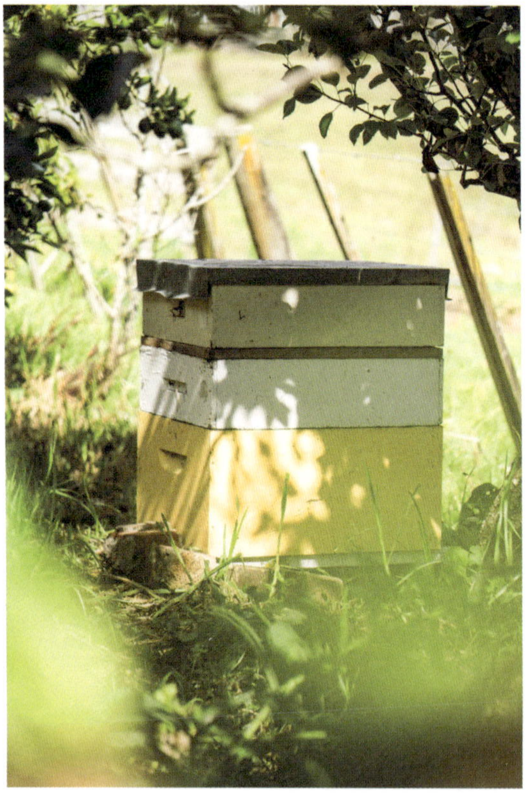

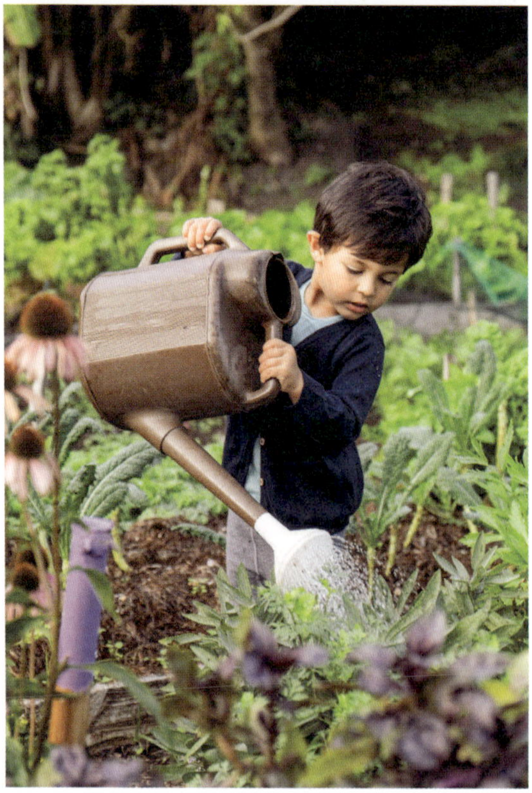

Suddenly you'll be roasting three whole bunches of radishes instead of just using three sliced in a salad, mashing up chickpeas and kumara for burger patties and spice rubbing and caramelising your cauliflower. And in the process, you'll feel happier and healthier that you're eating lots more of the good stuff. And maybe even treading a bit more lightly on the planet.

It really excites me that there's a definite wave of change happening, a growing desire amongst us to cook and eat a more 'vegful' way. So, with that, enjoy these recipes and all the amazing extra veg you'll be eating.

Nadia x

A few notes:

— At the top of each recipe it is stated whether a recipe is gluten-free (GF), dairy-free (DF) or vegan (VEGAN) or how to make adjustments to make them that way.
— The nutrition information for each recipe (calories, kilojoules, fat, carbohydrate, protein etc.) can be found in the back of the book.
— There are lots of fantastic dairy-free/vegan substitutes for cheeses and milk these days, like nut cheeses and mylks. So if you like, feel free to use them directly in place of their dairy counterparts.
— In some baking recipes (e.g. muffins, loaves, pikelets and cupcakes) you can also use flax eggs as a replacement to eggs (see page 291 on how to do this).
— Some recipes would go nicely with a little meat or fish added for a more 'flexitarian' style of meal, so add a little of these things if you so desire.

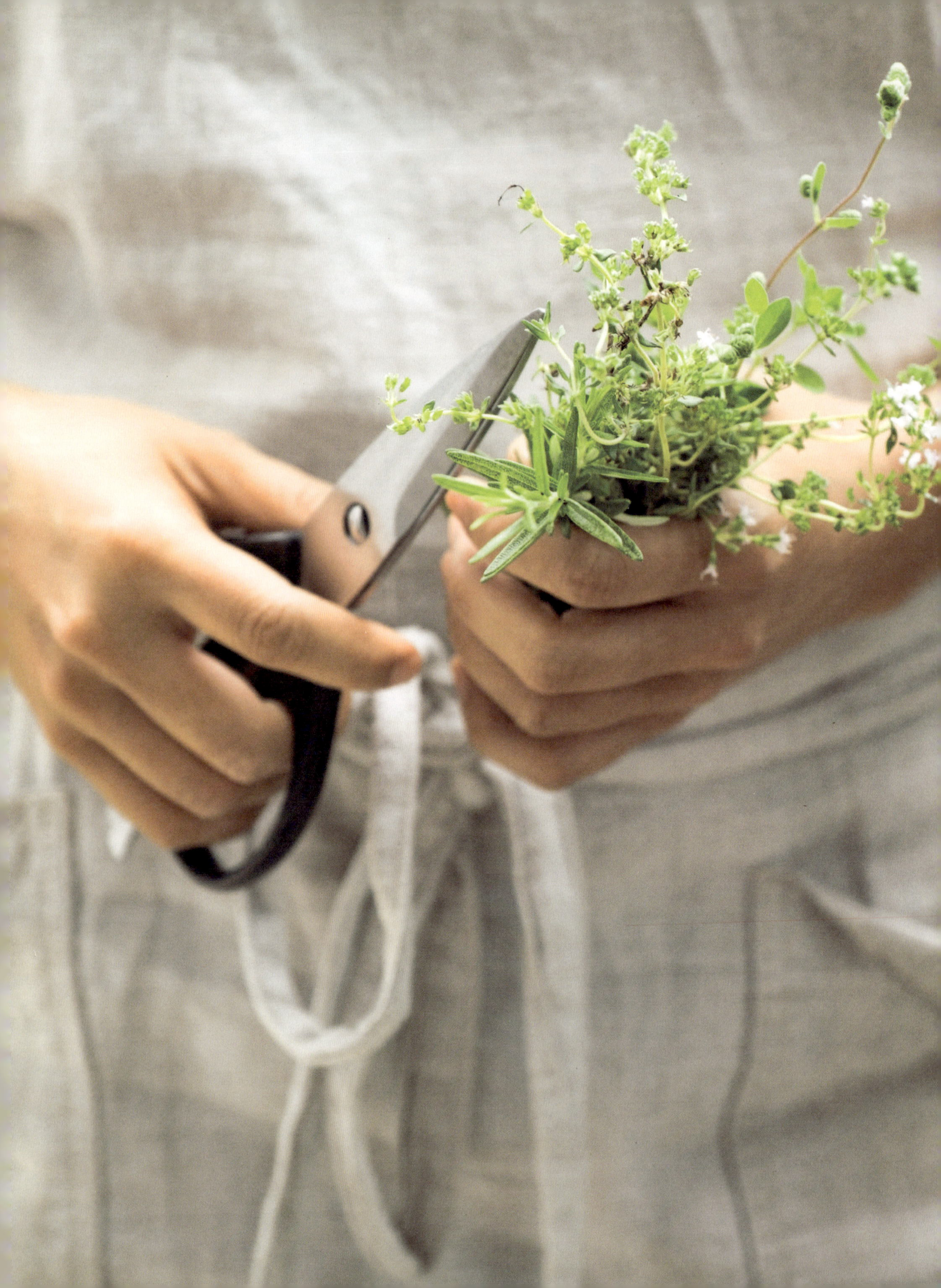

A SEASONAL GUIDE

TO SOME OF MY FAVOURITE
VEGETABLES & HERBS

A SEASONAL GUIDE

SUMMER

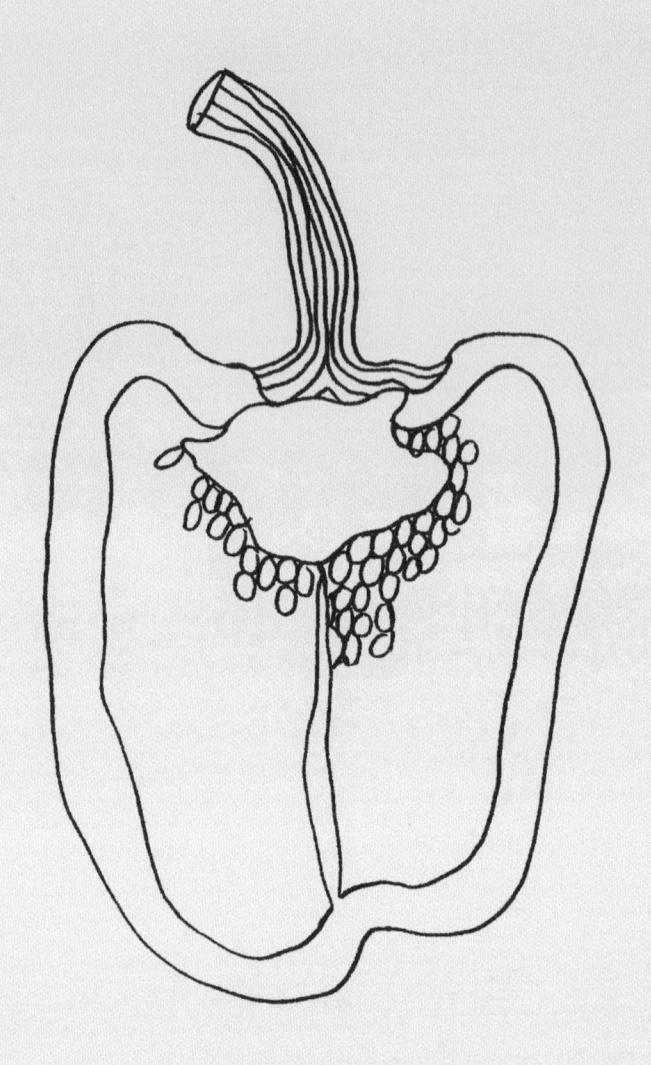

CAPSICUM

One of the best ways to eat capsicums is roasted — place whole capsicums on a tray and roast at 220°C until their skins are charred and blistered (about 30 minutes), then leave to cool and peel off their papery skins. The resulting soft, roasted flesh has a sweet, caramelised flavour and is amazing added to pasta, salads, blended into dips, sauces or soup, or piled on top of bruschetta.

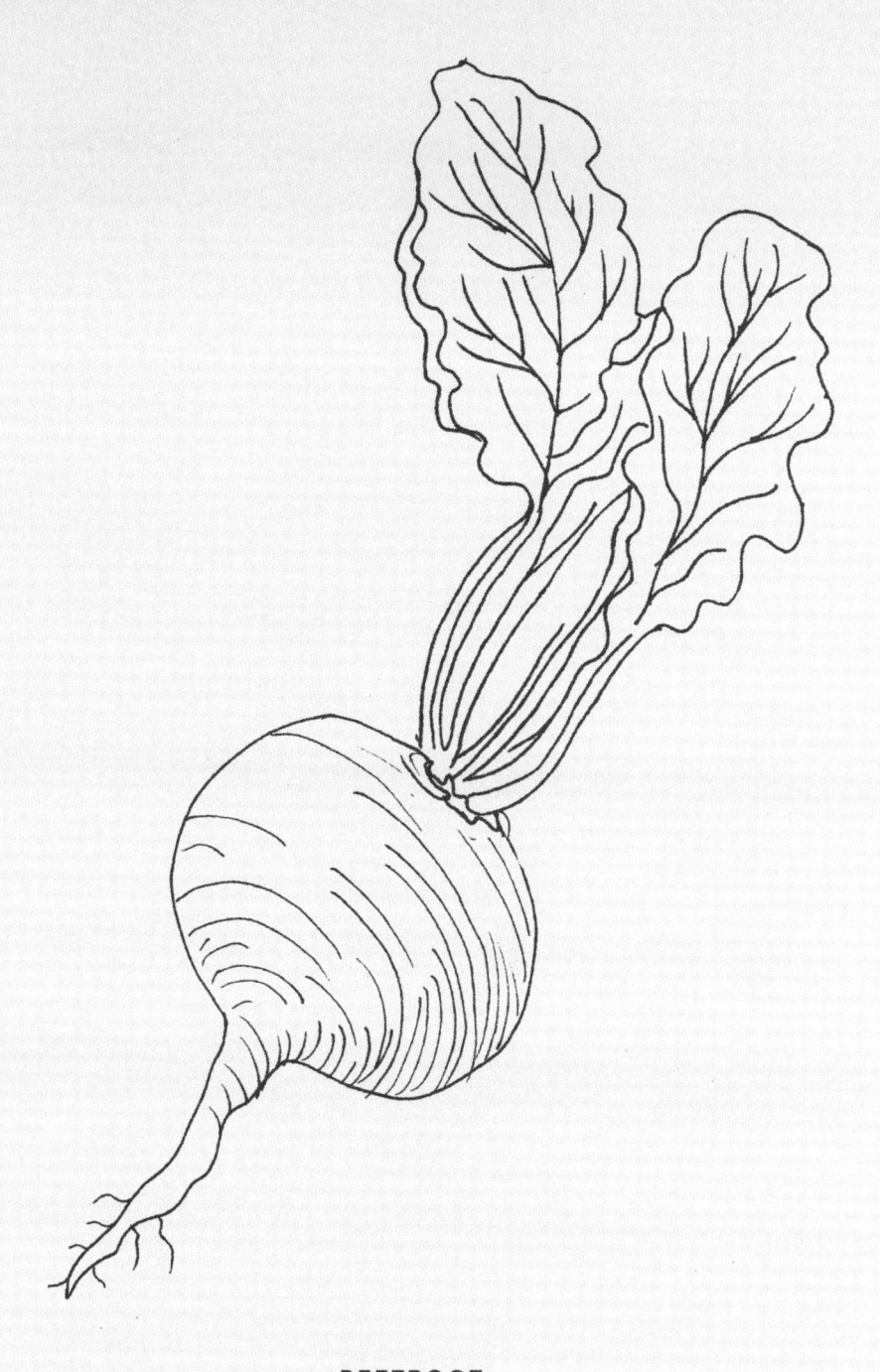

BEETROOT

Beetroot's stunning purple-red hue is thanks to the powerful antioxidant betacyanin, just one of the many reasons it is so incredibly good for you. The leaves are edible too and great in salads. I love beetroot raw (coarsely grated in a slaw), roasted (with olive oil and a drizzle of maple syrup to bring out its natural sweetness), and even in a delicious, moist chocolate cake (page 307).

COURGETTE

Courgettes are so clever at disguising themselves (grated in omelettes, frittata and pasta) that they've even made their way into sweet recipes like my Spiced Courgette, Date and Apple Loaf (page 291), and Courgette and Choc Chip Buttermilk Pikelets (page 297)! Choose smaller courgettes that are firm with dark green, glossy, unblemished skin — they're fresher, younger and tastier. They are at their best sliced and grilled on the barbecue, or stir-fried (skip boiling them as they go too mushy!).

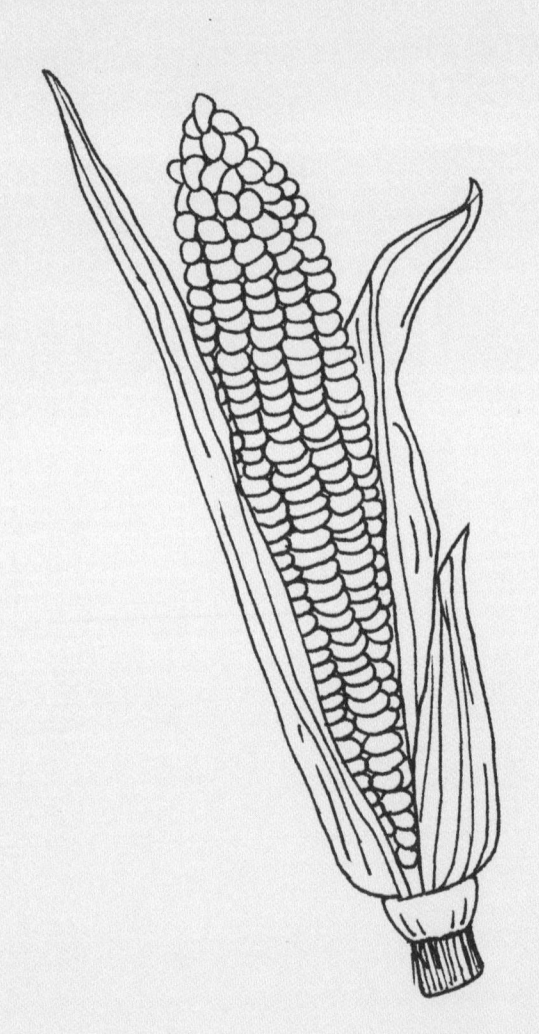

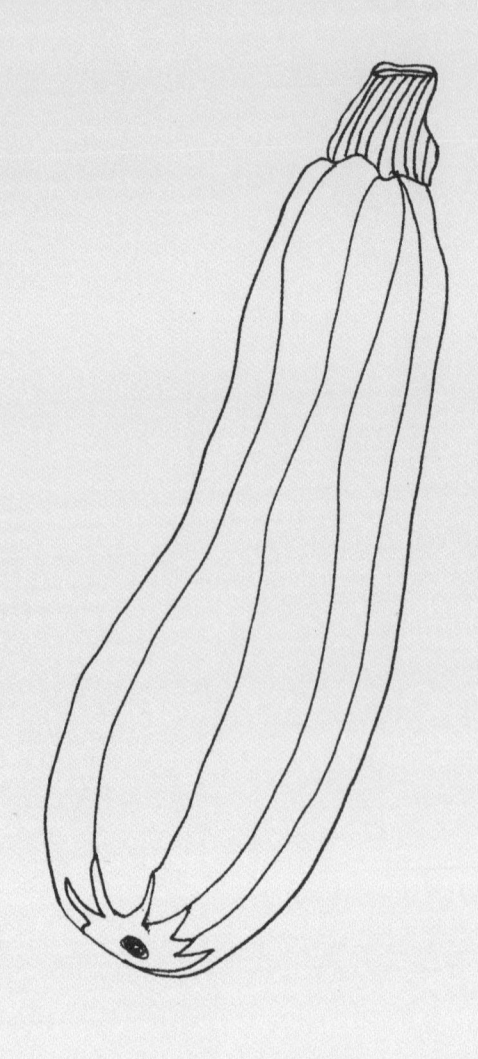

SWEET CORN

To choose the freshest, plumpest corn, make sure the husk (the outside) is bright green, wrapped tightly against the corn and slightly damp and the tassels should be light brown or gold, and slightly sticky to the touch. Avoid dry or black tassels, or husks that feel dry or are starting to yellow, which is a sign that the corn is old.

BASIL

Plant your own basil and cut your shopping bill significantly in summer. If you have a surplus, make pesto or basil oil. To make basil oil, place basil leaves in a bowl, pour over boiling water then drain immediately and plunge into iced water. Drain and blend with olive oil and a pinch of salt — it will keep in the fridge for a few days or freeze in ice cube trays.

LAVENDER

Yes, you can eat lavender! Just make sure it hasn't been sprayed. To make lavender syrup that can be used in drinks and desserts, simply boil a handful of lavender heads with seeds from a vanilla bean pod, a few strips of lemon zest, and equal parts sugar and water, until syrupy. Leave to cool and store in the fridge. Fold through whipped cream or yoghurt, drizzle over fruit, or shake up in a cocktail!

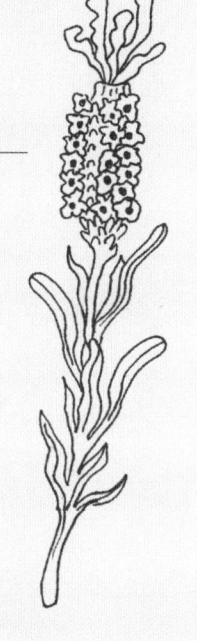

MINT

Plant mint in your garden and it will grow like crazy! It's a herb I can't do without; there is no other herb that is as versatile or brings so much freshness — in particular, it brings Asian and Middle Eastern dishes alive. Try using mint in pesto (instead of the usual basil) and making a pot of fresh mint tea by steeping a generous handful of mint leaves in boiling water and sweetening with honey.

A SEASONAL GUIDE

SPRING

LEAFY GREENS

It's quick and easy to grow leafy greens and you can't compare freshly picked to bought — as well as growing fresh lettuces, I love mizuna (a Japanese green that grows super quick), sorrel (best described as 'lemony spinach'), cavolo nero (like kale, the young leaves are tender and sweet), rocket (to add a bit of pepperiness to your salads) and young beetroot leaves are some of my favourites in the garden.

DILL

I love dill's delicate, feathery green leaves, they make a beautiful garnish. The anise-like liquorice flavour of dill works especially well with eggs and potatoes — try tossing boiled baby potatoes with lemon, dill and parsley, or adding to scrambled eggs or omelette. It's also essential to tzatziki (page 156), which makes a great creamy, tangy, cooling yoghurt condiment for lots of dishes.

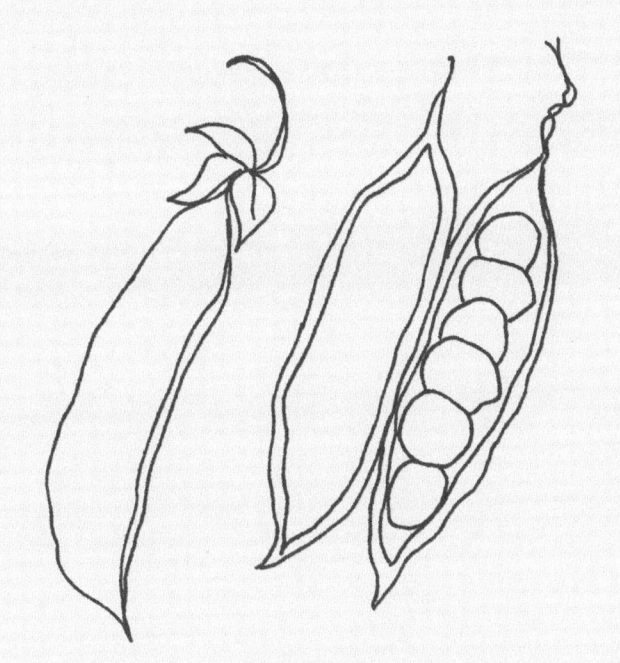

PEAS

The taste of fresh peas is a special one that makes the fiddly job of podding them worth it; however, our freezer always has a bag of peas in it for convenience, and the kids like to eat them frozen too, just like lollies! One of my favourite easy peas-ey (ha ha!) dishes that the kids love is fettuccine with sautéed onion, defrosted peas, chopped ham and sour cream tossed through.

ASPARAGUS

Asparagus is such a fleeting seasonal pleasure, so I make sure I get my fix for a solid six weeks while it's at its best. The spears of the first harvest are the fattest and often sweetest, before they start getting thinner. The bottom ends can be tough and woody, so snap or cut them off before cooking. Lightly boil (for no more than 2 minutes) or toss with olive oil and barbecue, or roast for 10 minutes or so at 220°C until bright green and just tender.

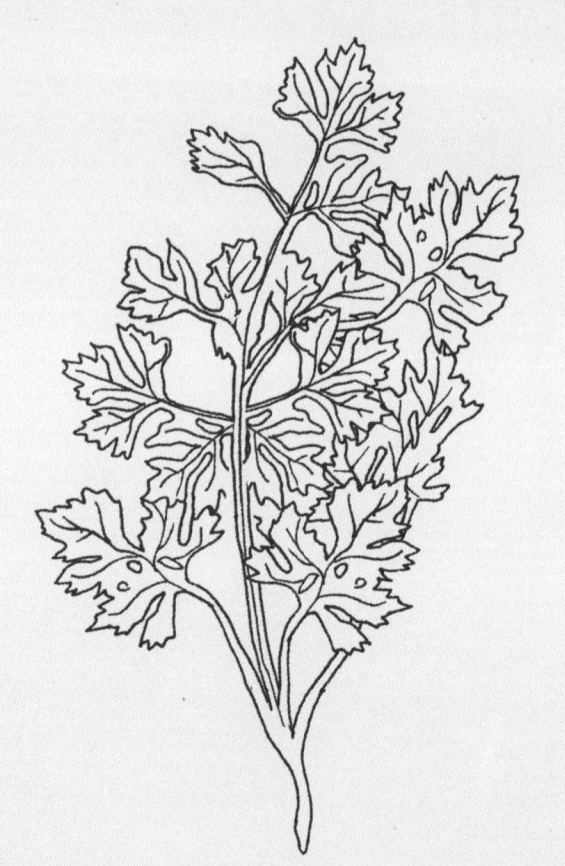

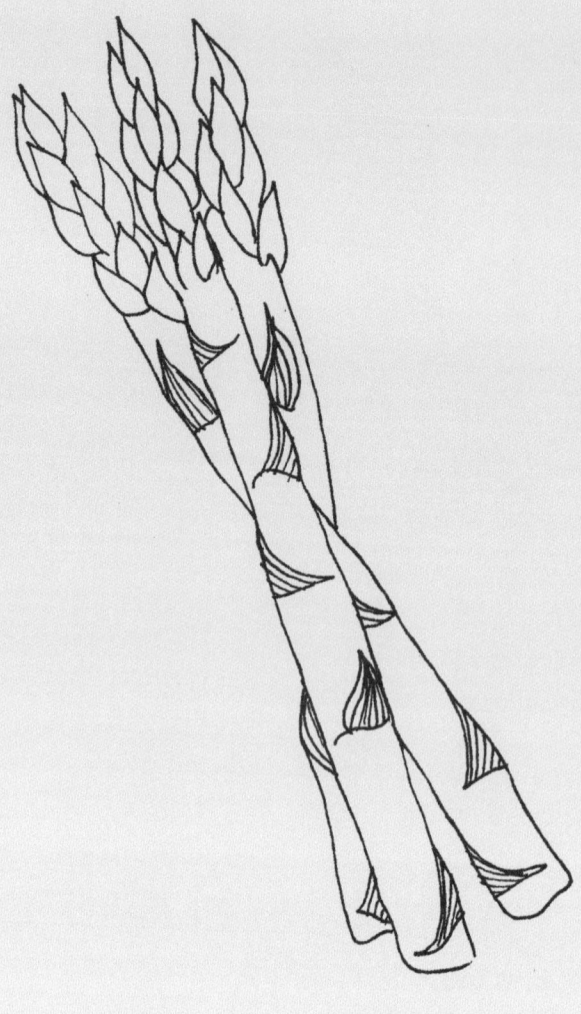

PARSLEY

Most of the time I prefer using flat-leaf parsley (instead of the curly variety) as it is a little more tender and easier to chop. To lift, liven and freshen a myriad of dishes, make and sprinkle over gremolata — sounds fancy, but it's just a mix of finely chopped fresh parsley, lemon zest and a little garlic and salt. I also mix mine with a little extra-virgin olive oil and lemon juice — it instantly adds vibrancy to dishes!

BROCCOLI

Some vegetables punch above their weight nutritionally and one of them is broccoli. Part of the super-nutritious brassica family, broccoli contains sulphuric compounds which act as powerful antioxidants with anti-cancer and liver detoxification properties. Avoid overboiling it until soft, instead lightly boil/steam or stir-fry until bright green and it still has some crunch, or enjoy it finely chopped raw (like in the Raw Vege Pilav on page 108) or lightly blanched and tossed in salads.

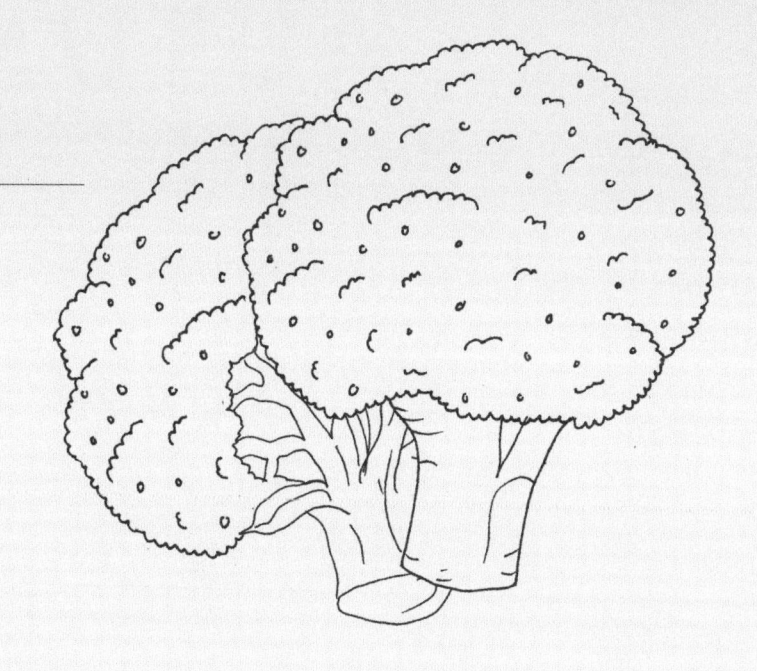

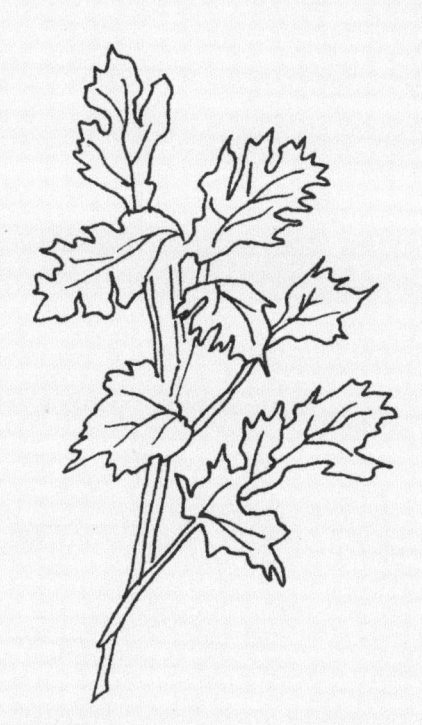

CORIANDER

I'm a coriander-lover so I grow lots of it. I leave my plants to go to seed (which they do quickly when it's hot and dry) and months later brand-new little coriander plants start popping up. I'll also harvest a jarful of the golden-brown dried seeds for my spice draw (they have much more flavour than what you can buy!) before they drop. Make sure you use the tender stalks as well as the leaves, as they're equally good for garnishing and flavour.

A SEASONAL GUIDE

AUTUMN

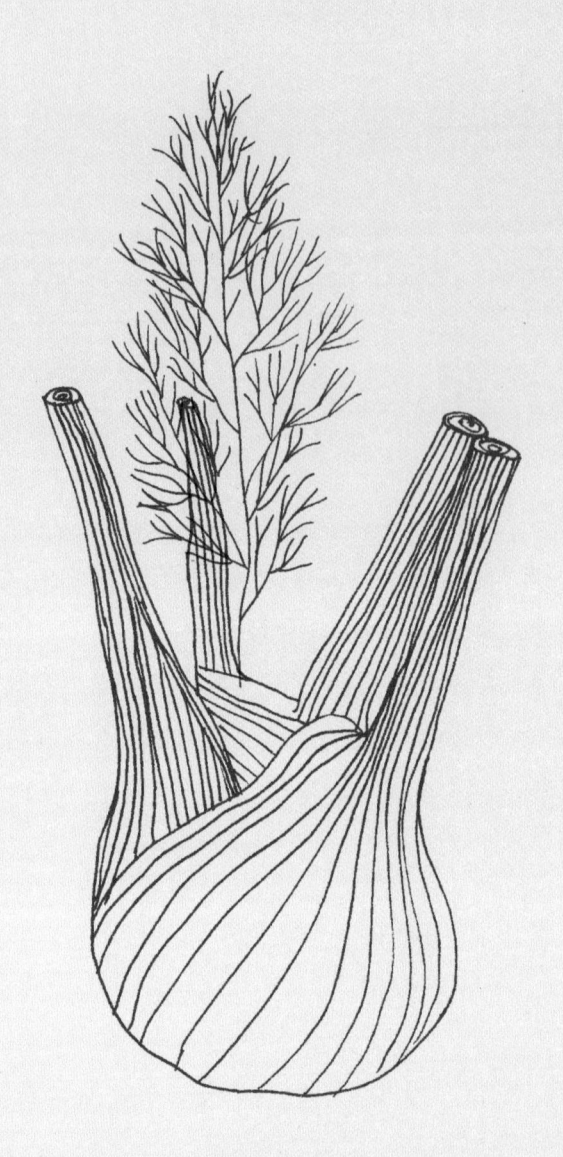

FENNEL

Its fresh crunch and subtle aniseed flavour makes fennel a great supporting partner in salads (rather than being the main component); slice it super thinly (pretty much shaved, if you can), and add to a cabbage slaw or toss with rocket leaves and orange segments and dress with lemon juice and extra-virgin olive oil. It is also excellent roasted and caramelised and blended up in a tomato pasta sauce (such as the Autumn Harvest Sauce on page 192).

EGGPLANT

Also called aubergine, eggplant is one of my favourite vegetables. Sliced and drizzled with olive oil and roasted until meltingly tender, roast eggplant becomes a delicious addition to salads, couscous and pasta dishes, or just dressed with lemon juice and herbs it's a fabulous side dish. Or mash it with natural yoghurt, herbs and lemon for a delicious dip with flat breads. Don't even get me started on how amazing it is in tagines and curries.

OREGANO

You can't cook Italian food without oregano. Unlike parsley, basil and coriander, which you can use liberally, fresh oregano has a strong flavour and is best used in smaller quantities. If you have a plant, dry some and keep in a jar — dried oregano is very handy when it comes to making a beautiful tomato pasta sauce, pizza sauce or casserole.

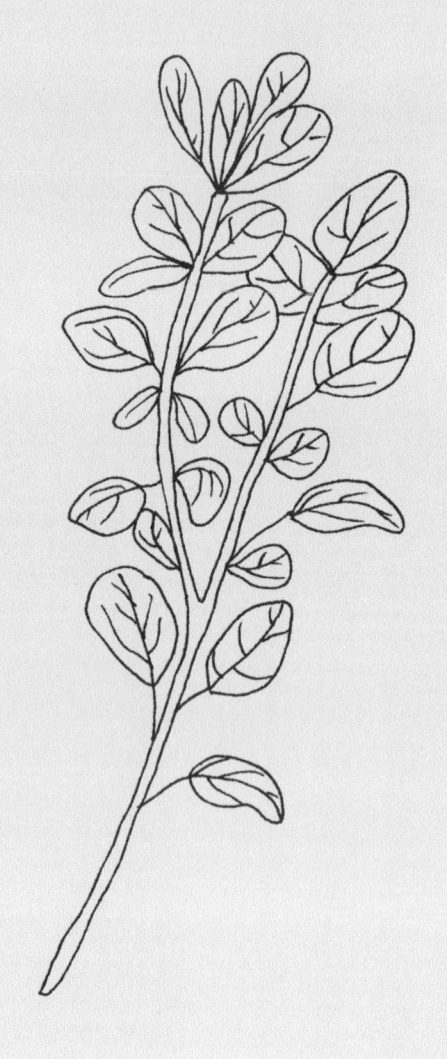

PUMPKIN

Pumpkin is such a versatile vegetable, but the thought of having to prepare it is what often puts people off. To make it easy to cut up pumpkin, I microwave the whole piece (skin and all) for about 5 minutes on High. This softens the skin, making it much easier and safer to cut off. The flesh will also be much softer and easier to cut.

MUSHROOMS

I am a big mushroom fan — I could have mushrooms on toast for breakfast, lunch and dinner. With their ability to add so much savoury depth and 'meaty' texture to dishes they're an essential ingredient in any vegetarian kitchen. Fresh shiitake mushrooms are now readily available (yay!) so get onto them. Don't wash your mushrooms as they will soak up water; instead, brush off any excess dirt with a pastry brush or paper towel.

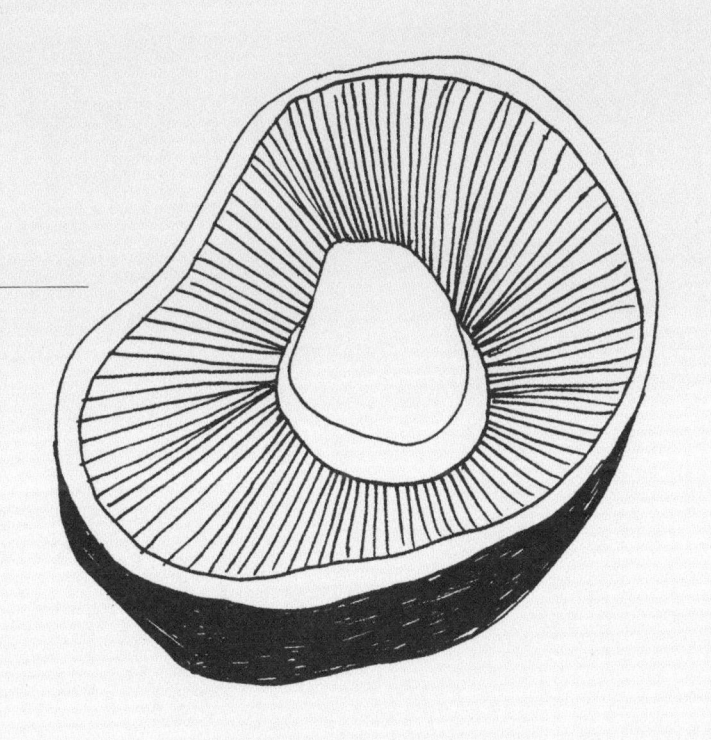

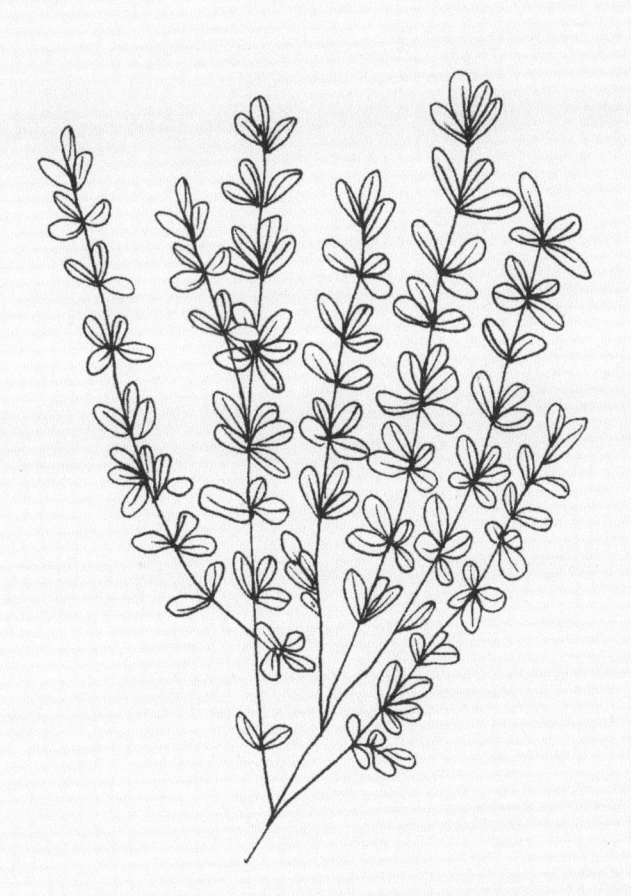

THYME

The fact I have five different varieties of thyme in my garden (Lemon, Chicken, Common, Pizza, French) demonstrates how much I love and use this herb (you'll find a lot of thyme in this book, so start growing some!). I almost always toss thyme with my vegetables before roasting. Its aromatic, almost-floral notes go well with sweet dishes too, à la the Thyme and Rosemary Citrus Tart (page 323). It also has amazing medicinal properties; thyme and honey tea helps soothe a sore throat.

A SEASONAL GUIDE
WINTER

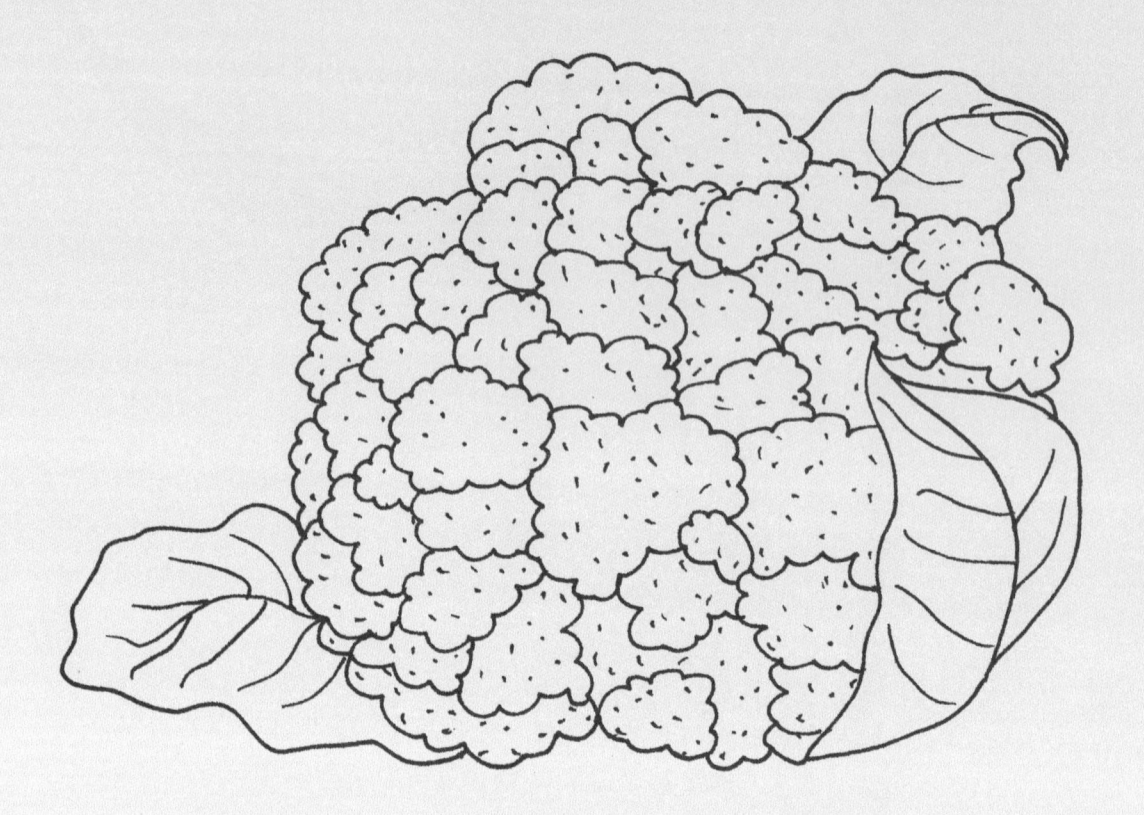

CAULIFLOWER

Seldom do I boil cauliflower (unless we're having cauliflower cheese) as it has so much more potential. It loves being roasted, especially with spices such as cumin and coriander, and feels at home in creamy curries like korma. And finely chopped it makes a fantastic raw, crunchy (and very healthy) salad. Believe it or not, the frozen florets make a fruit smoothie thick and creamy (without any cauliflower taste) — go on, try it!

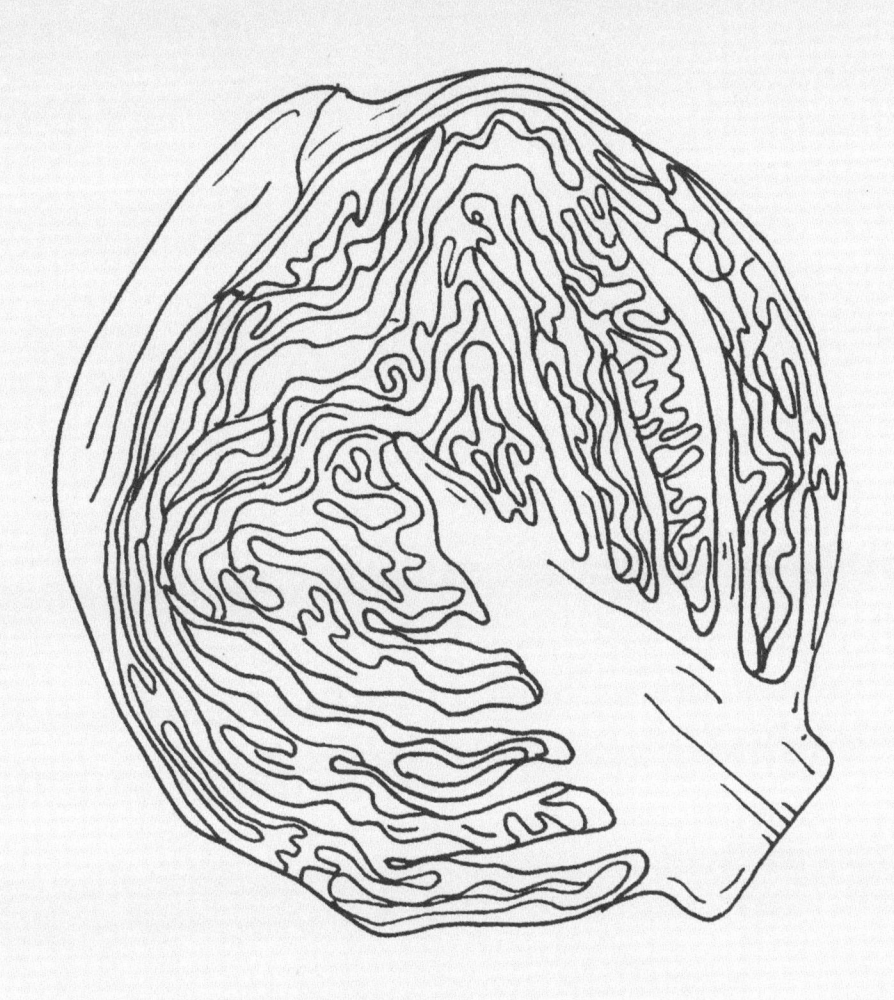

CABBAGE

Humble, yet so handsome — the veiny texture of a savoy cabbage and intricate maze of a cut red cabbage wows me every time. Not to mention its amazing magenta colour, which makes a beautiful natural blue food dye (great for kids' birthday cakes). Cabbage is another vegetable I avoid boiling (it just goes limp, bland and lifeless) and is far more exciting than many give it credit. I most often sauté it (in butter or olive oil, depending) or, in warmer weather, very finely shred it raw for slaws.

SILVERBEET

One of the best vegetables to grow at home. My nan religiously picked fresh silverbeet from her garden every night to cook with dinner. I love it simply sautéed (including the finely sliced stalks) in a drizzle of olive oil and knob of butter, with a pinch of salt, for about 5 minutes until tender and deep green. Sometimes I'll squeeze in a little orange juice for orange-buttered silverbeet. A more nutrient-dense substitute, try it in recipes that call for spinach.

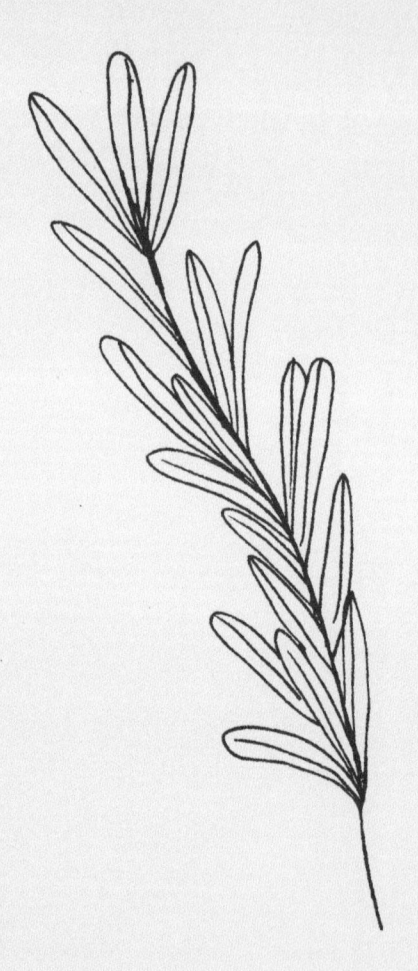

ROSEMARY

You should never have to buy rosemary as it grows prolifically and can be found in every neighbourhood. We have so much of it that we use its gorgeous long sprigs in a vase as a centrepiece for the table. And its smell, oh its smell. My kids love rubbing it between their fingers and holding it to their noses. You can never go wrong with adding it to your roast potatoes, kumara, vegetables or in a braise or casserole.

SAGE

How beautiful is sage with its soft, dusty jade-green leaves? Savoury, pungent and earthy, its smell and flavour remind me of a winter (or Christmas) roast with stuffing. It's a bit too overpowering to have raw, so is best used during cooking (and finely chopped). One of the best ways to enjoy it is fried in butter when the butter starts to brown and turn sweet and nutty. You can also dry it, and even freeze the whole leaves in a little zip-lock bag.

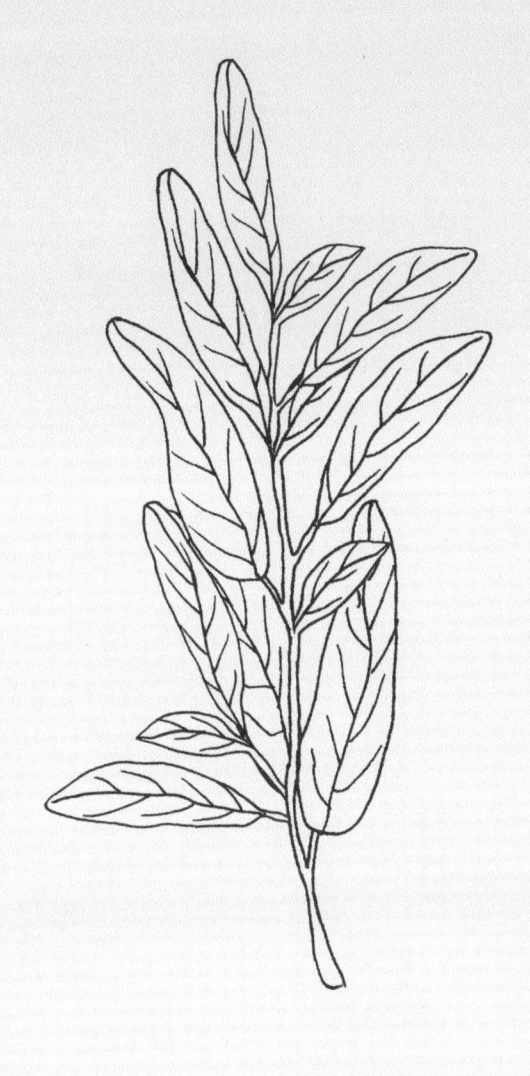

CHIVES

Chives' relation to onion, leeks and garlic is evident in its taste. However, it's best to add them, finely chopped, at the end of cooking, otherwise its flavour is almost entirely lost. Chives add much freshness, particularly to creamy dishes; they're the perfect finish to creamy mushrooms, a creamy cauliflower soup, or potatoes tossed with sour cream or mayo. Very handy to have growing in the garden indeed.

fea
Shar

CHAPTER ONE — P. 33

sts &
ing

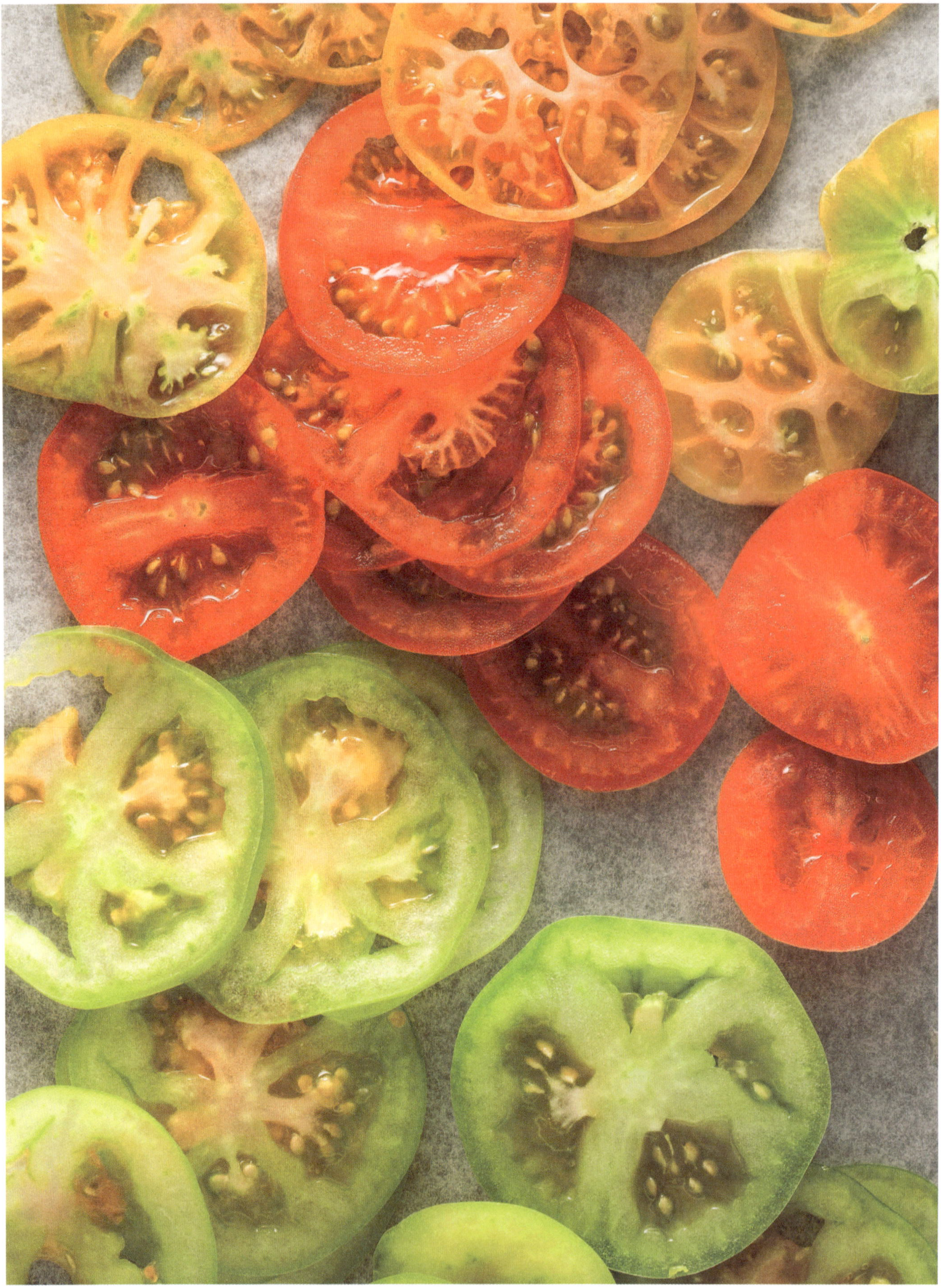

What do you make to eat when you have people coming over? It's something I still deliberate when we've asked a group of friends around.

In summer we fire up the barbecue, prep burger patties and marinate kebabs ahead, then lay out a sea of salads and condiments for everyone to help themselves to. For a casual catch-up in the afternoon sun, a big platter of colourful dips, crackers and fresh vegetables to dip, and maybe a few other easy nibbles always go down well. If we're going around to Mum's house, I might make dumpling filling and my brother, sister, their partners, Mum, Carlos and I will sit around the dining table and fill and fold dumplings until we have a heap ready to cook.

If you're asked to bring a plate, why not bring the marinated veggie kebabs along instead of steak for the barbie? I can guarantee they'll be gone in a flash; everyone will appreciate having some delicious veg-filled choices. Or surprise and delight everyone with just how flavourful and hearty vegetarian burgers and nachos can be at your next gathering.

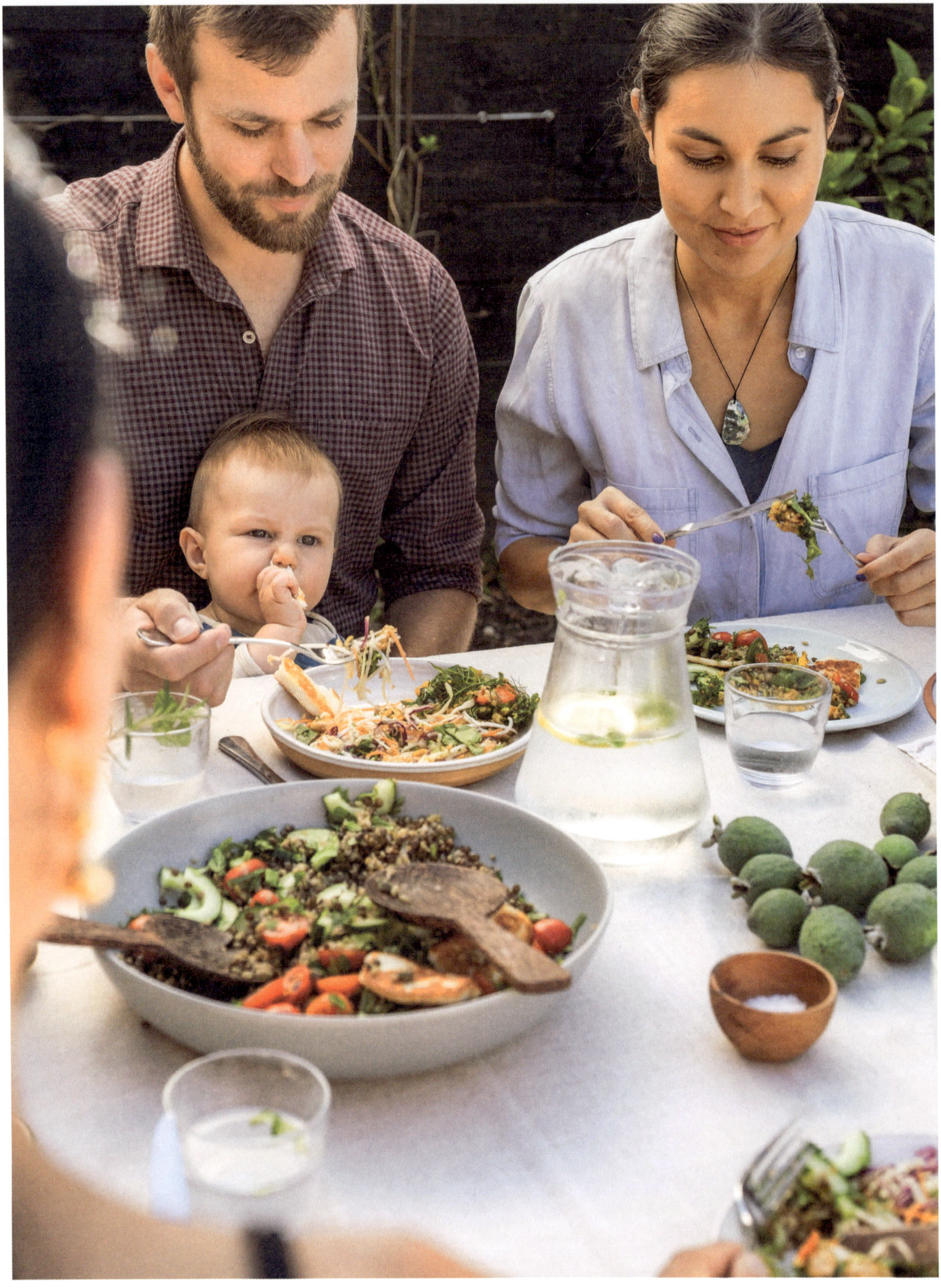

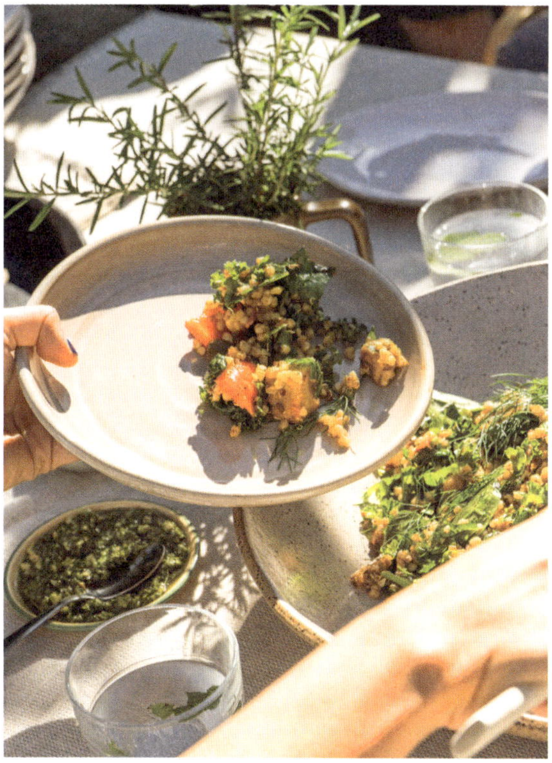

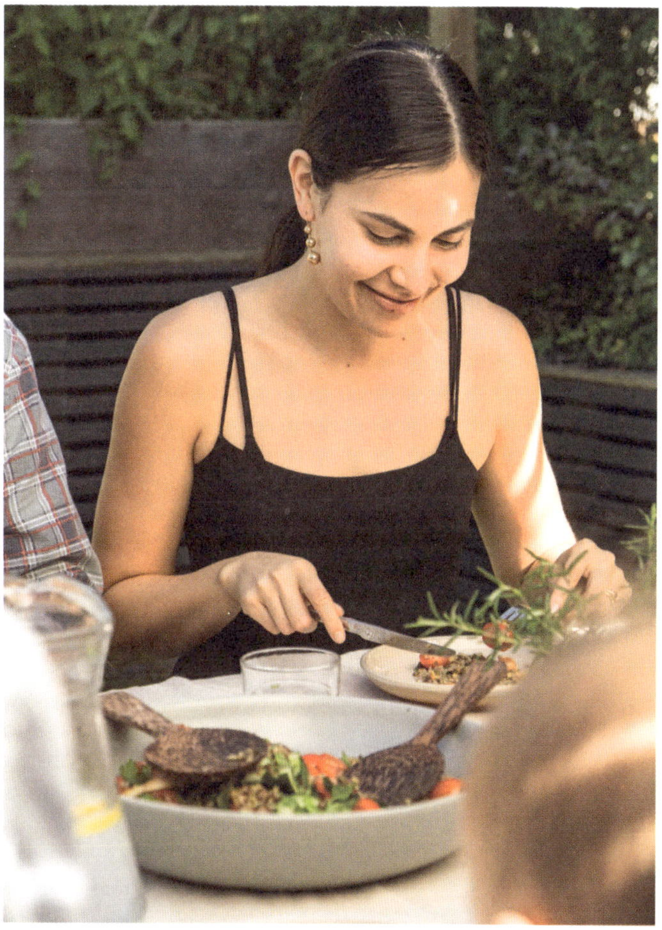

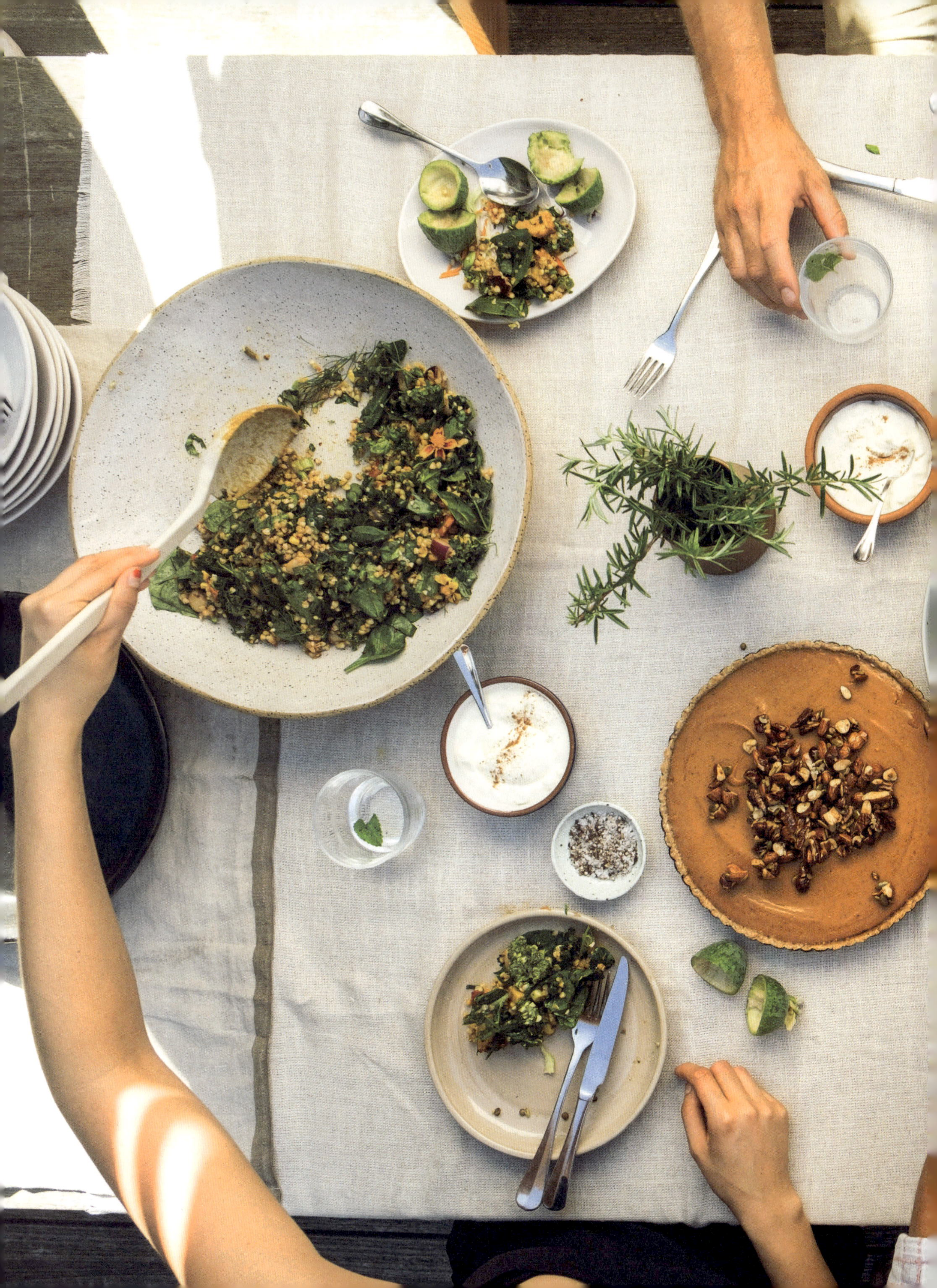

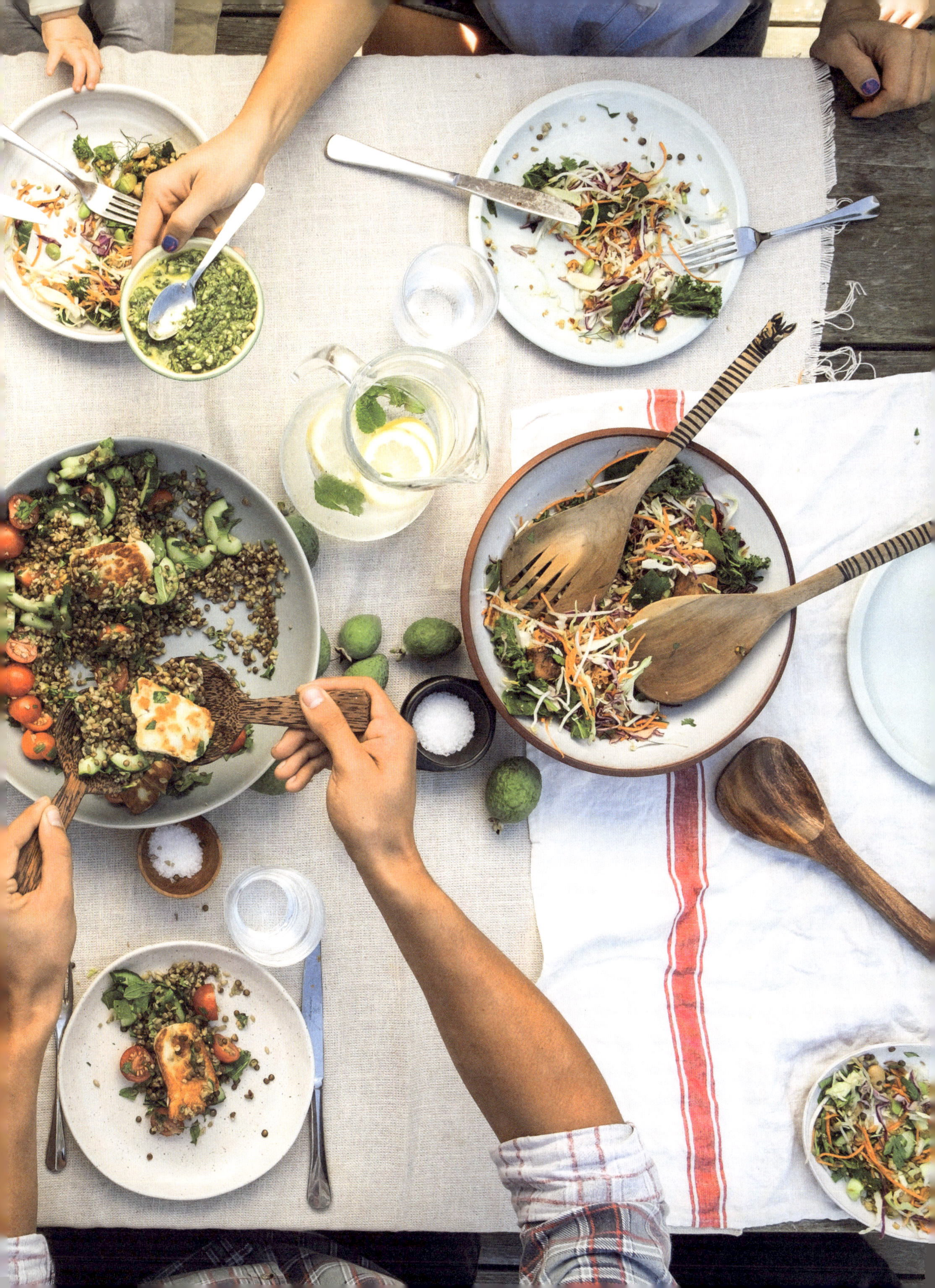

GF use GF breadcrumbs and burger buns | DF omit cheese |
VEGAN omit cheese, use vegan mayo and flax egg

KUMARA, CHICKPEA & MUSHROOM BURGERS

SERVES 6
Prep time: 30 minutes
Cook time: 20 minutes

PATTIES
250–300g red kumara, peeled and diced 2–3cm
2 tablespoons olive oil
250g Portobello mushrooms, stalks removed then diced
1 onion, finely chopped
3 cloves garlic, finely chopped
1 tablespoon curry powder
1 teaspoon ground cumin
zest of 1 lemon
400g can chickpeas, rinsed and drained
¾ cup breadcrumbs
1 free-range egg (or flax egg, page 291)
¾ teaspoon salt
⅓ cup finely chopped basil, parsley and/or coriander

OPTIONAL EXTRAS
6 Portobello mushrooms
6 slices eggplant

TO SERVE
6 slices cheddar
6 burger buns, split in half
tomato relish or Moroccan Apricot and Tomato Chutney (page 158)
pickles
2–3 tomatoes, sliced
½ red onion, thinly sliced into rings
6 fancy lettuce leaves
⅓ cup mayonnaise
1½ teaspoons curry powder

These burgers are so packed full of flavour and so satisfying that they'll please any burger lover, vegetarian or otherwise. Cook the patties (and Portobello mushrooms and/or eggplant if you're going all out) on the barbecue for a smoky flavour. The curry mayo is delicious and the perfect addition, so don't skip it. Make sure you use red (or gold) kumara, not orange kumara (which has a higher water content).

1. Cook kumara in boiling salted water for about 10 minutes or until soft. Drain well, tip back into pot and place over low heat to 'dry off' for a few minutes.

2. Heat olive oil in a large fry pan on medium to high heat. Cook mushrooms and onion, with a good pinch of salt, for 6–8 minutes or until soft and all the moisture in the pan (from the mushrooms) has evaporated. Add another drizzle of oil, garlic, curry powder, cumin and lemon zest and continue cooking for 1 minute more.

3. Add mushroom and onion mixture to pot of kumara, along with chickpeas, breadcrumbs, egg, salt and herbs. Use a potato masher to mash everything together and season with pepper.

4. Divide and roll mixture into six large balls (about ¾ cup mixture each). Flatten and shape each ball into patties 1.5cm thick. Place in the fridge to firm up a little while you prepare everything else.

5. Oil each patty and cook on preheated barbecue hotplate or a large fry pan over medium to high heat for a few minutes each side until golden and cooked through. If you're using Portobello mushrooms or eggplant as well, drizzle with olive oil and season with salt and pepper and cook for a few minutes each side until soft and golden.

6. Top each patty with cheese and melt under the grill, if desired. Lightly toast buns.

7. To assemble burgers, spread bottom half of each bun with relish/chutney, top with pickles, a patty and cheese, eggplant/mushroom (if using), tomato, onion and lettuce. Mix mayonnaise and curry powder together and spread top half of each bun with curry mayo.

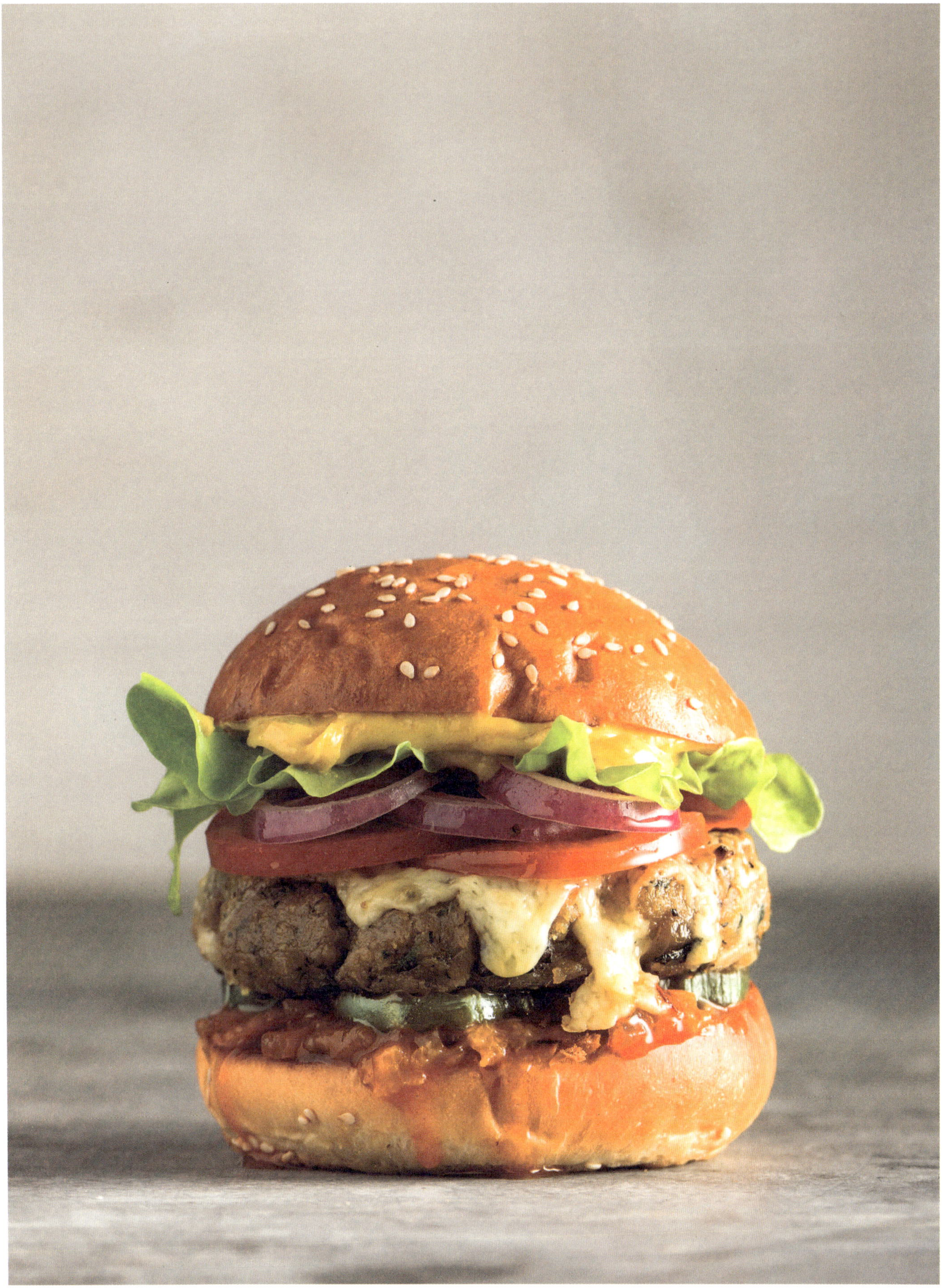

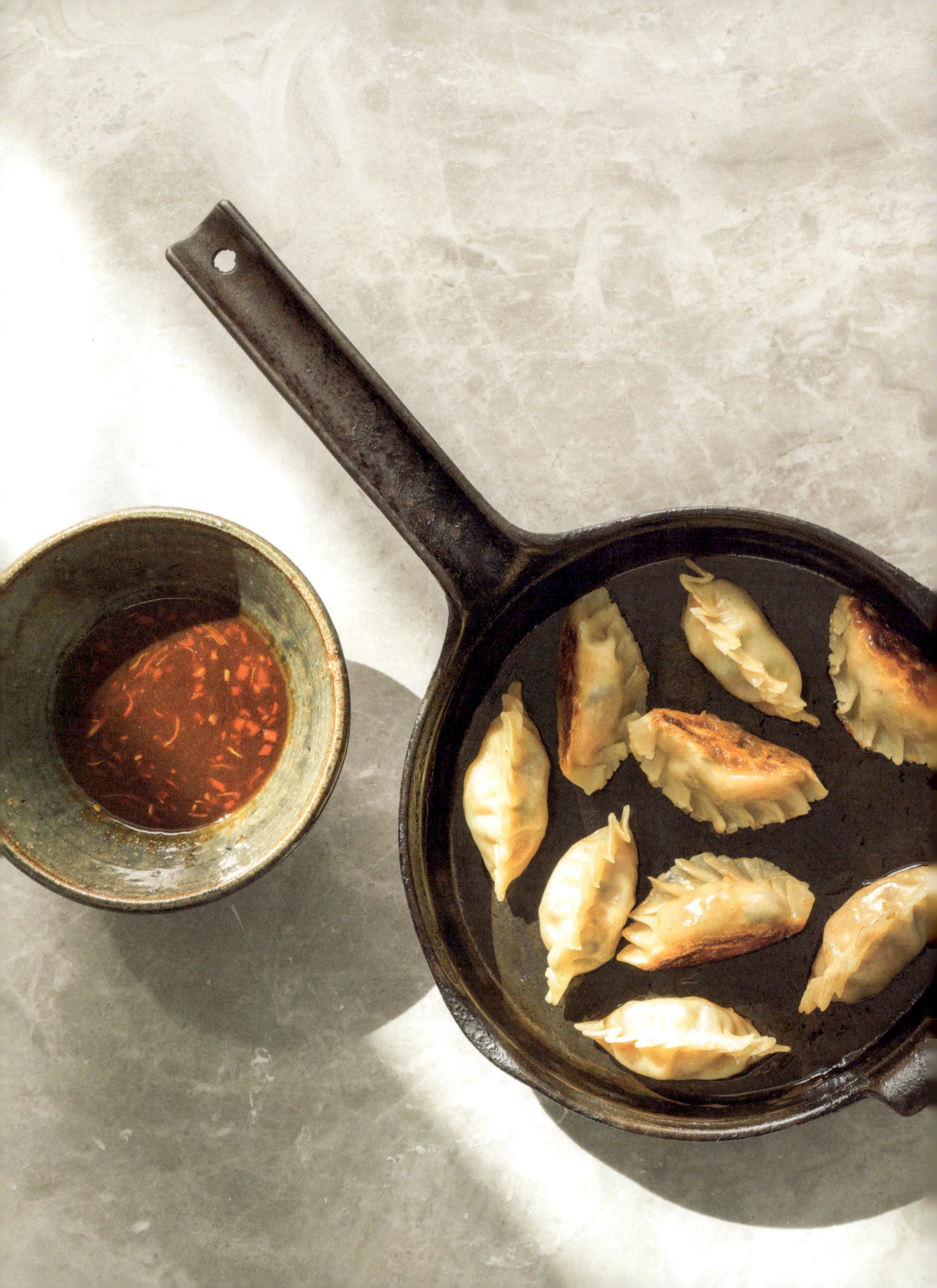

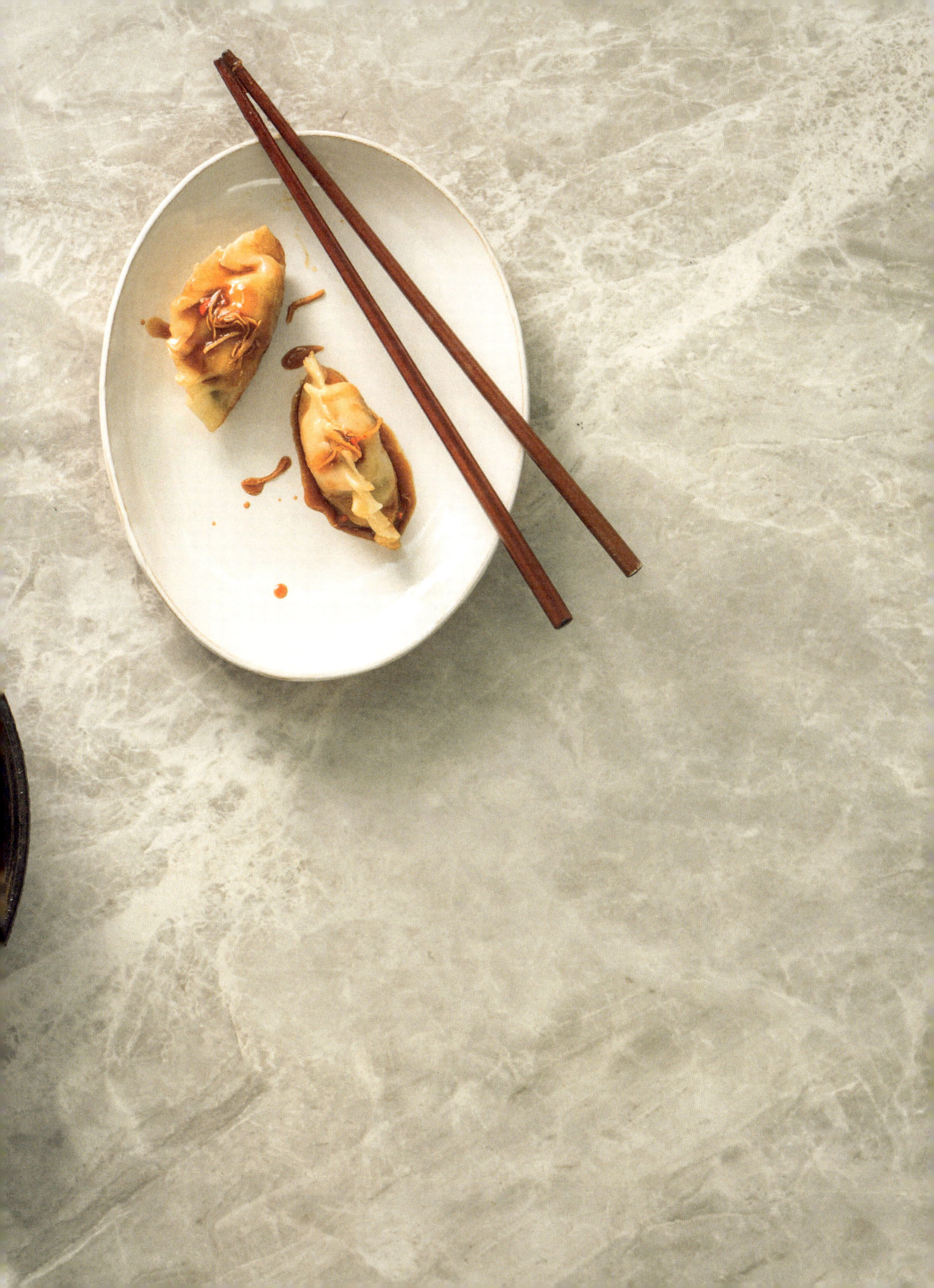

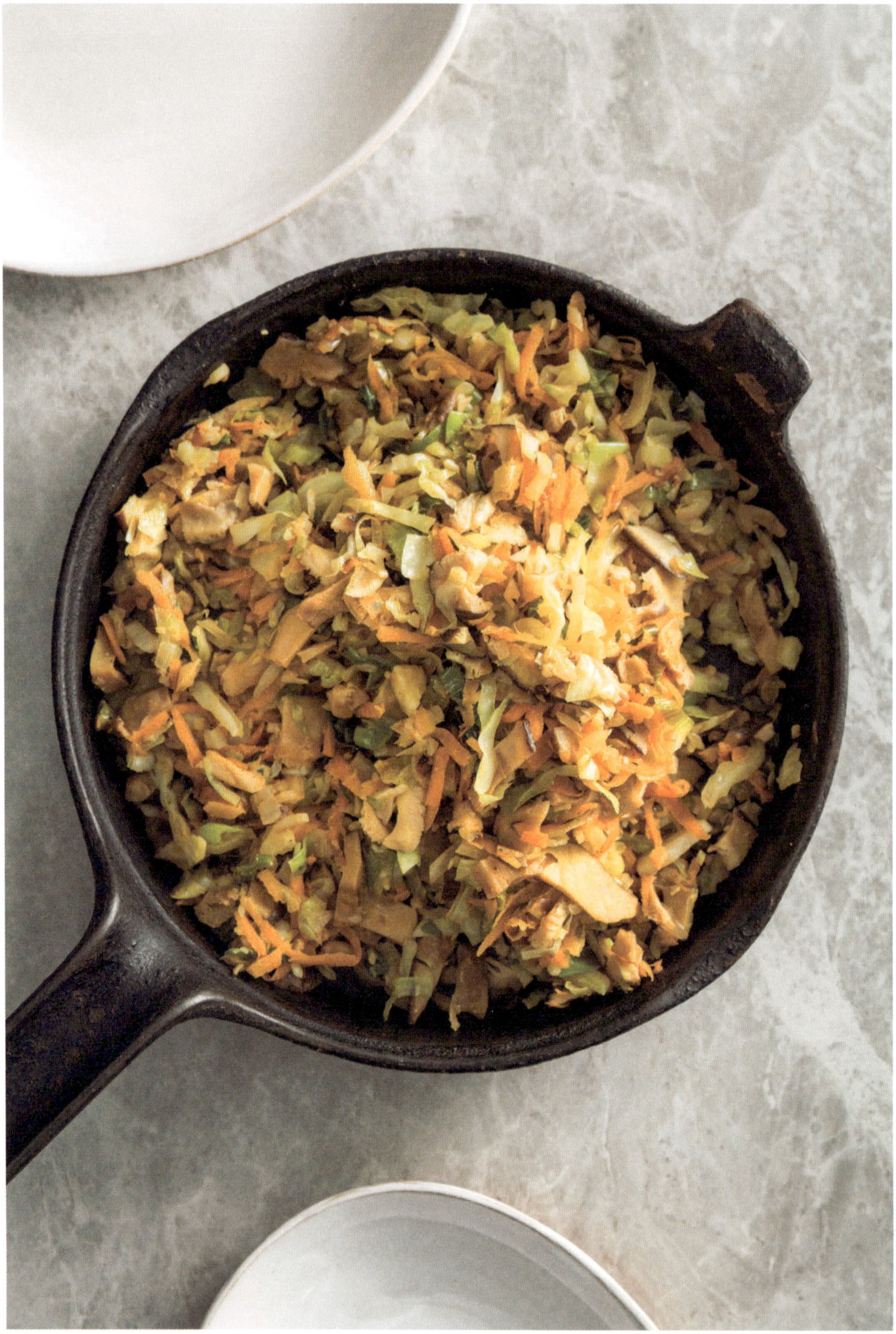

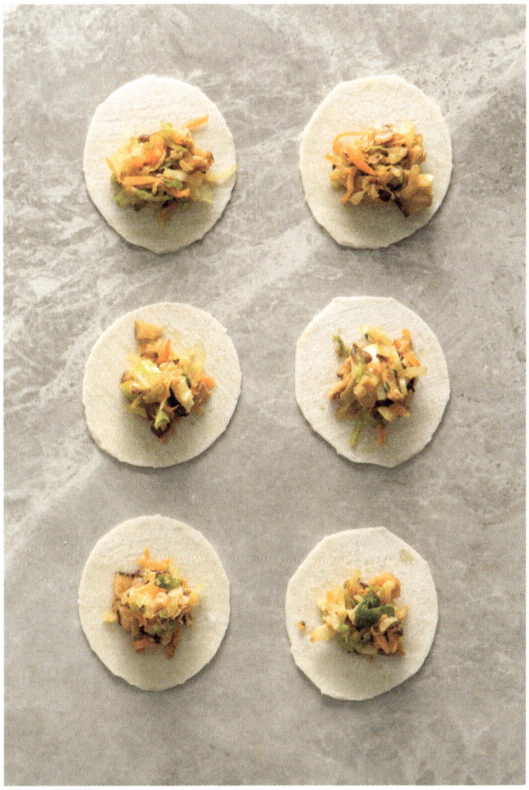
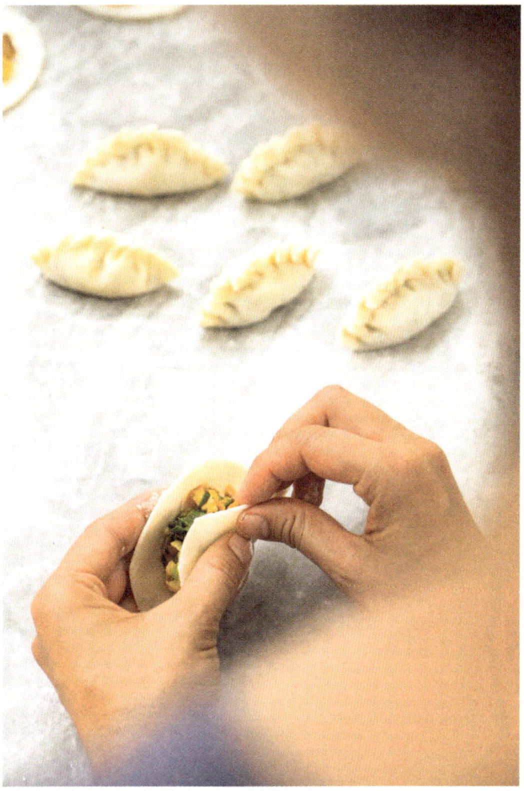
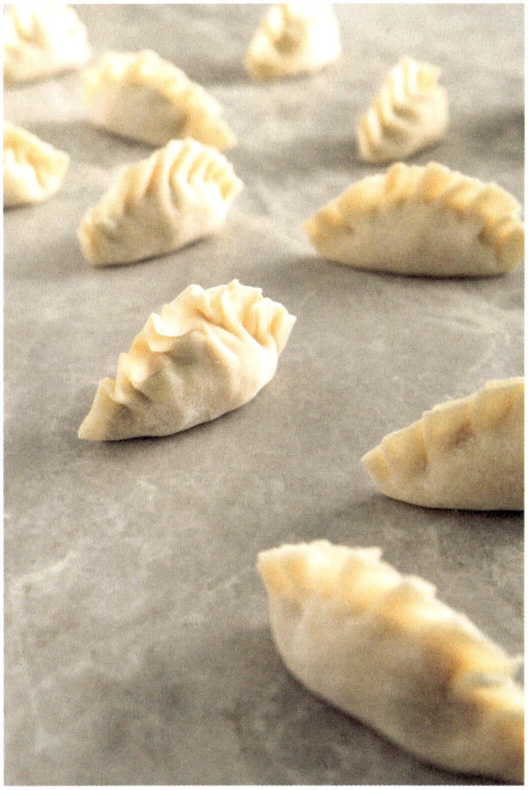
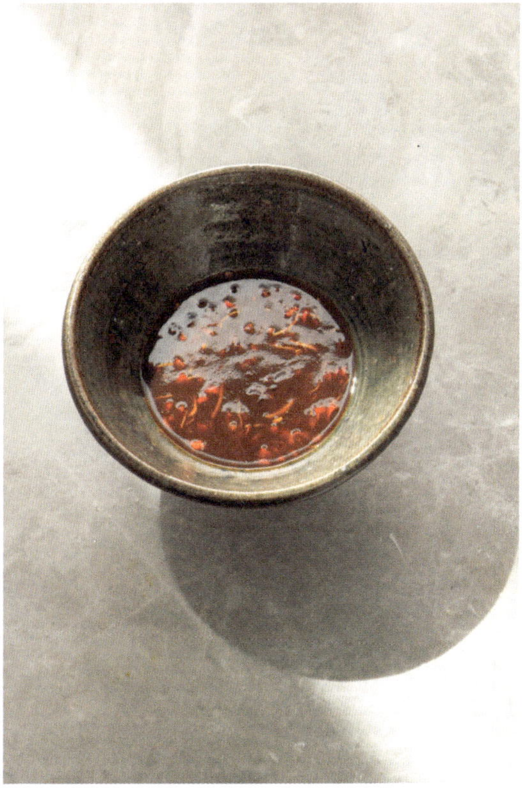

DF | VEGAN

VEGETABLE GYOZA (DUMPLINGS)

SERVES 4 (makes 30 dumplings)
Prep time: 45 minutes
Cook time: 20–25 minutes

2 tablespoons oil
1 onion, finely chopped
3–4 cloves garlic, finely chopped
1 tablespoon finely grated fresh ginger
3 cups finely chopped cabbage
4 spring onions, sliced
1 cup grated carrot
200g fresh shiitake mushrooms, stalk removed, finely diced
1 tablespoon miso paste
1 tablespoon soy sauce
½ teaspoon sesame oil
½ cup chopped coriander
30 dumpling pastry (gow gee) wrappers (300g packet)
oil, to cook dumplings
1–1½ cups hot vegetable stock, to cook dumplings

DIPPING SAUCE
1 tablespoon Hoisin sauce
1 tablespoon soy sauce
1 tablespoon rice vinegar
½ teaspoon sesame oil
½ teaspoon brown sugar
1 teaspoon finely grated fresh ginger
1 teaspoon finely chopped chilli or chilli sauce (optional)

Fresh, hand-made dumplings beat any pre-made ones you can buy, hands down. Many think they must be tricky and time-consuming to make, but you'd be surprised! Making the filling is easy, and then you can turn the dumpling filling and folding process into a fun, social affair where everyone sits around the table and helps out.

1. Heat oil in a large fry pan on medium to high heat. Cook onion, garlic and ginger for 1 minute, then add cabbage, spring onion, carrot and mushrooms. Stir-fry for 5–7 minutes until cabbage is soft. Add miso, soy sauce and sesame oil and continue cooking for a further 1–2 minutes. Turn off the heat and stir through coriander. Season to taste with salt and pepper. Transfer to a bowl and refrigerate to cool slightly.

2. Fill a small bowl with water. Dip your middle finger in the water and wet all around the edge of a dumpling wrapper. Place a teaspoonful of filling in the middle of the wrapper, then fold in half to form a semi-circle. Pinch the sides of the wrapper to seal. Crimp the seal to form pleats or use the prongs of a fork. Place dumplings, seam-side up, on a clean dry plate as you make them.

3. Heat 1–2 tablespoons of oil in a large cast-iron or non-stick fry pan on medium heat. Add 10–15 dumplings, seam-side up, and cook for 3–4 minutes until their bottoms are golden brown. Carefully pour ½ cup hot stock into the pan (be careful as it may splatter) and cover with a lid to steam for 1–2 minutes. Then uncover and continue cooking until most of the liquid has evaporated. Transfer dumplings to a serving plate.

4. Mix all dipping sauce ingredients together.

5. Serve dumplings with a small bowl of the dipping sauce.

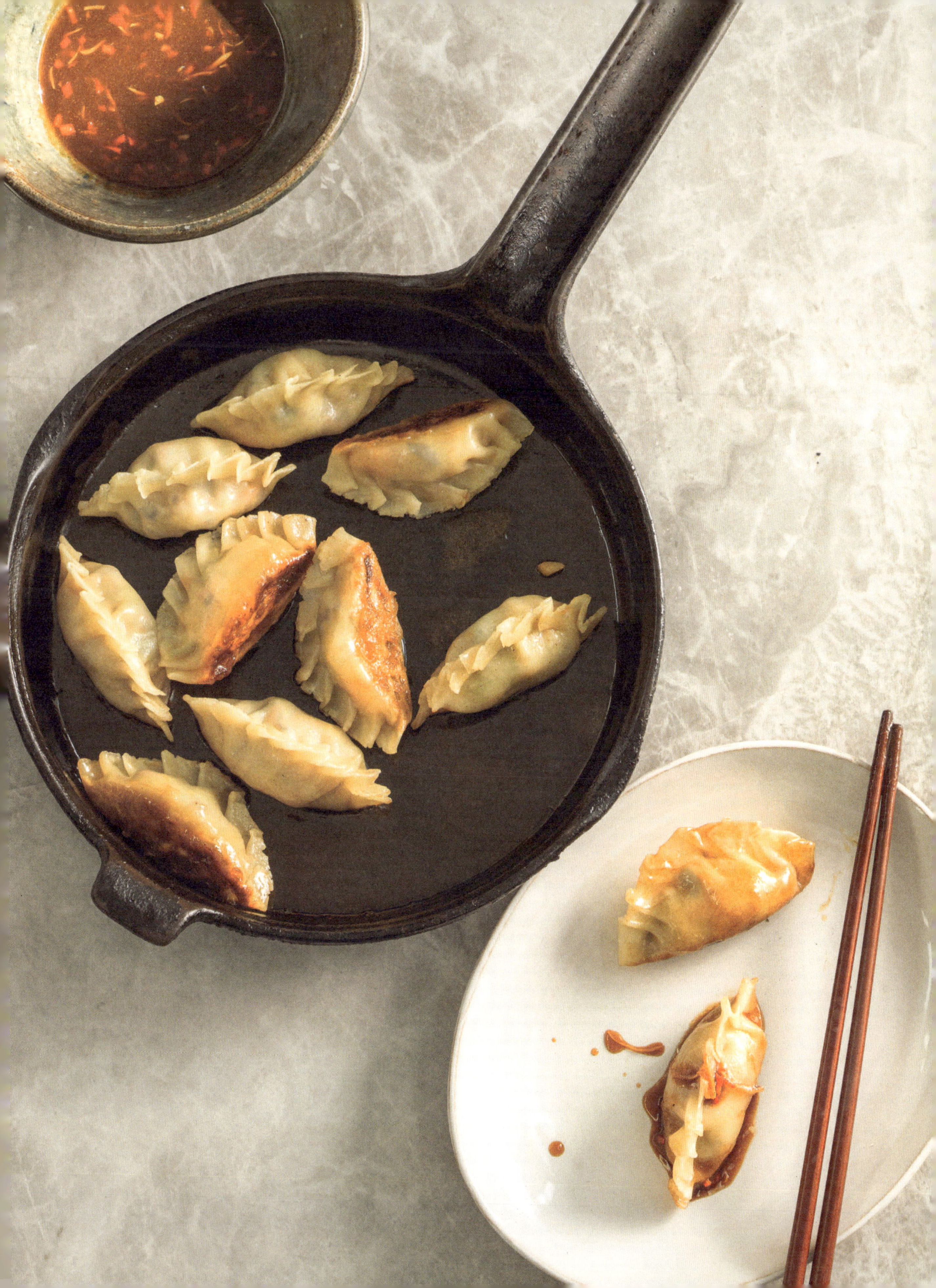

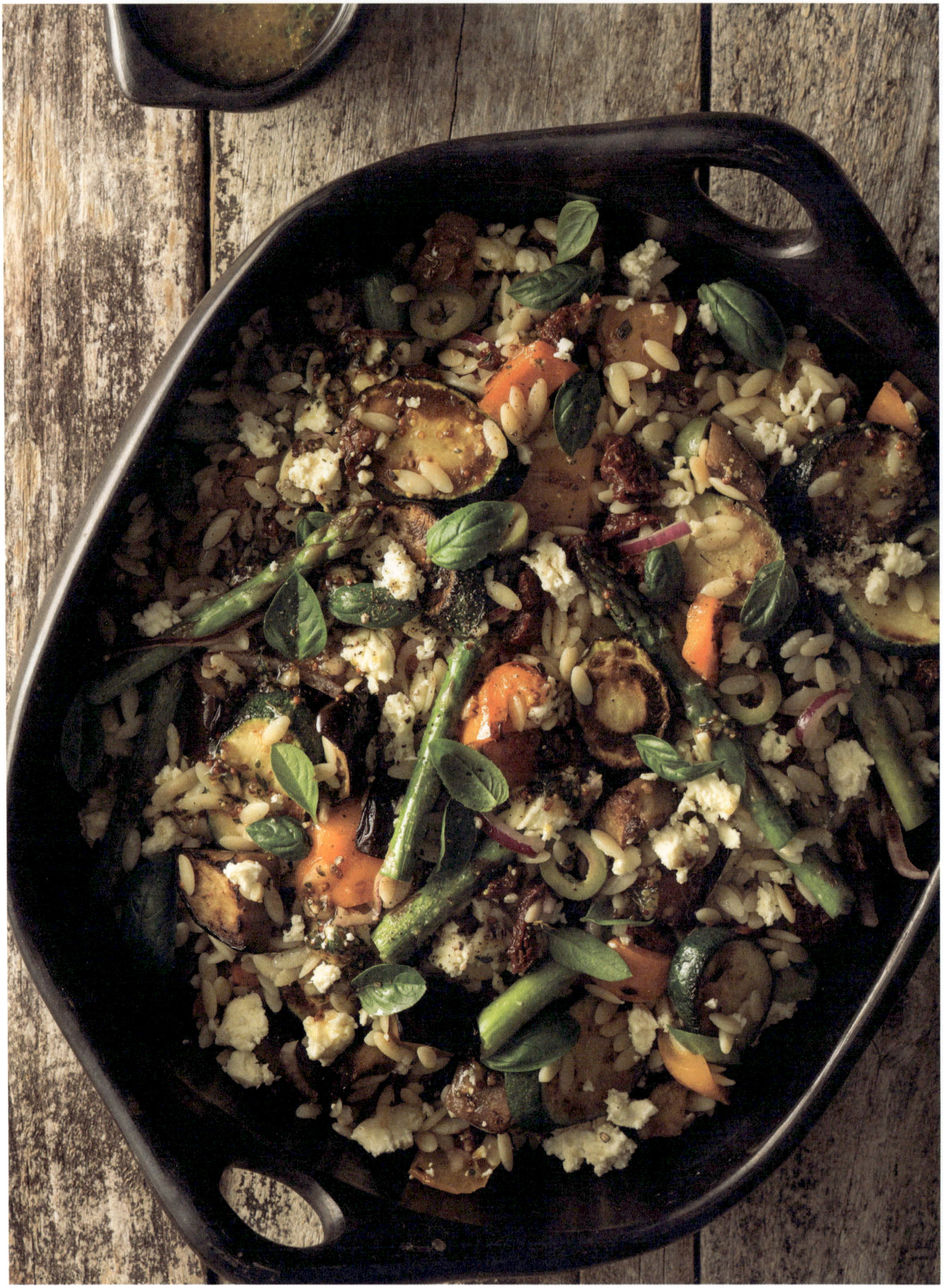

GF use GF pasta | DF use cashew feta | VEGAN use cashew feta

BBQ ORZO PASTA SALAD

SERVES 6
Prep time: 20 minutes
Cook time: 15–20 minutes

DRESSING
4 tablespoons olive oil
zest of 1 lemon
2 teaspoons wholegrain mustard
1 teaspoon honey
2 cloves garlic, crushed
1 tablespoon finely chopped thyme or rosemary leaves

SALAD
1 cup orzo/risoni pasta
1 small eggplant, diced 2cm
2 capsicums (red, yellow or orange), cored and cut into 2–3cm pieces
2 courgettes, sliced 1cm-thick on an angle
1 bunch asparagus spears or 150g green beans, trimmed
½ red onion, finely sliced
½ cup chopped sundried tomatoes
¼ cup pitted olives, sliced or 2 tablespoons roughly chopped capers (optional)
150–200g feta, crumbled
good handful of basil leaves

This one is perfect to take to a barbecue. Just pack the dressing separately and toss together before serving. Instead of pasta you can toss the vegetables with freekeh, bulghur or quinoa.

1. Bring a pot of well-salted water to the boil. Preheat barbecue (alternatively, preheat oven to 220°C).

2. Mix all dressing ingredients together.

3. Cook pasta in boiling water for 8–10 minutes or until al dente (just cooked). Drain and run under cold water (to cool and stop pasta sticking together).

4. Place eggplant, capsicums, courgettes and asparagus/green beans in a large bowl. Toss with a generous glug of olive oil and season with salt and pepper. Grill vegetables on the barbecue until soft and slightly charred (or roast in the oven for about 20 minutes, tossing once after 15 minutes). Allow to cool to room temperature.

5. Return grilled vegetables to large bowl, along with cooked pasta, red onion, sundried tomatoes, olives/capers (if using) and feta and toss with dressing. Season to taste with salt and pepper and toss with basil leaves just before serving.

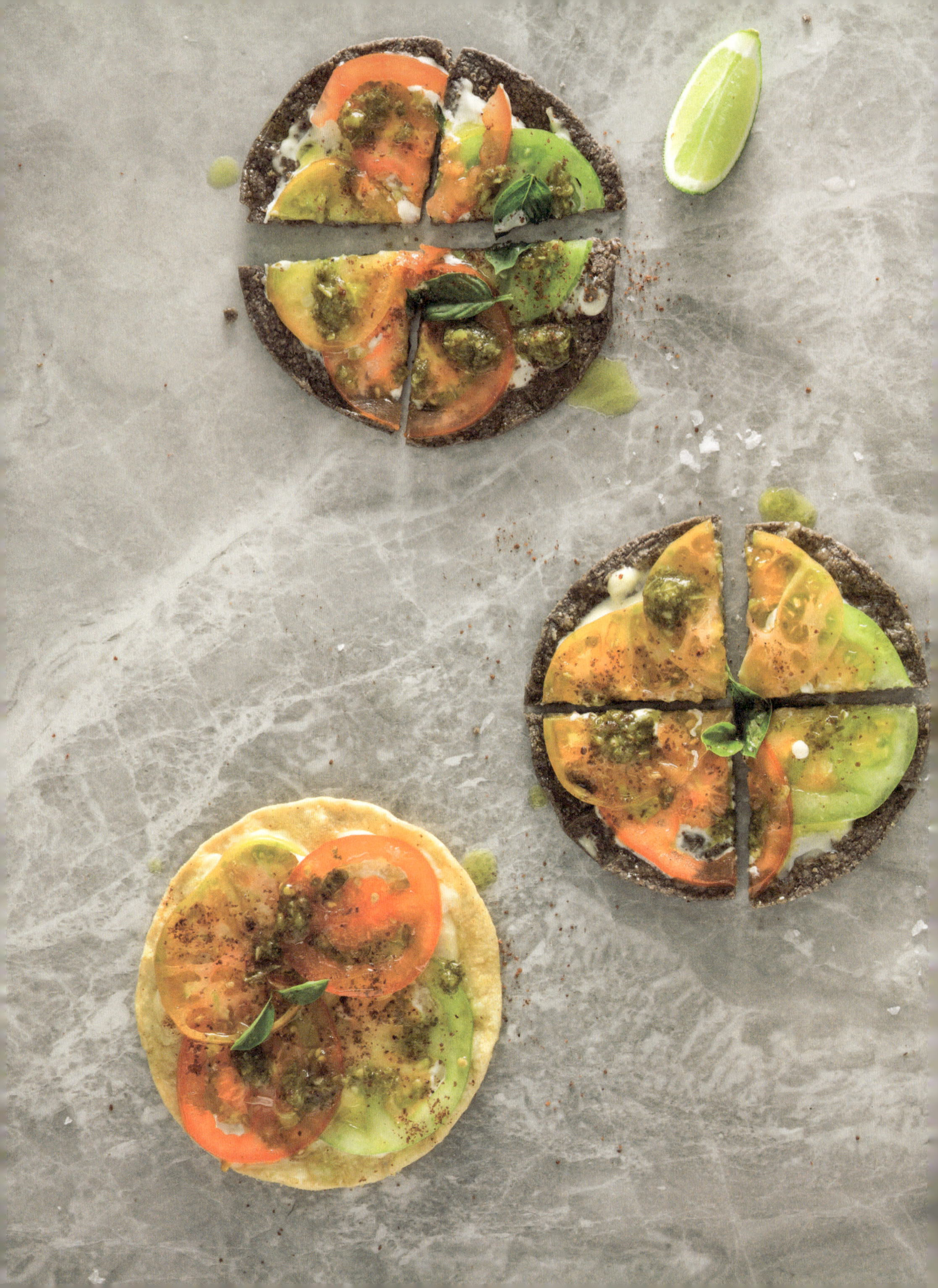

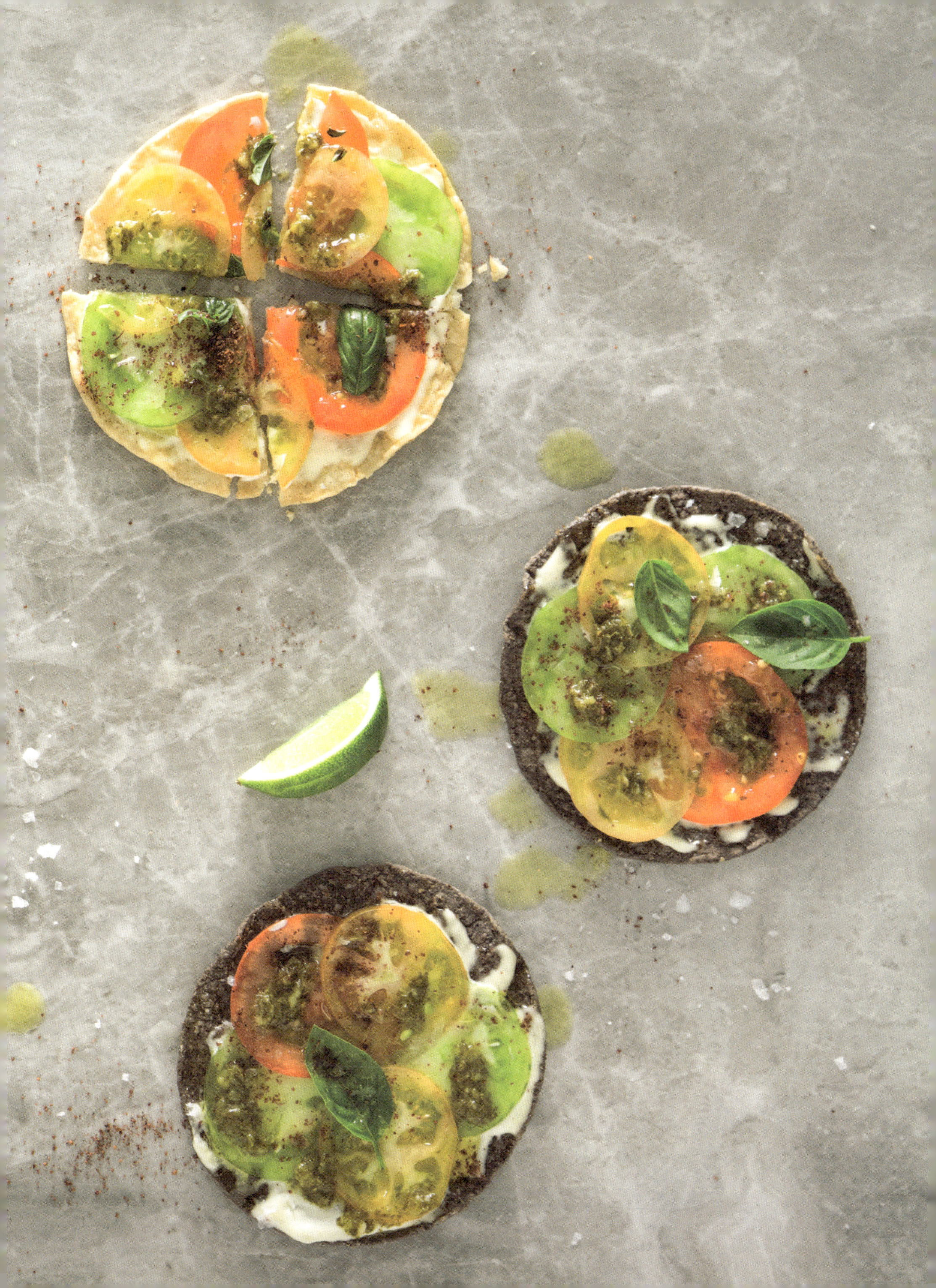

GF | DF | VEGAN use vegan mayo

TOMATO TOSTADAS WITH LIME MAYO

SERVES 4–6 (as a starter)
Prep time: 15–20 minutes

4 tablespoons Japanese Kewpie mayonnaise
juice and zest of 1 lime
12 tostadas
8–10 firm tomatoes (a mix of red, yellow and green, if you can)
flaky sea salt
good pinch of sumac (optional)
Jalapeño Chermoula (page 57), to drizzle
extra-virgin olive oil, to drizzle (ideally lemon-infused, if you have some)
baby basil leaves, to garnish

Tostadas are corn tortillas which have been either deep-fried or toasted — they make the perfect, crunchy corn chip-like base for a variety of tasty toppings. Sometimes you can buy them pre-made, but if not they're also easy to make — just brush small corn tortillas with oil on both sides and bake at 200°C for 12–15 minutes until crispy and allow to cool before topping.

1. Whisk mayonnaise and lime zest and juice until smooth.

2. Using a very sharp knife (or a serrated knife) very finely slice each tomato.

3. Spread 1 teaspoon of lime mayo over each tostada, then arrange slices of tomato on top. Season with flaky sea salt and sumac (if using), drizzle with Jalapeño Chermoula and a little extra-virgin olive oil. Garnish with basil leaves.

4. Leave for a few minutes to soften ever so slightly (which makes them easier to cut), before using a sharp, heavy knife to cut each tostada into quarters. Serve on a big wooden board.

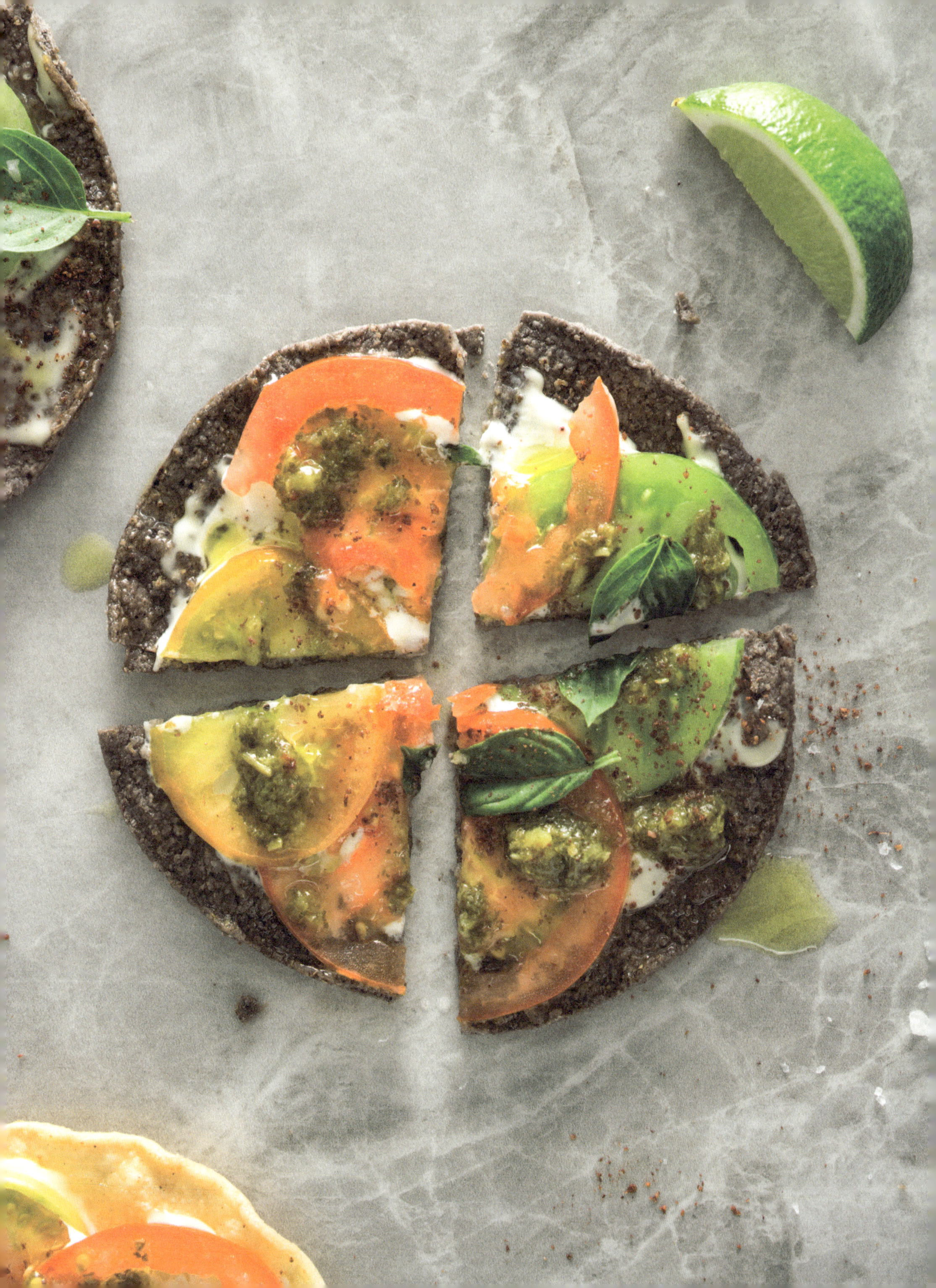

GF | DF omit haloumi and use coconut yoghurt | VEGAN omit haloumi and use coconut yoghurt

MARINATED VEGGIE KEBABS

SERVES 4–5
Prep time: 20 minutes
Cook time: 15 minutes

16 bamboo skewers

MARINADE AND DRESSING
¼ cup olive oil
zest and juice of 1 lemon
1 clove garlic
1 teaspoon ground coriander
¼ teaspoon ground cumin
½ teaspoon sweet or smoked paprika
½ teaspoon salt
2 tablespoons pickled jalapeños (from a jar, optional)
1 cup chopped parsley
1 cup chopped coriander

1 punnet cherry tomatoes
2 capsicums (red, yellow or orange), cut into 2–3cm pieces
1 red onion, cut into 2–3cm pieces
1 eggplant, cut into 2–3cm pieces
2 courgettes, sliced 1cm thick
200–250g haloumi, cut into 16 cubes
½ cup natural, unsweetened yoghurt, to serve

Marinating the vegetables and haloumi makes these kebabs all the more succulent and delicious, and cooking them on the barbecue will add a subtle smokiness. You can't have a barbecue without these on the menu and, what's more, kids love them too!

1. Soak bamboo skewers in a dish of water for at least 20 minutes while you prepare the marinade and vegetables.

2. Place all marinade ingredients, except parsley and coriander, in a food processor or high-speed blender and blend until smooth. Add parsley and coriander and pulse a few times until the herbs are finely chopped. Reserve 2 tablespoons of marinade for the yoghurt dressing.

3. Place vegetables and haloumi in a large bowl or zip-lock bag and add marinade. Toss to combine and coat the vegetables. If you have time, leave to marinate in the fridge for 4–6 hours.

4. Preheat barbecue or oven grill. Thread vegetables onto wet skewers, so that the vegetables are lightly touching each other. I like to place a piece of courgette on first, followed by capsicum, eggplant, haloumi, red onion, another piece of courgette, and finally a cherry tomato.

5. Brush skewered vegetables with oil. Grill kebabs for 10–15 minutes, turning once or twice, until vegetables are soft and haloumi is golden.

6. Arrange kebabs on a platter. Mix reserved marinade with yoghurt and drizzle over kebabs just before serving.

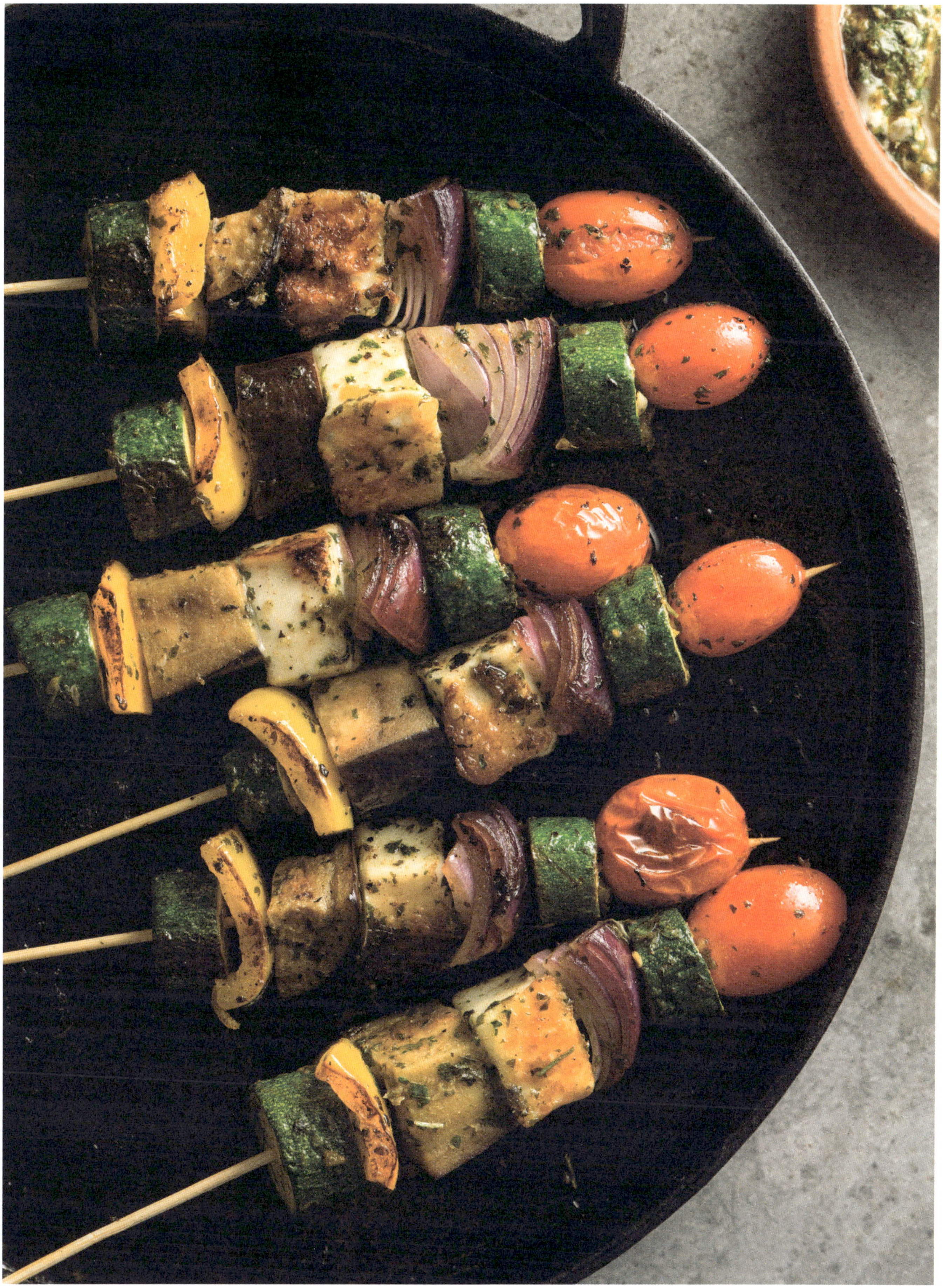

GF

CUCUMBER, CHUTNEY & HALOUMI CANAPÉS

SERVES 4–6 (makes 20 canapés)
Prep time: 10 minutes
Cook time: 5 minutes

2 Lebanese cucumbers or 1 thin telegraph cucumber
¼ cup Moroccan Apricot and Tomato Chutney (page 158) or similar store-bought chutney
200g haloumi
baby basil or mint leaves

These are a great little vegetarian canapé that's quick, simple and easy to put together. And super tasty!

1. Peel cucumber but leave a few 'stripes' of skin on. Cut cucumber into 1cm-thick rounds.

2. Top each cucumber round with ½ teaspoon chutney.

3. Pat haloumi dry with paper towels and slice 1cm thick, then cut each slice into 4 squares. Heat a drizzle of olive oil in a non-stick fry pan on medium to high heat. Pan-fry pieces of haloumi on each side until golden (about 1 minute each side).

4. Top each canapé with a piece of haloumi and garnish with basil/mint leaves.

GF | DF | VEGAN

MINT CHERMOULA

MAKES A GENEROUS ½ CUP

1 packed cup mint leaves
¼ packed cup chopped coriander or flat-leaf parsley
¼ cup extra-virgin olive oil
finely grated zest and juice of 1 lemon
1 clove garlic, chopped

Useful as a dressing or marinade, and to drizzle.

1. Blend all ingredients together in a blender or food processor until well combined. Season to taste with salt and pepper.

Jalapeño Chermoula
Use ¾ packed cup mint leaves and ¾ packed cup coriander and add ¼ cup fresh or pickled jalapeños (from a jar).

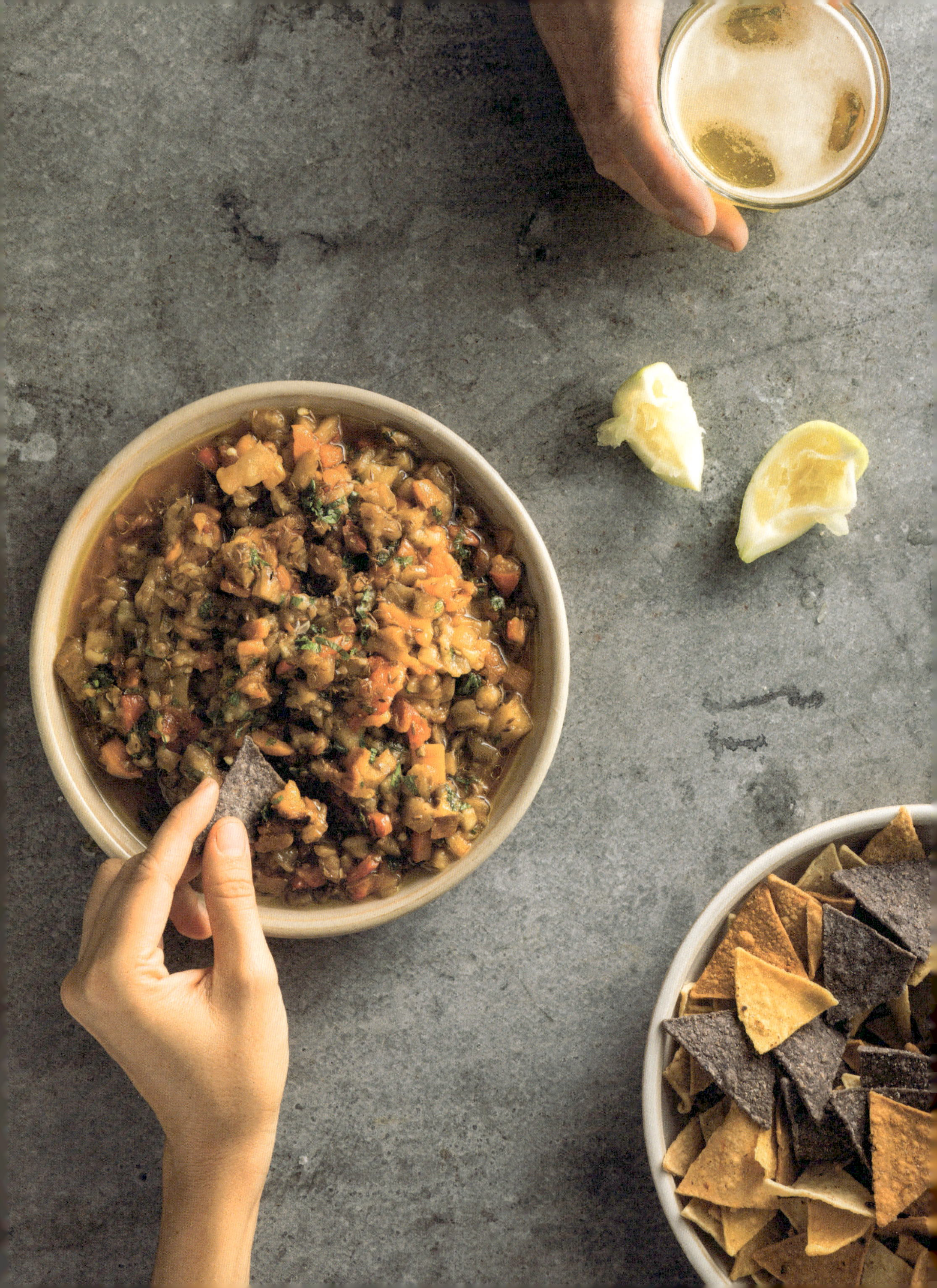

GF | DF | VEGAN

CHARRED EGGPLANT, CAPSICUM & MINT

SERVES 4 (as a starter)
Prep time: 10 minutes
Cook time: 30 minutes

1 medium eggplant
2 capsicums (red and/or yellow)
1 teaspoon toasted and crushed cumin seeds
½ teaspoon smoked paprika
juice of 1 lemon
2 tablespoons chopped mint leaves
2–3 tablespoons extra-virgin olive oil

This delicious dip, sauce, condiment or whatever you might call it was inspired by my travels in Turkey where they served something very similar with toasted pita bread. Charring the eggplant and capsicum gives a smoky flavour, although it's fine to roast them in the oven if you prefer. Delicious piled on top of bruschetta (page 191), or with flatbreads or corn chips, or part of a platter with crackers, olives, dips and cheese.

1. Prick eggplant in several places with the tip of a sharp knife. Barbecue whole eggplant and whole capsicums for about 30 minutes, turning about halfway through cooking, or until skin is charred, blackened and the eggplant flesh is very soft inside. You can also char them over a naked flame, turning them occasionally with metal tongs, until their skins are blackened and blistered. Alternatively, you can cook the eggplant and capsicums (whole) in a 220°C oven for about 45 minutes until they are soft and their skins are charred and blistered. Set aside to cool for about 5 minutes.

2. Peel capsicums — the skin should come off easily. Remove seeds and dice soft flesh. Cut eggplant in half lengthways, scoop out soft flesh with a spoon and dice.

3. Place eggplant and capsicum in a bowl with cumin and smoked paprika and mix to combine. Mix in lemon juice, mint and extra-virgin olive oil and season to taste with salt and freshly ground black pepper.

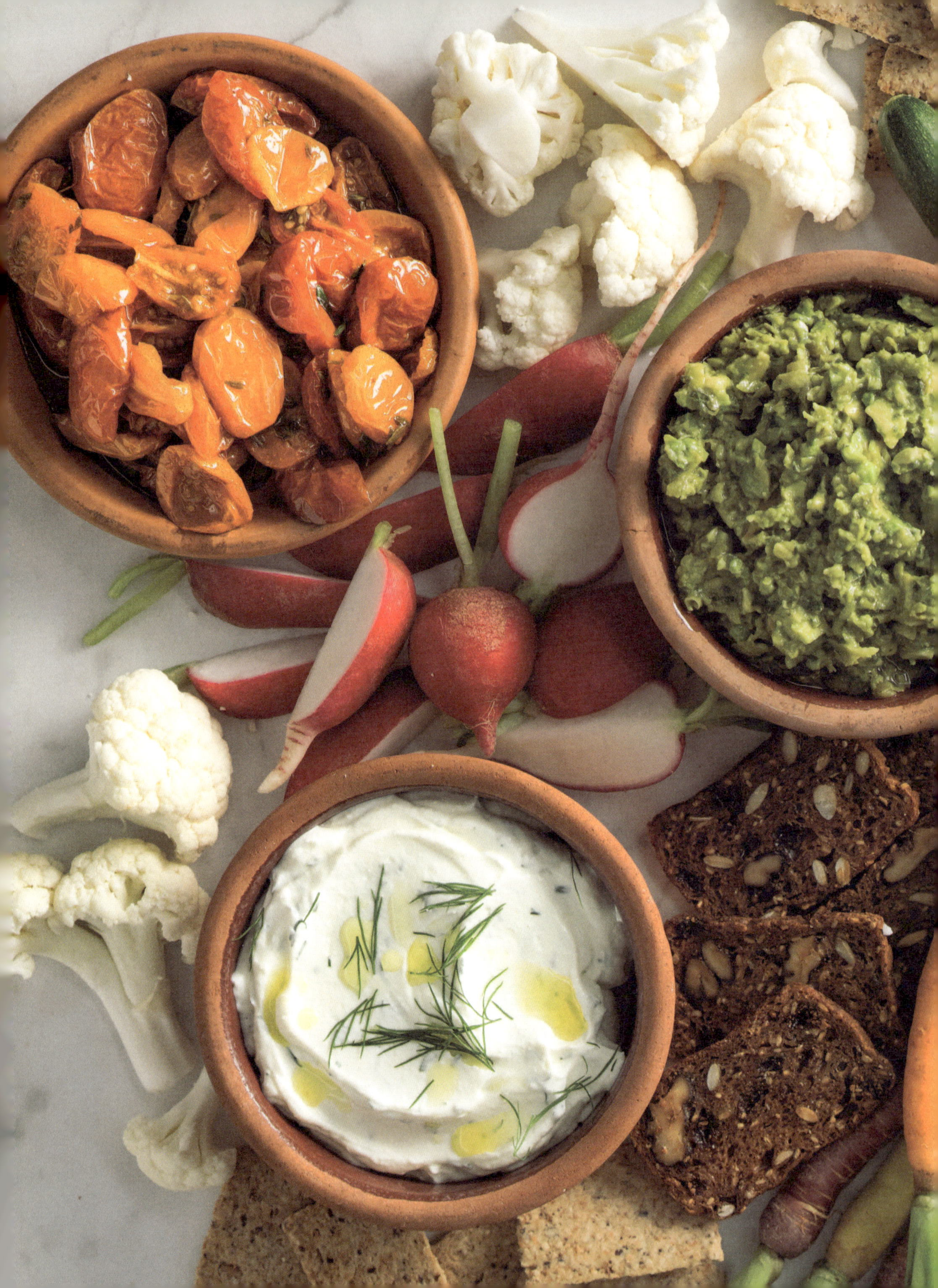

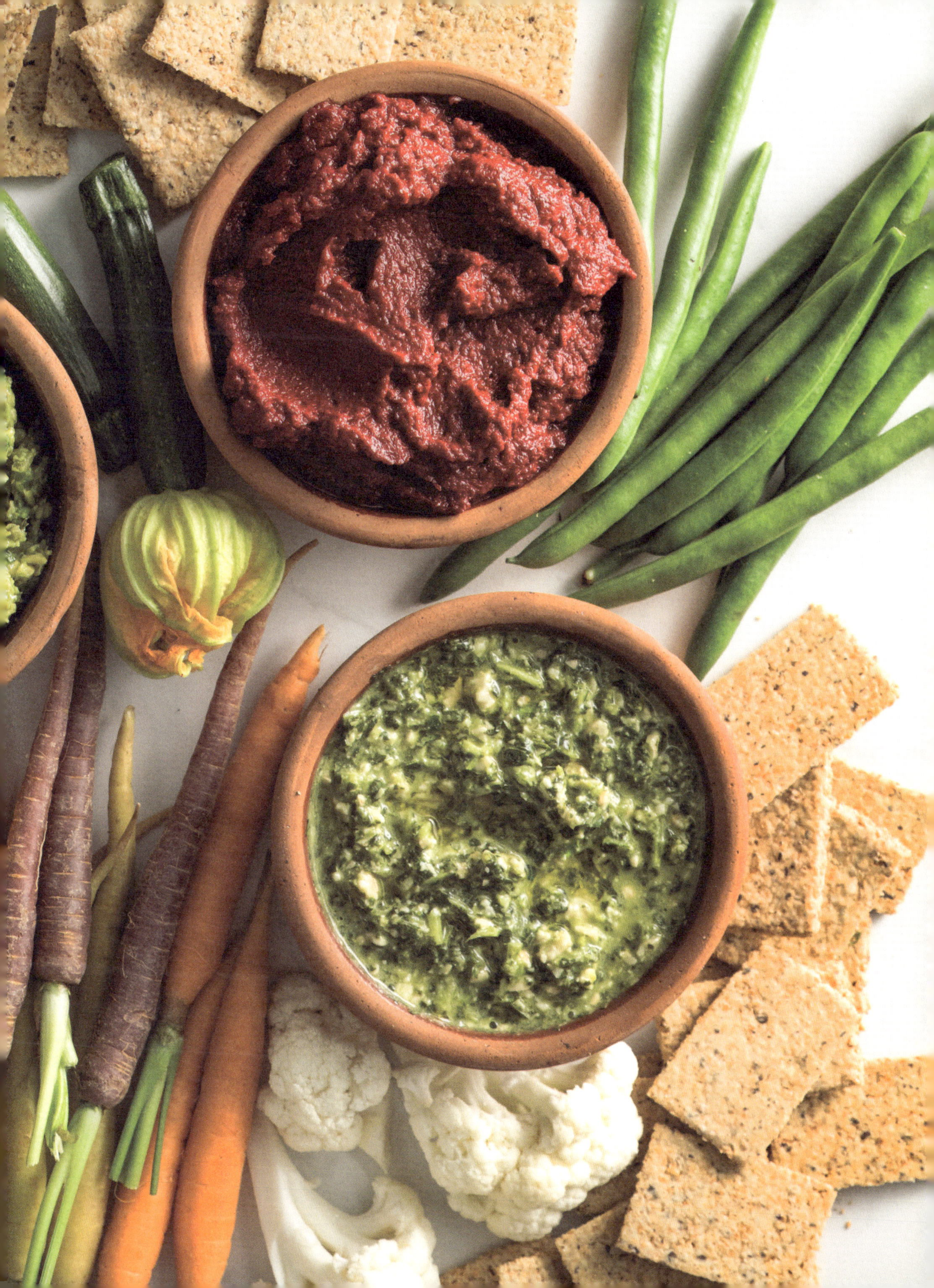

GF | DF use coconut yoghurt | VEGAN use coconut yoghurt and maple syrup

BEETROOT & CRÈME FRAÎCHE DIP

MAKES 1½–2 CUPS
Prep time: 10 minutes
Cook time: 25–30 minutes

2 medium beetroot, peeled and cut into 3cm pieces
2 teaspoons olive oil
2 teaspoons honey or maple syrup
1 teaspoon ground cumin
1 teaspoon ground coriander
½ teaspoon fennel seeds
juice of ½ lemon
1 clove garlic, chopped
zest of ½ orange
⅓–½ cup crème fraîche, sour cream, unsweetened Greek yoghurt or coconut yoghurt

A delicious creamy beetroot dip.

1. Preheat oven to 180°C.
2. Toss beetroot with olive oil, honey/maple syrup, cumin, coriander and fennel seeds in a baking dish, season with salt and pepper and roast for 25–30 minutes until tender. Leave to cool in the fridge.
3. Blitz cold beetroot with lemon juice, garlic and orange zest until smooth.
4. Add crème fraîche and pulse a few times until just combined. Season to taste with salt and pepper.

GF | DF | VEGAN

LEMONY PEA & AVOCADO DIP

MAKES 1½–2 CUPS
Prep time: 5 minutes

1 cup peas, broad beans or edamame beans (fresh or defrosted from frozen)
½–¾ cup mint leaves
zest and juice of 1 juicy lemon
1 small or ½ large ripe avocado, chopped

You can use fresh or frozen peas, broad beans or edamame beans.

1. Place peas/beans, mint and lemon zest and juice in a food processor and pulse a few times until finely chopped.
2. Add avocado and a good pinch of salt and pulse a few more times to combine.
3. Season to taste with more salt and lemon juice, if needed.

GF | DF | VEGAN

CORIANDER, LIME & CASHEW PESTO

MAKES ABOUT 1 CUP
Prep time: 10 minutes

1½ cups chopped coriander (leaves and stalks)
½ cup chopped parsley
½ clove garlic, chopped
1 kaffir lime leaf, stem removed and finely chopped
⅓ cup roasted cashew nuts
zest of 1 and juice of 2 juicy limes (or 1 lemon)
¼ cup extra-virgin olive oil

A zesty take on pesto. It will keep in the fridge for up to a few days or can be frozen in a small resealable bag.

1. Place coriander, parsley, garlic, kaffir lime leaf and cashew nuts in a food processor and pulse a few times until finely chopped, scraping down the sides of the bowl as necessary to make sure everything is incorporated.

2. Add lime zest and juice, extra-virgin olive oil and a pinch of salt, and pulse a couple more times until combined. Season to taste with more salt and lime/lemon juice, if needed.

GF | DF use coconut yoghurt | VEGAN use coconut yoghurt

LABNE

MAKES ABOUT 1½ CUPS
Prep time: 6–8 hours

500g natural, unsweetened, thick yoghurt or coconut yoghurt

HERBED LABNE
Mix labne with 2 tablespoons chopped parsley, coriander or basil and 2–3 teaspoons finely chopped thyme or rosemary, and season with salt and pepper.

SWEET LABNE
Mix labne with 1–2 tablespoons honey and zest of 1 lime (optional).

Labne is simply yoghurt that has been strained, removing the whey and leaving a thick, spreadable yoghurt dip that's tangy and creamy, and superb in both a sweet and savoury scenario.

1. Line a large sieve with muslin cloth or a clean tea towel or paper towels and place over a large (deep) bowl.

2. Place yoghurt in the lined sieve, cover well with a plate or clingfilm (so it doesn't take on any fridge smells or flavours) and leave in the fridge for at least 6 hours, or overnight, until whey has strained away leaving behind a very thick, spreadable yoghurt (labne).

3. Flavour with herbs, or honey and lime zest (see left).

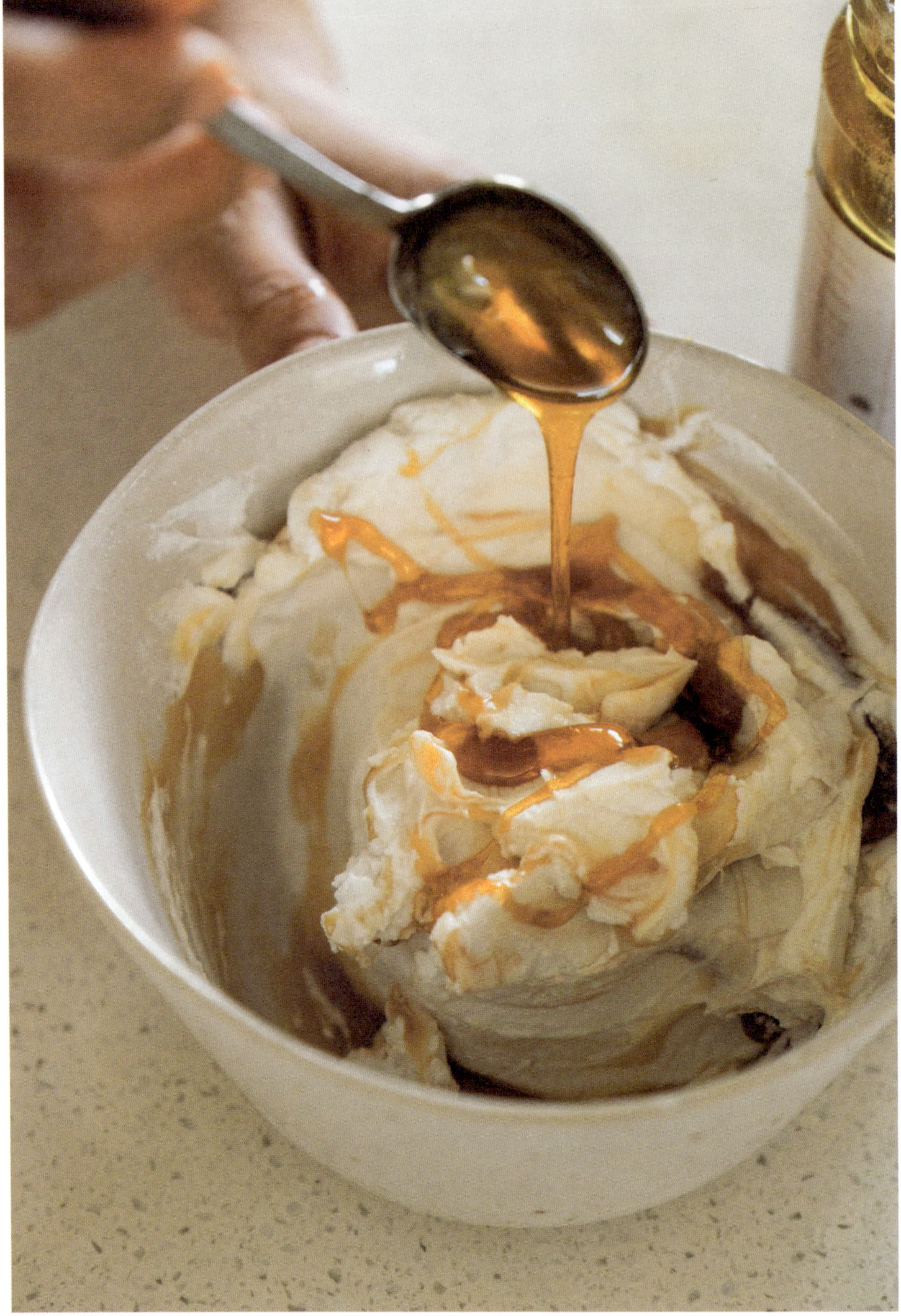

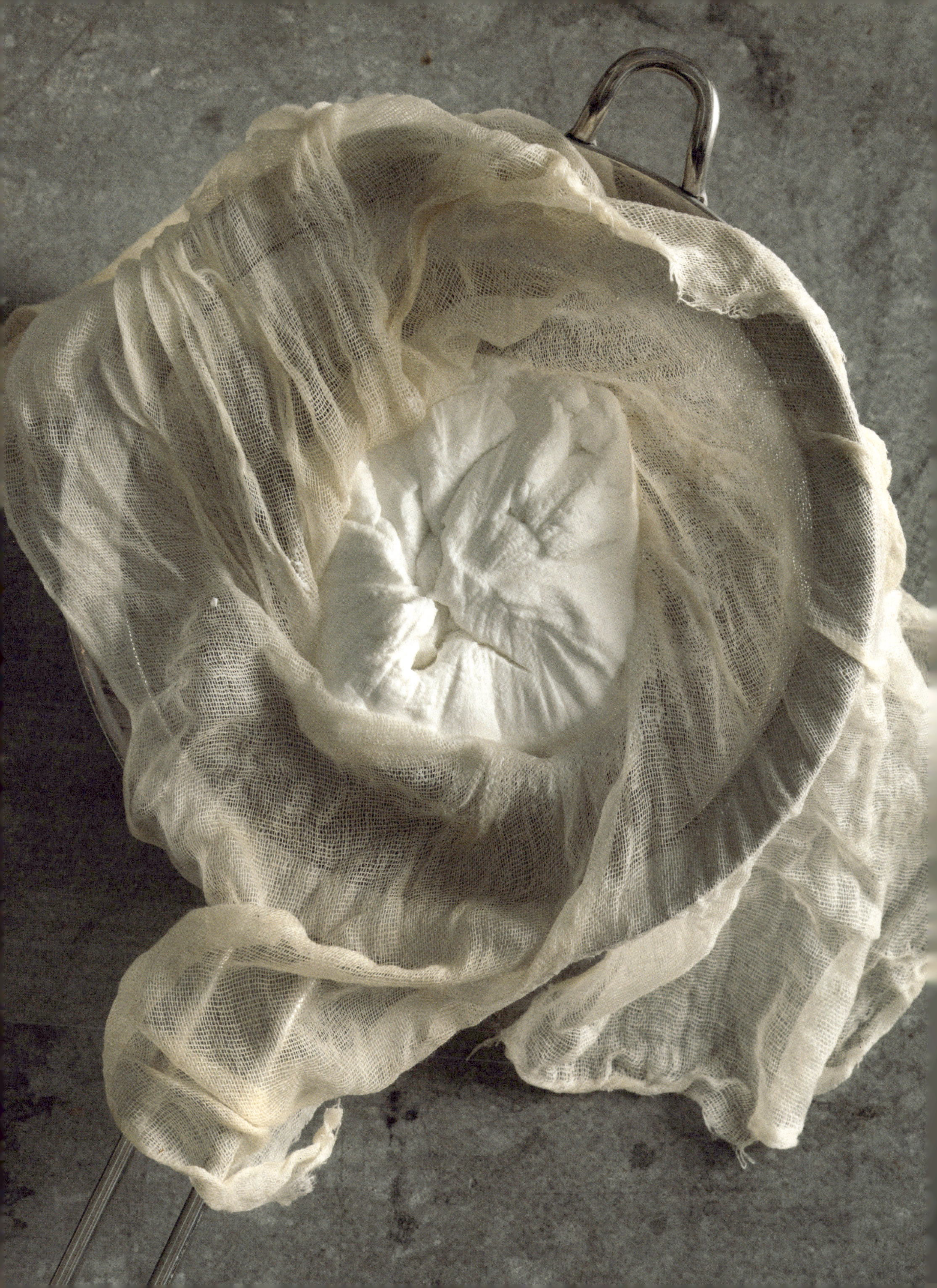

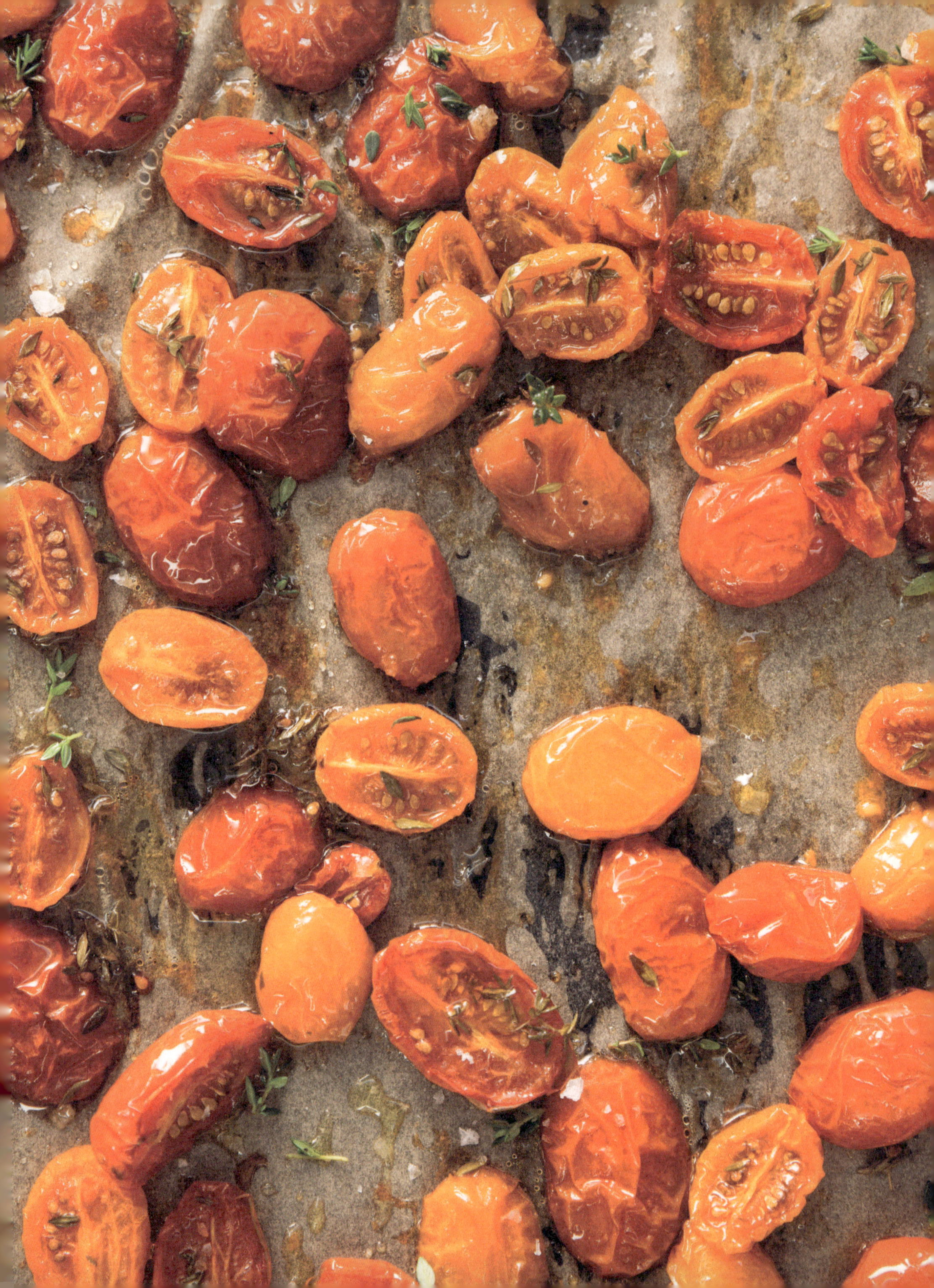

GF | DF | VEGAN use maple syrup instead of honey

HONEY & THYME ROAST TOMATOES

SERVES 4–6 (as part of a platter)
Prep time: 10 minutes
Cook time: 2 hours

2 punnets (500g) cherry tomatoes, cut in half
1½ tablespoons olive oil
1½ tablespoons liquid honey
2 tablespoons thyme leaves

Sweet, tangy, juicy and sticky, these roast tomatoes are bursting with flavour. They complement just about any dish and are fantastic simply piled on bruschetta (page 191), tossed through pasta or salads, or as part of a platter with dips, crackers and cheese.

1. Preheat oven to 120°C. Line an oven tray with baking paper.

2. In a large bowl, toss tomatoes with olive oil, honey and thyme.

3. Tip onto lined tray and spread out in a single layer. Season with salt and pepper. Roast for about 2 hours or until tomatoes are soft and shrivelled, but still a little juicy.

4. Serve as part of a platter with herbed labne (page 63), dips, crackers, bread and cheese.

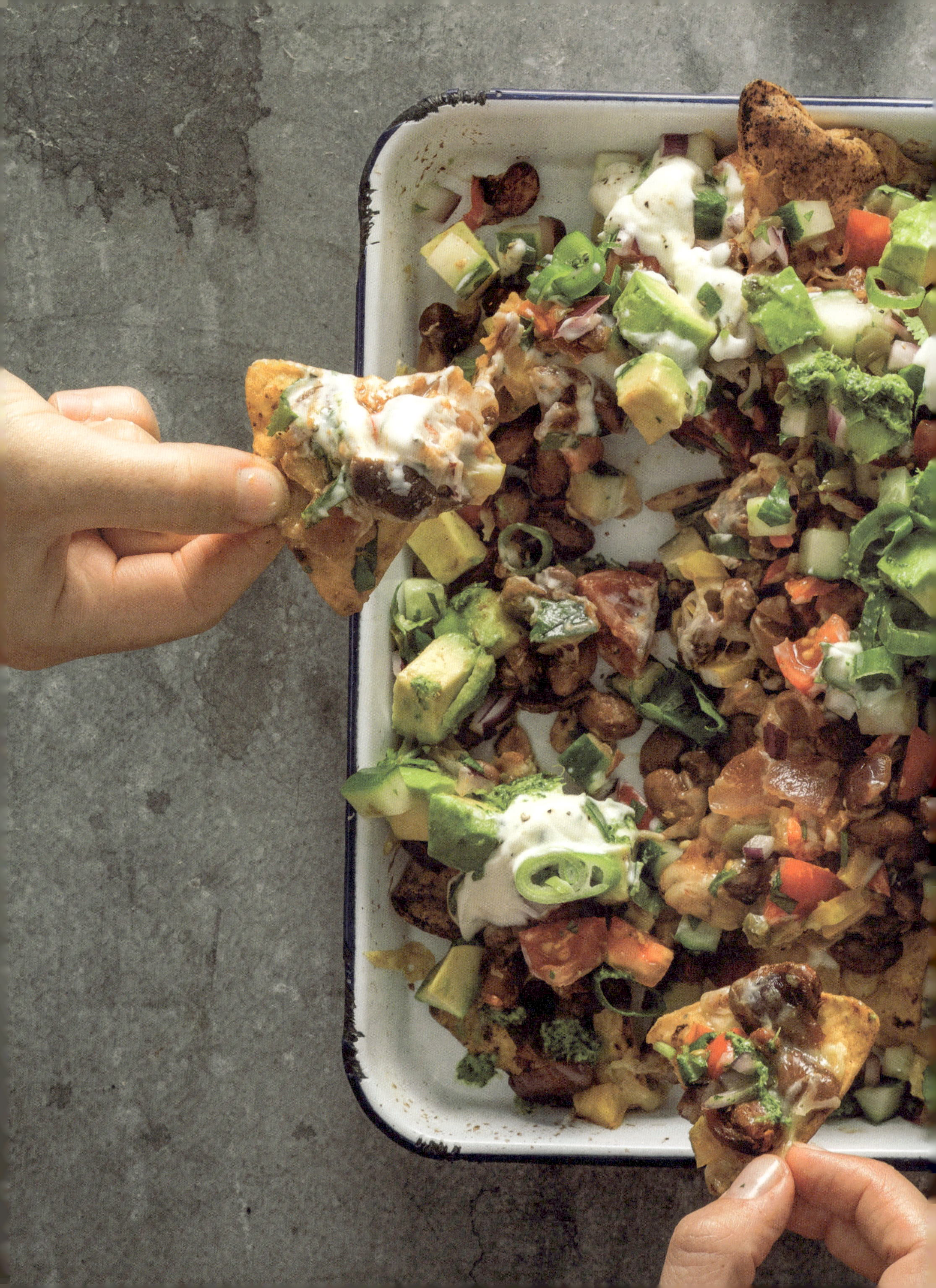

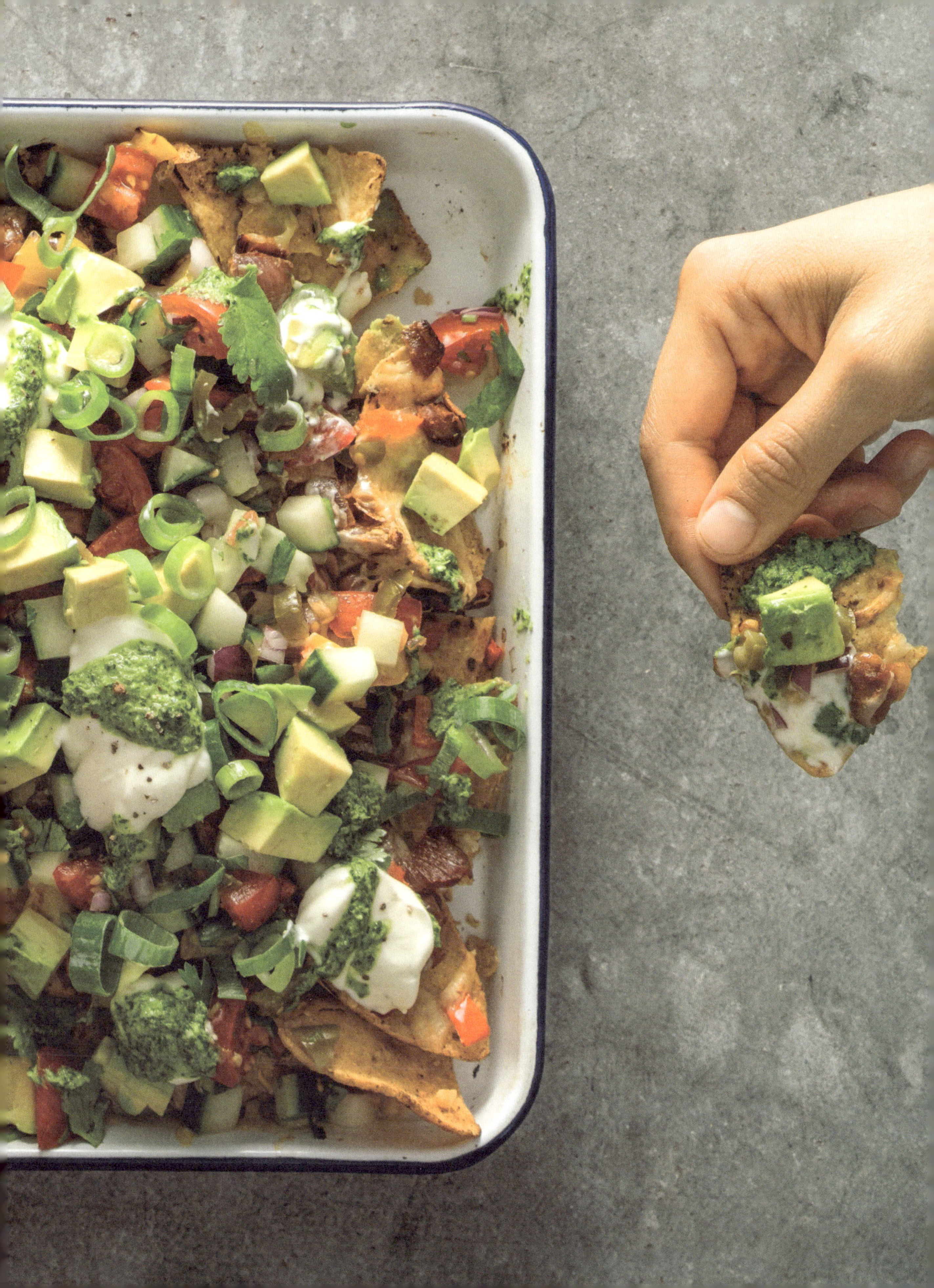

GF | DF omit cheese | VEGAN omit cheese, use coconut yoghurt

ZINGY NACHOS

SERVES 4
Prep time: 20 minutes
Cook time: 20 minutes

BEAN MIXTURE
2 tablespoons olive oil
1 large red onion, finely chopped
2 cloves garlic, finely chopped
1 teaspoon ground cumin
½ teaspoon smoked paprika
good pinch of cayenne pepper or ground chilli (optional)
400g can pinto beans, black beans or kidney beans, rinsed and drained
2 tablespoons tomato paste
2 tablespoons chipotle sauce

CHIPS AND TOPPINGS
150–200g good-quality corn chips
1 red capsicum or Palermo capsicum, cored and diced
1 yellow or green capsicum, cored and diced
1 cup grated cheese

TO SERVE
Tomato, Jalapeño and Coriander Salsa (page 190)
1 just-ripe avocado, diced
2 spring onions, finely sliced
¾ cup natural, unsweetened Greek yoghurt or sour cream
¼ cup Jalapeño Chermoula (page 57, optional)
1 lime, cut into wedges

You may or may not know that I'm a nachos fanatic. I have lots of different versions of nachos that I make and enjoy, but what they all have in common is freshness — they have to be super loaded with fresh veg, avocado and herbs, and these nachos are no exception! Plus they have lots of zing from the Jalapeño Chermoula! They don't even necessarily need cheese as there is so much flavour going on without it, so they're easy to make dairy-free and vegan.

1. Preheat oven to 180°C.

2. Heat olive oil in a large fry pan on medium heat. Cook onion and garlic, with a pinch of salt, for 4–5 minutes, until soft. Add cumin, paprika and cayenne/chilli (if using) and cook for a further minute. Add beans, tomato paste and chipotle sauce, and continue cooking for a further 5 minutes.

3. Tip corn chips into a large flat baking dish. Dollop with bean mixture, sprinkle with capsicum and cheese. Bake for 10 minutes then switch to grill for a few minutes until cheese is bubbly and golden.

4. Top with dollops of sour cream/yoghurt, Tomato, Jalapeño and Coriander Salsa, avocado and spring onions. Drizzle with Jalapeño Chermoula (if using) and serve with lime wedges to squeeze over. Eat immediately.

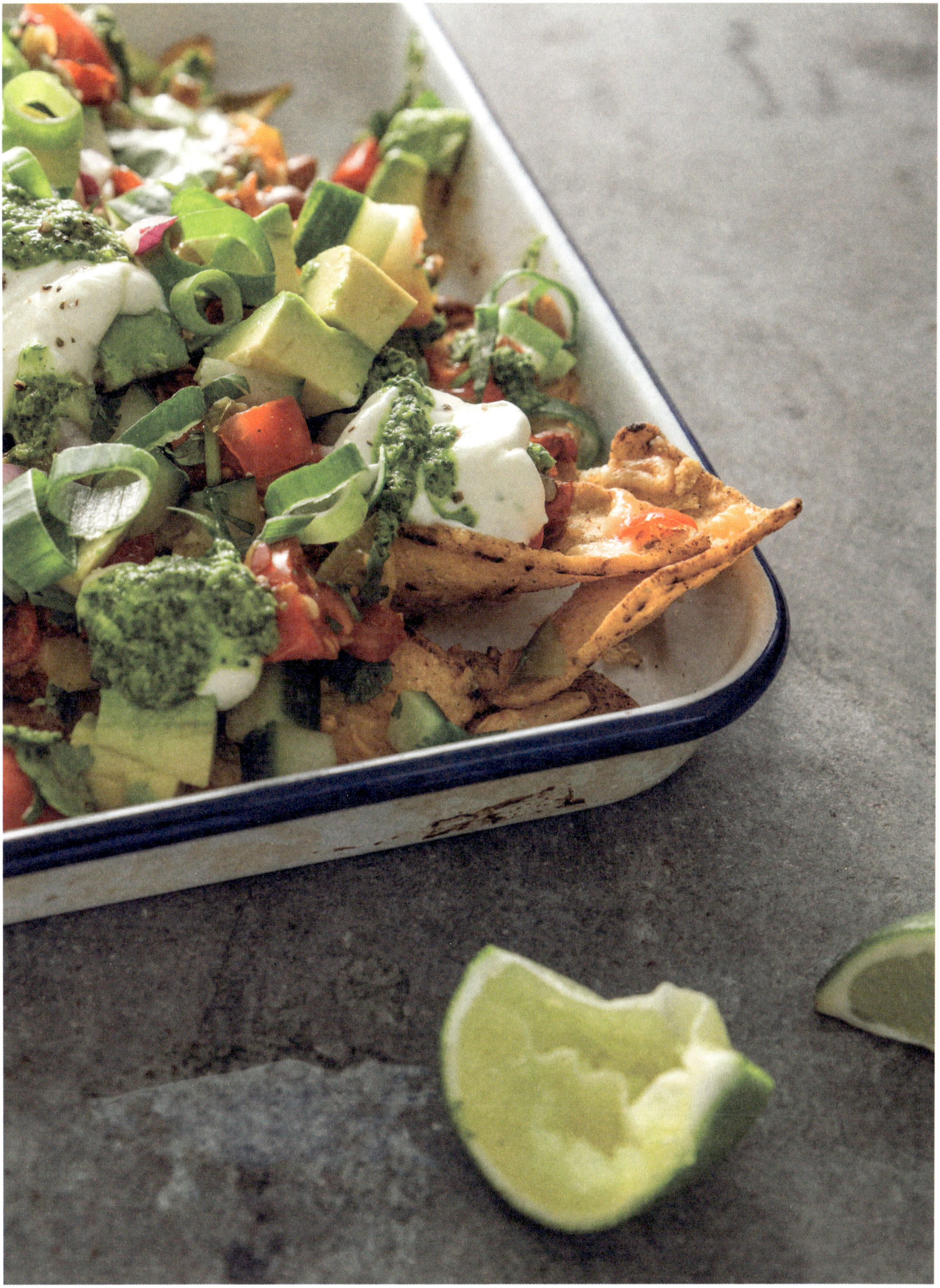

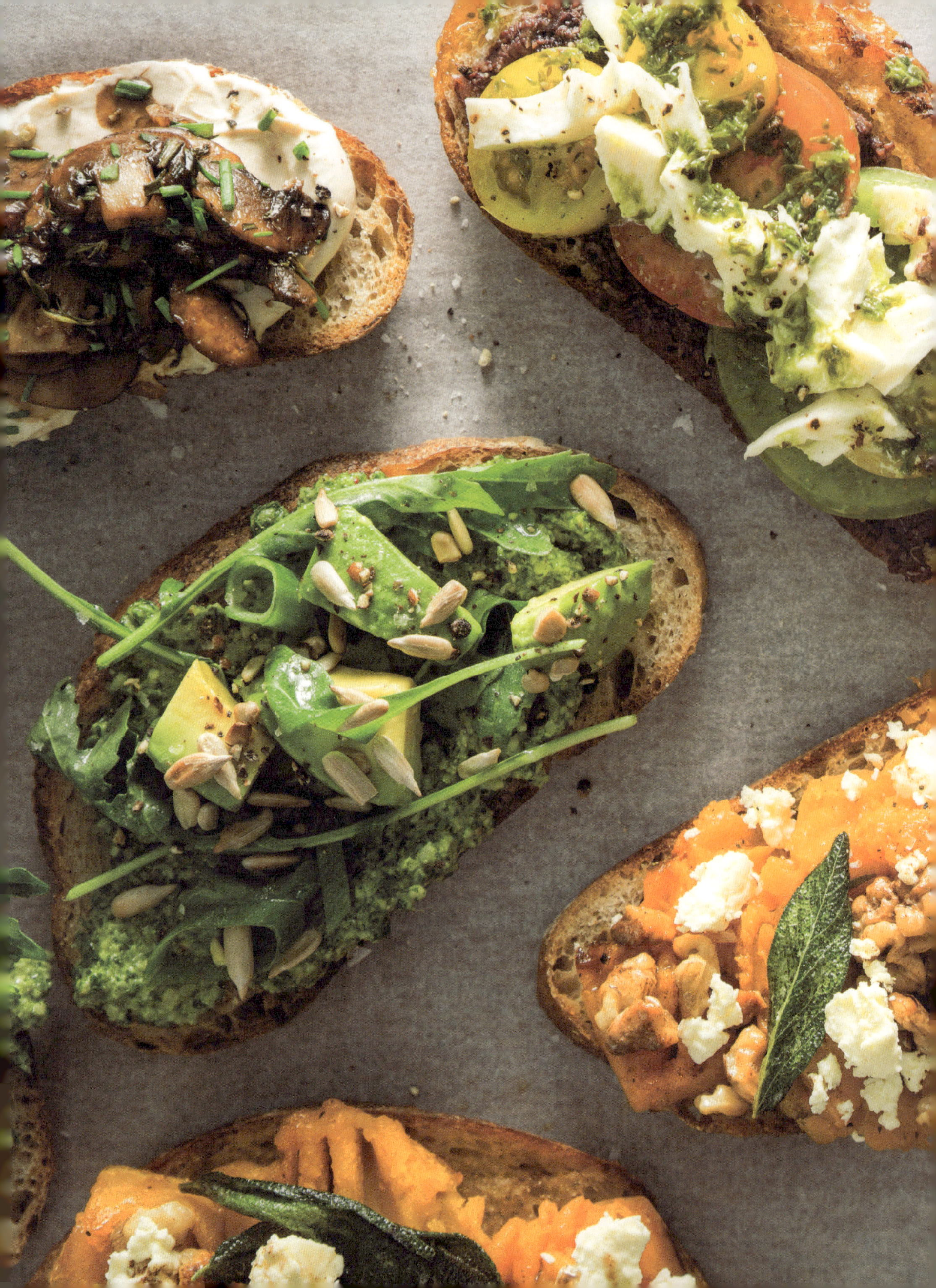

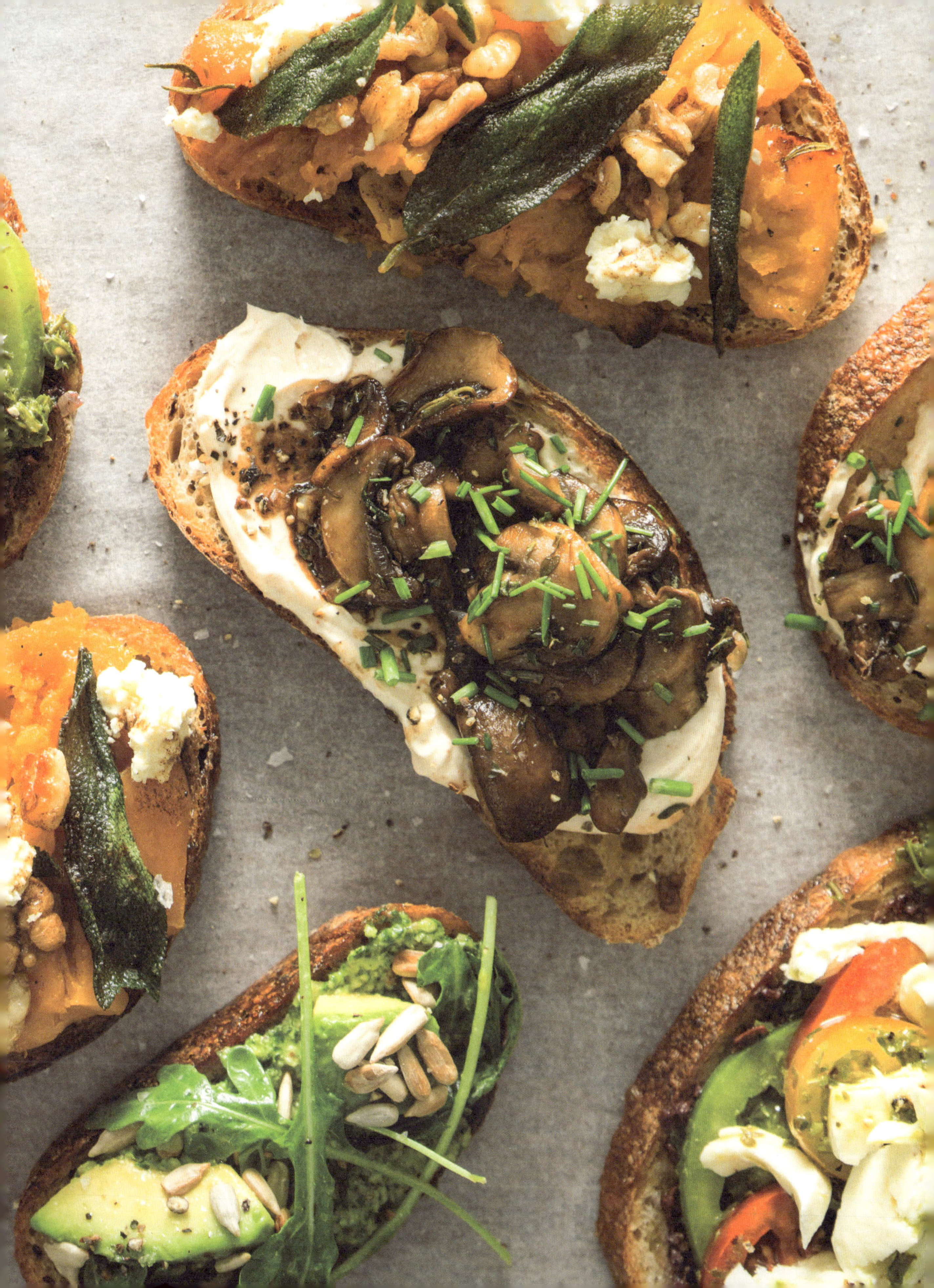

GF use GF bread | DF | VEGAN

SPRING BRUSCHETTA

SERVES 8
Prep time: 10 minutes
Cook time: 12–15 minutes

SPRING
handful of baby greens (e.g. baby rocket or spinach), sliced
1–2 spring onions, finely sliced
1 medium just-ripe avocado, diced
drizzle of extra-virgin olive oil
juice of ½ lemon
8 Bruschetta Bases (page 191)
1 cup Coriander, Lime and Cashew Pesto (page 63) or
store-bought pesto
¼ cup toasted sunflower seeds

Pesto, avocado, rocket and lemon — the fresh flavours of spring.

1. In a bowl, toss greens, spring onion and avocado with extra-virgin olive oil and lemon juice, allowing the avocado to get slightly mushed up. Season with salt and pepper.
2. Spread Bruschetta Bases with pesto.
3. Top with avocado and greens and sprinkle with toasted sunflower seeds.

GF use GF bread | DF omit mozzarella | VEGAN omit mozzarella

SUMMER BRUSCHETTA

SUMMER
500g assortment of tomatoes, sliced
3–4 tablespoons Mint Chermoula (page 57)
8 Bruschetta Bases (page 191)
¼ Olive Tapenade (page 190 or store-bought) or basil pesto
200g fresh mozzarella, torn into bite-sized pieces

Olives, tomatoes, basil and mozzarella — the juicy flavours of summer.

1. In a large bowl, toss tomatoes with Mint Chermoula and season with salt and pepper.

2. Spread Bruschetta Bases with Olive Tapenade or pesto. Top with slices of marinated tomato and mozzarella. Spoon over any extra Mint Chermoula from the bowl.

GF use GF bread

AUTUMN BRUSCHETTA

AUTUMN
700g pumpkin or butternut, peeled and diced 2cm
1–2 tablespoons olive oil
1–2 tablespoons maple syrup
leaves of 1 sprig thyme or rosemary
¼ cup chopped walnuts
25g butter
¼ cup sage leaves
8 Bruschetta Bases (page 191)
100g creamy blue cheese or feta

Maple-roast pumpkin (I use butternut), thyme, rosemary and sage, toasted walnuts, burnt butter and blue cheese — the sweet, nutty flavours of autumn.

1. Preheat oven to 200°C. Line an oven tray with baking paper.

2. Toss pumpkin/butternut with olive oil, maple syrup and thyme/rosemary on lined tray and season with salt and pepper. Roast for about 20 minutes until soft and caramelised.

3. Toast walnuts in small fry pan (with no oil) for 1–2 minutes over medium heat, then set aside. Add butter to pan and when it bubbles and starts to turn brown, add sage leaves and sizzle for 1–2 minutes until crispy. Turn off the heat.

4. Roughly squash roast pumpkin onto Bruschetta Bases and top with walnuts, sage and blue cheese/feta. Drizzle with brown butter from the pan.

GF use GF bread

WINTER BRUSCHETTA

WINTER
3 tablespoons butter or olive oil
250g button mushrooms, sliced
2–3 cloves garlic, finely chopped
1½ tablespoons chopped thyme and/or rosemary leaves
3 tablespoons balsamic vinegar
1 teaspoon liquid honey
¼ cup chopped chives
200g crème fraîche
2 tablespoons lemon juice
½ teaspoon smoked paprika
8 Bruschetta Bases (page 191)

Smoked paprika, lemon, rosemary and sweet balsamic mushrooms — the warming, comforting flavours of winter.

1. Heat butter/olive oil in a large fry pan on medium heat. Cook mushrooms, garlic and thyme/rosemary, with a good pinch of salt, for 5–8 minutes until mushrooms are soft and almost all liquid has evaporated.

2. Add balsamic vinegar and honey to the pan and continue cooking for a further 1–2 minutes. Season with salt and freshly ground black pepper. Stir through half of the chives and a drizzle of extra-virgin olive oil.

3. Mix crème fraîche with lemon juice and smoked paprika. Season with salt and pepper.

4. Spread crème fraîche mixture over Bruschetta Bases and top with mushrooms and remaining chives.

Hearty & S

CHAPTER TWO — P. 79

salads
soups

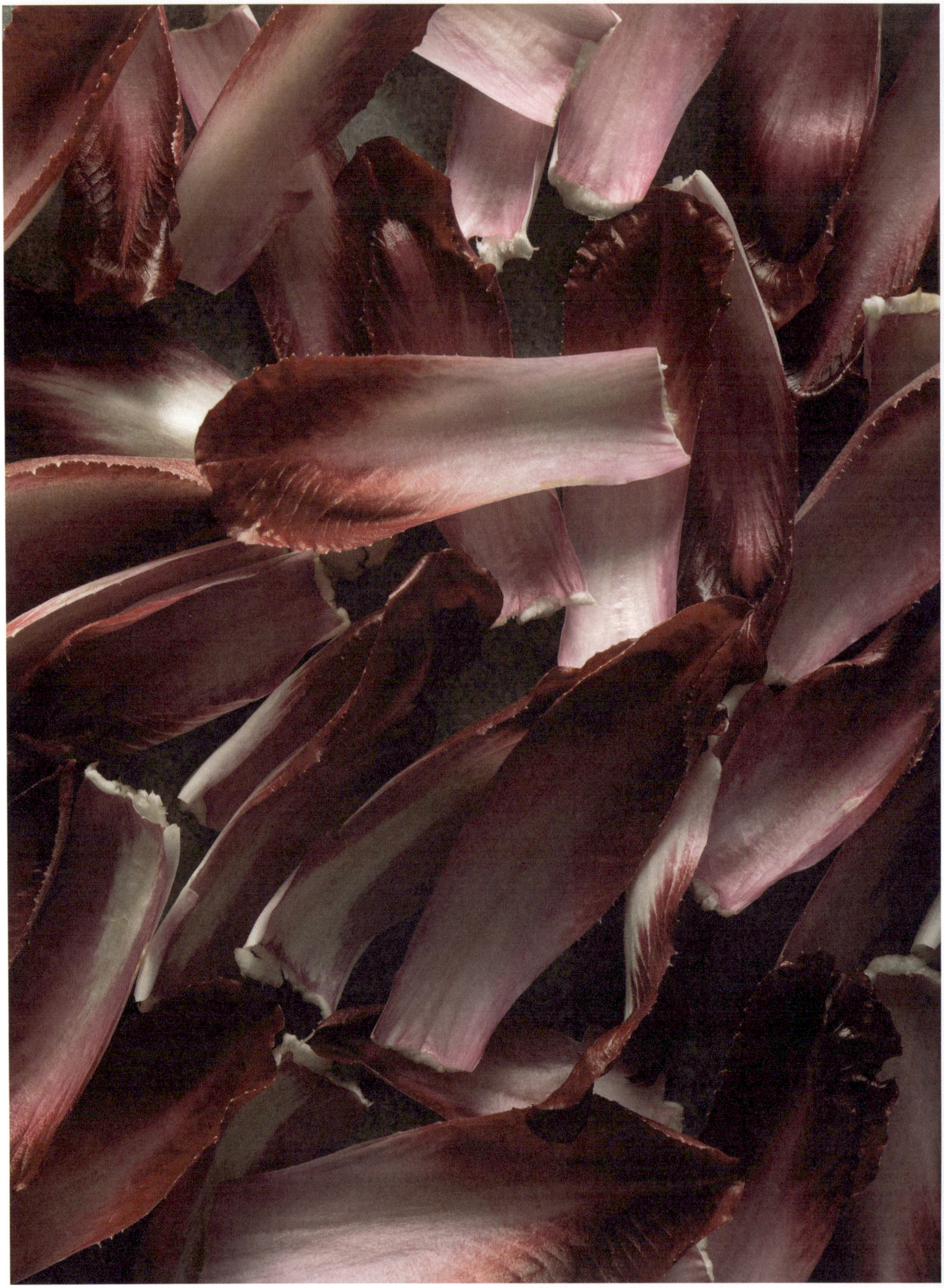

I love how the definition of 'salad' has far surpassed a handful of green leaves and a dressing as I knew it to be when I was growing up. Now, often the most exciting and intriguing item on the menu is a salad — for lunch or dinner, or even breakfast! Instead of being something on the side, hearty salads are wholly tempting and satisfying.

There is a bit of a rhythm to composing a hearty salad. Starting with a starchy base, like chickpeas, lentils, barley, freekeh, rice, quinoa or root vegetables. Add lots of fresh, colourful, crunchy notes in the form of leafy greens, fresh herbs, raw veg, cooked veg, fruit... Some kind of fat or protein, whether avocado, cheese or eggs, can further boost its satiety but is not always needed. Then a final scattering of nuts or seeds (maybe crispy croûtons) and a great dressing is all else that is needed to create your chef-d'oeuvre.

And soup. How I love a flavourful, hearty soup, the equivalent colder weather satisfier. Here are a few of my favourites ranging from a roast and caramelised veg soup (roasting and caramelising makes all the difference) to a chunky garden veg soup and a Moroccan-style lentil soup. Whether you go for hearty soup or salad, I find it's always a win-win result where you feel satisfied but not weighed down.

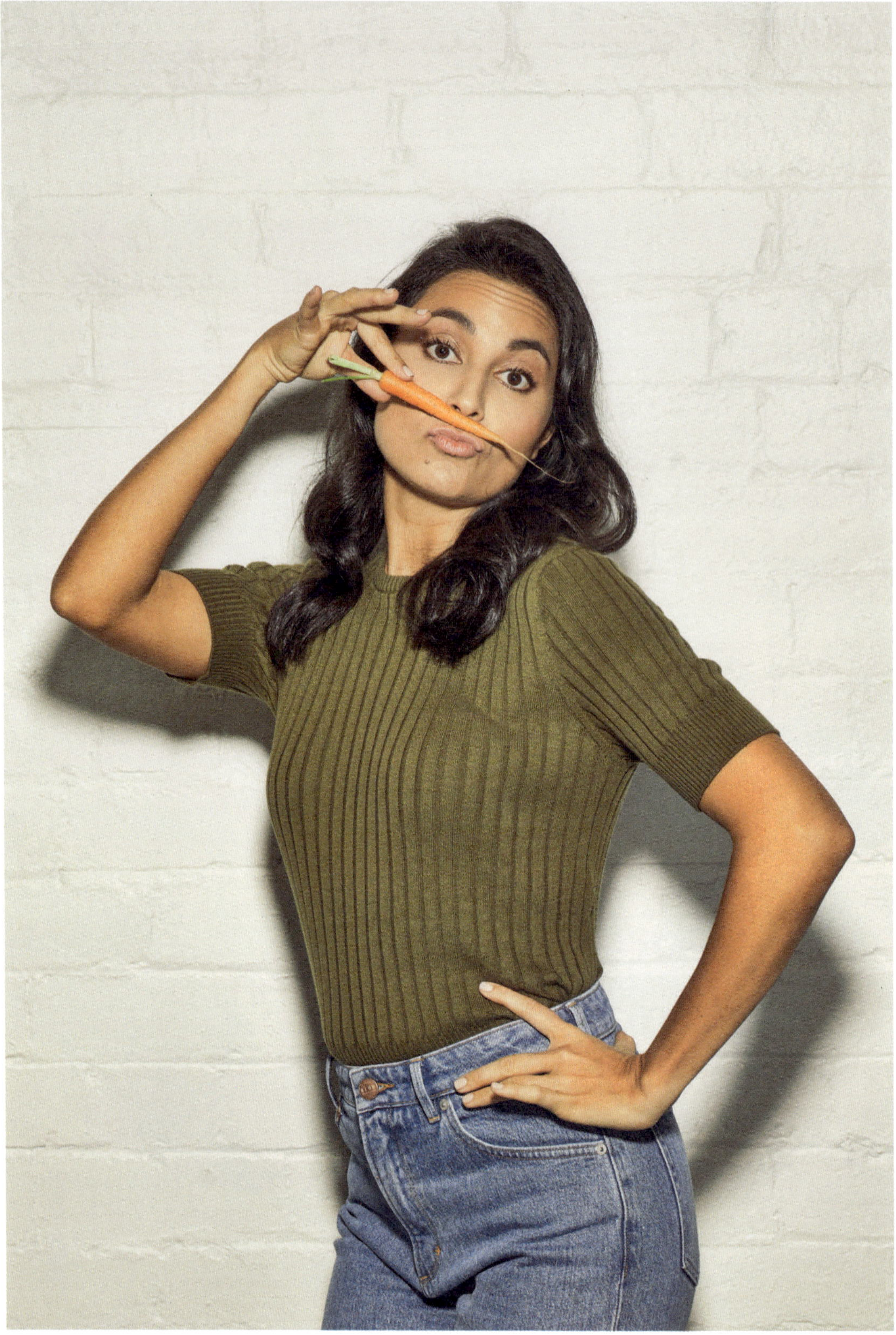

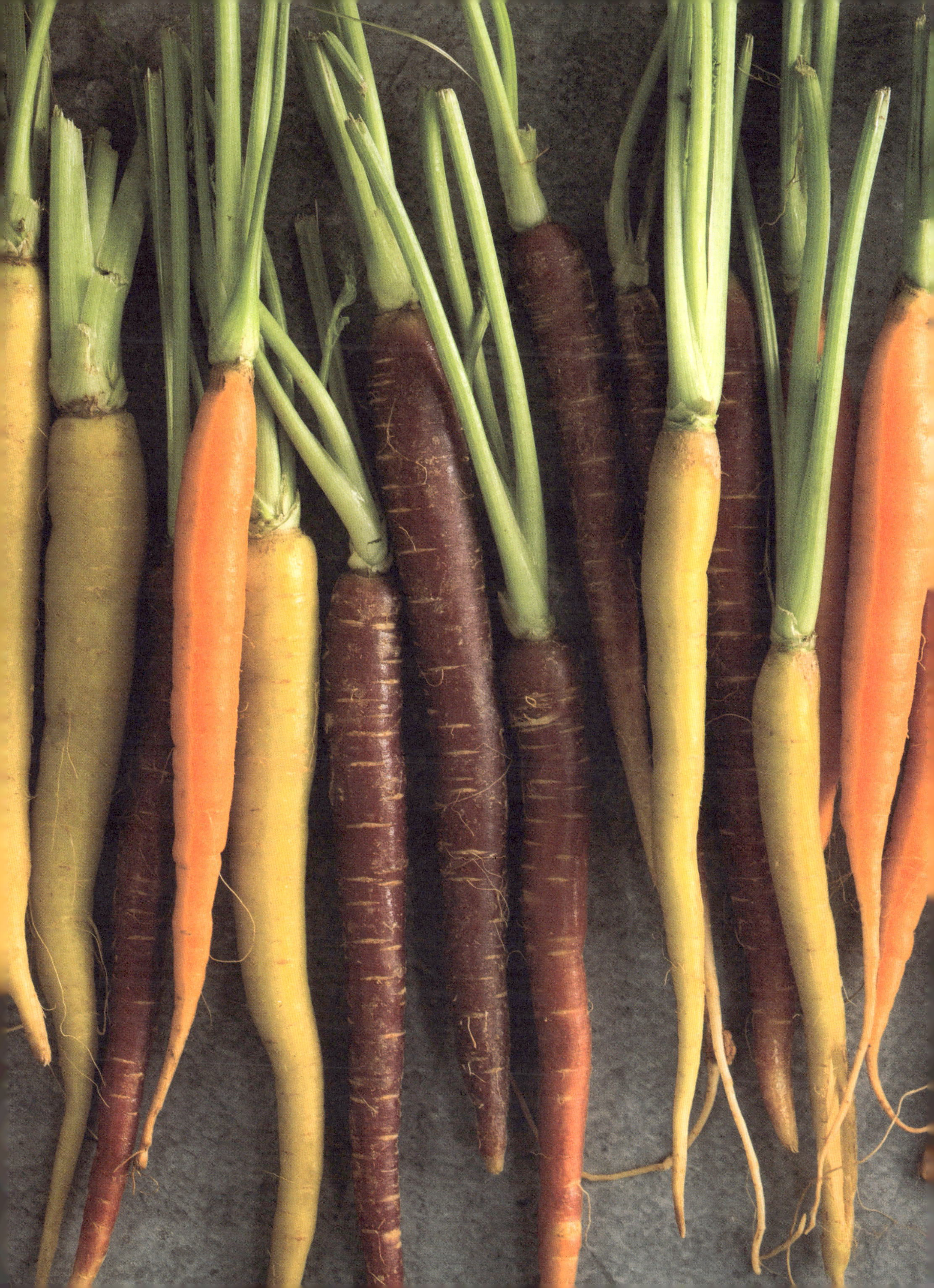

GF | DF omit haloumi | VEGAN omit haloumi and add cashew feta, and use maple syrup instead of honey

BALSAMIC ROAST BEETS, LENTILS & HALOUMI

SERVES 4
Prep time: 20 minutes
Cook time: 20–30 minutes

2 tablespoons olive oil
2 tablespoons balsamic vinegar
1½ tablespoons maple syrup or honey
1 tablespoon chopped thyme or rosemary leaves
3 red onions, cut into 1–2cm-thick wedges
3 medium beetroot, scrubbed, cut into 1cm-thick wedges
¾ cup dried Puy lentils (French green lentils)
200g haloumi, cut into 12 thin slices
2 tablespoons red wine vinegar
2 teaspoons honey
1 head radicchio, leaves separated and sliced
½ cup chopped parsley
½ lemon, cut into wedges, to serve

This is one of my favourite salads. We have it at all times of the year, winter or summer, for a lighter, veg-filled dinner — it's hearty and has a great balance of flavours and textures. Make sure you use Puy (also known as French green) lentils as this variety holds their shape when cooked (instead of going mushy like others). If you don't enjoy the bitter taste of radicchio, use another type of lettuce — for example, endive, or even just cos, baby spinach or rocket.

1. Preheat oven to 200°C. Line an oven tray with baking paper and bring a medium pot of water to the boil.

2. Mix olive oil, balsamic vinegar, maple syrup/honey and thyme/rosemary together. Toss half of this mixture (reserve the rest for the lentils) with onion and beetroot wedges on lined oven tray and season with salt and pepper. Roast for 20–30 minutes until tender and starting to caramelise.

3. Meanwhile, cook lentils in a pot of unsalted boiling water for 12–15 minutes until al dente/just tender. Drain well.

4. In a large bowl, toss lentils with remaining balsamic mixture, roast vegetables and all their juices. Season to taste with salt and pepper.

5. Heat a drizzle of olive oil in a large non-stick fry pan on medium heat. Pat haloumi slices dry with paper towels. Cook haloumi for 1–2 minutes on each side until golden. Set aside on a plate. Keep pan on the heat and add red wine vinegar and honey to the pan. Stir with a wooden spoon and allow to bubble for 1–2 minutes until thick.

6. Just before serving, gently toss roast vegetables and lentils with radicchio and parsley. Tip onto a serving platter, top with slices of haloumi and drizzle with glaze from the pan. Serve with lemon wedges to squeeze over just before eating.

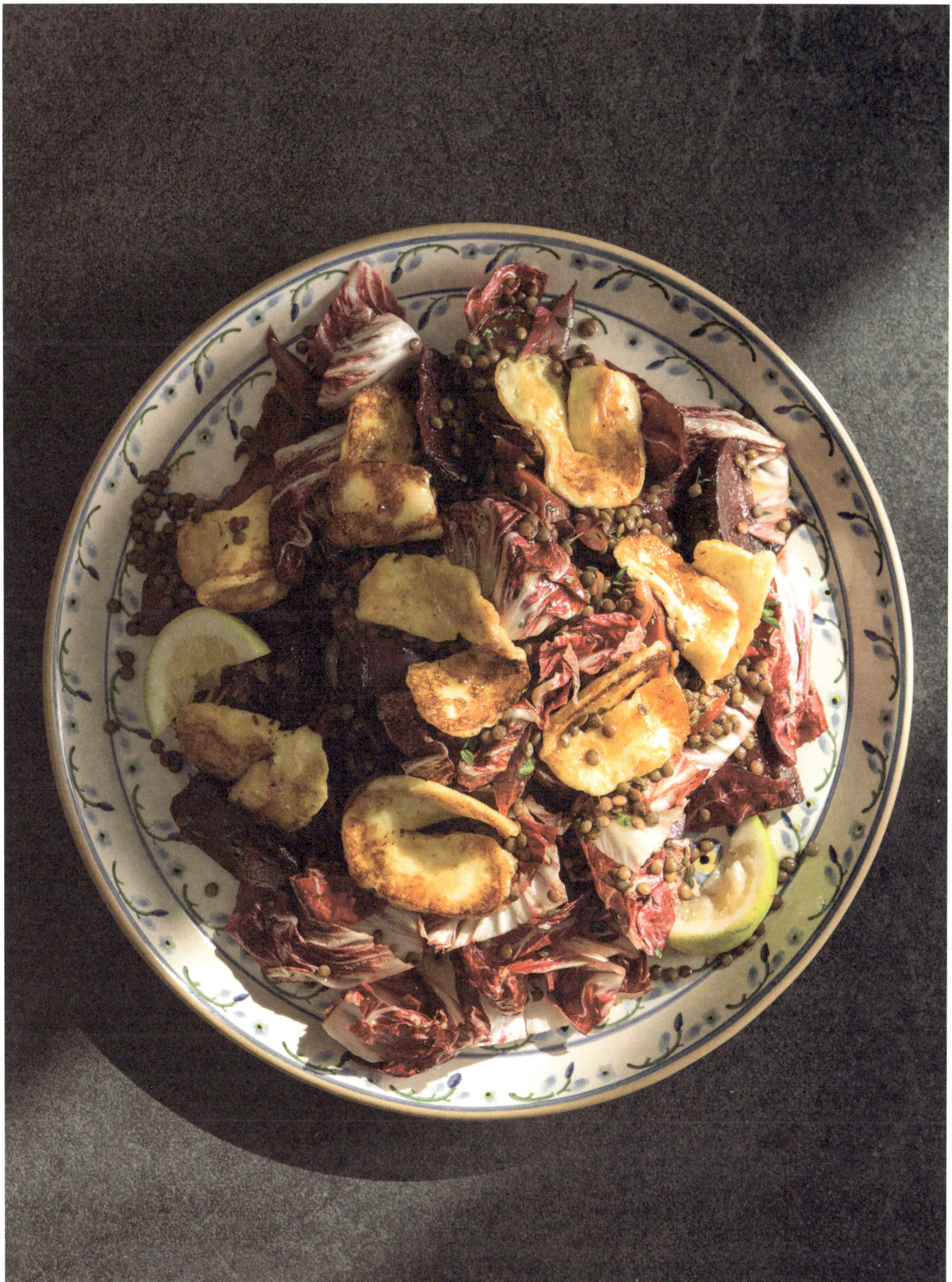

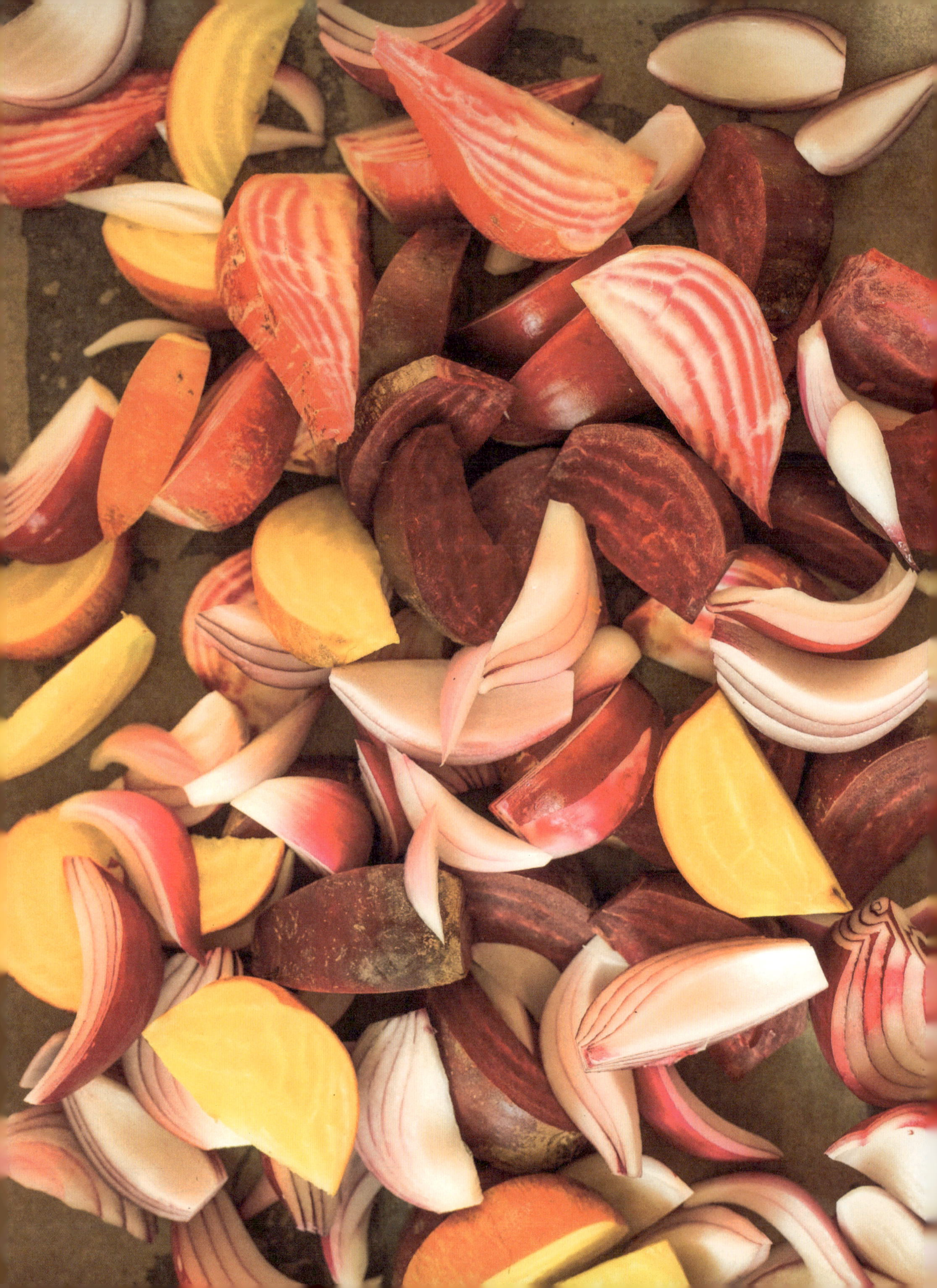

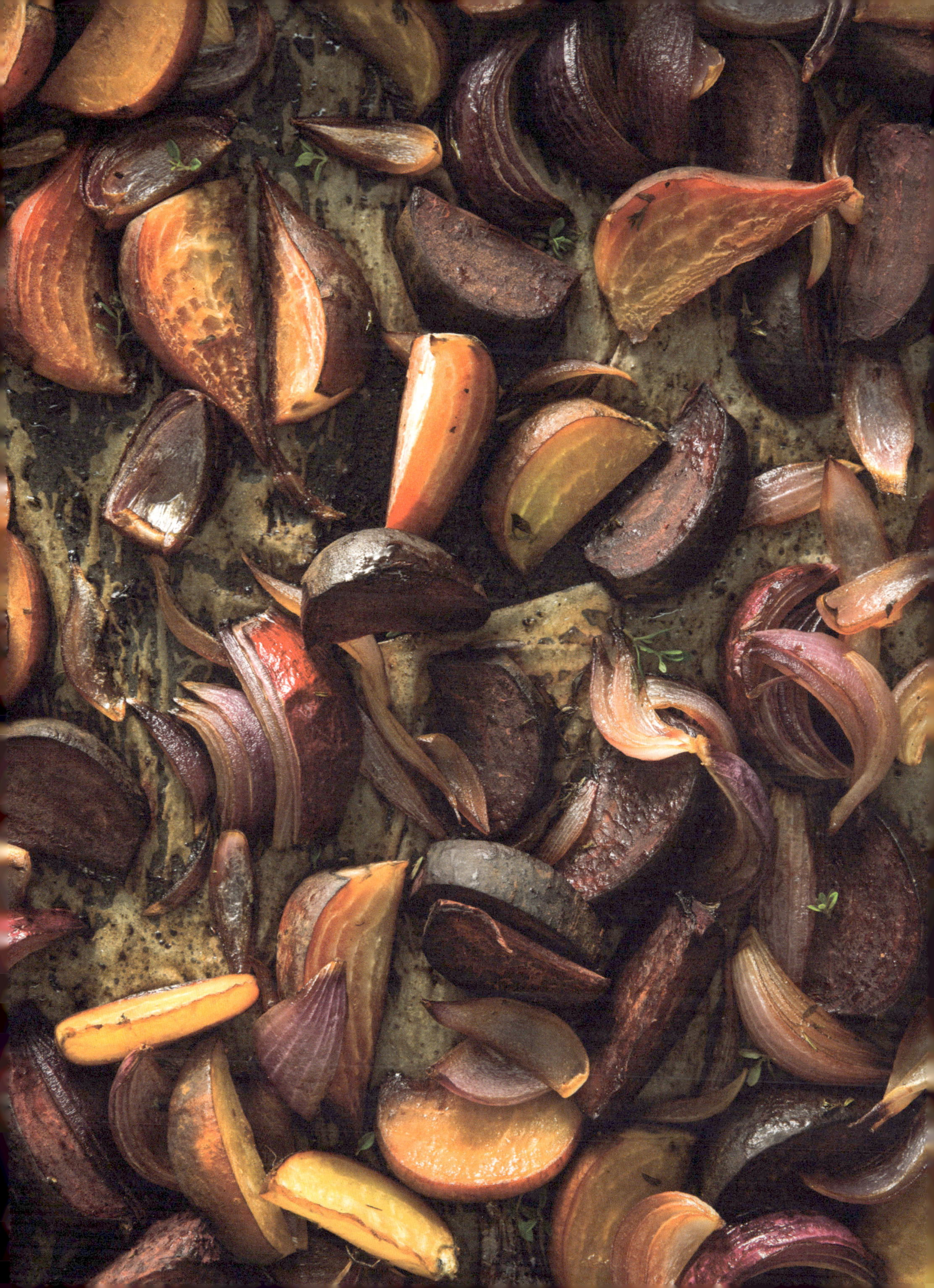

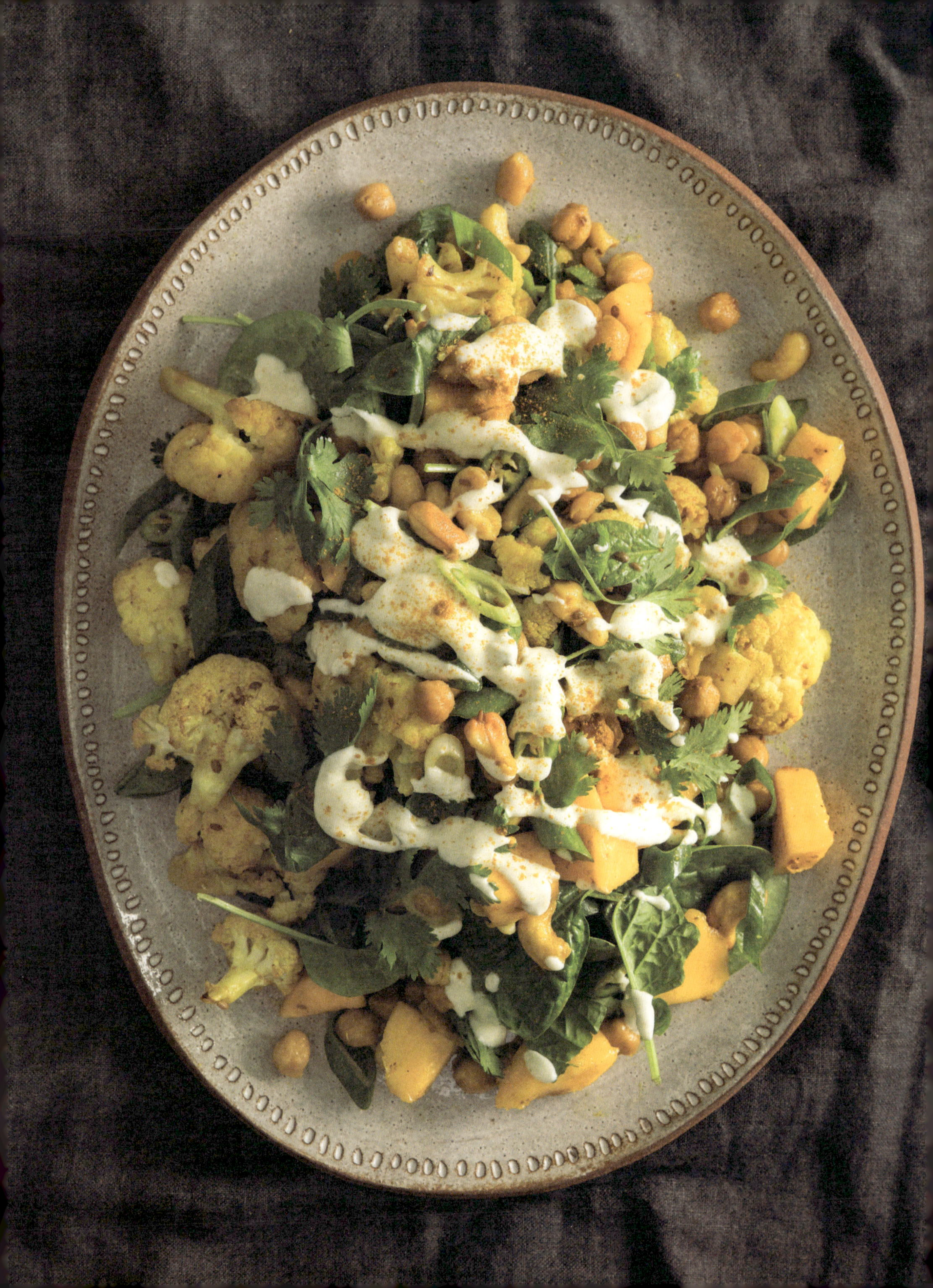

GF | DF | VEGAN

CURRIED CAULIFLOWER, CHICKPEA & MANGO SALAD WITH COCONUT YOGHURT DRESSING

SERVES 4-5
Prep time: 15 minutes
Cook time: 15-20 minutes

1 small head cauliflower, chopped into florets
400g can chickpeas, rinsed, drained and patted dry with paper towels
1 cup natural cashew nuts
3 tablespoons olive oil
1¼ teaspoons curry powder
1¼ teaspoons cumin seeds, crushed
1¼ teaspoons coriander seeds, crushed
2-3 cloves garlic, finely chopped
2 tablespoons maple syrup
1 ripe mango, peeled and diced
3 handfuls of baby spinach
1 red or green chilli, finely sliced
2 spring onions, finely sliced (mostly green part)
½ cup chopped coriander

COCONUT YOGHURT DRESSING
½ cup natural unsweetened coconut yoghurt
juice of 1 lime
¼-½ teaspoon curry powder

Chickpeas love a good spicing; otherwise they can be a bit bland and boring. Then they make a great base for filling, hearty, flavour-packed salads like this one with spice-roasted cauliflower, fresh mango, a kick of chilli and a creamy coconut dressing. There's a bit of Pacific and Indian fusion going on here and the result is sublime.

1. Preheat oven to 220°C. Line an oven tray with baking paper.

2. In a large bowl, toss cauliflower, chickpeas and cashew nuts with olive oil, curry powder, cumin and coriander seeds, garlic and maple syrup. Season with salt and pepper, tip onto lined tray and roast for about 15-20 minutes until cauliflower is just tender and golden.

3. Mix all dressing ingredients together and season with a little salt.

4. Set roast cauliflower mixture aside to cool slightly. Just before serving, toss with mango, baby spinach, chilli, spring onion and coriander and drizzle with the dressing.

GF use quinoa

CHARRED CORN, FETA & BARLEY SALAD WITH CHIPOTLE LIME DRESSING

SERVES 4
Prep time: 15 minutes
Cook time: 20 minutes

4 large corn cobs, silk and husks removed
2 large red capsicums, cored and cut into 3cm pieces
¾ cup barley (or orzo pasta, Israeli (pearl) couscous, or even quinoa)
1 punnet cherry tomatoes, cut in half
2–3 spring onions, thinly sliced
1 large just-ripe avocado, diced
100g feta, crumbled
2 large handfuls of baby spinach, rocket or mesclun

CHIPOTLE LIME DRESSING
juice of 1 lime
¼ cup sour cream, crème fraîche, natural Greek yoghurt or mayonnaise
2 teaspoons chipotle sauce

Barley gives a nice nutty flavour and texture, although you could also use orzo pasta, Israeli (pearl) couscous or quinoa. A great summer salad for a barbecue, this would be great served with the Marinated Veggie Kebabs on page 54.

1. Preheat barbecue grill to high and bring a medium pot of salted water to the boil.

2. Lightly brush corn with oil. Drizzle and toss capsicum with a little oil. Cook corn and capsicum on barbecue for about 10 minutes, turning every now and again, until lightly charred and corn kernels are bright yellow.

3. When cool enough to handle, stand each corn cob on its end on a chopping board and run a sharp knife down the edges to remove the kernels in chunks.

4. Cook barley in boiling water for about 10 minutes until just tender/al dente (or pasta, couscous or quinoa according to packet instructions). Drain and run under cold water to stop cooking process.

5. In a large bowl, toss together barley, corn, capsicum, tomatoes, spring onion, avocado, feta and leafy greens.

6. Whisk all dressing ingredients together in a small bowl until smooth. Season with salt and pepper. Loosen with a little water to a drizzling consistency, and drizzle over salad just before serving.

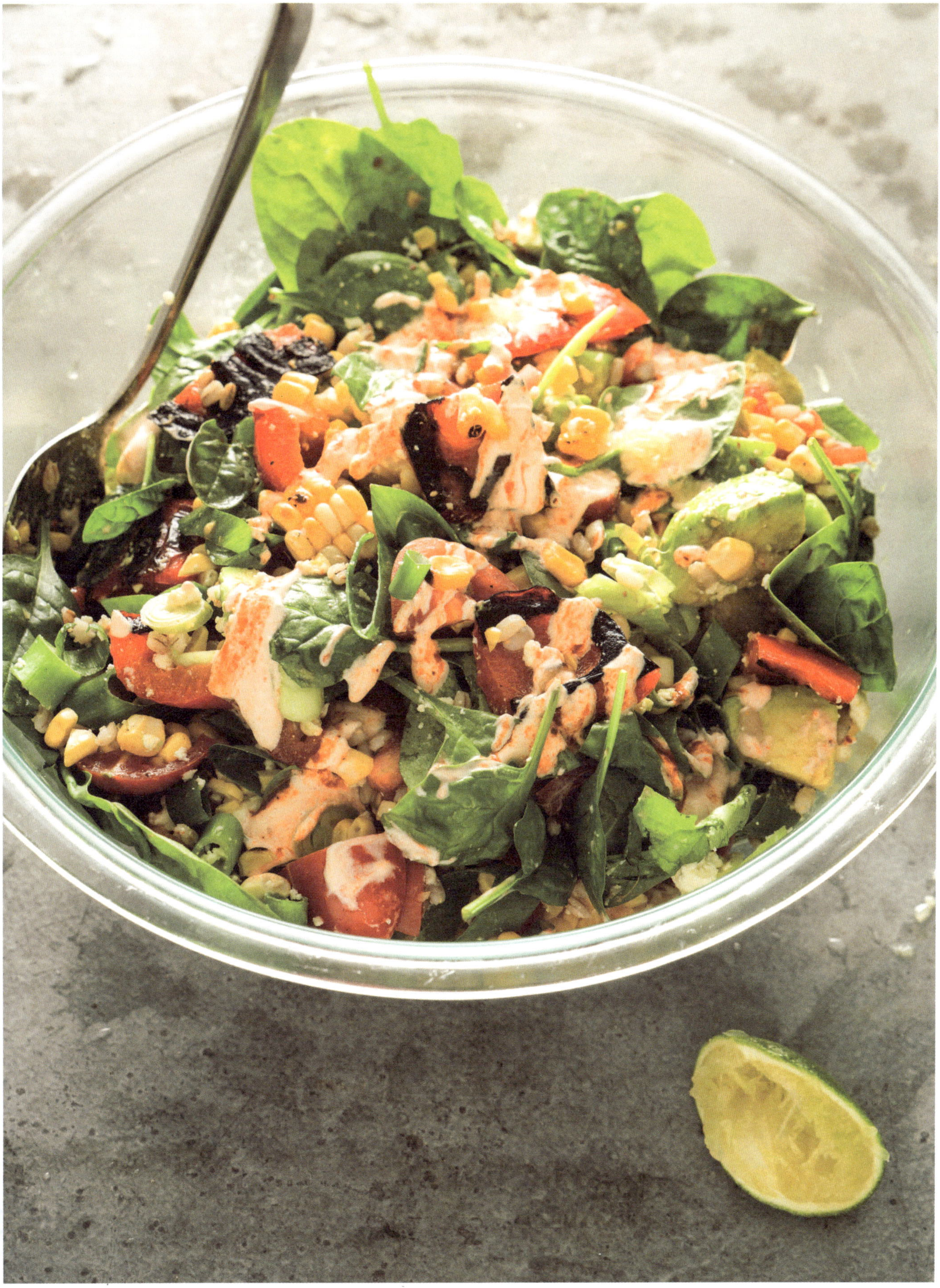

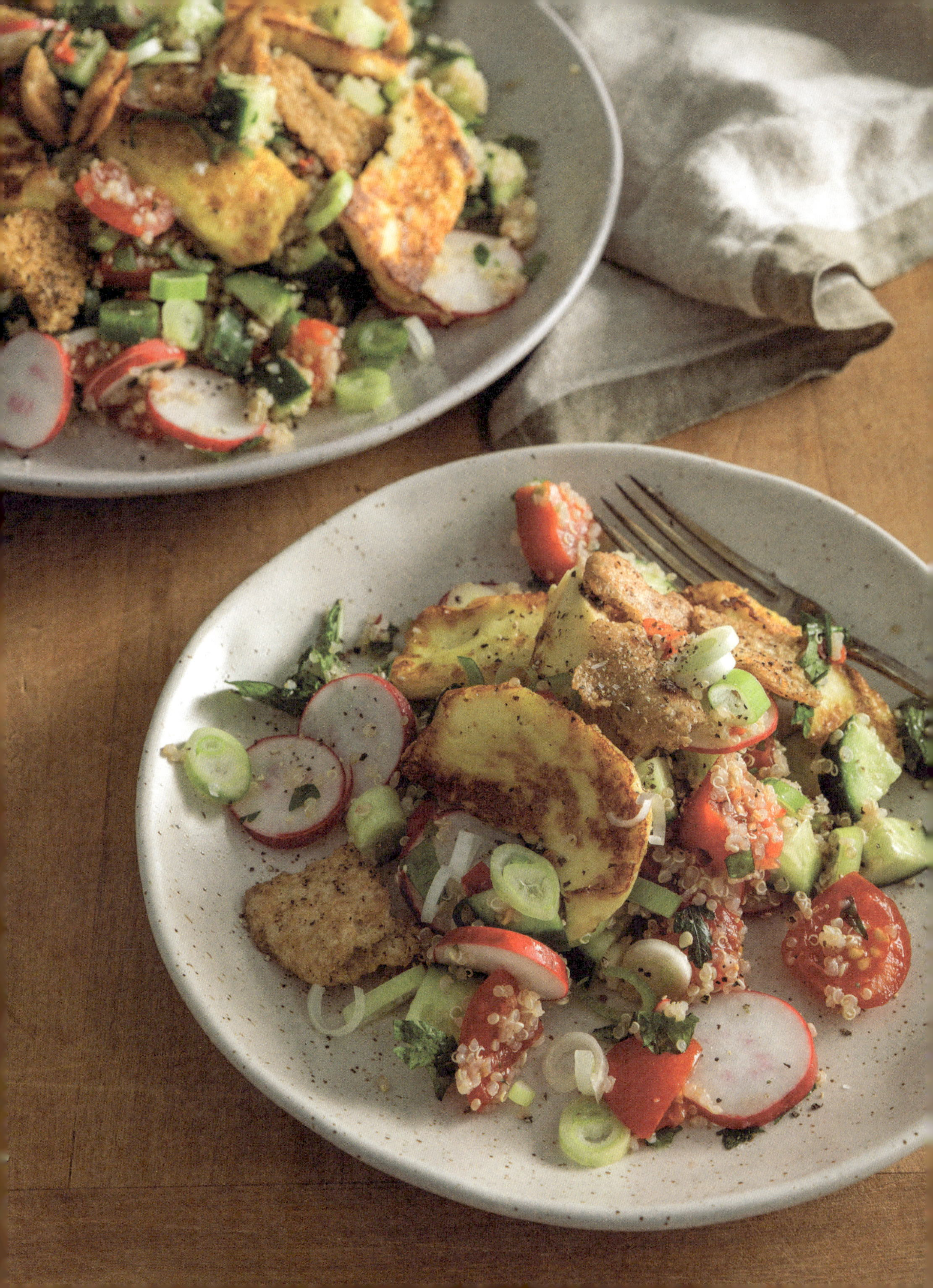

GF use GF bread | DF omit haloumi | VEGAN omit haloumi

MIDDLE EASTERN QUINOA SALAD WITH HALOUMI & CRISPY PITA

SERVES 4
Prep time: 20 minutes
Cook time: 25 minutes

¾ cup quinoa
2¼ cups water or vegetable stock
6 vine-ripened tomatoes
2 Lebanese cucumbers
3 baby radishes
2 spring onions
½ cup chopped flat-leaf parsley
½ cup chopped mint leaves
1 chilli, finely chopped (optional)
3 tablespoons extra-virgin olive oil
juice of ½ lemon
200g haloumi, sliced 0.5cm thick

CRISPY PITA
3 tablespoons olive oil
2 pita bread (or the equivalent sourdough, ciabatta, or baguette), torn or chopped into small bite-sized pieces
1 teaspoon sumac (optional)
flaky sea salt

Here is another one of my favourite salads that I'll never tire of eating — think a cross between tabbouleh and fattoush, but with quinoa and haloumi to bulk it out and provide some fatty, salty goodness. Sumac gives a wonderful lemony tanginess so, like I've said in other recipes, I recommend getting your hands on some as you'll love using it in lots of other dishes, even if just sprinkling over vegetables before roasting.

1. Place quinoa and water/stock in a small pot, cover and bring to the boil. Reduce heat to low and cook (with lid on) for 12 minutes. Turn off the heat and leave to finish steaming, still covered, for a further 5 minutes or so before fluffing up grains with a fork. Leave to cool.

2. To make the Crispy Pita, heat olive oil in a large fry pan on medium heat. Cook bread in the olive oil until golden and crispy, about 5 minutes. Turn off the heat and sprinkle with sumac (if using) and a pinch of flaky sea salt.

3. Dice tomatoes and cucumber and thinly slice radishes and spring onions. Place in a bowl. Add cooled quinoa, parsley, mint, chilli (if using), olive oil and lemon juice and toss together. Season to taste with salt and pepper.

4. Heat a drizzle of olive oil in a large non-stick fry pan on medium heat and cook haloumi for 1–2 minutes each side until golden.

5. Divide salad between serving plates and top with Crispy Pita and haloumi.

GF | DF | VEGAN use maple syrup

ROAST ROOTS & CARAMELISED ONION SOUP WITH LEMON, CHILLI & PARSLEY

SERVES 4
Prep time: 20 minutes
Cook time: 40 minutes

1 large kumara (gold, orange or red), peeled and chopped into 2–3cm pieces
2 large parsnips, peeled and chopped into 2–3cm pieces
2 large carrots, peeled and chopped into 2–3cm pieces
1 swede, peeled and chopped into 2–3cm pieces
1 tablespoon olive oil
2 teaspoons liquid honey or maple syrup
2 onions, sliced
1 tablespoon balsamic vinegar
¼ cup water
2 teaspoons brown sugar
1.5 litres vegetable stock

LEMON, CHILLI AND PARSLEY
zest of 1 lemon
1 red chilli, chopped
¼ cup chopped parsley
1 tablespoon extra-virgin olive oil

This is the king of all root vegetable soups. It has a mix of various root vegetables that are roasted until sweet, tender and intensified in flavour, blended up with caramelised onions (because caramelised onions just make everything taste better!) and a sprinkle of lemon, chilli and parsley to liven it up even more. If swede is unavailable/not in season, use more kumara, carrot or parsnip (or even pumpkin).

1. Preheat oven to 200°C. Line an oven tray with baking paper.

2. Toss kumara, parsnips, carrots and swede with olive oil and honey in lined tray. Season with salt. Roast for 30–40 minutes until tender and starting to caramelise.

3. While vegetables are roasting, make caramelised onions. Heat a good drizzle of olive oil in a large fry pan on medium heat. Cook onions for 8–10 minutes until soft and starting to caramelise. Add balsamic vinegar, water and brown sugar. Reduce heat and continue to cook for a further 2–3 minutes.

4. Tip roasted vegetables and caramelised onions into a large pot and pour in stock. Blend with a hand-held blender until smooth (add a little water, if needed, to get the desired thickness). Season to taste with salt and pepper. Heat on the stovetop if you're planning on eating the soup now, or store in a container in the fridge to eat later.

5. Place lemon zest, chilli and parsley all together in a pile on a chopping board and finely chop up together. Put in a small bowl, stir in olive oil and season with salt.

6. To serve, ladle hot soup into bowls and drizzle with lemon, chilli and parsley oil.

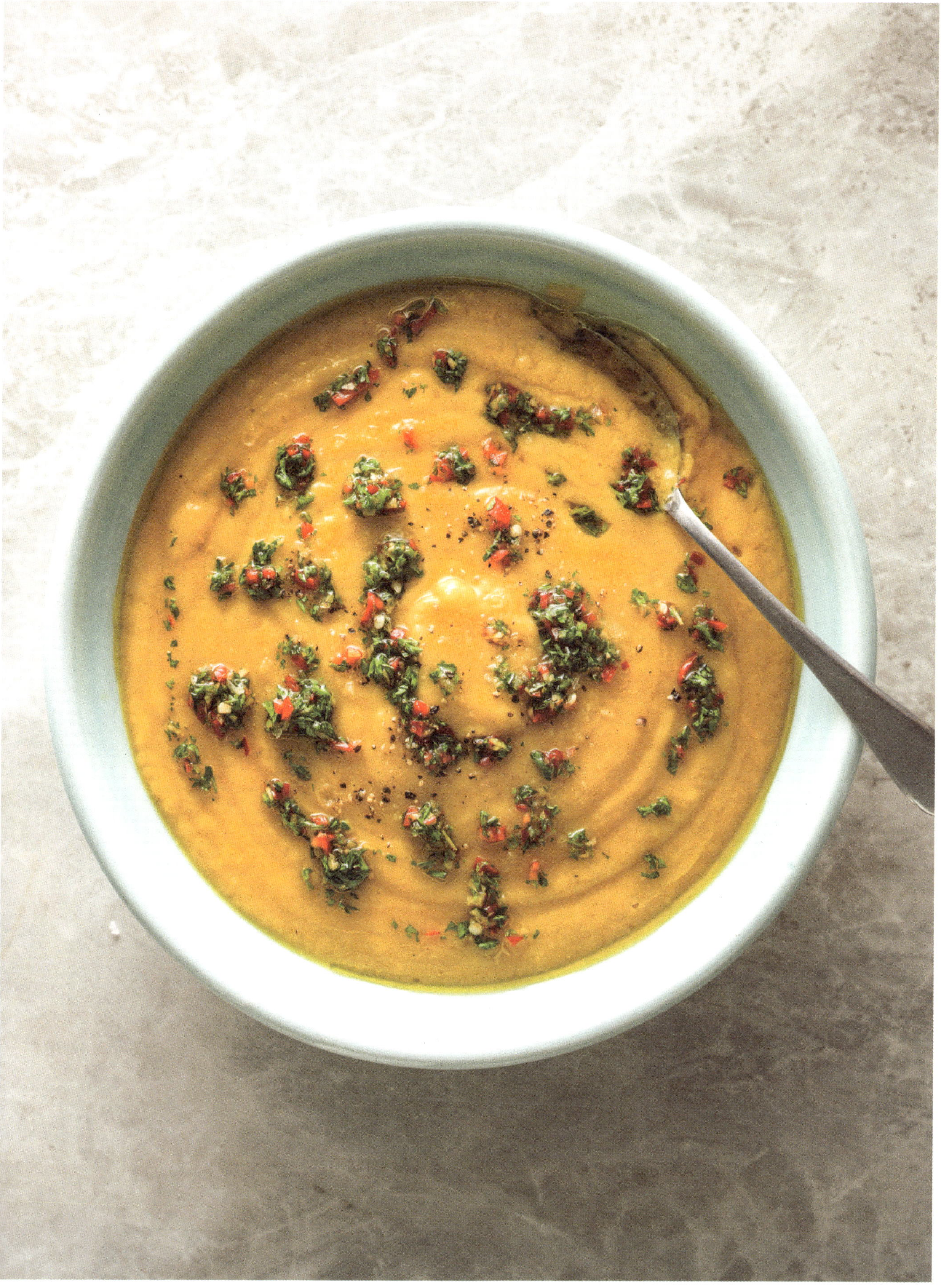

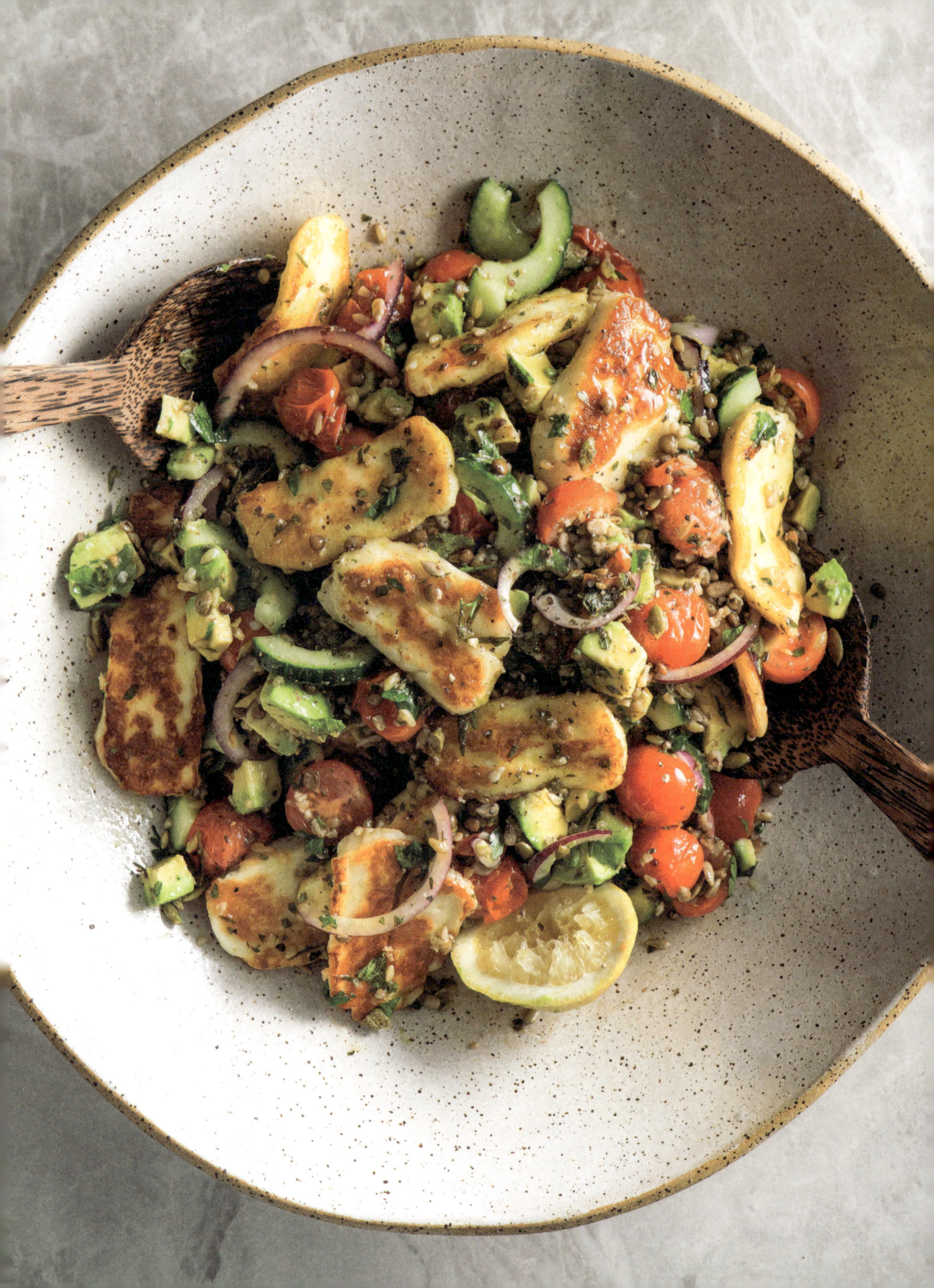

DF omit haloumi | VEGAN omit haloumi and use maple syrup instead of honey

CYPRIOT LENTIL & FREEKEH SALAD WITH HONEY-GLAZED HALOUMI

SERVES 4
Prep time: 20 minutes
Cook time: 25 minutes

½ cup dried Puy lentils (French green lentils)
½ cup cracked freekeh (or bulghur)
3 tablespoons sunflower seeds
3 tablespoons pumpkin seeds
½ large telegraph cucumber
½ red onion, finely sliced
½ punnet cherry tomatoes, cut in half
½ cup each chopped flat-leaf parsley and mint
2 tablespoons chopped capers
flesh of 1 firm-ripe avocado, diced

DRESSING
zest of ½ lemon
juice of 1 lemon
¼ cup chopped oregano leaves
¼ cup extra-virgin olive oil
1 clove garlic, finely chopped
2 teaspoons liquid honey
¼ teaspoon salt and freshly cracked black pepper

HONEY-GLAZED HALOUMI
400g haloumi, sliced 0.5cm-thick
½ punnet cherry tomatoes
leaves from a few sprigs of thyme or rosemary
zest and juice of ½ lemon
1 tablespoon liquid honey

This salad was scored a unanimous, definitive 10/10 by a group of friends over for lunch. Freekeh — a young, green wheat, most similar to bulghur — is a delicious grain to incorporate in your diet; it has a fantastic subtle smoky, nutty flavour and is a little chewy. The combination of freekeh, lentils, sunflower and pumpkin seeds lends heaps of texture and nuttiness to this summery salad. It's hands down one of my favourite salads and is incredibly filling.

1. Bring a medium pot of water to the boil. Cook lentils for 5–10 minutes then add freekeh and continue cooking for a further 10–15 minutes or until lentils and freekeh are tender. Drain and run under cold water to cool and stop the cooking process.

2. Place sunflower and pumpkin seeds in a small fry pan (with no oil) and toast on low to medium heat for a few minutes, stirring frequently to avoid burning. Set aside.

3. Place all dressing ingredients in a jar, screw the lid on and shake well to combine.

4. Cut cucumber in half lengthways, scrape seeds out with a teaspoon (and discard), then slice. Place in a large bowl. Add cooled lentils and freekeh along with toasted seeds, all remaining salad ingredients and dressing. Toss together and season to taste with a little more salt and pepper, if needed.

5. Heat a drizzle of olive oil in a large non-stick fry pan on medium heat. Cook haloumi for 1–2 minutes each side until golden. Transfer to a plate and keep pan on the heat.

6. Place cherry tomatoes and thyme/rosemary in the pan and cook, shaking every now and again, for a few minutes, until tomatoes are blistered. Add lemon zest and juice, let it bubble, then add honey and turn off the heat. Transfer blistered tomatoes to plate of haloumi and pour over the juices and herbs from the pan.

7. Top salad with haloumi, blistered tomatoes and honey glaze and juices.

GF use rice instead of barley and GF bread | DF omit parmesan | VEGAN omit parmesan

CHUNKY VEGETABLE & BARLEY SOUP WITH GARLIC SOURDOUGH CROÛTONS

SERVES 4
Prep time: 30 minutes
Cook time: 30–35 minutes

3 tablespoons olive oil
1 large onion, chopped
white part of 1 leek, finely sliced
2 stalks celery, sliced (reserve a handful of celery leaves)
2 carrots, peeled and diced 2cm
3–4 cloves garlic, chopped
2 tablespoons chopped thyme and/or rosemary
400g peeled pumpkin, diced 2cm
½ cup barley, rinsed and drained
400g can crushed tomatoes
1 tablespoon chipotle sauce
1 litre vegetable stock
2 courgettes, sliced 1cm-thick
150g green beans, chopped
handful of chopped spinach or silverbeet leaves (optional)
1–2 tablespoons lemon juice
½–1 cup mixed chopped herbs (e.g. parsley, coriander, oregano, marjoram)
extra-virgin olive oil to drizzle

GARLIC SOURDOUGH CROÛTONS

4 slices sourdough bread, cut or torn into 2cm pieces
2 tablespoons olive oil
4 cloves garlic, finely chopped
2 teaspoons chopped thyme leaves
¼ cup finely grated parmesan

Is there any dish more humble and nourishing than a vegetable soup? With ten different vegetables and loads of fresh herbs stirred in at the end, this soup is packed to the brim with goodness. Make sure you use some fresh oregano and marjoram if you have it. The addition of barley makes it substantial enough for a main course; you could also use orzo pasta or cannellini beans. Then all that's needed is a drizzle of good-quality extra-virgin olive oil and some crunchy, garlicky croûtons. It keeps well in the fridge over a few days and freezes well for those nights you need instant warming up.

1. Heat olive oil in a large pot on medium heat. Cook onion and leek for 6–8 minutes until soft.

2. Add celery, carrot, garlic, thyme/rosemary and pumpkin and continue to cook for a further 4–5 minutes.

3. Add barley, tomatoes, chipotle sauce and vegetable stock, simmer for about 15 minutes until pumpkin and barley are tender.

4. While soup is cooking, toss sourdough with olive oil, garlic, thyme and parmesan on a tray lined with baking paper and season with salt and pepper. Bake at 180°C for 15 minutes until golden and crispy.

5. Add courgettes, green beans and spinach/silverbeet (if using) to soup and continue simmering for 3–4 minutes until tender. Stir through lemon juice and herbs and season to taste with salt and pepper.

6. Ladle soup into bowls, drizzle with extra-virgin olive oil and top with croûtons.

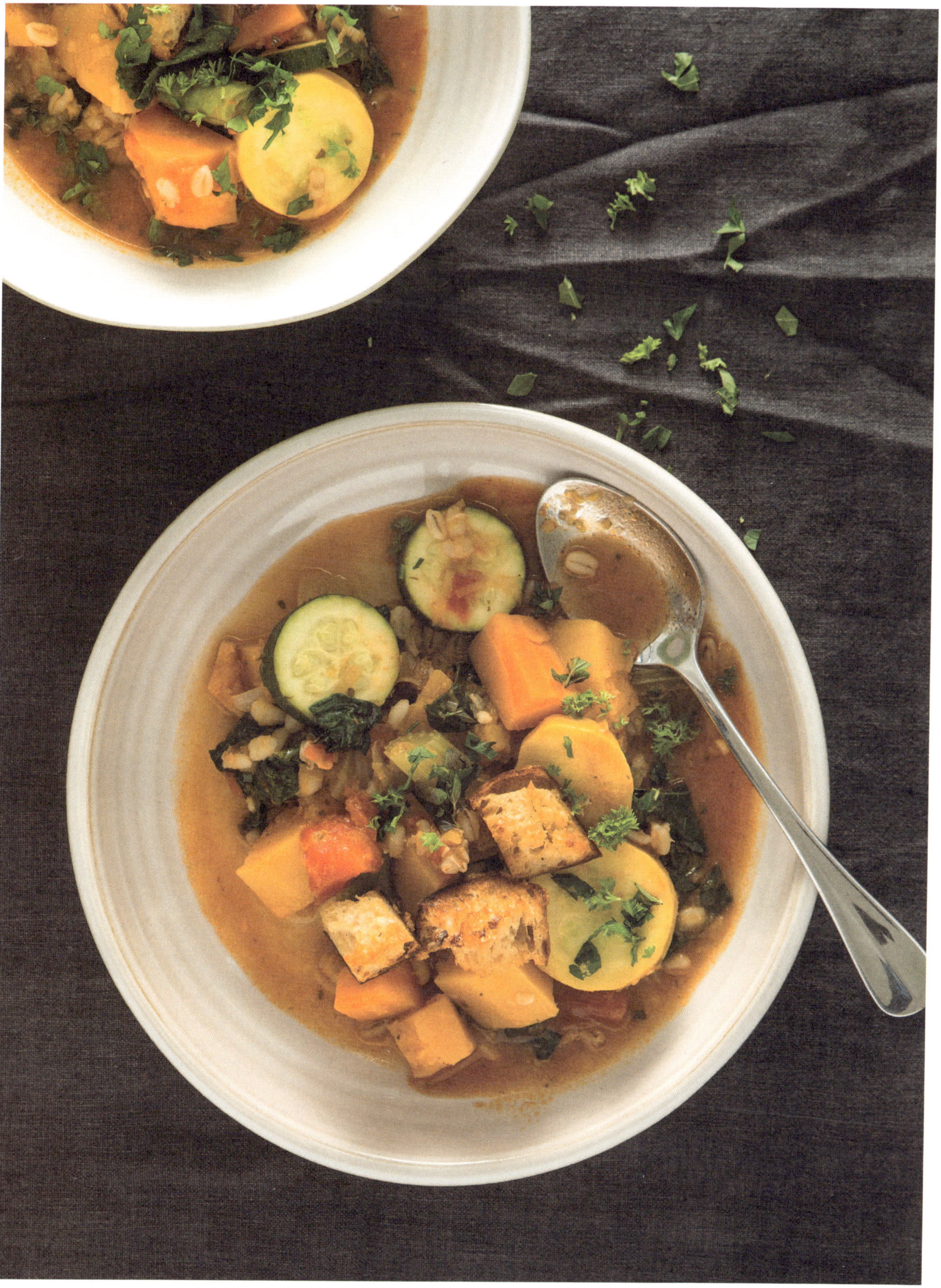

GF | DF | VEGAN use maple syrup

MOROCCAN ROAST CARROTS WITH QUINOA, DATES, LIME & CHILLI

SERVES 4
Prep time: 20 minutes
Cook time: 20 minutes

ROAST CARROTS
450–500g baby carrots, scrubbed and tops trimmed (or larger carrots, scrubbed and cut into batons)
2 tablespoons olive oil
1 tablespoon liquid honey or maple syrup
1½ teaspoons Moroccan Spice Mix (page 195)

QUINOA
2 tablespoons olive oil
1 red onion, diced
2 cloves garlic, chopped
2 teaspoons Moroccan Spice Mix
1 cup white quinoa, rinsed
1½ cups vegetable stock
zest of 2 limes
6 pitted medjool dates, chopped
1 red chilli, finely chopped
1 cup chopped parsley and/or coriander

TO SERVE
2 handfuls of rocket or baby spinach leaves
¼ cup toasted sliced/chopped almonds and/or pine nuts
1 lime or ½ lemon, cut into wedges

Roasting carrots with a delicious combination of spices makes all the difference; you can just buy a Moroccan spice mix or there is a recipe for one on page 195 to make your own. The quinoa is cooked in stock for extra flavour.

1. Preheat oven to 200°C. Line an oven tray with baking paper.

2. Toss carrots with olive oil, honey and spice mix. Roast for about 20 minutes until tender.

3. Heat olive oil in a medium pot on medium heat. Cook onion and garlic for 3–4 minutes until soft. Add spice mix and continue cooking for 30–60 seconds more.

4. Add quinoa and stock and bring to the boil. Stir, cover with a lid and reduce heat to low. Cook, covered, for 15 minutes. Turn off heat and leave quinoa to finish steaming for 5 minutes before uncovering and fluffing up with a fork.

6. Toss quinoa with roasted carrots (and any juices from the roasting tray), lime zest, dates, chilli and parsley/coriander. Season to taste with salt and pepper.

7. Just before serving toss rocket/spinach with roasted carrots and quinoa, and scatter with nuts. Squeeze over lime wedges just before eating.

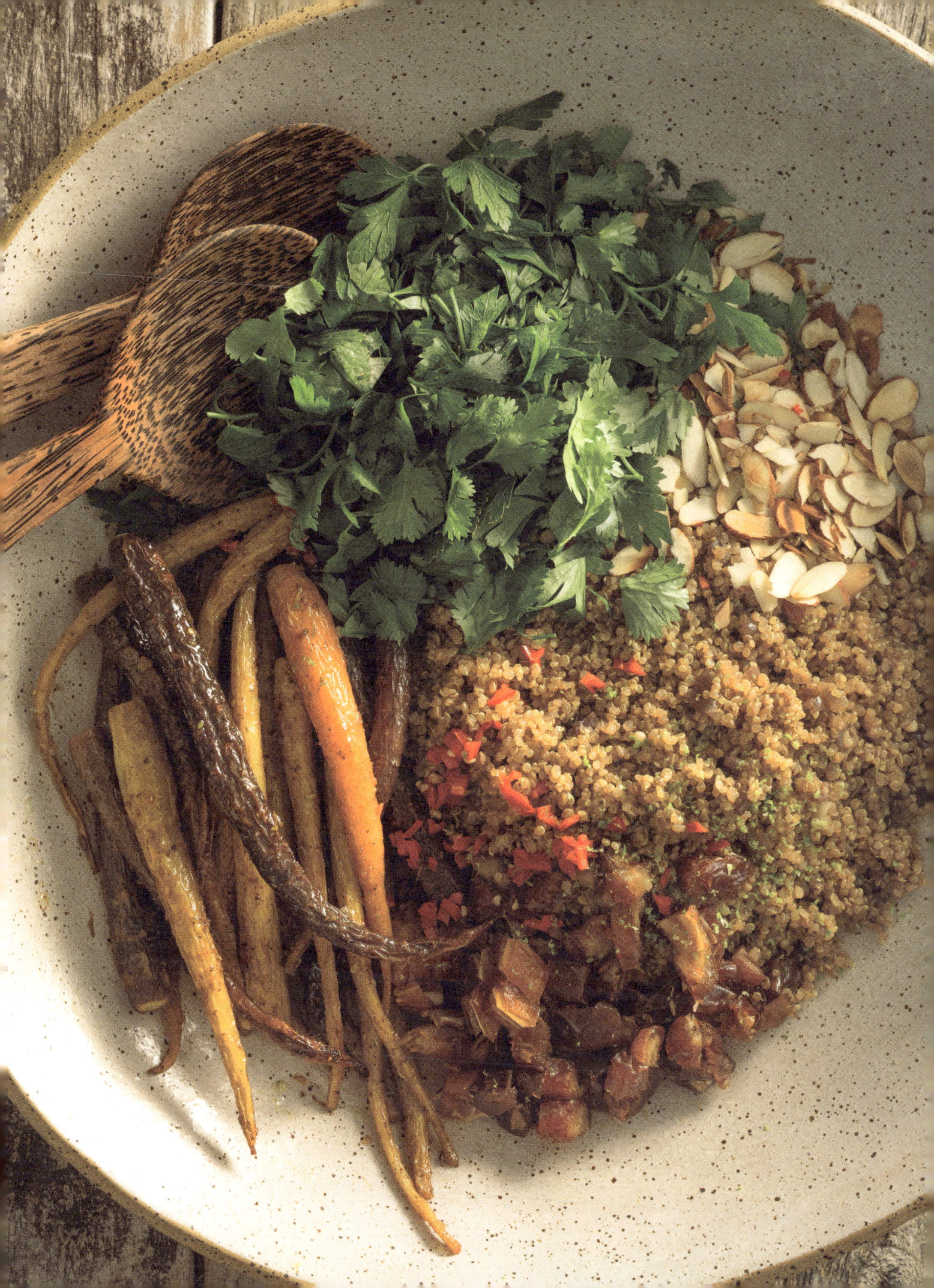

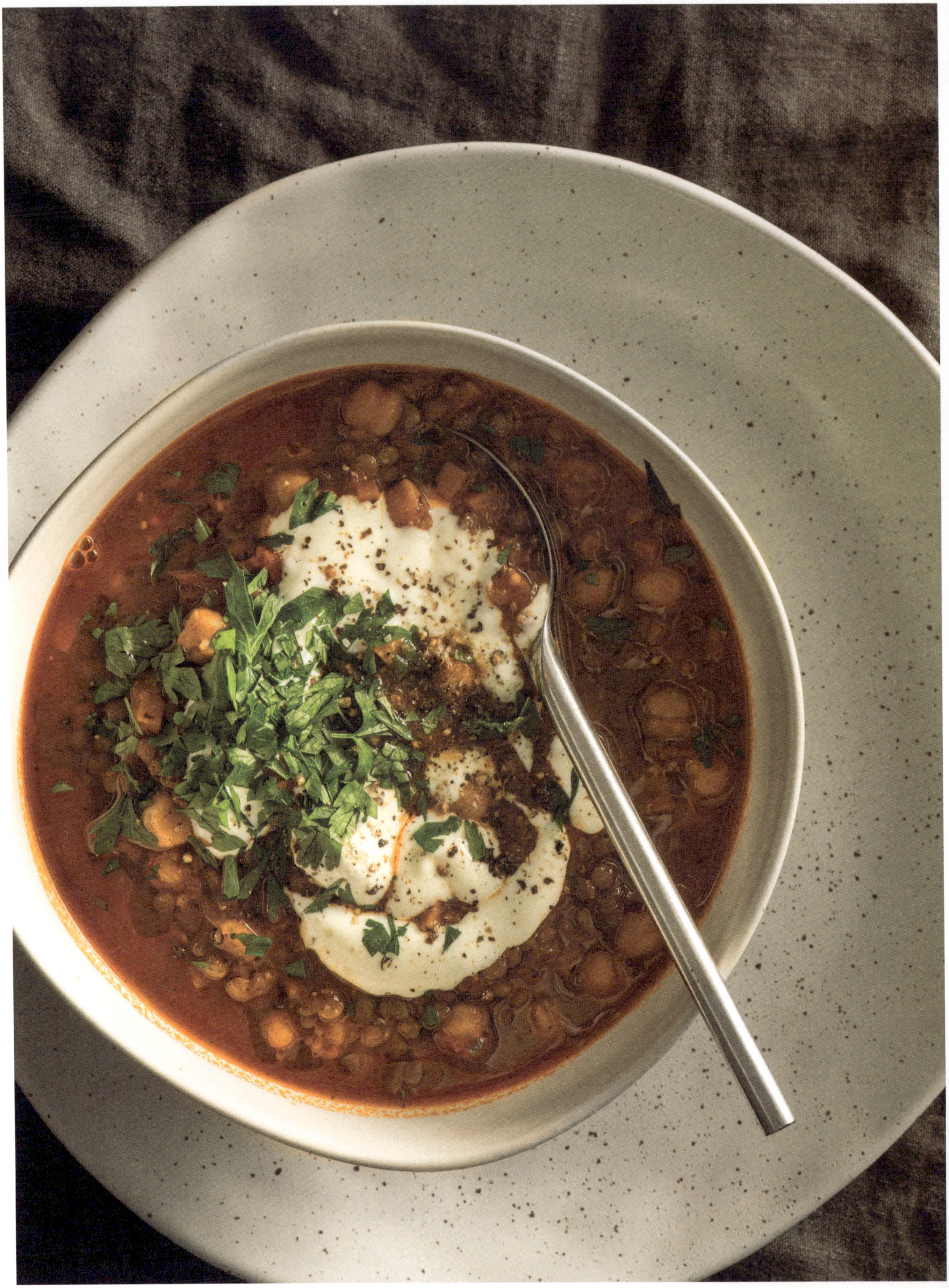

GF | DF use coconut yoghurt | VEGAN use coconut yoghurt and maple syrup

HARIRA

SERVES 4
Prep time: 15 minutes
Cook time: 45 minutes

2 tablespoons olive oil
1 onion, finely diced
2 carrots, peeled and finely diced
2 stalks celery, finely diced
2 cloves garlic, minced
1 tablespoon finely grated fresh ginger
2 tablespoons harissa paste (store-bought or page 216)
1 tablespoon tomato paste
1 tablespoon ground cumin
2 teaspoons ground coriander
2 teaspoons smoked paprika
1 tablespoon chopped fresh thyme
400g can crushed tomatoes
½ teaspoon honey or maple syrup
½ cup dried Puy lentils (French green lentils), rinsed
1.5 litres (6 cups) vegetable stock
400g can chickpeas, rinsed and drained

TO SERVE
¼ cup natural, unsweetened yoghurt
½ cup chopped coriander and/or parsley

Harira is a hearty Moroccan soup full of flavour. I love brothy legume soups like this one when it's cold outside. They're the ultimate way to warm yourself up from the inside out! Harissa is a North African spice mix. Buy harissa paste from a gourmet supermarket, or make it yourself with the recipe on page 216.

1. Heat oil in a large pot over medium heat. Cook onion, carrots, celery, garlic and ginger until soft, about 6 minutes.

2. Add harissa paste, tomato paste, cumin, coriander and smoked paprika. Cook for 2 minutes until fragrant.

3. Add thyme, tomatoes, honey, lentils and stock and bring to the boil. Simmer for about 25 minutes, then add chickpeas and continue simmering for a further 10–15 minutes or until lentils are cooked through (tender, but still firm to the bite).

4. Season soup to taste with salt and pepper. Ladle into bowls and dollop with yoghurt and sprinkle with herbs.

GF use GF tamari soy sauce | DF | VEGAN

PEANUT, LIME & SESAME DRESSED SLAW

SERVES 4 (or 6 as a side)
Prep time: 20 minutes

¼ (red, green or savoy) cabbage
1 large carrot
2–3 baby bok choy
1–2 spring onions
2 handfuls of baby kale or torn kale leaves
2–3 handfuls of mung bean sprouts

PEANUT LIME DRESSING
2 tablespoons peanut butter (smooth or crunchy)
2 tablespoons lime juice
1 teaspoon finely grated fresh ginger
1 teaspoon sesame oil
2 teaspoons tamari soy sauce
1 tablespoon sweet chilli sauce or 1 ½ teaspoons sugar
2 teaspoons rice vinegar

TO SERVE
¼ cup roughly chopped roasted peanuts
2–3 teaspoons toasted sesame seeds
handful of coriander and/or mint leaves

This fresh, crunchy slaw reminds me of the flavours in Vietnam (a country I've travelled to four times now!). The delicious virtues of raw bok choy are not known to everyone (it's almost always cooked) — it has a mild, fresh flavour and crunch similar to mung bean sprouts (which are also in this salad). To turn this into a meal, toss through some noodles and crispy fried tofu.

1. Very finely slice cabbage. Shred or coarsely grate carrot. Cut bottom 2cm off bok choy stems and discard. Wash remaining stems and leaves well, then finely slice. Finely slice spring onions. Place all in a large bowl and add kale and mung bean sprouts.

2. Whisk all dressing ingredients together. Thin out with a little water to get a drizzling consistency.

3. Add dressing to vegetables, along with peanuts and sesame seeds and toss together just before serving. Scatter with coriander and mint.

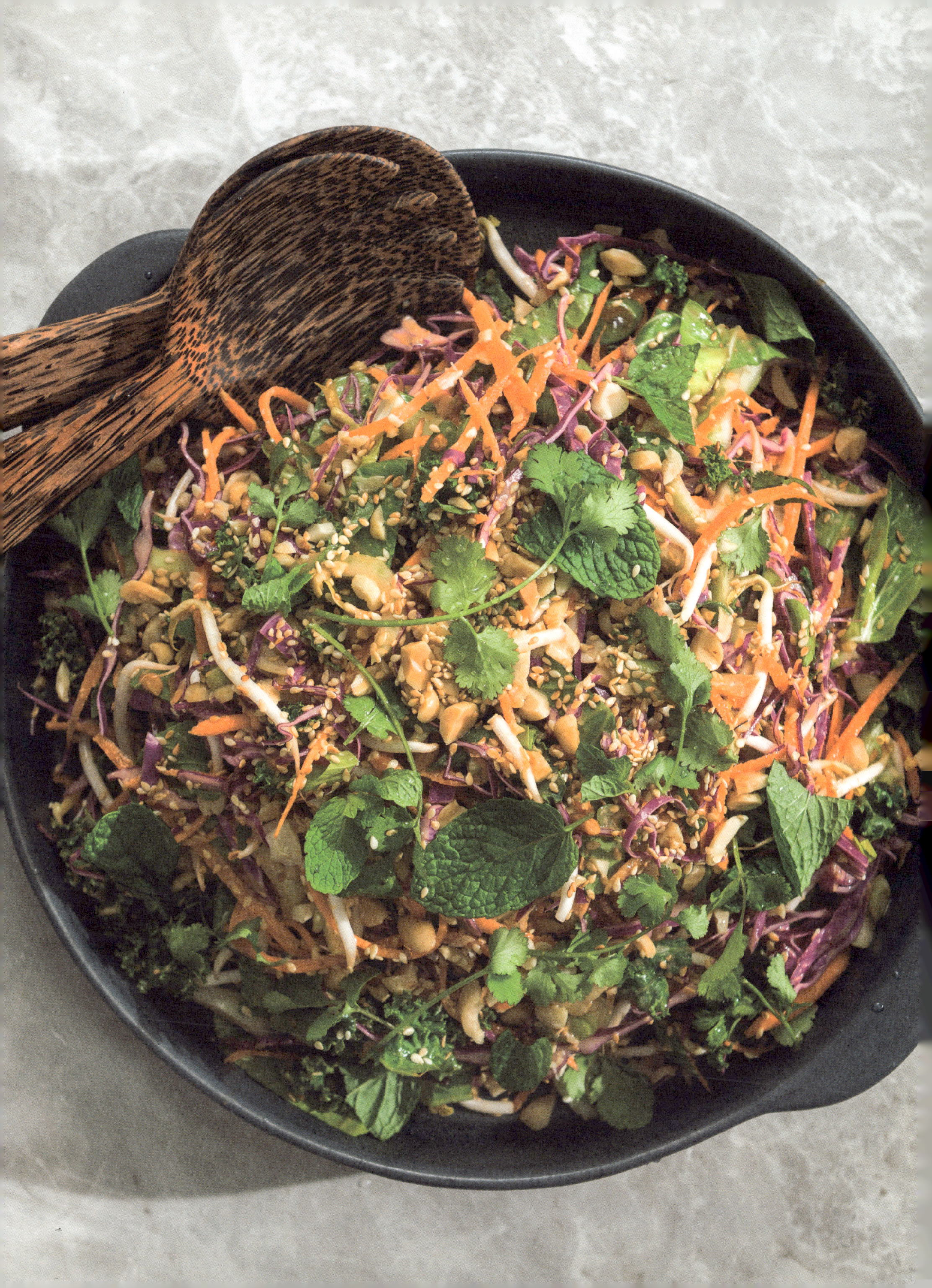

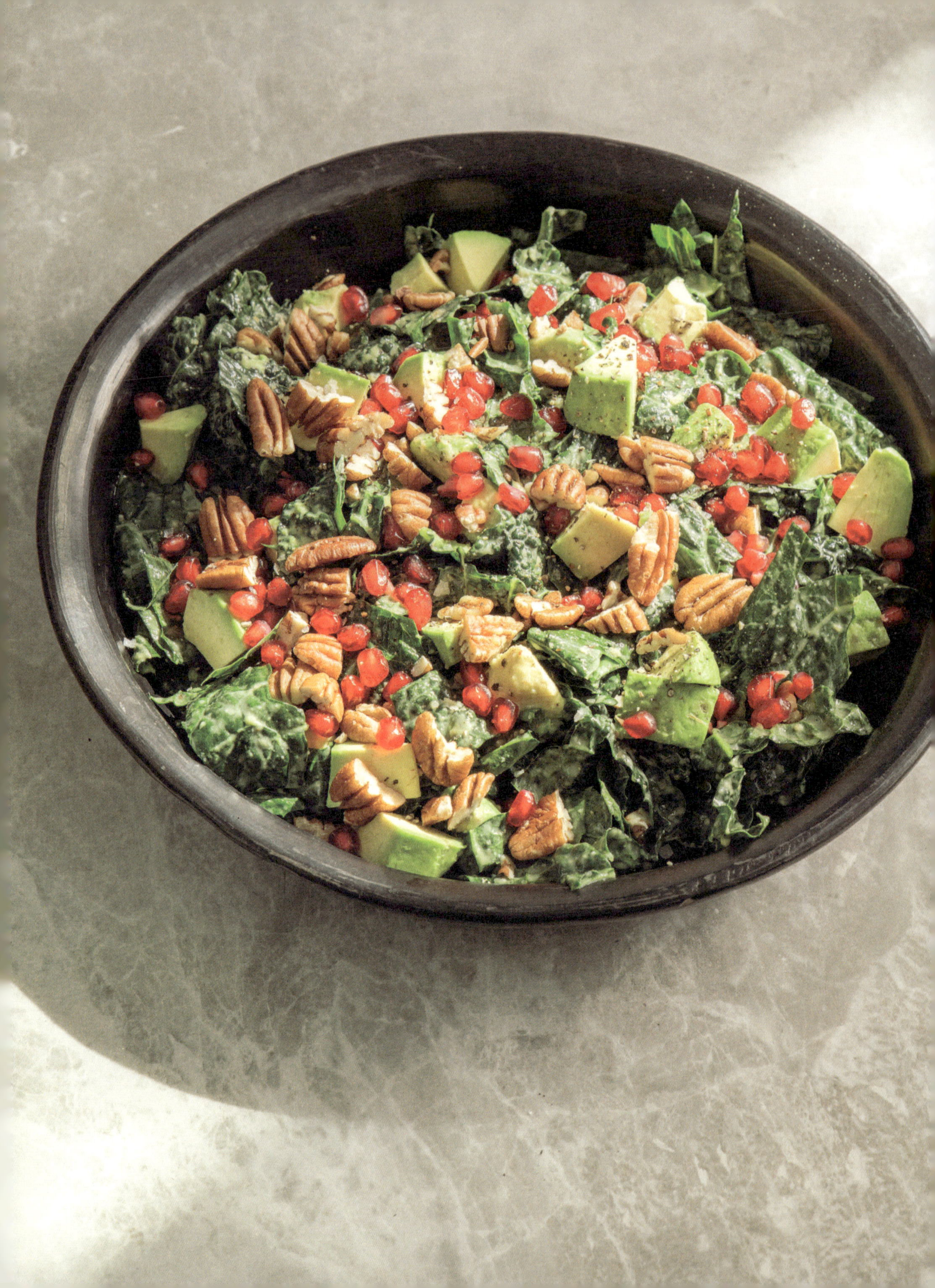

GF | DF | VEGAN use maple syrup

JASMIN'S CHRISTMAS SALAD

SERVES 4 (or 6 as a side)
Prep time: 15 minutes

1 large bunch cavolo nero (aka dinosaur kale)
flaky sea salt
½ ripe avocado, diced

DRESSING
juice of ½ lemon
½ teaspoon liquid honey or maple syrup
1 teaspoon Dijon mustard
1 heaped tablespoon macadamia or cashew nut butter
1½ tablespoons extra-virgin olive oil

TO SERVE
¼–½ cup lightly toasted pecans, roughly chopped
seeds of ½ pomegranate (about ½ cup seeds)
½ ripe avocado, diced

My sister Jasmin makes this salad for our Christmas feast (a very welcome addition to the other richer, heavier dishes). It looks right at home on the Christmas table with its dark green leaves and bright red pomegranate seeds, and the pecans add a warm, toasty, nutty touch. Of course, it's not just a good one for Christmas, but for any time of the year. Thanks for the recipe Jaz!

1. Wash cavolo nero and tear leaves from the stalks (discard stalks). Chop leaves and place in a large bowl. Sprinkle with a good pinch of flaky sea salt.

2. Whisk all dressing ingredients together until smooth and drizzle over cavolo nero. Use clean hands to thoroughly 'massage' the dressing and sea salt into the cavolo nero for a few minutes with your fingertips — this helps to soften the leaves (making them easier to eat) and takes away any bitter taste. The leaves should be well coated, feel softer and have a glossy sheen.

3. Add first half of avocado and lightly 'massage' it through so that the very soft part of the avocado lightly coats the leaves, but there are still chunks of avocado.

4. Transfer to a serving bowl and top with remaining diced avocado, pecans and pomegranate seeds. Toss just before serving.

GF | DF | VEGAN use maple syrup

RAW VEGE PILAV

SERVES 4 (or 6 as a side)
Prep time: 15 minutes

¼ cup pine nuts
¼ cup chopped pistachios
1 large carrot, peeled and roughly chopped
½ head cauliflower, roughly chopped
½ head broccoli, roughly chopped
4–5 pitted medjool dates, finely chopped
zest of 1 lemon
¼ cup finely chopped flat-leaf parsley
¼ cup chopped mint leaves
seeds of ½ pomegranate

DRESSING
¼ cup freshly squeezed lemon juice
3 tablespoons extra-virgin olive oil
1½ teaspoons maple syrup or liquid honey

Raw, crunchy, fresh and full of vigour. I love its texture (its important you don't over-pulse the vegetables as you still want them coarse and crunchy!), and the little bursts of sweet and sour that you get from the dates, lemon and pomegranate. This is perfect as a high-veg alternative to couscous or rice.

1. Place pine nuts and pistachios in a medium-sized fry pan on medium heat for a few minutes, shaking pan frequently, until pine nuts are lightly toasted. Take off the heat and tip into a bowl to cool.

2. Place carrot, cauliflower and broccoli into the bowl of a food processor and pulse a few times until vegetables are finely chopped, about the size of rice grains.

3. Tip vegetables into a large bowl and toss with dates, lemon zest, parsley, mint and pomegranate seeds.

4. Mix all dressing ingredients together and season with salt and pepper. Toss with salad just before serving.

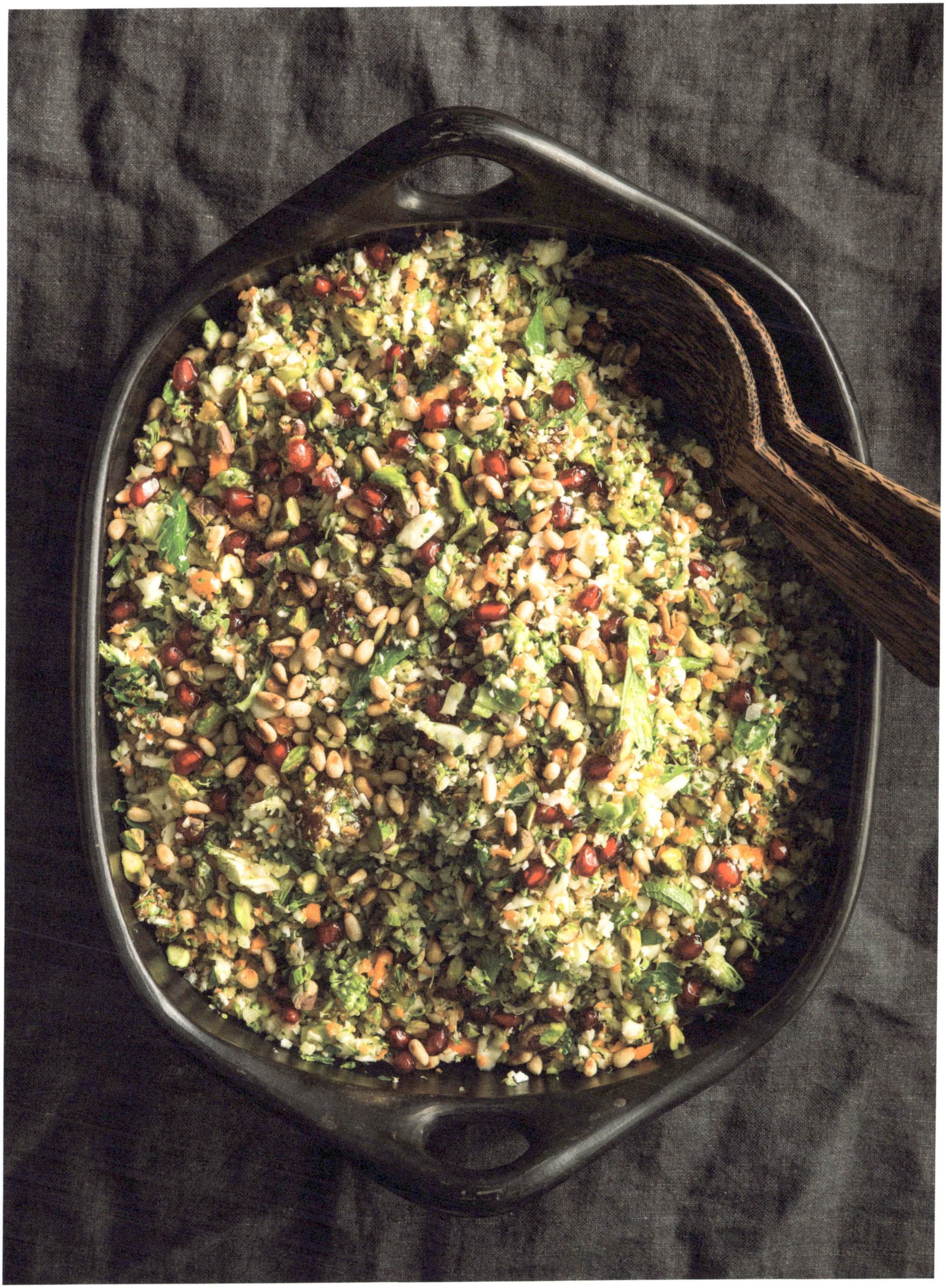

Lunc
din

CHAPTER THREE — P. 111

h & her

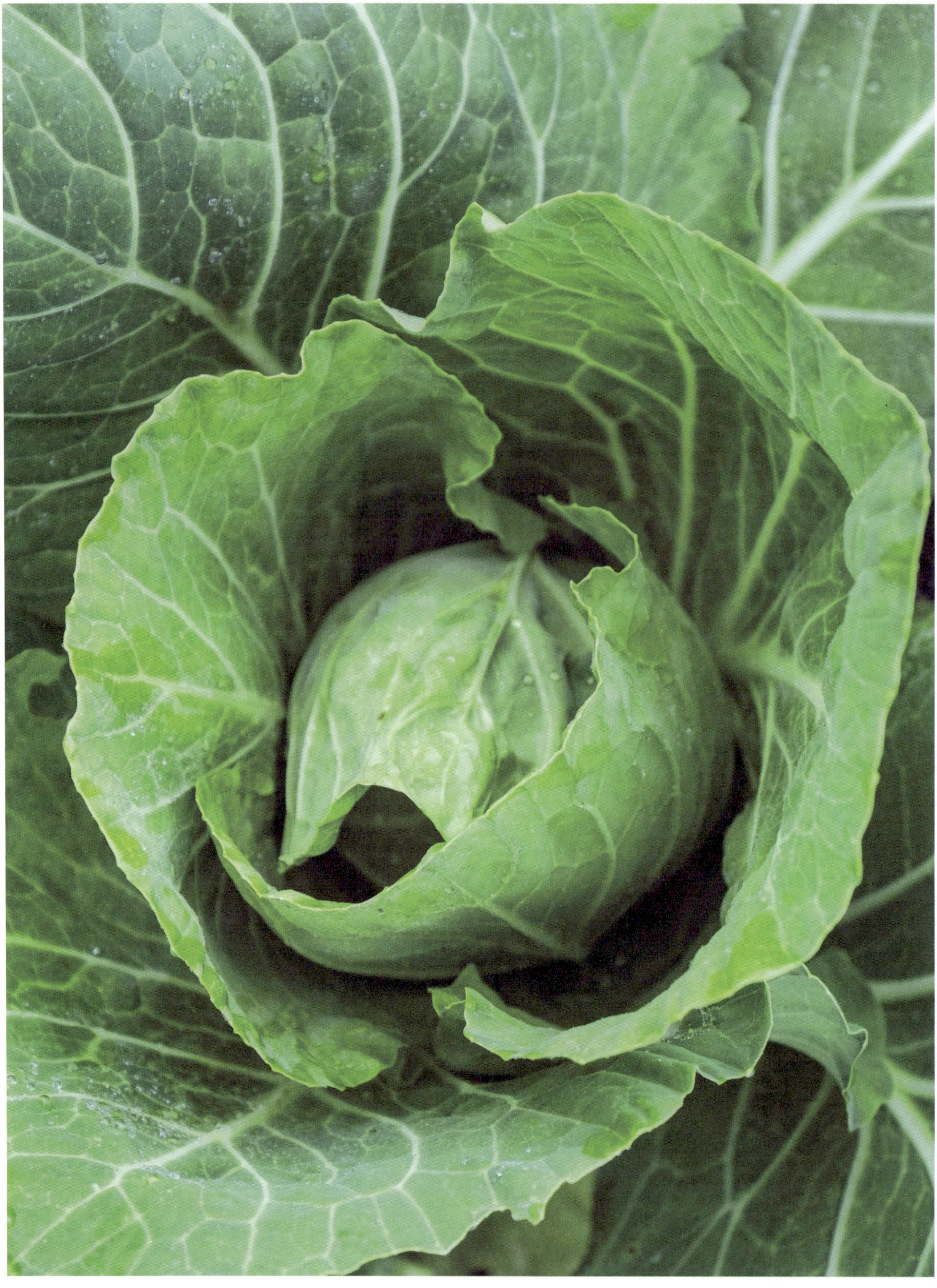

There is so much deliciousness awaiting in the following pages that I'm excited for you, particularly if you have been wanting to enjoy more meat-free meals.

Vegetables take centre stage in these recipes, no longer in traditional supporting roles to meat. And I can assure you that any fear you have of feeling deprived or not fully satisfied without meat on your plate will be gone once you try these recipes.

I challenge you to invite some omnivores over for a meal and serve them a wholly vegetarian feast, sit back and enjoy their overwhelmingly positive response (it's very likely that, for some, it will be a revelation). I must admit the first time I cooked an all vegan and vegetarian special-occasion dinner I had my doubts. But now, I revel in the opportunity to bring out more vegetarian and vegan dishes for omnivores, vegetarians and vegans alike.

These, hand over heart, are some of my favourite meals and I know that some will become reliable, gratifying favourites in your home too, and inspire you to eat and love more meat-free meals.

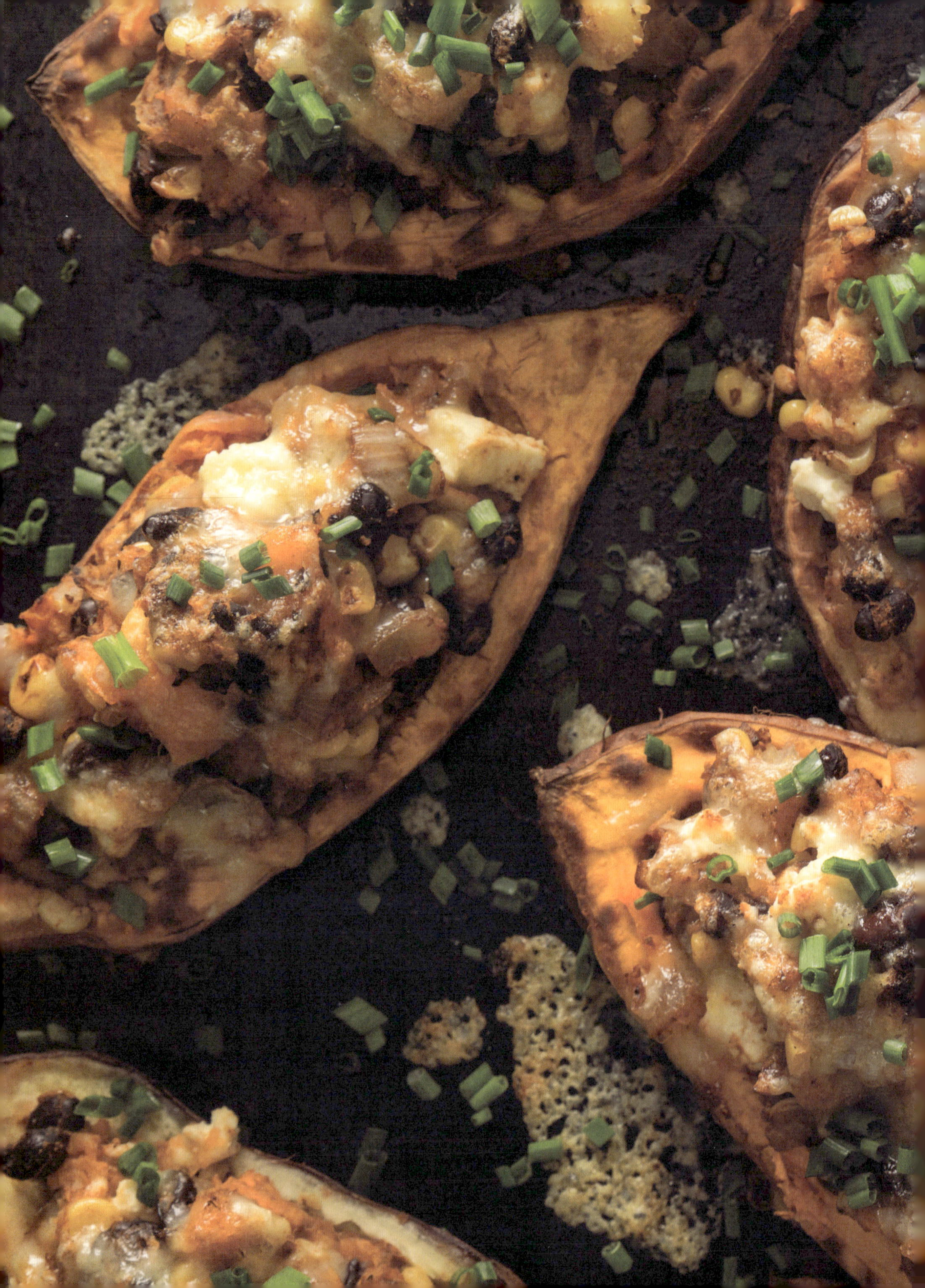

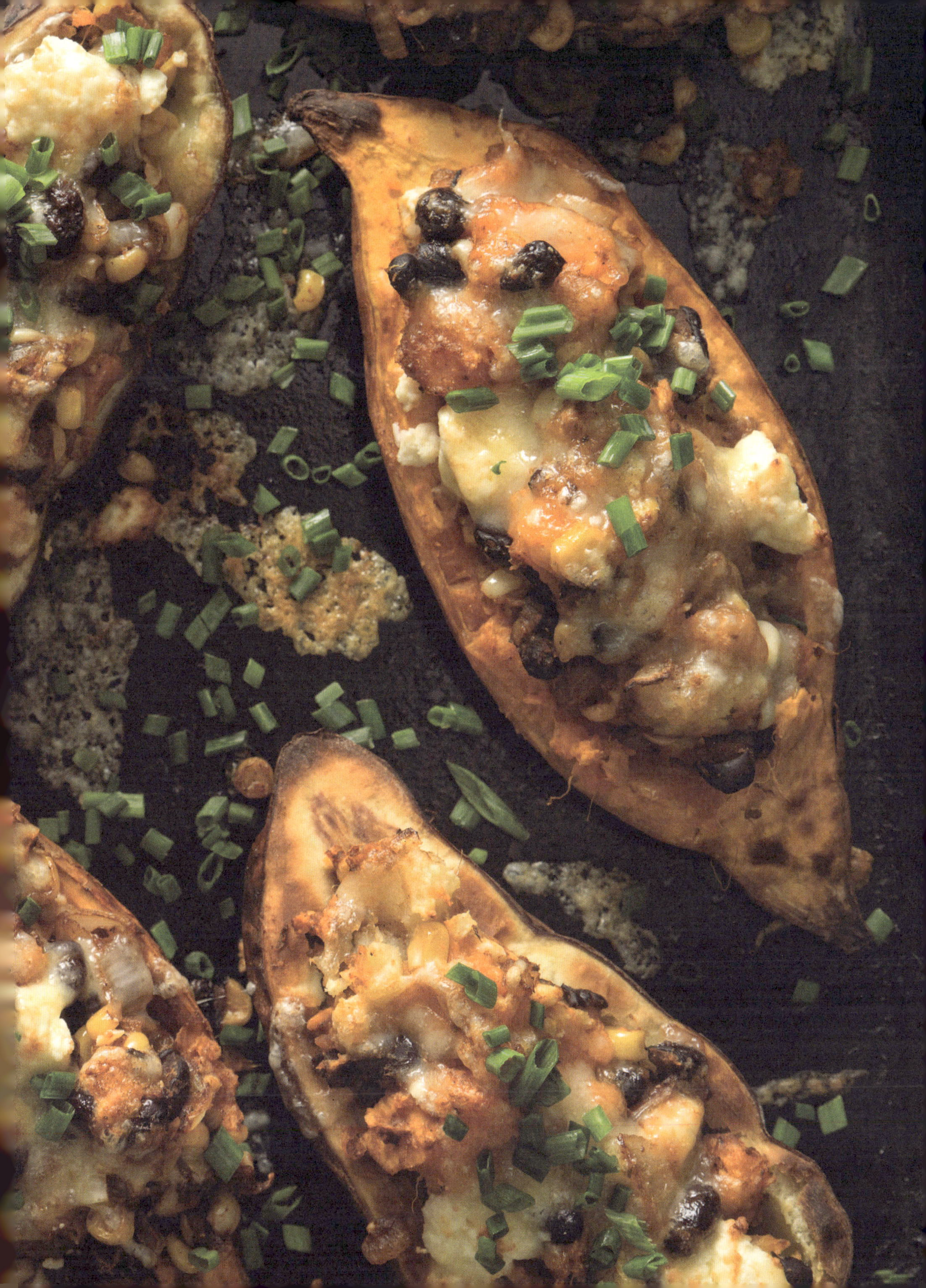

GF

MEXICAN STUFFED KUMARAS

SERVES 4–6
Prep time: 25 minutes
Cook time: 45 minutes

4 medium-sized kumara (red, gold or orange), scrubbed
kernels of 2 corn cobs (or 1½ cups canned or frozen and defrosted corn kernels, patted dry)
2 tablespoons olive oil
1 red or brown onion, diced
1½–2 tablespoons Mexican spice mix (store-bought or page 195)
2–3 cloves garlic, finely chopped
400g can black beans, rinsed and drained
3 tablespoons chipotle sauce
50g feta, crumbled or 100g cream cheese (optional)
1–1½ cups grated cheese

TO SERVE
½ cup chopped chives, coriander, parsley or basil
sour cream or natural Greek yoghurt
Salsa (store-bought or page 195)

Tender, sweet baked kumara, piled high with a tasty Mexican-inspired filling and covered in melted cheese. As with other Mexican dishes (e.g. nachos or tacos), you can go all out with the accompaniments — I suggest serving with salsa and sour cream (or natural Greek yoghurt) at the very least. But if you want to step it up, add guacamole, pink pickled onions (page 180), jalapeños, and whatever else you like!

1. Preheat oven to 220°C.

2. Cut kumara in half lengthways and place on a baking tray, cut-side up. Drizzle with olive oil and season with salt and pepper. Bake for 40 minutes or until flesh is tender (test by poking into the centre with a knife tip or fork).

3. Heat a large (preferably heavy-based, cast iron) fry pan on medium to high heat. Add corn kernels (without any oil) and cook, stirring occasionally, until slightly charred. It helps if you leave them for a few minutes before stirring at all. Transfer to a bowl; keep pan on the heat.

4. Add olive oil to the pan. Cook onion for a few minutes until starting to soften. Add spice mix and garlic and continue cooking for a further 1–2 minutes. Add to bowl of charred corn, along with black beans and chipotle sauce.

5. When kumara are ready, remove from oven. Switch oven to grill. Use a spoon to carefully scoop out kumara flesh, leaving 1cm thickness of flesh from the skin. Add kumara flesh to bowl along with feta or dots of cream cheese (if using). Gently toss everything together to combine. Season to taste with salt and pepper.

6. Loosely fill kumara skins with the filling. Sprinkle with grated cheese and grill for about 5 minutes until cheese is golden and bubbly.

7. Serve scattered with chopped herbs and sour cream/yoghurt, salsa and salad on the side.

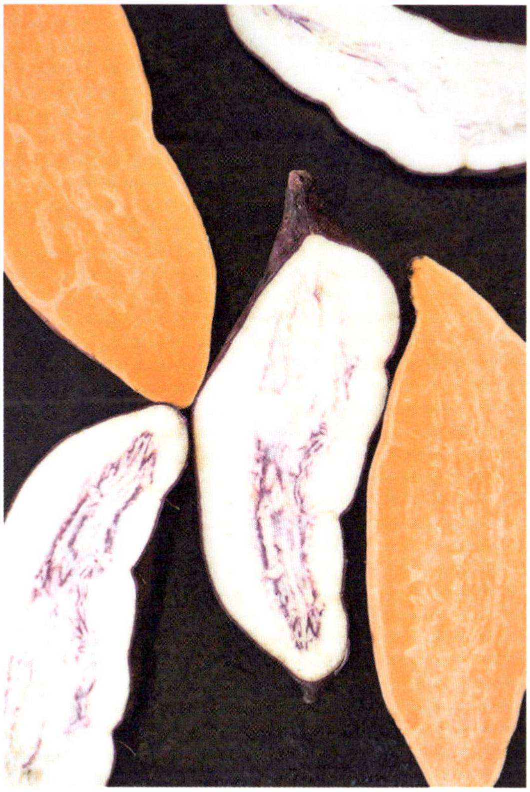
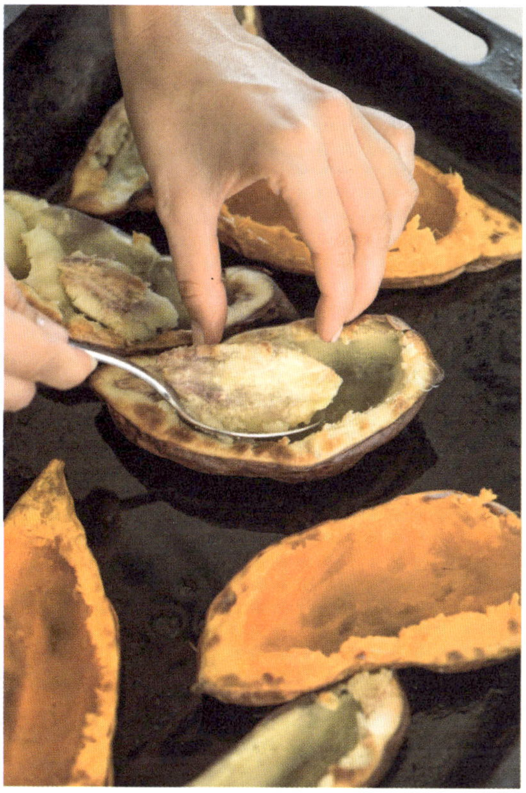
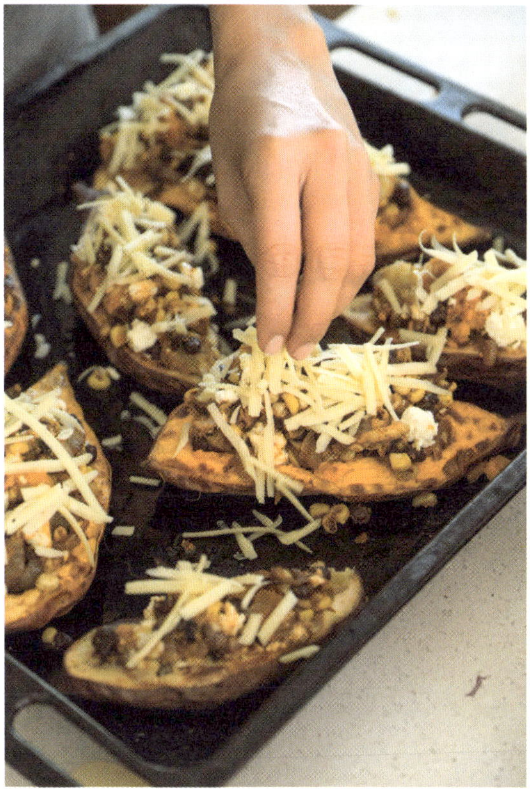
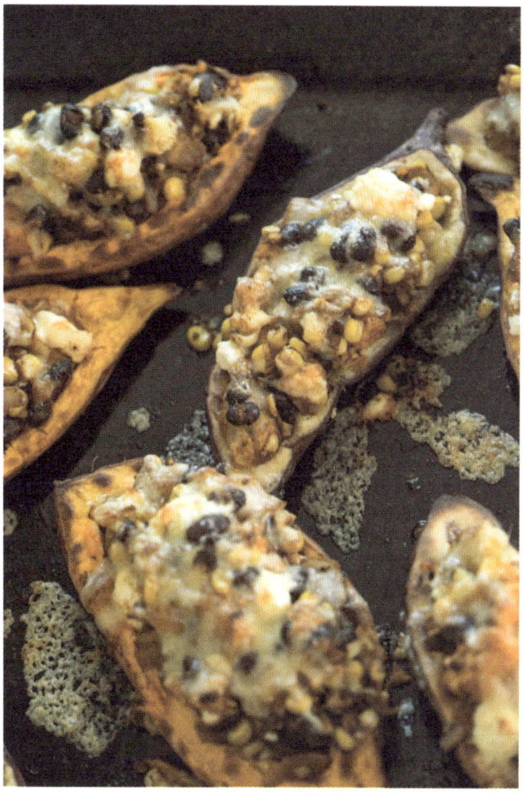

DF | VEGAN

CARAMELISED ONION & BEETROOT TART WITH SOFT CASHEW CHEESE

SERVES 4–6
Prep time: 15 minutes
Cook time: 50 minutes

3 medium beetroot, scrubbed
1 tablespoon olive oil
1 tablespoon maple syrup
1 quantity Olive Oil Pastry (page 157) or 1 square sheet store-bought shortcrust pastry
1 cup Caramelised Onions (page 159 or use store-bought)

TO SERVE
Soft Cashew Cheese (page 156 or a store-bought cashew cheese, e.g. cashew feta), or crème fraîche or sour cream
pea tendrils and/or baby rocket
2–3 tablespoons lightly toasted pine nuts
2–3 tablespoons Mint Chermoula (page 57) or store-bought pesto (optional)

This delicious tart is always a hit with everyone and it's completely vegan! The light, crumbly pastry is made from olive oil (instead of butter) and then it is dolloped with home-made soft cashew cheese which is very easy to make. You could, of course, use store-bought pastry if you wanted, and a soft goats cheese in place of the cashew cheese. For a super-quick (however not vegan) version, use store-bought pastry, cheese/crème fraîche and pesto!

1. Preheat oven to 190°C. Slice beetroot into 0.5cm-thick rounds. Place on an oven tray lined with baking paper and drizzle with olive oil and maple syrup, and season with salt and pepper. Roast for 20–25 minutes, until tender.

2. On a piece of baking paper, roll pastry dough out into a large circle, about 3–4mm thick (or you can leave as a square if you prefer). Prick in a few places with a fork and bake for 20–25 minutes until light golden brown.

3. Warm up Caramelised Onions. Remove pastry base from oven and spread with Caramelised Onions and arrange beetroot on top. Top with dollops of Soft Cashew Cheese, rocket/pea tendrils, pine nuts and pesto or Mint Chermoula (if using).

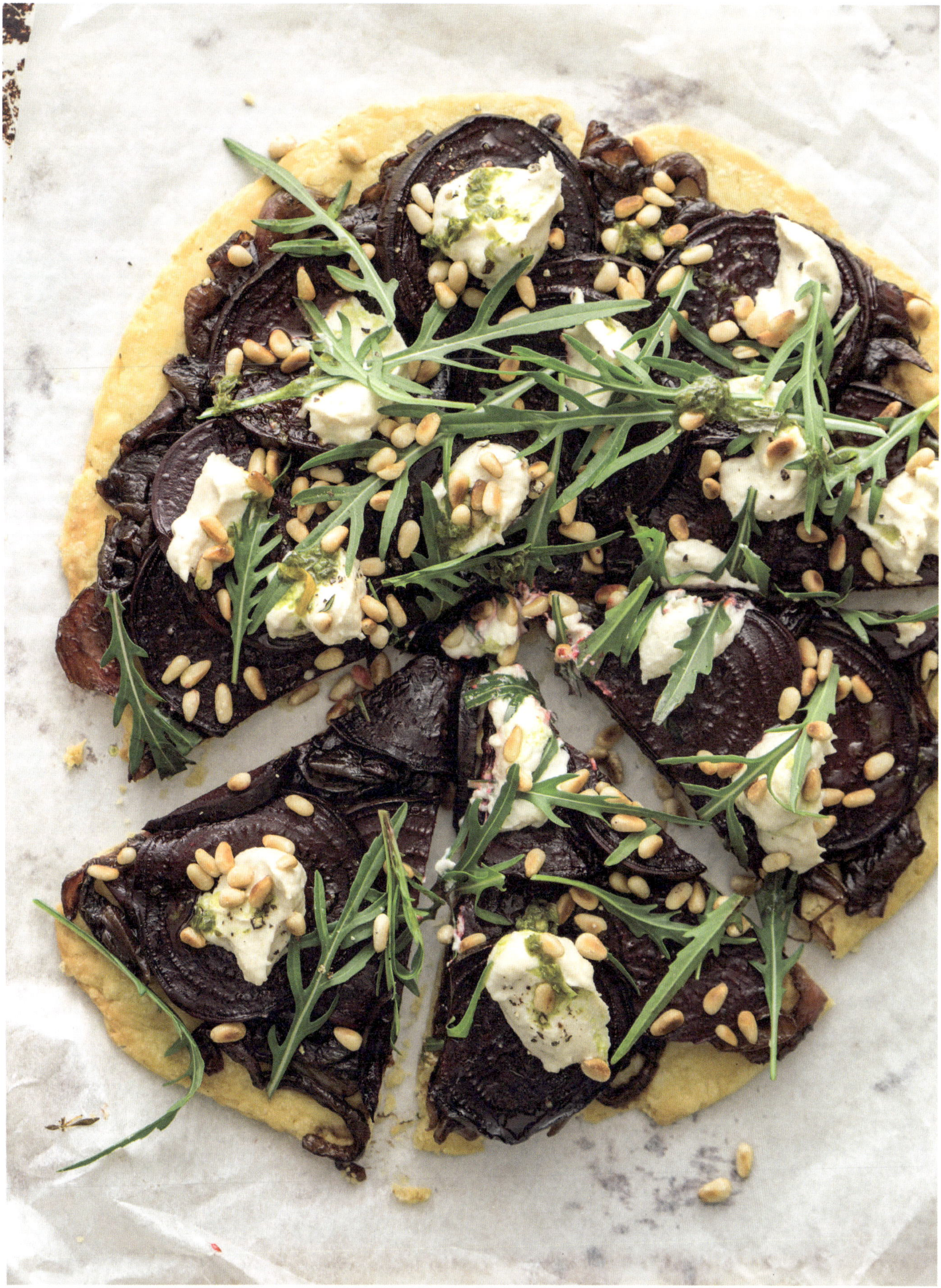

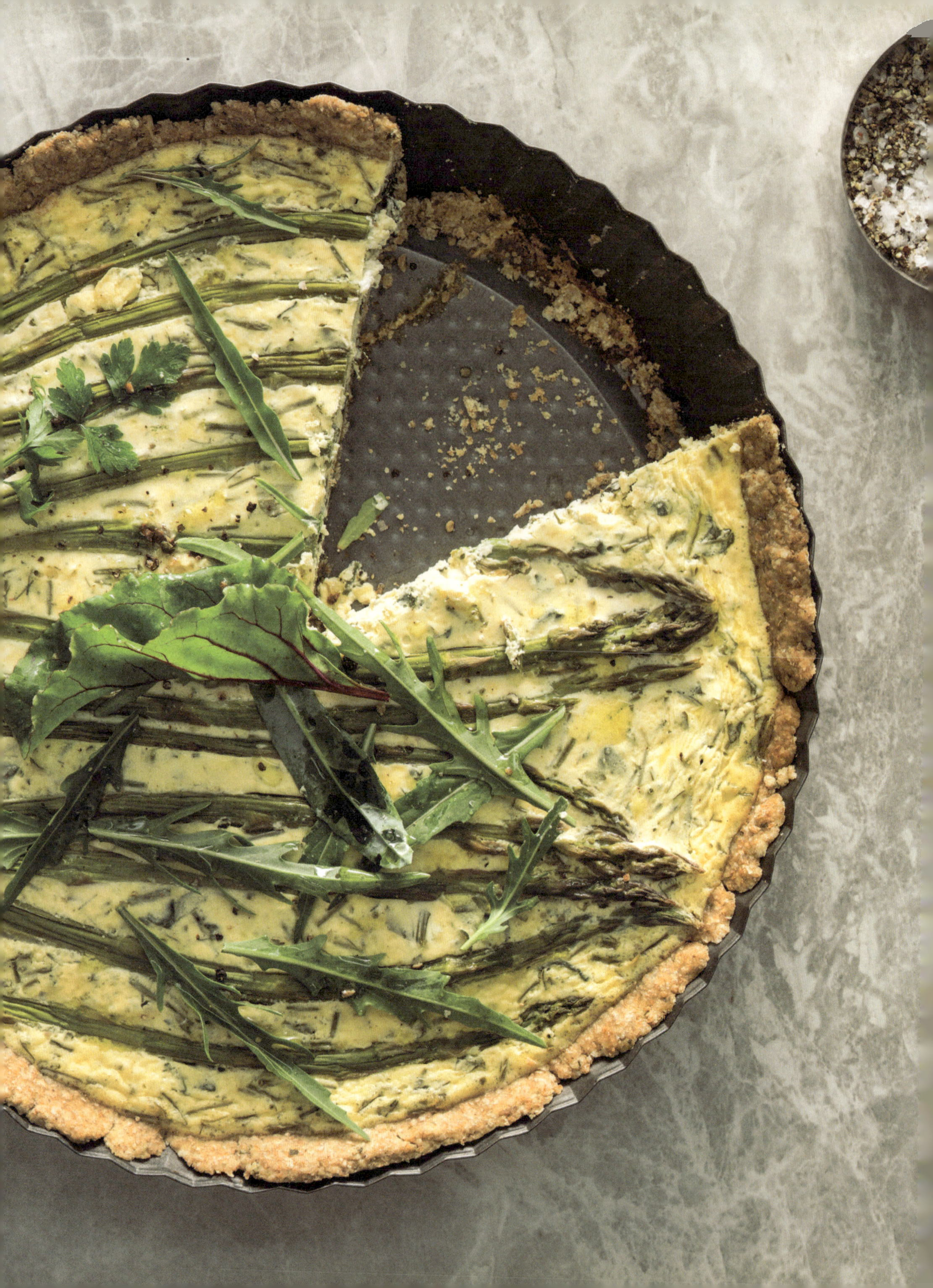

CREAMY ASPARAGUS, SPINACH, HERB & GOATS CHEESE TART

SERVES 6
Prep time: 30 minutes
Cook time: 35–40 minutes

WHOLEMEAL HERB PASTRY
225g wholemeal flour
1 tablespoon chopped fresh thyme and/or rosemary
1 small clove garlic, chopped
1 teaspoon salt
125g cold butter, cubed

FILLING
1 bunch (10–12) spears of asparagus, tough ends trimmed
100g spinach, chopped
3 large free-range eggs
200g sour cream or crème fraîche
½ cup cream or full cream milk
100–125g soft goats cheese or feta
1–1¼ cups mixed chopped soft herbs (e.g. chives, parsley, tarragon, dill, chervil)
finely grated zest of ½ lemon
2 teaspoons lemon juice

This tart uses a homemade wholemeal herb pastry. However, you can just use store-bought shortcrust pastry if you prefer/wanted to make this quickly. It makes the perfect lunch or light meal — all you need is a green salad and a dollop of tomato relish on the side. And a glass of pinot gris would go down well too!

1. Preheat oven to 180°C. Grease a 27–28cm fluted tart tin with butter or oil. Bring a kettle of water to the boil.

2. To make the pastry, place ingredients in a food processor and blitz until crumbly then, with the motor still running, drizzle in 2–3 tablespoons of cold water until mixture holds together when pressed between your fingers. Alternatively, if you don't have a food processor, rub butter in with your fingertips until mixture resembles fine breadcrumbs, then add 2–3 tablespoons water and mix to a firm dough. Use your hands to bring dough together into a big ball, wrap in clingfilm and allow to rest on the bench for 15 minutes while you start preparing the filling.

3. Place asparagus and spinach in a large heatproof bowl or dish and cover with boiling water, leave for 1–2 minutes then drain. When cool enough to handle, use your hands to squeeze out as much excess water from the spinach as you can, then finely chop.

4. On a clean, dry, lightly floured surface (or on a sheet of baking paper), roll out the pastry and use to line the base and up the sides of the greased tin. Don't worry if the pastry tears a little in places; just press and patch it back together. Refrigerate for 5 minutes or so. Bake for 12–15 minutes until lightly browned. Remove from oven and set aside to cool.

5. Whisk eggs, sour cream/crème fraîche and cream/milk together until smooth. Finely crumble in goats cheese/feta. Add herbs, lemon zest and juice, and spinach. Season with salt and freshly ground black pepper.

6. Pour filling into pastry crust and arrange asparagus spears on top, pushing down to slightly submerge in the filling. Bake for 20–25 minutes or until just set. Leave to stand for at least 15 minutes before removing from tin. Cut into six slices and serve with salad and tomato relish or chutney.

DF omit feta or use cashew feta | VEGAN omit feta or use cashew feta

MOROCCAN EGGPLANT BOATS

SERVES 4
Prep time: 15 minutes
Cook time: 40–45 minutes

2 large or 3 smaller eggplants
2 tablespoons olive oil
1 red onion, diced
1 capsicum, diced
2 cloves garlic, chopped
1 cup pearl couscous
   (Israeli couscous)
2 teaspoons Moroccan Spice Mix
   (store-bought or page 195)
zest of ½ lemon
1¾ cups water or vegetable stock
¼ cup chopped dried sweet apricots
2 tablespoons dried currants
½–¾ cup chopped parsley
100g creamy feta
4 tablespoons chutney (e.g.
   Moroccan Apricot and Tomato
   Chutney (page 158) or similar
   style store-bought chutney)

TO GARNISH
2–3 tablespoons lightly toasted
   pine nuts or slivered almonds
chopped parsley or coriander

I love cooking and serving these baked and stuffed eggplant boats as part of a Moroccan or Middle Eastern-style feast. Add a colourful salad or two, like the Moroccan Roast Carrots with Quinoa, Dates, Lime and Chilli (page 100) or the Middle Eastern Quinoa Salad with Haloumi and Crispy Pita (page 93), and you have a real feast for the senses. You can stuff the eggplants with lots of things other than pearl couscous, from rice to lentils and chickpeas... even cubes of cooked potato!

1. Preheat oven to 200°C.

2. Cut eggplants in half lengthways, leaving stems intact. Place cut-side up on a baking tray, drizzle with olive oil and season with salt. Bake for about 35 minutes until soft and lightly browned.

3. Heat olive oil in a medium pot on medium heat. Cook onion, capsicum and garlic for 3–4 minutes until soft. Add couscous, Moroccan Spice Mix and lemon zest and cook for a further 1 minute.

4. Add water/stock and a pinch of salt. Bring to the boil, stir and cover with a lid. Reduce heat to low and cook, covered, for 8–10 minutes until couscous is tender.

5. Turn off heat and leave couscous to finish steaming for 10 minutes before uncovering and tossing with dried apricots, currants and parsley. Season with salt and pepper.

6. When eggplants have finished baking, remove from oven and lightly scoop out soft flesh with a spoon, leaving about a 1cm border from the skin. Roughly chop flesh, then add to couscous and gently toss together.

7. Loosely fill hollowed out eggplant halves with couscous. Top with feta and dollops of chutney. Return to the oven to bake for 6–8 minutes until heated through.

8. Sprinkle with toasted nuts and parsley/coriander. Serve with a salad on the side.

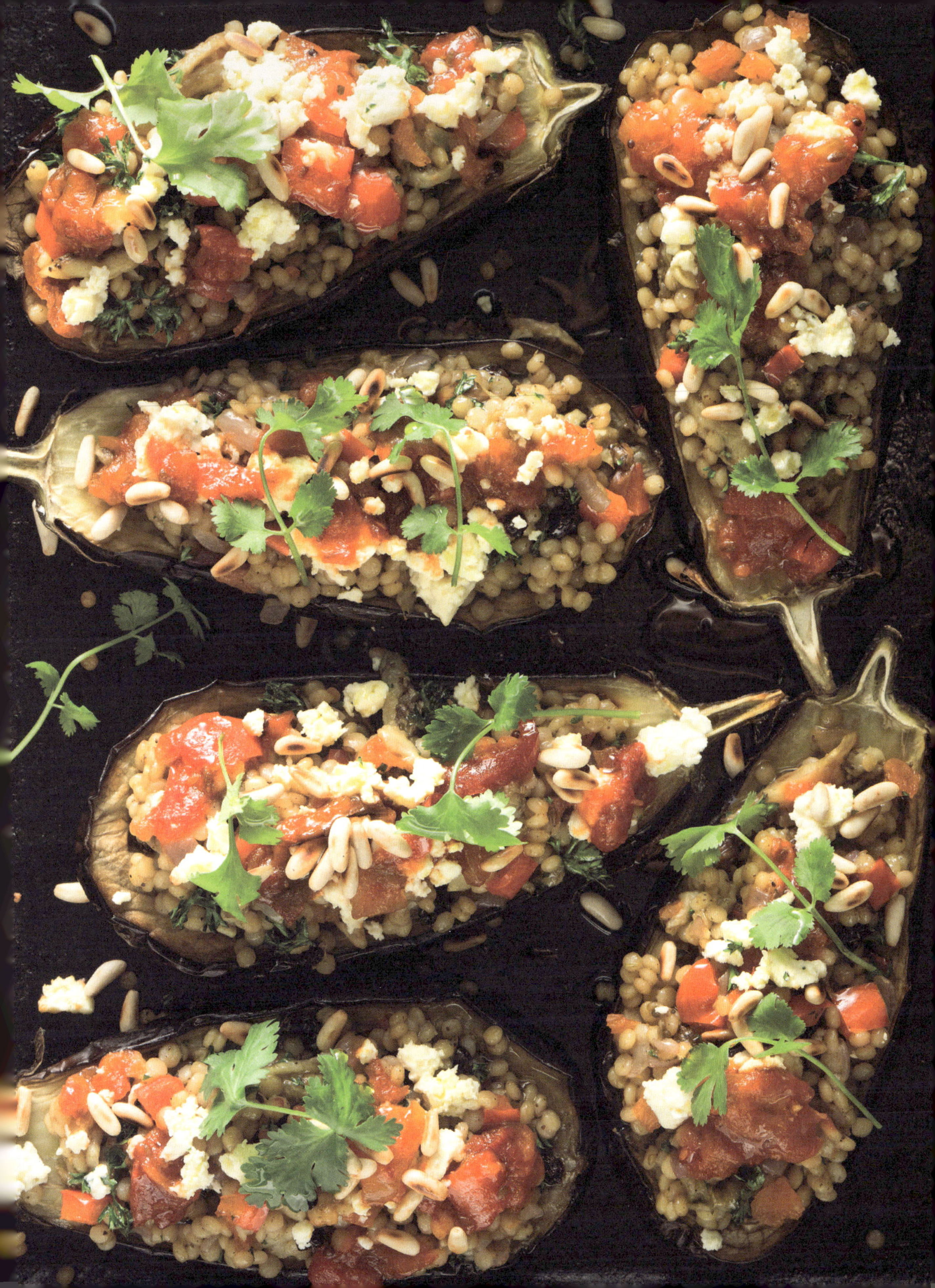

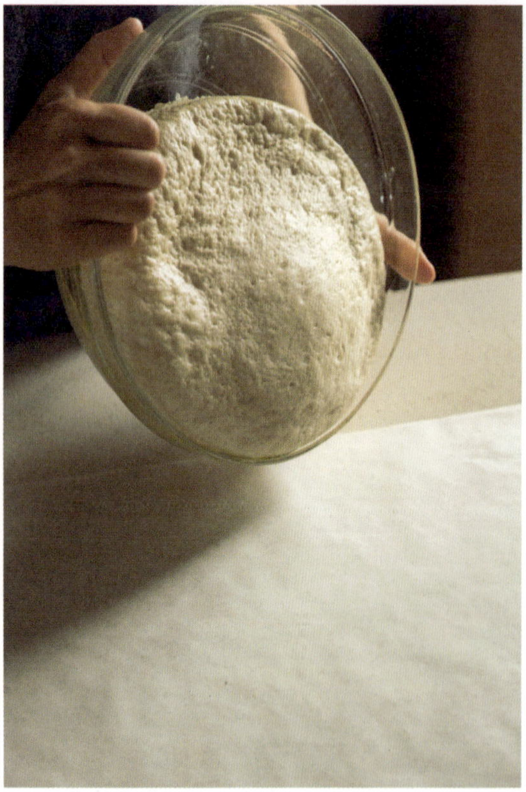
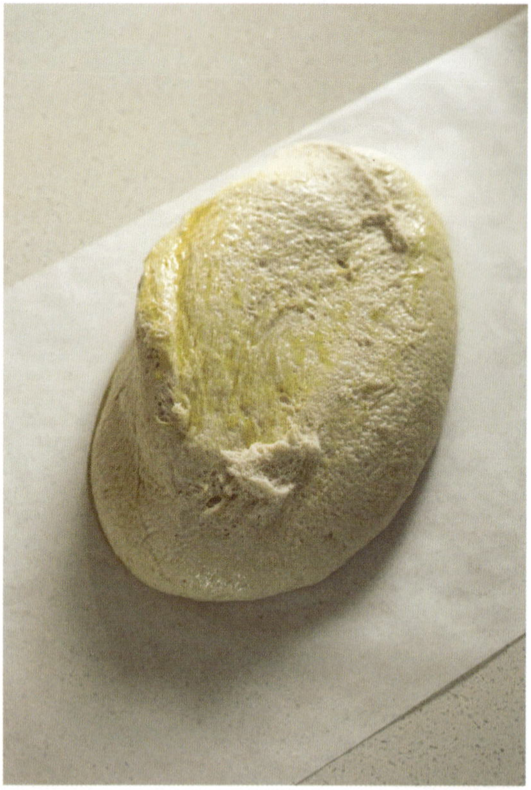
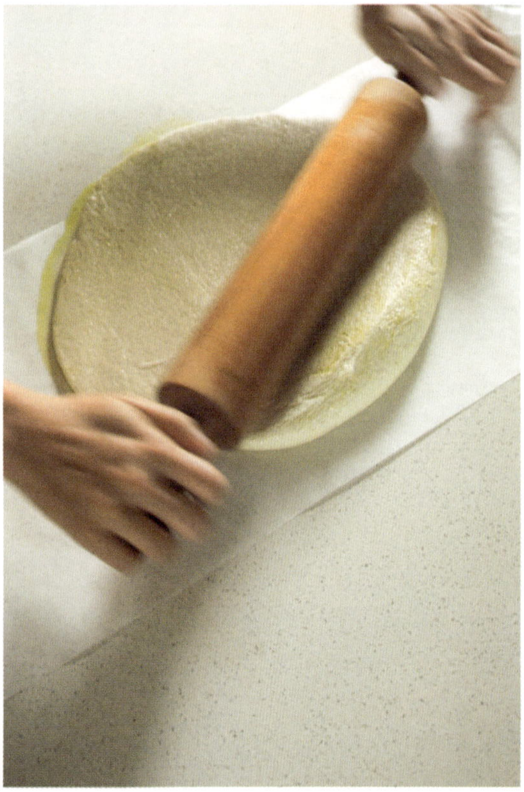
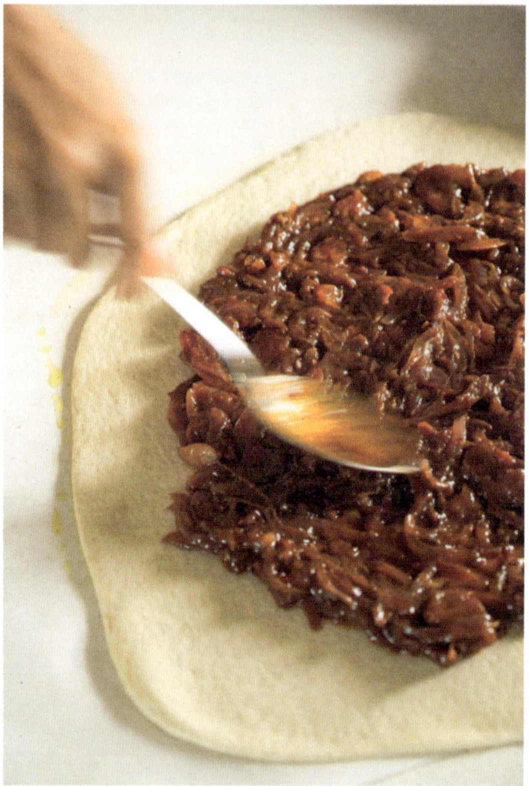

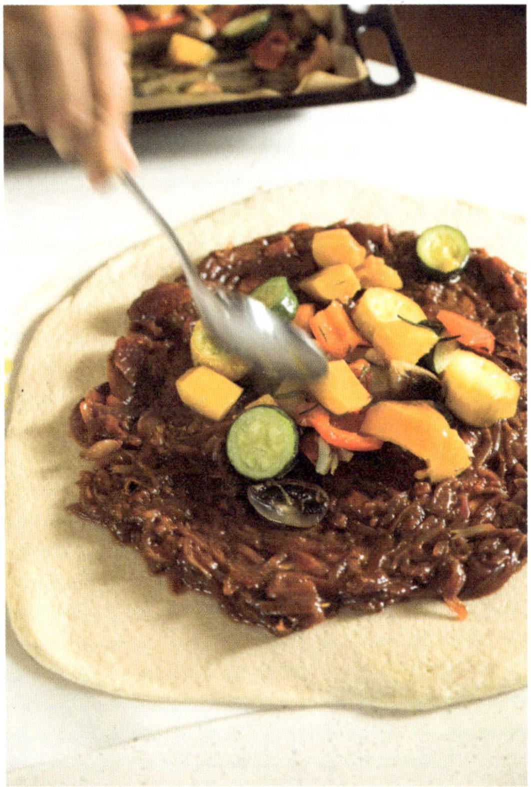
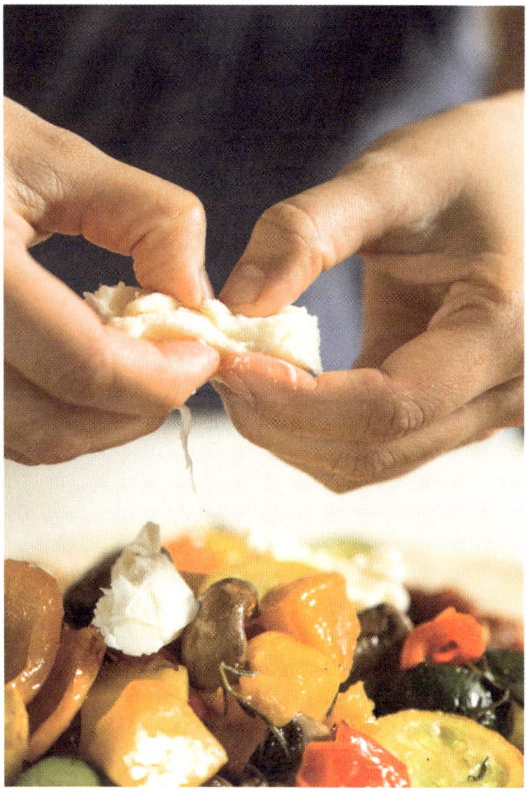
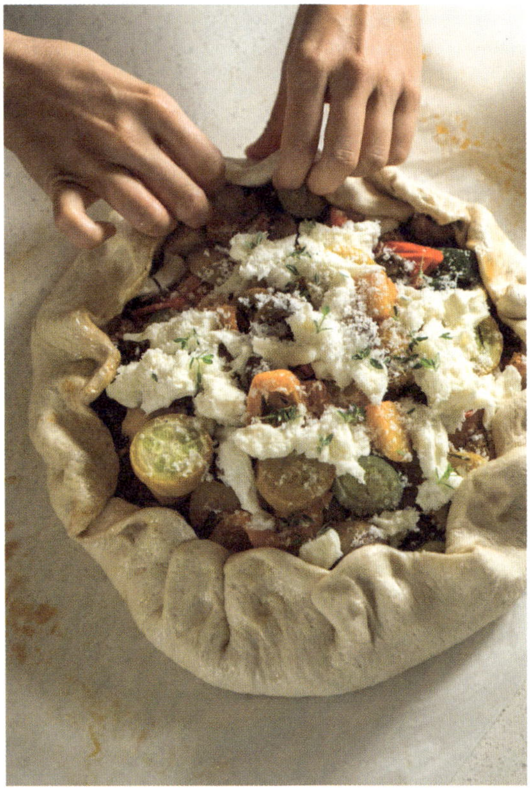
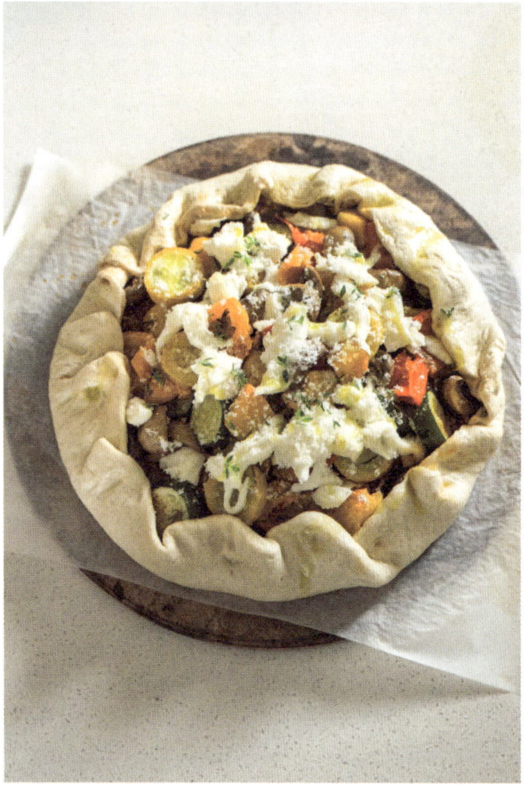

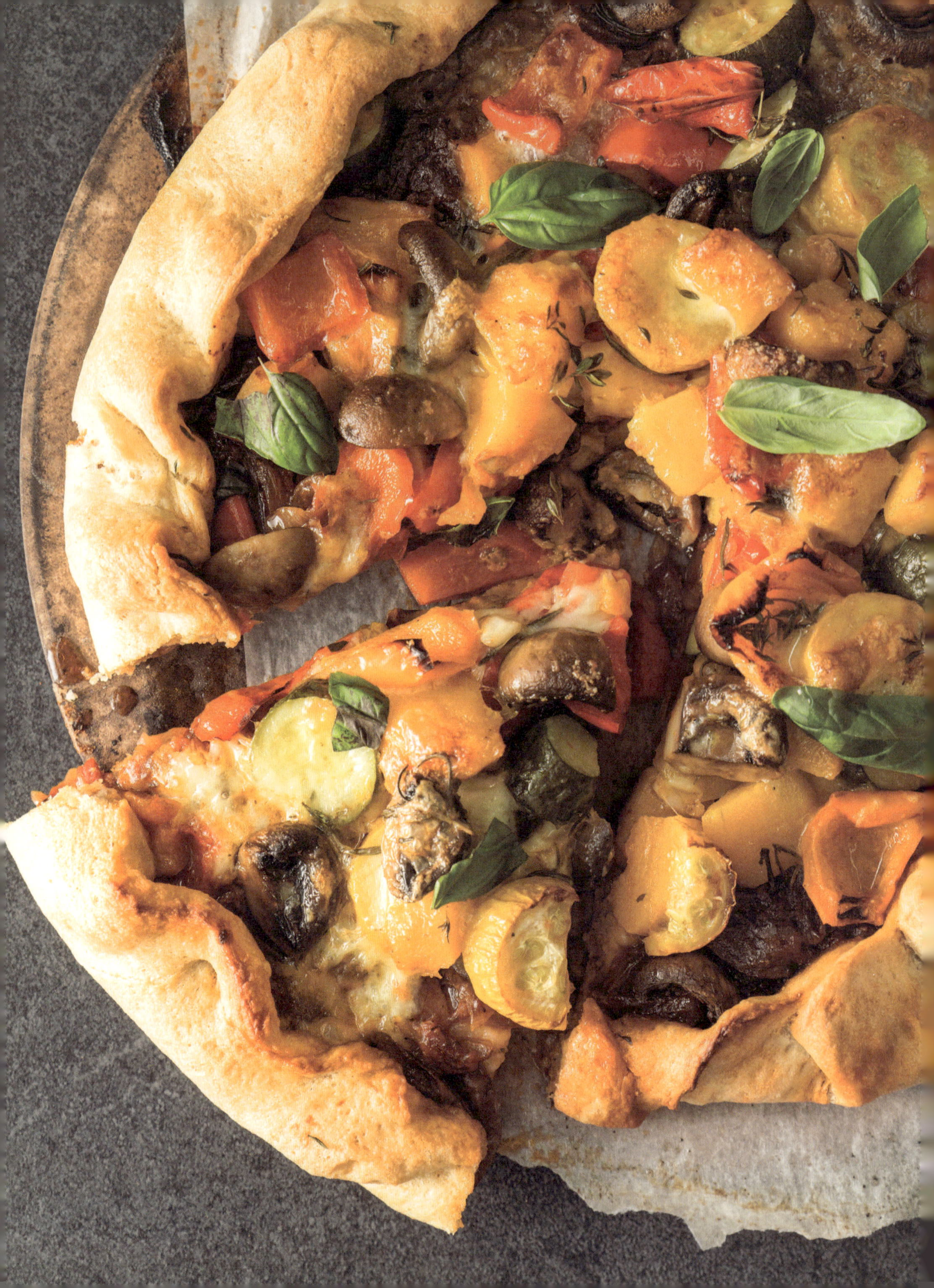

DF omit cheese | VEGAN omit cheese

RUSTIC VEGETABLE PIZZA PIE

SERVES 4–6
Prep time: 30 minutes
(+ 45 minutes to make pizza dough)
Cook time: 1 hour

1 quantity Pizza Dough (page 157)

TOMATO CARAMELISED ONIONS
3 tablespoons olive oil
3 red onions, thinly sliced
2 tablespoons brown sugar
3–4 tablespoons balsamic vinegar
1 teaspoon dried mixed herbs or oregano
400g can crushed tomatoes

600g peeled butternut or pumpkin, diced 2cm
800g vegetables (e.g. courgette, capsicum, mushrooms etc. — all the ones you'd be happy to put on a pizza!), cut into 2cm pieces
2 tablespoons olive oil
2–3 tablespoons chopped rosemary and/or thyme leaves
4 cloves garlic, chopped
1½ cups grated or shredded mozzarella cheese
½ cup grated parmesan
basil leaves and extra-virgin olive oil, to serve

Is it a pizza, or is it a pie? It's a bit of both! I start with my good ol' pizza dough, smother it with tomato caramelised onions and load it up with roast vegetables (the great thing is, you can use whatever you fancy on a pizza, like capsicum, mushrooms or courgette). Scatter some cheese on top (or go dairy-free), then bake in the oven and wait for the tempting smell of pizza wafting out of your kitchen. If you have a pizza oven, of course you'd cook it in that instead!

1. Start by making the Pizza Dough on page 157.

2. For the caramelised onions, heat olive oil in a large fry pan on medium heat. Cook onions until very soft and starting to caramelise, about 10 minutes. Add brown sugar, balsamic vinegar, dried herbs and tomatoes. Simmer for 10–12 minutes or until thick and reduced, like chutney. Stir in a drizzle of extra-virgin olive oil and season to taste with salt and pepper. Set aside to cool.

3. Preheat oven to 220°C. On a large oven tray lined with baking paper, toss butternut/pumpkin, and vegetables with olive oil, rosemary/thyme and garlic. Season with salt and pepper. Roast for about 20 minutes until vegetables are tender and slightly caramelised. If you don't have a very large oven tray, divide vegetables over two trays instead.

4. Reduce oven to 200°C and preheat a pizza stone if you have one, or an oven tray. Place pizza dough on a large sheet of baking paper on the bench. Roll out dough to a 35–40cm diameter circle, 4–5mm thick. Spread with Tomato Caramelised Onions, leaving a 5cm border around the edge. Place roast vegetables (make sure you drain off any liquid to avoid soggy pizza base) on top and sprinkle with cheeses.

5. Gather edge of the dough and drape back over the edge of the filling to create a ruffled look. Carefully transfer to preheated pizza stone or oven tray by holding the edges of the baking paper and lifting paper and pizza into the oven. Bake for 35–40 minutes or until crust is golden brown.

6. Transfer to a large serving board, scatter with basil and drizzle with a little extra-virgin olive oil. Serve with salad.

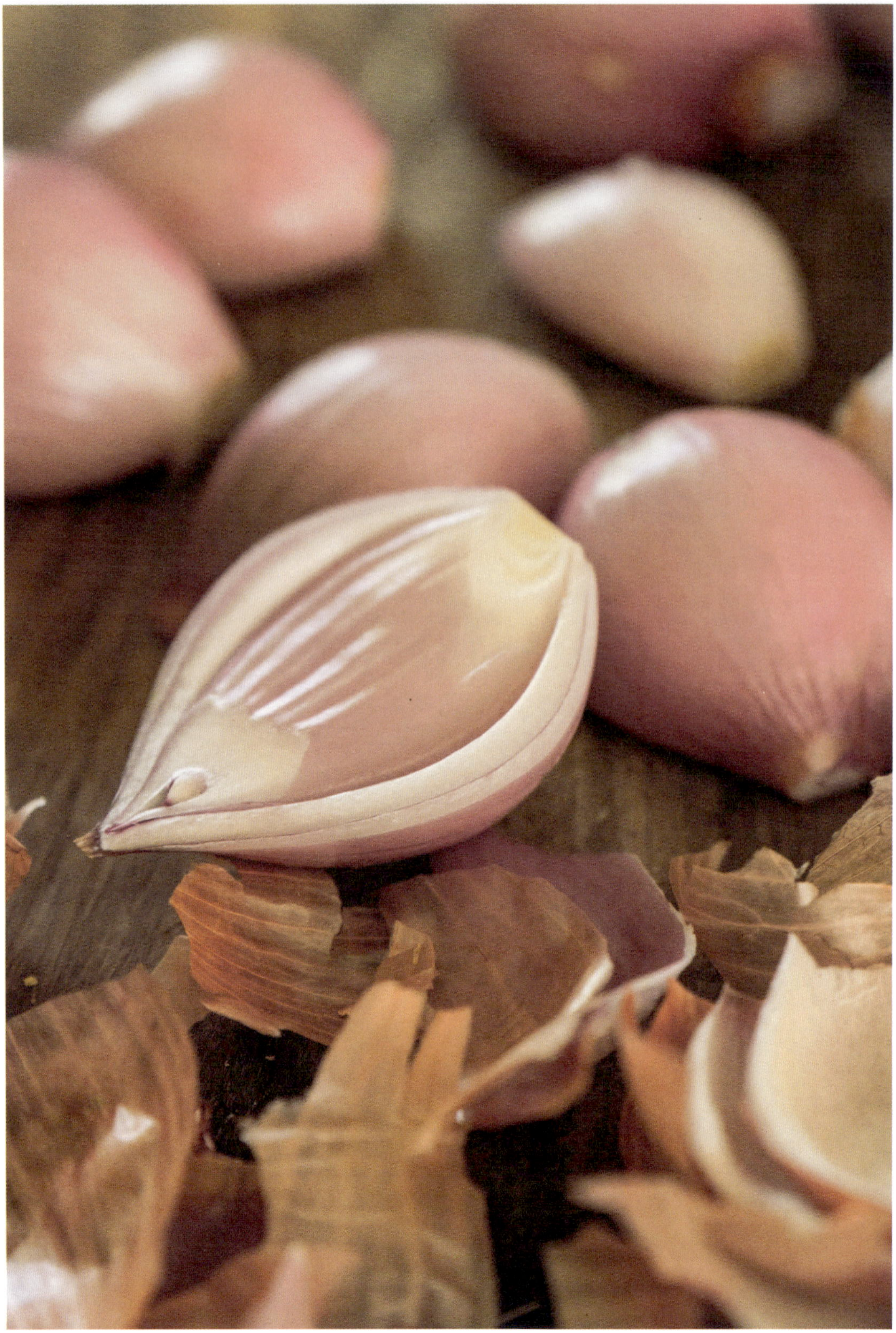

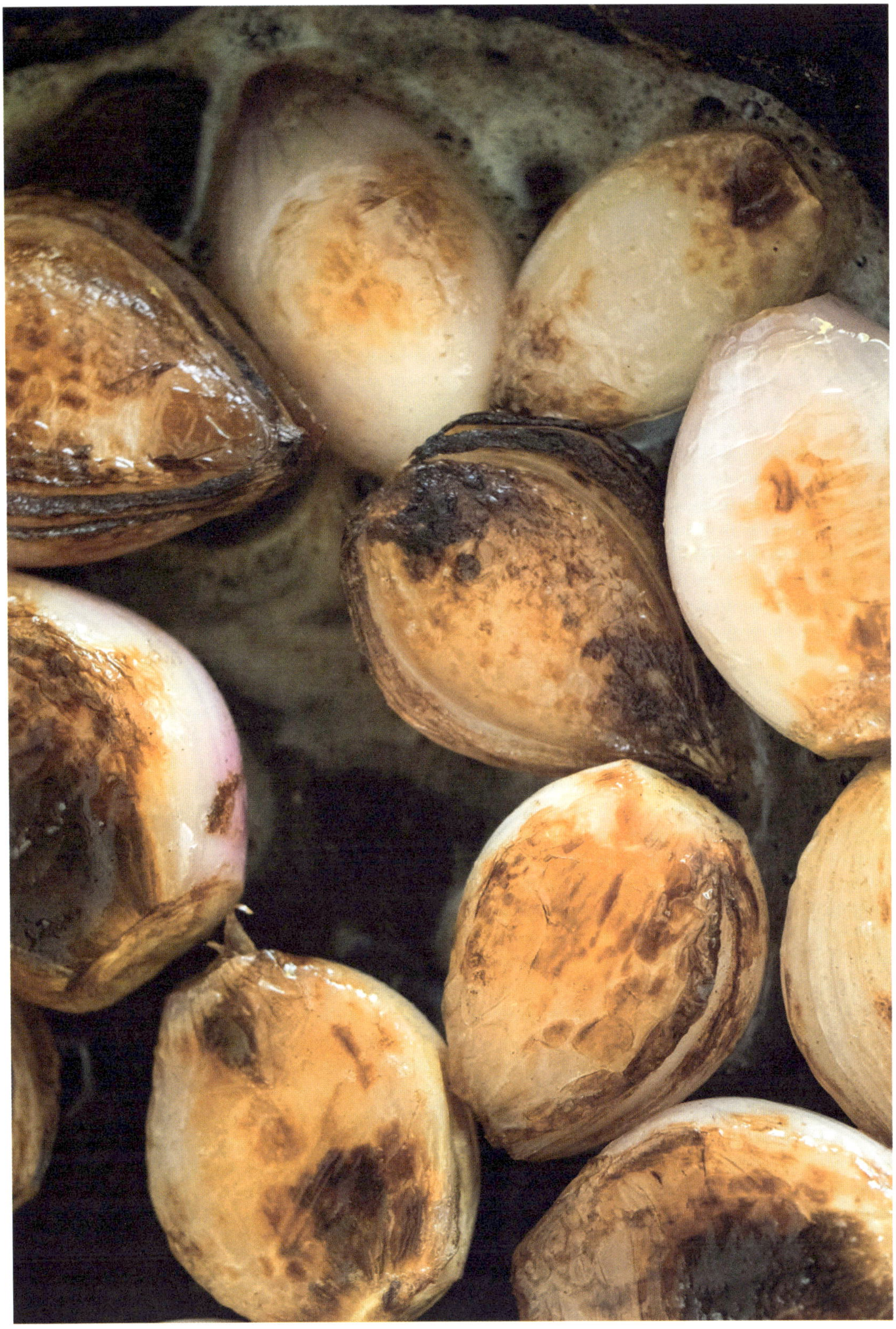

CARAMELISED SHALLOT & THYME TARTE TATIN

SERVES 3–4 (as a light meal)
Prep time: 20 minutes
Cook time: 40–45 minutes

500g shallots
2 tablespoons olive oil
25g butter
4 tablespoons balsamic vinegar
3 tablespoons brown sugar
½ cup water
1 heaped tablespoon tomato relish or chutney (optional)
2 tablespoons thyme leaves
1 square sheet or 200–250g puff pastry

Shallots are even sweeter than onion when cooked and caramelised until soft and golden. They make an amazing savoury twist on the upside-down tart classic. Carlos gave this a solid 10/10 and said he could easily eat the whole tart... and another! The Pear, Radish, Blue Cheese and Rocket Salad on page 242 makes the perfect partner for a fabulous meal.

1. Peel shallots by making a cut through the paper skin and first outer layer. Break each shallot into its two bulbs.

2. Heat olive oil and butter in a heavy-based ovenproof pan on medium heat. Use a pan that the shallots will fit in a single layer (I use a heavy, 25cm diameter, cast-iron pan). Add shallots, flat-side down first, and cook for 4–5 minutes on each side until starting to brown.

3. Mix balsamic vinegar, brown sugar, water and chutney/relish (if using) together and pour into the pan with the shallots. Simmer for about 10 minutes, adding more water if you need to, until the shallots are completely cooked through and the vinegar and sugar has reduced, becoming sticky and caramelised. Scatter with thyme leaves and season with salt and pepper. Set pan aside to cool slightly.

4. Preheat oven to 200°C. Roll out pastry and roughly cut a circle a little larger than the pan. Lay pastry over the shallots and tuck in down the sides with the help of a fork to enclose the shallots. Prick pastry with a fork in a few places. Place in oven for 22–25 minutes until pastry is puffed and golden.

5. To flip tart out onto a plate, place a plate (face down) on top of the pan and use oven mitts or a tea towel to hold the pan and plate together (so you don't burn yourself) and carefully flip it over in one smooth movement. The tart will fall out onto the plate — ta da!

6. Cut tart into wedges and serve with salad.

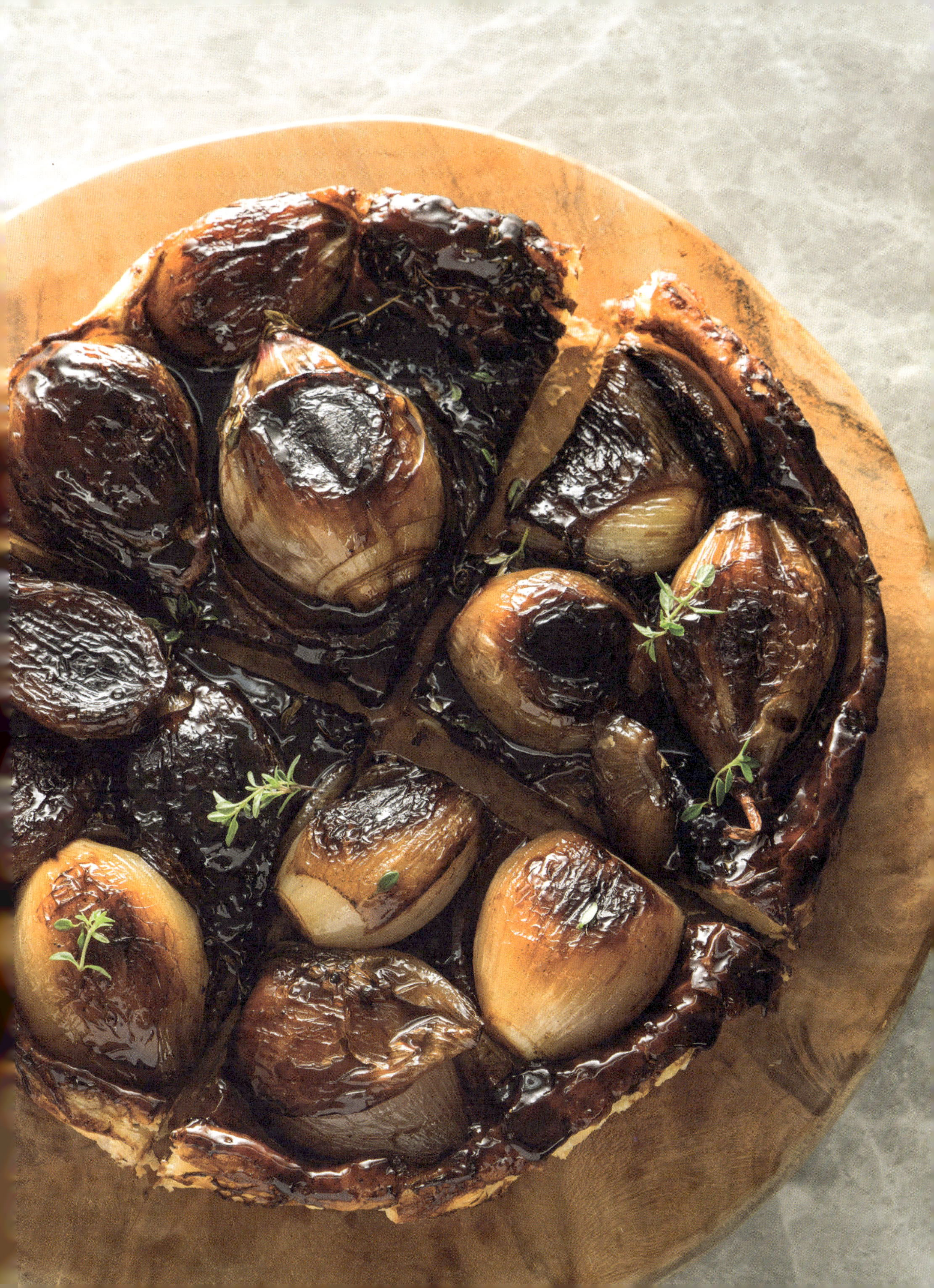

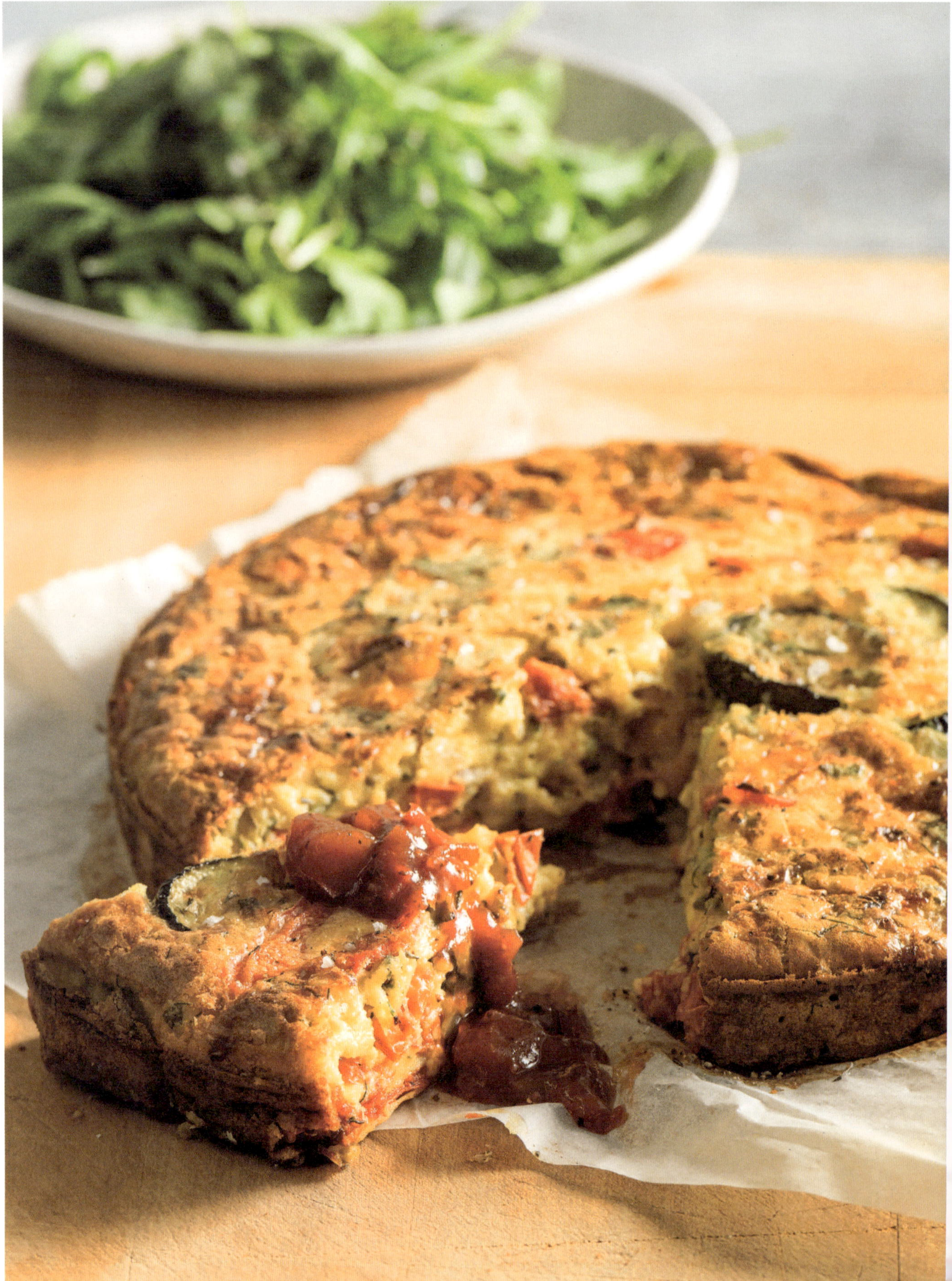

GF use GF self-raising flour

SELF-CRUSTING SUMMER VEGETABLE QUICHE

SERVES: 6
Prep time: 20 minutes
Cook time: 40–45 minutes

2 medium courgettes, sliced 1cm-thick
2 capsicums (red, yellow or orange), cored and cut into 3cm pieces
1 punnet cherry tomatoes, cut in half
2 tablespoons olive oil
25g butter
1 leek (white and pale green part), finely chopped
1 onion, finely chopped
3–4 cloves garlic, finely chopped
2 tablespoons finely chopped rosemary and/or thyme leaves
6 large (or 7 medium) free-range eggs
¾ cup cream, sour cream or crème fraîche
1 heaped teaspoon Dijon mustard
½ cup chopped fresh soft herbs (e.g. basil, parsley, sage, chives, dill, fennel)
½ cup self-raising flour
1½ cups grated cheese
75–100g feta

A self-crusting quiche requires no pastry yet forms a lovely outer crust layer as it bakes. This makes a lovely summer picnic meal. Make it in advance (it keeps in the fridge for a couple of days and reheats well) and bring a jar of chutney and simple leafy green salad along. There is also a pumpkin, spinach and feta version on the next page.

1. Preheat oven to 220°C. Line an oven tray with baking paper.

2. Toss courgettes, capsicums and cherry tomatoes with olive oil on lined tray. Season with salt and pepper. Roast for about 25 minutes until lightly browned.

3. While vegetables are roasting, prepare filling. Grease a 21–23cm round metal flan tin, pie dish or cake tin and line the base with baking paper. Heat butter in a large fry pan on medium heat. Cook leek and onion for 6–8 minutes until softened. Add garlic and rosemary/thyme and continue cooking for a further 2 minutes.

4. Use a fork to whisk together eggs, cream, mustard and herbs in a large mixing bowl. Stir in cooked leek and onion and season well with salt and pepper.

5. Sift in flour and stir with fork until just combined (be careful not to overmix). Gently stir in cooked vegetables (drained of any liquid), cheese and feta.

6. Pour into prepared tin and bake for 25–35 minutes or until puffed up, golden brown and set (check that there is no wobble in the middle). Leave for 5 minutes before removing from tin and slicing. Serve with relish or chutney and salad.

GF use GF self-raising flour

PUMPKIN, SPINACH AND FETA SELF-CRUSTING QUICHE

SERVES: 6
Prep time: 20 minutes
Cook time: 40–45 minutes

500g peeled pumpkin or butternut, cut into 2cm cubes
25g butter
1 leek (white and pale green part), finely chopped
1 onion, finely chopped
3–4 cloves garlic, finely chopped
2 tablespoons finely chopped rosemary and/or thyme leaves
250g spinach
6 large (or 7 medium) free-range eggs
¾ cup cream, sour cream or crème fraîche
1 heaped teaspoon Dijon mustard
½ cup chopped fresh soft herbs (e.g. basil, parsley, sage, chives, dill, fennel)
½ cup self-raising flour
1 cup grated cheese
150–200g feta

Here is another version of a self-crusting quiche that is equally delicious. It keeps well in the fridge for a couple of days and reheats well.

1. Preheat oven to 220°C. Line an oven tray with baking paper. Bring a full kettle of water to the boil.

2. Toss pumpkin with a drizzle of olive oil on lined tray and season with salt and pepper. Roast for 20–25 minutes until lightly browned.

3. Grease a 21–23cm round metal flan tin, pie dish or cake tin with butter and line the base with baking paper. Heat butter in a large fry pan on medium heat. Cook leek and onion for 6–8 minutes until softened. Add garlic and rosemary/thyme and continue cooking for a further 2 minutes.

4. Wash spinach and roughly chop. Place in a large heatproof bowl and cover with boiling water. Leave for a few minutes until wilted, then drain and run under cold water to cool. Squeeze out as much water from the spinach as you can (to do this, place in a clean tea towel and wring out the excess water, or just squeeze with your clean hands). Chop finely.

5. Use a fork to whisk together eggs, cream, mustard and herbs in a large mixing bowl. Stir in cooked leek and onion and season well with salt and pepper.

6. Sift in flour and stir with fork until just combined (be careful not to overmix). Gently stir in roast pumpkin, spinach, cheese and feta.

7. Pour into prepared tin and bake for 25–35 minutes or until puffed up, golden brown and set (check that there is no wobble in the middle). Leave for 5 minutes before removing from tin and slicing. Delicious served with a little relish or chutney and a side salad.

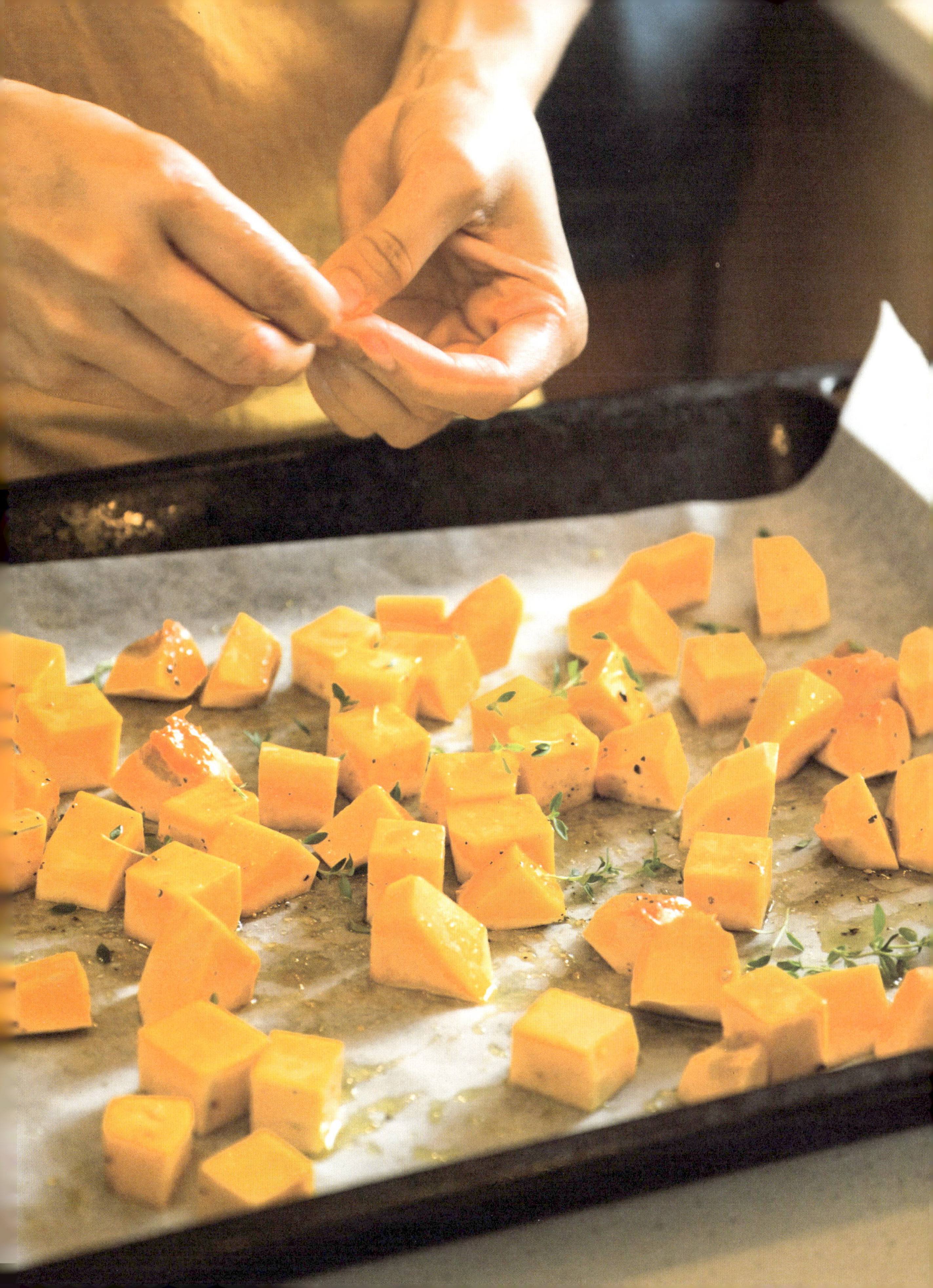

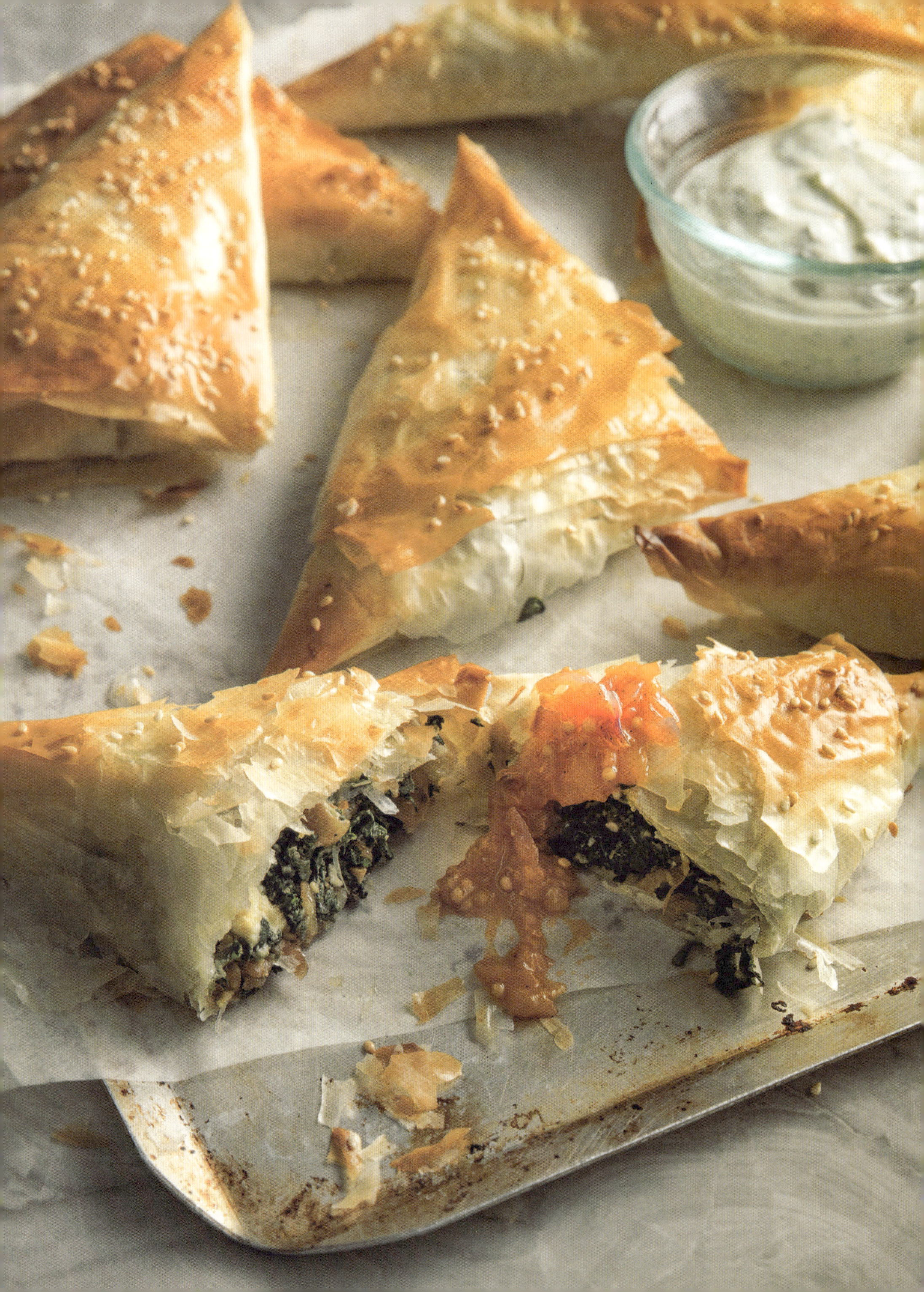

SPINACH, CARAMELISED ONION & FETA FILO PARCELS

SERVES 4–6
(or 8 as a light meal)
Prep time: 40 minutes
Cook time: 20 minutes

2 tablespoons olive oil or butter
2 onions, diced
3 cloves garlic, finely chopped
1 tablespoon chopped fresh thyme
2 teaspoons brown sugar
1 tablespoon balsamic vinegar
300g chopped spinach (fresh or frozen and defrosted)
1 free-range egg
200g feta, roughly crumbled
zest of ½ lemon
½ cup chopped herbs (e.g. flat-leaf parsley, oregano and dill)
¼ teaspoon salt
¼ teaspoon freshly ground black pepper
16 sheets filo pastry
100–125g butter, melted
1–2 teaspoons sesame seeds (optional)

TO SERVE
Moroccan Apricot and Tomato Chutney (page 158) or store-bought tomato or fruit chutney
Dill Tzatziki (page 156)

These are a twist on the Greek classic, spanakopita, with caramelised onions and a generous amount of fresh herbs adding loads of flavour to these spinach-packed, crispy, buttery, flaky parcels. They keep well in the fridge for a couple of days and reheat well, crisping back up in a 150°C oven for 10–15 minutes.

1. Preheat oven to 200°C. Bring a full kettle of water to the boil.

2. Heat oil/butter in a fry pan over medium heat. Cook onion for about 5 minutes, until golden and soft. Add garlic and thyme and keep cooking for a few more minutes. Then add brown sugar and balsamic vinegar and cook for a further 5 minutes or so. Set aside to cool.

3. Place spinach in a large heat-proof bowl and pour over boiling water to cover. Leave for a few minutes until wilted, then drain and run under cold water to cool. Squeeze out as much water from the spinach as you can (to do this, place in a clean tea towel and wring out the excess water, or just squeeze with your clean hands). Make sure you squeeze out as much moisture as you can to avoid soggy pastry.

4. In a large bowl, mix egg, feta, lemon zest, herbs, salt and pepper together.

5. Chop the spinach roughly and add to the egg mixture, along with the caramelised onions, and mix well.

6. Lay a sheet of filo pastry on a clean, dry, flat bench or board. Brush with melted butter. Place another sheet of filo on top and brush with melted butter. Fold in half lengthways (so you now have a long rectangle, 4 sheets thick). Brush with melted butter. Place (roughly) an eighth of the filling in the middle of the first third of the pastry rectangle. Fold bottom left corner diagonally to meet top edge of filo strip, making a triangular parcel. Continue folding until you get to the end of the pastry and you have a neat triangular parcel.

7. Repeat with remaining pastry and filling, arranging parcels on the lined baking tray as you go. Brush parcels with more butter and sprinkle with sesame seeds (if using). Bake for 20 minutes or until golden and crispy.

8. Serve with chutney and Dill Tzatziki, and salad.

GF use GF pasta sheets and flour

RATATOUILLE, BUTTERNUT & LENTIL LASAGNE

SERVES 4–6
Prep time: 35 minutes
(+ 2 hours to slow-roast vegetables)
Cook time: 45 minutes

RATATOUILLE SAUCE
1 quantity Slow-roasted Eggplant, Capsicum and Courgette (page 228)
2 tablespoons olive oil
1 onion, diced
250g button mushrooms, sliced
3–4 cloves garlic, finely chopped
2 tablespoons chopped thyme, oregano or rosemary leaves (or 1 teaspoon dried herbs)
400g can crushed tomatoes or tomato passata
2 tablespoons tomato paste
1 teaspoon sugar
200–250g silverbeet or spinach leaves, chopped
400g can brown lentils or black beans, rinsed and drained

CHEESE SAUCE
50g butter
2½ tablespoons plain flour
2 cups milk
1½ cups grated cheese

TO LAYER LASAGNE
500–600g peeled butternut or other pumpkin
400g fresh or dried lasagne sheets
½ cup grated parmesan

This lasagne is full of different vegetables — eight different ones in fact! The vegetable sauce is incredibly rich and flavourful thanks to the slow-roasted vegetables (which are quick to prepare before leaving them alone to slow-roast in the oven), and the lentils add a 'meaty' bite and texture. All will love this delicious lasagne; it's a big winner with my kids too and it gets lots of veggies into them!

1. Start by making the Slow-roasted Eggplant, Capsicum and Courgette. Preheat oven to 200°C.

2. Place silverbeet/spinach in a heatproof bowl and pour over boiling water to cover, leave for 2–3 minutes then drain and run under cold water to cool. Use your hands to squeeze out excess water, then finely chop.

3. Heat olive oil in a large fry pan on medium heat. Cook onion, mushrooms and garlic for 4–5 minutes until soft. Add herbs, crushed tomatoes, tomato paste and sugar. Simmer for 6–8 minutes until starting to thicken. Stir through roast vegetables, silverbeet/spinach and lentils/black beans. Simmer for a few more minutes and season to taste with salt and pepper.

4. Heat butter in a medium-sized pot on medium heat. Add flour and stir with a wooden spoon until frothy. Whisk in ½ cup of the milk until smooth, then gradually whisk in remaining milk, ½ cup at a time, until smooth. Simmer for a few minutes, letting it bubble gently, whilst whisking often, until it has thickened. Whisk in half of the cheese until smooth (leave the remainder for sprinkling on top). Season to taste with salt and pepper.

5. Very thinly slice butternut into 3–4mm thick slices – make sure they are not too thick so that they cook through.

6. Spread the bottom of a large lasagne or square/rectangular baking dish with 2 spoonfuls of vegetable sauce. Arrange a sheet of lasagne on top (you may have to cut the pasta to fit). Spread with half of the remaining sauce and arrange half of the butternut slices on top. Layer with another sheet of lasagne and repeat with remaining sauce and butternut. Finish with a final layer of lasagne. Pour cheese sauce on top and sprinkle with remaining cheese and parmesan.

7. Bake for about 30 minutes until golden and bubbly. Allow to stand for at least 10 minutes before cutting.

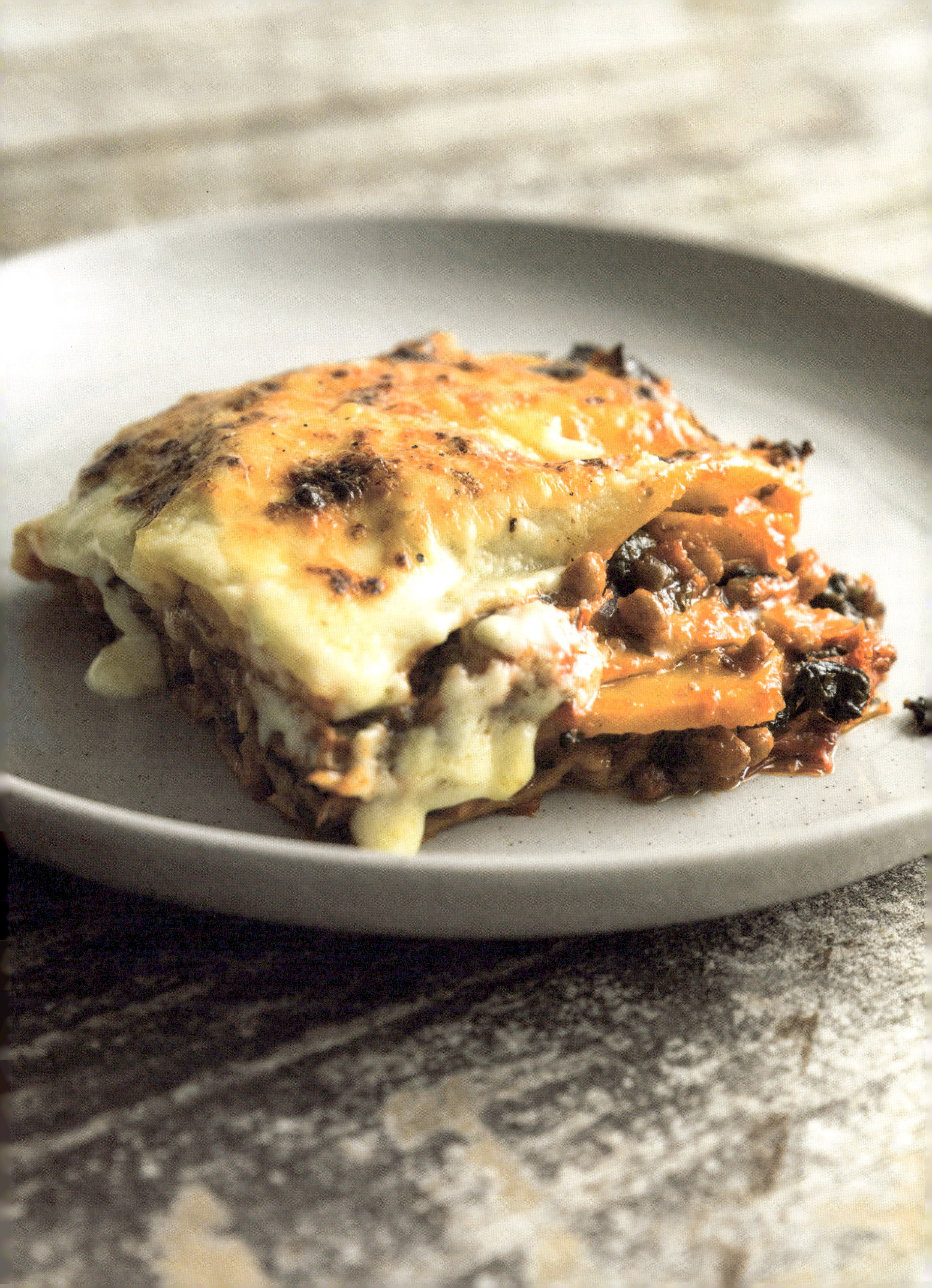

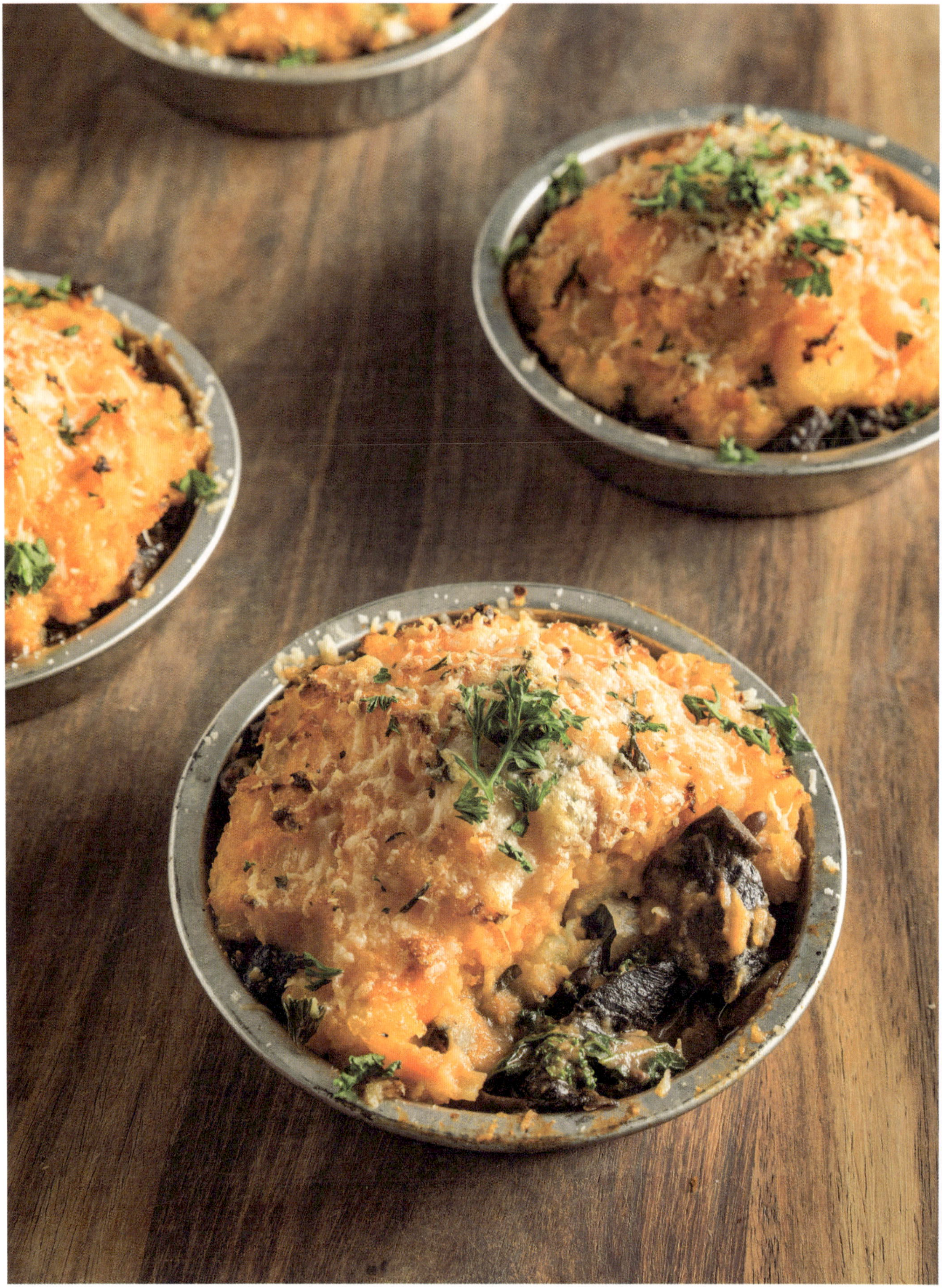

GF | DF use Cashew Cream and omit butter, milk and cheese from mash |
VEGAN use Cashew Cream and omit butter, milk and cheese from mash

CREAMY TOMATO, MUSHROOM, KALE & BLACK BEAN SHEPHERD'S PIE

SERVES 4–6
Prep time: 20 minutes
Cook time: 35 minutes

125g chopped kale leaves (with tough stem removed) or 250g spinach, or a mix of both
2 tablespoons olive oil
1 onion, diced
2–3 cloves garlic, chopped
1½ tablespoons chopped thyme leaves
½ teaspoon ground cumin
500g mushrooms (e.g. button and/or Portobello), sliced
3 tablespoons tomato paste
1 cup cream or Cashew Cream (page 217)
400g can black beans, rinsed and drained

TOPPING
800g–1kg mix of agria potatoes, kumara and carrots, peeled and chopped
knob of butter
2–3 tablespoons milk
1 cup grated cheese
½ cup grated parmesan
¼ cup finely chopped curly parsley

A vegetarian version of the classic, it's a winter comfort food favourite in our house. The creamy tomato mushroom filling, bulked out with greens and black beans, could also be topped with pastry to make pot pies. Either way, it'll warm you up on a cold night!

1. Preheat oven to 200°C. Bring a medium pot of salted water to the boil, and a full kettle of water to the boil.

2. Place kale/spinach in a large heatproof bowl and pour over boiling water to cover. Leave for a few minutes until bright green and wilted, then run under cold water to cool and drain well. Use your hands to squeeze out excess water, then chop.

3. Cook potatoes, kumara and carrot in boiling salted water for 10–15 minutes until tender. Drain well and mash with butter and milk. Season to taste with salt and pepper.

4. Heat olive oil in a large fry pan on medium heat. Cook onion, garlic and thyme, with a good pinch of salt, for 2–3 minutes or until onion is soft.

5. Add cumin, mushrooms, a drizzle more olive oil and continue cooking for 4–5 minutes until soft and most of the moisture has evaporated.

6. Stir in tomato paste, cream, cooked greens and black beans and season to taste with salt and pepper. Simmer for 4–5 minutes until thickened.

7. Spoon filling into a large dish or individual ramekins or pie dishes. Top with mash, and sprinkle with cheeses and parsley. Bake for 15–20 minutes until cheese is bubbly and golden.

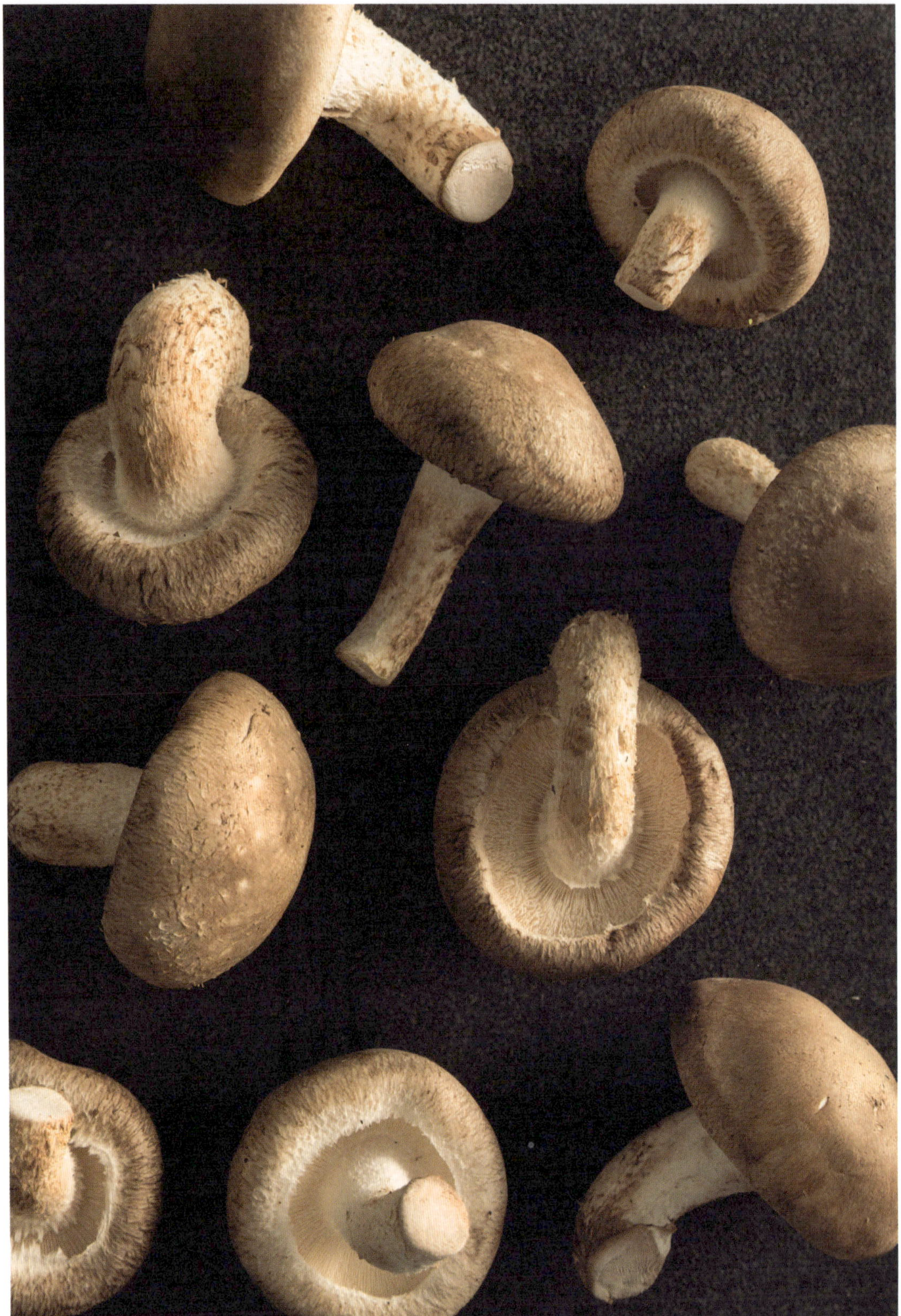

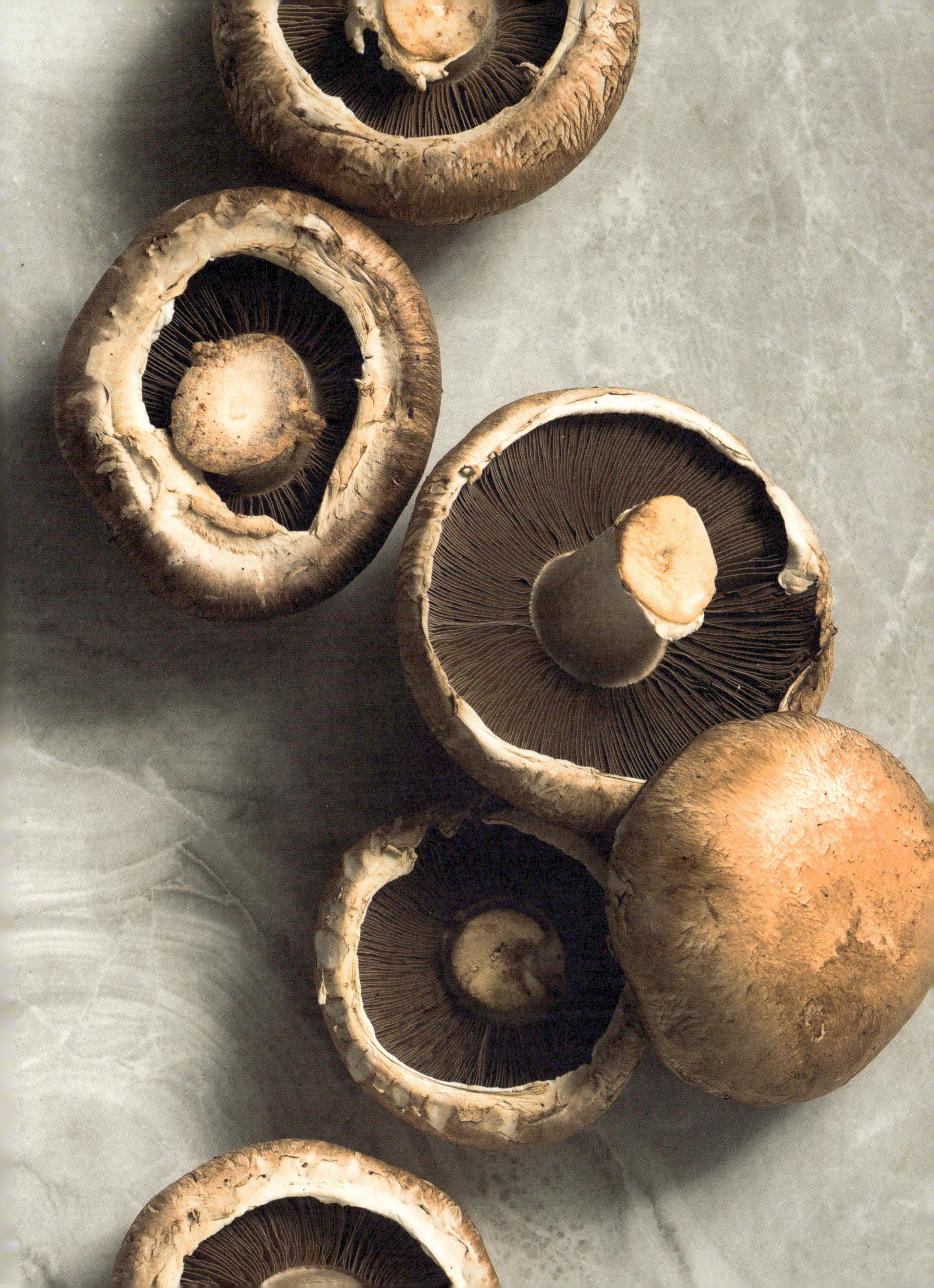

PORTOBELLO MUSHROOM & BRIE WELLINGTON

SERVES 4–6
Prep time: 40 minutes
Cook time: 1 hour

6 very large or 12 medium Portobello mushrooms
1 large square sheet puff pastry
1–1 ½ cups Caramelised Onions (page 159 or use store-bought)
300g brie, camembert or gruyère, sliced 0.5–1cm-thick
1 free-range egg
25g butter
about 20 sage leaves

This is the perfect centrepiece for a vegetarian dinner party, or even Christmas table. It's so delicious and special that meat-eaters will be more than happy! It's important to make sure the caramelised onions have cooled, so you don't melt the pastry when it comes to assembling the Wellington.

1. Brush any excess soil off mushrooms with a pastry brush or paper towels (do not wash the mushrooms as they will soak up too much moisture). Trim stalks. Heat a good drizzle of oil in a large fry pan on medium to high heat. Cook the mushrooms in batches, skin-side down, for about 5 minutes (add more oil in between batches as needed). Use a fish slice to flatten mushrooms whilst cooking in the pan; aim to get almost all the moisture out of them. Gently flip and cook for a further 5 minutes, until golden. Transfer to a plate lined with paper towels and place in fridge to cool.

2. Preheat oven to 200°C. Line an oven tray with baking paper and lay puff pastry sheet on it. Roll it out a little to make it slightly thinner. Pat mushrooms with paper towels, gently pressing them flat between paper towels to absorb excess moisture.

3. Spread half of the caramelised onions down the middle length of the pastry, leaving a 1cm gap at the left and right ends. Top onions with half of the cheese, then half of the mushrooms, slightly overlapping. Top with another layer of mushrooms, then cheese, then onions. You should have a kind of log shape in the middle of your square of pastry.

4. Lift the pastry from the bottom end to cover the filling (use the baking paper to help guide you), followed by the top end. Use your fingers to gently seal the pastry together. Then seal the ends by folding over and gently pinching. Roll the Wellington over so that it is seam-side down.

5. Make an egg wash by lightly whisking egg with 2 tablespoons of milk. Brush lightly over the Wellington and bake for 30–40 minutes, or until the pastry is puffed, golden and cooked through. Cheese may ooze out but don't worry — those golden, crusty bits of bubbly cheese are so delicious — just serve it with the rest of the Wellington.

6. Melt butter in a fry pan until starting to bubble, add sage leaves and fry for 1–2 minutes until crispy.

7. Garnish Wellington with crispy sage leaves, let it rest for a few minutes then use a serrated knife to cut into 4–6 slices. Serve with relish or chutney and salad.

Tip: Keep pastry cold (defrosted in fridge) until ready to use — it will make it much easier to work with.

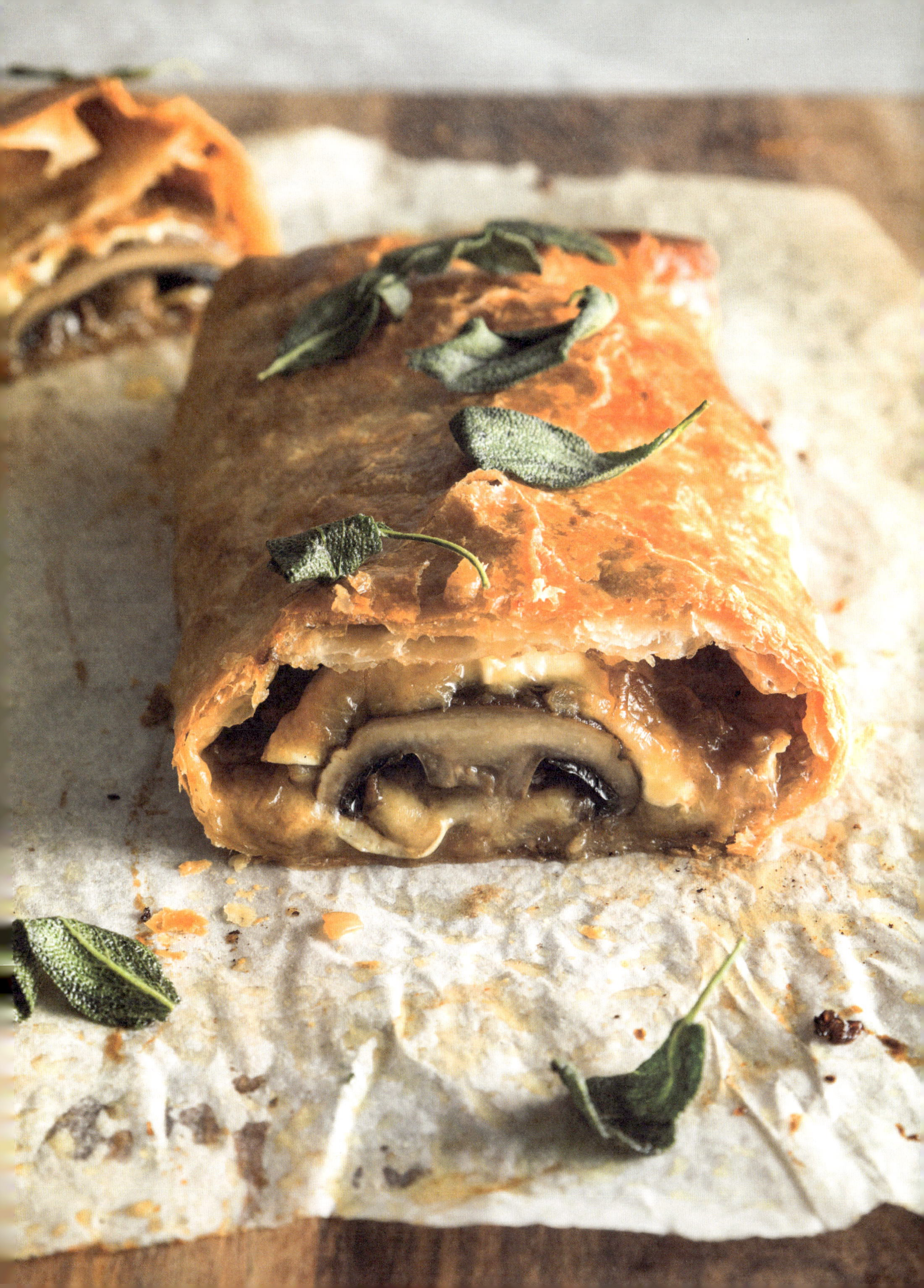

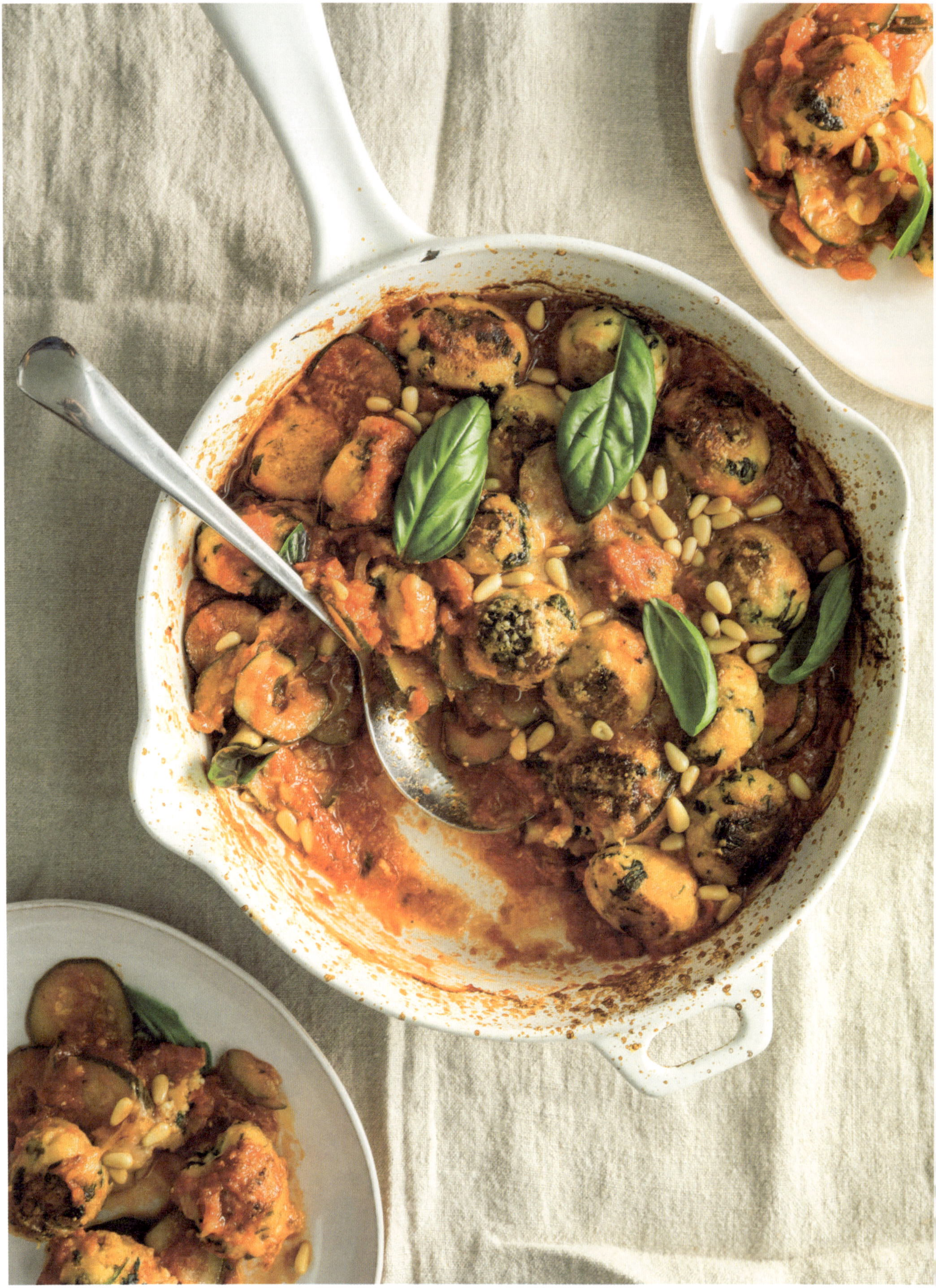

SPINACH & RICOTTA DUMPLINGS WITH TOMATO COURGETTE SAUCE

SERVES 4
Prep time: 20 minutes
Cook time: 25 minutes

150g spinach or baby spinach
400g ricotta
70g (1¼ cups) finely grated parmesan + 30g (½ cup) extra for sprinkling
2 free-range egg yolks
¼ teaspoon freshly grated nutmeg (optional)
¾ teaspoon salt
75g plain flour

TOMATO COURGETTE SAUCE
2 tablespoons olive oil
1 onion, finely chopped
2–3 cloves garlic, finely chopped
3 small courgettes, thinly sliced
400g can crushed tomatoes
2 tablespoons tomato paste
¼ cup water
¼ teaspoon dried mixed herbs or oregano
½ teaspoon sugar

TO SERVE
handful of basil leaves
2–3 tablespoons toasted pine nuts

These plump little dumplings (often called 'gnudi') are the lighter, ricotta-instead-of-potato version of gnocchi (which there is also a recipe for on page 150). They're usually boiled; however, I much prefer them pan-fried to get a delightful golden crust. Plonked in a rich tomato sauce and grilled with cheese, this dish is seriously good comfort food.

1. Preheat oven grill. Bring a full kettle of water to the boil.

2. Place spinach in a heatproof bowl or pot and cover with boiling water. Leave for a few minutes until spinach has wilted, then drain well and rinse under cold water to cool. Use your hands to squeeze out as much excess moisture as you can, then finely chop spinach.

3. Combine spinach with ricotta, parmesan, egg yolks, nutmeg (if using) and salt in a large bowl. Add flour and stir until just combined.

4. Squeeze and roll tablespoons of mixture into slightly oval balls and place on a plate. Refrigerate for 10 minutes or so to firm up while you make the sauce.

5. Heat olive oil in a large fry pan (use an ovenproof one if you can) on medium heat. Cook onion, garlic and courgettes, with a good pinch of salt, for 5–10 minutes, until soft. Stir in tomatoes, tomato paste, water, dried herbs and sugar and simmer for about 5 minutes until sauce has thickened. Stir in a good glug of extra virgin olive oil and season to taste with salt and pepper. Spoon into an ovenproof dish (or leave in the pan if it is ovenproof).

6. Heat a drizzle of olive oil or knob of butter in a separate, non-stick fry pan on medium to high heat. Pan-fry dumplings (in batches) for a few minutes, gently shaking around the pan to brown evenly on both sides. Place dumplings in the tomato sauce.

7. Drizzle with extra-virgin olive oil and sprinkle with extra parmesan. Grill for about 5 minutes until golden. Garnish with basil and pine nuts.

Tip: If your ricotta is quite wet (some brands are more so than others) it helps to squeeze out some of the excess moisture by gently wringing it in muslin cloth or a clean tea towel first.

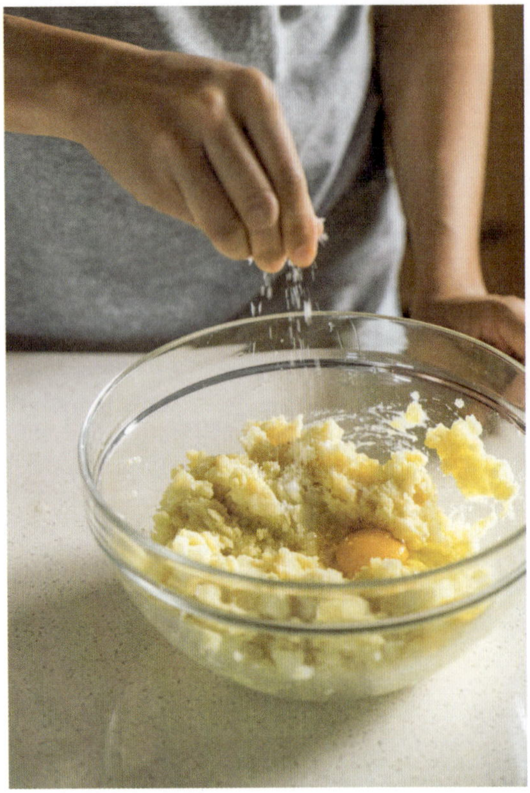
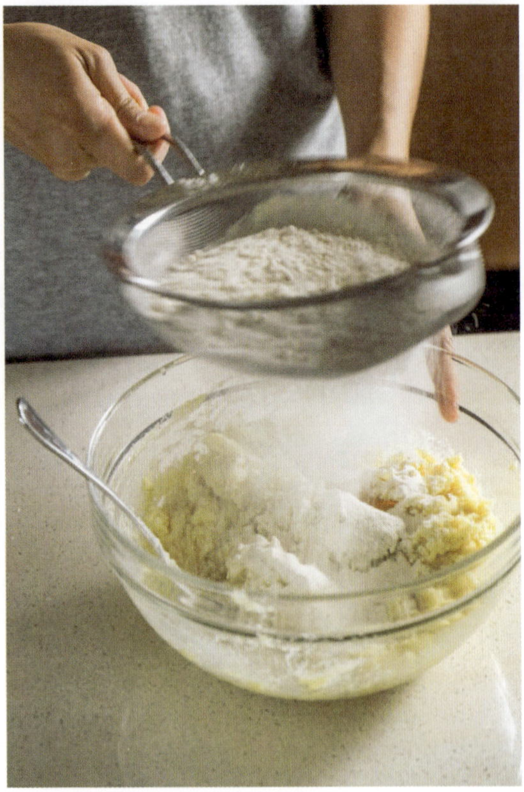
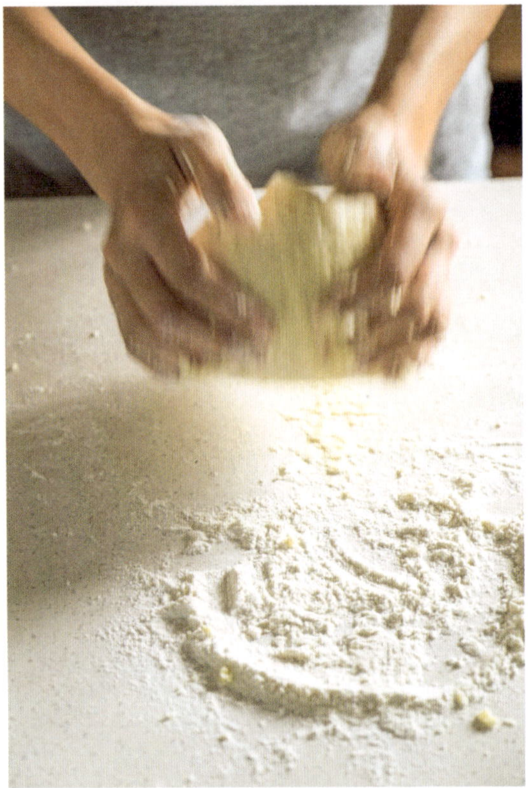
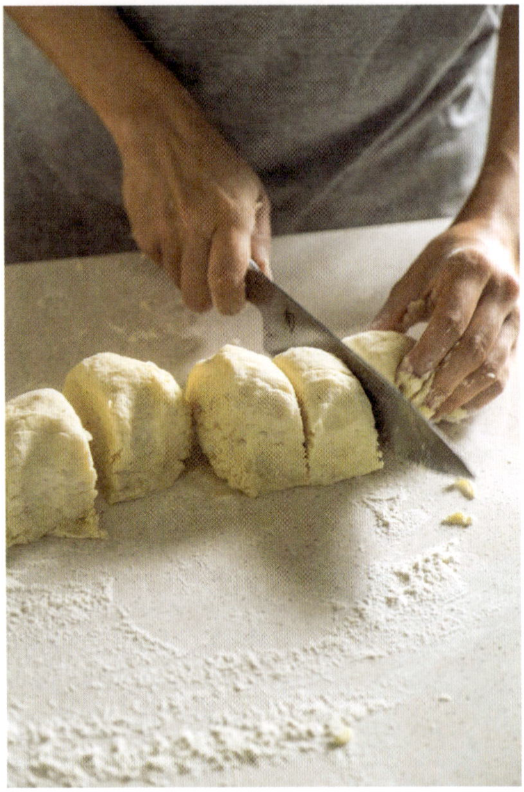

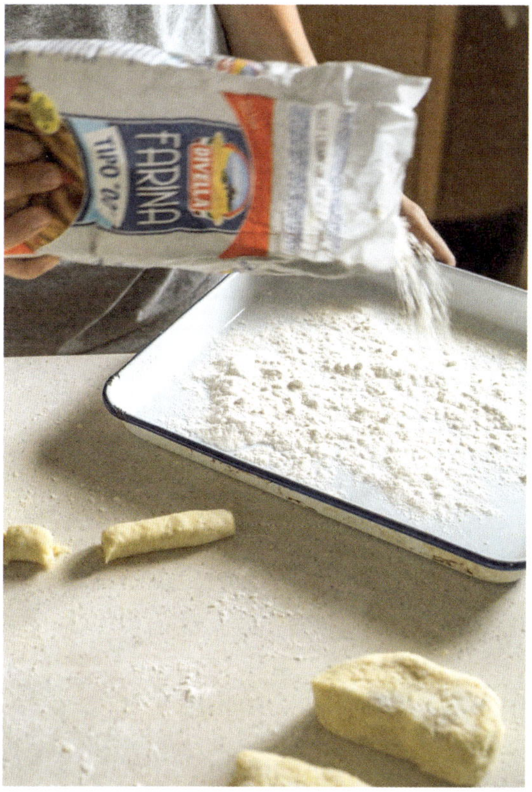
DIVELLA
FARINA
TIPO "00"
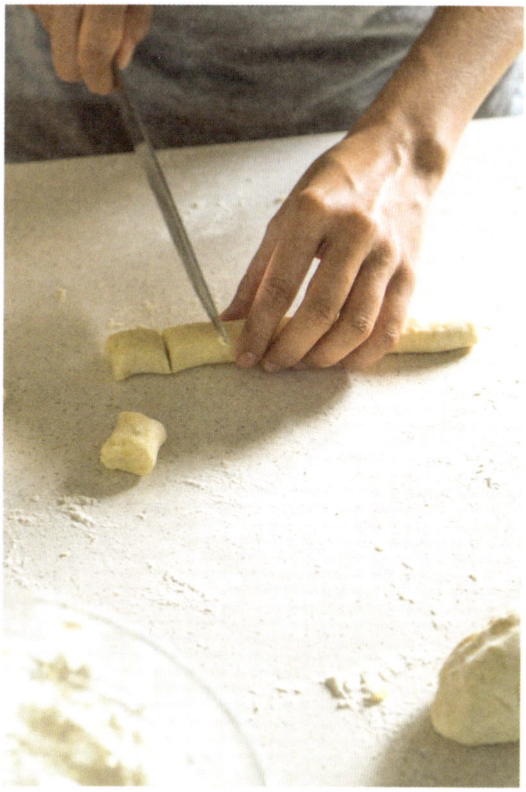
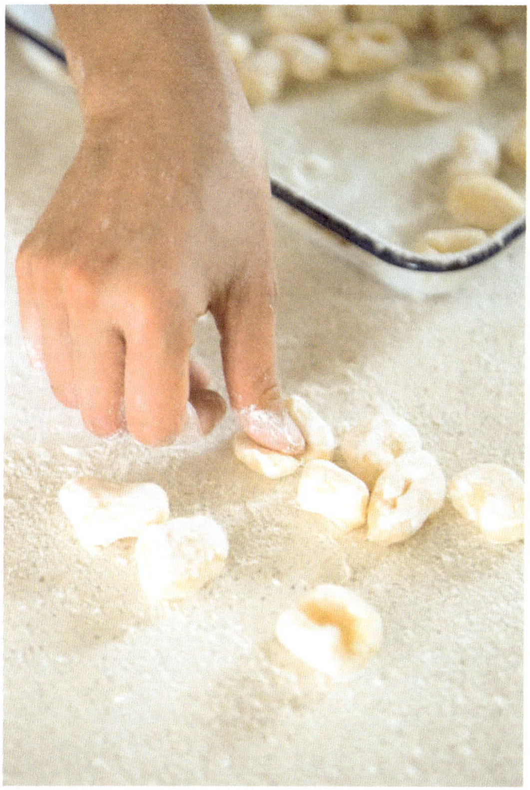
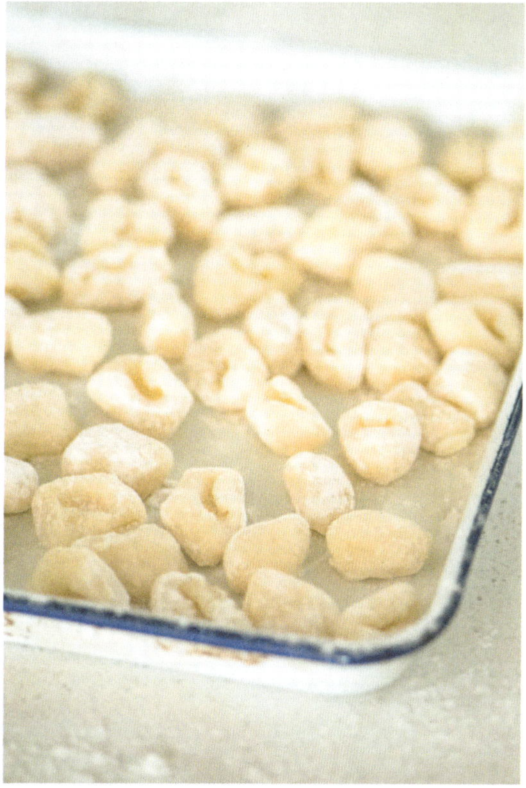

CIRO'S GNOCCHI

SERVES 4
Prep time: 30 minutes
Cook time: 15 minutes
(+ 1 hour to roast potatoes)

700–800g agria potatoes, scrubbed (leave skin on)
1 free-range egg
¾ teaspoon salt
150g '00' Italian flour

TOMATO BASIL SAUCE
¼ cup olive oil
4 cloves garlic, sliced
1½ 400g cans Italian crushed tomatoes
very generous handful of basil leaves
150g fresh mozzarella
handful of grated parmesan

In my teens I worked as a waitress in an Italian restaurant run (very authentically) by Ciro Sanino from Naples and he made THE best fresh gnocchi. Up until that point I'd always thought gnocchi was overrated because I'd only had dense, bland and chewy stuff out of a packet. Home-made gnocchi is entirely different — soft, silky, delicate little mouthfuls of potato-ey pasta. And you'll be pleasantly surprised at how easy and satisfying it is to make. Whilst you can use plain flour, '00' Italian flour (which is very finely milled) works best and is easy to find these days.

1. Preheat oven to 200°C. Place whole potatoes on an oven tray and bake for about 1 hour (depending on the size of potatoes) until very tender — test with a skewer or tip of a sharp knife; it should poke right through with no resistance.

2. Cut potatoes in half and peel off the skins while still warm. Push warm potato flesh through a potato ricer or a sieve (with the help of the back of a large spoon) into a large bowl. This ensures light gnocchi; whatever you do, do not mash the potato.

3. Add egg and salt and mix in with a fork. Sift in flour and use your hands to bring together as a soft dough. Add a little more flour if needed — it should feel dry to the touch, but not crumbly. Knead a few times, then divide into six pieces.

4. On a lightly floured surface, roll each piece out into a log about 30cm long, then cut into bite-sized 2cm pieces. Gently push the tip of your thumb or finger into the centre of each piece to make a little indent (this makes the perfect little hollow for sauce to pool in). Place in a large dish or on a tray (with a lip) dusted with flour, and shake pieces around to coat. Set aside until ready to cook.

5. Bring a large pot of well-salted water to the boil and preheat oven to grill. While water is coming to the boil, make the sauce. Heat olive oil in a large heatproof fry pan on medium heat. Sizzle garlic for 1–2 minutes (but do not let it brown), then stir in crushed tomatoes. Simmer for 5–8 minutes until thickened, and season to taste with salt and pepper. Stir through basil.

6. Drop about half of the gnocchi (one by one) into the boiling water and cook for a couple of minutes, scooping them out with a slotted spoon as they bob to the surface. Transfer straight into the pan of hot tomato sauce.

7. Once all the gnocchi are in the pan, gently toss to coat in sauce and top with mozzarella and parmesan. Place under the oven grill for about 5 minutes or until sauce is bubbling and mozzarella is melted. Serve immediately.

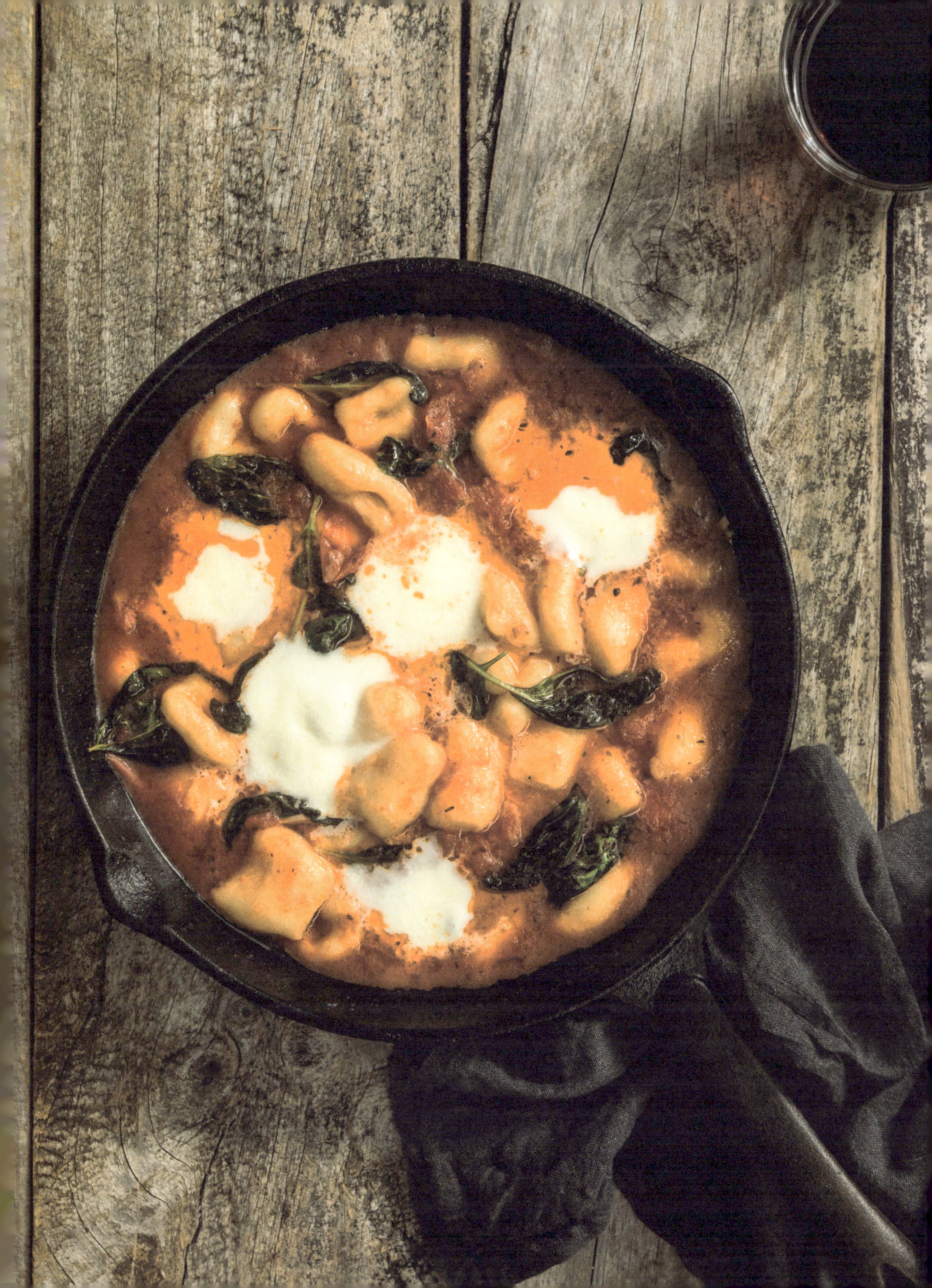

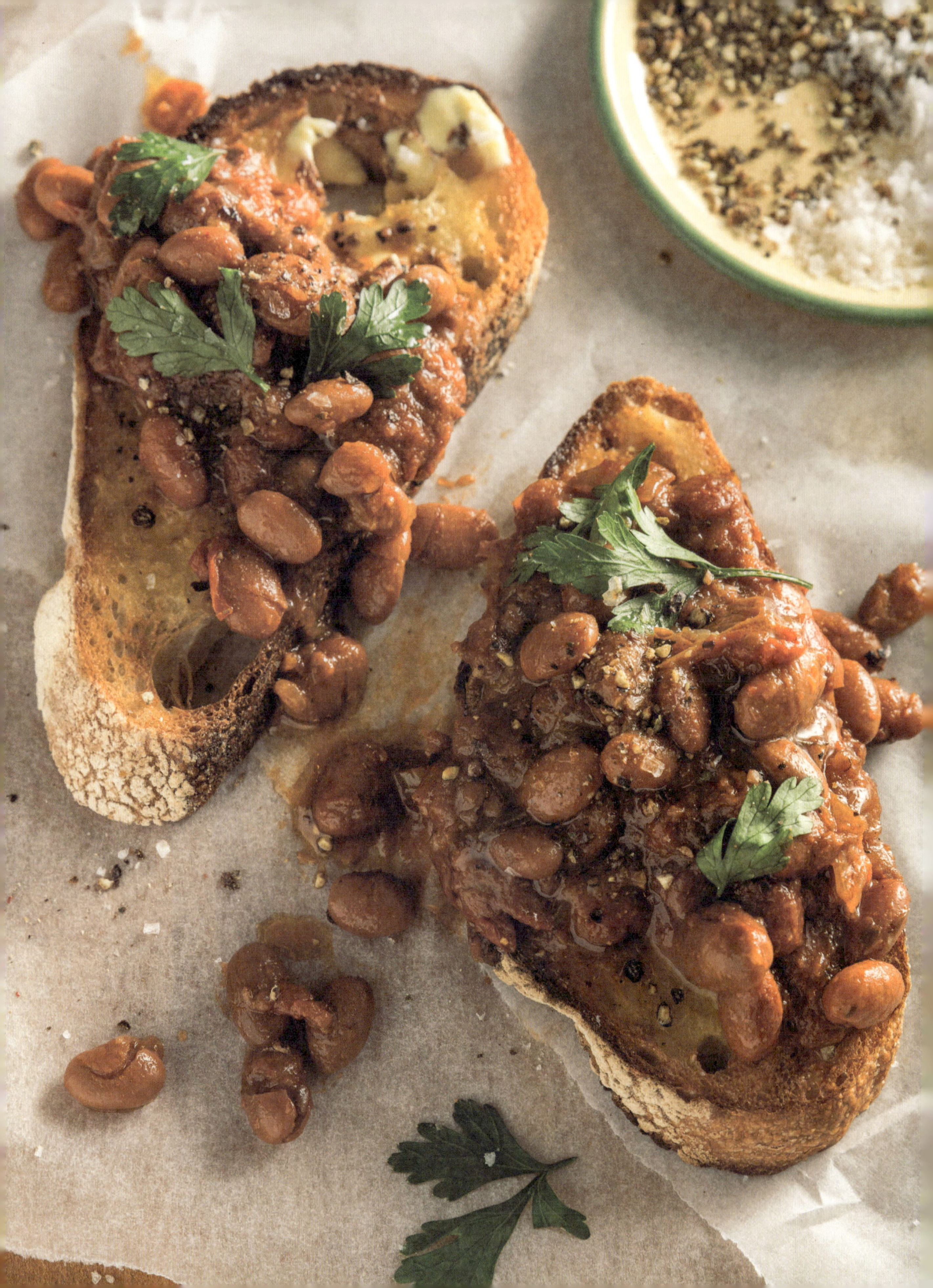

GF use apple cider vinegar | DF | VEGAN

SLOW-COOKED SMOKY BEANS

SERVES 6

Prep time: 5 minutes
(+ time to soak the beans)
Cook time: 2½–3 hours

2 tablespoons olive oil
1 onion, diced
3 cloves garlic, chopped
2 tablespoons thyme leaves
leaves from 1 sprig rosemary
1 teaspoon each ground cumin, coriander and smoked paprika
200g dried beans (e.g. pinto, haricot, kidney) soaked in water for a few hours (or overnight), drained
3 cups Autumn Harvest Sauce (page 192) or tomato passata
6–8 tablespoons smoky barbecue sauce
2 tablespoons tomato sauce
1–2 tablespoons chipotle sauce (optional)
1–2 tablespoons brown sugar
1 tablespoon malt vinegar
3 cups vegetable stock

I use dried beans in this recipe which are slow-cooked to perfection, soaking up all the flavours and maintaining a texture superior to canned beans. Make sure you soak the beans in water for at least a couple of hours (or overnight) before cooking to help slightly soften them (it improves their texture and reduces cooking time).

These beans are delicious in many ways — nachos, burritos or enchiladas, or simply on hot buttered toast with a poached egg. For an extra veg hit, stir through chopped or baby spinach at the end until wilted, or even cooked eggplant, courgette or roast pumpkin.

1. Preheat oven to 150°C.

2. Heat olive oil in a large, heavy-based, flame-proof, ovenproof casserole dish or Dutch oven, or a fry pan with a lid. Cook onion, garlic, thyme and rosemary for 3–4 minutes until onion is soft and starting to brown a little. Add spices and continue cooking for 30 more seconds.

3. Add all remaining ingredients, stir, cover with a tight-fitting lid and place in the oven to cook for 3½–4 hours until beans are soft and sauce has thickened. Check on the beans after 2–2½ hours and top up with a little water if it looks like it is drying out.

4. Once beans are cooked, season to taste with salt and pepper. If the sauce is not quite thick enough, simmer the beans and sauce on the stovetop for about 5 minutes or until it thickens.

GF | DF | VEGAN

VEGETABLE STOCK

MAKES 2–2½ LITRES
Prep time: 10 minutes
Cook time: 1–1½ hours

2–3 tablespoons miso paste
3 litres water
2 onions, chopped
2 carrots, chopped
2 stalks celery, chopped
2 cloves garlic, crushed
small handful of dried shiitake mushrooms (optional)
1 teaspoon peppercorns
a bunch of parsley stalks (you can reserve the leaves for other recipes, or use both leaves and stalks)
10 sprigs of thyme

Here's a simple recipe for home-made vegetable stock, which is much fresher and lighter in taste than concentrated/powdered stock. This is a basic recipe, but you can add other vegetables (or their off-cuts) such as fennel, spring onion, capsicum or leek if you like.

1. Mix miso paste with ⅓ cup of the water until dissolved, then pour into pot. Add remaining water and all other ingredients.

2. Bring to the boil, then reduce heat and leave to simmer, partially covered, for 1–1½ hours. Season to taste with salt.

3. Pour into a sieve over a large heatproof bowl or jug and leave to cool. Keep in the fridge (for up to 5 days) or freeze until ready to use.

Other vegetables and herbs that are great additions:
Parsley (I usually only add the stalks as I reserve the leaves for other recipes)
Sprigs of thyme
Bay leaves
Leek tops (make sure to wash these well as they tend to trap a lot of sand)
Capsicum
Courgettes
Mushrooms
Spring onions
Shallots
Rosemary
Fennel
Tomato
Basil
Dried mushrooms

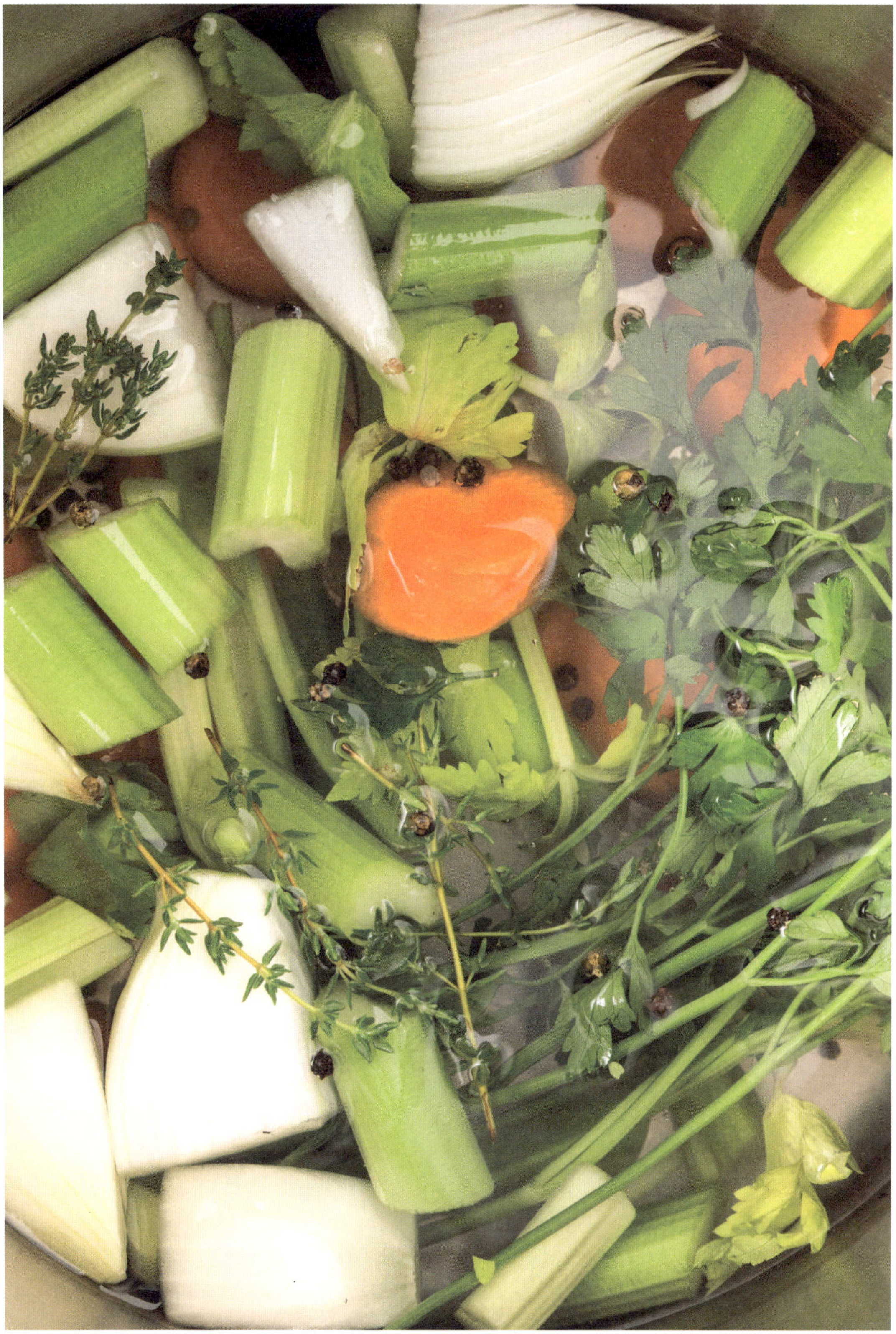

GF | DF | VEGAN

SOFT CASHEW CHEESE

MAKES ABOUT 1 CUP
Prep time: 5 minutes
(+ 6–8 hours to soak cashew nuts)

1 cup natural (raw, unsalted) cashew nuts
1 tablespoon extra-virgin olive oil
¼ cup cold filtered water
½ teaspoon salt
juice of ½ lemon
2 teaspoons yeast flakes or nutritional yeast (optional – it gives a more savoury 'cheesy' flavour)

Cashew cheese is a delicious creamy non-dairy alternative to the likes of cream cheese, sour cream and crème fraîche; for example, on the Caramelised Onion and Beetroot Tart on page 118. Its texture is somewhere between ricotta and hummus. To this basic cashew cheese, you can add chopped herbs or a little garlic powder for extra flavour.

1. Place cashew nuts in a bowl and add enough cold filtered water to completely cover. Leave to soak in the fridge for 6–8 hours or overnight.

2. Drain cashews and rinse well. Place all ingredients in a high-speed blender (a standard blender might struggle to break them down fully) or food processor and blitz until smooth and creamy, scraping down the sides as necessary. It will take at least a couple of minutes for the cashew nuts to break down completely. Add a little more water as needed to get a smooth, thick, creamy consistency. Transfer to a bowl and set aside. It will keep for up to 5 days in an airtight container, in the fridge.

GF | DF use coconut yoghurt | VEGAN use coconut yoghurt

DILL TZATZIKI

MAKES 1 CUP
Prep time: 5 minutes

1 cup thick, Greek-style natural unsweetened yoghurt or labne (page 63)
2 tablespoons lemon juice
2 tablespoons finely chopped dill
1 small clove garlic, minced

A simple condiment/dip of yoghurt, lemon and dill — it goes great with lots of Mediterranean or Middle Eastern couscous, lentil, quinoa or rice dishes, or tagines, or the filo parcels (on page 137) — just dollop, drizzle or dip... yum!

1. Mix all ingredients together and season to taste with salt and pepper.

DF | VEGAN

OLIVE OIL PASTRY

MAKES ENOUGH FOR 1 TART
Prep time: 10 minutes

200g plain flour
   + extra to dust
½ teaspoon salt
6 tablespoons olive oil
   + extra to grease
¼ cup cold water

Made with olive oil instead of butter, this pastry is very useful if you are dairy-free or have dairy-free guests. It's lovely, flaky and crumbly, and crisps and browns really well just like butter pastry.

1. Mix flour and salt together in a mixing bowl. Add olive oil and stir with a fork until it resembles breadcrumbs.

2. Stir in cold water (you may need a little more, but only add 1–2 teaspoons at a time if needed) until mixture forms a soft dough.

3. Bring dough together with your hands, wrap in clingfilm and allow to rest in the fridge for 15 minutes before using.

DF | VEGAN

PIZZA DOUGH

MAKES ENOUGH FOR 4 PIZZA BASES
Prep time: 15 minutes (+ 40 minutes to rise)

1 cup (250ml) warm water
1 tablespoon active dried yeast
1 teaspoon sugar
400–450g plain flour
1 teaspoon salt
2 tablespoons olive oil

My good ol' pizza dough recipe — it's featured in a number of my cookbooks!

1. Pour warm water into a large mixing bowl and add yeast and sugar. Stir gently. Stand in a warm place for about 10 minutes until frothy. Mix well.

2. Add flour, salt and olive oil to yeast mixture and mix well to form a dough — don't worry if there is a little leftover flour in the bowl, that's fine. However, if the dough seems too sticky, add a little more flour.

3. Bring together with your hands and knead dough for 5–10 minutes until smooth and elastic, then place in an oiled bowl (so it doesn't stick), cover with a tea towel and leave in a warm place to rise until doubled in size (about 40 minutes). Your pizza dough is now ready to use!

GF use apple cider or red wine vinegar | DF | VEGAN

MOROCCAN APRICOT & TOMATO CHUTNEY

MAKES 2½–3 CUPS
Prep time: 5 minutes
Cook time: 15–20 minutes

1 tablespoon olive oil
1 onion, diced
1 red capsicum, cored and diced
3cm piece fresh ginger, finely grated
1 teaspoon each fennel, coriander and cumin seeds, crushed
½ teaspoon ground turmeric
¼ teaspoon smoked paprika
1 cinnamon stick
400g can crushed tomatoes
400g can apricots in juice/syrup
1 tablespoon hot chilli sauce (e.g. sriracha)
1½ tablespoons vinegar (e.g. malt, red wine)
3–4 tablespoons sugar

This delicious spiced apricot and tomato chutney goes with just about anything from the burgers (page 40) to the haloumi canapés (page 56), Moroccan Eggplant Boats (page 122) and filo parcels (page 137). Super handy to have in the fridge.

1. Heat olive oil in a fry pan on medium heat. Cook onion and capsicum for a few minutes until soft.

2. Add ginger and crushed fennel, coriander and cumin seeds, and cook for a further 1–2 minutes.

3. Add remaining ingredients and simmer for 10–15 minutes, stirring often, until thick and 'jammy'. Whilst cooking, roughly mash apricots in the pan with a potato masher to break them up. Season to taste with salt and pepper. The chutney will keep in the fridge for up to a week.

GF | DF | VEGAN

CARAMELISED ONIONS

MAKES ABOUT 2 CUPS
Prep time: 5 minutes
Cook time: 25 minutes

3 tablespoons olive oil
3 red onions, thinly sliced
2 tablespoons brown sugar
3–4 tablespoons balsamic vinegar
¼ cup water
1 tablespoon chopped thyme leaves

'Caramelised onions make any meal taste better' was something my nan believed and, as such, she would fry up onions every night to have with dinner. Whilst her meals were very basic, I remember them tasting (and smelling!) really good. All thanks to those onions. Caramelised onions add a sweet and savoury depth of flavour to loads of dishes — everything from stews and casseroles to the base of tarts and pies. Or even gourmet mousetraps!

1. Heat olive oil in a large fry pan on medium heat. Cook onions until very soft and starting to caramelise, about 10 minutes.

2. Add brown sugar, balsamic vinegar and water, reduce heat and continue to cook until you have a jam-like consistency, about 12–15 minutes. Stir in thyme and season to taste with salt and pepper. Will keep in the fridge for up to 5 days.

Quick, & Let

CHAPTER FOUR — P. 161

easy
lovers

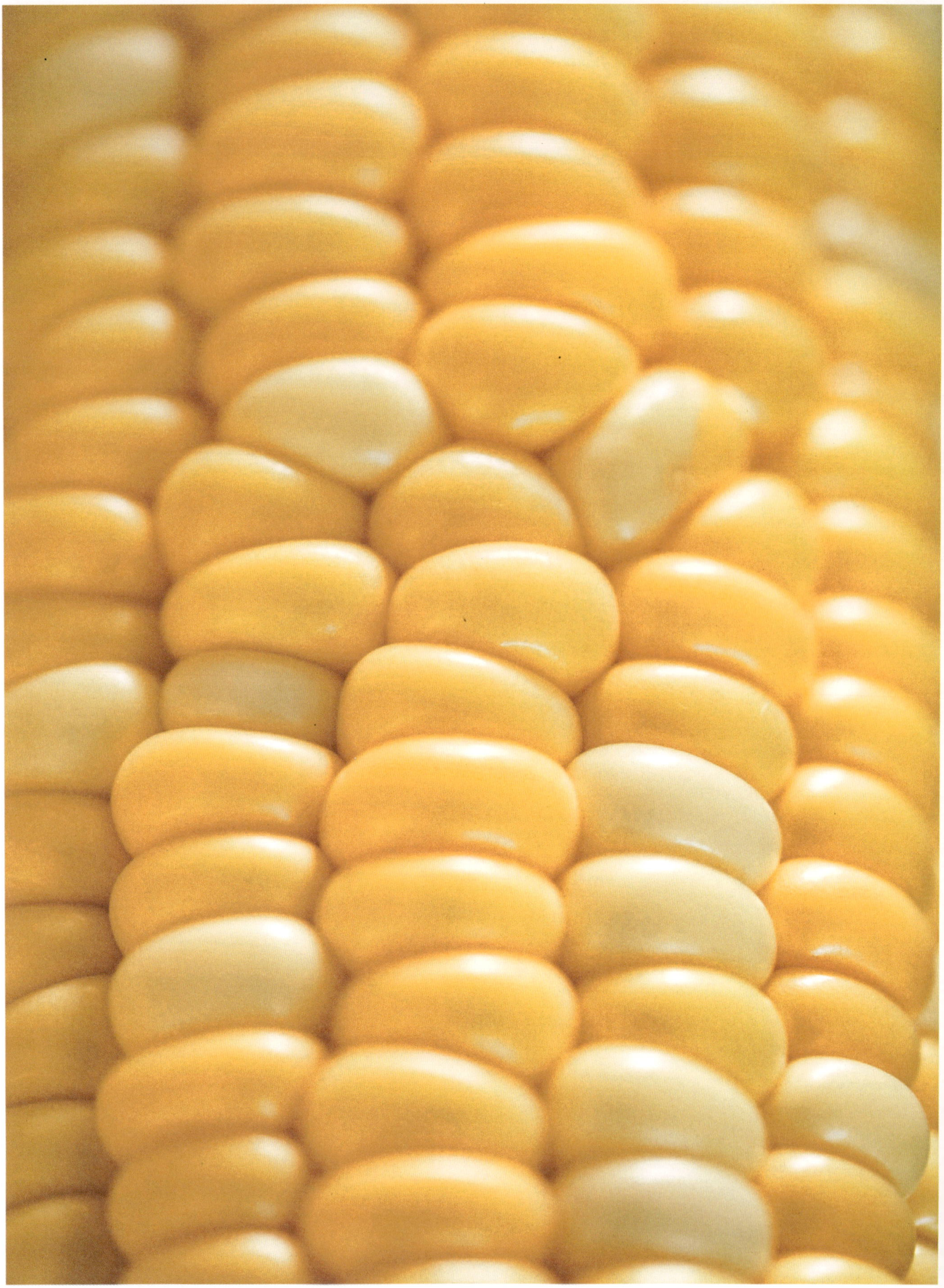

This is the kind of chapter I personally want in a cookbook, a reflection of the lack of time, inspiration and energy I sometimes have at the end of the day to get something on the table quickly to avoid 'hangry' kids (and me snacking!). So here are some quick and easy no-fuss recipes, and others that use up leftover cooked veg.

It's a great idea to roast extra vegetables, or cook extra rice, beans or lentils when you're making dinner so that you can use them in a quick frittata, tart or hearty salad (check out that chapter) or fried rice the next day, saving you time and effort — and thinking! Leftovers often make the tastiest meals, and I love how resourceful and satisfied you feel when you use up what's in the fridge, transforming yesterday's remnants into a whole new dish.

Most of these (easily scaled down) recipes are also perfect for a simple dinner-for-one. When it's just me, I love having a Gourmet Mousetrap with pickles and chutney for a simple meal or one of my reliably gratifying dinners for one, the Winter Greens with a fried egg and parmesan.

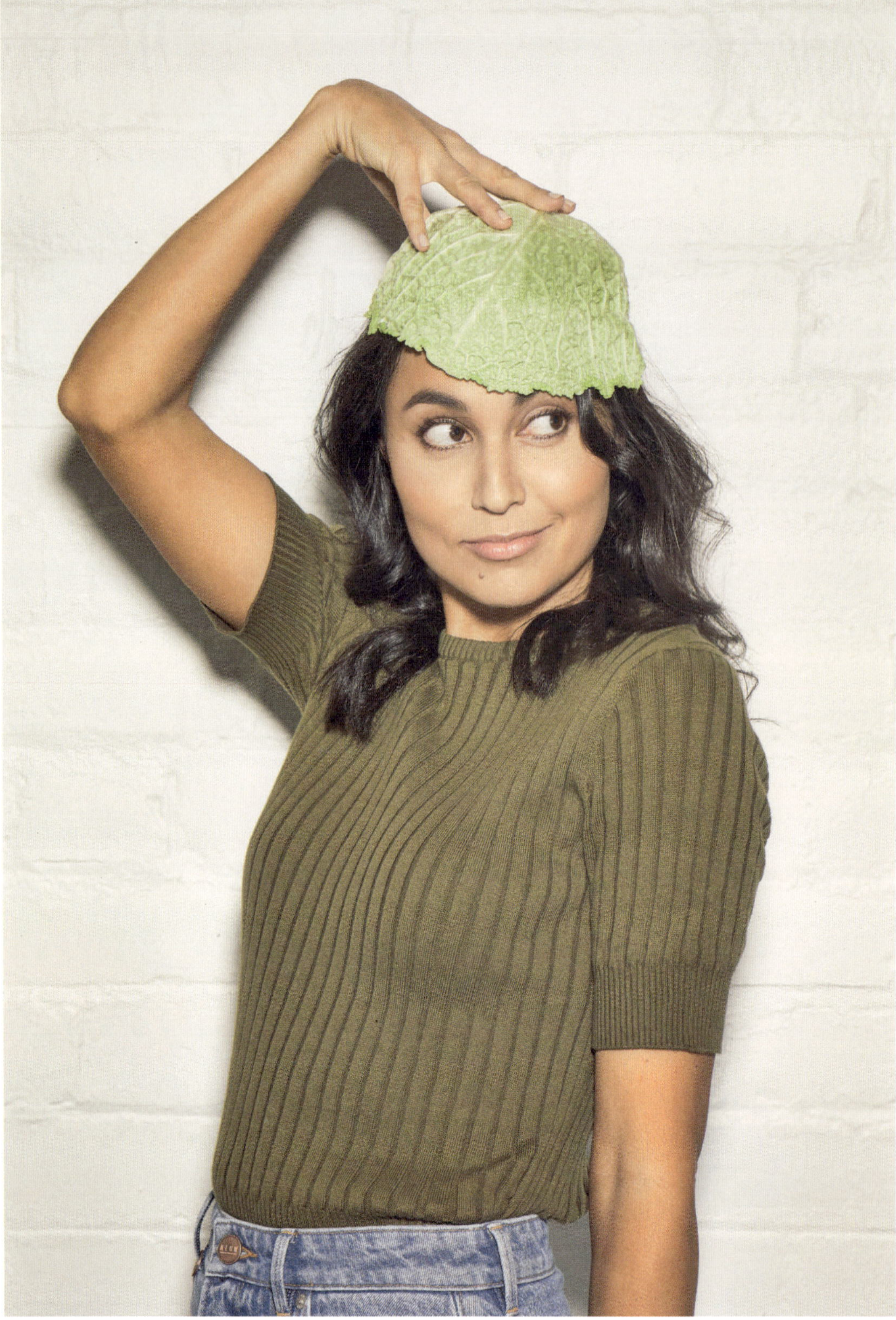

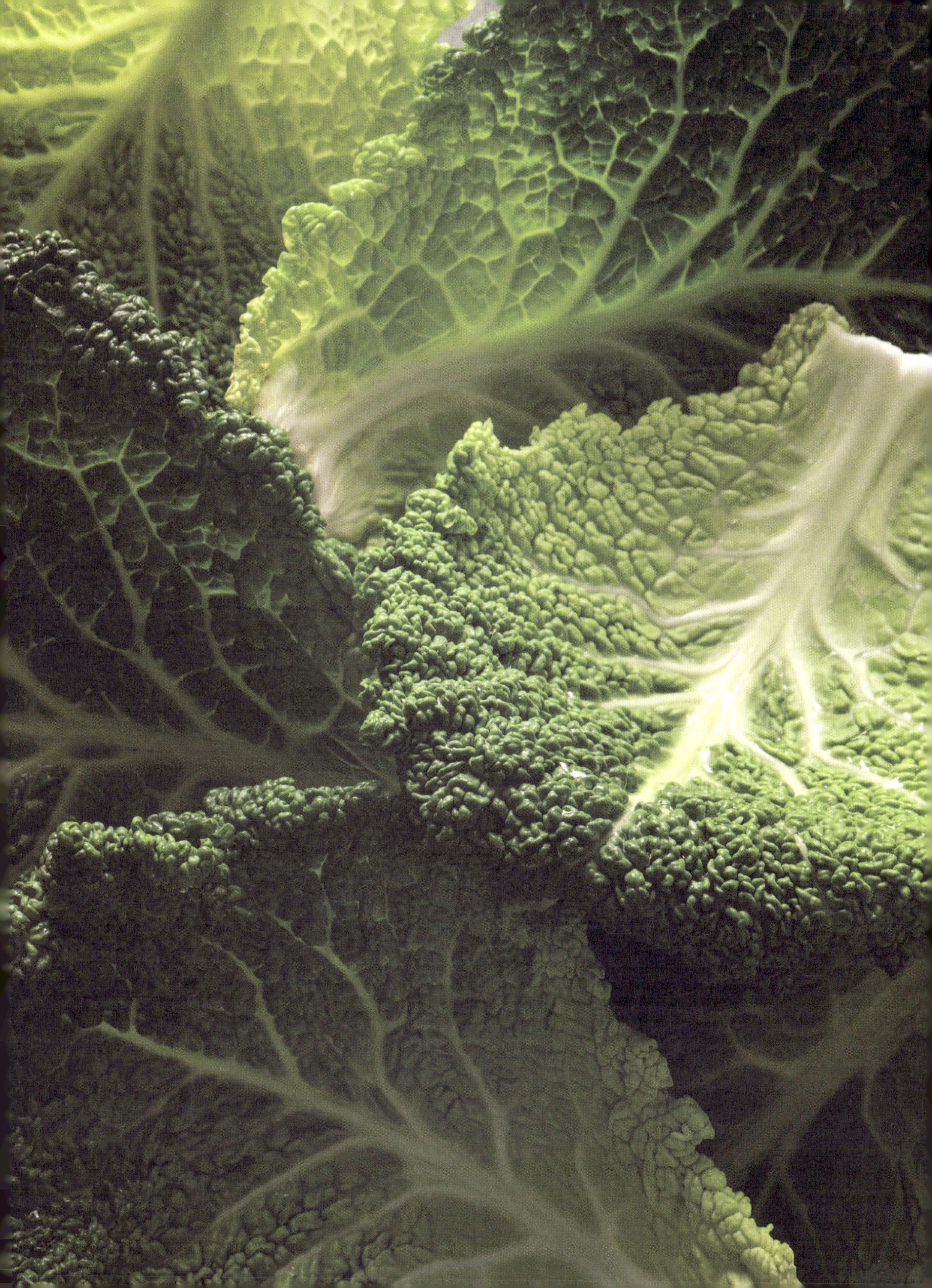

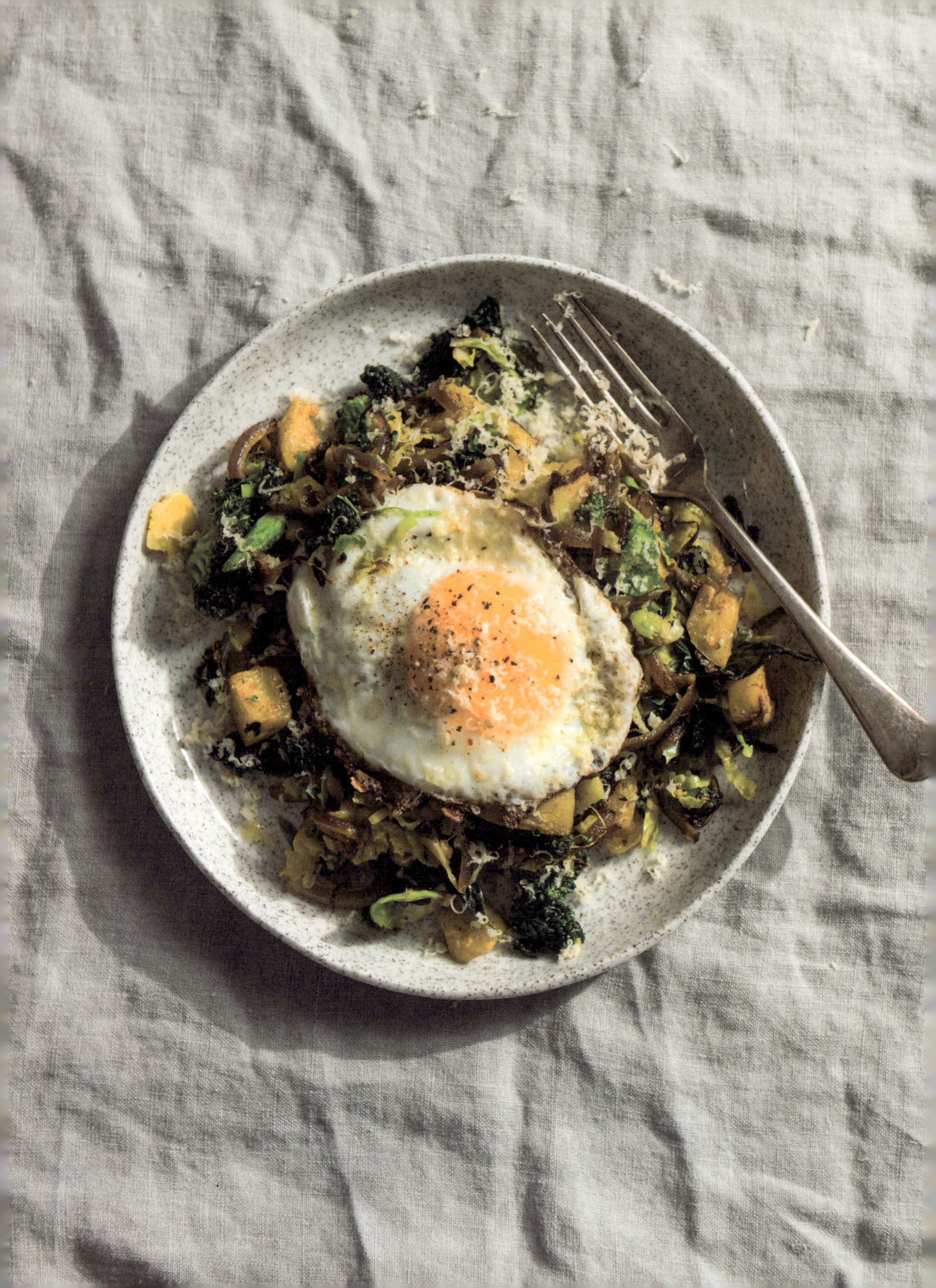

GF | DF omit butter and parmesan | VEGAN omit butter, eggs and parmesan

WINTER GREENS WITH A FRIED EGG & PARMESAN

SERVES 2
Prep time: 10 minutes
Cook time: 15 minutes

olive oil and butter, to cook
1 red or brown onion, finely sliced
1 teaspoon mild curry powder
1 large (about 300g) cooked agria potato, or swede, kumara or yams, chopped
4 stems broccolini, trimmed and chopped
6 Brussels sprouts, thinly sliced
4 cavolo nero or 2 large kale leaves, stripped from tough stem
2 free-range eggs
grated parmesan, to serve

This makes an easy, wholesome lunch or light dinner for one or two. I often make it just for myself and keep the remaining potato and greens mixture in the fridge for the next day. It's a great way to use up leftover cooked potatoes, kumara, swede, yams and the like, and whatever greens you have handy — my favourite is cavolo nero, but you could use finely sliced kale leaves, silverbeet, mustard greens or spinach.

1. Heat a drizzle of olive oil and knob of butter in a large fry pan. Cook onion, with a good pinch of salt, for about 5 minutes until golden. Add curry powder and cook for 30 seconds, then add potatoes and another drizzle of olive oil. Cook potatoes, tossing with the onions, for about 5 minutes until heated through. Roughly crush potatoes with a wooden spoon or a fork while they are cooking in the pan. Set mixture aside.

2. Add another drizzle of olive oil and little knob of butter to the pan. Cook broccolini, Brussels sprouts and cavolo nero/kale for about 5 minutes until soft. Return potato mixture to pan, toss together and season to taste with salt and pepper. Keep warm.

3. Heat a drizzle of oil and a little butter in a non-stick fry pan. Crack in eggs and cook until whites are set but yolk is still runny.

4. Divide potatoes and greens between plates and top with a fried egg. Season egg with salt and pepper and grate a little parmesan on top.

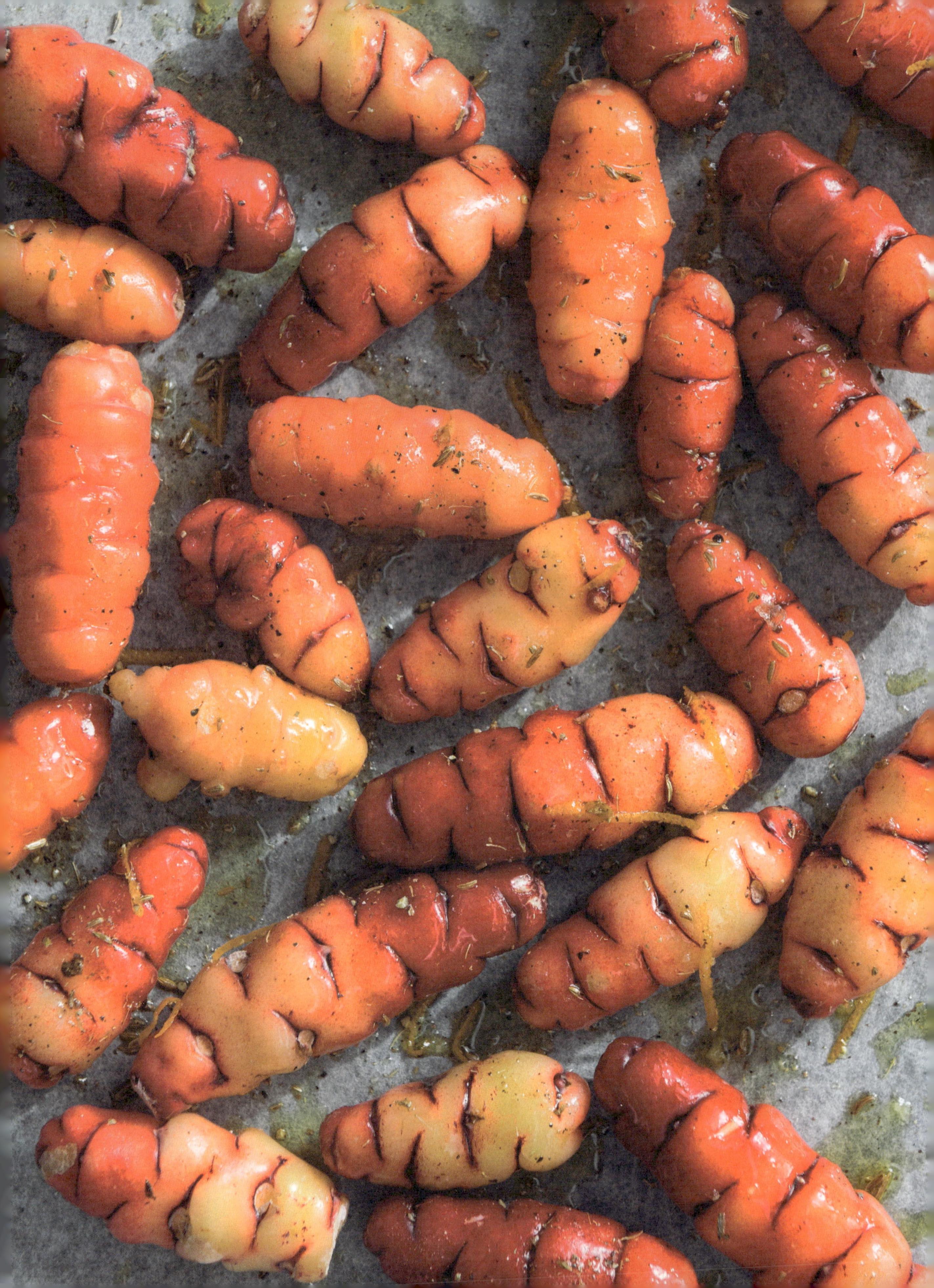

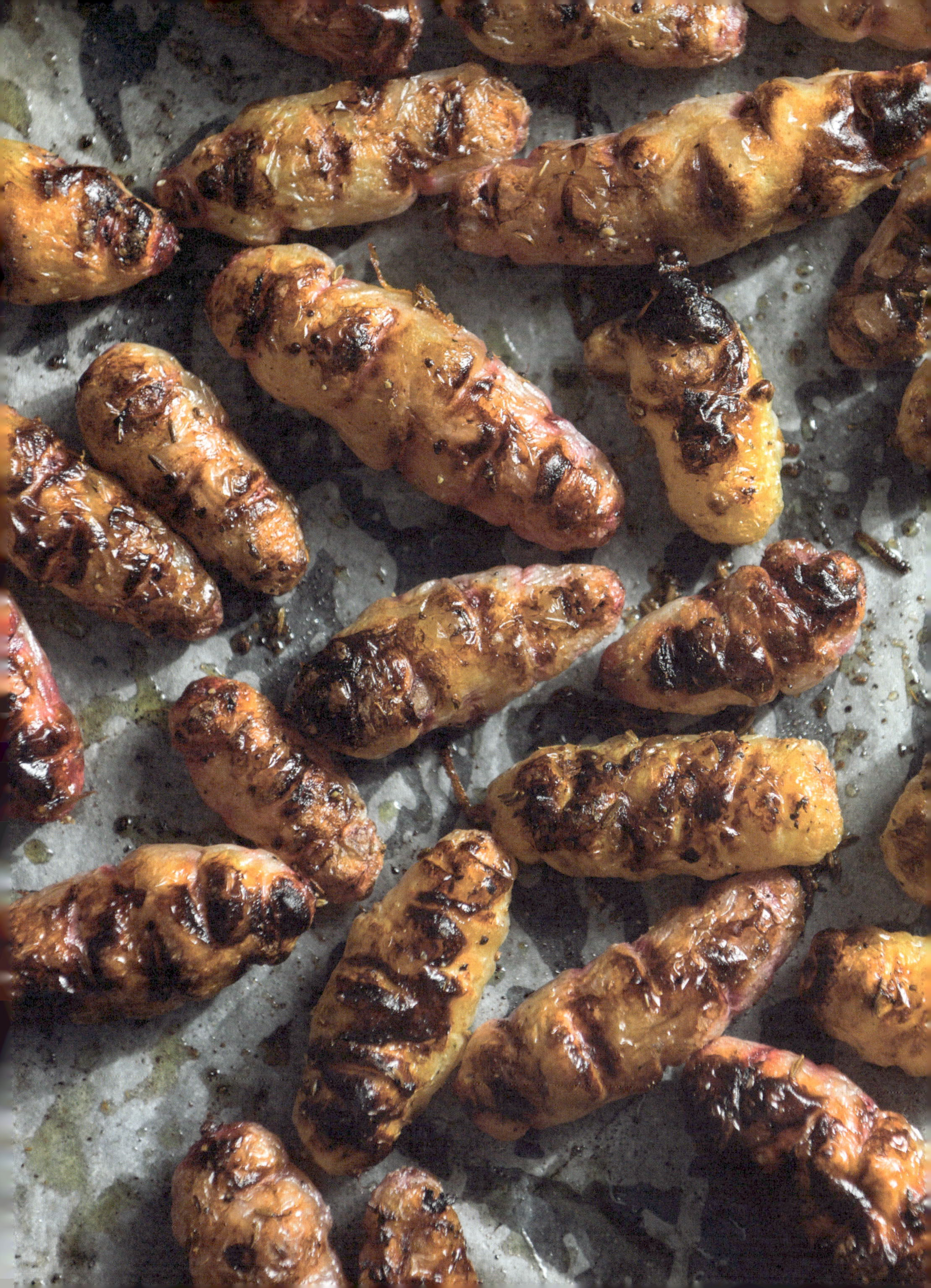

DF | VEGAN

BOK CHOY & SHIITAKE MUSHROOM MISO NOODLE SOUP

SERVES 2
Prep time: 10 minutes
Cook time: 10 minutes

120–150g dried ramen or soba noodles
750ml (3 cups) vegetable stock
3cm piece fresh ginger, peeled and thinly sliced
1 long red chilli, cut in half lengthways
1 clove garlic, bashed
2 tablespoons white miso paste
1–2 tablespoons oil
½ small onion, thinly sliced
100–120g fresh shiitake mushrooms, stalks trimmed, thinly sliced
1 small carrot, cut into matchsticks
1–2 spring onions, finely sliced (keep white and green part separated)
2cm piece fresh ginger, peeled and cut into fine matchsticks
1–2 teaspoons soy sauce
1 teaspoon sesame oil
2 baby bok choy or pak choy, sliced

This quick, easy and soul-nourishing soup is a winner on a cold day or night. Like all broths, it relies on the quality of stock used (either your own home-made stock, or a good-quality — ideally fresh — bought one). Shiitake mushrooms have much more 'umami' (savoury) flavour than button or Portobellos, hence I've specified to use them in this recipe as they help flavour the broth as well as have a great 'meaty' texture. This recipe is perfect for halving to serve one or doubling to serve four.

1. Cook noodles in a medium-sized pot of boiling water according to packet instructions (they cook very quickly, so be careful not to overcook). Drain and divide between serving bowls.

2. Place stock, sliced ginger, chilli and garlic in the same pot the noodles were cooked in and bring to the boil. Whisk in miso paste until dissolved.

3. Heat oil in a large fry pan on medium to high heat. Stir-fry onion, shiitake mushrooms, carrot, white part of spring onion (reserve the green for garnish) and matchstick ginger for 2–3 minutes until mushrooms are soft. Add soy sauce and sesame oil and continue cooking for a further 1–2 minutes.

4. Add bok choy to boiling broth and cook for 30 seconds before turning off the heat.

5. Divide mushroom mixture and bok choy between serving bowls. Remove sliced ginger, chilli and garlic from broth (with a slotted spoon), then ladle hot broth over noodles and vegetables. Garnish with green spring onion and eat while piping hot.

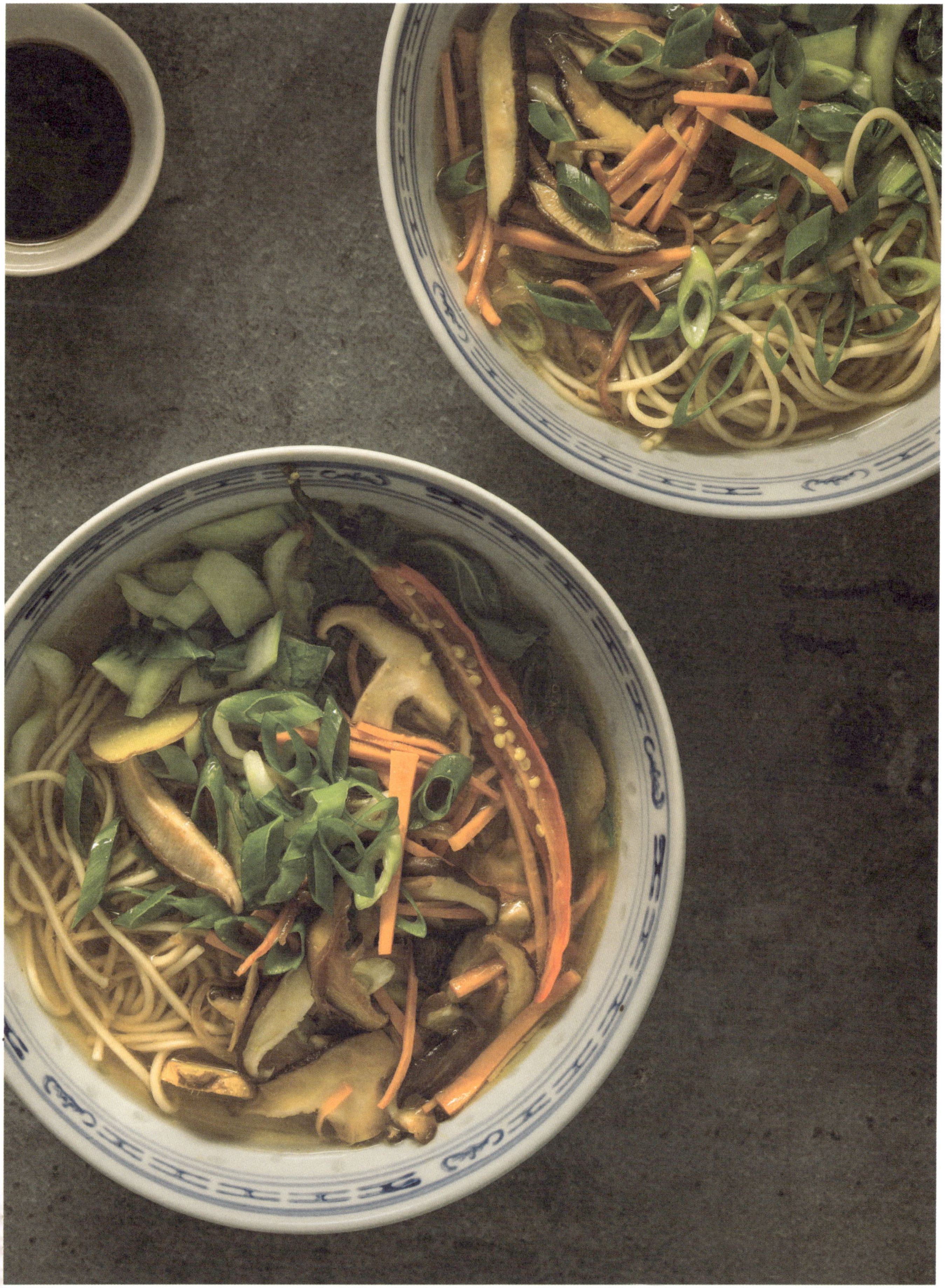

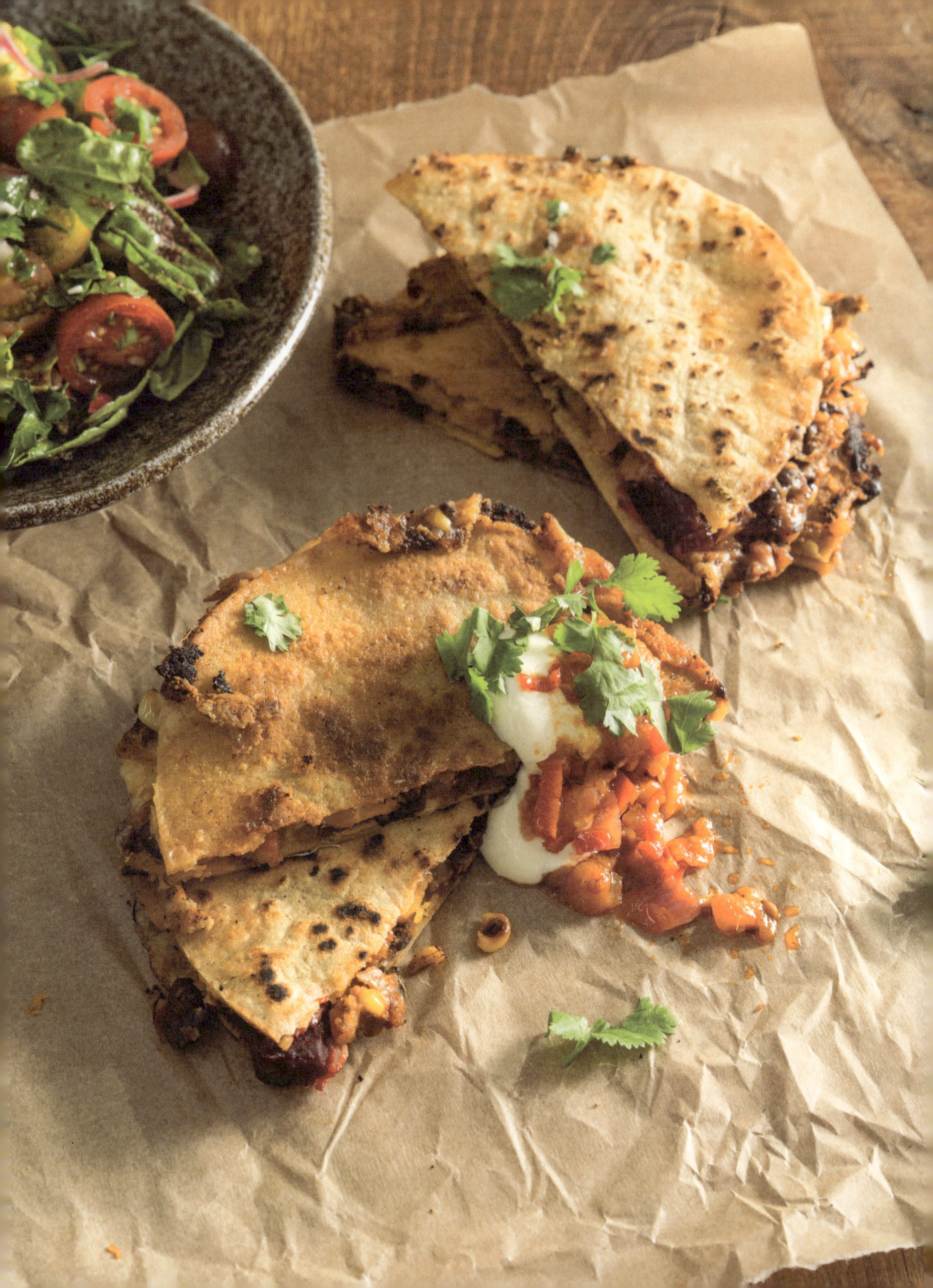

GF use GF corn tortillas

VEGGIE QUESADILLAS

SERVES 4-6
Prep time: 20 minutes
Cook time: 35 minutes

1 tablespoon oil
1 onion, finely chopped
1 clove garlic, finely chopped
2 cups raw or cooked vegetables (e.g. grated courgette or carrot, finely diced capsicum, sliced mushrooms, diced cooked pumpkin, eggplant etc.)
1 cup corn kernels (fresh, frozen or canned and drained)
1 teaspoon smoked paprika
1 teaspoon ground cumin
1 tablespoon tomato paste
400g can black beans or kidney beans, rinsed and drained
3 tablespoons chipotle sauce
10 small corn or wheat tortillas
2½–3 cups grated cheese (I like to use a mix of mozzarella and cheddar, but any grated cheese is fine)

TO SERVE
chopped coriander, parsley or basil
sour cream or thick, Greek-style natural, unsweetened yoghurt
Jalapeño Chutney (page 191), or store-bought chilli jam or relish

Who doesn't love a good quesadilla? Tortillas sandwiched together with a tasty Mexican bean and veg-packed filling (a great way to use up leftover veggies), smoky sauce and cheese, pan-fried until crispy and golden, and the cheese is all melted and oozy. Take your time to get them nice and golden in the pan, and you can keep them warm in the oven if cooking a lot at a time. Served with salsa or my Jalapeño Chutney (page 191), they are the ultimate crowd pleaser and a favourite with everyone, whether vegetarian or not.

1. Heat oil in a fry pan on medium heat. Cook onion until soft, 3–4 minutes. Add garlic and vegetables. Continue cooking for a further 4–5 minutes or until cooked through and all moisture from the pan has evaporated.

2. Add corn, paprika and cumin and continue cooking for a further minute. Add tomato paste and cook for another minute.

3. Take off the heat and mix in beans and chipotle sauce. Use a fork to roughly crush everything together. Season to taste with salt and pepper.

4. Lay a tortilla on a clean, dry surface. Sprinkle with about ¼ cup grated cheese, spoon about ⅔ cup bean and veg mixture on top, and sprinkle with another ¼ cup grated cheese. Top with another tortilla and press down gently but firmly. Repeat with remaining tortillas and filling.

5. Heat a drizzle of oil in a large fry pan (preferably cast-iron or non-stick) on low to medium heat. Cook each quesadilla for 2–3 minutes on one side, until golden brown and slightly crispy on the outside and cheese has melted. Press down on the quesadilla with a fish slice while cooking to help flatten it and make sure the filling sticks. Carefully flip over and cook for a further 2 minutes until golden brown on the other side. Repeat with remaining quesadillas.

6. To serve, cut each quesadilla into four and pile onto a large plate or wooden board. Sprinkle with herbs. Serve with sour cream/yoghurt and Jalapeño Chutney on the side.

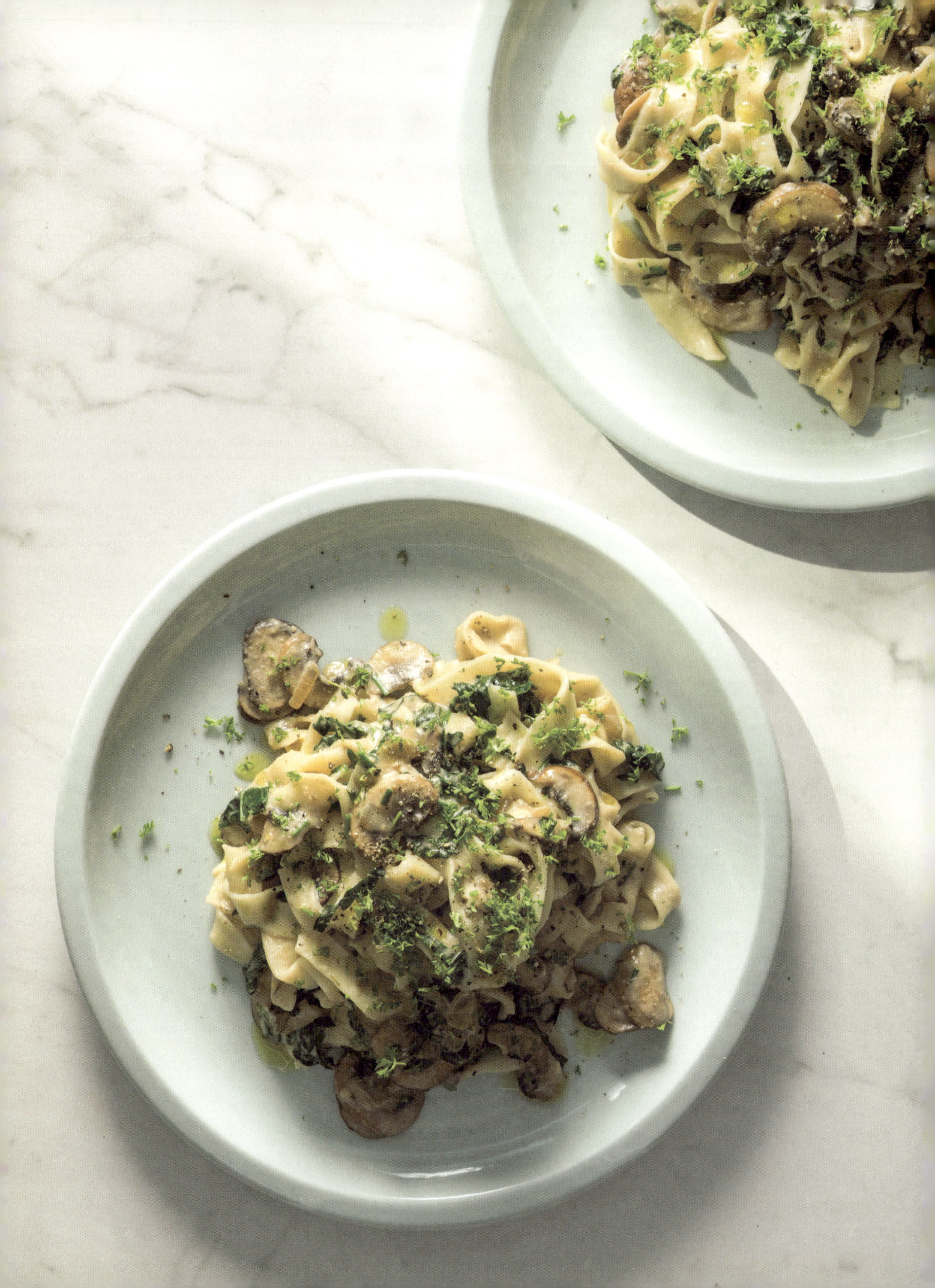

GF use GF pasta | DF | VEGAN

MUSHROOM & HERB FETTUCCINE WITH CASHEW CREAM SAUCE

SERVES 4
Prep time: 20 minutes
Cook time: 15–20 minutes

2 tablespoons olive oil or butter
1 onion, finely chopped
500g Swiss brown and/or button mushrooms, stalks removed, sliced
2 cloves garlic, chopped
1 tablespoon chopped thyme leaves
1–2 teaspoons soy sauce
1 cup vegetable stock
400g fresh or 250g dried fettuccine or other pasta (e.g. spaghetti or penne)
150g chopped spinach, cavolo nero or kale leaves, stems discarded
1½ cups Cashew Cream (page 217 or store-bought)
¼ cup chopped chives
3–4 tablespoons finely chopped parsley, to serve
extra-virgin olive oil or truffle oil, to serve

Creamy mushroom pasta is one of my favourite comfort foods, but it's easy to feel like a glutinous sloth after eating a bowl of it, so here is my lighter, healthier, dairy-free version using cashew nut cream (which is super easy to make, or you can buy it pre-made from some places). It's just as rich and creamy, and with more flavour.

1. Bring a large pot of well-salted water to the boil. Heat olive oil/butter in a large fry pan on medium heat. Cook onion, mushrooms, garlic and thyme, with a good pinch of salt, for 5–10 minutes until mushrooms and onion are soft.

2. Add soy sauce and vegetable stock to the mushrooms and continue cooking for a further 5 minutes or so until the mushrooms have soaked up most of the stock.

3. Cook pasta in boiling water until al dente. Add spinach/cavolo nero/kale to the pasta pot to cook in the last 1–2 minutes.

4. Stir Cashew Cream and chives into the mushrooms and bring to a gentle simmer to heat through. Stir in a little more vegetable stock to loosen the sauce, if needed. Season to taste with salt and pepper.

5. Drain pasta and greens and tip back into the pot. Add creamy mushroom sauce and toss together.

6. Divide between bowls, scatter with parsley and drizzle with a little extra-virgin olive oil or truffle oil.

GF use GF bread

GOURMET MOUSETRAPS

SERVES 1
Prep time: 5 minutes
Cook time: 5 minutes

1 slice grainy bread
butter, to spread
Marmite or Vegemite, to spread
2 button mushrooms, sliced
a few thin slices of red onion
½ tomato or 3 cherry
    tomatoes, sliced
1 teaspoon store-bought pesto
small handful of grated cheese
chopped chives or parsley

This recipe needn't be a recipe as it's so simple. It makes the best 3pm or after-school snack, or even a great simple lunch or dinner with a salad and whatever pickles, chutney or relish you have hanging about in the fridge.

1. Preheat oven to 200°C.

2. Place bread on a baking try and spread with butter and Marmite/Vegemite. Top with mushrooms, red onion and tomato.

3. Dot with pesto and sprinkle with grated cheese. Bake for 5 minutes, then switch to grill for 1–2 minutes until cheese is bubbly and golden.

4. Sprinkle with chives or parsley and serve with whatever pickles, chutney and salad you have in the fridge!

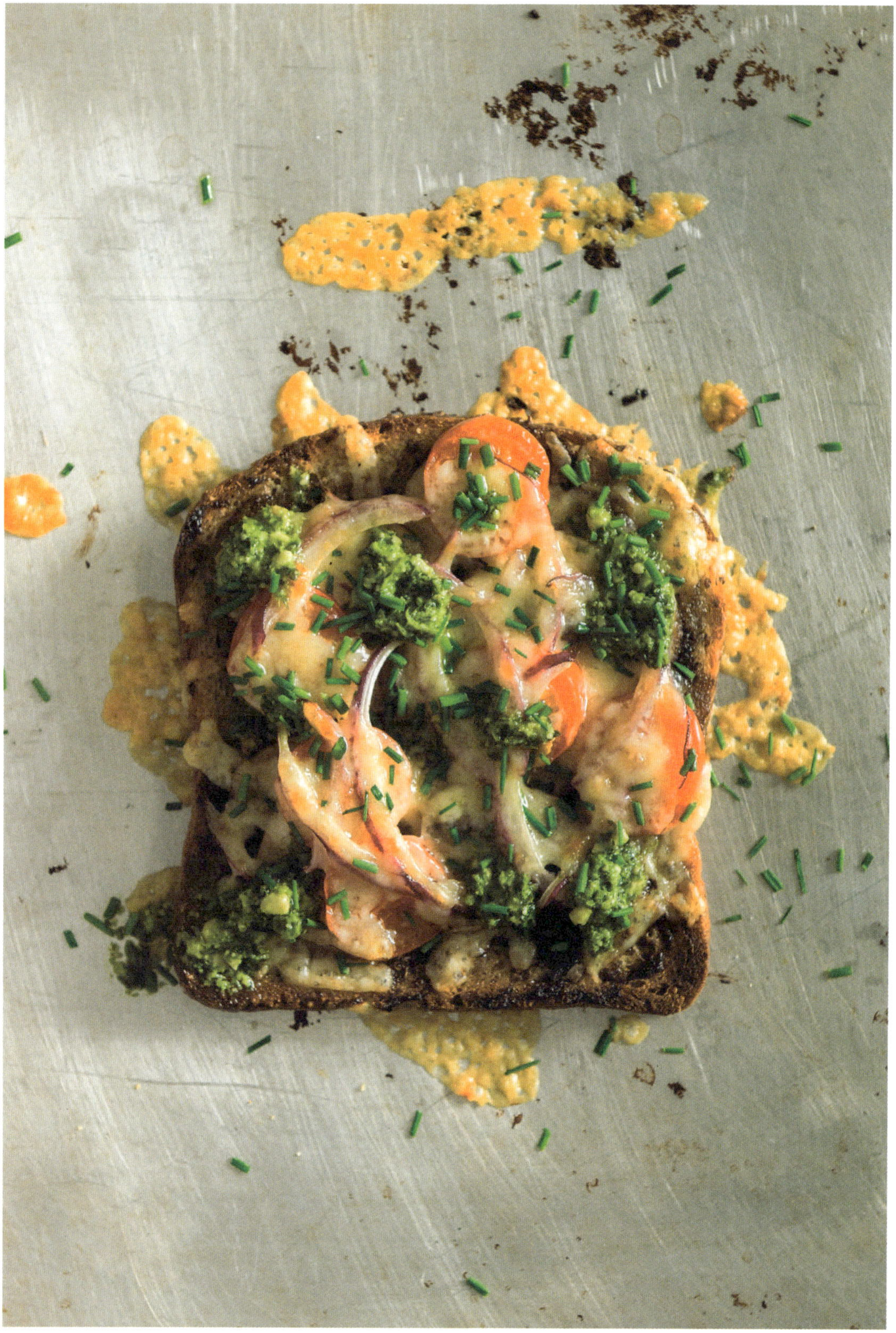

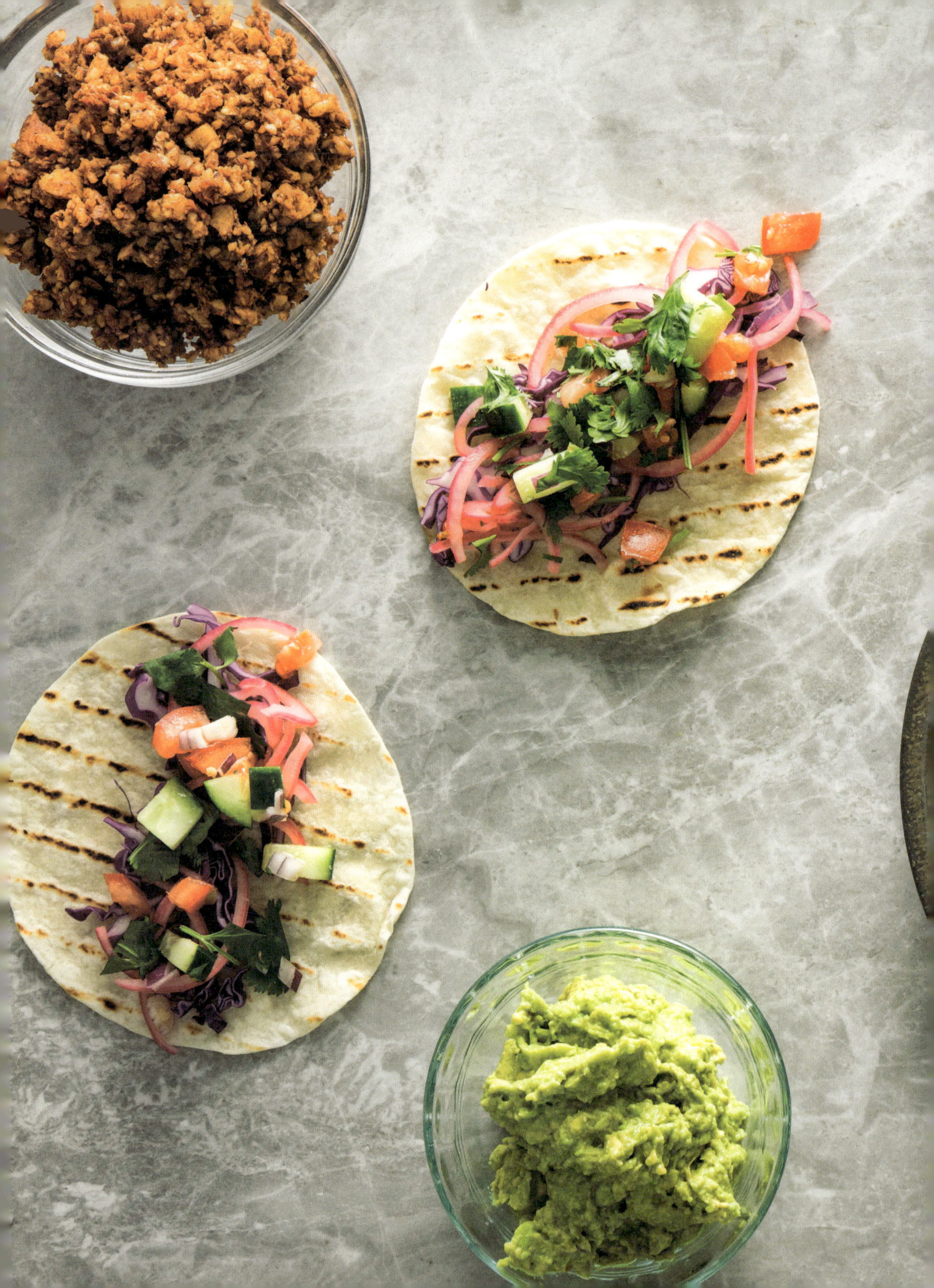

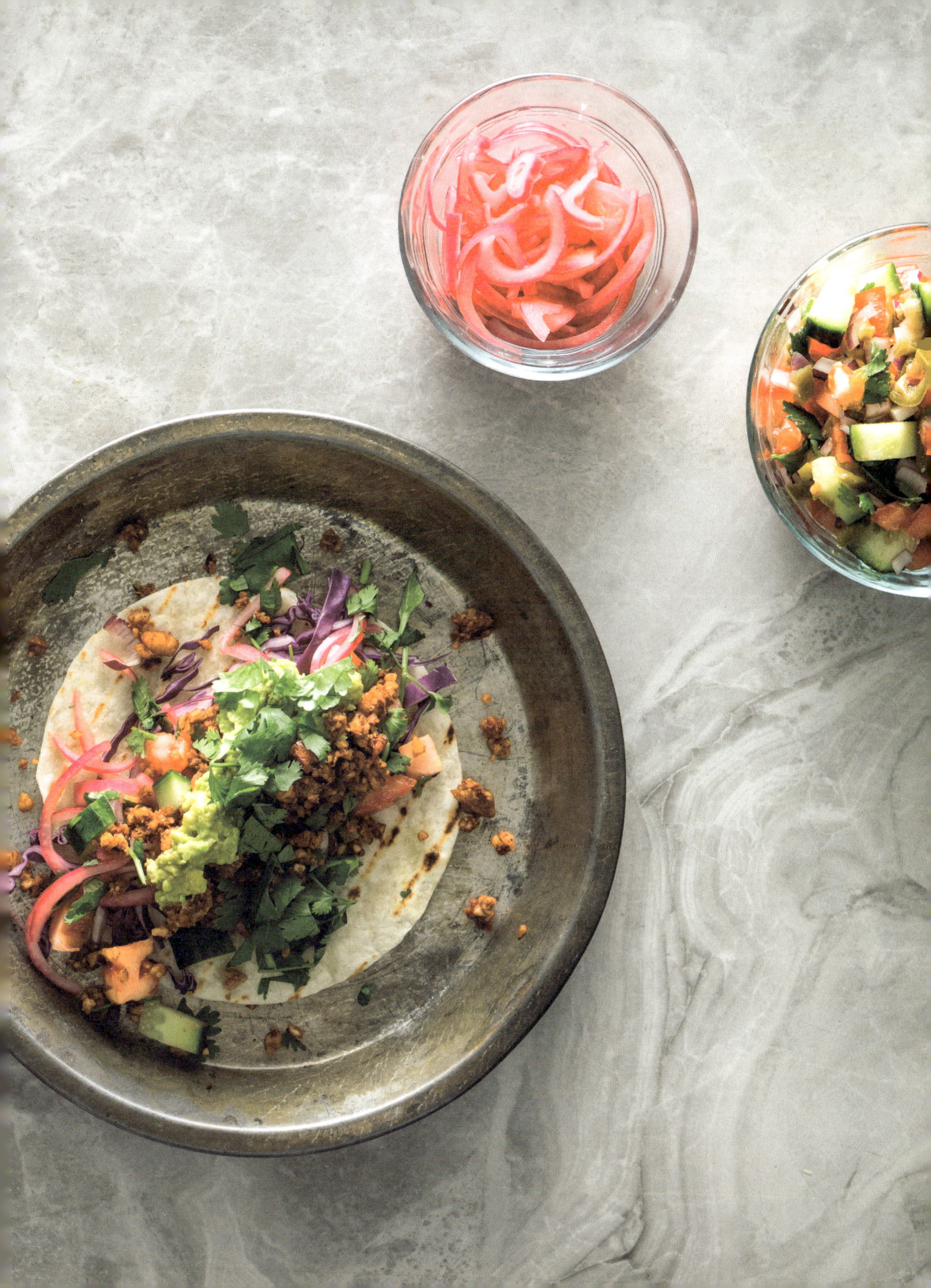

GF use GF tamari soy sauce and GF corn tortillas | DF | VEGAN

TACOS WITH WALNUT & ALMOND CHILLI & GUACAMOLE

SERVES 4
Prep time: 30 minutes

PINK PICKLED ONIONS
¼ cup red wine vinegar
1 teaspoon sugar
1 red onion, very thinly sliced

WALNUT AND ALMOND CHILLI
¾ cup walnuts
¾ cup roasted almonds
½ cup chopped sundried tomatoes
1 small clove garlic, minced
1 teaspoon smoked paprika
½ teaspoon ground cumin
½ teaspoon ground coriander
¼ teaspoon ground chilli or cayenne pepper
1½ tablespoons soy sauce or tamari
1 tablespoon balsamic vinegar

GUACAMOLE
flesh of 2 just-ripe avocados
3–4 tablespoons lime or lemon juice

TO SERVE
2–3 cups shredded red or green cabbage
12 soft corn tortillas or crispy corn taco shells
Tomato, Jalapeño and Coriander Salsa (page 190)

These tacos are amazing; they absolutely taste as good as they look! The Walnut and Almond Chilli is so simple and quick to make and has a delicious savoury flavour and texture, and it almost looks as if it could be mince! You can use it with other dishes, like the Burrito Bowls (over on the next page), too. And it will last in an airtight container in the fridge for up to 5 days. Make sure you slice the red onion very thinly so you don't end up with chunky bits (no one likes chunky bits of raw onion!).

1. Mix red wine vinegar and sugar in a bowl. Add red onion and toss to combine. Leave to marinate for at least 15 minutes while you make the rest of the meal. Drain before using.

2. Place all Walnut and Almond Chilli ingredients in a food processor and pulse a few times until ingredients are crumbly and just combined — be careful not to over-process the mixture or it will be too smooth. The texture should resemble that of crumbly cooked mince.

3. Mash avocado and lime or lemon juice together, and season to taste with salt and pepper. Toss cabbage with a drizzle of extra-virgin olive oil, a squeeze of lemon or lime juice and a pinch of salt.

4. Heat tortillas or taco shells according to packet instructions.

5. To serve, place all components of the meal in the middle of the table for people to help themselves.

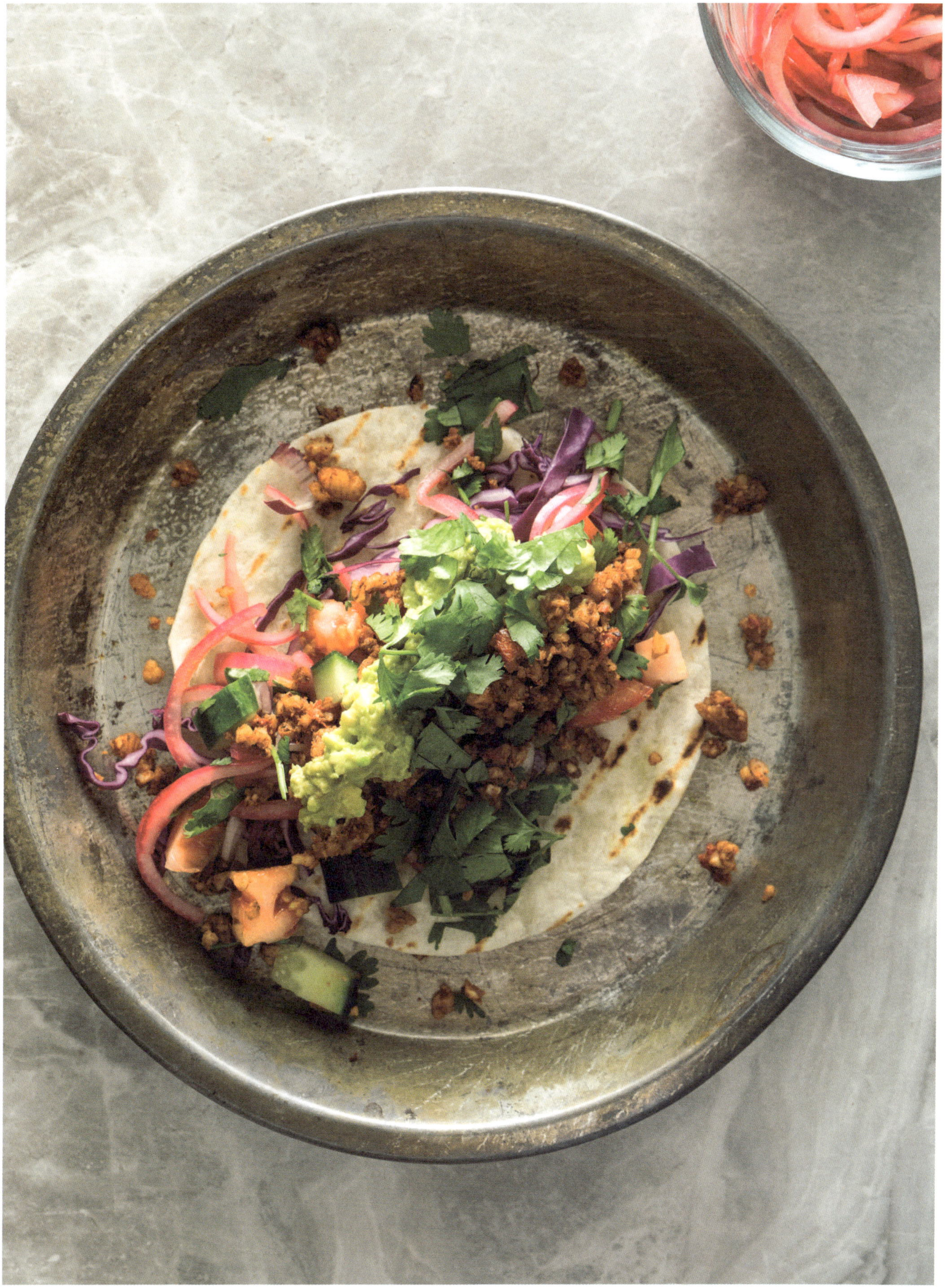

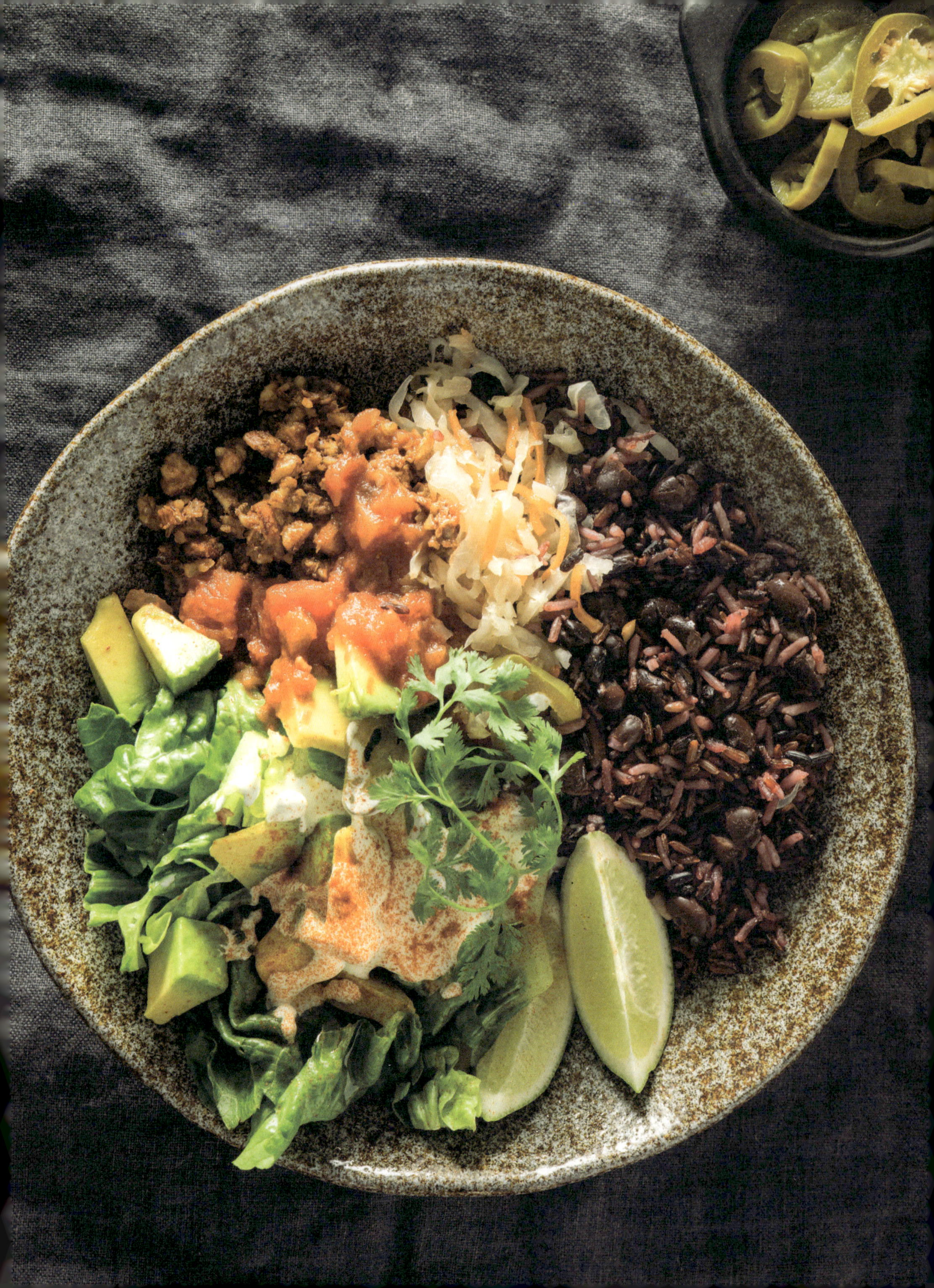

GF use GF tamari soy sauce | DF use coconut yoghurt |
VEGAN use coconut yoghurt

BURRITO BOWLS

SERVES 4
Prep time: 10 minutes
Cook time: 25 minutes

1 cup rice (e.g. brown, red, or wild rice)
1½ cups water
400g can black beans or kidney beans, rinsed and drained

TO SERVE
Walnut and Almond Chilli (page 180)
1 cos lettuce (or ½ iceberg), chopped
juice of ½ lemon
1 just-ripe avocado, diced
½ cup sauerkraut
Quick Salsa (page 195 or store-bought)
sour cream or Greek-style natural, unsweetened yoghurt
¼ cup pickled jalapeños (from a jar)
1 lime, cut into wedges

If you have some Walnut and Almond Chilli in the fridge (page 180), simply cook some rice and you can whip up this delicious bowlful of goodness in far less time than it takes to pick up Mexican takeaways.

1. Combine rice, water and a pinch of salt in a pot and bring to the boil. Cover with a tight-fitting lid and reduce to low heat. Cook for 15 minutes, then turn off the heat and leave to finish steaming, still covered, for 10 minutes.

2. While rice is cooking, make Walnut and Almond Chilli.

3. Toss lettuce with avocado, a drizzle of extra-virgin olive oil and lemon juice. Season with a pinch of salt.

4. Uncover rice, add beans and toss together.

5. To serve, divide rice and beans between bowls. Top with Walnut Almond Chilli, avocado salad, sauerkraut, salsa, a dollop of sour cream/yoghurt and jalapeños. Serve with lime wedges to squeeze over.

GF use GF puff pastry

LEFTOVER VEG TARTS

SERVES 4
Prep time: 10 minutes
Cook time: 20 minutes

1 large square sheet puff pastry
4 heaped tablespoons relish
   or chutney
3 cups leftover cooked vegetables
   (e.g. pumpkin, carrot, kumara,
   onion, beetroot, broccoli,
   courgette, capsicum, anything
   you've got really!)
½ red onion, thinly sliced
leaves from a few sprigs of thyme
   or 1 sprig of rosemary
1½ cups grated cheese, or
   8 slices cheese such as brie,
   camembert or even blue cheese
chopped parsley and/or chives

Thaw some pastry from the freezer, top with whatever leftover veg you have, a bit of chutney or relish, sliced onion, herbs and cheese (of any kind), whack in the oven and in 20 minutes you have a satisfyingly tasty meal.

1. Preheat oven to 200°C. Line a baking tray with baking paper.

2. Place pastry on lined baking tray and cut into four squares. Separate each pastry square from the others a little. Use a knife to lightly score a 0.5–1cm border inside each pastry square.

3. Spread chutney/relish on each square of pastry, within the border. Then top with vegetables, red onion, thyme/rosemary leaves and cheese.

4. Bake for about 20 minutes or until pastry is puffed and golden. Garnish with parsley/chives. Serve with tomato chutney or relish, and salad.

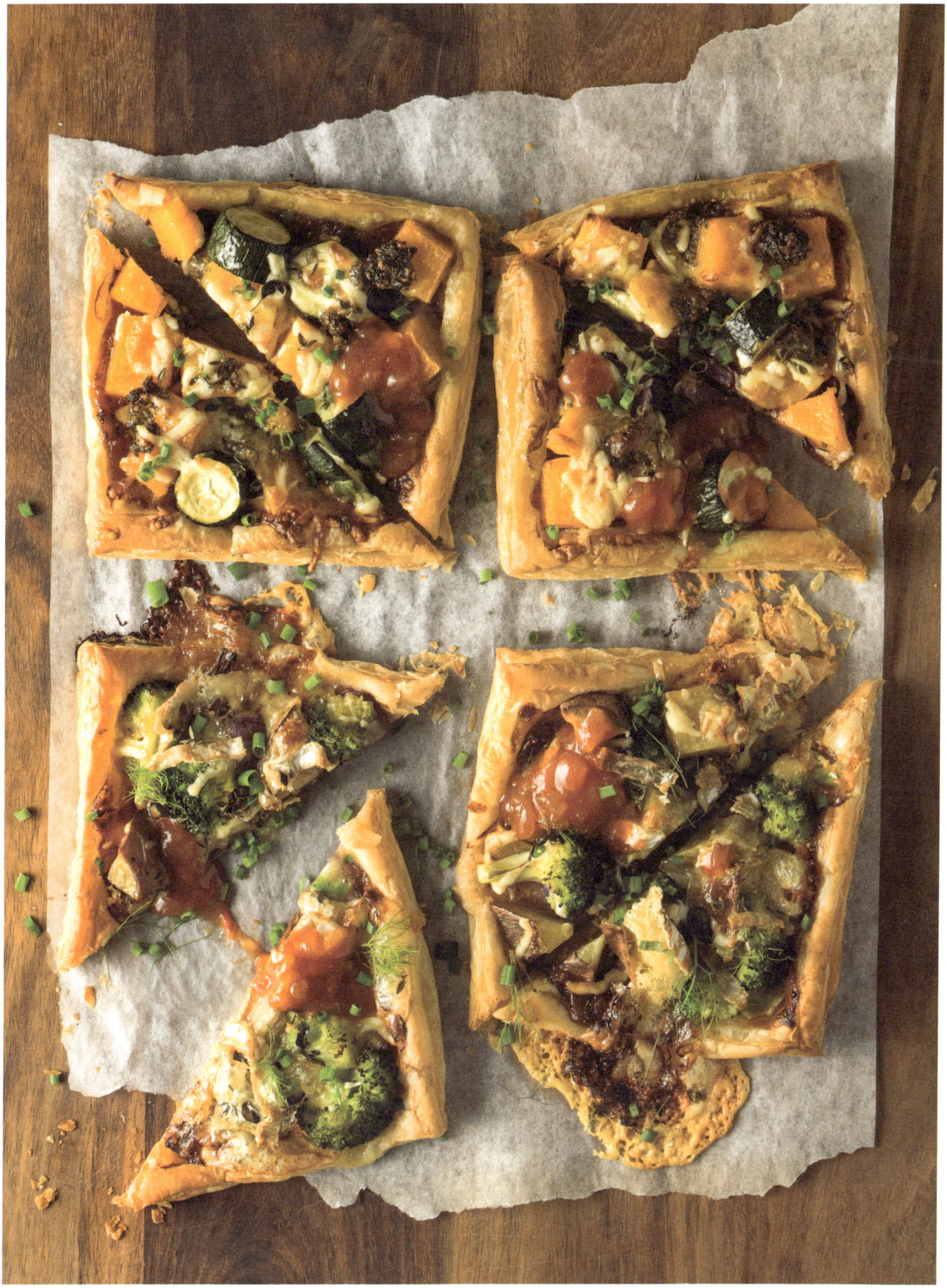

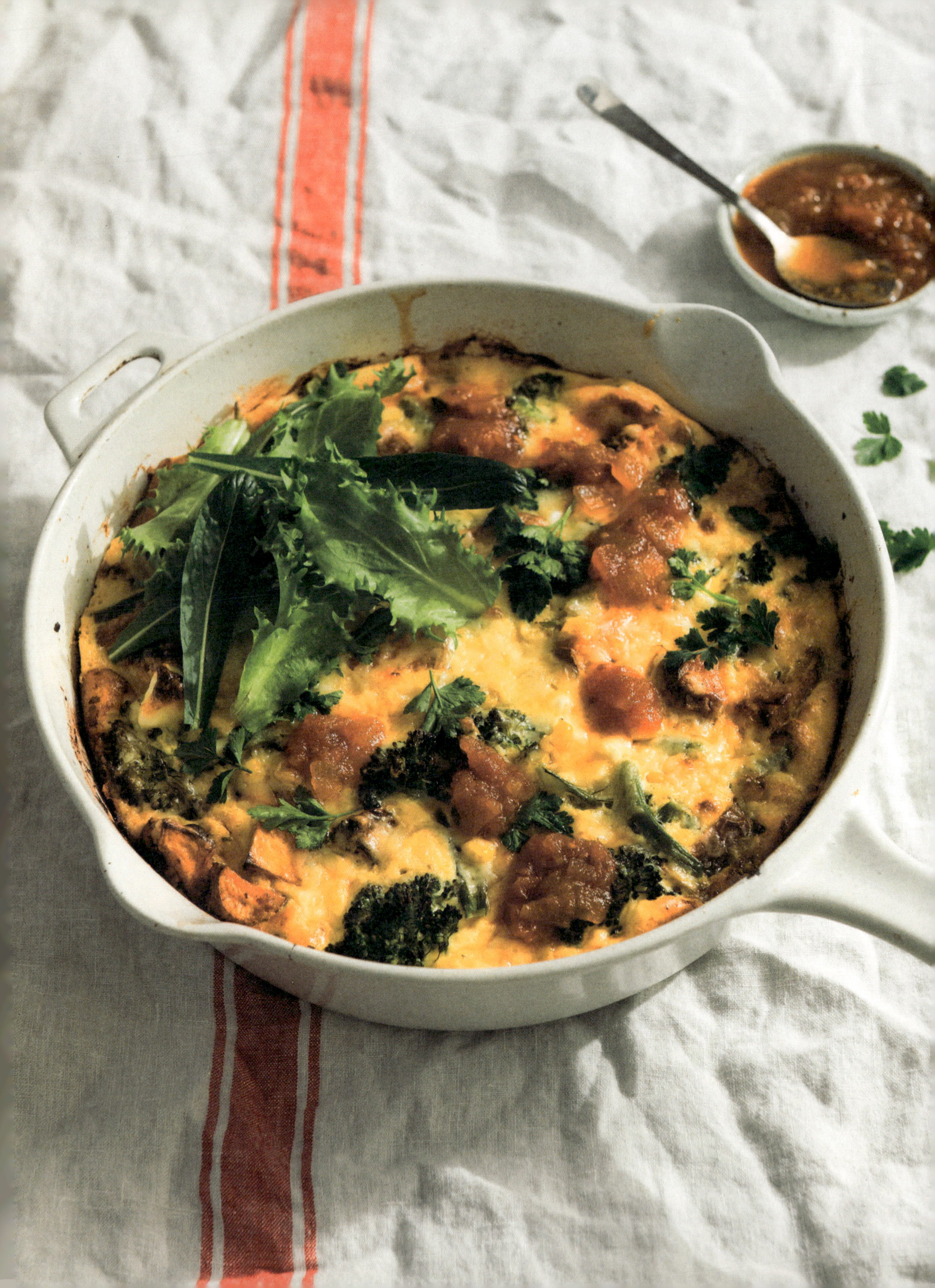

GF

ANYTHING VEGGIE FRITTATA

SERVES 4–6
Prep time: 15 minutes
Cook time: 45 minutes

6 free-range eggs
½ cup sour cream, cream or crème fraîche
150g feta, crumbled
1 tablespoon chopped thyme leaves
2–3 spring onions, sliced
kernels from 2 corn cobs (or 1½ cups canned or defrosted frozen corn kernels)
2–3 cups diced roast pumpkin, kumara or potato
2 cups chopped asparagus spears, green beans or broccoli florets
1 cup grated cheese

Mix and match almost any vegetables you have in this versatile frittata — it's one of those meals that is great for using up leftover vegetables and can be easily adapted to what you have. I've suggested using corn and asparagus, beans, or broccoli. But feel free to swap with other vegetables, although if the veggies have a high water content (e.g. eggplant, mushrooms, courgette) it is best if they are precooked/roasted first.

1. Preheat oven to 220°C.

2. In a large bowl, whisk eggs and sour cream together until smooth. Stir in feta and thyme and season with salt and pepper.

3. Heat a drizzle of olive oil in a large, heavy-based, ovenproof fry pan (e.g. a cast-iron pan) on medium heat. Cook spring onion and corn for 1–2 minutes. Remove from heat and toss through roast kumara/pumpkin/potato and asparagus/beans/broccoli.

4. Pour in egg mixture and sprinkle with cheese. Bake for about 20 minutes until frittata is set.

5. Stand in the pan for 5 minutes before cutting into wedges. Serve with tomato relish or chutney and salad.

GF use GF tamari soy sauce | DF | VEGAN

SAUCY PAD THAI

SERVES 2
Prep time: 15 minutes
Cook time: 10–15 minutes

150g dried rice-stick noodles (about 1cm thickness)
2 tablespoons oil
1 stalk lemongrass, tough outer leaves removed, finely chopped
2 medium-sized kaffir lime leaves, tough central stem removed, very finely shredded
100–150g fresh shiitake mushrooms, sliced
2 spring onions, sliced (white and green part separated)
1 cup sliced green beans and/or red capsicum
2 large handfuls of mung bean sprouts
½ red chilli, finely sliced (optional)

SAUCE
2 tablespoons soy sauce
3 tablespoons sweet chilli sauce
1 teaspoon brown sugar
2 teaspoons lime juice
1 teaspoon sesame oil
½ cup coconut milk

TO SERVE
¼ cup chopped roasted peanuts
handful of chopped coriander
½ lime, cut into wedges

Here's my yummy vegan version of one of the world's most popular street food dishes, which is also super quick and easy to make!

1. Cook noodles in a pot of boiling water for about 5 minutes or until just soft (be careful not to overcook them), then drain and run under cold water to stop the cooking process (this also helps to prevent them from sticking together).

2. Mix all sauce ingredients together and set aside.

3. Heat oil in a wok or your largest non-stick fry pan on medium to high heat. Fry lemongrass, kaffir lime leaves, mushrooms, white part of spring onions, beans and/or capsicum for 4–5 minutes until mushrooms are starting to turn golden.

4. Add drained noodles, green part of spring onions, bean sprouts, chilli (if using) and sauce. Stir-fry, tossing everything together, for about 5 minutes until noodles are well coated in the sauce and heated through.

5. Top noodles with peanuts and coriander. Serve with lime wedges to squeeze over just before eating.

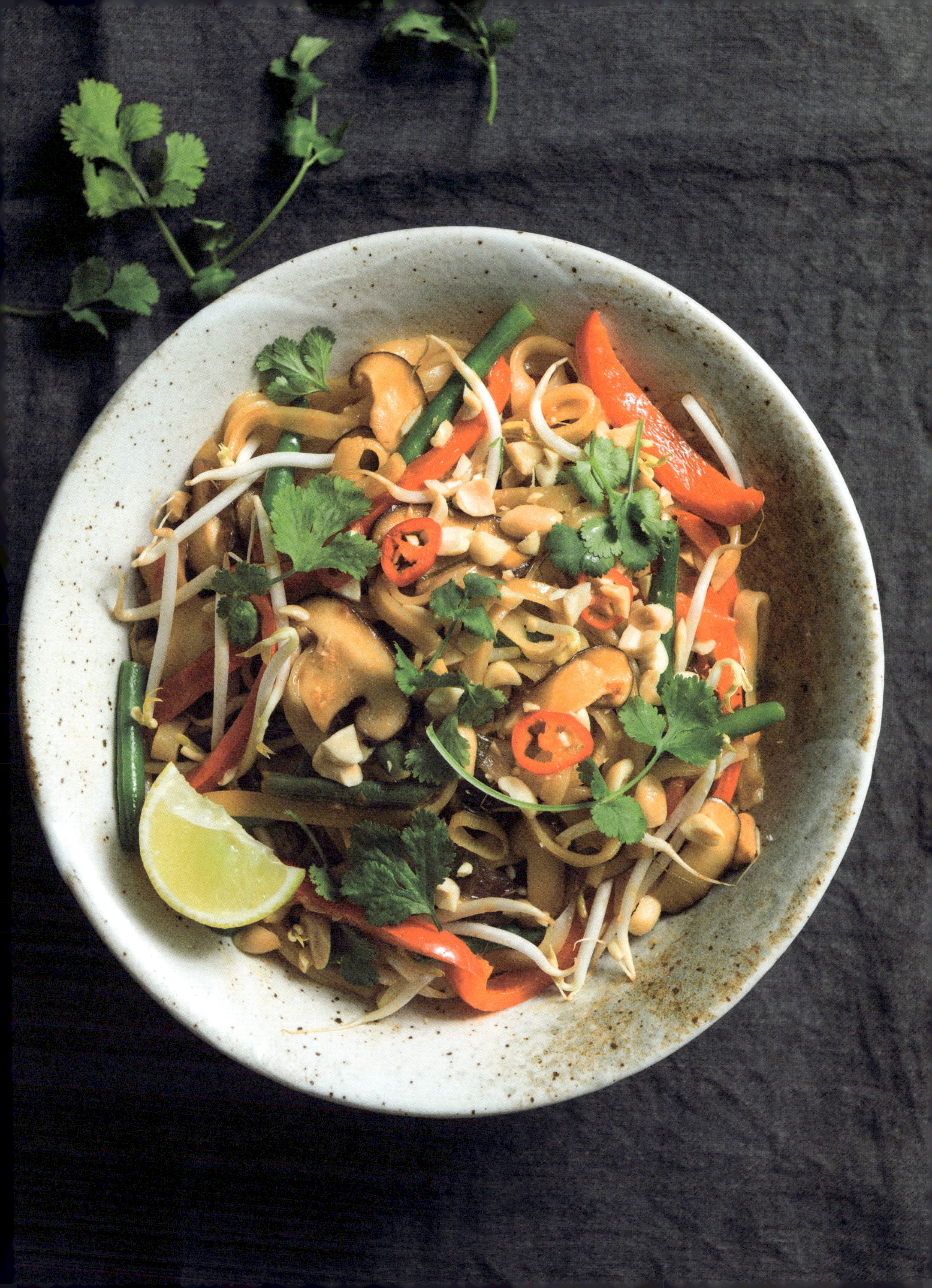

GF | DF | VEGAN

OLIVE TAPENADE

MAKES ¾ CUP
Prep time: 5–10 minutes

1 cup pitted olives
   (black and/or green)
1 teaspoon capers
1 small clove garlic, chopped
juice of ½ lemon
¼ cup chopped parsley
¼ cup extra-virgin olive oil

Delicious tossed through pasta or boiled potatoes, on bruschetta, as a dip for vegetables, tossed through vegetables in a salad, a dollop on soup, and more!

1. Place all ingredients, except olive oil, in a food processor and blitz until finely chopped. Scrape down the sides of the food processor to make sure everything gets incorporated.
2. With the motor still running, drizzle in the olive oil and blitz until combined.

GF | DF | VEGAN

TOMATO, JALAPEÑO & CORIANDER SALSA

MAKES 3–4 CUPS
Prep time: 10 minutes

6–8 vine-ripened tomatoes, diced
1 Lebanese cucumber (or
½ telegraph cucumber), seeds
   removed then diced
¼ cup finely diced red onion
2–4 tablespoons finely chopped
   pickled jalapeños (from a jar)
juice of ½ lemon
drizzle of extra-virgin olive oil
½ cup chopped coriander

This amazing fresh salsa livens up any dish. The pickled jalapeños are key so make sure you include them!

1. Mix all ingredients together in a bowl and season to taste with salt.

GF | DF | VEGAN

JALAPEÑO CHUTNEY

MAKES 1 LARGE CUP
Prep time: 2 minutes
Cook time: 8–10 minutes

1 tablespoon olive oil
400g can crushed tomatoes
¼ cup pickled jalapeños
   (from a jar), chopped
2 teaspoons honey or brown sugar

Like a chilli jam or chutney, but with pickled jalapeños instead — makes a great condiment for quesadillas and other Mexican dishes, or on a cheese platter.

1. Mix all ingredients in a pot and simmer for 8–10 minutes until thick and jam-like. Season with salt and pepper.

GF use GF bread | DF | VEGAN

BRUSCHETTA

MAKES 8–10 BRUSCHETTA BASES
Prep time: 5 minutes
Cook time: 10 minutes

½ sourdough or ciabatta baguette
¼ cup olive oil
2–3 cloves garlic, cut in half

Bruschetta makes one of the best starters (or antipasto as it is called in Italy). Slices of bread grilled or toasted with olive oil, rubbed with garlic and topped with all sorts of delicious things — check out pages 59, 67, 74–77 and 228 for ideas.

1. Slice baguette about 1cm-thick into 8–10 slices. Place on a baking tray and drizzle or brush with olive oil. Bake at 180°C for 12–15 minutes until light golden and crisp.

2. When cool enough to handle, but still warm, rub each piece of toast with garlic to impart a subtle garlicky flavour. They're now ready to be topped with all sorts of delicious things!

GF | DF | VEGAN

AUTUMN HARVEST SAUCE

MAKES ABOUT 6 CUPS
Prep time: 15 minutes
Cook time: 2–2½ hours

2 teaspoons chopped thyme and/or rosemary leaves
4 tablespoons olive oil
¼ cup tomato paste
1½ tablespoons sugar
½ teaspoon salt
1 red chilli, finely chopped (optional)
800g–1kg ripe tomatoes, cut into wedges
1 small eggplant, cut into 2cm pieces
2 red, yellow or orange capsicums, cored and cut into 2cm pieces
1 large red onion, cut into 2–3cm pieces
1 bulb fennel, sliced
4 cloves garlic, peeled

This super-useful, rich, tomato-based vegetable sauce is handy to have in the fridge to whip up quick pasta dishes, bakes, casseroles and the like, to add a delicious rich flavour. An abundance of autumn vegetables — eggplant, tomatoes, onion, capsicum and fennel (and a little chilli) — are roasted to sweeten and concentrate their flavours, before being blended into a velvety sauce.

1. Preheat oven to 160°C. Line a large oven tray or roasting dish with baking paper.

2. Mix thyme/rosemary, olive oil, tomato paste, sugar, salt and chilli (if using) together.

3. Toss tomatoes, eggplant, capsicum, onion, fennel and garlic with olive oil/tomato paste mixture in lined tray.

4. Spread out in a single layer and roast for 2–2½ hours until vegetables are soft and slightly caramelised.

5. Once vegetables are cooked, purée half of them then mix through the rest for a beautiful sauce that goes with lots of different dishes!

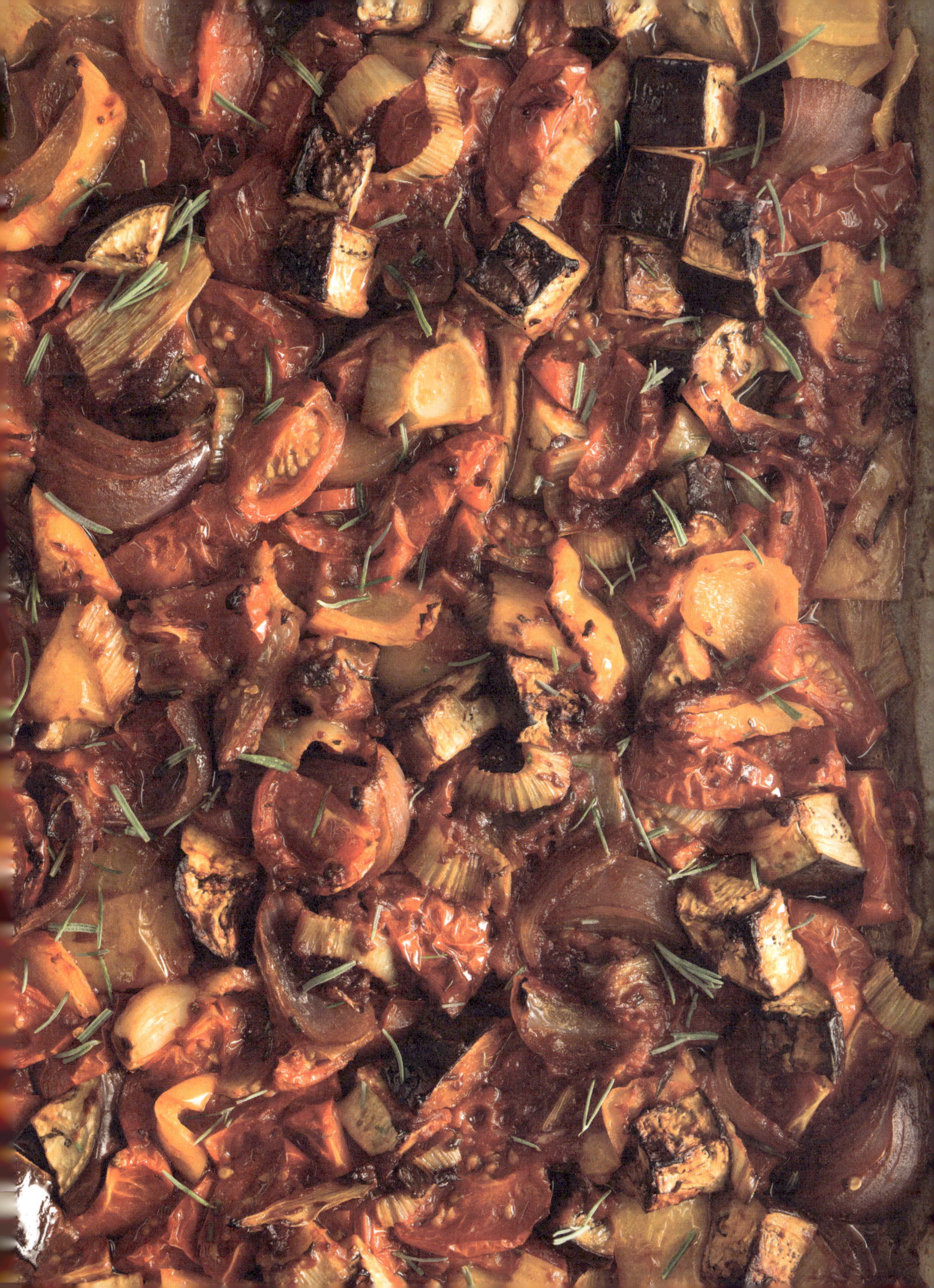

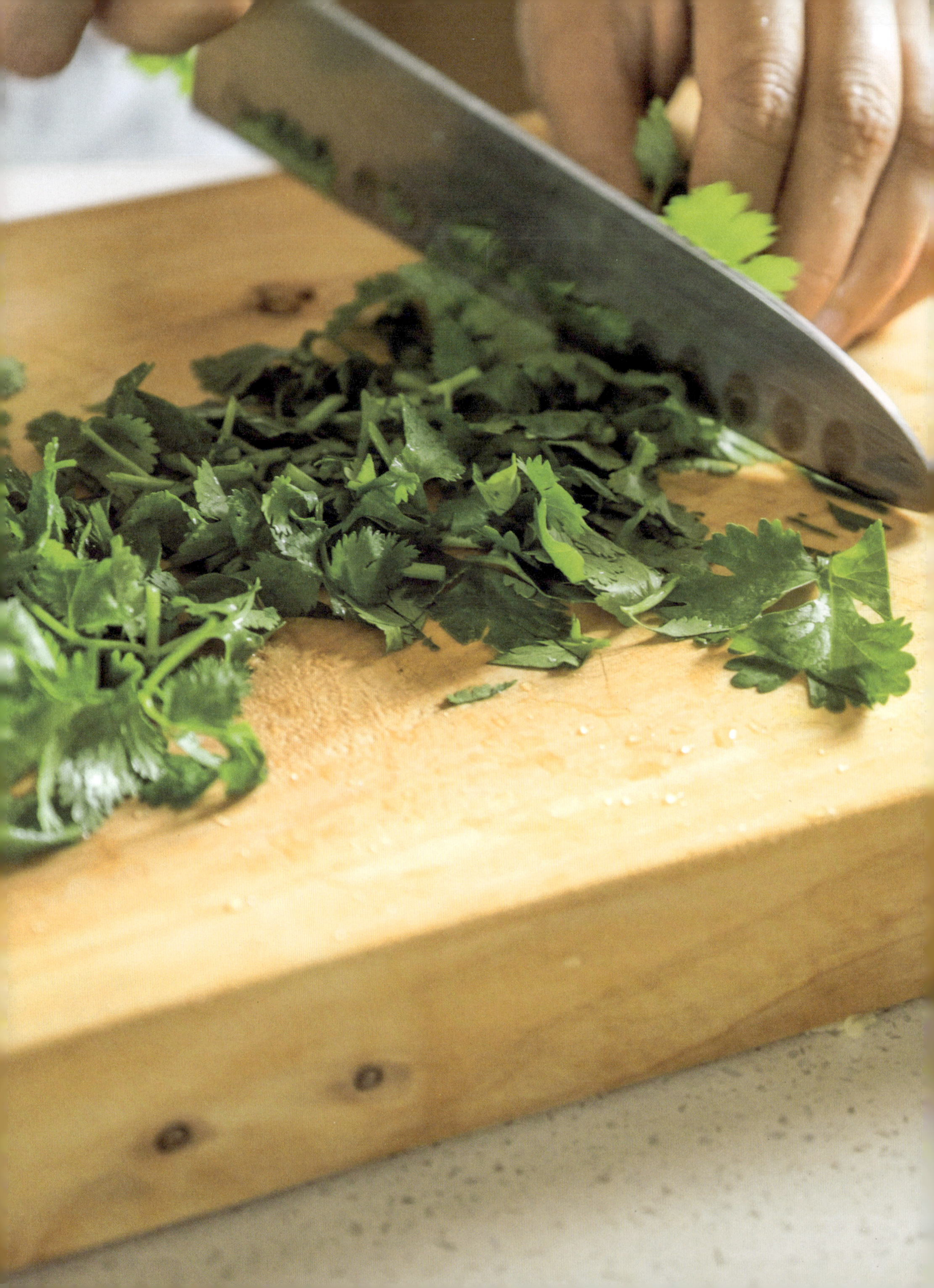

GF | DF | VEGAN

SPICE MIXES

MOROCCAN SPICE MIX
4 teaspoons paprika
2 teaspoons ground cumin
1 teaspoon ground coriander
1 teaspoon ground cinnamon
4 teaspoons sumac

MEXICAN SPICE MIX
1 teaspoon paprika
1 teaspoon smoked paprika
1 teaspoon ground cumin
1 teaspoon ground coriander
1 teaspoon dried oregano or mixed herbs
¼ teaspoon ground chilli or cayenne pepper
½ teaspoon each garlic and onion powder
1 teaspoon brown sugar
½ teaspoon salt

These popular spice blends are readily available in supermarkets, so feel free to just buy them. But if you'd prefer to make your own, here's how.

1. Mix all ingredients together and store in an airtight container.

GF | DF | VEGAN

QUICK SALSA

MAKES 1 CUP
Prep time: 3 minutes

400g can crushed tomatoes
½ chilli, finely chopped (or pinch of chilli flakes)
drizzle of extra-virgin olive oil
½ teaspoon sugar
2 tablespoons finely diced red onion (optional)
3–4 tablespoons chopped coriander or basil (optional)

This super-quick salsa uses canned tomatoes instead of fresh and is more like the type of salsa you'd buy in a jar. It's perfect for adding as a quick condiment to lots of Mexican dishes.

1. Tip canned tomatoes into a sieve over a bowl or the sink to allow excess liquid to drain away.
2. Mix with all remaining ingredients and season to taste with salt.

Spic
Ex

CHAPTER FIVE — P. 197

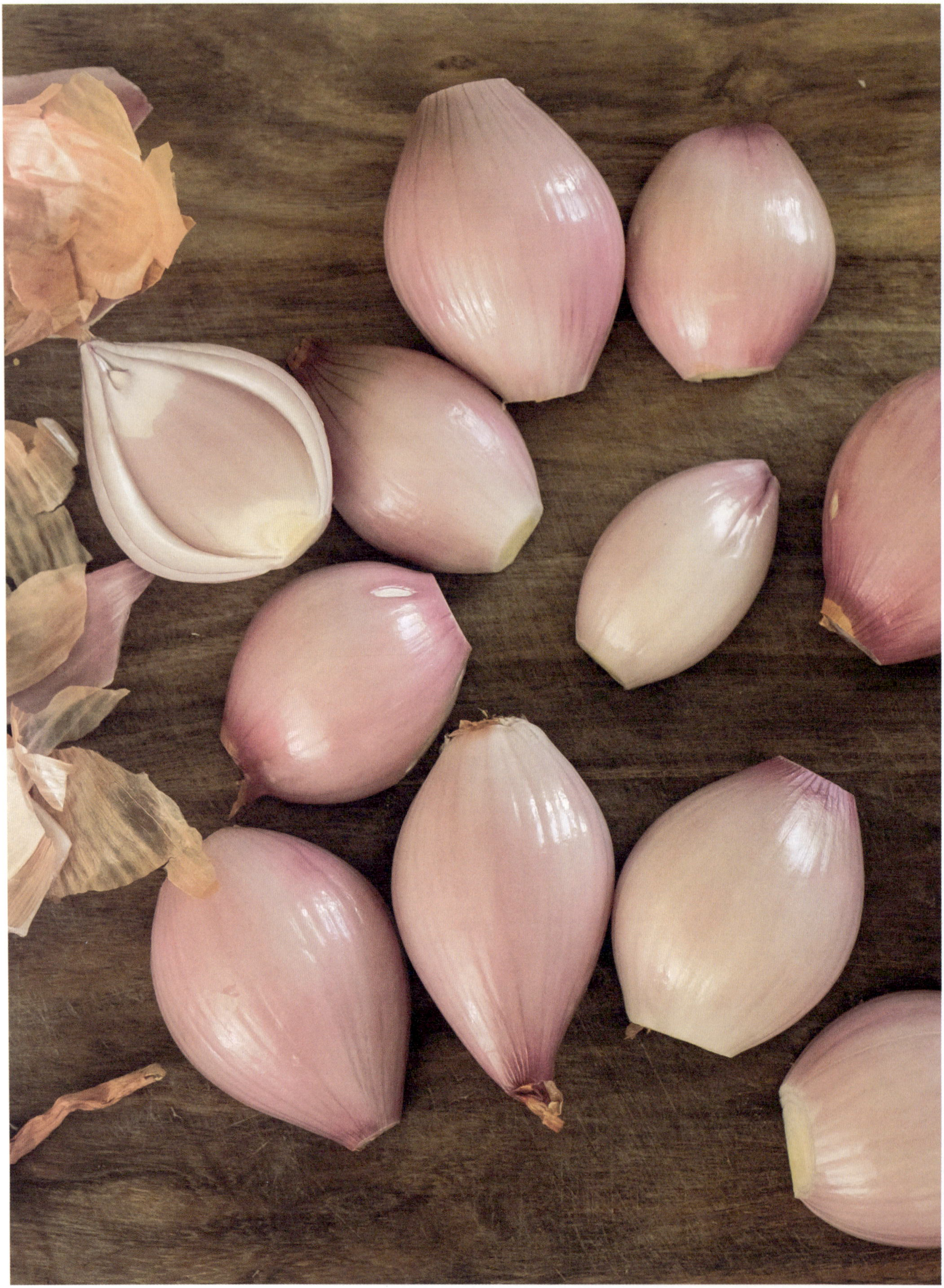

It's no secret that arguably THE best vegetarian food in the world can be found in South East Asia. I could have easily (and very happily) been vegetarian, even vegan, for months on end and never missed eating meat whilst in India. So, it seemed fitting to highlight some of my favourite spicier and more exotic vegetarian dishes that come from this part of the globe.

There are lots of great store-bought curry pastes available these days that have a rich, authentic flavour and no bad additives, so a lot of the time I just use pre-made pastes (as in the laksa and korma). It saves time and money and you get a great result, so I reckon there's no need to bother making your own pastes in this instance.

If you don't like chilli at all, leave it out. But if you do like a little kick of heat, add a pinch of dried chilli flakes or a fresh medium-heat chilli (with the seeds removed). And if you LOVE chilli, by all means leave the seeds in and add more. It's entirely up to you how spicy you go!

GF use rice stick or vermicelli noodles | DF | VEGAN omit eggs

VEGETABLE COCONUT LAKSA

SERVES 4
Prep time: 30 minutes
Cook time: 15–20 minutes

1 tablespoon oil
½ cup store-bought laksa paste
2 x 400g cans coconut milk
2 kaffir lime leaves, torn
2 cups vegetable stock
500g butternut, pumpkin or kumara, peeled and diced 1–2cm
400g fresh egg noodles (or 150g dried rice stick or vermicelli noodles)
2 cups green beans and/or sliced capsicum
2 cups chopped cauliflower and/or broccoli florets
300g fried tofu puffs, cut in half (or firm tofu, diced)
2 baby bok choy, finely sliced
100g snow peas, sliced, or mung bean sprouts
2 spring onions (green part), finely sliced
4 hardboiled eggs, peeled and cut in half
1 red chilli, finely sliced (optional)
handful of fresh Asian herbs (e.g. coriander, Thai basil and Vietnamese mint)
¼ cup roughly chopped roasted cashew nuts (optional)
¼ cup crispy fried shallots (optional)

I love a bowl of steaming hot, fragrant laksa on a cold night. There are so many good pre-made laksa pastes available now that I don't bother making my own. You can use egg noodles, rice noodles, vermicelli, or even kelp noodles (just cook according to packet instructions) and vary the vegetables you add too.

1. Bring a full kettle of water to the boil.

2. Heat oil in a large pot over medium heat. Cook laksa paste with a few tablespoons of the coconut milk, stirring with a wooden spoon, for 2–3 minutes until very fragrant.

3. Add kaffir lime leaves, remaining coconut milk, stock and butternut/pumpkin/kumara and bring to a gentle boil. Simmer for 8–10 minutes or until vegetables are tender.

4. Cook noodles according to packet instructions. Drain and divide between serving bowls.

5. Add beans/capsicum, cauliflower/broccoli, tofu and bok choy to laksa broth and continue to simmer for a few minutes until just cooked through. Season to taste with salt or soy sauce and a pinch of sugar, if needed.

6. Ladle hot laksa broth and contents over noodles and top with snow peas/bean sprouts, spring onion, egg, chilli (if using), herbs, cashew nuts and fried shallots (if using).

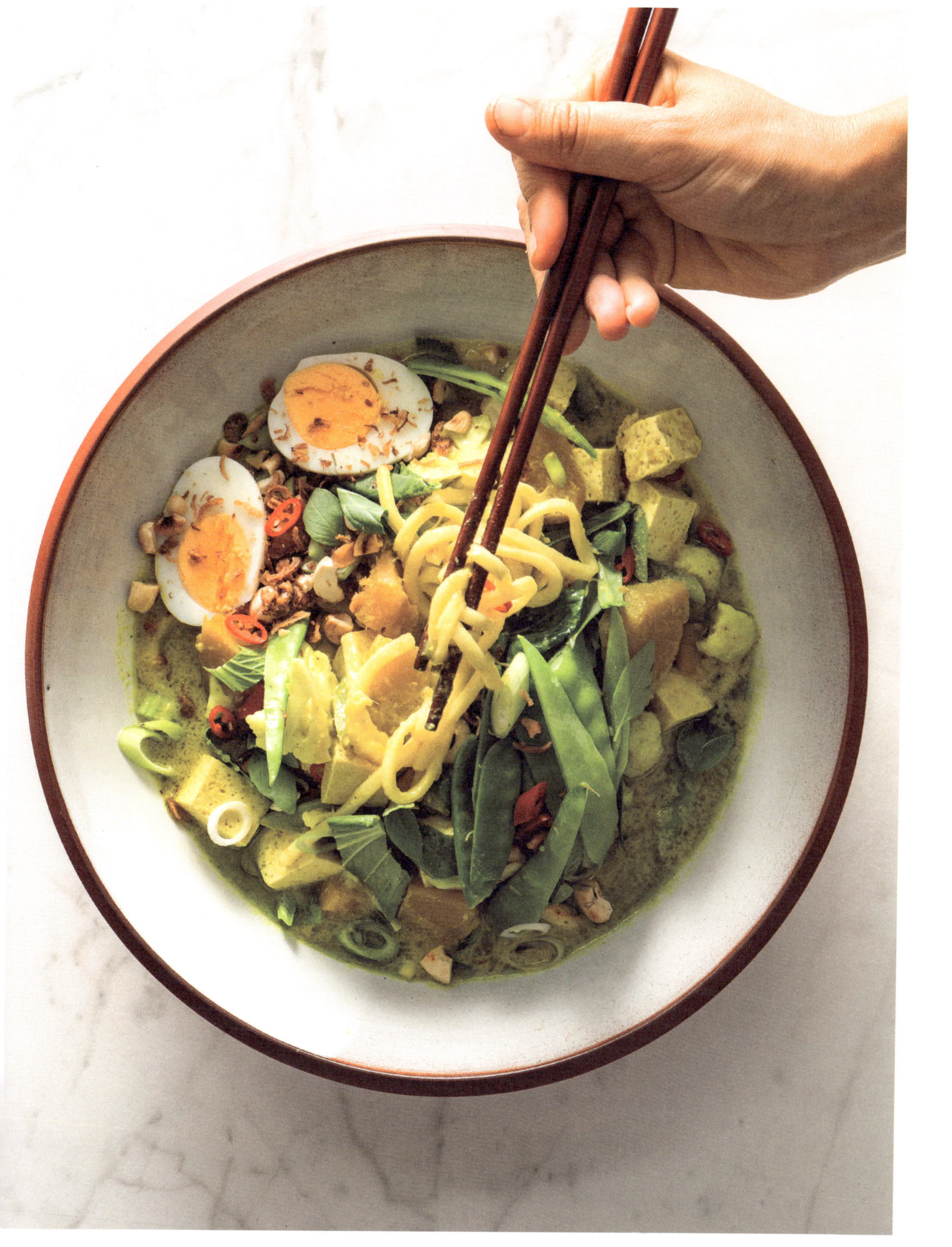

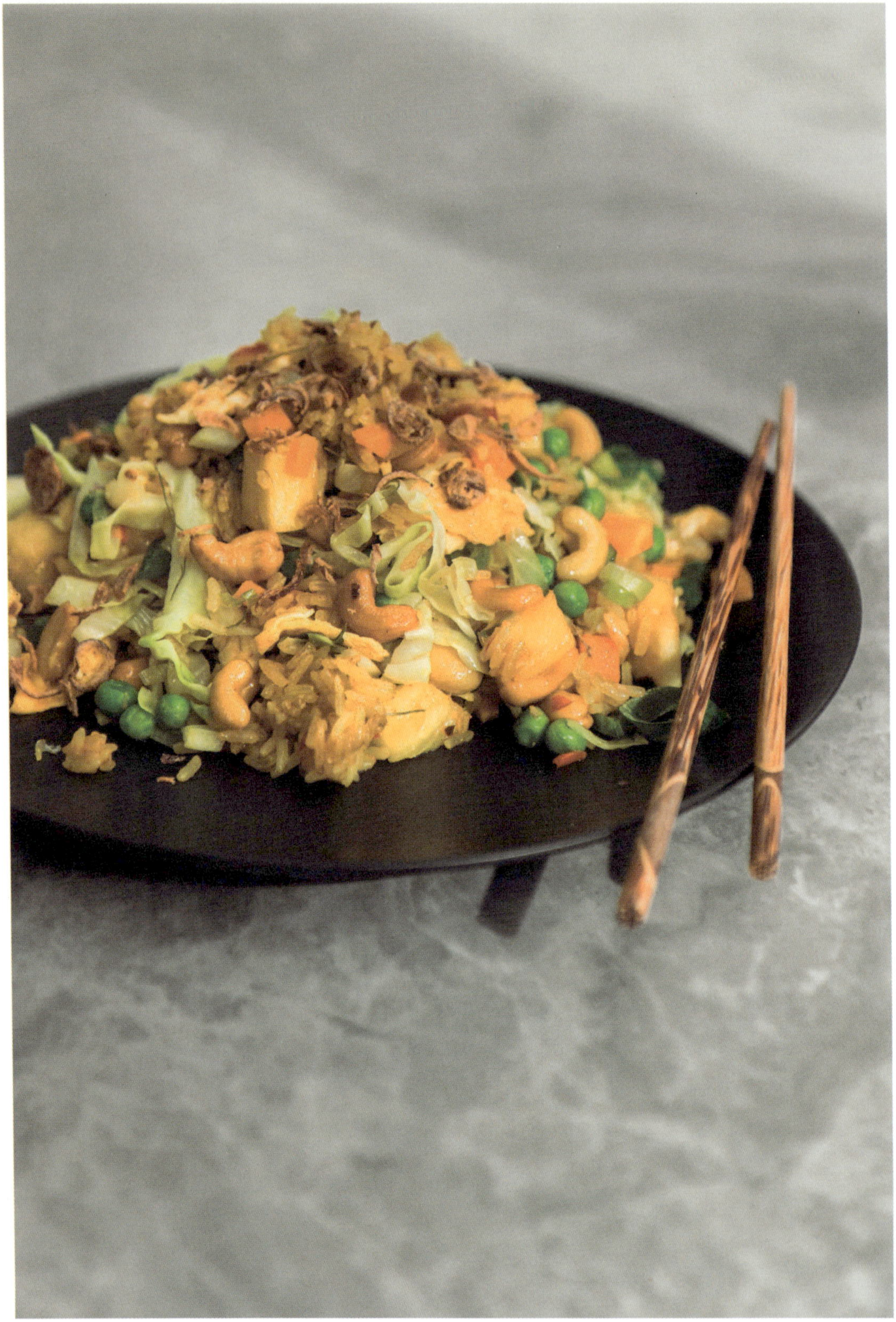

GF | DF | VEGAN omit eggs

PINEAPPLE FRIED RICE

SERVES 4–5
Prep time: 30 minutes
Cook time: 25 minutes

2 tablespoons oil
1 onion, finely chopped
1 carrot, peeled and diced
2 spring onions, finely sliced (white and green part separated)
3 cloves garlic, chopped
3 cups finely sliced cabbage
1 cup peas, corn kernels (fresh or frozen and defrosted) or sliced green beans
½ teaspoon ground turmeric
½ teaspoon ground coriander
1 teaspoon curry powder
pinch of chilli flakes
2 kaffir lime leaves, stems removed and finely sliced
1 stalk lemongrass, finely chopped
4–5 cups cooked coconut rice (see Note) or plain rice
1½ cups diced pineapple (fresh or canned)
½ cup roasted salted cashew nuts
1 red chilli, finely chopped (optional)
1½–2 tablespoons sweet chilli sauce
2 tablespoons soy sauce
1 teaspoon sesame oil
4 free-range eggs
¼ cup crispy fried shallots

This was always a childhood favourite whenever we visited a Thai restaurant. The best fluffy fried rice is made with rice that is a day old (and has been kept in the fridge, giving it some time to cool and dry out). However, if using freshly cooked rice it will help if you spread it out in a large dish and cool it in the freezer while you prepare the remaining ingredients. Coconut rice (see Note) makes this dish extra delicious, but plain rice is fine to use. While the fried rice is cooking, it's nice if you can let it stick to the bottom of the pan to brown and form a bit of a crust (then break it up and stir through) — those golden crusty bits are extra yummy!

1. Heat oil in a wok or your largest fry pan on high heat. Cook onion, carrot, white part of spring onions, garlic, cabbage and peas/corn/green beans for about 5 minutes. Then set aside in a large bowl. Keep pan on the heat.

2. Add another drizzle of oil to the pan. Add spices, kaffir lime leaves and lemongrass and sizzle for 30 seconds, then add cooked rice, pineapple, cashew nuts, chilli (if using), sweet chilli sauce, soy sauce and sesame oil. Stir-fry everything for about 5 minutes until well combined and heated through. Toss through green part of spring onions and cooked vegetable mixture.

3. Spoon fried rice into a large serving bowl. Whisk eggs with a pinch of salt in a bowl. Heat a drizzle of oil or sesame oil in a non-stick fry pan on medium heat and add eggs. Push from the outside to the middle with a wooden spoon or spatula, then allow to set (like an omelette). This will take about 2 minutes. Once just set, roughly break up into pieces and toss through or scatter on top of the rice.

4. Taste rice and season with more soy sauce and sweet chilli sauce, if needed. Sprinkle over crispy fried shallots.

Note: To make coconut rice, cook your rice with a 50/50 mix of coconut milk and water.

GF | DF | VEGAN

CAULIFLOWER & CHICKPEA KORMA

SERVES 4
Prep time: 15 minutes
Cook time: 25 minutes

2 tablespoons olive oil
1 large onion, diced
1 large carrot, peeled and diced
¾ teaspoon garam masala
200g (1 cup) store-bought korma curry paste (see *Tip*)
450–500g cauliflower, chopped into small florets
400g can chickpeas, rinsed and drained
1½ cups Coconut Cashew Cream (page 217)
1 cup vegetable stock or water
2 tablespoons tomato paste
pinch of chilli flakes (optional)
150g chopped spinach or baby spinach
juice of ½ lemon

TO SERVE
½ cup Coconut Cashew Cream
½ cup chopped coriander

Coconut Cashew Cream thickens and enriches this creamy curry without having to use dairy cream. There are lots of fantastic pre-made korma curry pastes around now, so I just buy mine rather than making it. Serve with the Currant and Nut Rice on page 219 and raita for a beautiful Indian meal.

1. Heat oil in a wok or large fry pan on medium heat. Cook onion and carrot for about 5 minutes, until softened. Add garam masala and curry paste and cook for a further 2 minutes or so, until fragrant.

2. Add cauliflower, chickpeas, Coconut Cashew Cream, stock or water, tomato paste and chilli flakes (if using). Bring to the boil, then reduce heat and leave to simmer, stirring occasionally, for 10–15 minutes until vegetables are tender and sauce has thickened.

3. Stir through spinach and lemon juice until wilted and season to taste with salt and pepper.

4. To serve, drizzle curry with Coconut Cashew Cream and garnish with coriander.

Tip: Double check the korma paste you are using – some brands are more concentrated than others, and you may not need to use as much as 200g. Use whatever is recommended for 4 servings.

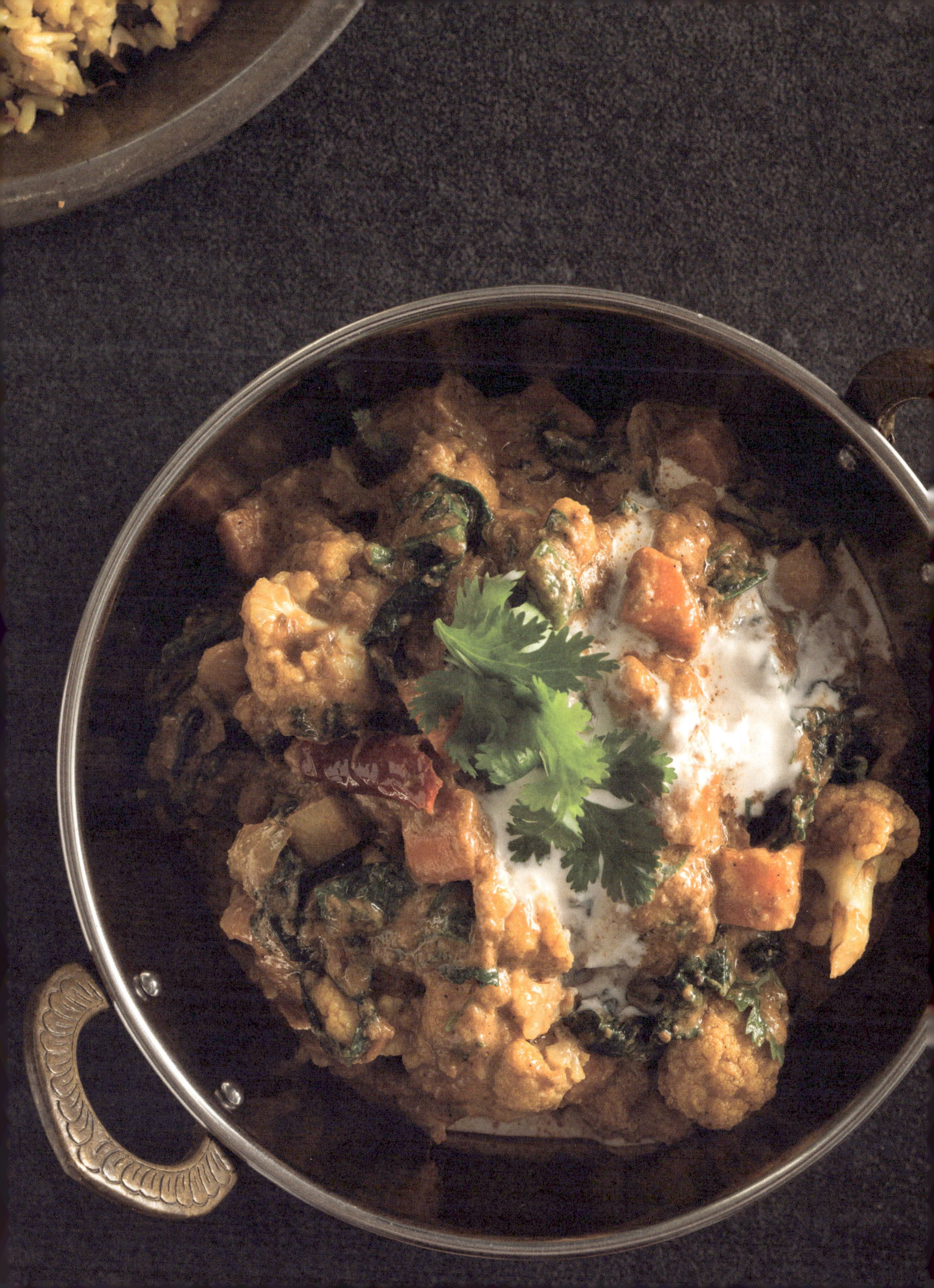

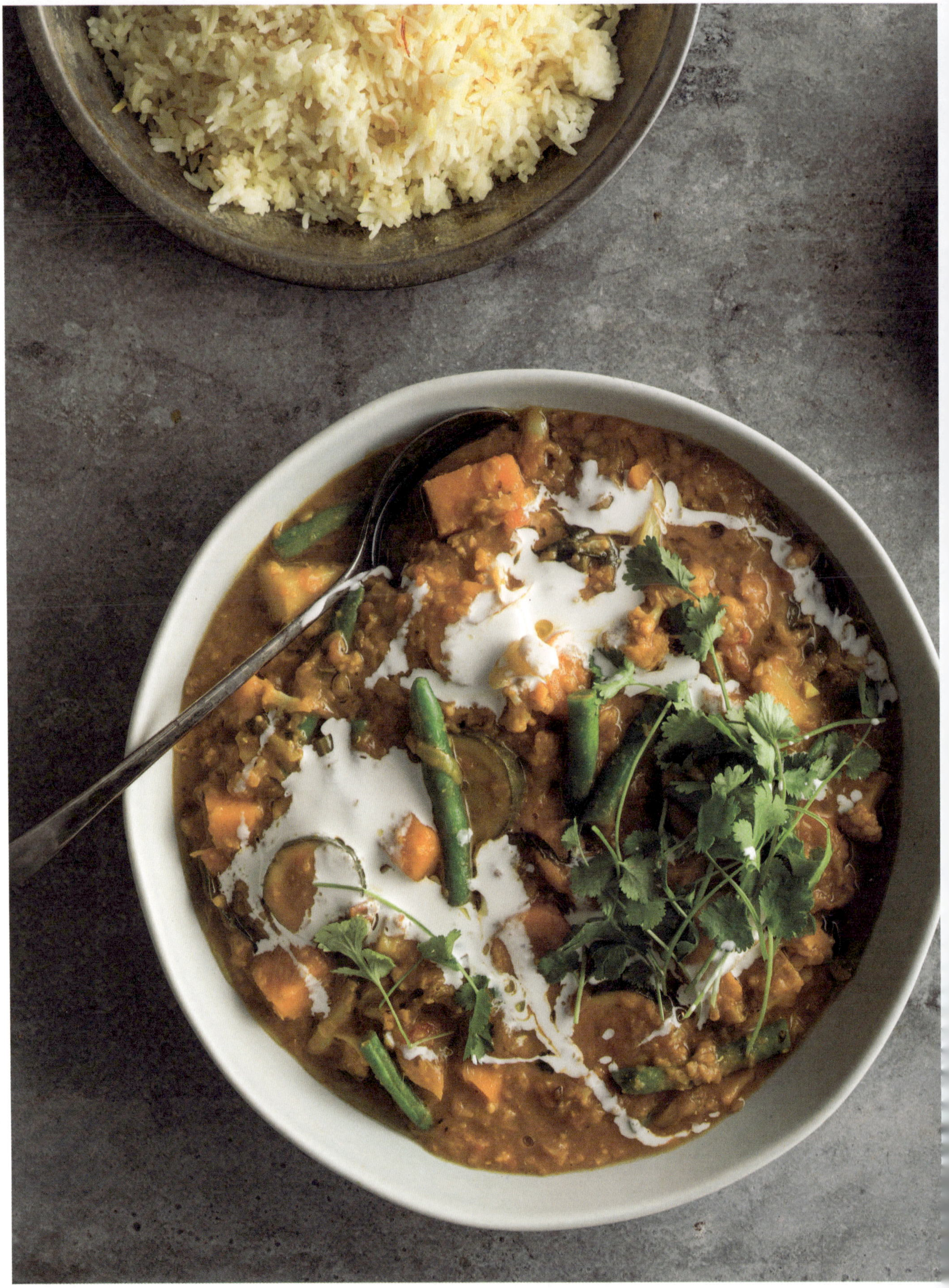

GF | DF | VEGAN

VEGETABLE DHAL (LENTIL CURRY)

SERVES 4-6
Prep time: 15 minutes
Cook time: 1 hour

1 cup dried red lentils
2 cups vegetable stock
1½ cups water
2 tablespoons oil
1 large onion, thinly sliced
3 cloves garlic, finely chopped
1 teaspoon mustard seeds (optional)
3–4cm piece fresh ginger, finely grated
1 teaspoon ground cumin
1 teaspoon ground coriander
1 teaspoon ground turmeric
½ teaspoon ground chilli
400g can crushed tomatoes
400g can coconut milk
½ teaspoon salt
6 cups mixed chopped vegetables, e.g. carrot or courgette (sliced into 1cm rounds), cauliflower or broccoli florets, kumara, potato, pumpkin or eggplant (cut into 1–2cm pieces), green beans (cut in half), chopped cabbage, etc.
2–3 handfuls of chopped spinach
juice of ½ lemon
chopped coriander, to serve

Lentils simmered with spices, tomatoes, coconut milk and vegetables make a warming, filling meal with rice or naan bread (or the flatbreads on page 216). You can use all sorts of vegetables in this dhal; some of my favourites are beans, eggplant, pumpkin and kumara.

1. Combine lentils, stock and water in a large pot and bring to the boil. Reduce heat, cover and simmer until lentils are soft and almost mushy, about 30 minutes.

2. Heat oil in a medium fry pan over medium heat. Add onion and cook for 6–8 minutes until starting to turn golden brown. Add a drizzle of oil, garlic, mustard seeds (if using), ginger and spices. Cook for a further 2–3 minutes until the mustard seeds start popping.

3. Add onion mixture, crushed tomatoes, most of the coconut milk (reserve ⅓ cup), salt and vegetables to the pot of lentils. Partially cover and simmer for 15–20 minutes until vegetables are tender. Stir a few times during cooking to avoid it catching and burning on the bottom of the pot. In the last few minutes, stir in spinach until wilted.

4. Once cooked, season dhal to taste with salt, pepper and lemon juice. Garnish with remaining coconut milk and coriander. Serve with rice, naan or flatbreads.

DF use coconut yoghurt | VEGAN use coconut yoghurt

QUICK MASALA DOSA

SERVES: 4 (2 dosa per person)
Prep time: 10 minutes
Cook time: 20 minutes

DOSA BATTER
1 cup chickpea (besan) flour
½ cup plain flour
½ cup rice flour or GF flour
1 teaspoon mustard seeds (optional)
½ teaspoon baking soda
½ teaspoon salt
450–500ml water
oil or ghee, to cook

TO SERVE
1 quanitity Masala Potatoes and Carrots (page 211)
½ cup natural, unsweetened yoghurt
2 tablespoons chopped mint leaves
mango and tamarind chutney (store-bought) or
Moroccan Apricot and Tomato Chutney (page 158)
½ cup chopped coriander

Anyone who has visited India knows how incredible dosa is! These marvellous savoury crêpes are usually stuffed with a spiced potato mixture and served everywhere in India. Get your dosa nice and crispy by spreading and cooking it paper thin in the pan. Stuff with Masala Potatoes and Carrots (page 211) and serve with mint yoghurt and chutney for a simply amazing meal.

1. Place flours, mustard seeds (if using), baking soda and salt in a large mixing bowl. Whisk in the water, about ½ cup at a time, until you have a smooth, runny batter, the consistency of pouring cream.

2. Heat about 1 teaspoon oil or ghee in a large cast-iron or non-stick fry pan on medium to high heat, then lightly wipe it around the pan and up the sides with a scrunched-up ball of paper towel or a clean cloth.

3. Add half a ladleful of batter to the pan whilst immediately twisting and swirling the pan around so it evenly coats the surface in a very thin layer (thinner means lighter, crispier dosa!).

4. When the surface of the dosa is covered in tiny bubbles and the base is crispy (it will take about 2 minutes), use a fish slice or spatula to gently flip it over to cook the other side for a minute or so. Transfer to a plate, top with a few heaped tablespoons of warm Masala Potatoes and Carrots and loosely roll up the dosa. Repeat with remaining batter.

5. Mix yoghurt with the mint.

6. Serve dosa with mint yoghurt, chutney and coriander scattered on top.

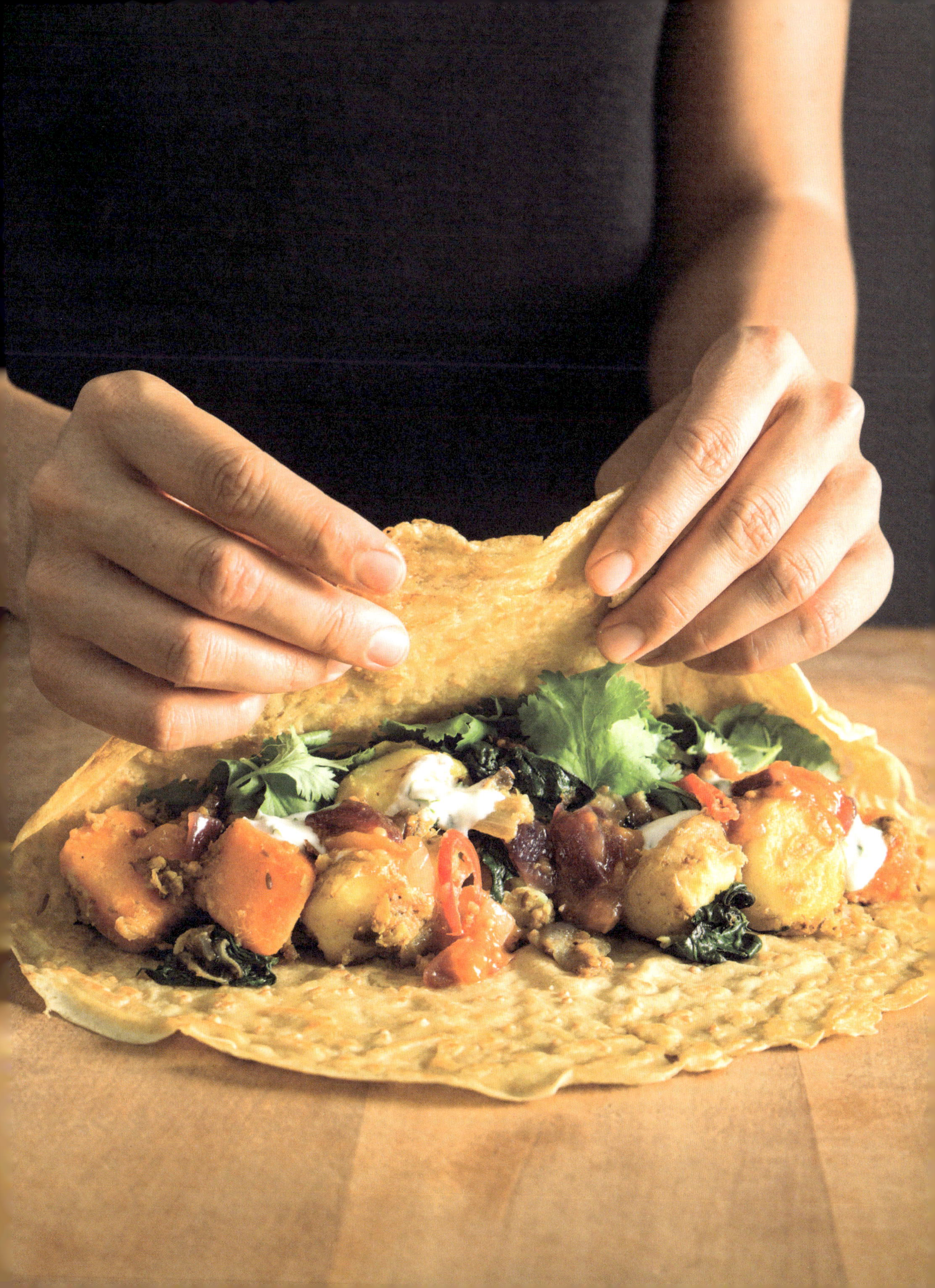

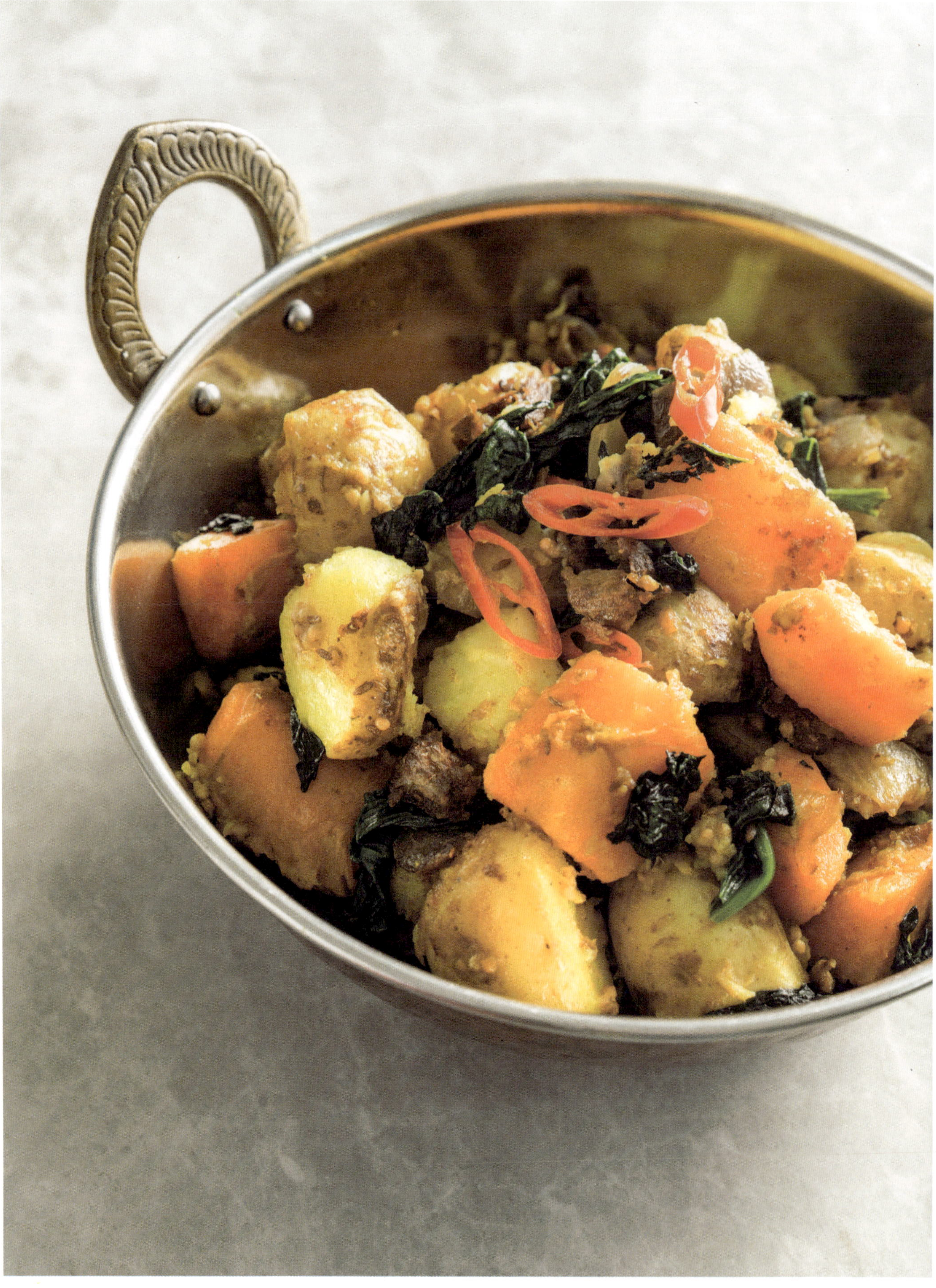

GF | DF | VEGAN

MASALA POTATOES & CARROTS

SERVES 4
Prep time: 10 minutes
Cook time: 25 minutes

700g agria potatoes, scrubbed (skin on) and cut into 2–3cm pieces
2 medium carrots, scrubbed and cut into 2–3cm pieces
2 tablespoons oil
1 large red onion, chopped
1½ teaspoons mustard seeds
1 teaspoon crushed cumin seeds
2 teaspoons curry powder
3cm piece fresh ginger, finely grated
½ teaspoon salt
2 handfuls of chopped spinach or silverbeet, or baby spinach
1 red or green chilli, finely sliced

This is used as the stuffing for the dosa on the previous page, or is a great dish to accompany others as part of an Indian-inspired feast. It is also delightfully satisfying as a simple, flavoursome meal on its own with a fried egg on top.

1. Place potatoes and carrots in a pot of well-salted water and bring to the boil. Cook for about 12 minutes, or until tender. Drain well, tip back into the pot and sit over a low heat for a few minutes to steam and 'dry off' the vegetables a little. Shake the pot and stir to 'rough and fluff up' the edges of the potatoes and carrots.

2. In a wok or your largest fry pan, heat oil and cook onion for 3–4 minutes until soft and starting to turn golden. Add another drizzle of oil, mustard seeds, cumin seeds, curry powder and ginger, and cook for 1 minute, until fragrant.

3. Add cooked potatoes, carrots and salt to the pan and toss to coat in the spiced oil and onions. Keep cooking for 6–8 minutes until potatoes are golden, tossing every now and again. (Try to get a little golden, crunchy crust on some of the potatoes if possible.)

4. Toss spinach/silverbeet and chilli through potatoes and carrots until spinach has wilted.

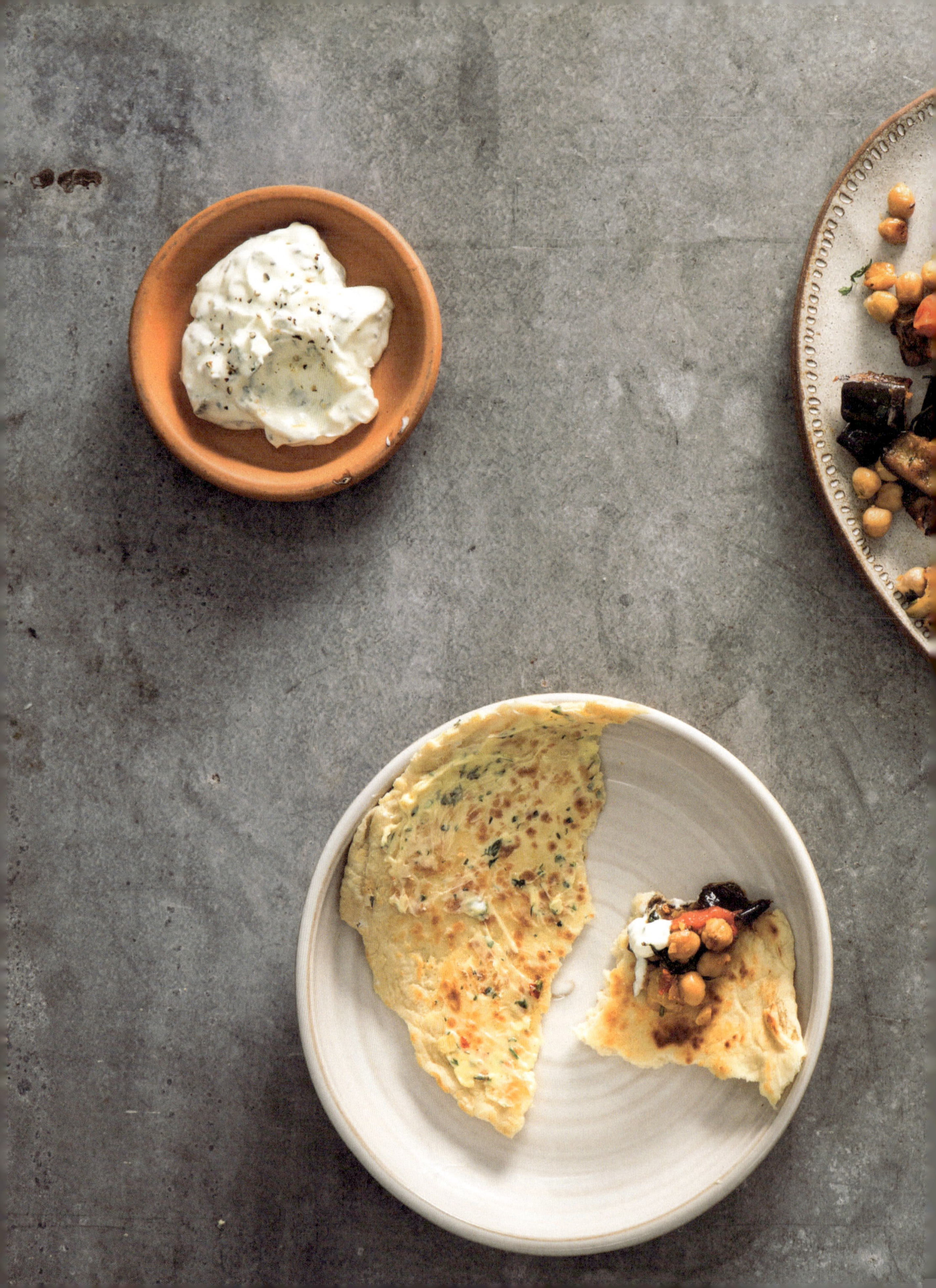

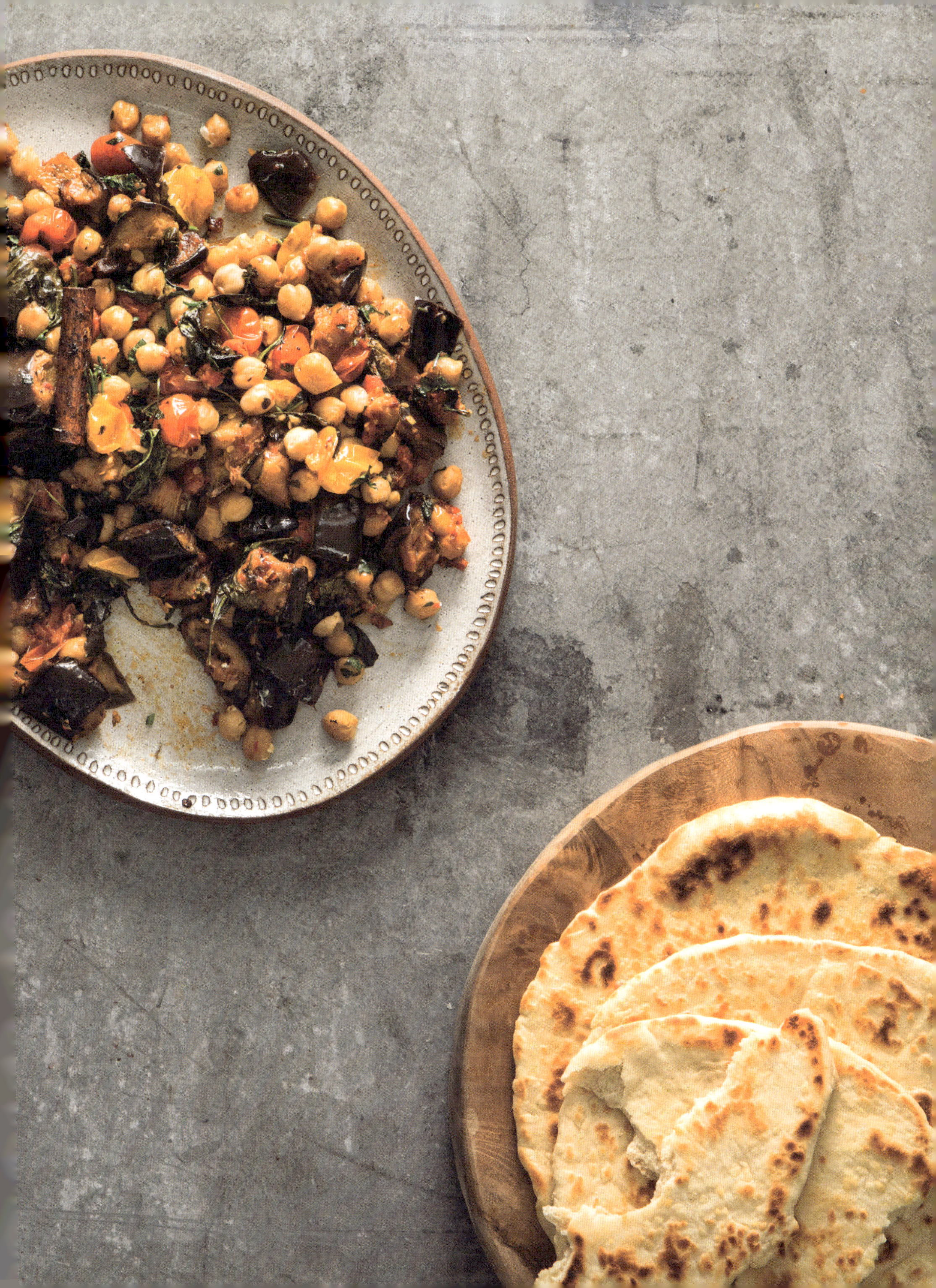

GF | DF use coconut yoghurt | VEGAN use coconut yoghurt

HARISSA EGGPLANT, TOMATOES & CHICKPEAS

SERVES 4–6
Prep time: 15 minutes
Cook time: 40 minutes

2 medium eggplants, diced 2cm
4 tablespoons olive oil
3–4 tablespoons harissa paste (page 216 or store-bought)
1 cinnamon stick
300–400g cherry tomatoes, cut in half
2 cloves garlic, chopped
400g can chickpeas, rinsed and drained
2 handfuls of chopped spinach or baby spinach
½ cup chopped parsley
good pinch of chilli flakes
zest of 1 lemon
juice of ½ lemon

TO SERVE
½ cup natural, unsweetened yoghurt
3 tablespoons chopped mint leaves
½ lemon, cut into wedges

Eggplant loves a good spicing and roasting until meltingly tender, making it one of my all-time favourite vegetables. This Moroccan-inspired dish will fit in as part of a Middle Eastern, Indian or even Spanish or Greek feast. Serve on the side, or as a main with rice or couscous or, my favourite way, with flatbreads and the Essential Summer Salad on page 245.

1. Preheat oven to 220°C and line an oven tray (with a lip) with baking paper.

2. Toss eggplant with olive oil, harissa and cinnamon stick on lined tray. Season well with salt and pepper. Roast for 15–20 minutes, tossing once during cooking, until soft and slightly charred.

3. Reduce oven temperature to 200°C. Add tomatoes, garlic and chickpeas, toss and continue cooking for 15 minutes.

4. Add spinach, parsley, chilli flakes and lemon zest and juice, toss and continue cooking for 5 minutes until spinach has wilted. Toss and season to taste with salt and pepper.

5. Mix yoghurt with mint.

6. Spoon into a serving dish and serve with mint yoghurt and lemon wedges on the side.

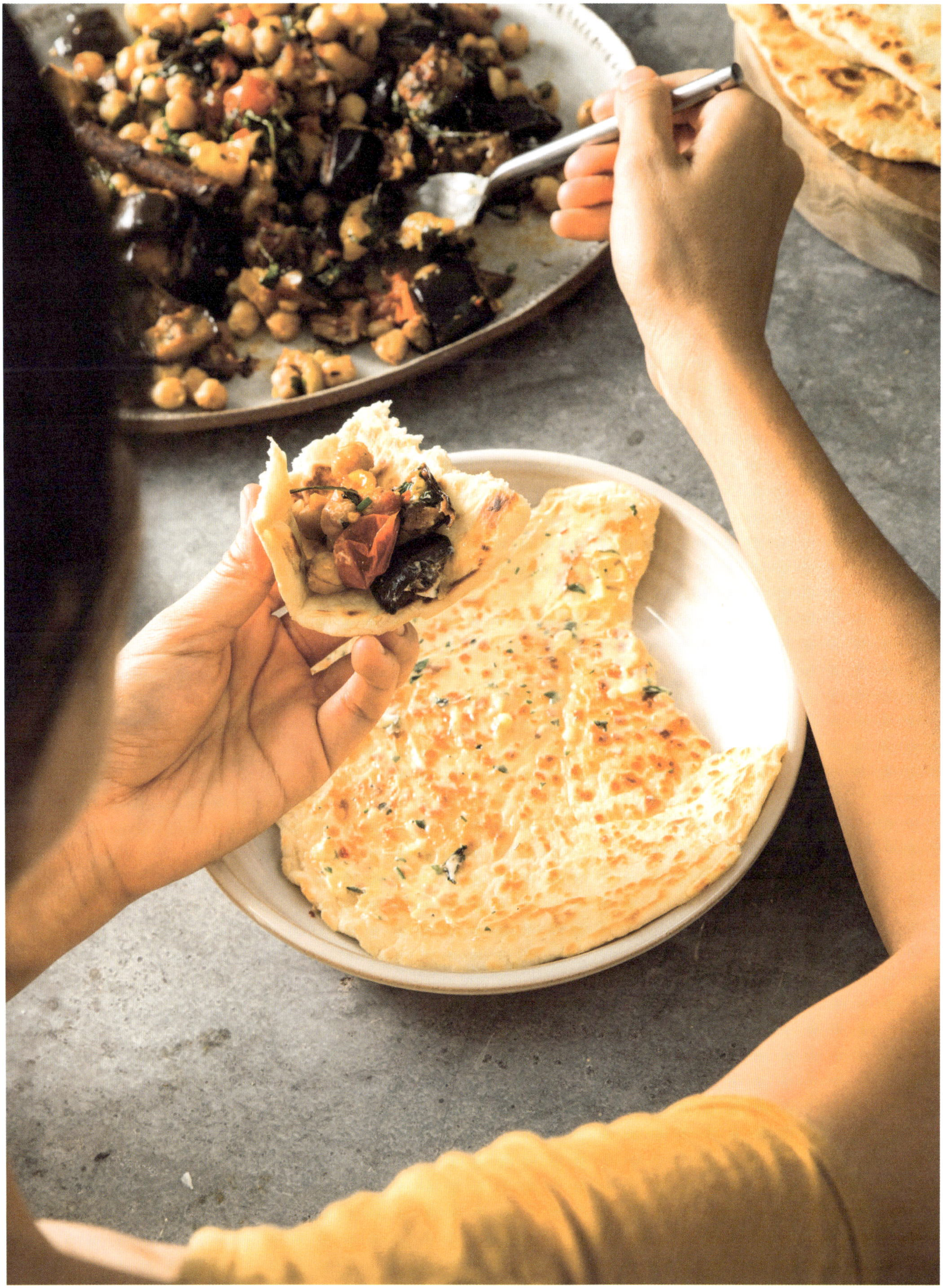

GARLIC & HERB FLATBREADS

SERVES 4
Prep time: 10 minutes
Cook time: 15 minutes

2 cups self-raising flour
¾ cup milk (of any kind)
1½ tablespoons olive oil
¼ teaspoon salt

GARLIC HERB BUTTER
25g butter, softened
1 teaspoon finely chopped rosemary or thyme leaves
2 cloves garlic, finely chopped

Home-made flatbreads – they're easy and satisfyingly fun to make, and don't contain any preservatives, as bought ones do. Give them a go!

1. Place flour, milk, olive oil and salt in a bowl and mix to combine.
2. Knead (on a lightly floured surface) for 5 minutes or until dough is smooth. Divide into four portions and leave to rest on the bench for 10 minutes or so.
3. Mix all Garlic Herb Butter ingredients together.
4. Heat a large, heavy-bottomed fry pan (such as a cast iron pan) on medium heat. Roll out a piece of dough into a 25cm circle and brush with olive oil. Place in the hot pan and cook for about 2 minutes each side until puffed and golden. Transfer to a chopping board and spread with 1 teaspoon Garlic and Herb Butter while hot. Repeat with remaining dough.

GF | DF | VEGAN

HARISSA

MAKES ¾ CUP
Prep time: 5–10 minutes

2½ teaspoons cumin seeds
2 teaspoons coriander seeds
3 cloves garlic, chopped
1–2 large red chillies, chopped
1 teaspoon brown sugar
1 teaspoon salt
juice of ½ lemon
2 tablespoons tomato paste
3–4 tablespoons olive oil

I've put this harissa recipe in several of my cookbooks, and here it is again because it's just so useful and delicious I couldn't do a cookbook without using it. Try mixing with a good drizzle of oil and brushing over vegetables (eggplant, courgette, capsicum, mushrooms, onions...) before barbecuing — it will transform them!

1. Crush cumin and coriander seeds with a mortar and pestle or in a spice grinder.
2. Add all ingredients to a high-speed blender or food processor and blitz until well combined. Alternatively, bash spices, garlic, chillies, brown sugar and salt with a mortar and pestle until a paste forms, then mix in remaining ingredients.

GF | DF | VEGAN

COCONUT CASHEW CREAM

MAKES 2 CUPS
Prep time: 5 minutes
(+ 6–8 hours to soak cashew nuts)

1 cup natural (raw, unsalted) cashew nuts
2 teaspoons lemon juice
400g can coconut milk

Amazing to use in creamy curries such as korma. Keeps in the fridge for up to 5 days.

1. Place cashews in a bowl and add enough cold filtered water to completely cover. Leave to soak in the fridge for 6–8 hours or overnight.

2. Drain cashews and rinse well. Place in a high-speed blender (a standard blender might struggle to break them down completely) or food processor with lemon juice, a pinch of salt and coconut milk and blend until very smooth and creamy — this will take at least a few minutes. Scrape down the sides of the processor/blender with a spatula as needed. Add more water or milk as required to achieve a pouring cream consistency.

GF | DF | VEGAN

CASHEW CREAM

MAKES 2–3 CUPS
Prep time: 5 minutes
(+ 6–8 hours to soak cashew nuts)

1 cup natural (raw, unsalted) cashew nuts
1 teaspoon lemon juice
1½ cups cold filtered water or almond milk

A fantastic dairy-free substitute for cream whether using in curries, creamy pasta sauces or desserts. So easy to make too. Keeps in the fridge for up to 5 days.

1. Place cashews in a bowl and add enough cold filtered water to completely cover. Leave to soak in the fridge for 6–8 hours or overnight.

2. Drain cashews and rinse well. Place in a high-speed blender (a standard blender might struggle to break them down completely) or food processor with lemon juice, a pinch of salt and 1 cup of the cold water and blend until very smooth and creamy — this will take a few minutes. Scrape down the sides of the processor/blender with a spatula as needed and add more water as required (about ½–1 cup) to achieve a pouring cream consistency.

Sweet Cashew Cream
Make cashew cream as above, adding 1½ tablespoons liquid honey or maple syrup, and ½ teaspoon vanilla essence/extract, or seeds scraped from ½ vanilla bean pod. Use as a pouring cream with desserts.

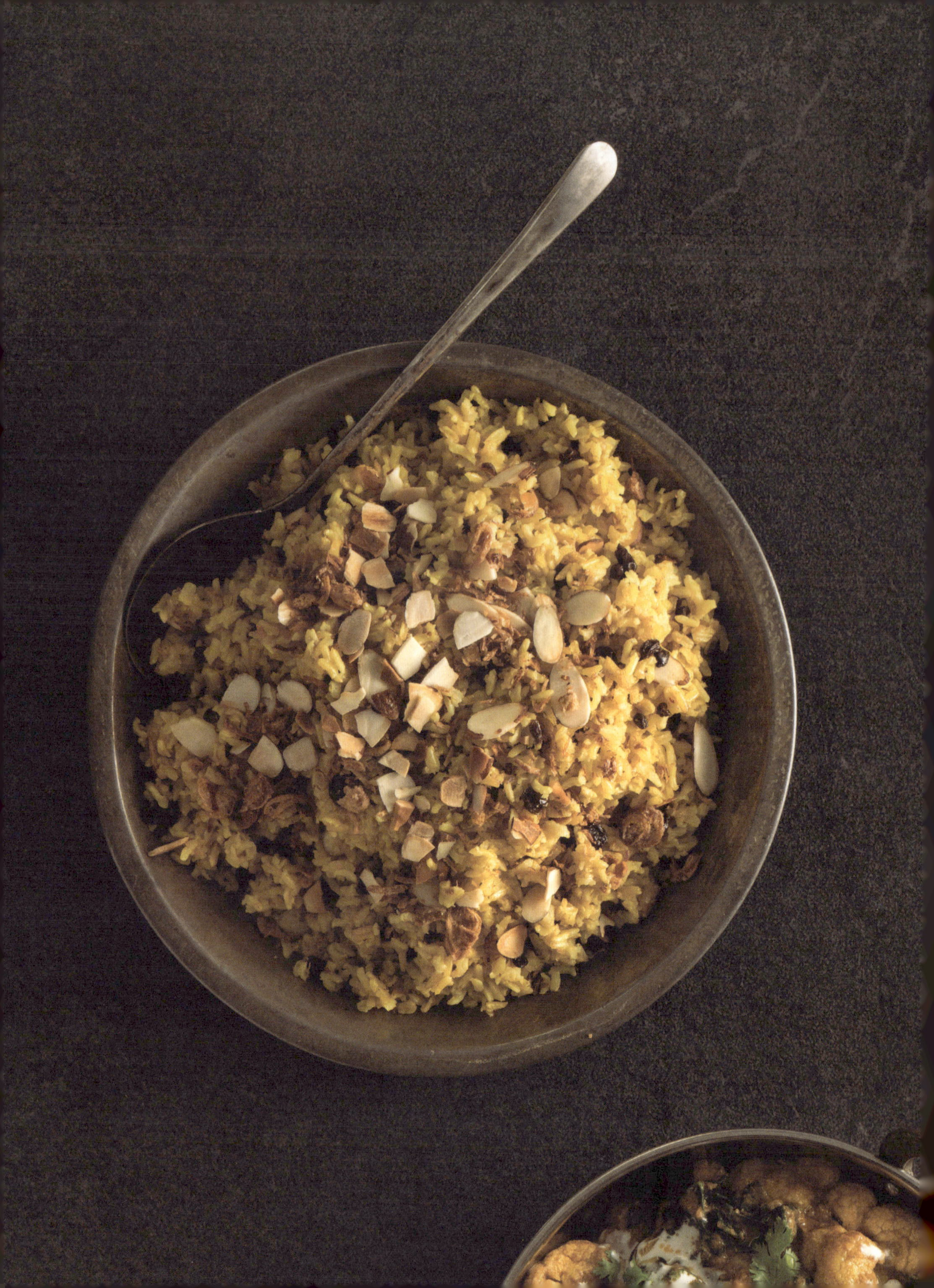

GF | DF omit butter | VEGAN omit butter

CURRANT & NUT RICE

SERVES 4 (as a side)
Prep time: 5 minutes
Cook time: 15 minutes

2 cups long-grain or basmati rice
3 cups water or vegetable stock
¼ teaspoon salt
¾ teaspoon ground turmeric or 2 good pinches of saffron threads
1 large knob butter
½ cup dried currants
½ cup toasted sliced almonds and/or chopped pistachios
¼ cup crispy fried shallots (optional)

A great rice dish to have with Indian and Middle Eastern meals. And it doesn't take any longer than cooking plain rice, so you may as well!

1. Combine rice, water/stock, salt and turmeric/saffron in a medium pot, cover with a lid and bring to the boil. As soon as it boils, reduce heat to low and cook for 12 minutes. Turn off the heat and leave rice, still covered, to finish steaming for 5 minutes.

2. Add butter, currants and nuts and toss to combine. Season to taste with salt and pepper. Spoon into a serving bowl and scatter crispy shallots on top (if using.)

Small &

CHAPTER SIX — P. 221

salads
sides

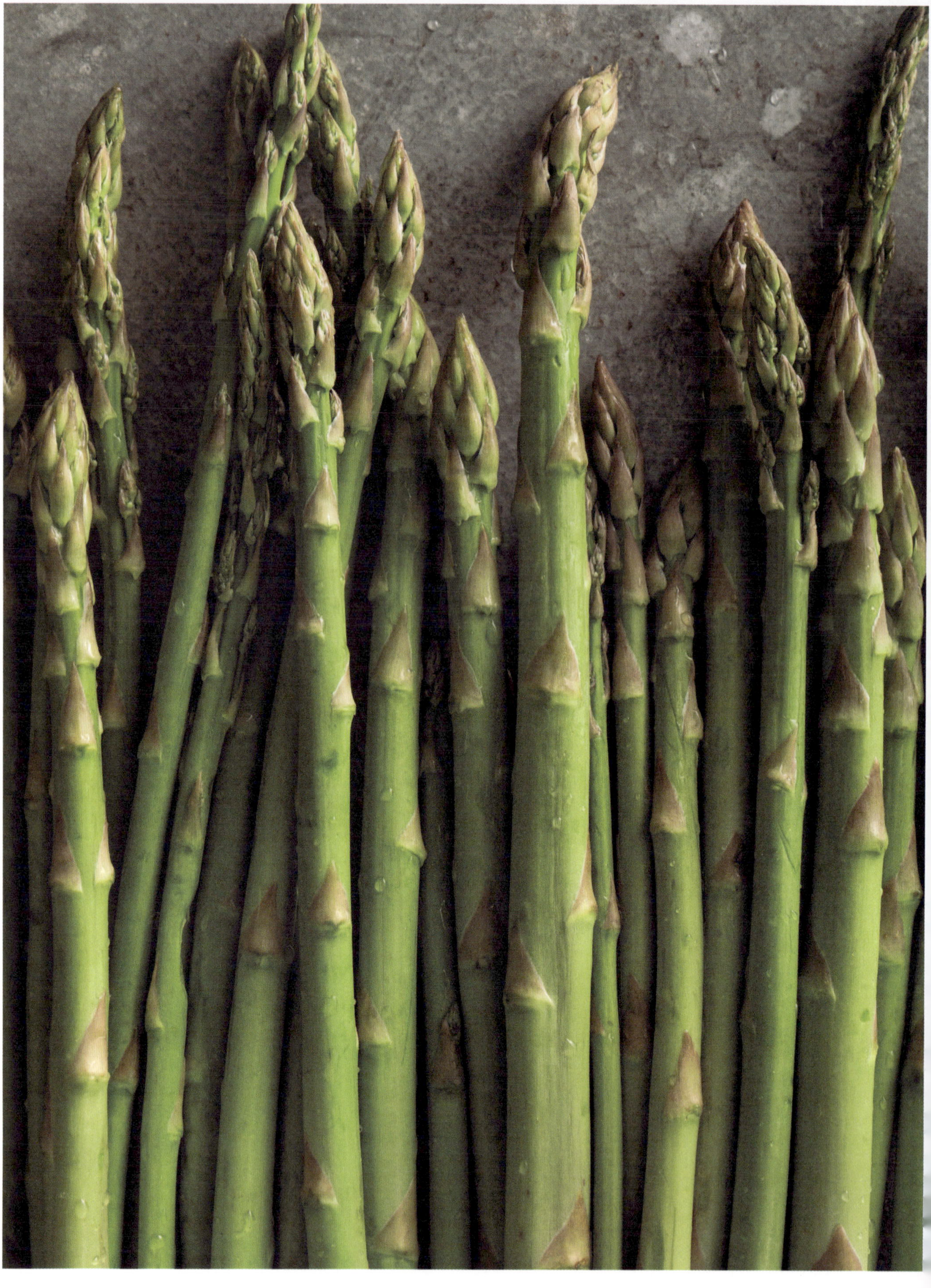

A lot of the time, a good side dish is the key difference between a good meal and an amazing one. The side(s) you choose play pivotal supporting roles to balance out and make the main dish shine. Imagine a rich, buttery onion tart by itself. Yum. But now imagine it served with fresh peppery rocket, sweet crisp pear and a little creamy blue cheese...

  Consider what kind of side will bring balance to the main dish — does it require something fresh and zesty to help balance out something rich and hearty, or something super simple to bring calm to a dish with lots going on? Or maybe the side dish has more going on, to accompany a main which is very simple.

  For many of the recipes in this book, all you'll need is a crisp leafy green salad or roasted or steamed vegetables, but this chapter has some side dishes with a bit more flair. In fact, they're even flavoursome and exciting enough to form a kind of mix-and-match feast, much like tapas or mezze, all by themselves.

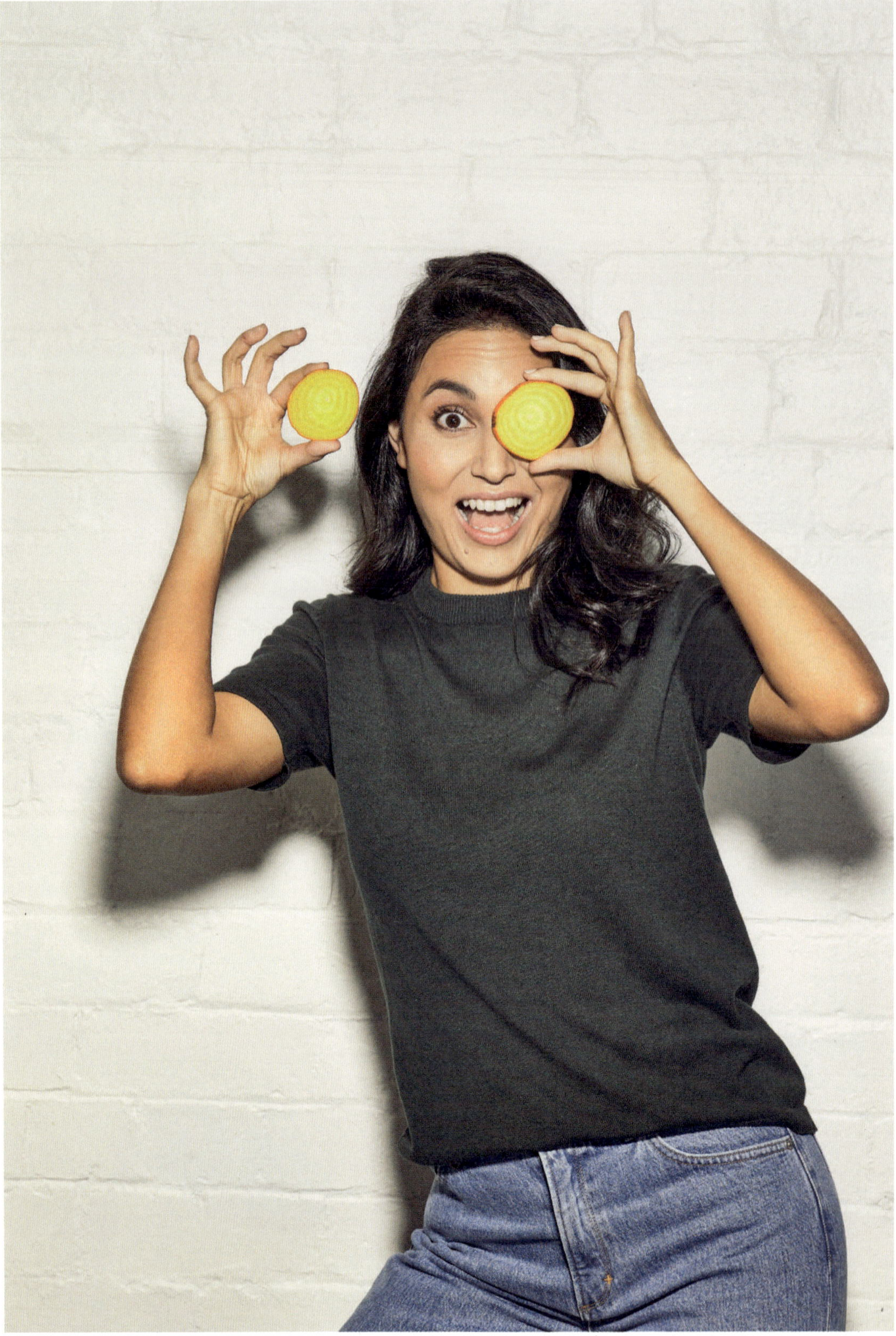

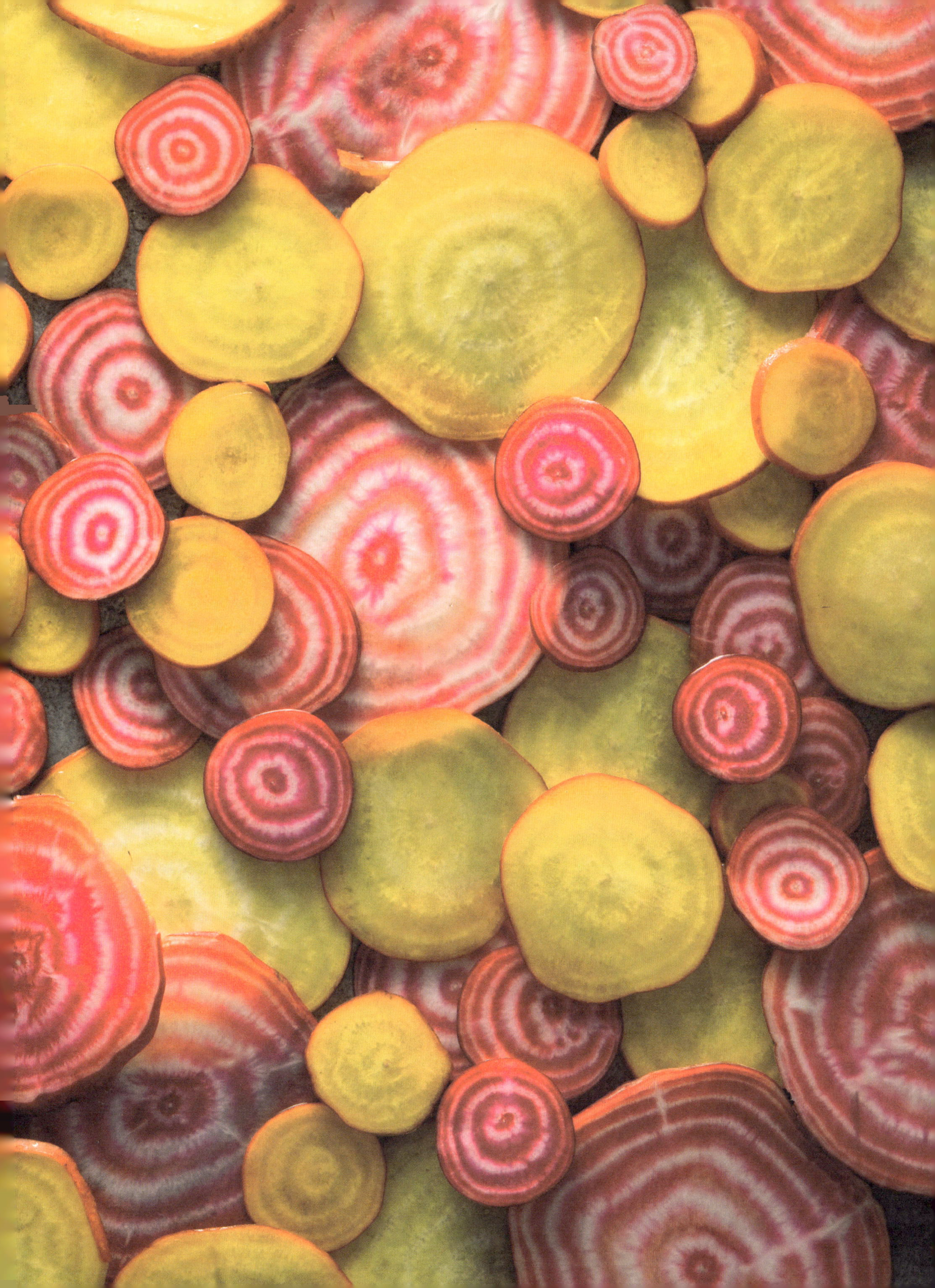

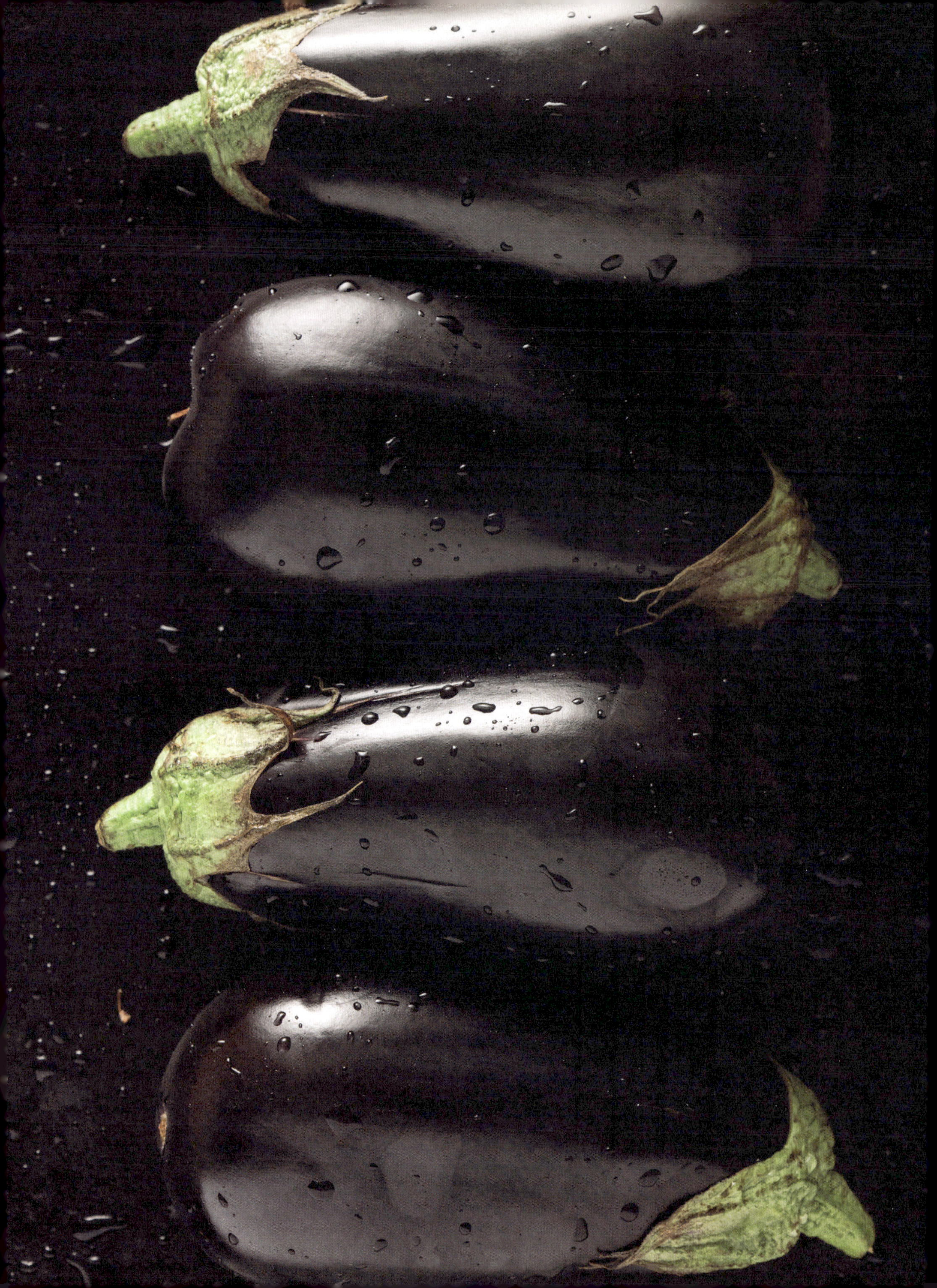

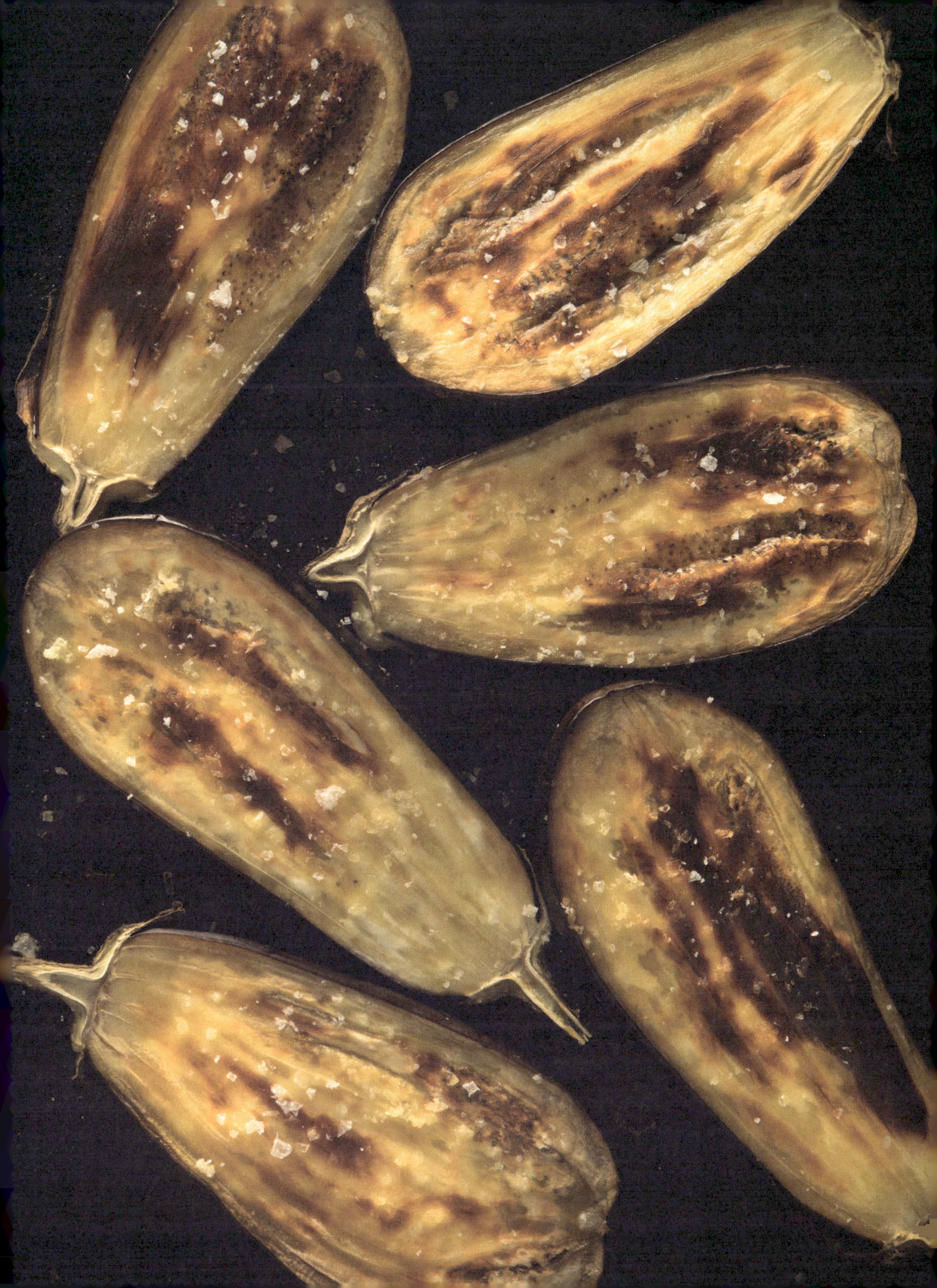

GF | DF omit feta or use cashew feta | VEGAN omit feta or use cashew feta

SLOW-ROASTED EGGPLANT, CAPSICUM & COURGETTE WITH LEMON, GARLIC & HERB OIL

SERVES 4
Prep time: 15 minutes
Cook time: 1 hour 45 minutes

1 large eggplant, thinly sliced into 0.5cm thick rounds
½ cup olive oil
1 sweet Palermo capsicum, chopped into 3–4cm pieces
2 capsicums (red and/or yellow), cored and chopped into 3–4cm pieces
3 courgettes, sliced into 1cm-thick rounds
2–3 cloves garlic
zest of 1 lemon
1 tablespoon chopped rosemary and thyme leaves
1–2 teaspoons chopped oregano and marjoram leaves (optional)
50g creamy feta or soft goats cheese (optional)

Slow roasting really intensifies the flavour of these vegetables. From this you can make so many different dishes, from topping bruschetta (page 191) to tossing through pasta or as the filling for a tart or even a hearty vegetable lasagne (page 138). Or simply serve as a fantastic vegetable side. A batch of this in the fridge means endless possibilities for scrumptious vegetarian meals over a few days!

1. Preheat oven to 160°C. Line a large oven tray with baking paper.

2. Layer eggplant on lined oven tray and drizzle with 2 tablespoons of the olive oil, season with salt and pepper. Top with capsicum and courgette and drizzle with another 2 tablespoons of the olive oil, season with salt and pepper. Roast for about 1 hour 45 minutes to 2 hours, or until vegetables are very soft and starting to caramelise a little. Spoon roasted vegetables into a bowl.

3. Heat remaining ¼ cup olive oil in a small pot on low heat. Add garlic, lemon zest and herbs and sizzle for 1 minute or so before taking off the heat and drizzling over the vegetables.

4. Dot feta/goats cheese over roast vegetables (if using.)

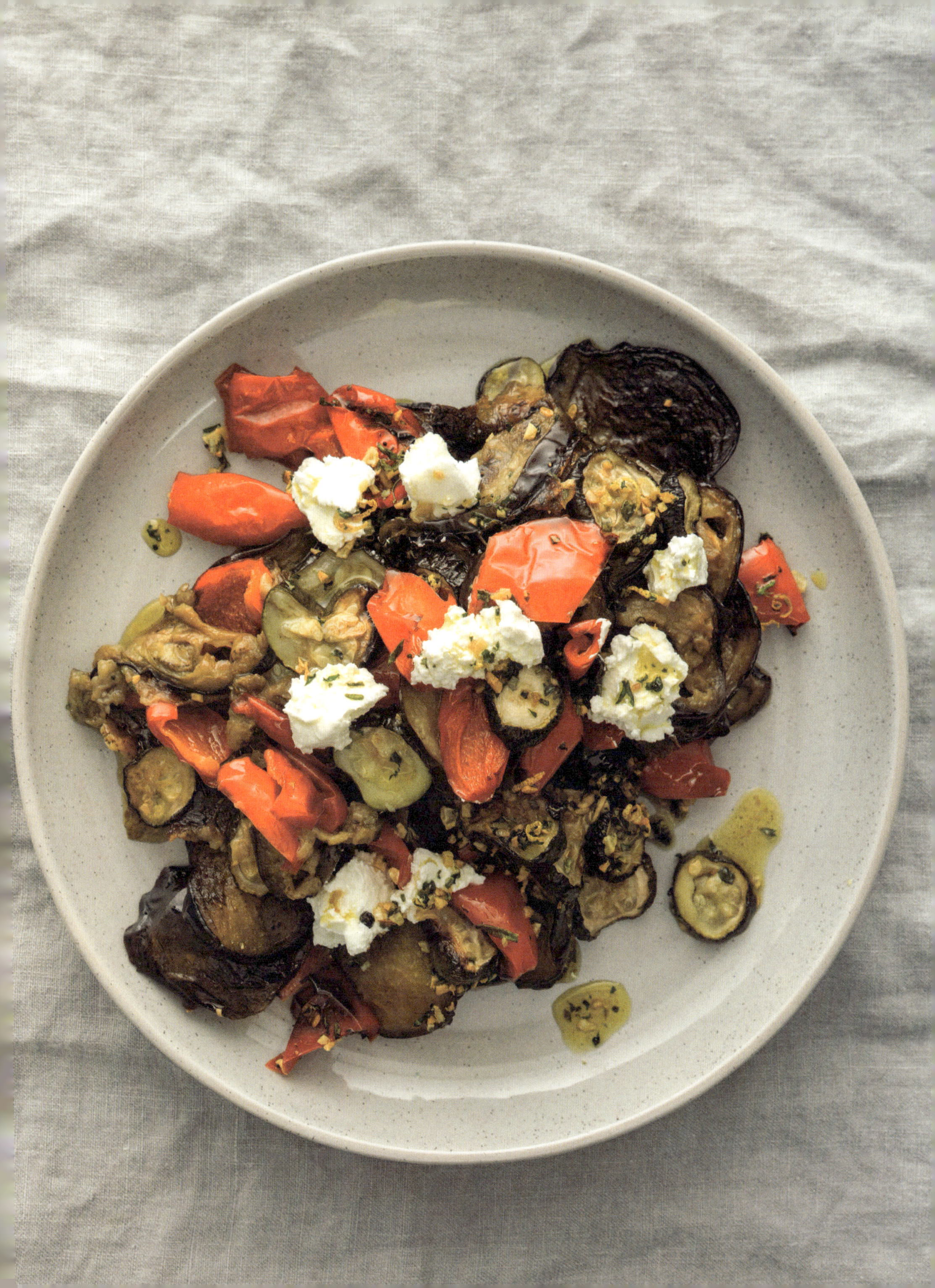

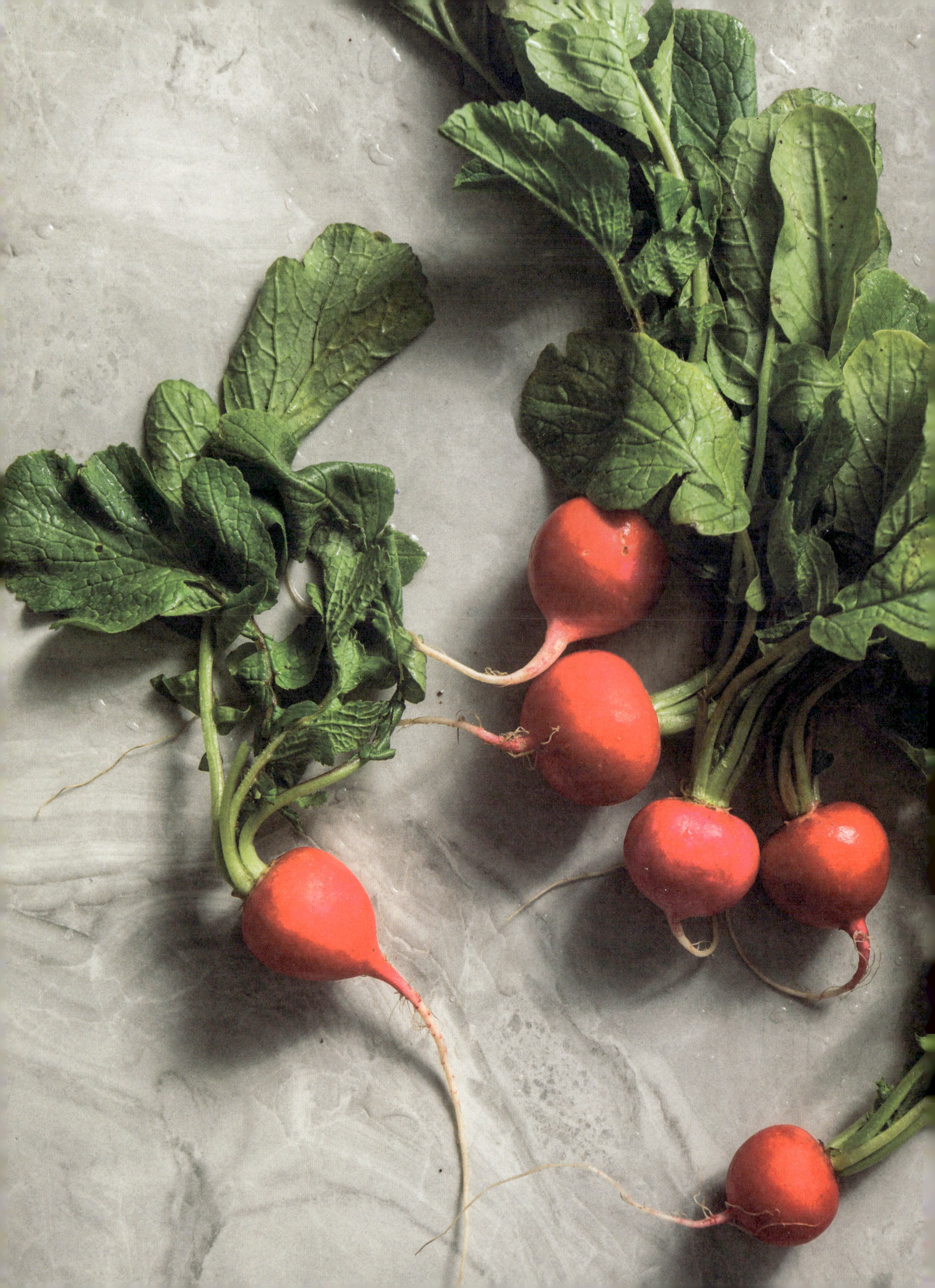

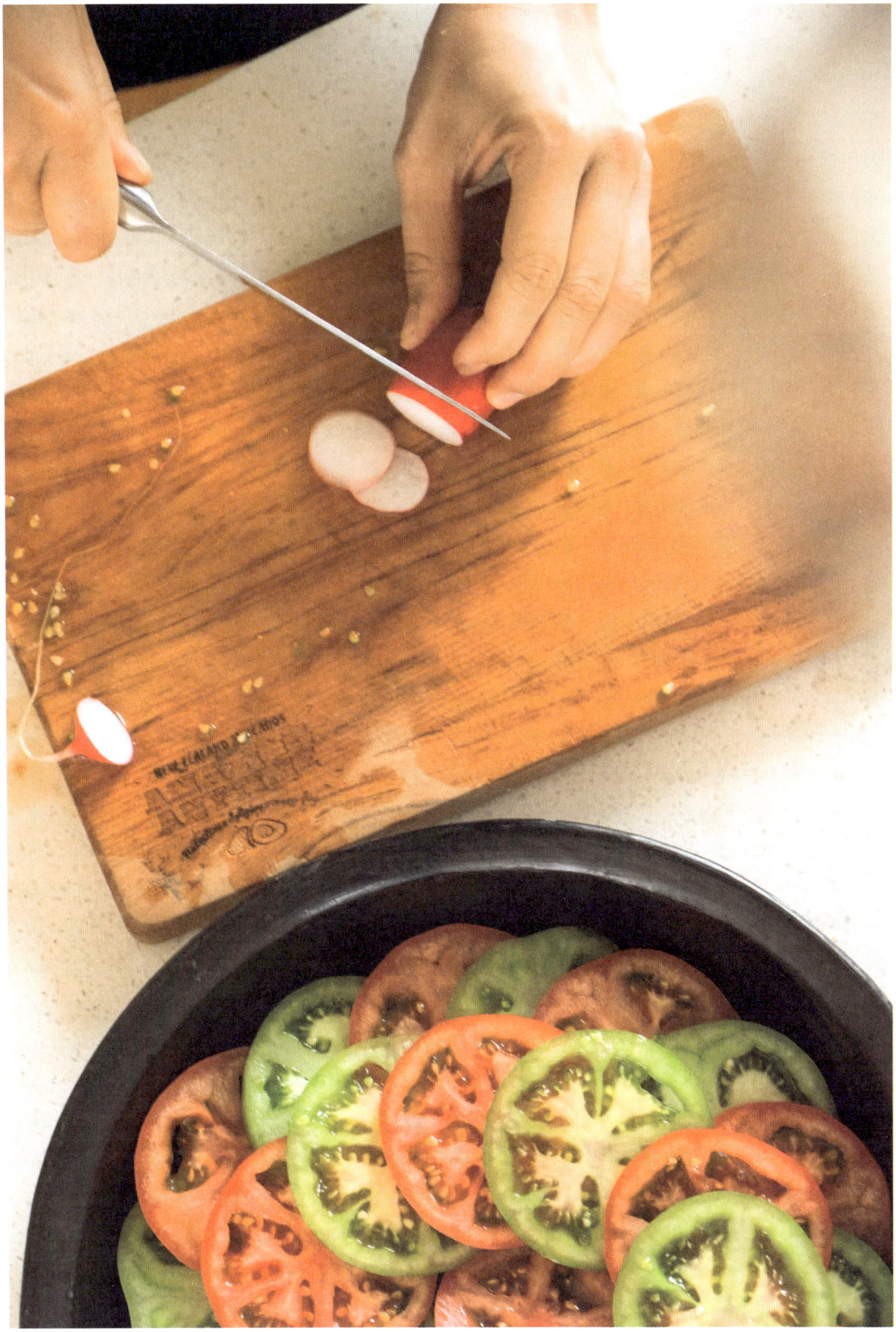

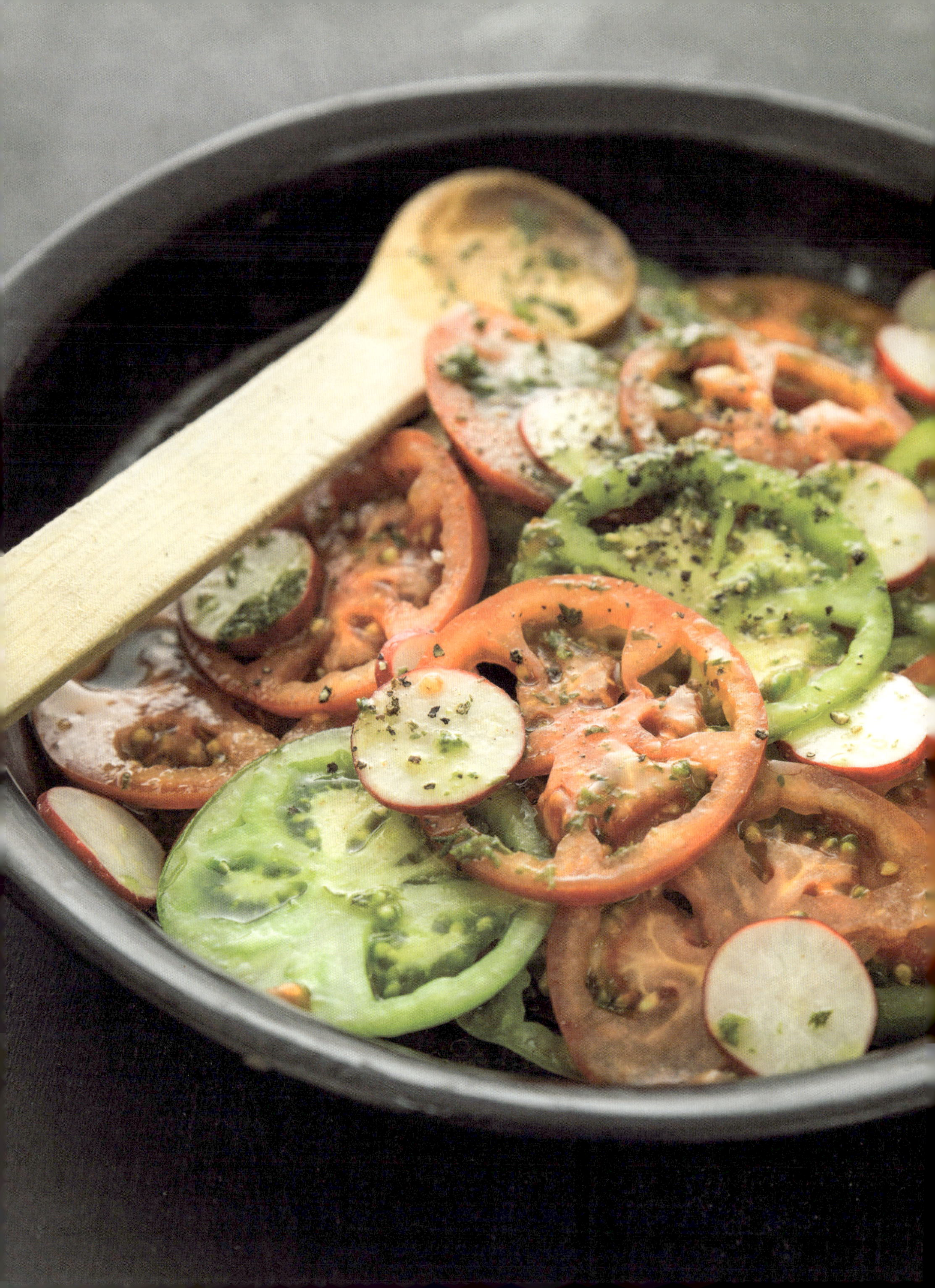

GF | DF | VEGAN

TOMATO & RADISH SALAD WITH MINT CHERMOULA

SERVES 4–6
Prep time: 10 minutes

800g assortment of tomatoes (I like to use some green, yellow and red ones; some larger, some cherry)
extra-virgin olive oil
flaky sea salt
freshly ground black pepper
3–4 radishes
2–3 tablespoons Mint Chermoula (page 57)
juice of ½ lemon

Tangy, juicy tomatoes and crunchy, peppery radishes, with a fresh and zingy herb dressing, make a great simple salad.

1. Thinly slice larger tomatoes and cut cherry tomatoes in half. Place in a large bowl and drizzle with extra-virgin olive oil and season with flaky sea salt and a grind of black pepper.

2. Thinly slice radishes and add to bowl.

3. Mix Mint Chermoula with lemon juice and a drizzle of extra-virgin olive oil and toss with tomatoes and radishes just before serving.

GF | DF | VEGAN use maple syrup instead of honey

BRUSSELS SPROUTS, APPLE & ALMOND SLAW

SERVES 4
Prep time: 15–20 minutes

300g Brussels sprouts
2 small young, firm, crisp apples
juice of ½ lemon
½ cup chopped roasted almonds
¼ cup chopped chives

HONEY MUSTARD DRESSING
1 tablespoon liquid honey
1½ tablespoons extra-virgin olive oil
1 heaped teaspoon wholegrain mustard
2 tablespoons apple cider vinegar
   or lemon juice

Raw Brussels sprouts make the best fresh, crunchy slaw, especially with sweet, crunchy apple and roasted almonds.

1. Finely slice Brussels sprouts as thinly as you can and place in a large bowl.
2. Core apples and thinly slice, add to the bowl of Brussels sprouts and squeeze lemon juice over the top to prevent browning.
3. Mix all dressing ingredients together and season with salt and pepper.
4. Just before serving, toss Brussels sprouts and apple with almonds, chives and dressing.

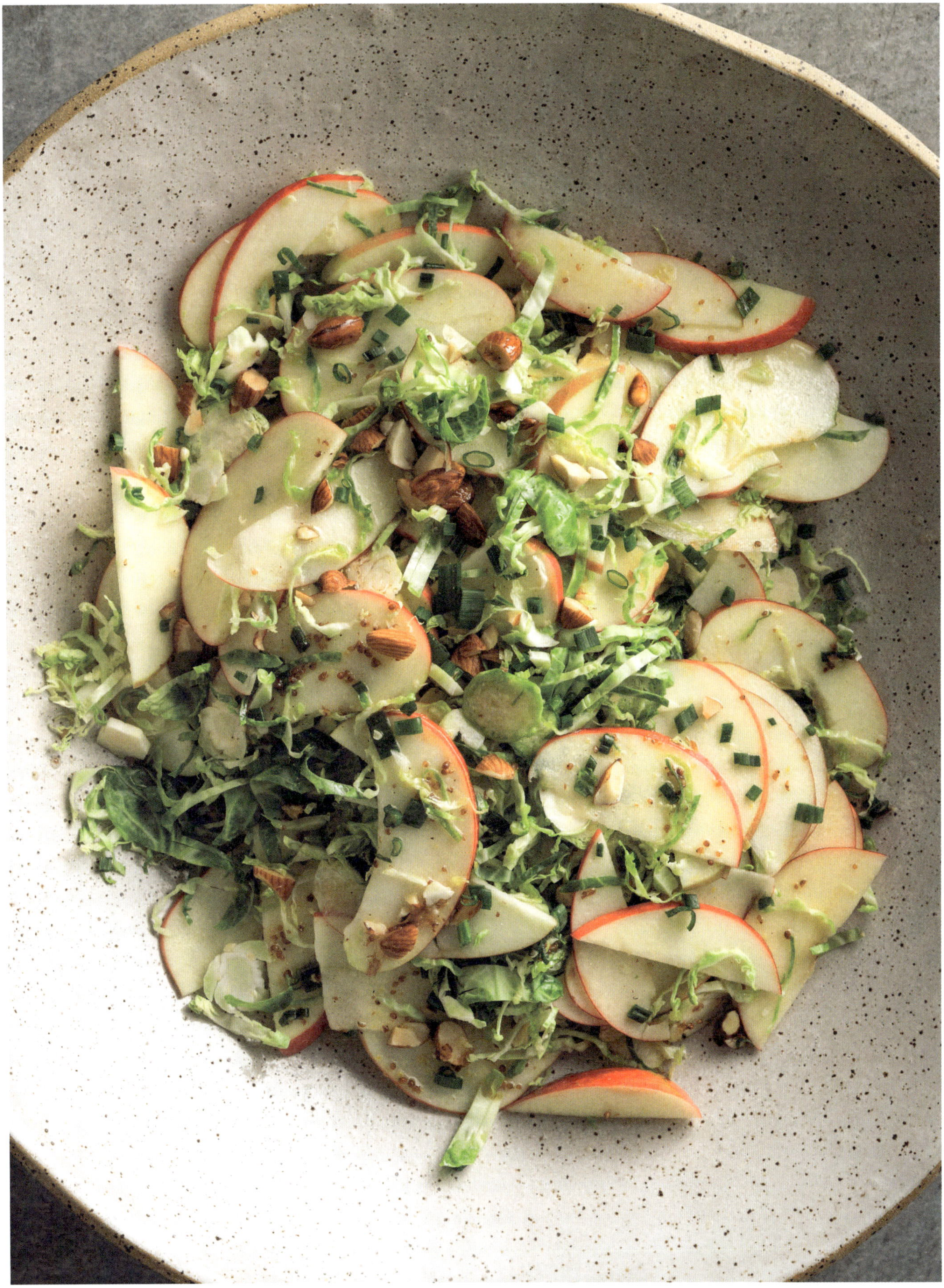

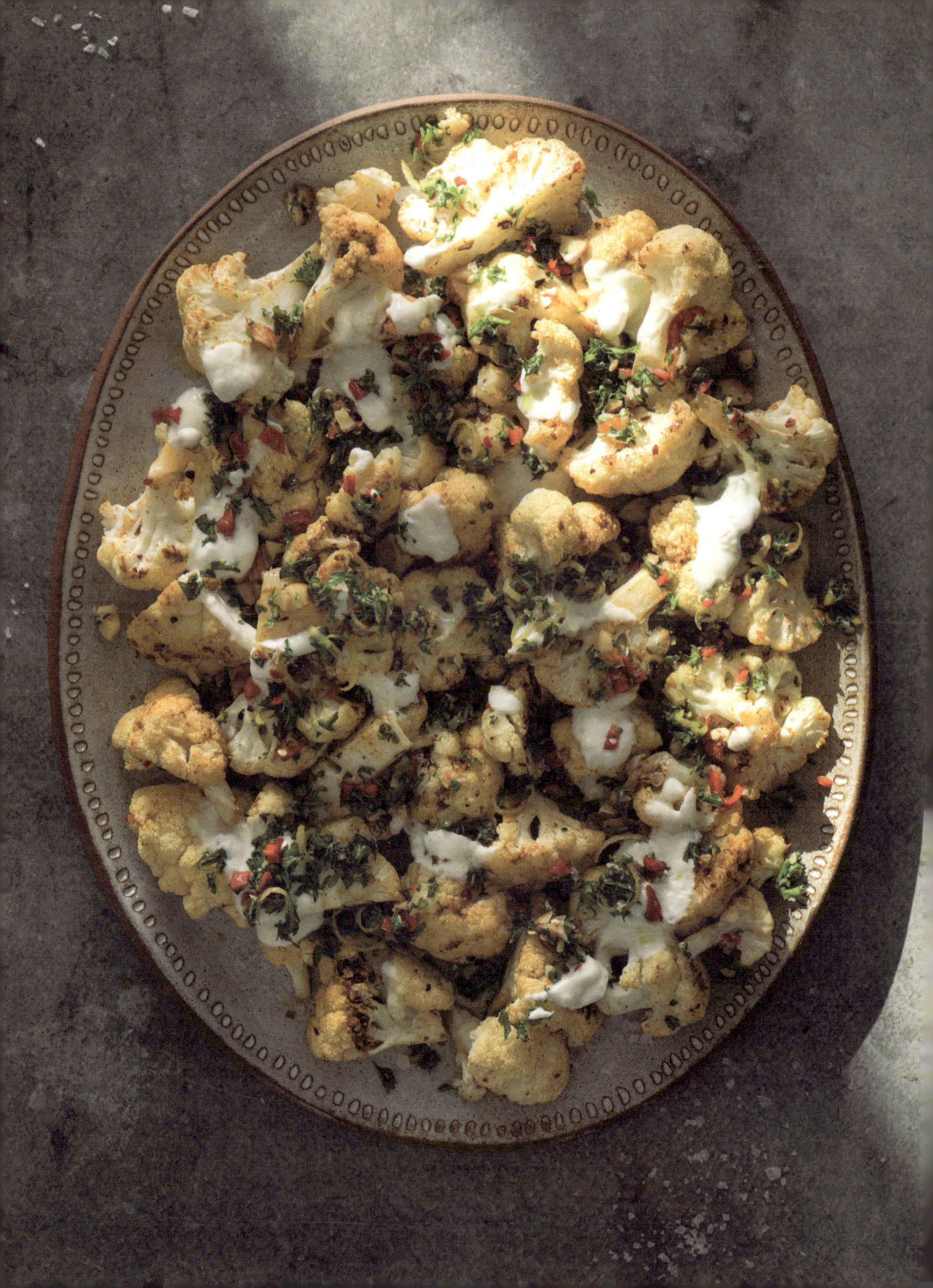

GF | DF use coconut yoghurt | VEGAN use coconut yoghurt

ROAST SPICED CAULIFLOWER WITH CARAMELISED GARLIC YOGHURT

SERVES 4
Prep time: 10–15 minutes
Cook time: 30 minutes

CARAMELISED GARLIC YOGHURT
1 whole bulb garlic (unpeeled)
½ cup natural, unsweetened yoghurt

ROAST CAULIFLOWER
2–3 tablespoons olive oil
1½ teaspoons ground cumin
1 teaspoon ground coriander
1 teaspoon ground turmeric
½ teaspoon ground cinnamon
½ teaspoon chilli flakes
1 teaspoon salt
zest of 1 lemon
1 large head cauliflower, chopped into bite-sized florets

CHILLI AND ALMOND GREMOLATA
3 tablespoons chopped roasted almonds
3 tablespoons finely chopped parsley
1 red chilli, finely chopped
zest of 1 lemon
drizzle of extra-virgin olive oil

TO SERVE
½ lemon, cut into wedges

Caramelised garlic yoghurt might just become your new favourite condiment — garlic roasted until sweet, sticky and caramelised, then mixed with cooling, tangy yoghurt. It's sublime drizzled over lots of things including roasted spiced cauliflower. A hit of fresh chilli, parsley and lemon at the end gives a fresh zing.

1. Preheat oven to 220°C.

2. Slice the top off garlic bulb to expose the cloves. Place on a square of tinfoil, drizzle with olive oil, season with salt, and wrap up loosely. Place parcel of garlic in the oven to cook for 20 minutes.

3. Mix oil, spices and salt and lemon zest together to a paste. In a large roasting dish, toss cauliflower florets with spice paste. Place in the oven (with the garlic parcel) to roast for 10–15 minutes or until cauliflower is slightly tender, but still has some bite. Switch to grill for a few minutes to get a nice colour on the cauliflower.

4. Mix all Gremolata ingredients together in a small bowl.

5. Carefully squeeze caramelised garlic out of its skin (without burning yourself; using paper towels helps) into a bowl. Mash garlic and mix in yoghurt. Season to taste with salt and pepper.

6. Arrange cauliflower on a serving platter and drizzle with Caramelised Garlic Yoghurt. Scatter with Chilli and Almond Gremolata. Serve with lemon wedges to squeeze over just before eating.

GF

GOLDEN PARMESAN PARSNIPS

SERVES 4
Prep time: 15 minutes
Cook time: 50–55 minutes

800g–1kg parsnips
2 tablespoons olive oil
3 cloves garlic, finely chopped
¾ cup finely grated parmesan
¼ cup finely chopped parsley

Like carrots, parsnips have this amazing natural sweetness that is really brought out when they are roasted. Add some salty parmesan and fresh parsley, and you have something very moreish you'll end up picking at before they get to the table. The cooking time is just a guide depending on your oven and how fat your pieces of parsnip are. Use your eye and make sure those parsnips are nicely caramelised.

1. Preheat oven to 200°C and line an oven tray with baking paper.

2. Peel parsnips. Cut in half; cut thinner half in half lengthways, and wider half into quarters lengthways so that they are roughly all the same thickness. Toss with olive oil and garlic in lined tray, season with salt and pepper, and roast for 40–45 minutes until starting to caramelise.

3. Sprinkle parsnips with parmesan and parsley, toss, and return to oven for a further 10 minutes or until parmesan is golden and crispy.

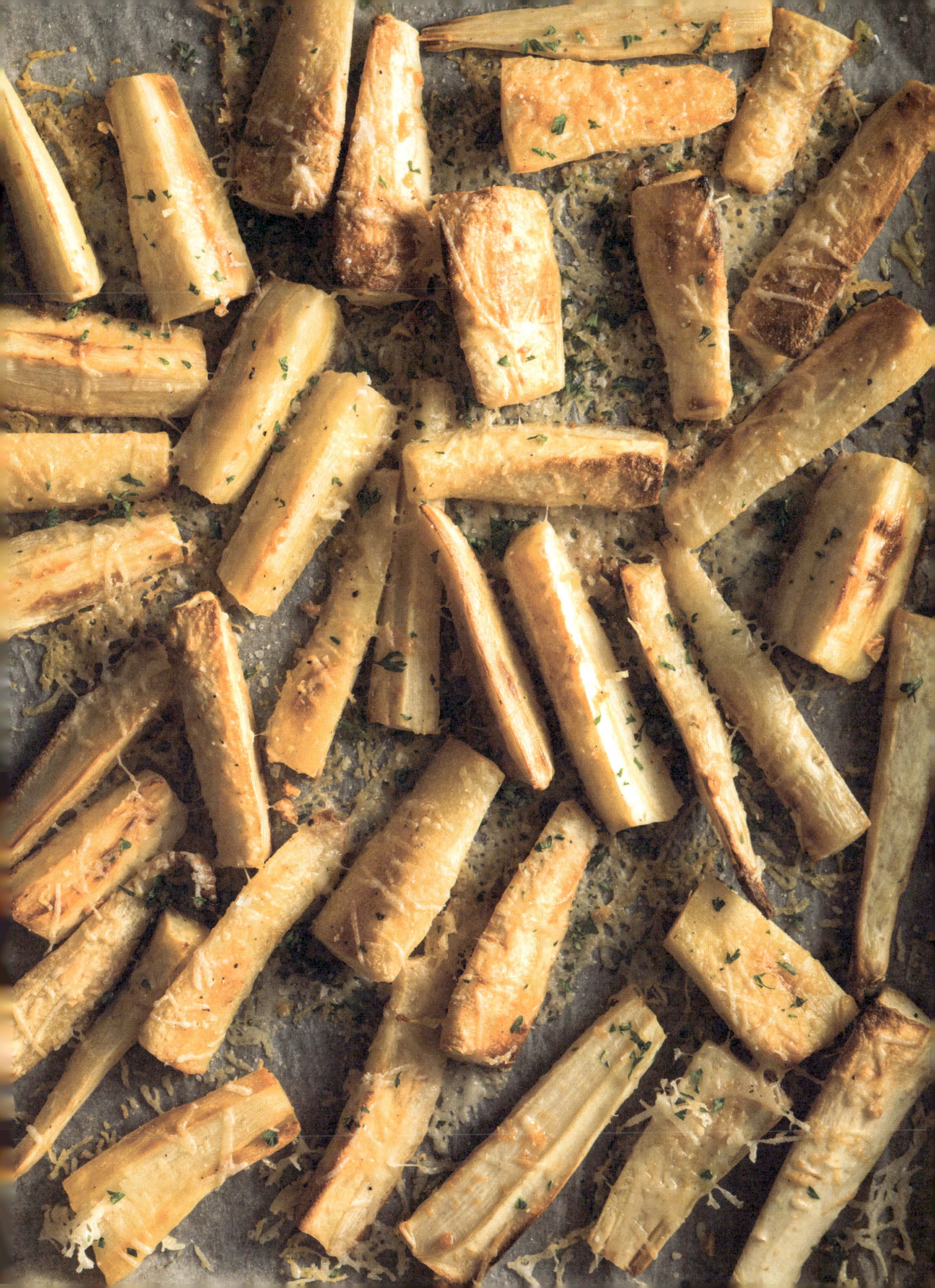

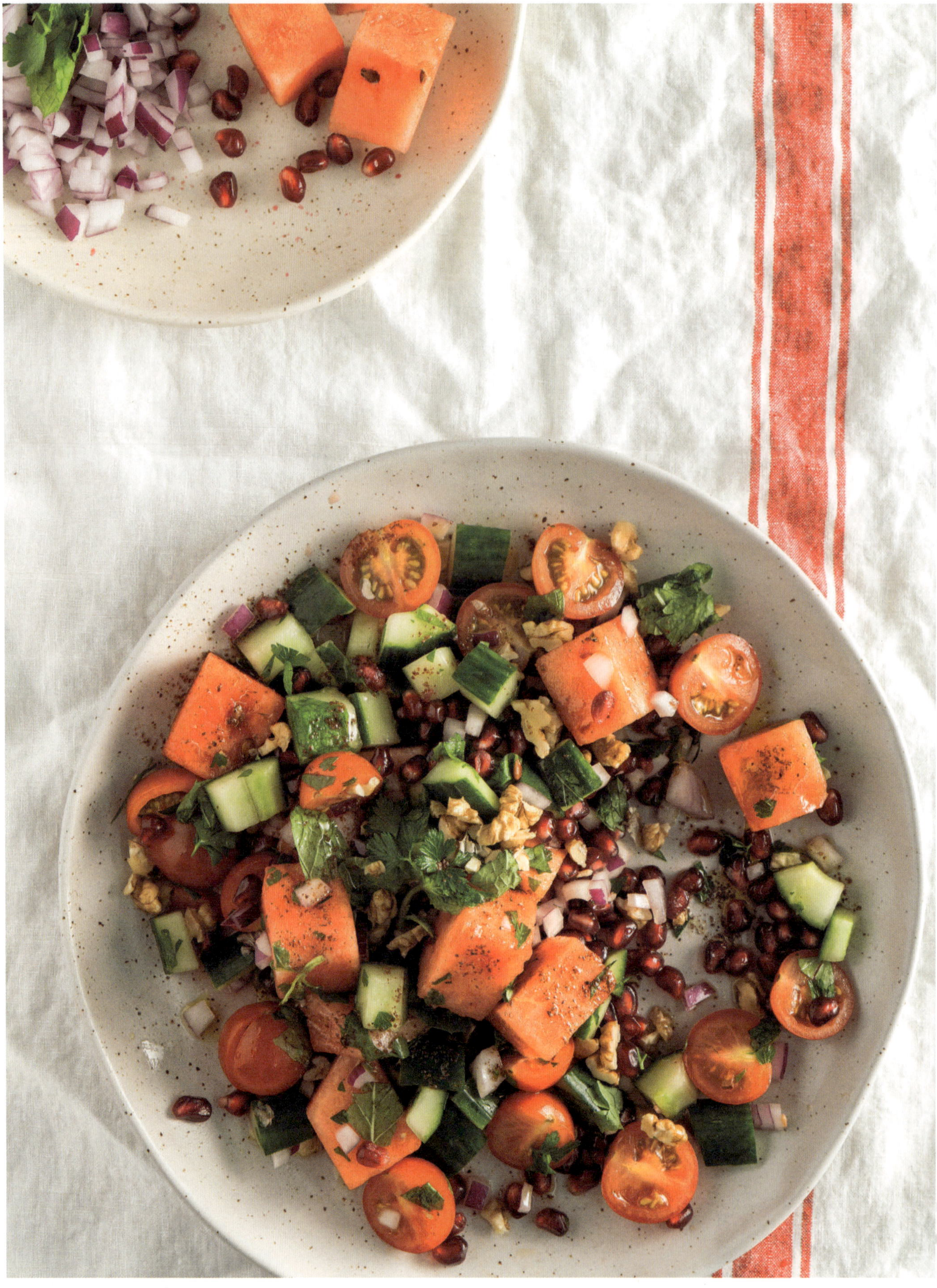

GF | DF | VEGAN

TURKISH SALAD WITH WATERMELON

SERVES 4
Prep time: 15 minutes

½ telegraph cucumber
1 punnet cherry tomatoes, cut in half
3 cups watermelon cubes (about ¼ large watermelon)
½ red onion, finely diced
seeds from 1 pomegranate
⅓ cup finely chopped walnuts
½ cup torn mint leaves
½ cup roughly chopped flat-leaf parsley
2–3 tablespoons extra-virgin olive oil
1½ teaspoons sumac
juice of 1 lemon

This is a wonderful dish for the summer table. To turn this salad into a meal of its own, top with pan-fried haloumi and avocado. Sumac is a quintessential ingredient in Turkish cuisine, and adds this amazing tartness and flavour to dishes, so I recommend finding it as you'll end up using it lots in other dishes too. However, if you can't get your hands on some, use a little finely grated lemon zest instead.

1. Cut cucumber in half lengthways and scrape out seeds using a teaspoon. Dice deseeded cucumber.

2. In a large bowl, toss cucumber with all remaining ingredients and season to taste with salt and freshly ground black pepper.

GF | DF omit blue cheese | VEGAN omit blue cheese

PEAR, RADISH, BLUE CHEESE & ROCKET

SERVES 4
Prep time: 5 minutes

4 handfuls of baby or wild rocket
1 just-ripe pear, thinly sliced
3–4 baby radishes, thinly sliced
25–50g blue cheese or feta, crumbled
drizzle of extra-virgin olive oil and lemon juice

I've been making this salad for as long as I can remember — it's always the perfect partner for a quiche or tart, like the Caramelised Shallot & Thyme Tart Tatin on page 130.

1. Place rocket in a bowl. Thinly slice pear and radishes, add to bowl.

2. Crumble in blue cheese/feta.

3. Just before serving, drizzle with extra-virgin olive oil and lemon juice, and season with salt and pepper. Toss everything together.

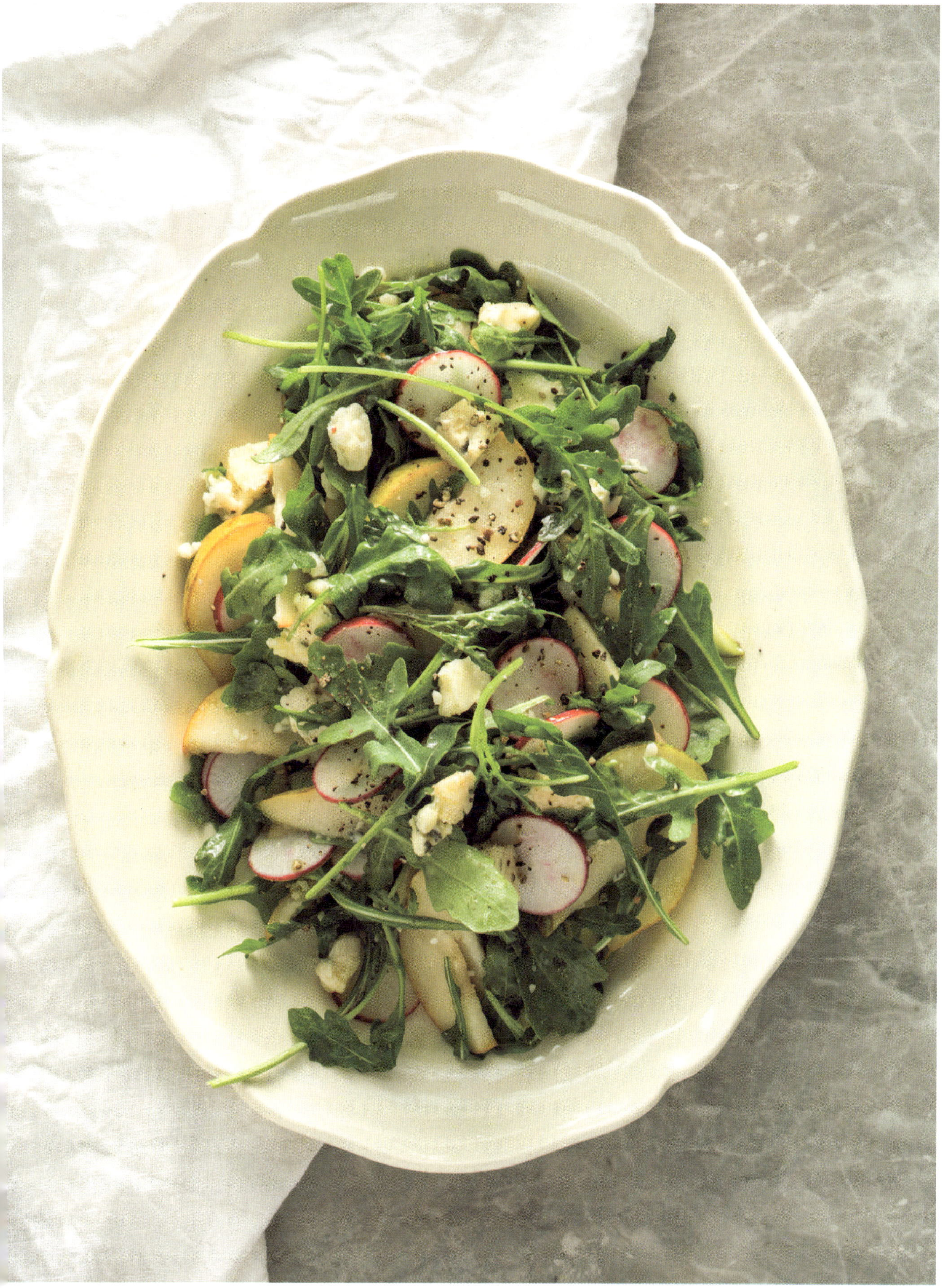

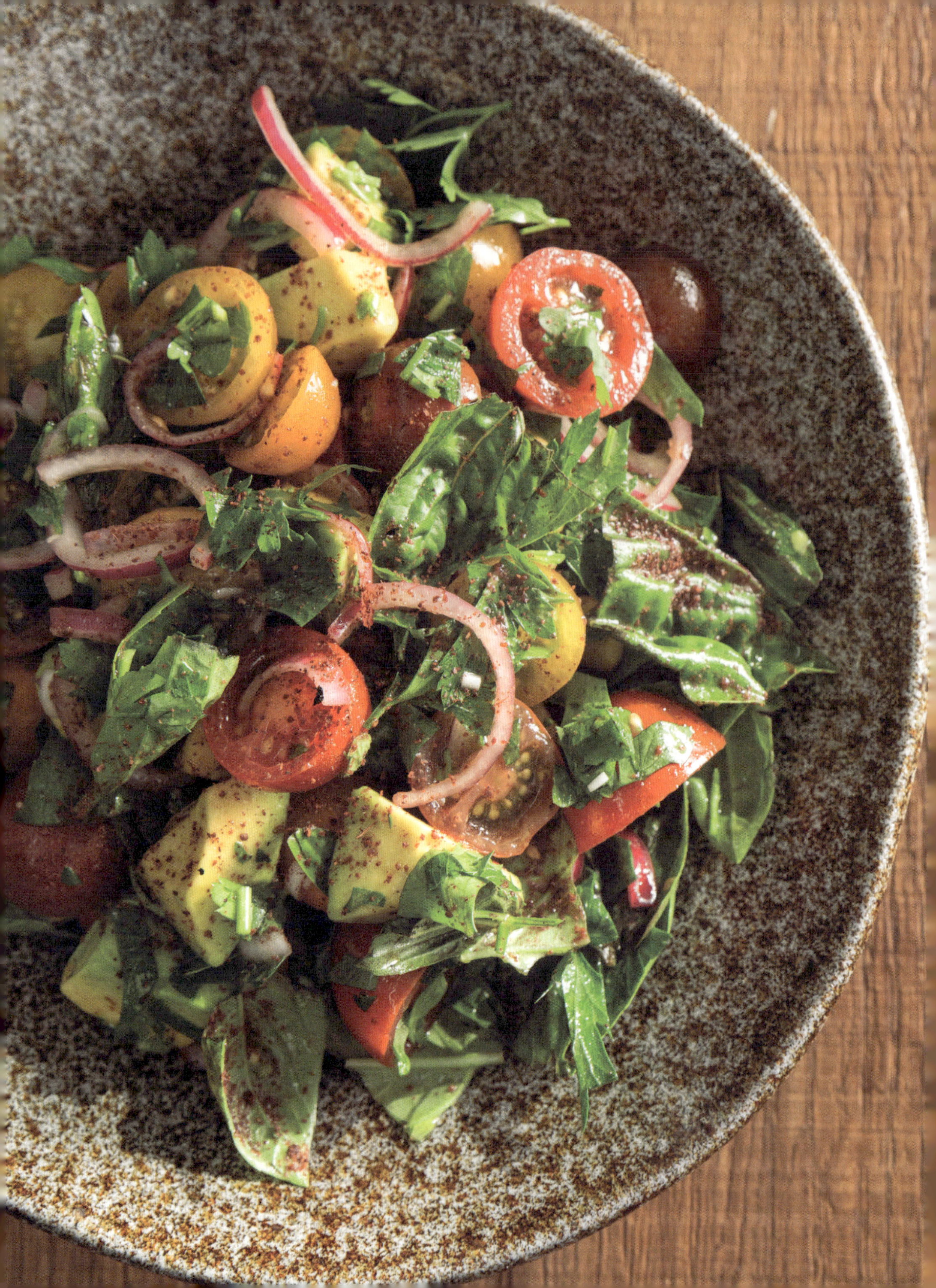

GF | DF | VEGAN

ESSENTIAL SUMMER SALAD

SERVES 4
Prep time: 10 minutes

½ red onion, thinly sliced
1 tablespoon red wine vinegar
pinch of sugar
1 punnet cherry tomatoes
1 large just-ripe avocado
½ cup torn basil leaves
½ cup chopped flat-leaf parsley
1½ tablespoons extra-virgin olive oil
½–1 teaspoon sumac (optional, but highly recommended)

This is an all-round perfect salad to accompany any summer meal. Marinating the red onion in vinegar first takes away the harsh, pungent flavour of raw onion.

1. Place onion in a large bowl, drizzle with vinegar and sprinkle with sugar. Leave for 5–10 minutes.

2. Cut cherry tomatoes in half. Peel and dice avocado. Add to the bowl of red onion, along with basil, parsley, extra-virgin olive oil and sumac (if using). Season with salt and freshly ground black pepper and toss to combine. Serve immediately.

GF | DF | VEGAN use maple syrup instead of honey

ASPARAGUS & STRAWBERRIES WITH BALSAMIC & BASIL

SERVES 4
Prep time: 10 minutes
Cook time: 5 minutes

3 tablespoons balsamic vinegar
3 tablespoons extra-virgin olive oil
1½ tablespoons liquid honey
2–3 bunches (24–36 spears) asparagus, tough ends trimmed
1 punnet (250g) strawberries, hulled and cut in half
2 tablespoons lightly toasted sliced almonds
handful of basil leaves

This is such a gorgeous, vibrant dish to make when asparagus and strawbs are in season. A great side as part of a feast or to accompany some lovely bread and cheese (I'd go with a brie or camembert) for a simple meal or picnic.

1. Put balsamic vinegar, olive oil and honey in a jar, season with salt and freshly ground black pepper. Screw the lid on tightly and shake until well combined.

2. Toss asparagus with a drizzle of olive oil and season with salt. Cook either on the barbecue or in a large fry pan on medium to high heat for a few minutes until tender and slightly charred.

3. In a serving bowl, toss strawberries, cooked asparagus and dressing together. Scatter with almonds and basil.

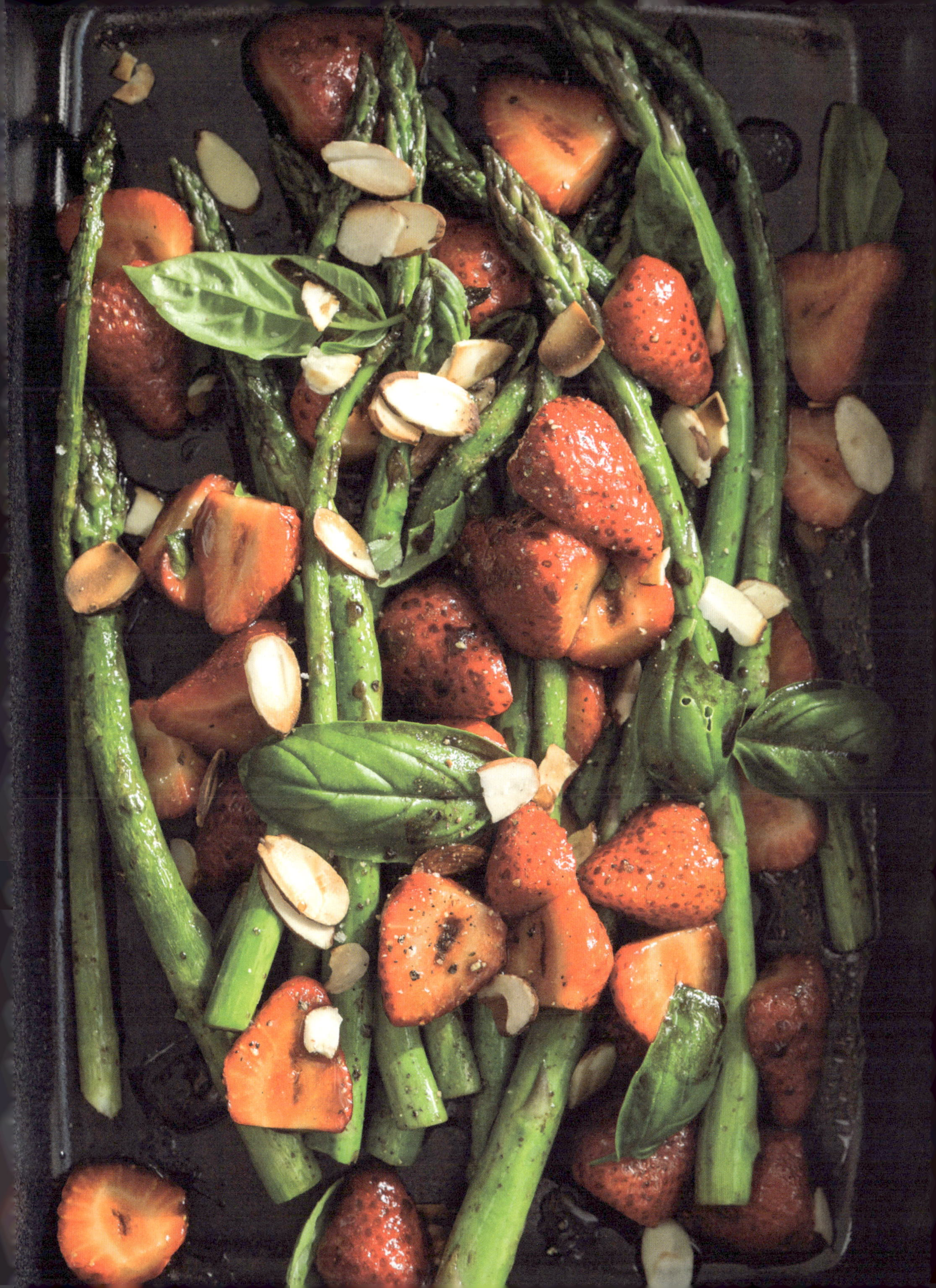

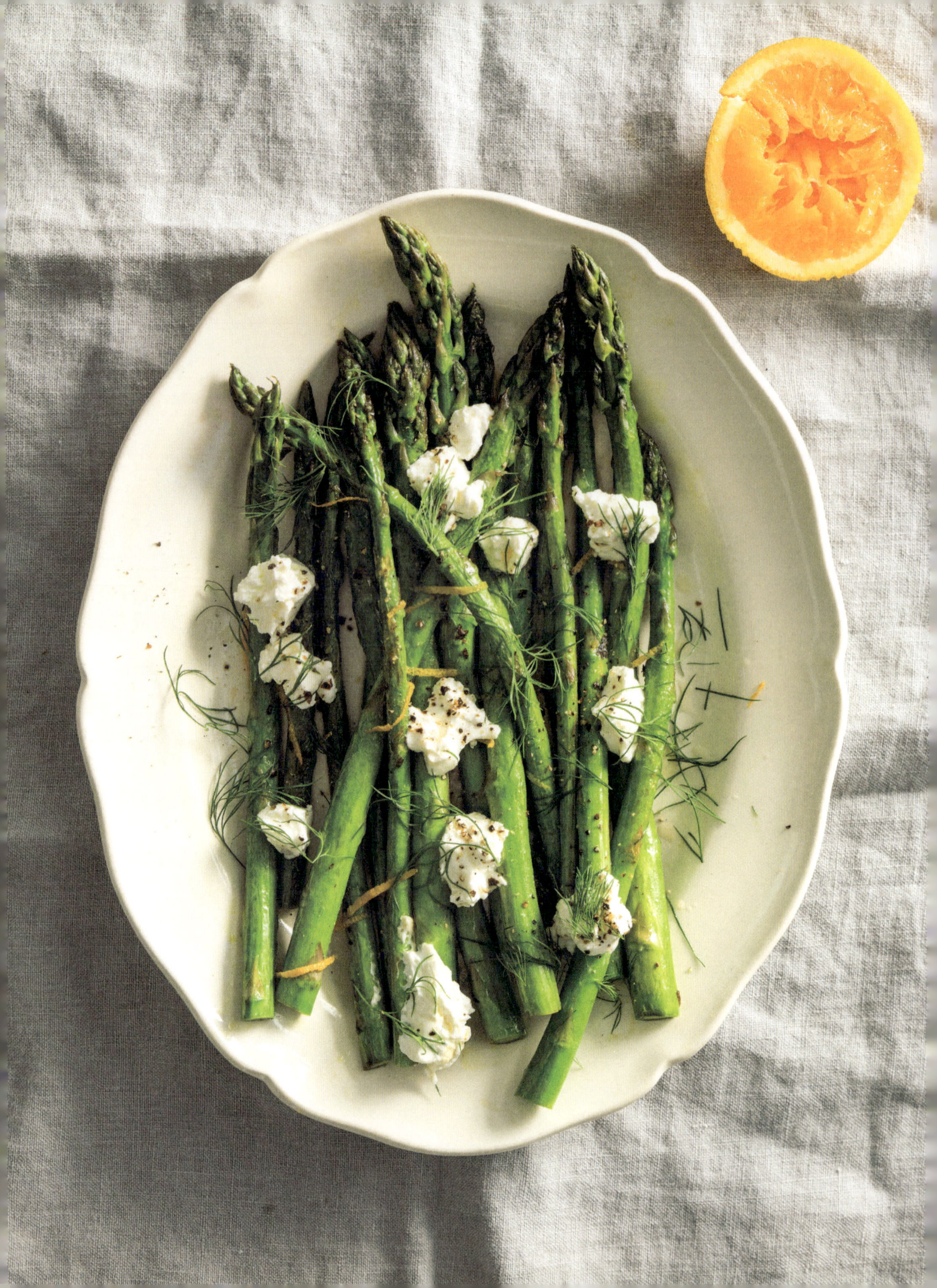

GF

ASPARAGUS, ORANGE, GOATS CHEESE & DILL

SERVES 4
Prep time: 5 minutes
Cook time: 5 minutes

2–3 bunches (24–36 spears) asparagus, tough ends trimmed
juice of 1 orange
zest of ½ orange
50g soft goats cheese (chèvre) or creamy feta
a few sprigs of dill

Orange, dill and a little goats cheese (or use feta if you're not into goats cheese) make tender, juicy spears of asparagus sing, particularly if you cook the asparagus on the barbecue until slightly charred and blistered.

1. Toss asparagus with a drizzle of olive oil and season with salt. Cook either on the barbecue grill or in a large fry pan on medium to high heat for a few minutes until tender and slightly charred.

2. If cooking in a pan, squeeze the orange juice over the asparagus and let it bubble, coating the asparagus in an orange glaze. If cooking on the barbecue grill, transfer asparagus to a plate and squeeze over the orange juice.

3. Sprinkle with orange zest, dot with goats cheese or feta, and garnish with dill. Grind over black pepper.

GF | DF omit butter | VEGAN omit butter

RED WINE-BRAISED CABBAGE WITH CURRANTS & SPICES

SERVES 4
Prep time: 5 minutes
Cook time: 30 minutes

2 tablespoons olive oil
1 tablespoon butter
700–800g (½ medium) red cabbage, finely sliced
2 cinnamon sticks
1 bay leaf
1 cup red wine
juice of 1 orange
2 tablespoons dried currants
1 tablespoon plum, cherry or blackberry jam or jelly
knob of butter

When we cook and eat this delicious braised cabbage it is almost always with wild venison. However, I can imagine it would be equally fantastic with some juicy, roasted Portobello mushrooms and roast potatoes.

1. Place olive oil, butter, cabbage, cinnamon sticks and bay leaf in a large heavy-based pot or fry-pan over medium to high heat. Cook, stirring often, for about 10 minutes, until cabbage is starting to soften.

2. Add wine, orange juice, currants and jam/jelly. Continue cooking for a further 20 minutes until cabbage is soft and liquid has reduced. Stir through butter and season to taste with salt and pepper.

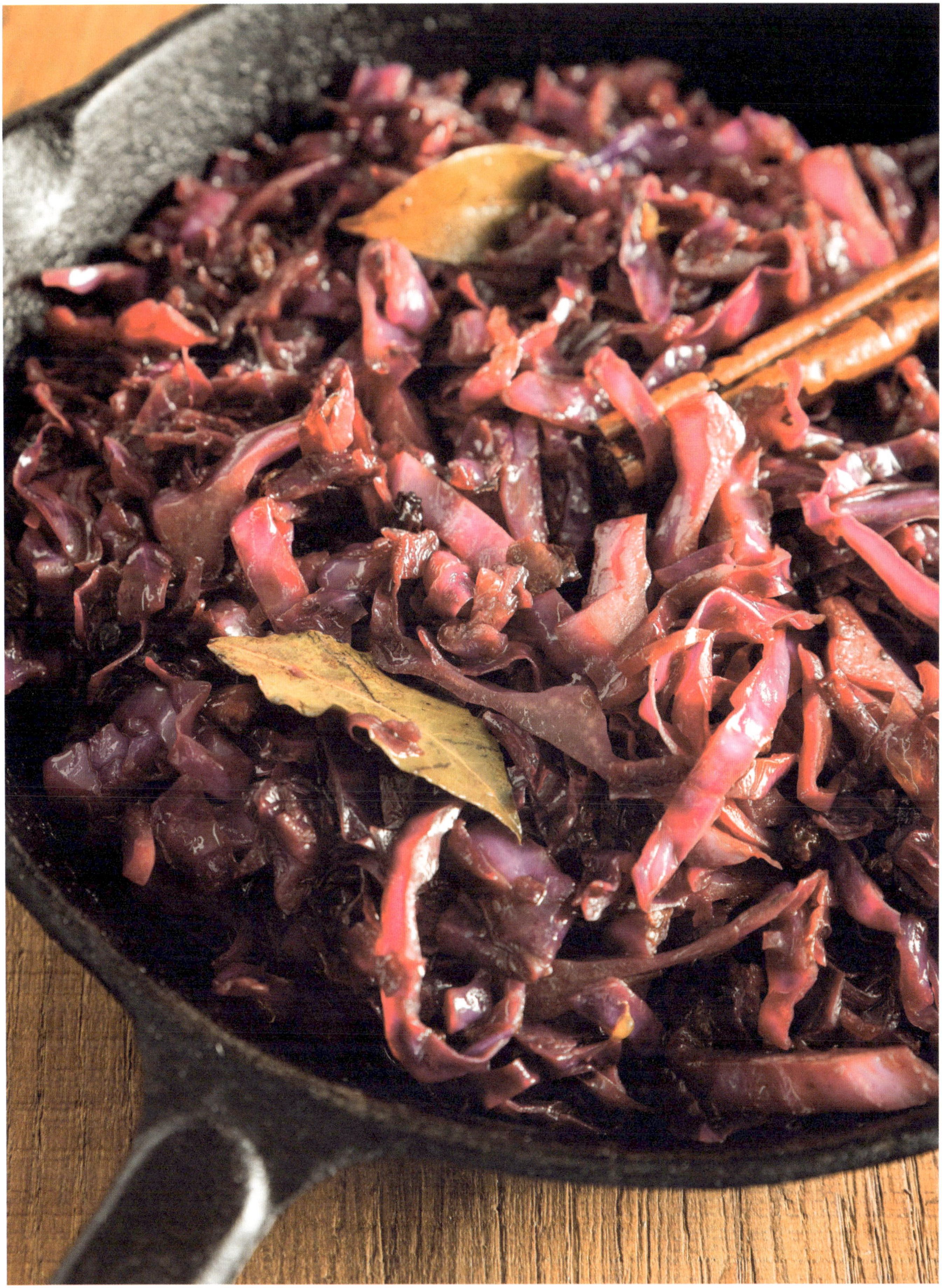

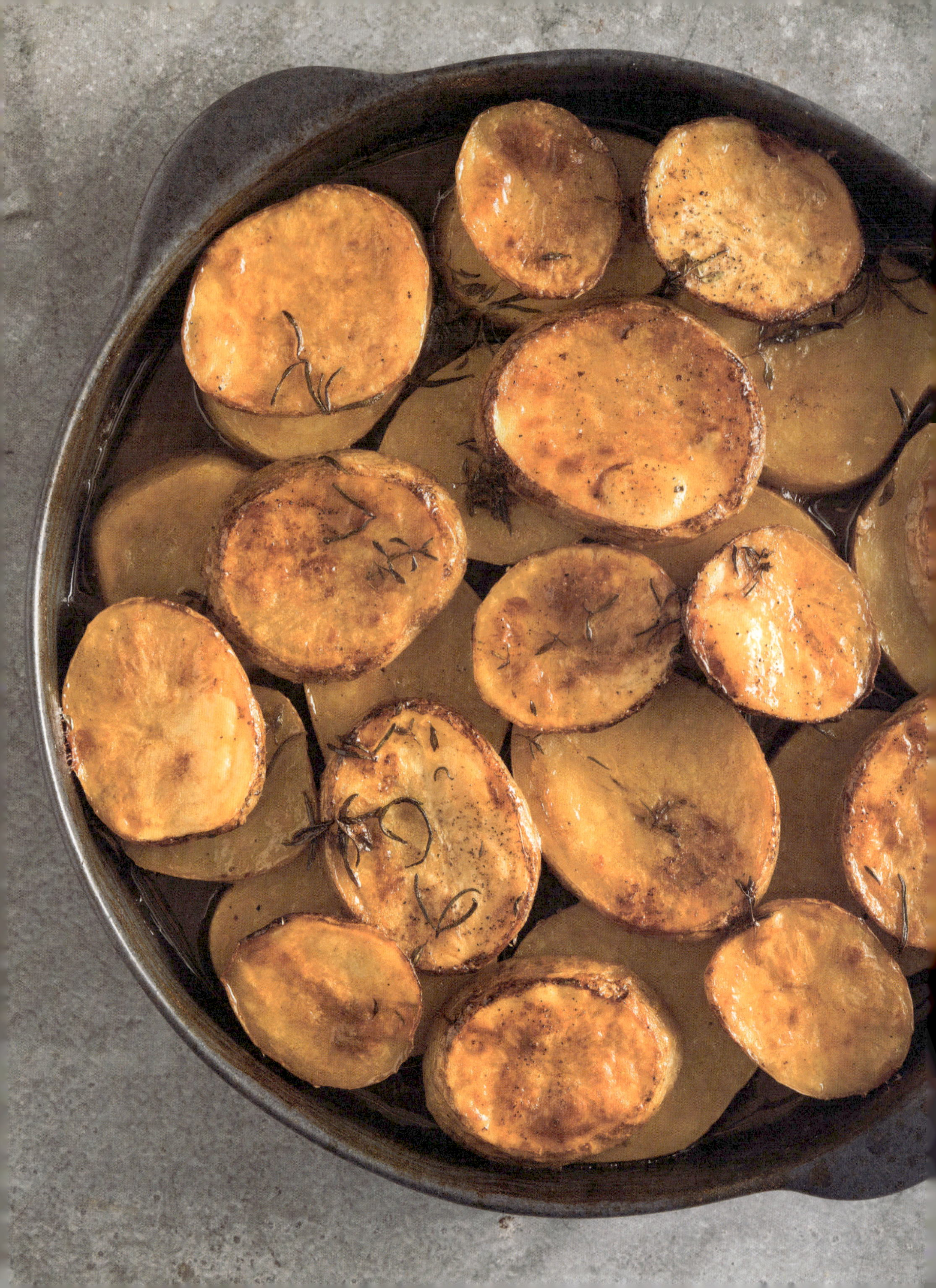

GF

FONDANT POTATOES

SERVES 4–6
Prep time: 5 minutes
Cook time: 40–60 minutes

800g–1kg agria potatoes, scrubbed
500–600ml vegetable stock
  (see Note)
leaves of 1 sprig thyme or rosemary
50g butter
finely chopped parsley, to garnish
  (optional)

You won't be able to get enough of these utterly scrumptious potatoes. Slow-cooking them in stock makes them meltingly tender and flavourful inside, whilst the tops turn golden brown in a glaze of butter and reduced stock.

1. Preheat oven to 220°C.

2. Slice potatoes into 1–1.5cm-thick rounds and place in a large baking or casserole dish, ideally in a single layer, but don't worry if you have to layer them a little.

3. Pour over stock. Sprinkle with thyme/rosemary and dot with butter. Bake, uncovered, for 40 minutes to 1 hour or until potatoes are golden and almost all the stock has been absorbed. Sprinkle with chopped parsley (if using).

Note: In this dish reconstituted, as opposed to fresh, stock works best.

GF | DF omit butter | VEGAN omit butter

ROAST RADISHES WITH BUTTER & LEMON

SERVES 4-6
Prep time: 2 minutes
Cook time: 15–20 minutes

2–3 bunches radishes
1 knob butter
1 tablespoon lemon juice
1 tablespoon chopped parsley (optional)

Chances are you haven't had roasted radishes before (I hadn't until a couple of years ago). Roasting takes away any harsh pepperiness, mellowing them out and making them sweet and juicy. They're so delicious it's easy to eat a lot of them — especially when roasted with butter and lemon — as if they were roast spuds. In fact, they are a great low carb alternative to roast potatoes!

1. Preheat oven to 220°C. Line an oven tray with baking paper.
2. Cut radishes in half lengthways (however, you can leave any very small ones whole). Drizzle and toss with olive oil on lined tray. Season with salt and pepper.
3. Roast for 10–15 minutes until tender and starting to caramelise. Add butter and lemon juice and toss together, then return to oven for a further 5 minutes.
4. Toss with parsley (if using) and serve.

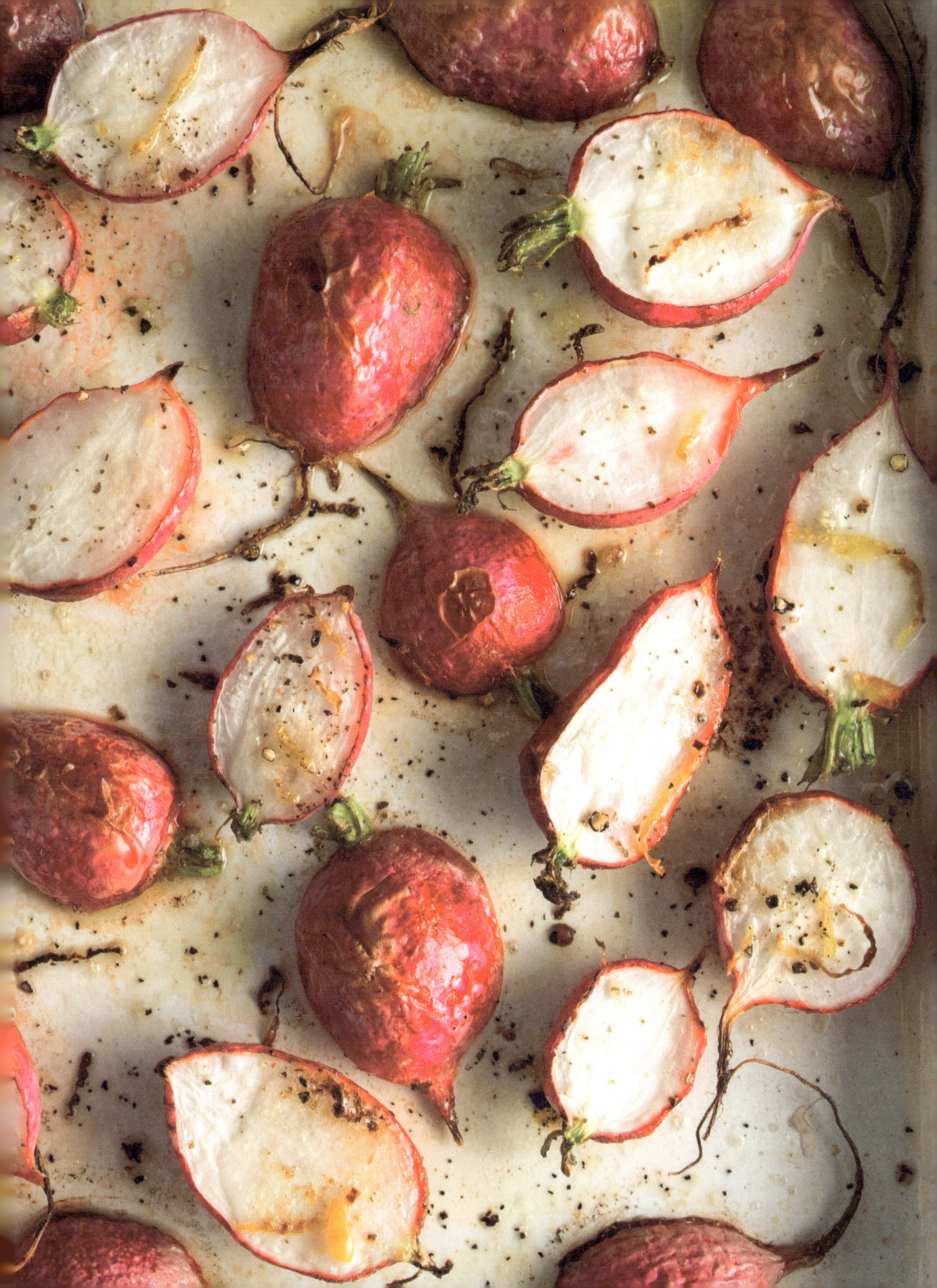

Swee
Ba

CHAPTER SEVEN — P. 257

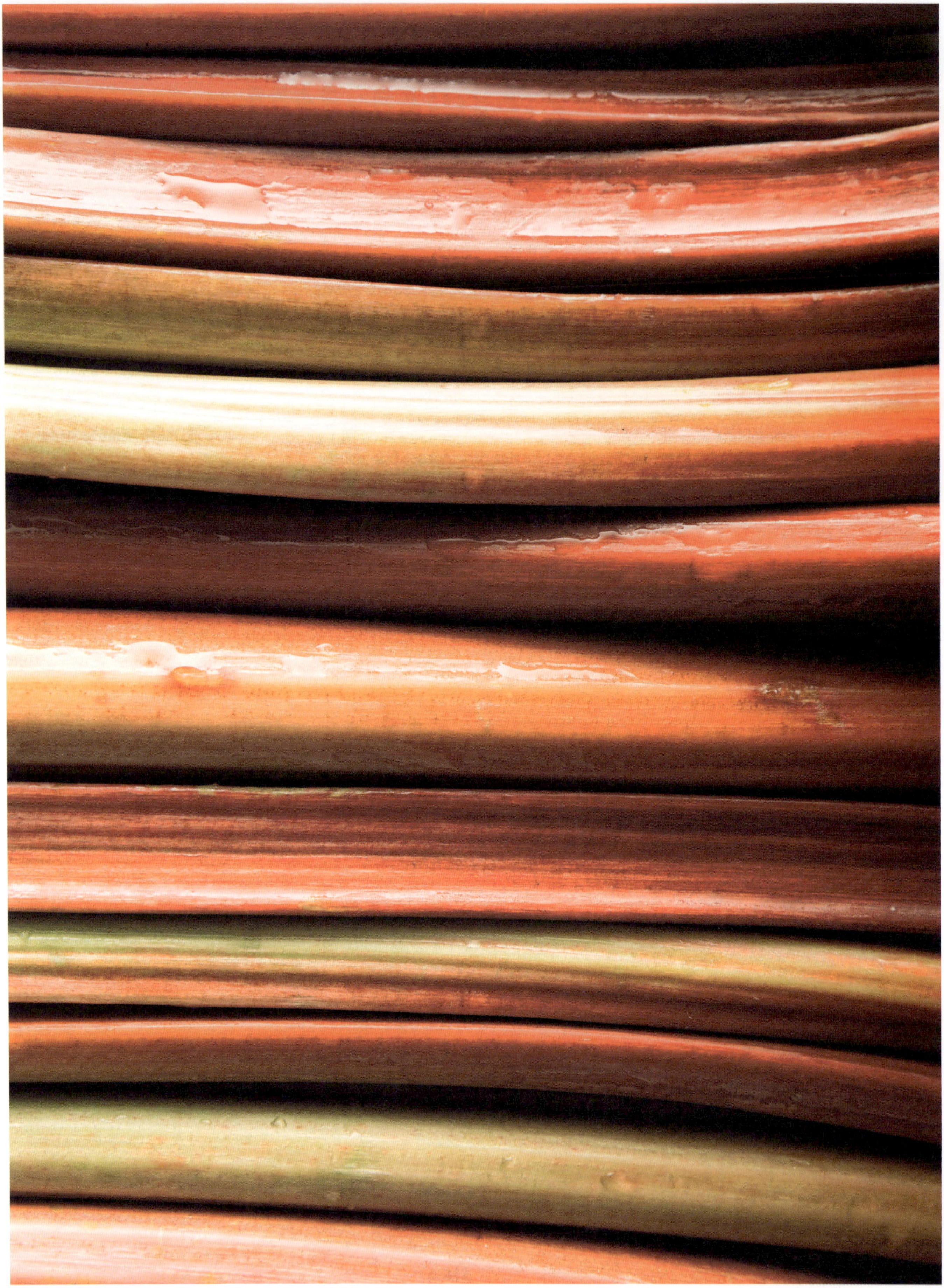

This chapter is full of treats that, like the other chapters, contain vegetables. I know, you probably weren't expecting to find such a chapter! But hopefully it demonstrates, again, just how clever and adaptable vegetables can be.

You'll be familiar with carrot cake, or even chocolate beetroot cake (of which there is an old favourite recipe in here), and the treats in this chapter are very much of the same kind: indulgent, occasional sweet treats that star vegetables.

Okay, I've stretched the definition of vegetable a little — there are some that are generally treated and eaten in a fruity way that are actually a vegetable (e.g. rhubarb), and some that are usually treated in a savoury way like a vegetable that are actually a fruit (e.g. avocado and pumpkin!). And then there is polenta (from corn) which I've used instead of flour in a couple of recipes (it gives a light crumbly texture, and makes baking gluten-free), and rosemary and thyme (not vegetables, I know!) have been added to some classics for a fragrant herbaceous note.

You'll find in some recipes the vegetable is a primary 'star' ingredient (à la my sweet potato pie), while in others they're more hidden… in some cases to try to get more greens into unsuspecting children!

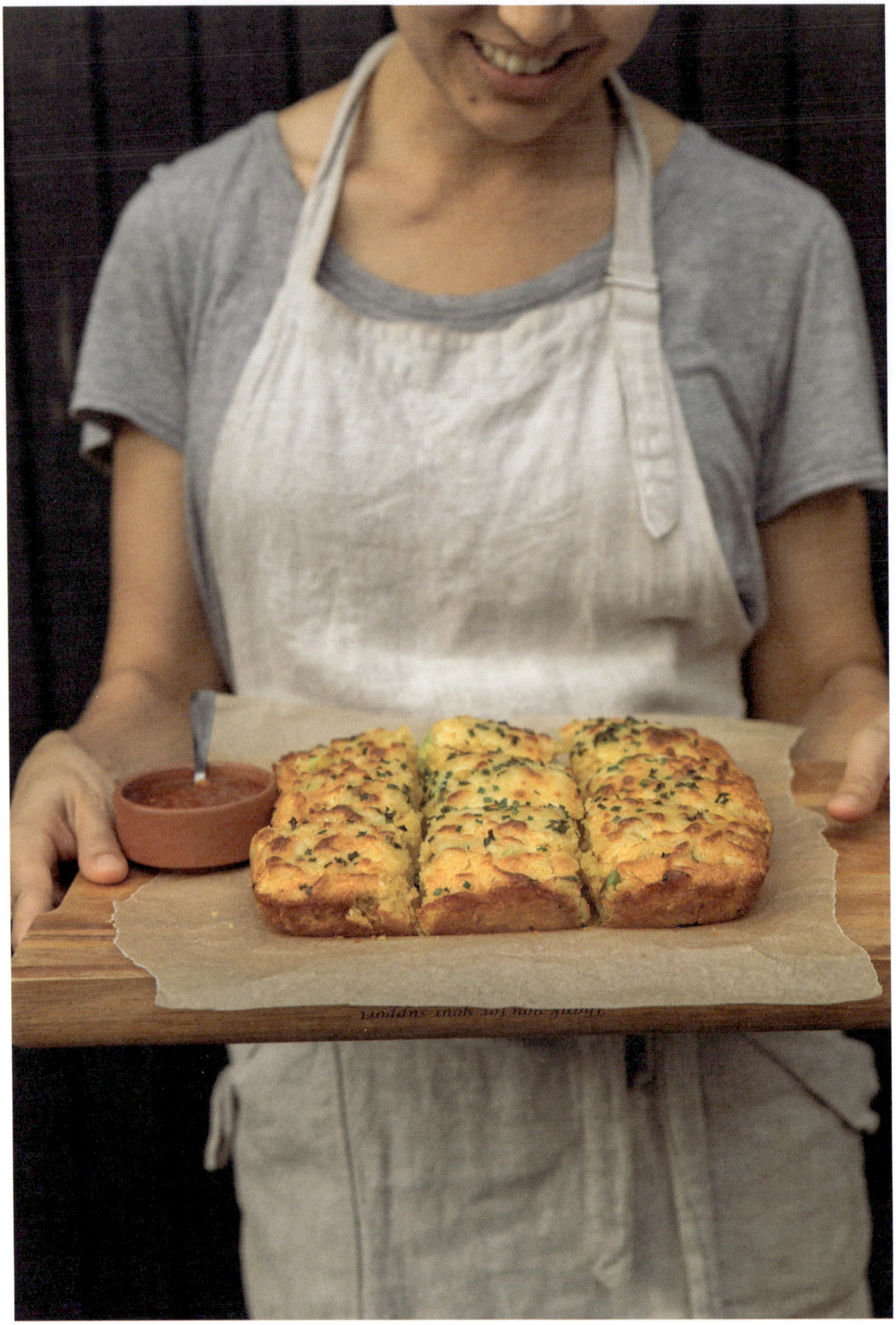

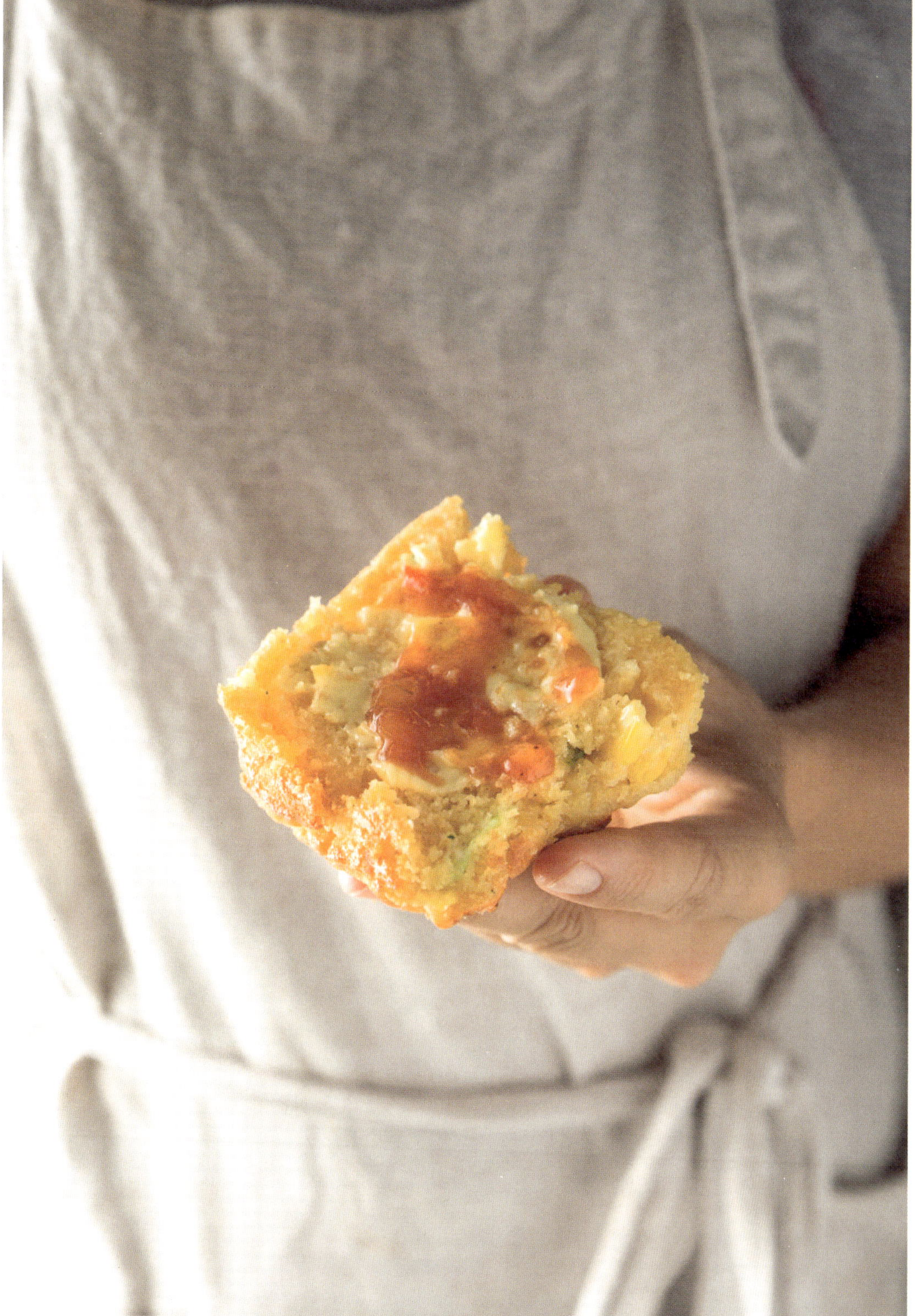

JALAPEÑO, CHEESE & SPRING ONION CORNBREAD

SERVES 9
Prep time: 15 minutes
Cook time: 30 minutes

kernels from 1 corn cob
2 free-range eggs (or flax eggs, see page 291)
1 cup milk + 3 tablespoons
115g butter, melted
185g plain flour
½ cup polenta (cornmeal)
1 tablespoon sugar
½ teaspoon paprika
1 tablespoon baking powder
½ teaspoon salt
150g tasty cheese, grated
⅓ cup sliced spring onions
1–2 tablespoons chopped jalapeños (fresh or pickled from a jar)

Thanks to My Food Bag for this scrumptious recipe. Much like a light, fluffy scone, cornbread is a quick bread made with cornmeal (polenta) and is a big part of Southern cuisine with lots of variations (this one is kind of 'Tex-Mex'). Packed with cheese, corn, spring onions and jalapeños for a little spicy kick, this cornbread is deeeelicious warm, spread with a little butter and tomato relish (and incredibly hard to stop eating).

1. Preheat oven to 200°C. Bring a full kettle of water to the boil. Grease a 20–25cm baking dish with butter or oil.

2. Place corn kernels is a heatproof bowl or pot and cover with boiling water, leave for 5 minutes until bright yellow, then drain.

3. In a large bowl, whisk eggs, milk and butter.

4. Into another bowl sift flour, then stir in polenta, sugar, paprika, baking powder and salt.

5. Tip flour mixture into egg mixture, along with corn, cheese (reserve ½ cup for topping), spring onions and jalapeños. Season with pepper and stir until just combined, being careful not to overmix.

6. Spoon batter into greased dish and sprinkle with remaining ½ cup grated cheese. Bake for about 30 minutes until a knife inserted into the centre comes out clean. Allow to cool in the dish for 10 minutes before cutting.

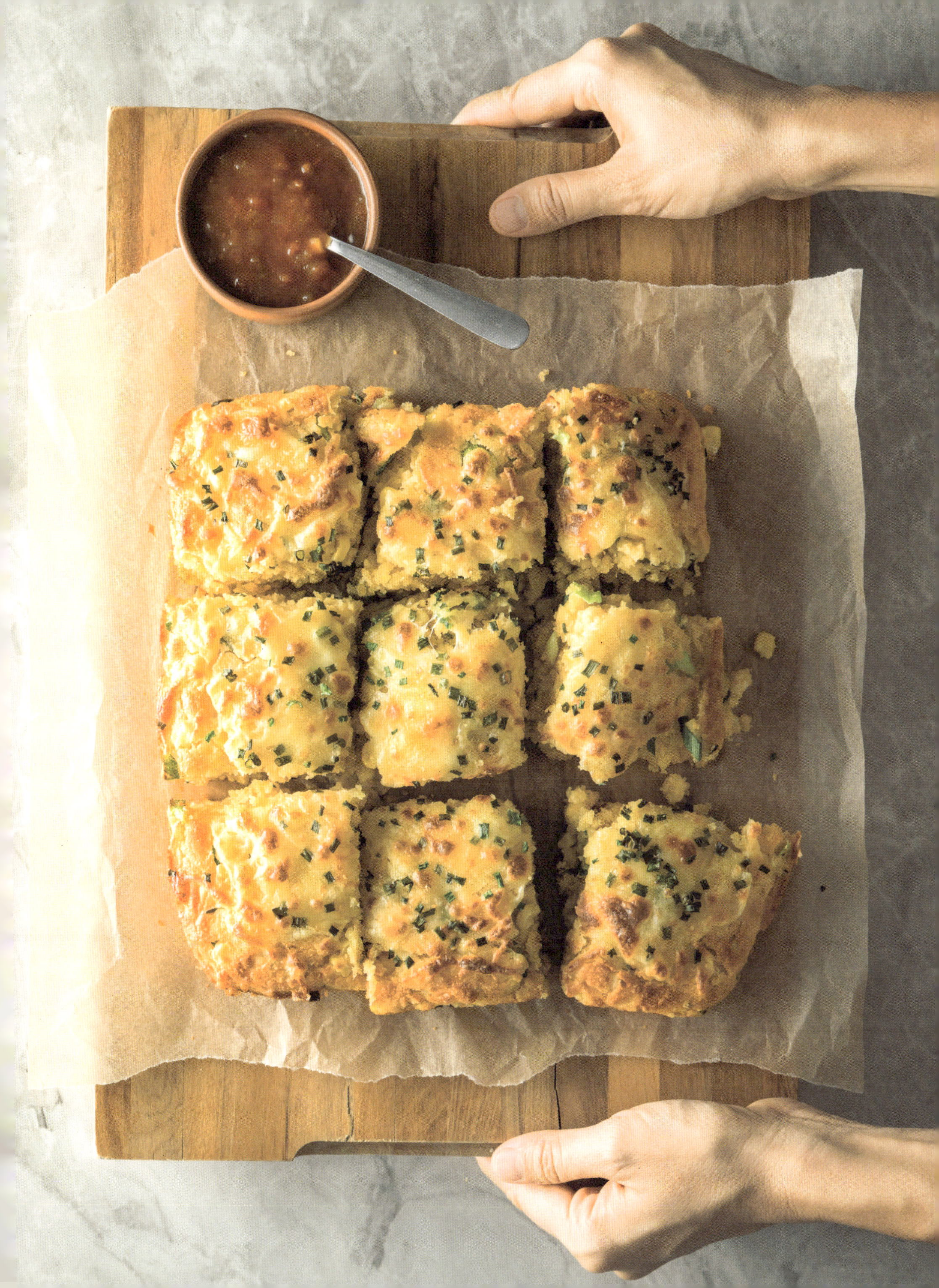

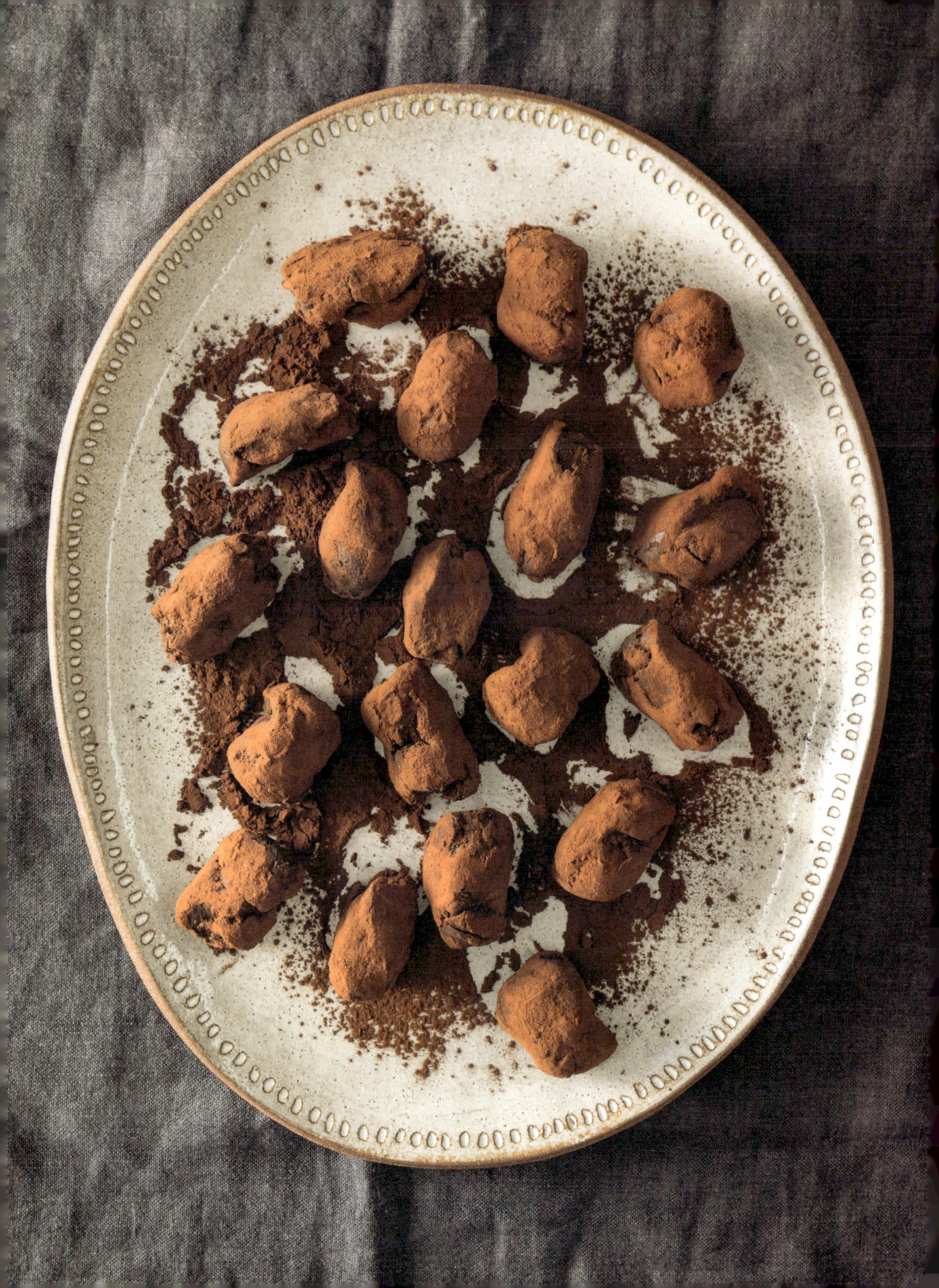

GF | DF use DF dark chocolate and coconut cream |
VEGAN use DF dark chocolate and coconut cream

AVOCADO CHOCOLATE TRUFFLES

MAKES ABOUT 30 TRUFFLES
Prep time: 20 minutes
Cook time: 5 minutes

250g good-quality dark (60%–70% cocoa) chocolate, chopped
flesh of 2 medium, just-ripe avocados, chopped
⅓ cup cream or coconut cream
4–5 tablespoons maple syrup
4 tablespoons Dutch cocoa or cacao powder + 2–3 tablespoons extra for dusting

Avocados are so clever that they even make incredible desserts, like these decadent truffles. You would never know their secret as the dark chocolate masks any avocado flavour — all the avocado really does is provide the rich, creamy texture of truffles, instead of copious amounts of butter and cream (so you could almost say they're good for you!) Go for a really good-quality dark eating (not baking) chocolate — the deliciousness of your truffles depends on it.

1. Melt chocolate in a double-boiler or in a glass bowl set above a pot of simmering water (just make sure the water does not touch the bottom of the bowl or the chocolate may overheat and risk becoming grainy), whilst stirring every now and again. Alternatively, melt chocolate in the microwave for 1–2 minutes, stirring every 30 seconds or so, until almost melted, then stir until smooth and glossy.

2. Place avocado, cream or coconut cream, maple syrup, cocoa and melted chocolate in a food processor and blend together until smooth. Transfer to a bowl and refrigerate for at least 1–2 hours to firm up.

3. When the mixture is firm, but still mouldable, remove from the fridge. Sieve extra cocoa onto a plate. Roughly shape teaspoon-sized balls of mixture to form even-sized truffles. Roll in cocoa and place on a plate or tray. Place back in the fridge to set, and store in an airtight container in the fridge until ready to eat. They'll last, refrigerated, for 2–3 days.

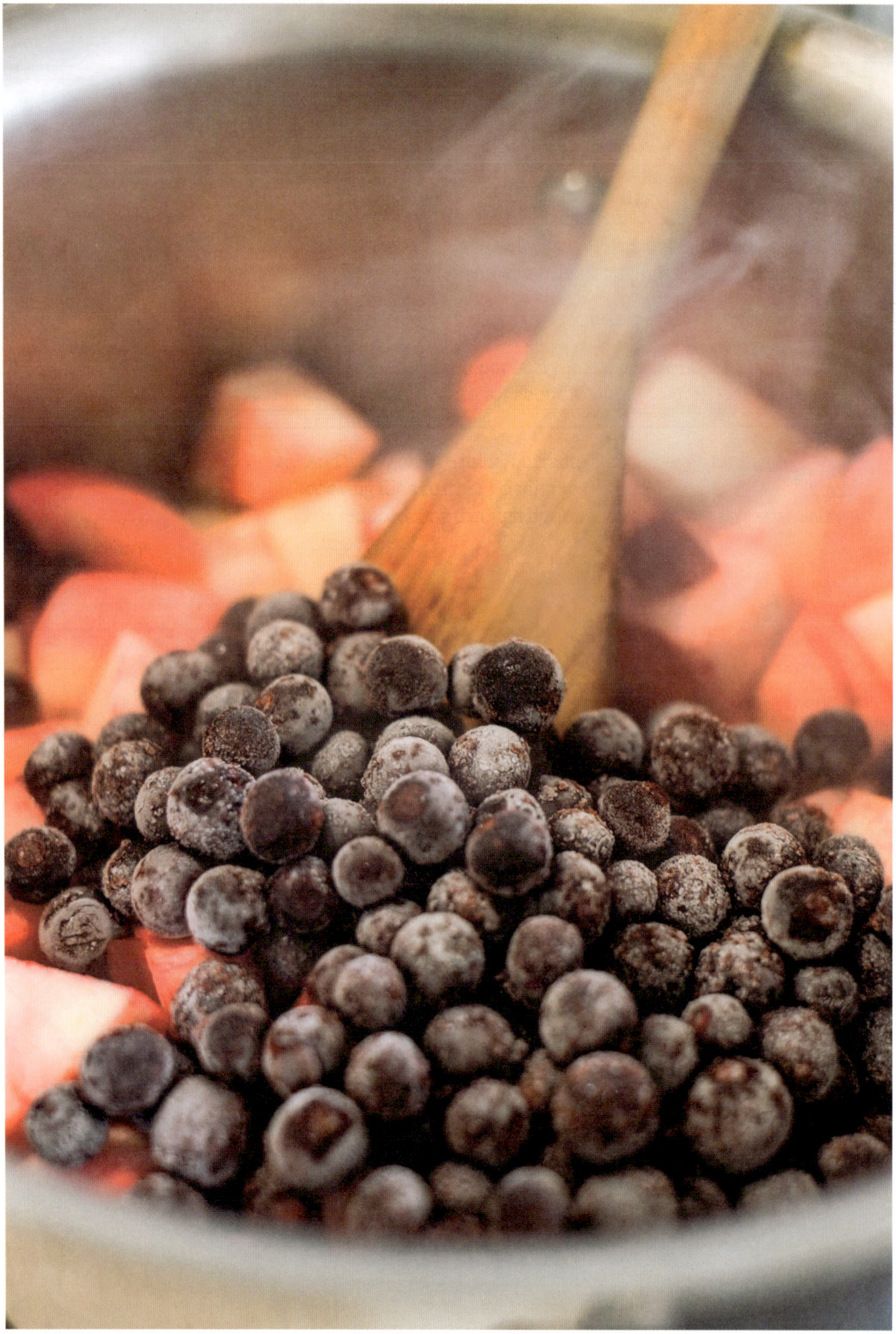

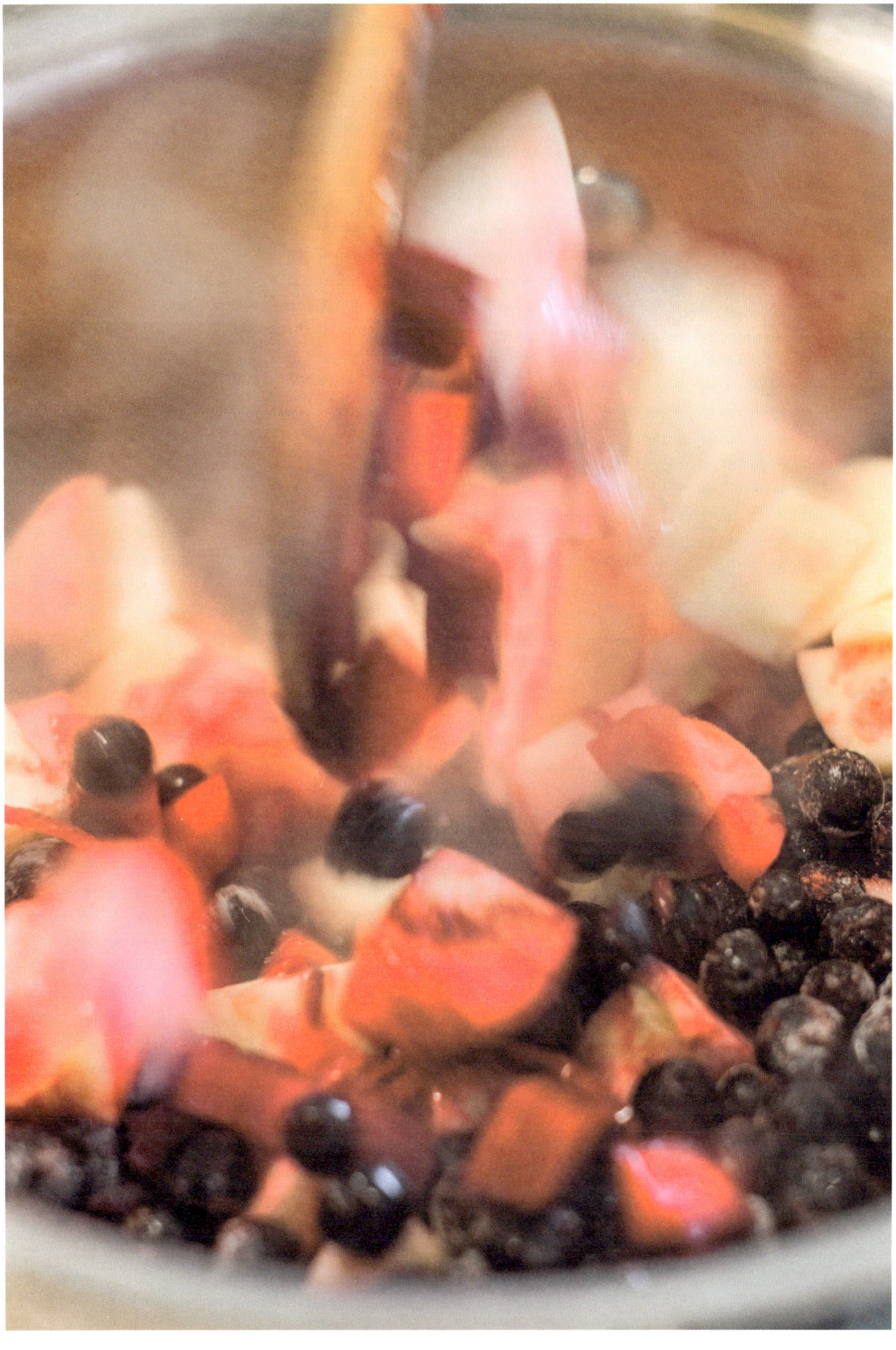

GF | DF | VEGAN

CARROT, BEETROOT, APPLE & BLACKCURRANT COMPÔTE

SERVES 6–8
Prep time: 15 minutes
Cook time: 10 minutes

1 medium carrot, peeled and diced 1cm
1 medium beetroot, peeled and diced 1cm
zest and juice of 1 lemon
2 cinnamon sticks
¼ cup water
6 apples (e.g. Braeburn or Royal Gala), cored, peeled and chopped
1½–2 cups frozen blackcurrants (or you could use raspberries)
3–4 tablespoons sugar, honey or maple syrup, to taste

Yes, you can add beetroot and carrot to your stewed fruit compôte — and it's delicious. When you think about it, it's not that surprising as beetroot and carrot are naturally sweet anyway. This is divine on your muesli, porridge, pancakes… you name it. Or use it in the crumble over on the next page. What a delicious way to get more veg in!

1. Combine carrot, beetroot, lemon zest and juice, cinnamon sticks and water in a medium to large pot. Cover and bring to a simmer. Cook on medium heat for about 3 minutes.

2. Add apples and blackcurrants, stir, and continue to cook, partially covered, for about 10 minutes or until fruit has softened. Sweeten to taste with sugar or honey. Leave cinnamon sticks in to infuse. Will keep in the fridge for up to 1 week.

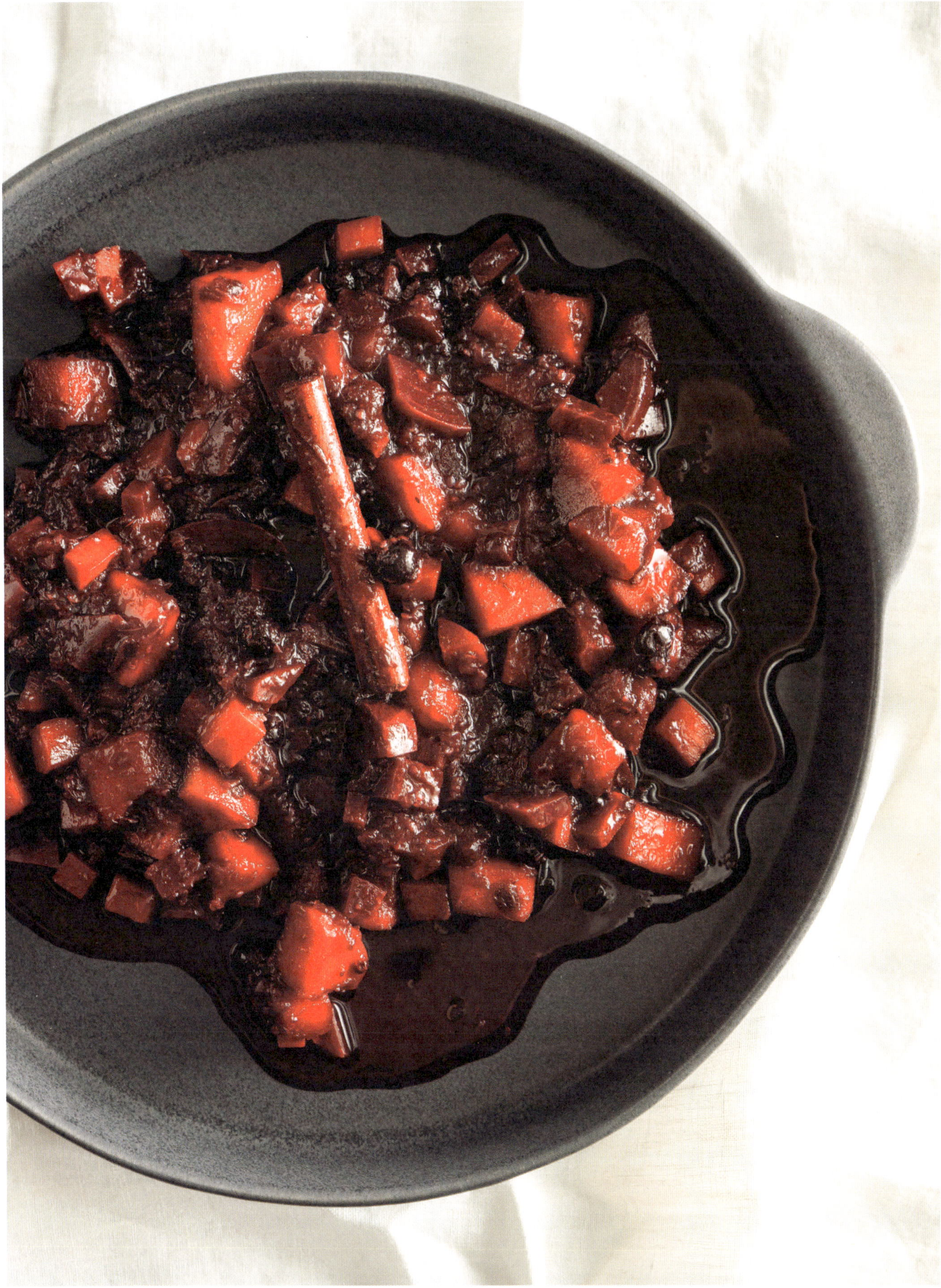

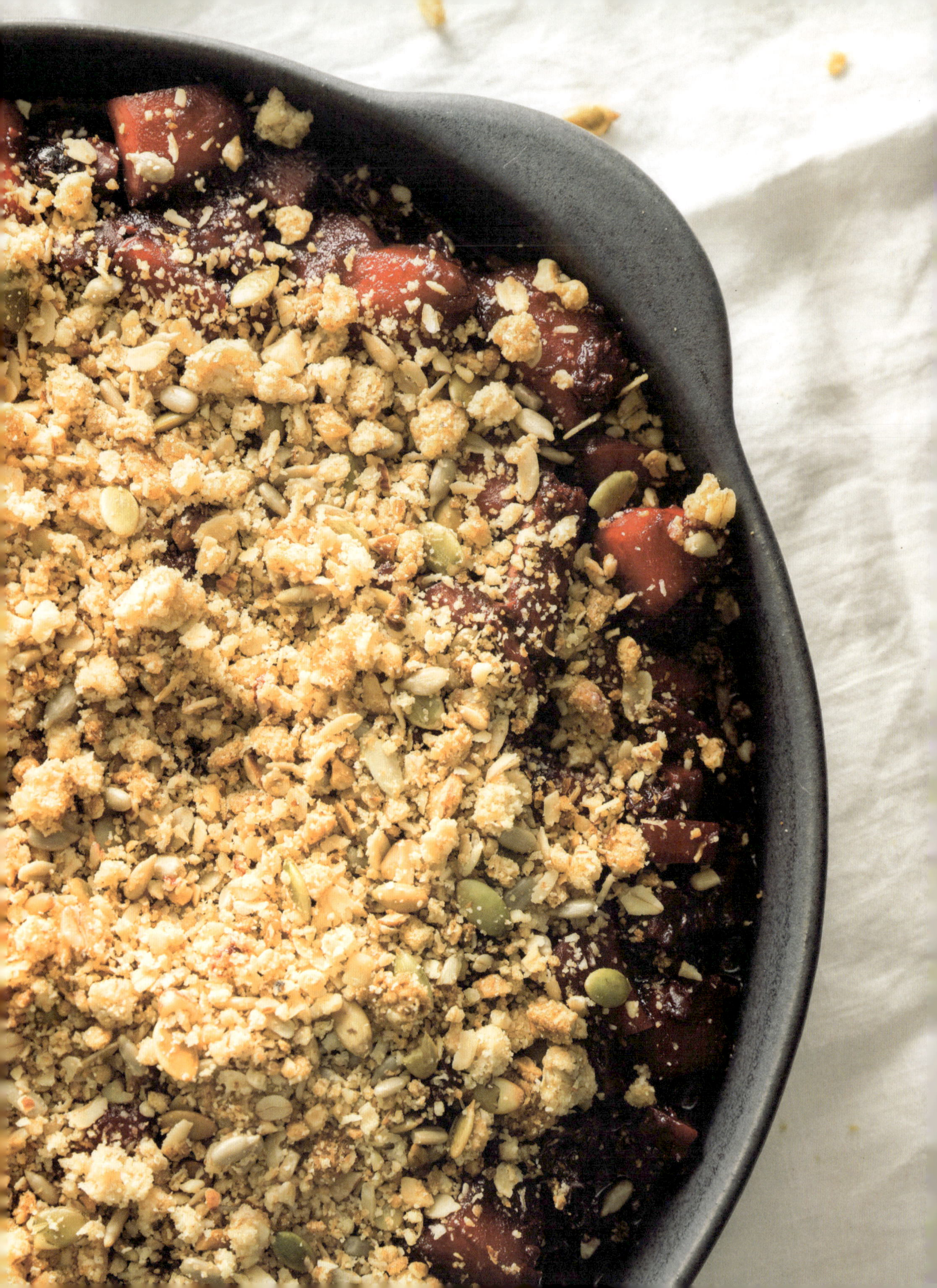

DF use coconut oil instead of butter | VEGAN use coconut oil instead of butter

SEED & NUT CRUMBLE

SERVES 6–8
Prep time: 10 minutes
Cook time: 15–20 minutes

75g butter
½ cup ground almonds or plain flour
½ cup rolled oats
¼ cup desiccated coconut
½ cup nuts (e.g. macadamias, walnuts, pecans, almonds), finely chopped
¼ cup brown sugar or maple syrup
¼ cup sunflower seeds
¼ cup pumpkin seeds
4 – 6 cups stewed fruit or Carrot, Beetroot, Apple and Blackcurrant Compôte (page 268)

This might be the best crumble topping ever — full of nuts and seeds and super light, crisp and crumbly… the trick is baking the crumble topping separately before sprinkling it over the top of the filling to avoid any soggy crumble. Use as the crumble topping for any stewed fruit or the Carrot, Beetroot, Apple and Blackcurrant Compôte on the previous page and serve with ice cream, yoghurt or cream (I like a mix of whipped cream and yoghurt sweetened with maple syrup and cinnamon).

1. Preheat oven to 180°C. In a medium-sized mixing bowl, rub the butter into the ground almonds/flour and oats with your fingertips until it resembles the texture of breadcrumbs. Then add remaining ingredients and mix well to combine. Alternatively add all ingredients, except sunflower and pumpkin seeds, to a food processor and blitz until crumbly, then pulse in seeds briefly to mix.

2. Spread crumble on an oven tray and bake for 10–15 minutes until golden and crunchy.

3. Toss on the tray. Sprinkle on top of hot stewed fruit or compôte filling and return to oven for a few more minutes to warm through. Serve warm with ice cream, yoghurt or cream.

GF | DF | VEGAN

FLASH-ROASTED RHUBARB & STRAWBERRIES

SERVES 6
Prep time: 5 minutes
Cook time: 10-15 minutes

4 large stalks rhubarb, cut into 3-4cm lengths
400-500g strawberries, hulled and cut in half
3 tablespoons caster sugar
1 orange

Rhubarb and strawberries take really well to being roasted, going soft, juicy and creating a sweet fragrant syrup of their own. They are divine by themselves with just a dollop of cream, or Sweet Cashew Cream (page 217) for a vegan dessert.

1. Preheat oven to 200°C. In a baking dish, toss together rhubarb, strawberries and sugar.

2. Roast for 10-15 minutes until rhubarb is tender (test with the sharp tip of a knife).

3. Cut orange in half and squeeze over fruit in the baking dish. Allow fruit to cool.

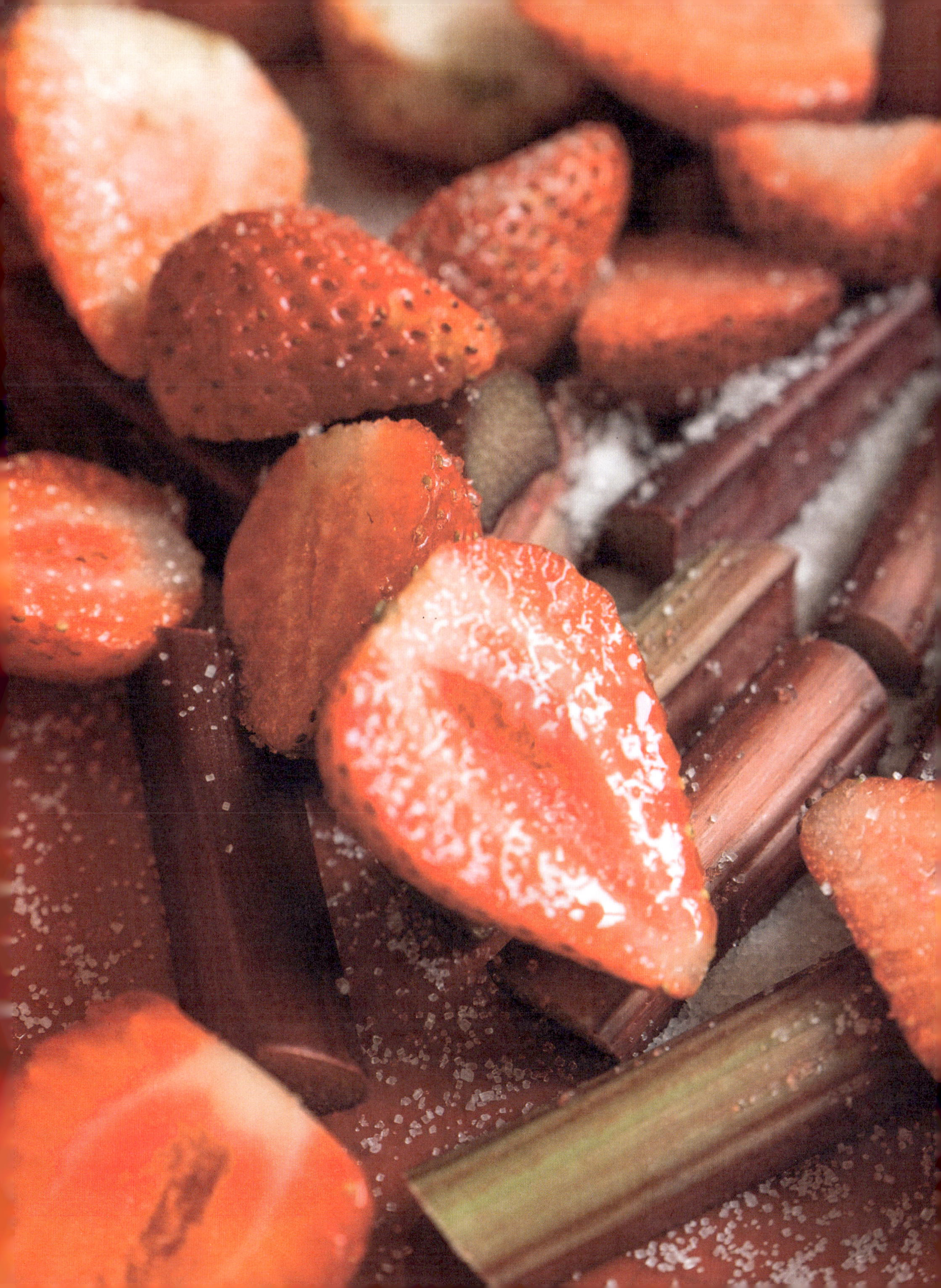

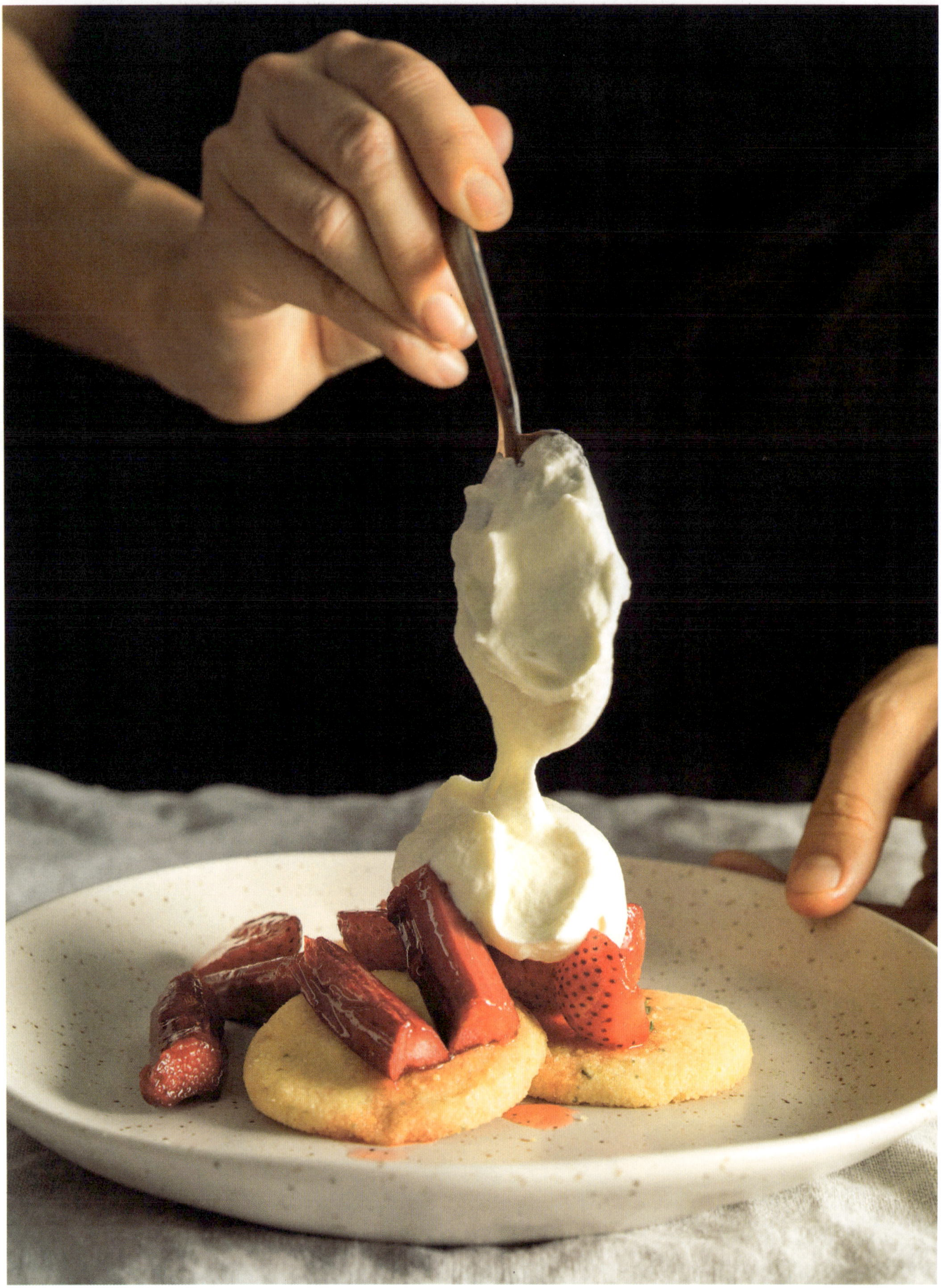

RHUBARB, STRAWBS 'N' CREAM LOADED SHORTBREAD

SERVES 6
Prep time: 10 minutes

500ml cream
2 tablespoons icing sugar
1 teaspoon vanilla bean paste or seeds of 1 vanilla bean pod
12–18 Thyme and Lemon Shortbread (page 278)
1 quantity Flash-Roasted Rhubarb and Strawberries (page 273)

Dessert doesn't get any better than this. The combination of crisp, crumbly thyme and lemon shortbread, juicy, sweet, fragrant roasted rhubarb and strawberries and whipped cream is simply heavenly. All I can say is be generous with the fruit and cream!

1. Whip cream to soft peaks, then fold in icing sugar and vanilla.

2. To serve, divide shortbread between plates and top with a generous amount of whipped cream and Flash-Roasted Rhubarb and Strawberries. Drizzle with syrup from the roasted fruit.

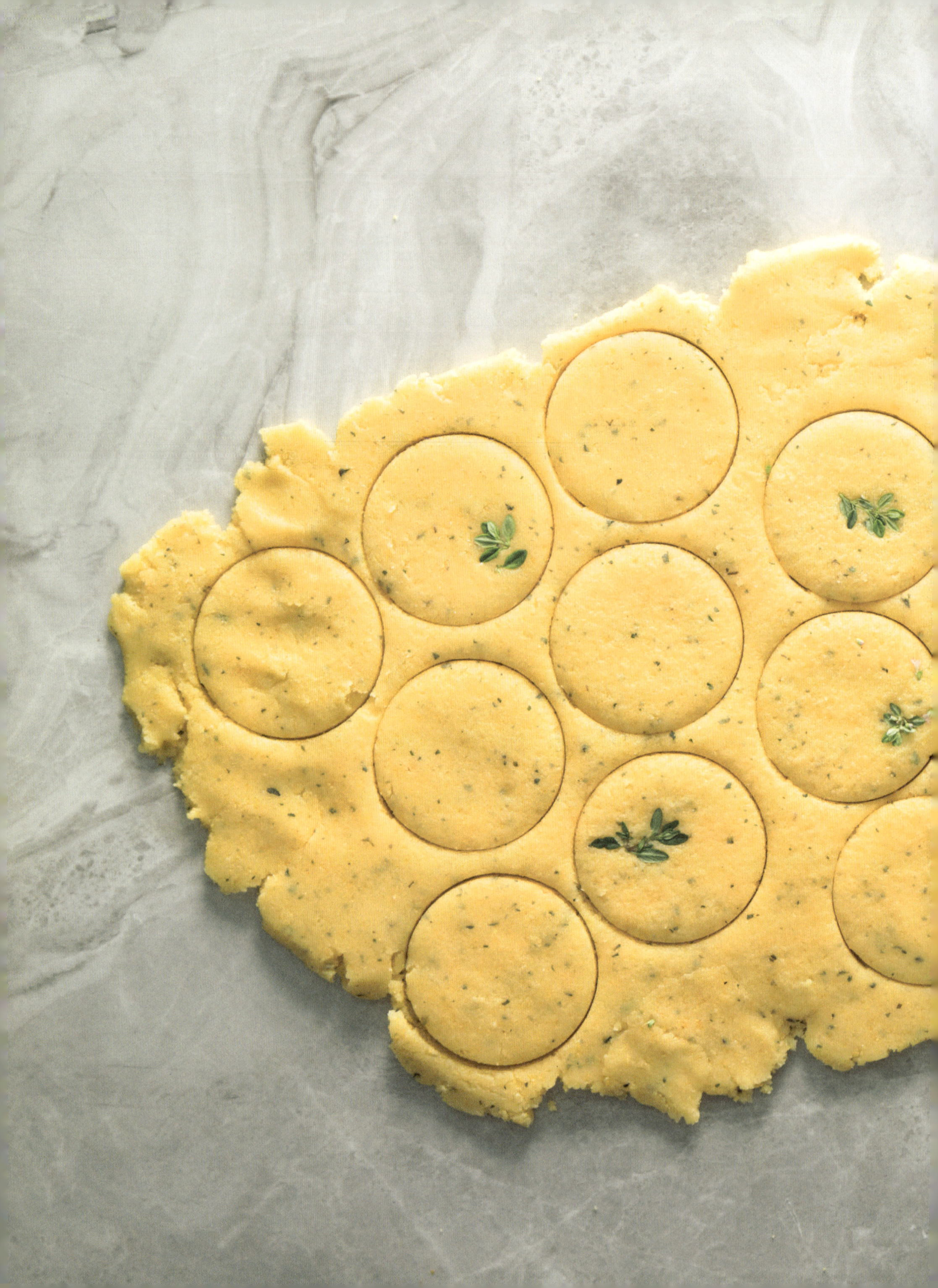

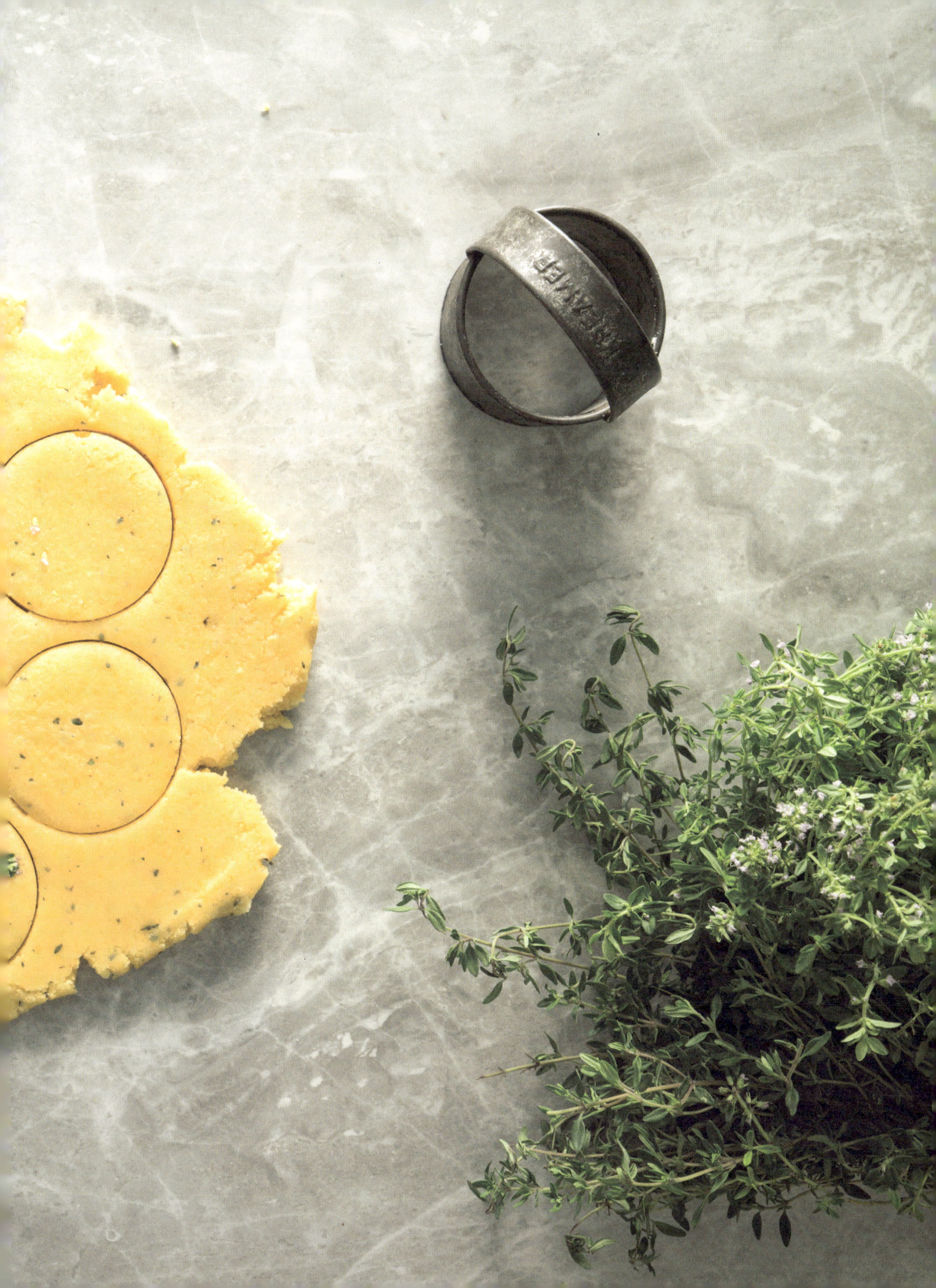

THYME & LEMON SHORTBREAD

MAKES ABOUT 18 SHORTBREAD
Prep time: 20 minutes
Cook time: 20–25 minutes

175g plain flour
⅓ cup caster sugar
75g fine polenta or semolina
1 free-range egg yolk
finely grated zest of 1 lemon
2–3 teaspoons finely
　chopped thyme leaves
175g cold butter, cubed (see Tip)

These shortbread are buttery, delicate, crumbly and crisp and spiked with lemon and thyme. Read the tips below for making the perfect shortbread.

1. Preheat oven to 150°C. Line two baking trays with baking paper.

2. Combine flour, caster sugar, polenta/semolina, egg yolk, lemon zest and thyme in a large bowl. Add butter and use your fingertips to gently rub it in until mixture resembles fine breadcrumbs. Alternatively, place ingredients in a food processor and pulse until mixture resembles breadcrumbs.

3. Bring dough together with your hands and shape into two balls. Wrap balls in clingfilm and refrigerate for 5 minutes to firm up a little.

4. On a clean, dry, lightly floured surface, roll a ball of dough out to 0.5–0.75cm thickness. Use a cookie cutter (approximately 6cm diameter) to cut into rounds. Whilst quite delicate to work with, shortbread dough is very forgiving. So, if the mixture starts crumbling or breaking up, don't fret as you can just press and patch it back together with your fingers — you can even add leftover bits of dough to help patch up cracked bits!

5. Transfer to the prepared trays with the help of a metal fish slice or edge of a knife. Bake for 20–25 minutes or until shortbread is light golden around the edges. Swap the trays around halfway through cook time, so that the batches cook evenly.

6. Remove from oven and allow to cool on the trays for a few minutes. Gently transfer shortbread to a wire rack to cool completely and let them crisp up. Store in an airtight container or cake tin — they will keep for a few weeks if they don't get gobbled up before!

Tips:
— The temperature of the butter is key — it must be cool or cold, not softened or melted, in order to get a flaky-textured shortbread.

— Avoid overmixing as it will result in a tough dough.

— It can help to put the (uncooked) shortbread in the fridge for about 15 minutes before baking to help create a crisp texture.

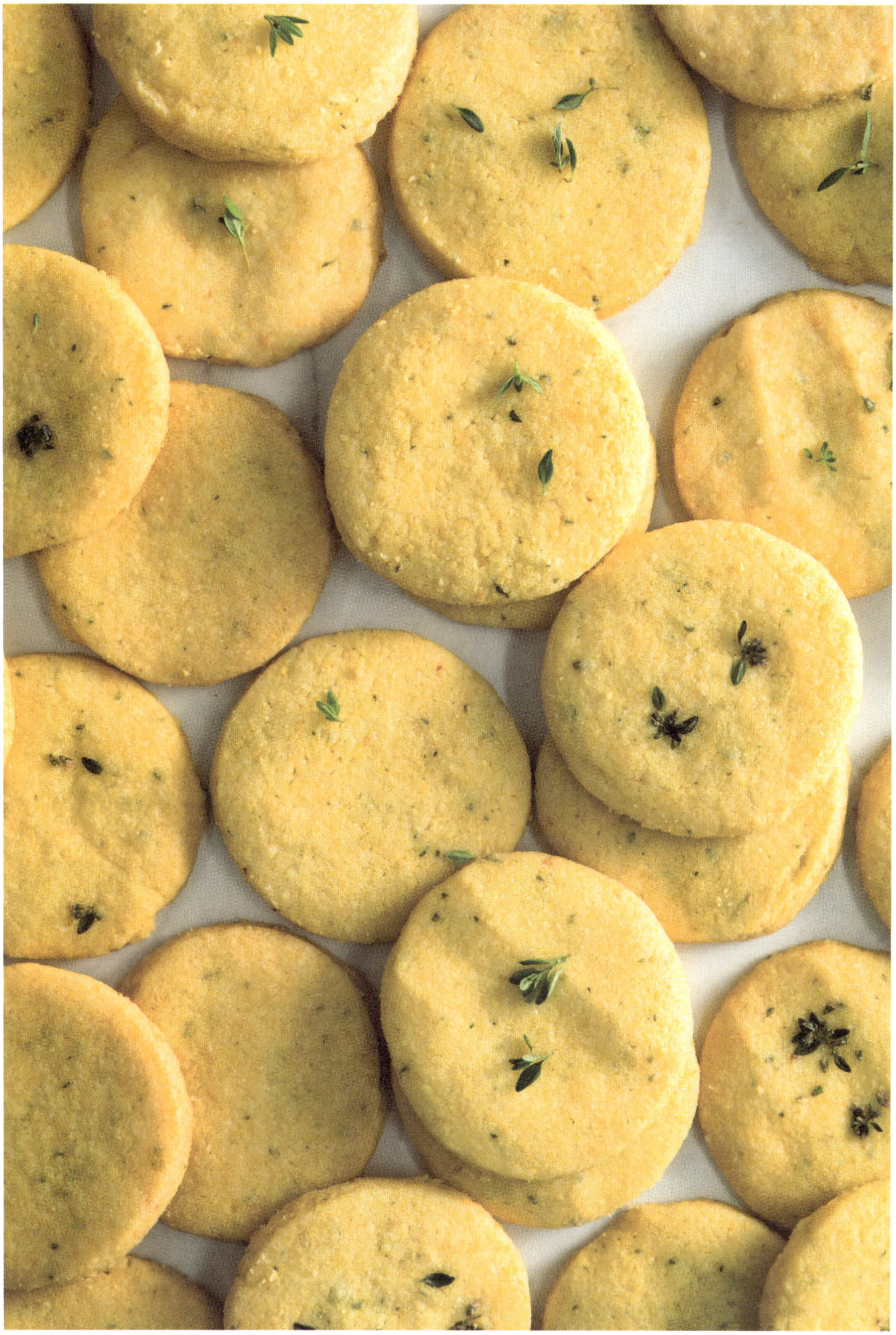

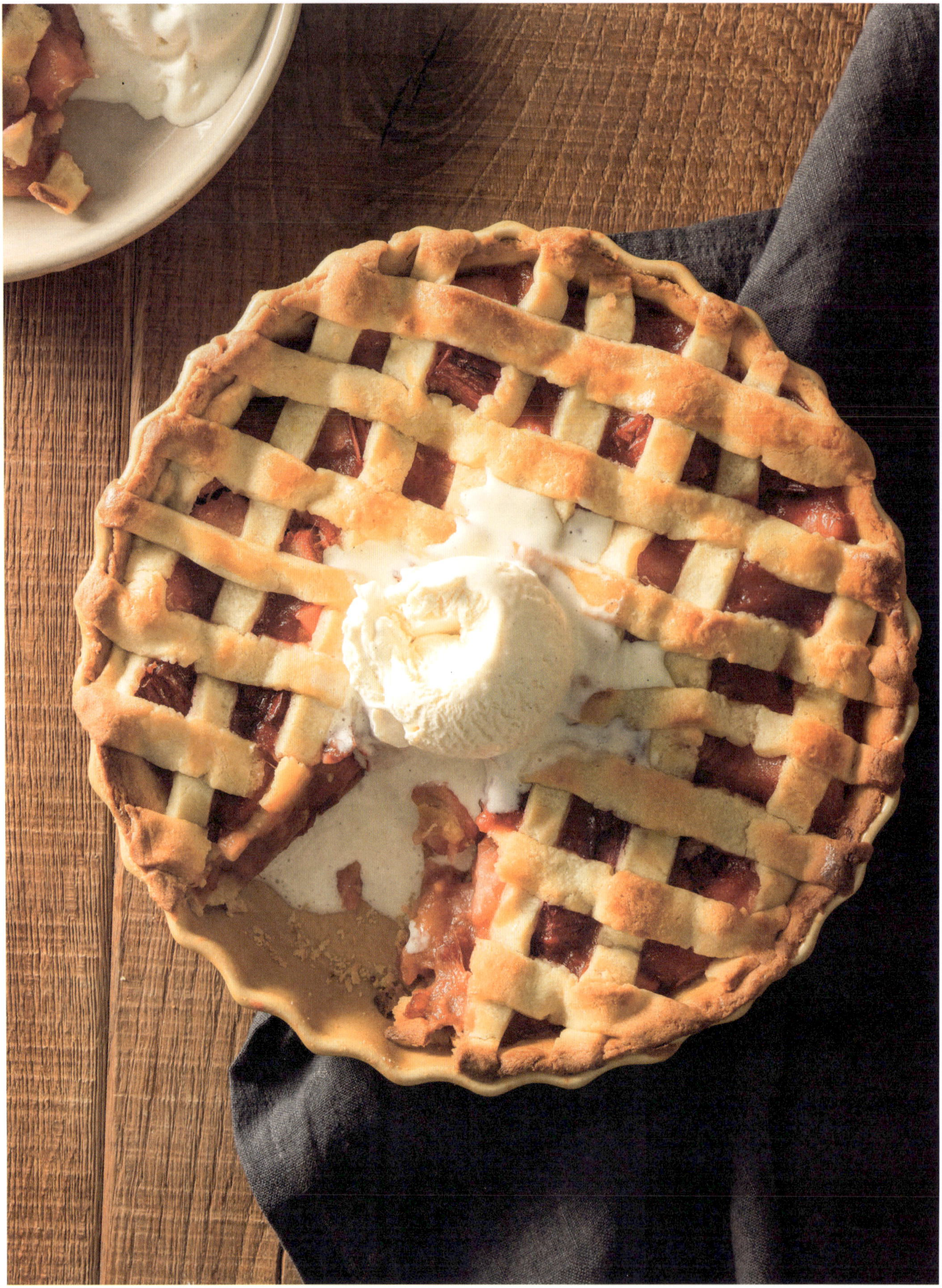

RHUBARB & APPLE PIE

SERVES 6–8
Prep time: 20 minutes
Cook time: 35–45 minutes

1½ tablespoons butter or coconut oil
4–5 large Granny Smith apples, peeled, cored and diced
4–5 large stalks rhubarb, diced 2cm
zest and juice of ½ orange
¼ teaspoon ground cinnamon
½ cup caster sugar
2 square sheets or 400–500g sweet shortcrust pastry divided into 2 portions
1 free-range egg
2 tablespoons milk

This rhubarb and apple pie is a hit with everyone, every time. It often comes out for dessert after a family Sunday dinner. It's easy to make and all you need to serve it with is some vanilla ice cream, or whipped cream or custard.

1. Preheat oven to 190°C.

2. Melt butter/coconut oil in a medium to large pot over medium heat. Add apple and cook for 4–5 minutes, stirring, until starting to soften, then add rhubarb, orange zest and juice and cinnamon. Continue cooking for a further 4–5 minutes until rhubarb is starting to soften. Stir in sugar until it has dissolved. Set aside to cool until you are ready to assemble the pie.

3. Roll out one sheet (or portion) of pastry on a clean, dry, flat surface to about 2–3mm thickness. Line a pie dish (about 25cm in diameter) with the pastry. Don't worry if it tears in places — shortcrust pastry is very forgiving, just squish and patch it back together. You may need to use some of the other sheet of pastry and bits of off-cuts to line the whole tin. Trim around the edges to create a neat flat edge. Whisk egg with milk in a small bowl. Prick pastry with a fork in a few places and brush with a little egg wash. Bake for about 15–20 minutes until golden. Remove pie base from oven and set aside to cool.

4. Fill pie base with cooled apple and rhubarb filling. Cut the remaining pastry into 1cm-thick strips and arrange on top of filling in a lattice.

5. Brush pastry lattice lightly with egg wash. Bake for 20–25 minutes or until pastry is crisp and golden. Serve warm with custard, ice cream or cream.

DF omit icing | VEGAN omit icing and use flax eggs

PARSNIP, PEAR, GINGER & WALNUT CAKE WITH CARAMEL CREAM CHEESE ICING

SERVES 10
Prep time: 35 minutes
Cook time: 40–45 minutes

1 large or 2 medium ripe pears, peeled
1 large or 2 medium parsnips, peeled
225g wholemeal flour
1 teaspoon baking powder
1½ teaspoons baking soda
1½ teaspoons ground cinnamon
1 teaspoon ground ginger
½ teaspoon salt
¾ cup desiccated coconut or ground almonds
3 large free-range eggs (or flax eggs, see page 291)
1 cup oil (e.g. sunflower or grapeseed)
1 cup golden syrup or maple syrup
zest of 1 lemon or orange + 2 tablespoons juice
1 tablespoon finely grated fresh ginger
¾ cup chopped walnuts

CARAMEL CREAM CHEESE ICING
50g unsalted butter, softened
125g softened cream cheese
2–3 tablespoons golden syrup or maple syrup
1 tablespoon brown sugar
½ teaspoon vanilla bean paste or extract

CANDIED MAPLE WALNUTS (OPTIONAL)
handful of walnuts
2–3 tablespoons maple syrup

This cake is up there with the best — super moist with loads of flavour. If you like carrot cake, then you'll love parsnip cake — as well as an earthy sweetness, parsnips have a slight creaminess to them. Just be sure to avoid grating too much of the tough inner core and use the surrounding creamy white flesh instead. It's a great cake to make in autumn and winter when parsnips are young and tender with creamy flesh, and pears are in season. The cake keeps well (in an airtight container, in a cool, dark place) for up to 5 days, with its flavour improving after a day or two. Feel free to mix and match pear for apple, and parsnip for carrot.

1. Preheat oven to 180°C. Grease and line a 23cm round spring-form cake tin with baking paper.

2. Grate pear and parsnip directly onto a clean tea towel, until you have approximately 1½ cups of each. Wring tea towel gently to squeeze out excess moisture.

3. Sift flour, baking powder, baking soda, spices and salt into a large bowl. Stir in coconut/ground almonds.

4. In a separate large bowl, whisk eggs, oil, golden/maple syrup, lemon/orange zest and juice, and fresh ginger together. Stir in grated pear and parsnip and walnuts.

5. Make a well in the flour and pour in wet mixture. Fold together with a large metal spoon until just combined (do not overmix), then pour into prepared tin. Bake for 40–45 minutes or until the cake springs back when lightly pressed in the centre.

6. Allow to cool in the tin for about 10 minutes before transferring to a wire rack to cool. Ice once cooled.

7. To make the Caramel Cream Cheese Icing, use an electric beater (or use a good amount of elbow grease) to beat all ingredients together in a mixing bowl until smooth, thick and creamy. Spread icing over the cake.

8. To make Candied Maple Walnuts, toast walnuts in a small fry pan (with no oil) on low to medium heat for a few minutes, then pour in maple syrup. Let it bubble, then turn off the heat and toss the walnuts in the maple glaze. Leave to cool before scattering over iced cake.

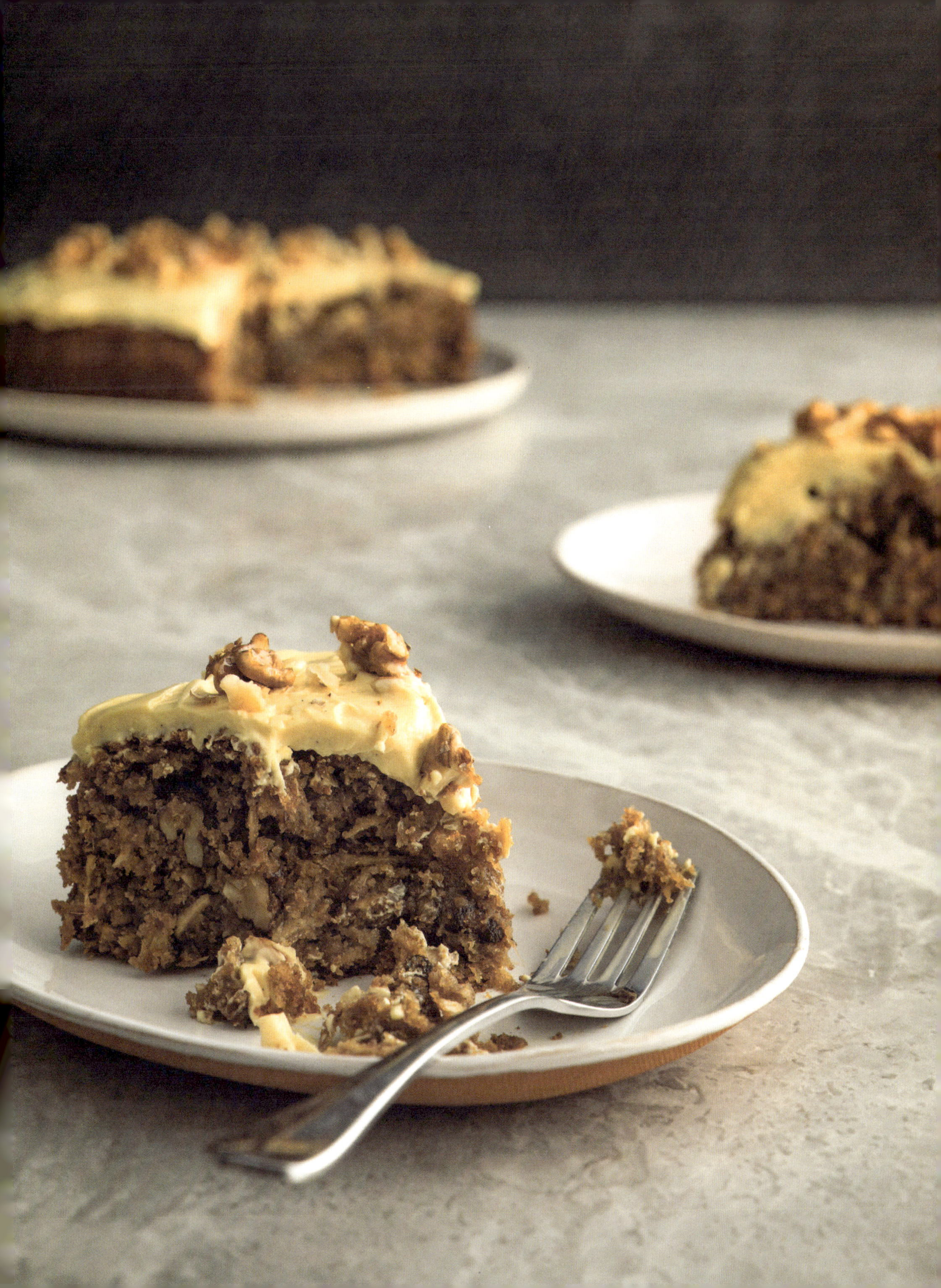

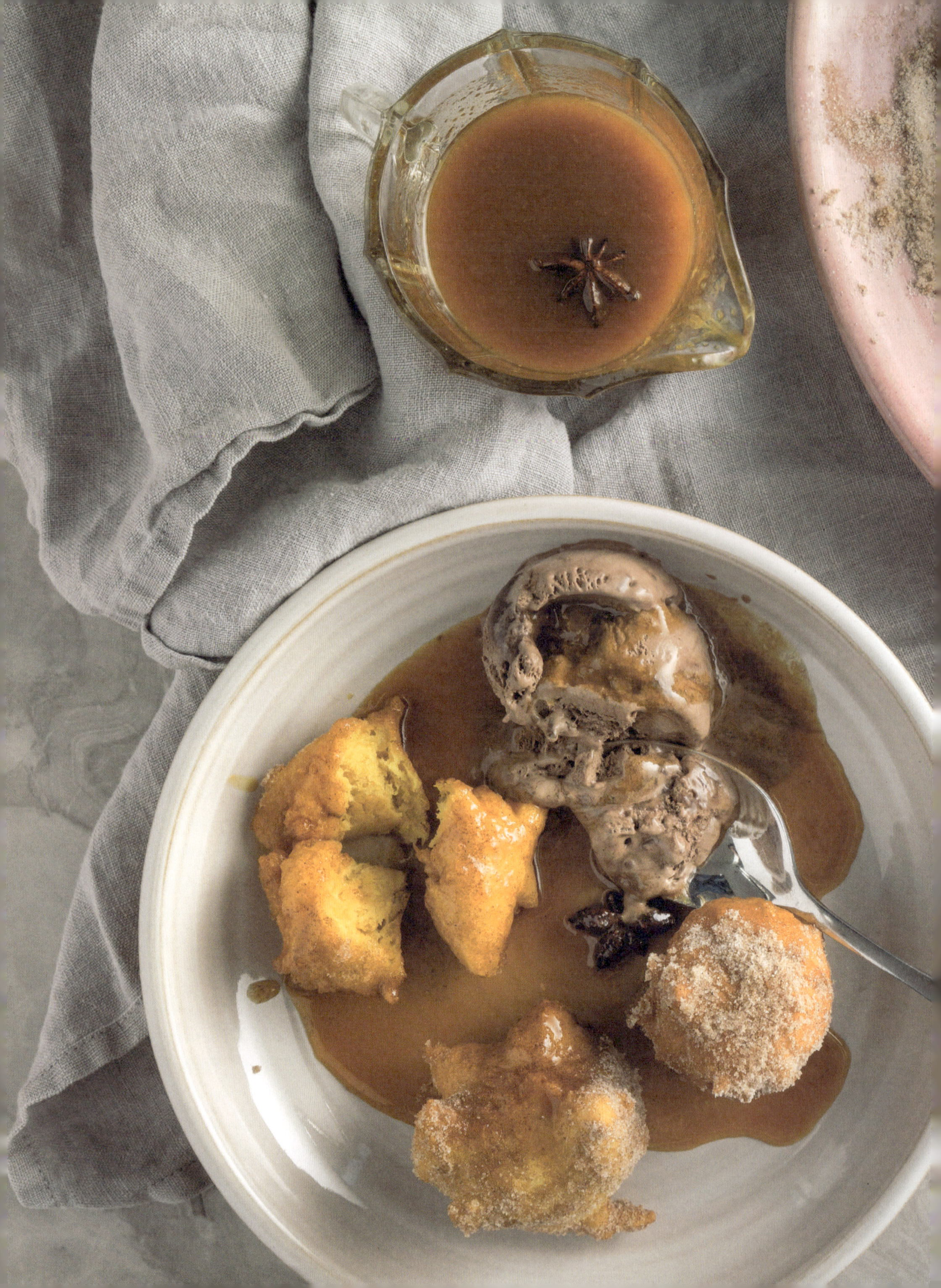

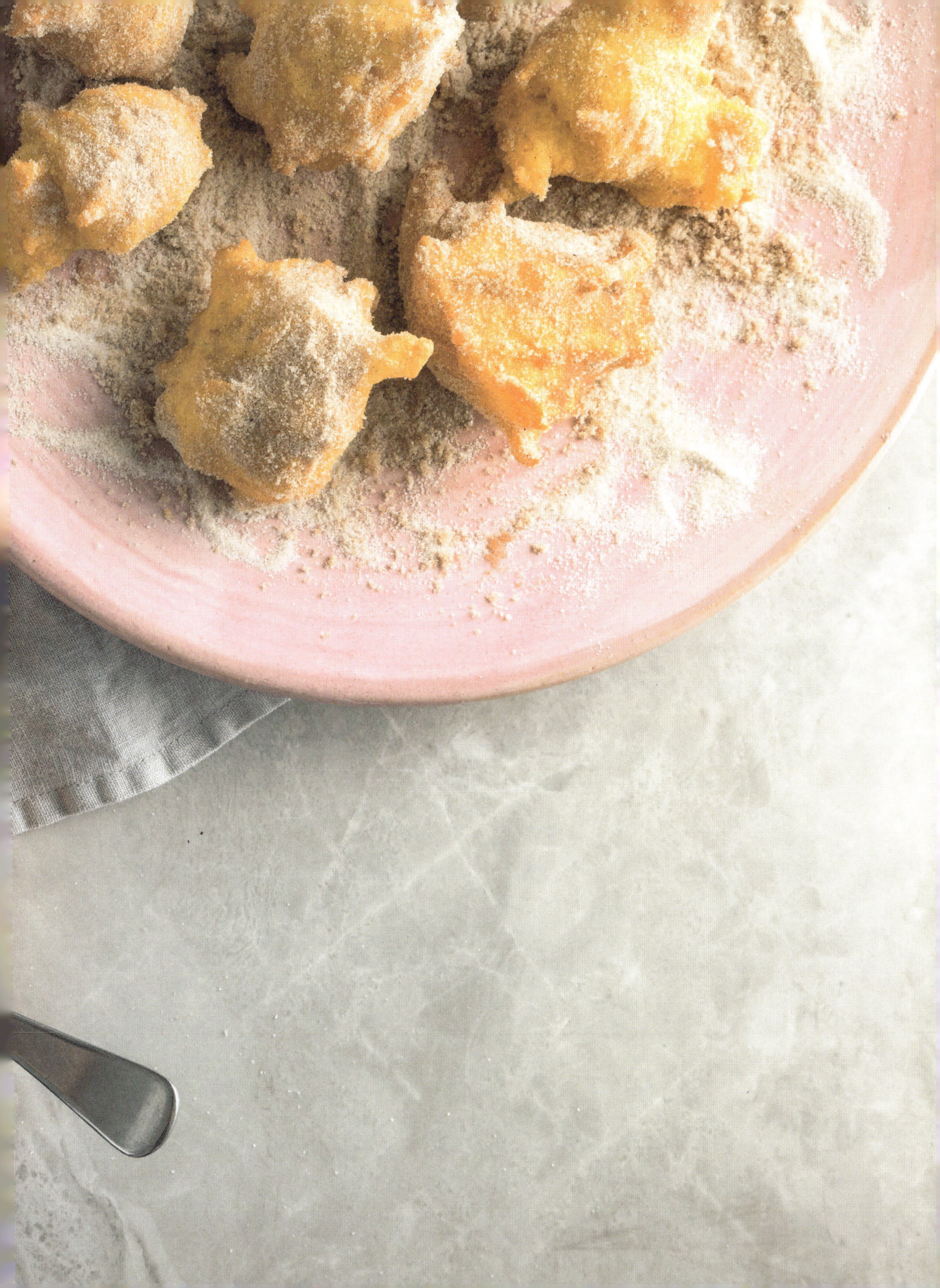

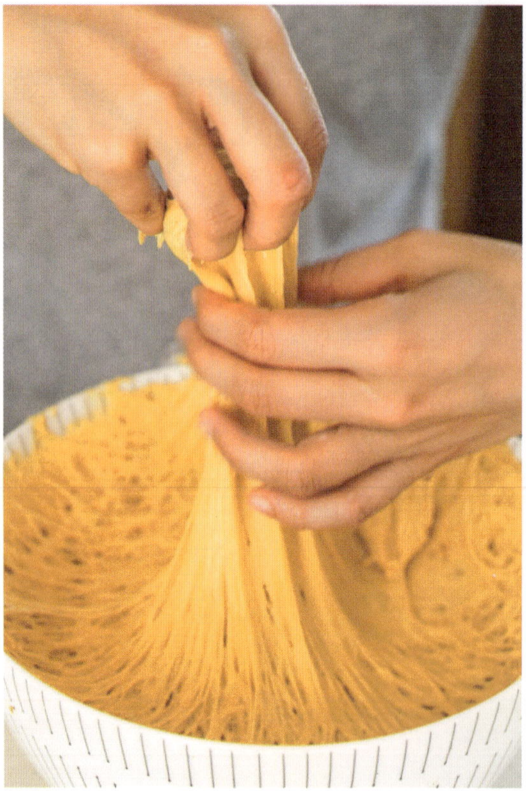
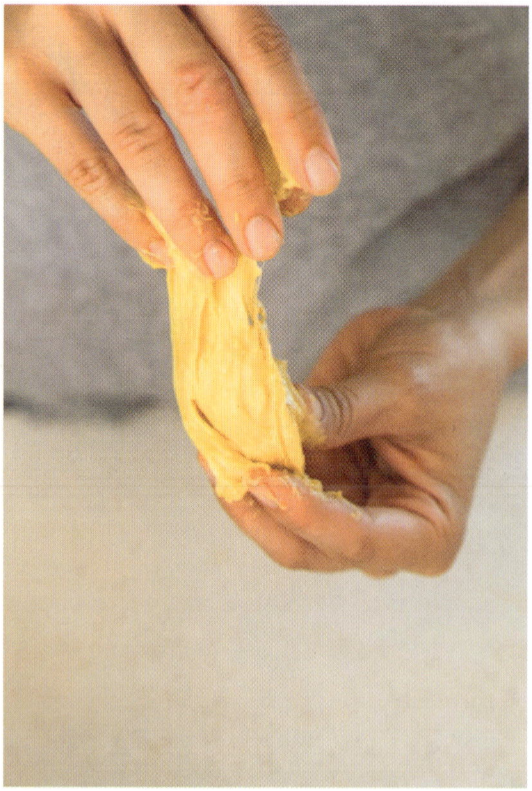
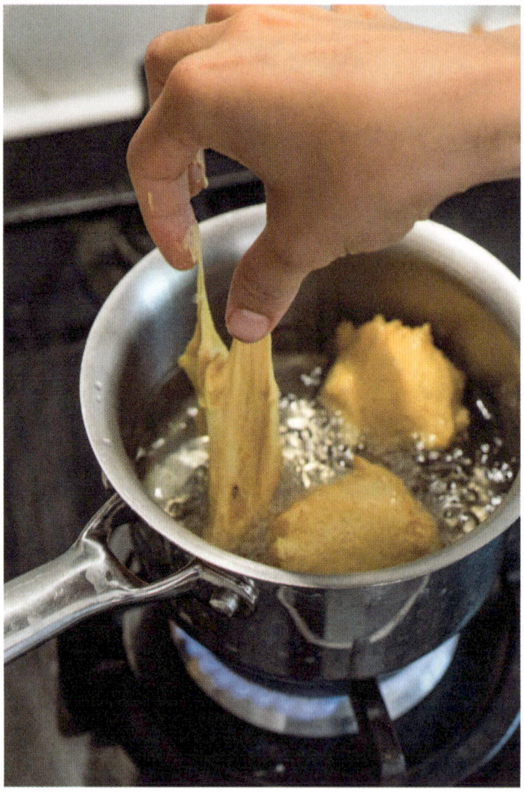
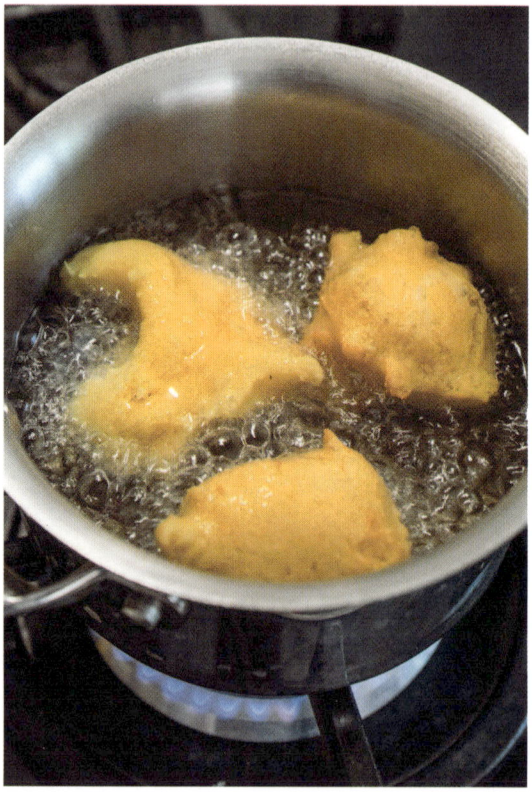

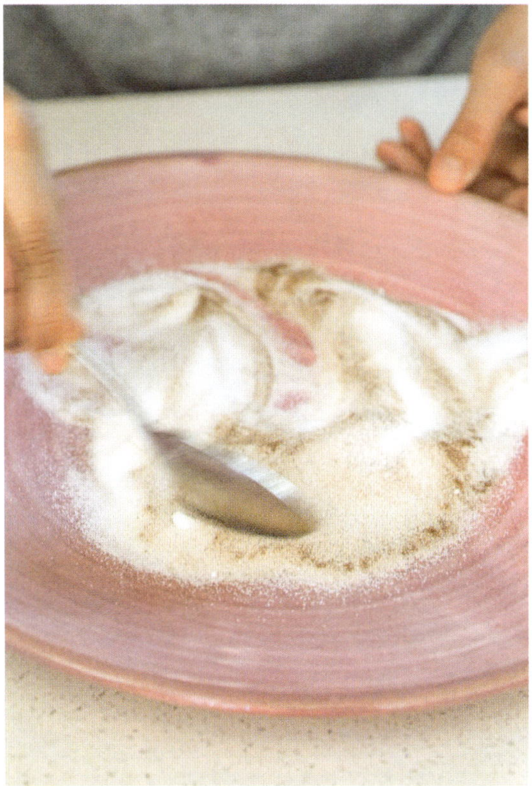
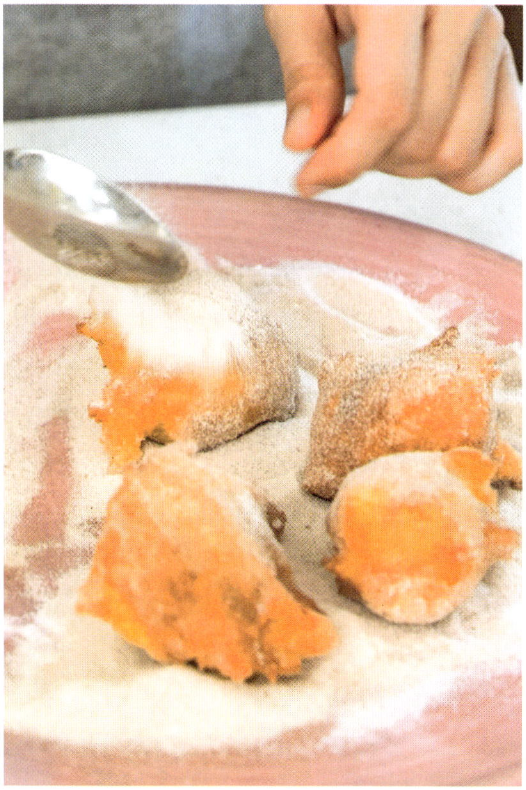
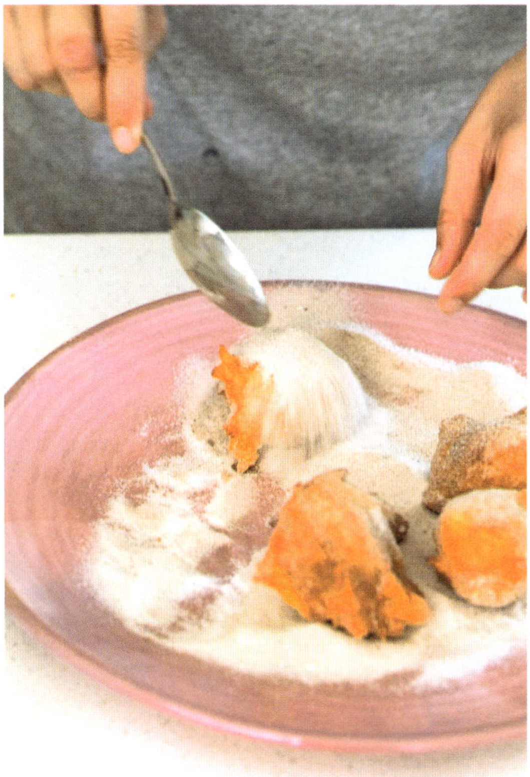
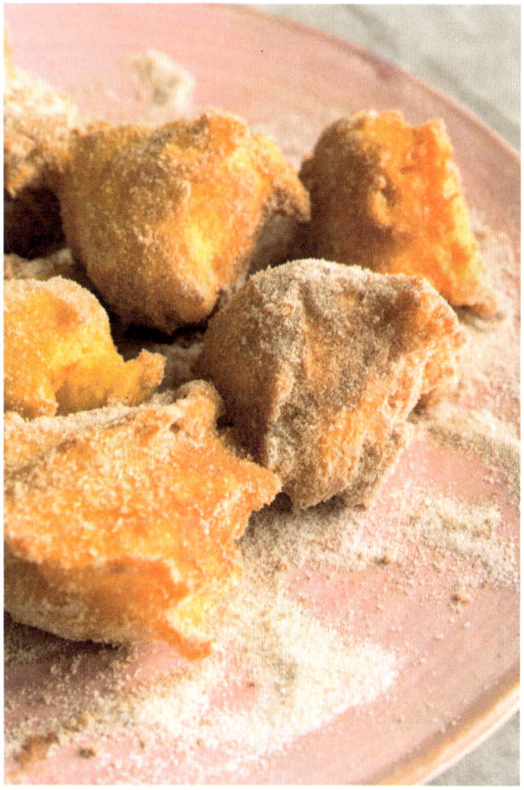

PUMPKIN & CINNAMON DONUTS

SERVES 8
Prep time: 15 minutes
(+ 2 hours or more to rise)
Cook time: 15–20 minutes

1 tablespoon active dried yeast
2 teaspoons caster sugar
½ cup warm water
2 free-range eggs, lightly whisked
½ teaspoon salt
1½ cups well-mashed roast pumpkin or orange kumara
3–4 cups self-raising flour
oil (e.g. canola, grapeseed, rice bran), for frying
½ cup caster sugar
2 teaspoons ground cinnamon

ORANGE CARAMEL SAUCE
3 tablespoons (45g) butter
2 tablespoons golden syrup
zest and juice of 1 orange
¼ cup brown sugar
2 tablespoons cream
pinch of flaky sea salt

Light fluffy donuts made with the addition of mashed pumpkin or orange kumara (sweet potato) doused in a caramel sauce (which I have spiked with orange, cinnamon and star anise) and served with ice cream. Drooool!

1. In a large mixing bowl, gently mix together yeast, 2 teaspoons sugar and warm water. Set aside in a warm place for about 10 minutes, or until frothy.

2. Add eggs, salt and mashed pumpkin/kumara and mix until combined.

3. Gradually add the flour (beginning with 3 cups), mixing until a smooth, sticky dough is formed. If the dough is very liquid, add a little more flour. Knead dough on a floured surface for 5–10 minutes (it doesn't matter if the dough is shaggy/sticky in texture and appearance), then cover and set aside in a warm place for about 2 hours (or up to 4 hours) until doubled in size.

4. On a plate, combine ½ cup sugar and cinnamon.

5. Once the dough is ready, heat about 6cm depth of oil in a small or medium-sized pot on medium heat. With wet hands, take small balls of dough (about the size of a walnut) and stretch them slightly so they are about 1cm thick, and carefully place in the hot oil — about 3–6 donuts can cook at the same time. Don't worry if you get all sorts of irregular/different shapes; lots of different-shaped donuts is cool! Cook for 1 minute or so until golden, then flip over with a metal spoon to continue cooking on the other side until golden and cooked through. Test one by breaking in half to ensure the dough is cooked all the way through and adjust cooking time as necessary. Briefly drain on paper towels before tossing in cinnamon sugar.

6. To make Orange Caramel Sauce, heat butter, golden syrup, orange zest and juice and brown sugar in a pot on medium heat. Simmer for 2–3 minutes, then remove from the heat and stir in cream and salt to taste. Set aside to cool.

7. Serve donuts warm, drizzled with Orange Caramel Sauce, vanilla or chocolate ice cream, custard or whipped cream.

Tip: The ideal frying temperature is 175°C; however if, like me, you don't have a thermometer, you can test it is the right temperature by adding a small piece of dough to the oil. If it floats and starts bubbling, and browns in 50–60 seconds, the oil is at the right temperature.

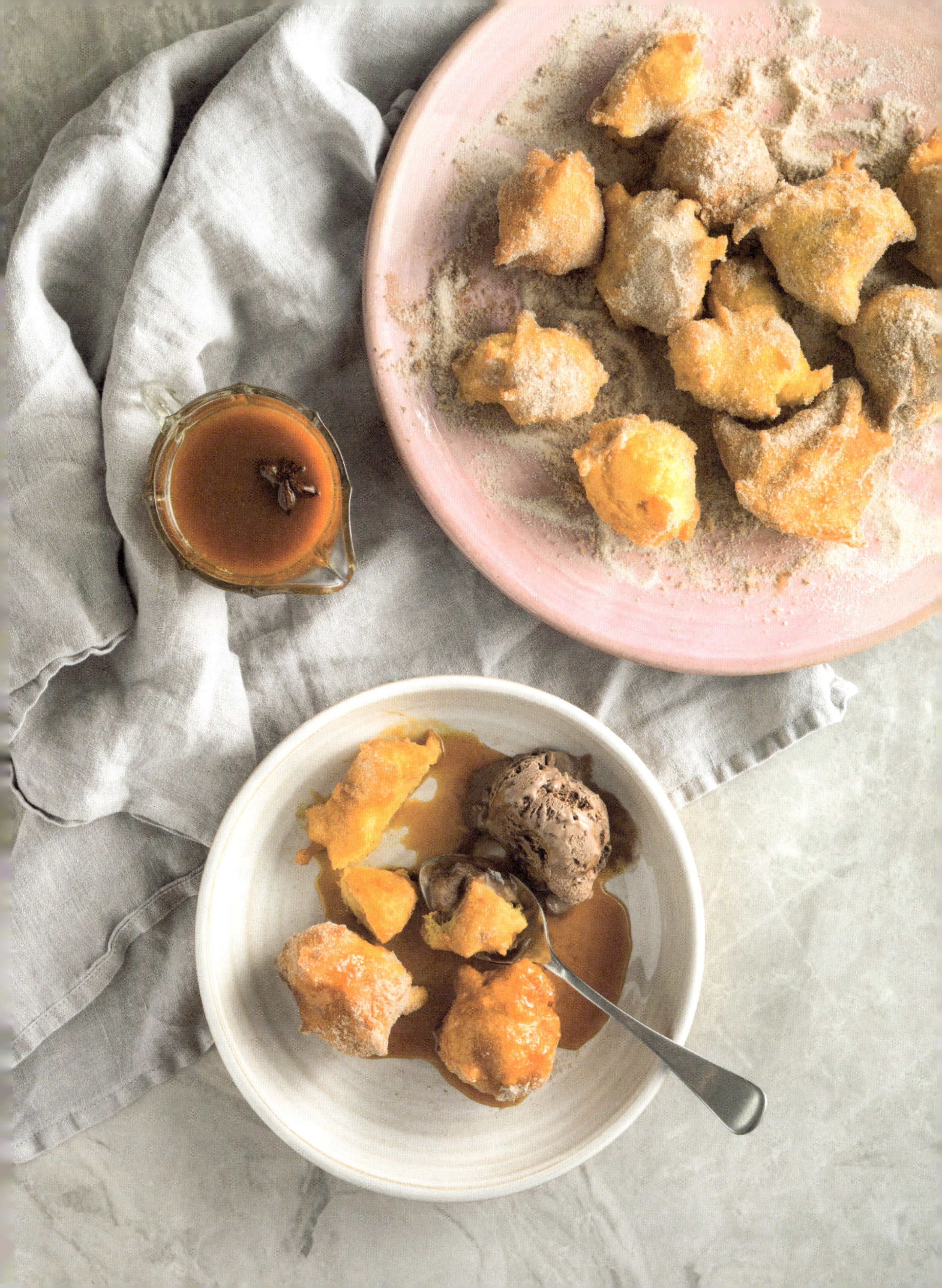

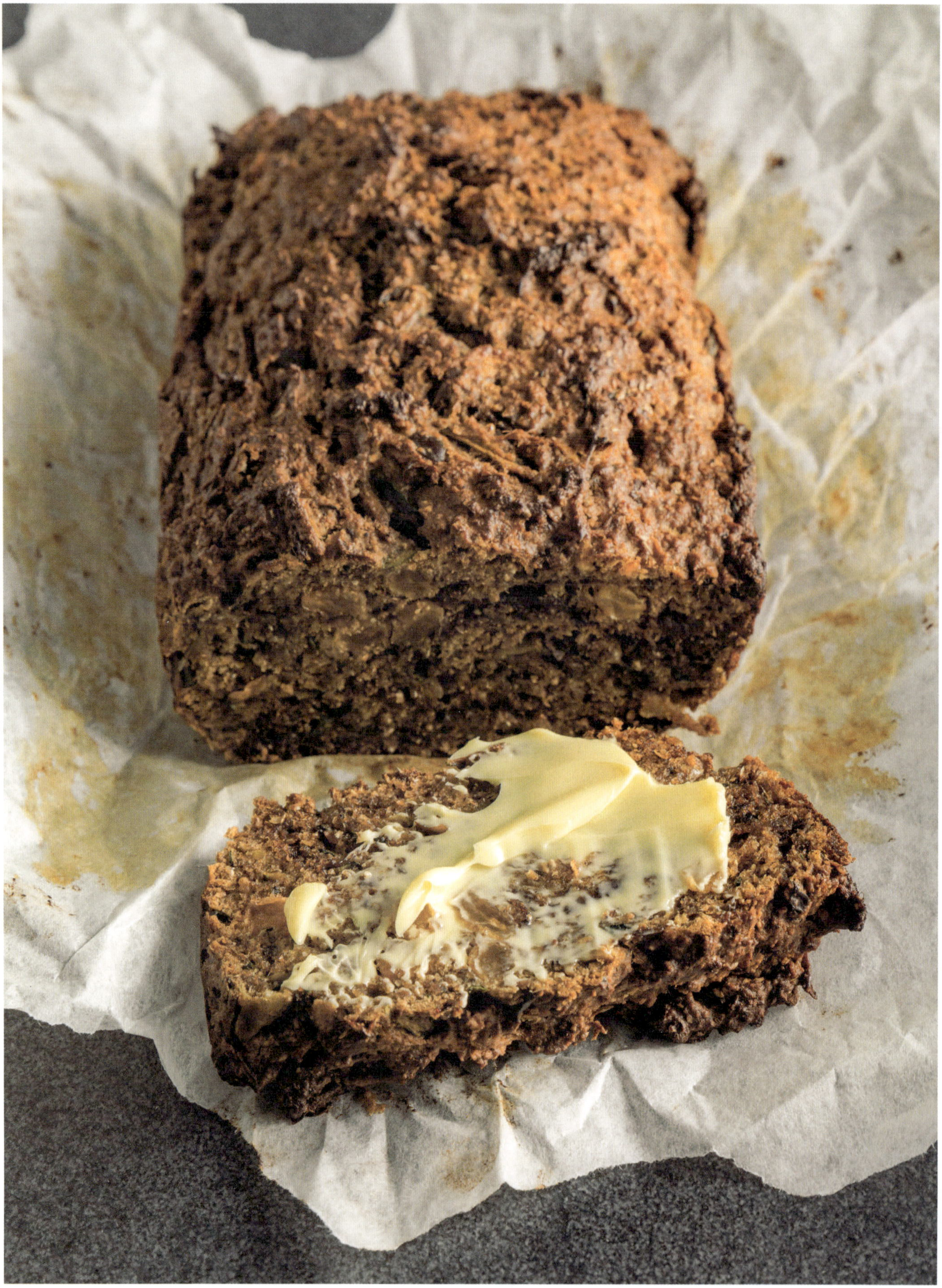

DF use coconut oil instead of butter |
VEGAN use coconut oil and flax eggs

SPICED COURGETTE, DATE & APPLE TEA LOAF

SERVES 10-12
Prep time: 20 minutes
Cook time: 1 hour

1 cup (175g) pitted dates
¼ cup water
1½ teaspoons baking soda
100g softened butter
2 tablespoons golden syrup or brown sugar
200g courgettes
200g apples (I like to use Braeburn)
2 teaspoons mixed spice
½ teaspoon ground cardamom or ginger or cinnamon
zest of 1 lemon
3 free-range eggs (or flax eggs, see below)
½ cup golden raisins or sultanas (or, for a less sweet version, use pumpkin and sunflower seeds)
1 cup (100g) ground almonds
150g wholemeal flour
1 teaspoon baking powder
¼ teaspoon salt

This is a lovely loaf to have with a cup of tea and have handy for guests. You can also use grated carrot or butternut in place of the courgette. It keeps (in an airtight container, in a cool, dark place) for up to 5 days or freeze in slices.

1. Preheat oven to 180°C. Line a large (8 cup capacity) loaf tin with baking paper.
2. Place dates and water in a medium pot. Boil for a few minutes until soft and mash with a potato masher until mushy. Stir in baking soda; it will froth a little.
3. Add butter and golden syrup/brown sugar and mix until well combined.
4. Grate courgette and apple directly onto a clean tea towel, then wring to squeeze out excess moisture.
5. Add courgette, apple and all remaining ingredients to date mixture. Stir until just combined — be careful not to overmix.
6. Spoon into prepared tin. Bake for 50 minutes to 1 hour or until a skewer inserted into the middle of the loaf comes out clean. Remove from oven and stand in tin for 10 minutes before transferring to a wire rack to cool.

FLAX EGGS

MAKES 1 FLAX EGG

1 tablespoon ground flaxseed (linseed)
2½ tablespoons hot water

Flax eggs make a great vegan replacement to eggs as a binder in lots of baking recipes such as muffins, loaves, pikelets and some cakes. One flax egg is equivalent to one egg.

1. To make a flax egg, simply mix ground flaxseed (linseed) with hot water for 1–2 minutes until it becomes gelatinous.

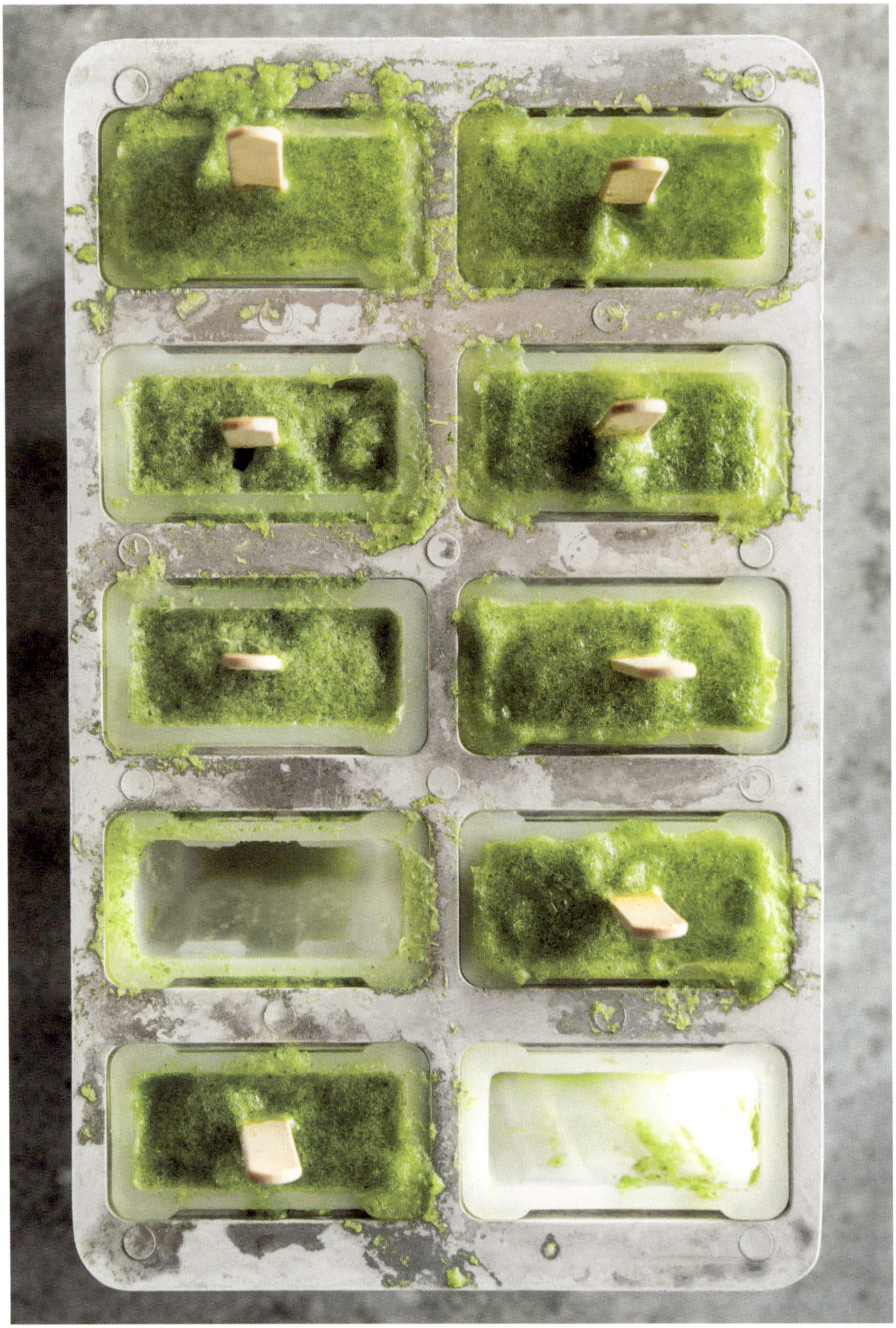

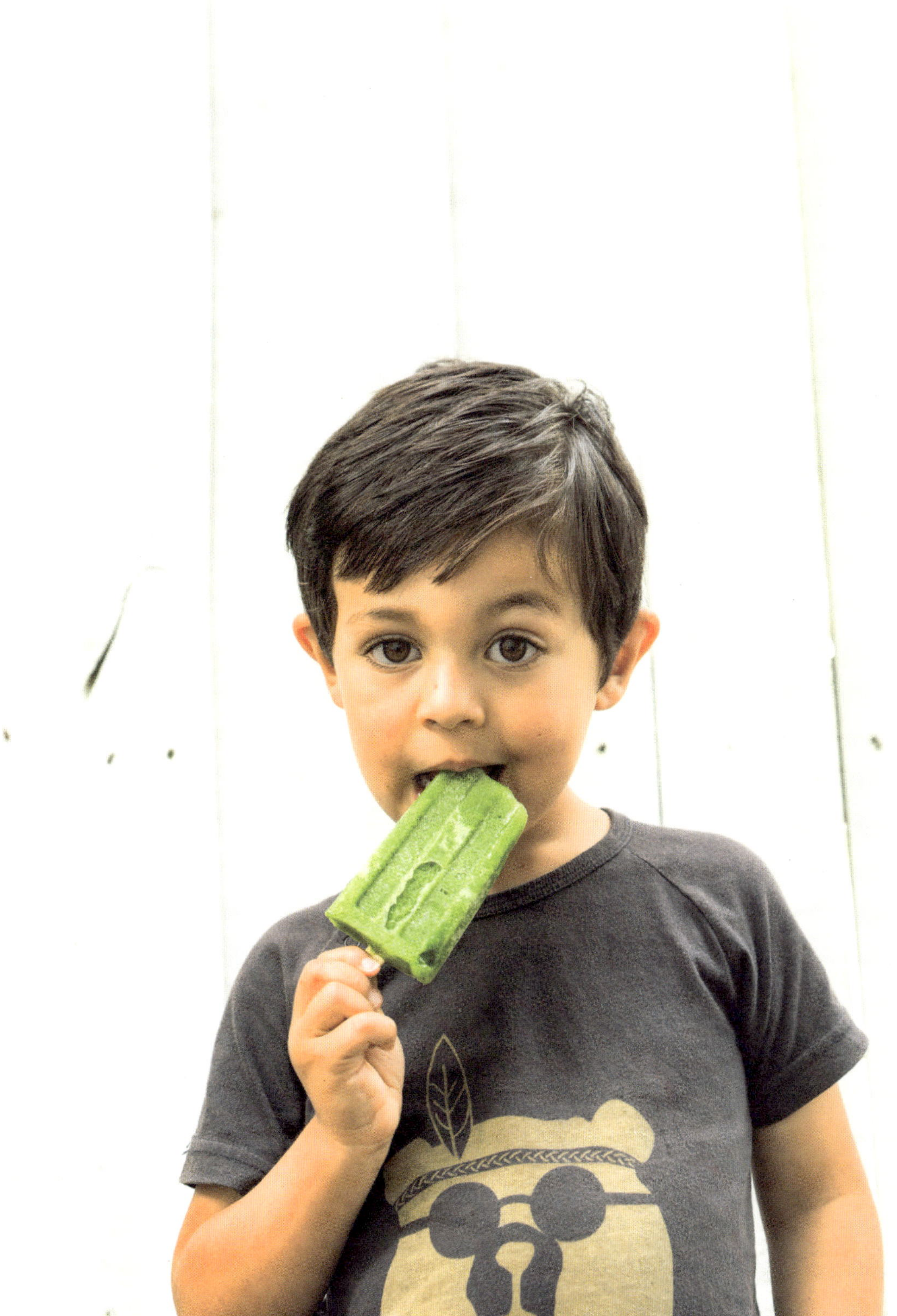

GF | DF | VEGAN

VEGGIE POPS

MAKES 8–10 ICE BLOCKS
Prep time: 10 minutes

½ ripe pineapple, skin cut off, cored and chopped
1 cup peeled and diced cucumber
2 handfuls of chopped spinach
1 green apple, peeled and chopped
½ cup coconut water or filtered water
handful of mint leaves

A delicious and refreshing way to get greens into kiddies. Both my boys love them!

1. Blend all ingredients in a blender until smooth.
2. Pour into ice block moulds and insert sticks.
3. Freeze for at least 8 hours or overnight until frozen solid.

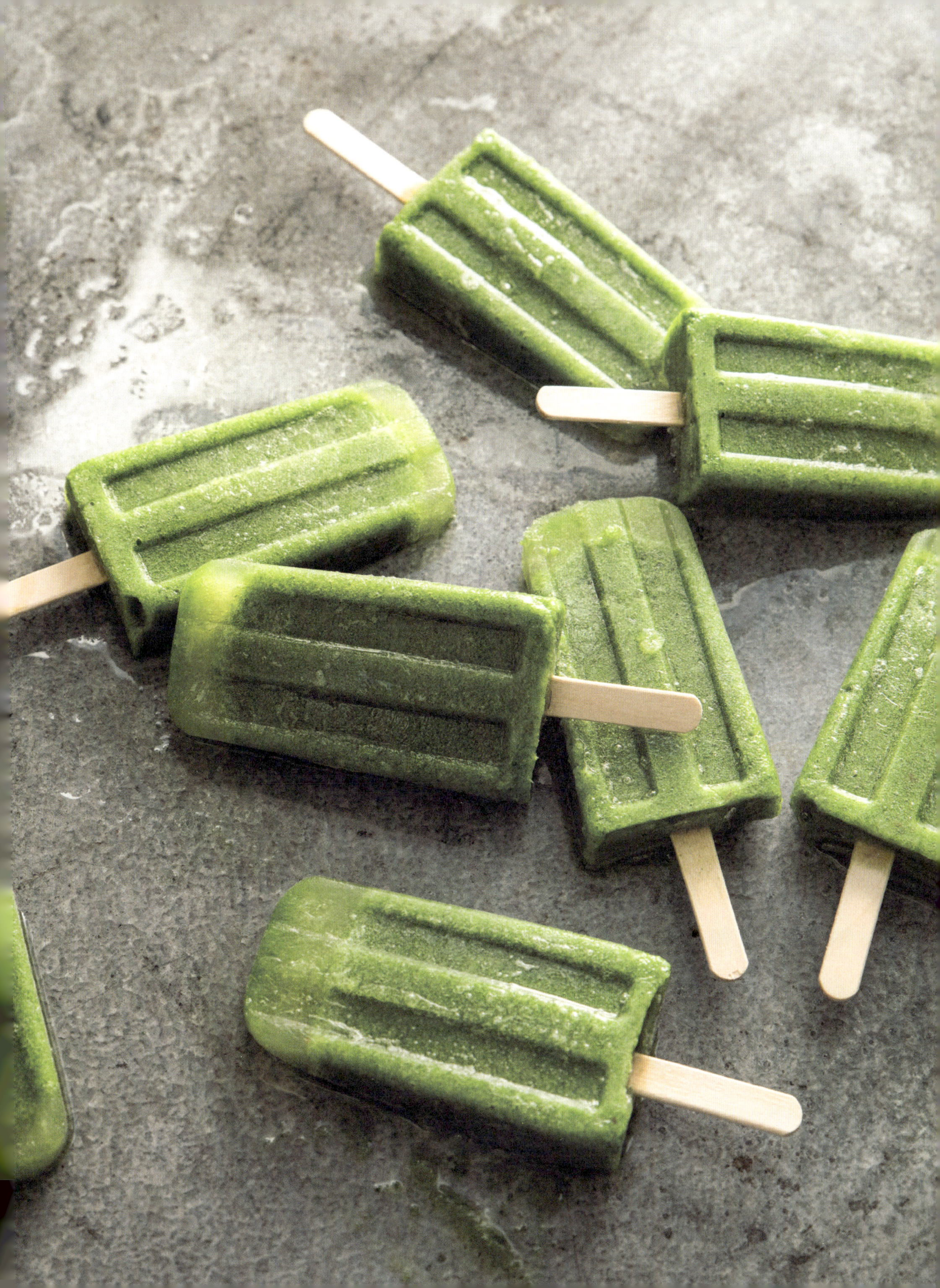

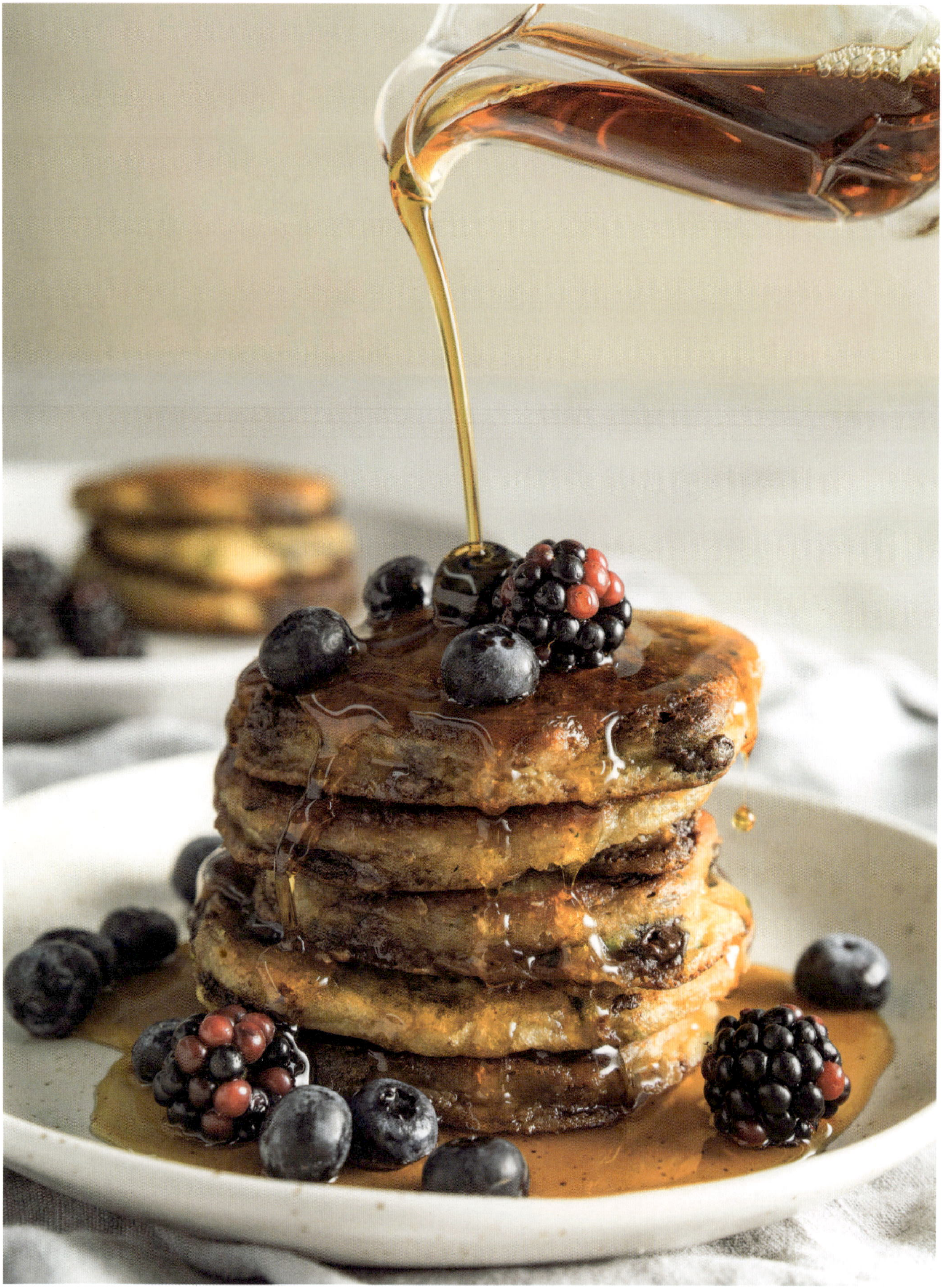

GF use GF self-raising flour | DF use coconut oil instead of butter and DF buttermilk |
VEGAN use coconut oil instead of butter, DF buttermilk and flax eggs

COURGETTE & CHOC CHIP BUTTERMILK PIKELETS

SERVES 4
Prep time: 10 minutes
Cook time: 15–20 minutes

1½ cups grated courgette (about 2 small to medium courgettes)
1 medium ripe banana
2 free-range eggs (or flax eggs, page 291)
1 tablespoon brown sugar
finely grated zest of 1 lemon
½ cup buttermilk
¾ teaspoon baking soda
good pinch of salt
175g self-raising flour
3 tablespoons (45g) cooled, melted butter
½ cup dark chocolate chips or 1 cup blueberries (fresh or frozen & defrosted)
coconut oil or butter, for cooking

TO SERVE
fresh fruit (e.g. berries or sliced banana)
maple syrup or liquid honey
yoghurt or whipped cream

You'd never guess there are vegetables in these light, fluffy, golden pikelets/little pancakes. The courgettes provide moisture, while the addition of buttermilk makes them light and fluffy. You can make either a chocolate chip or blueberry version. My kids love them!

1. Preheat oven to 50°C.

2. Coarsely grate courgette directly onto a clean tea towel, then wring tea towel firmly to squeeze out excess moisture.

3. Place banana, eggs, brown sugar, lemon zest, buttermilk, baking soda and salt in a blender and blend until smooth. Add courgette and pulse a few times to combine.

4. Pour mixture into a large mixing bowl. Sift in flour and stir until just combined (be careful not to overmix).

5. Fold through cooled melted butter and then chocolate chips/blueberries.

6. Melt a knob of butter or coconut oil in a large non-stick fry pan on medium heat and swirl around to coat. Dollop spoonfuls of batter into the pan and cook for about 2 minutes on one side until bubbles start to appear, then use a spatula or fish slice to flip over and continue cooking for a further 1–2 minutes until golden and cooked through. Transfer to a plate and keep warm in the oven.

7. Serve with fruit, a drizzle of maple syrup or honey, and a dollop of yoghurt or cream, if desired.

Note: To make DF buttermilk, mix ½ tablespoon lemon juice or vinegar with ½ cup soy or coconut milk and let it sit for 10 minutes until it curdles.

GF

AVOCADO MINT CHOC CHIP ICE CREAM

SERVES 8–10
Prep time: 15 minutes

½ cup (tightly packed) mint leaves
395g can sweetened condensed milk
1 tablespoon vanilla bean paste or seeds of 1 vanilla pod
pinch of salt
flesh of 1 large or 2 small to medium ripe avocados
1 teaspoon peppermint essence
2 cups (500ml) double cream
1 cup dark chocolate chips or chopped dark chocolate

This beautiful mint-green ice cream is a real decadent treat. You'll be amazed at how smooth, creamy and rich it is, yet it has a lovely freshness to it from the fresh mint and avocado (which is very subtle in taste).

1. Place mint leaves in a bowl, cover with boiling water for 1 minute, then plunge into cold water (this helps to brighten and soften the mint leaves). Drain well.

2. Blend condensed milk, vanilla, salt, avocado, peppermint essence and blanched mint leaves in a blender or food processor until smooth.

3. In a large bowl, whip cream (with a hand whisk or an electric beater) to soft peaks.

4. Spoon avocado mixture into the bowl of whipped cream, add chocolate, and fold everything together with a large metal spoon until combined, taking care not to overmix in order to keep mixture as light and fluffy as possible.

5. Spoon into a large loaf tin or medium dish, cover with clingfilm touching the surface of the ice cream (this helps to avoid oxidisation and therefore discolouration) and freeze for at least 6–8 hours, or overnight, until firm.

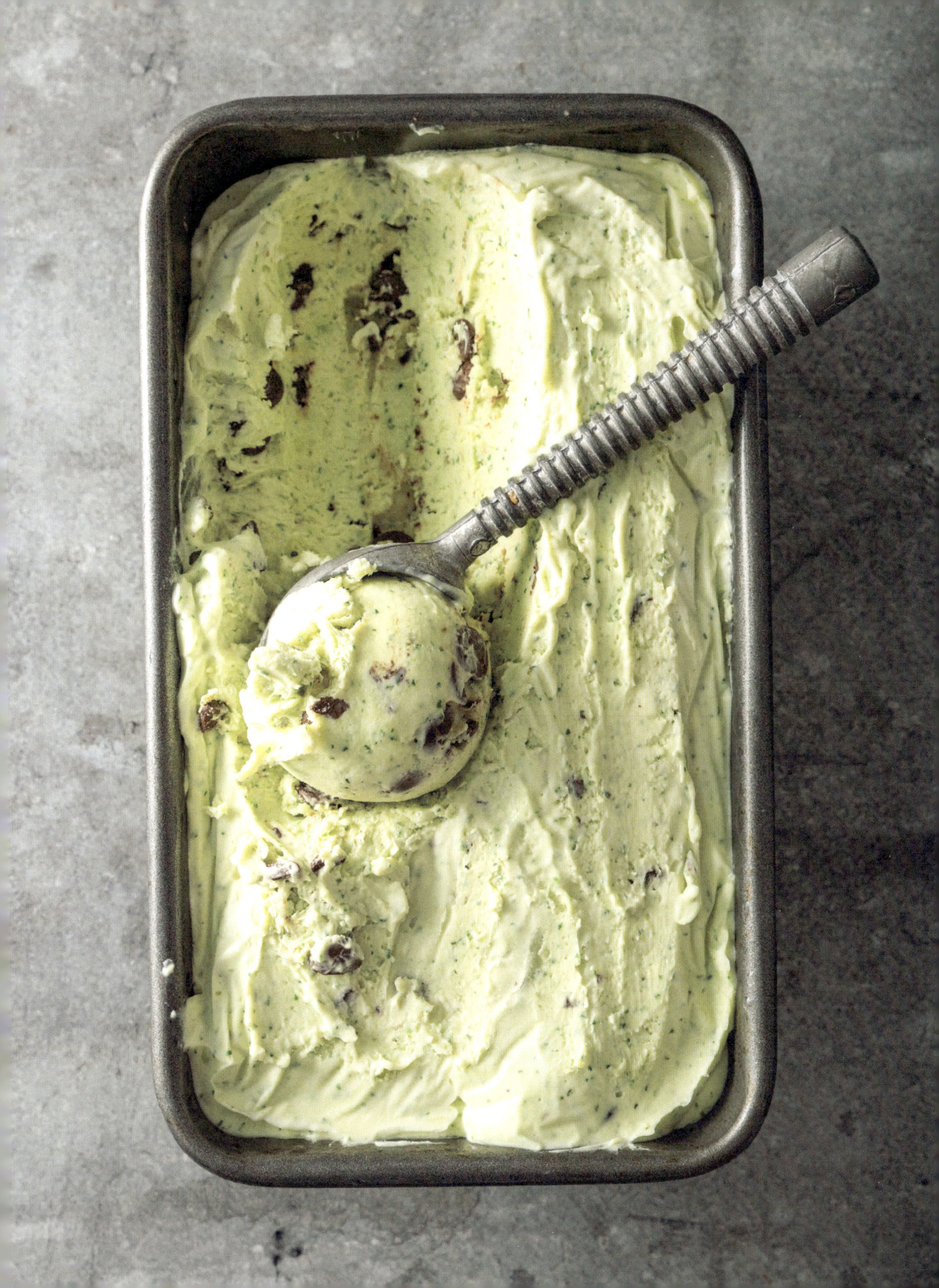

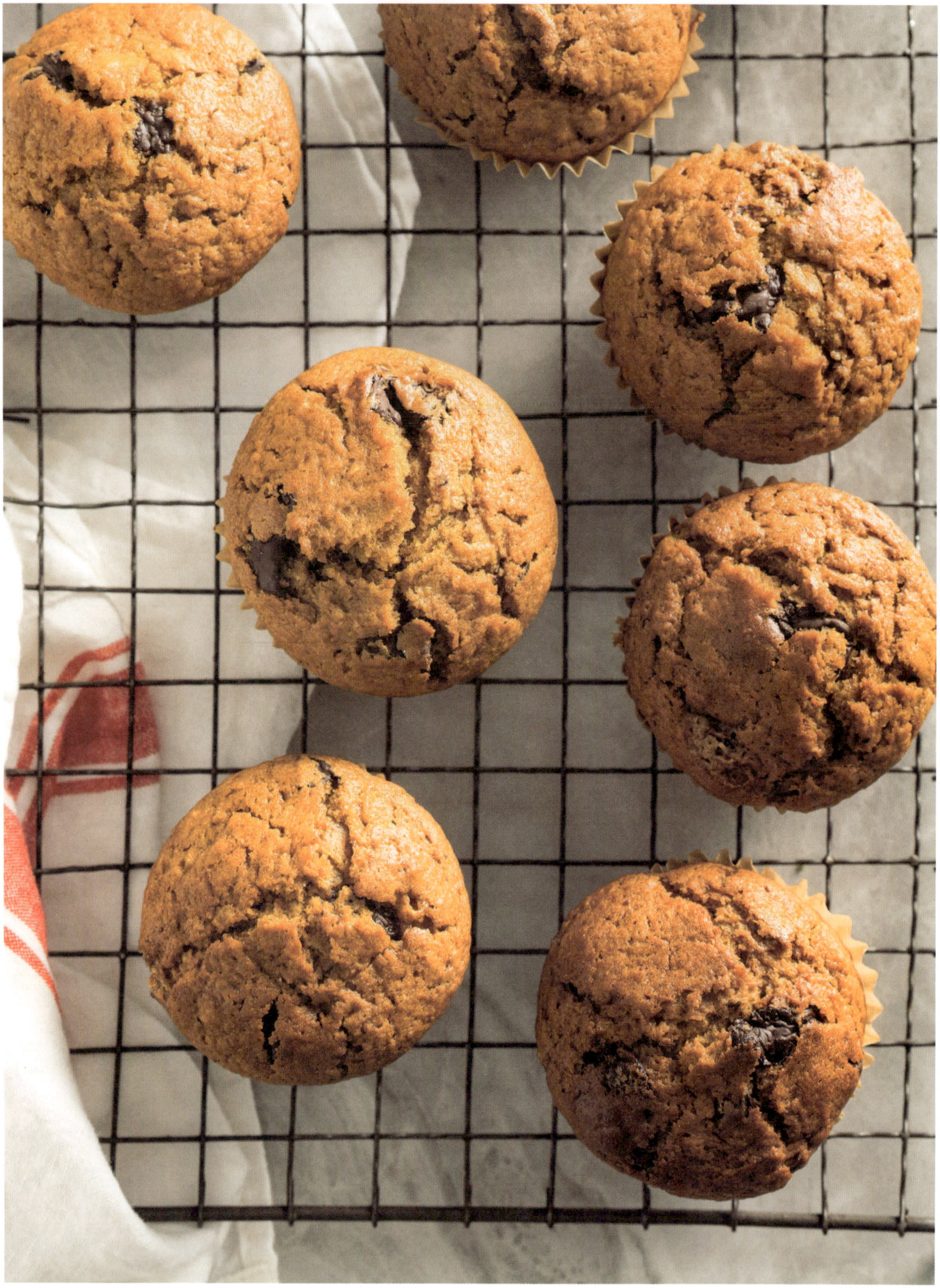

GF use GF flour | DF use DF milk and dark chocolate, coconut oil instead of butter | VEGAN use DF milk and dark chocolate, coconut oil instead of butter and flax eggs

ANNABEL'S PUMPKIN & CHOCOLATE CHUNK MUFFINS

MAKES 12 MUFFINS
Prep time: 20 minutes
Cook time: 20 minutes

½ cup full fat milk
2 tablespoons freshly squeezed orange juice (reserving zest)
100g butter
3 tablespoons golden syrup
250g plain flour
2 teaspoons baking powder
1 teaspoon baking soda
2 teaspoons ground cinnamon
½ teaspoon mixed spice
¾ cup lightly packed brown sugar
½ cup chopped milk or dark chocolate
1 cup roasted pumpkin purée (see Note), at room temperature
2 free-range eggs, (or flax eggs, see page 291)
zest of 1 orange

This recipe comes from my friend Annabel Inglis who is a brilliant cook and baker. The muffins are light and have a lovely treacley flavour from the roast pumpkin and golden syrup, made even more yummy by the hint of orange and warming spices. And chunks of chocolate!

1. Preheat oven to 200°C. Line a 12-hole standard-sized muffin tin with muffin/cupcake liners.

2. Place milk and orange juice in a small bowl and set aside while you prepare the dry ingredients. The mixture may curdle slightly over this time (giving it the moistening qualities typical of buttermilk).

3. Heat butter and golden syrup in a small pot over medium heat until just melted. Remove from heat and allow to cool slightly.

4. Sift flour, baking powder, baking soda, cinnamon and mixed spice into a large mixing bowl. Add brown sugar and use your fingertips to combine, ensuring there are no remaining lumps of brown sugar. Add the chocolate and make a well in the centre of the dry ingredients.

5. In a separate mixing bowl, whisk together pumpkin purée, eggs, orange zest, butter/golden syrup mixture and milk/orange juice mixture until smooth. Pour into the dry ingredients and stir with a large spoon until just combined — do not overmix (don't worry about a few lumps, it will ensure a lighter muffin).

6. Divide mixture between muffin cases, filling almost to the top. Bake for about 20 minutes, until light golden. Allow to cool in the tin for about 5 minutes before transferring to a wire rack. Enjoy warm or at room temperature.

Note: To make roasted pumpkin purée, preheat oven to 200°C. Chop 600g Crown pumpkin into 5cm pieces. Place on a lined tray and dry roast (without oil) for about 40 minutes, or until soft enough to be easily pierced with a skewer. When cool enough to handle, scoop away the orange flesh, discarding seeds, skin and any green-tinged flesh (which will be bitter) or charred bits. Mash very well using a fork.

DF use coconut oil, coconut cream and serve with coconut yoghurt

SWEET POTATO PIE WITH MAPLE-GLAZED NUTS

SERVES 8–10
Prep time: 20 minutes
Cook time: 40–45 minutes
(+ 20–25 minutes to cook sweet potato)

OAT AND NUT CRUST
1¼ cup instant rolled oats
1 cup nuts (e.g. almonds, walnuts, hazelnuts, pecans or a combination)
½ cup (125g) melted butter or coconut oil
2 tablespoons maple syrup
pinch of salt
1 free-range egg white (from one of the eggs used below)

FILLING
1½ cups roughly mashed orange kumara or butternut (see Note)
1 cup double cream or coconut cream
1½ teaspoons vanilla essence or extract
2 free-range egg yolks
½ cup maple syrup
1 teaspoon custard powder or cornflour
good pinch of salt
½ teaspoon mixed spice
1 teaspoon ground cinnamon
¼ teaspoon ground or freshly grated nutmeg

MAPLE-GLAZED NUTS
½ cup roughly chopped nuts (e.g. almonds, walnuts, hazelnuts, pecans or a combination)
2 tablespoons pumpkin seeds
3 tablespoons maple syrup
good pinch of salt

CINNAMON YOGHURT CREAM
½ cup cream
½ cup natural unsweetened yoghurt
¼ teaspoon ground cinnamon

Pumpkin pie is very American (I'd make a bet that every American has eaten it!), but a bit of a foreign concept to us Kiwis. Yet we love our kumara (or sweet potato) so much, so why not have a version of this famous pie using our beloved tuber? You can either make the Oat 'n' Nut Crust or, if you want to save some time, just use store-bought sweet shortcrust pastry. This pie is lovely served at room temperature or cold, with Cinnamon Yoghurt Cream, coconut yoghurt or ice cream.

1. Preheat oven to 170°C. Lightly grease a 27cm fluted edge flan or pie dish with butter or coconut oil.

2. Place all crust ingredients in a food processor and blitz until it comes together as a sticky dough.

3. Press dough mixture into the base and up the sides of greased pie dish with the help of the back of a spoon. Brush crust with egg white (this helps to 'seal' it) and bake on a lower rack in the oven for 8–10 minutes until light golden around the edges. Remove and use a spoon to press down the crust again, flattening and pushing it up the sides. Set aside to cool while you make the filling.

4. To make the filling, place all ingredients in a food processor or a blender and blitz until smooth. Pour filling into the crust. Place on a lower rack in the oven and bake for 40–45 minutes until the filling is just set, like custard — it should still have a slight wobble in the middle. Leave pie to cool to room temperature before serving or refrigerate for a few hours to eat cold.

5. Place nuts and pumpkin seeds in a small fry pan on medium heat and toast for 1–2 minutes. Add maple syrup and salt, stir to coat the nuts and let it bubble for 1 minute or so, then take off the heat and spoon nuts and syrup over the pie.

6. To make Cinnamon Yoghurt Cream, whip cream to soft peaks, then fold in yoghurt and cinnamon. Cut pie into pieces and serve with Cinnamon Yoghurt Cream on the side.

Note: Peel and chop 600g orange kumara or butternut into 2–3cm cubes. Toss with a drizzle of maple syrup on an oven tray lined with baking paper. Roast at 200°C for 25–35 minutes or until soft and mash with a fork.

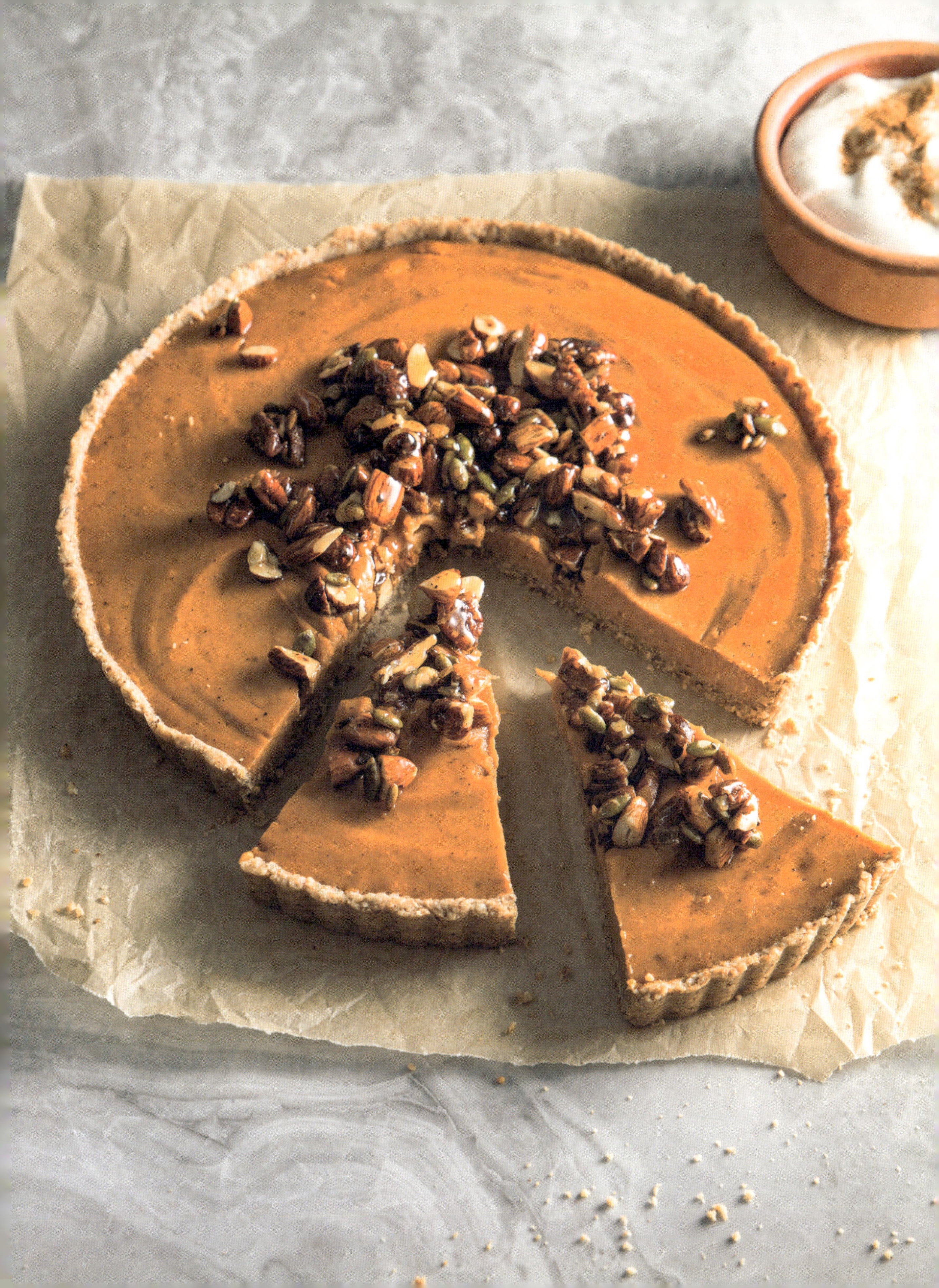

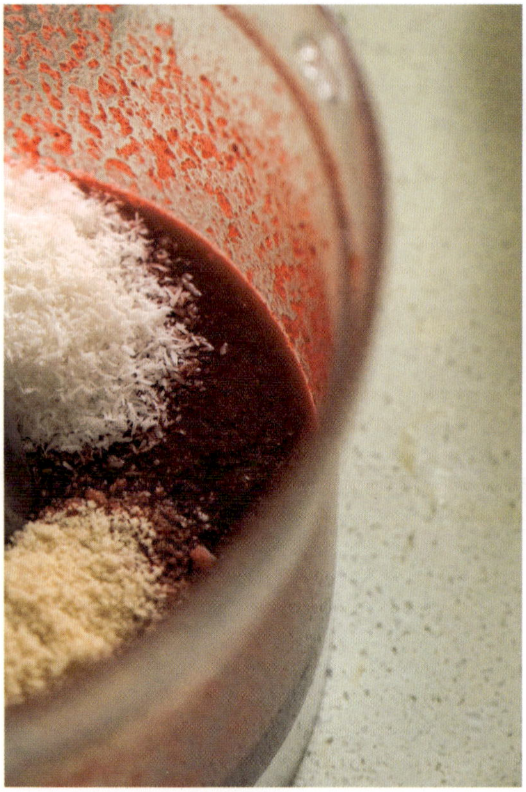
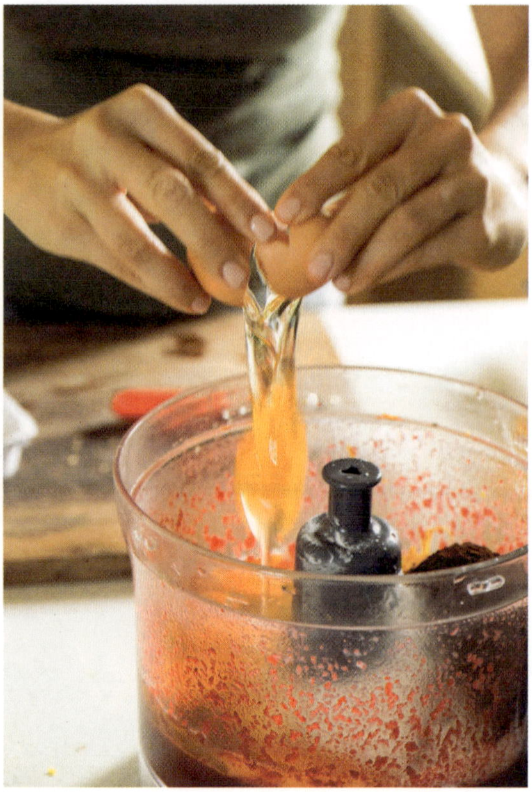
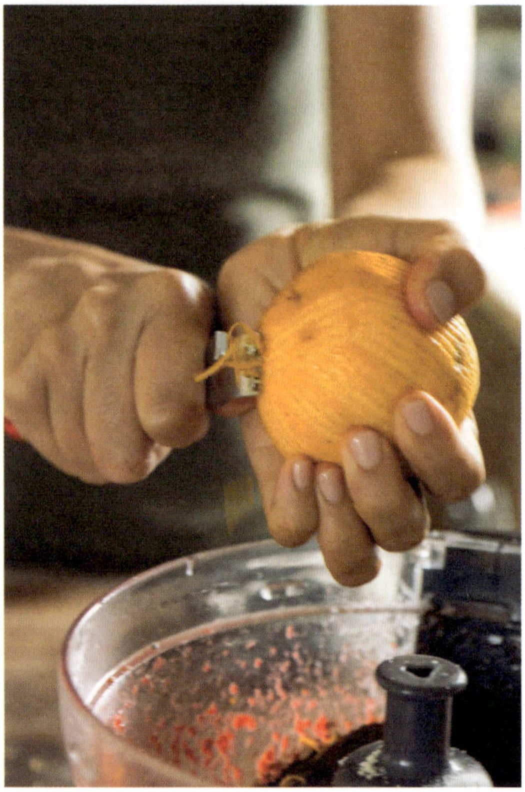
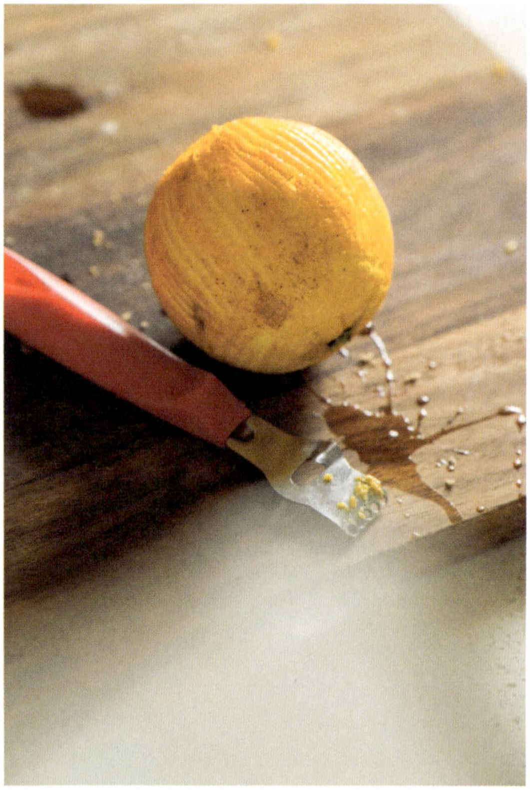

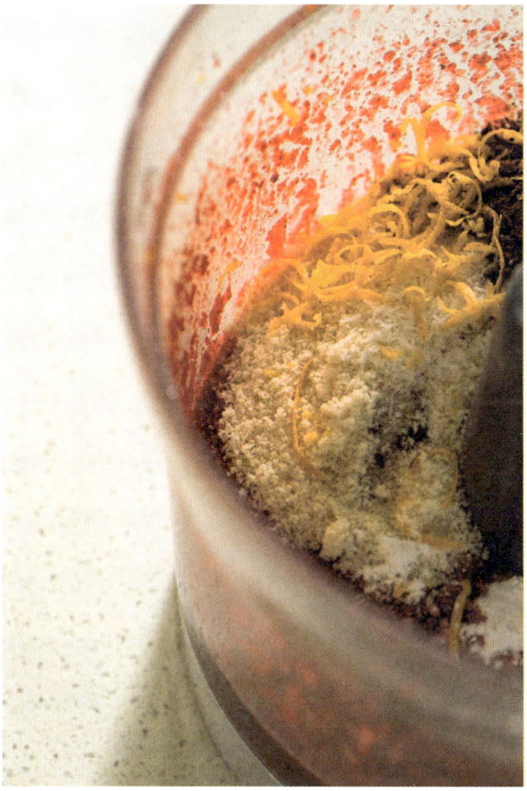
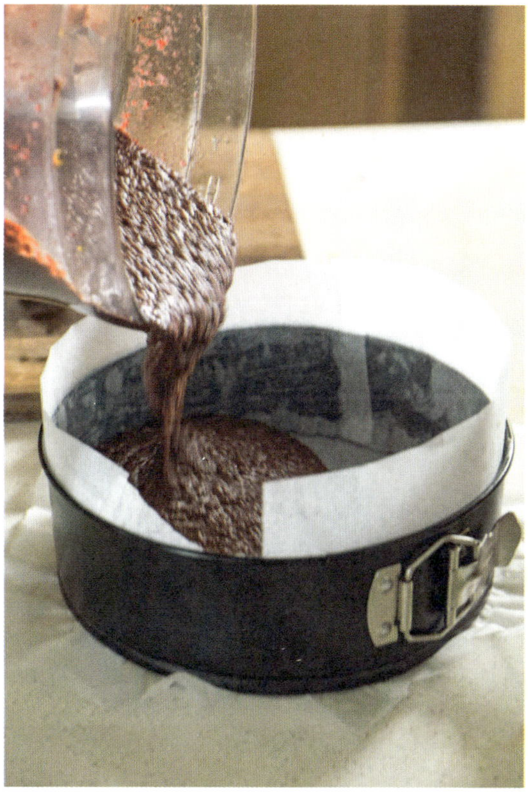
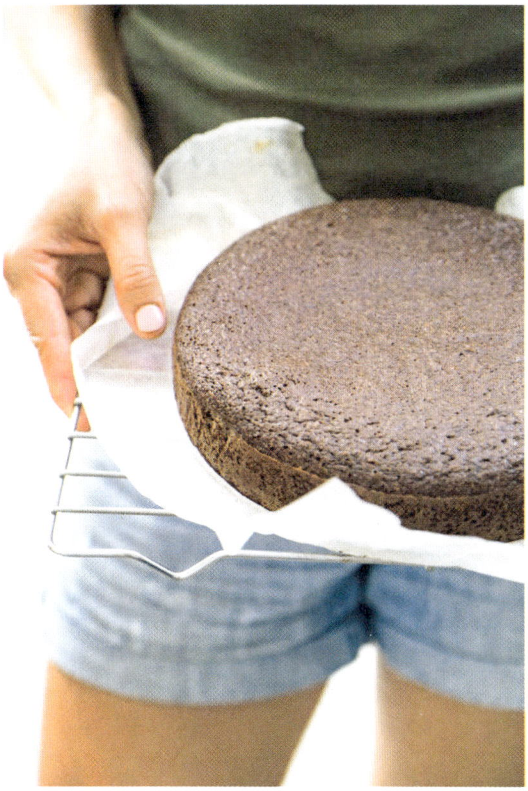
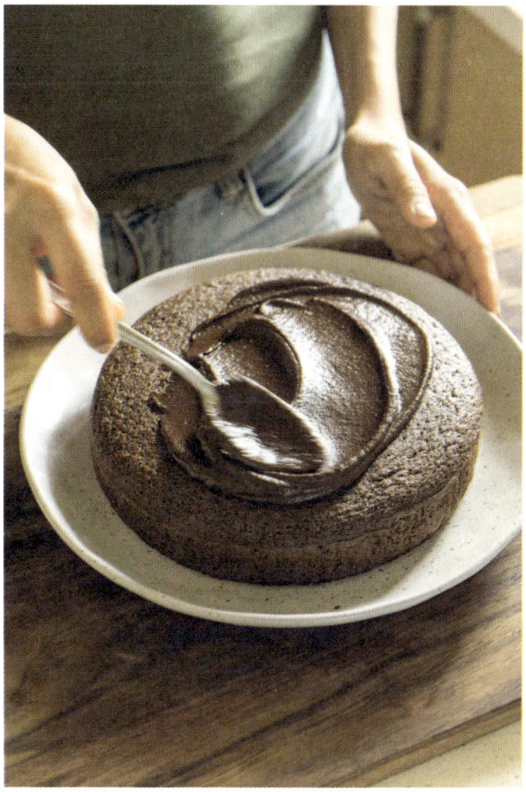

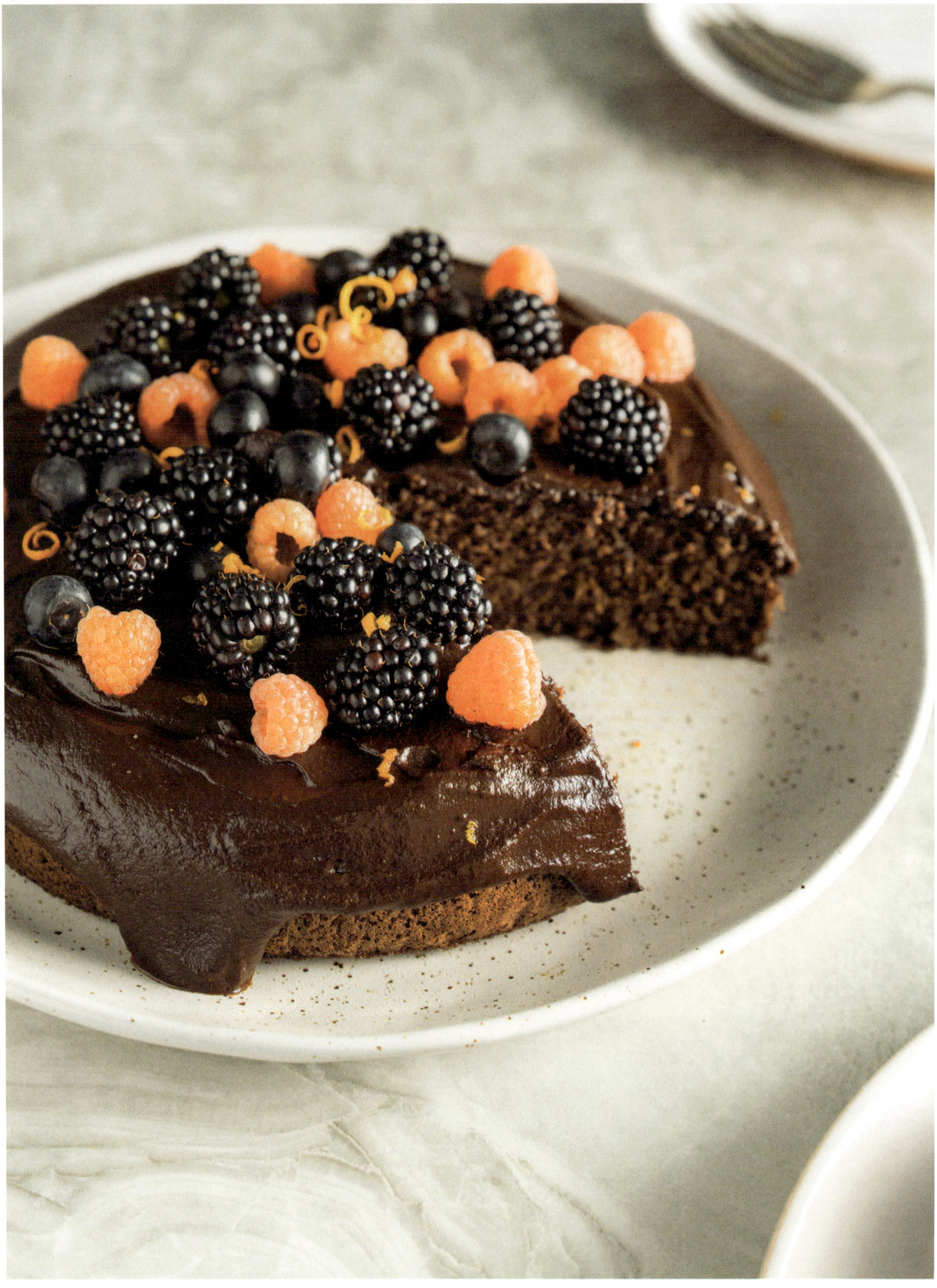

GF | DF use coconut oil and cream and DF dark chocolate |
VEGAN use coconut oil and cream, DF dark chocolate and flax eggs

BEETROOT, CHOCOLATE & ORANGE CAKE

SERVES 8–10
Prep time: 20 minutes
Cook time: 1 hour

350–400g beetroot, peeled and chopped
¼ cup coconut oil or melted butter
1 cup brown sugar
1 teaspoon vanilla essence or extract
1 cup (100g) ground almonds
1¼ cup (100g) desiccated coconut
finely grated zest of 1 orange
3½ tablespoons dark cocoa or cacao powder
1 teaspoon baking powder
5 free-range eggs (or flax eggs, see page 291)

CHOCOLATE GANACHE
85g dark chocolate, chopped
⅓ cup cream or coconut cream

1 punnet fresh berries, to garnish

This light, almost sponge-like cake is one that is great as a morning or afternoon tea-type cake by itself (as it's not overly sweet or rich), or you can make it more decadent and special with the chocolate ganache and fresh berries. This recipe makes a smaller cake, enough to serve 8–10 nicely.

1. Preheat oven to 170°C. Lightly grease and line the base and sides of a 20–21cm cake tin with baking paper.

2. Boil beetroot for 10–15 minutes until tender.

3. Drain beetroot well and place in a food processor or blender along with coconut oil/butter, brown sugar and vanilla. Blend until smooth.

4. If using the food processor, add ground almonds, coconut, orange zest, cocoa, baking powder and eggs, and continue blending until mixture is smooth and well combined. Otherwise, pour mixture into a large bowl, add other ingredients and whisk until smooth and well combined.

5. Pour into prepared cake tin and bake for 1 hour or until cake is just set. Leave to cool for at least 10 minutes before removing from tin and transferring to a cake rack, then allow to cool completely before icing.

6. To make ganache, place chocolate and cream/coconut cream in a heatproof bowl and melt together in the microwave in 30-second bursts, then stir until smooth and glossy. Alternatively, place bowl above a small pot of barely simmering water and stir gently every now and again until melted. Allow ganache to cool slightly before using.

7. Spread ganache over the top of the cake and a little down the sides and top with fresh berries.

GF use GF self-raising flour | DF | VEGAN use flax eggs and maple syrup

CARROT, PINEAPPLE & BANANA CUPCAKES

MAKES 12–15
Prep time: 15 minutes
Cook time: 20–25 minutes

2 medium very ripe bananas
1 cup grated carrot (about
   1 medium to large carrot)
235g can crushed pineapple,
   lightly drained
⅔ cup oil (e.g. coconut,
   grapeseed, sunflower or canola)
1½ teaspoons vanilla essence
   or extract
2 large free-range eggs
   (or flax eggs, see page 291)
1 level teaspoon baking soda
¾ cup desiccated coconut
⅔ cup sugar
2 tablespoons liquid honey
   or maple syrup
good pinch of salt
225g self-raising flour
¾ teaspoon ground cinnamon

These tropical-flavoured cupcakes are delicious as is, although if you'd like them iced for something a bit more decadent and special, use the Caramel Cream Cheese Icing on page 282 or Sweer Labne (made with coconut yoghurt) sweetened with honey on page 63. This recipe would also bake and ice nicely as a whole cake.

1. Preheat oven to 200°C. Line a 12-hole standard-sized muffin tin with muffin/cupcake liners.

2. In a large mixing bowl, mash bananas. Add carrot, pineapple, oil, vanilla, eggs, baking soda, coconut, sugar, honey/maple syrup and salt and mix until well combined.

3. Sift in flour and cinnamon. Use a large metal spoon to fold ingredients together until just combined, being careful not to overmix.

4. Divide mixture between muffin cases, filling almost to the top. Bake for 20–25 minutes until risen and golden and the cakes spring back when lightly pressed in the centre.

5. If icing cupcakes, wait until they have cooled before icing.

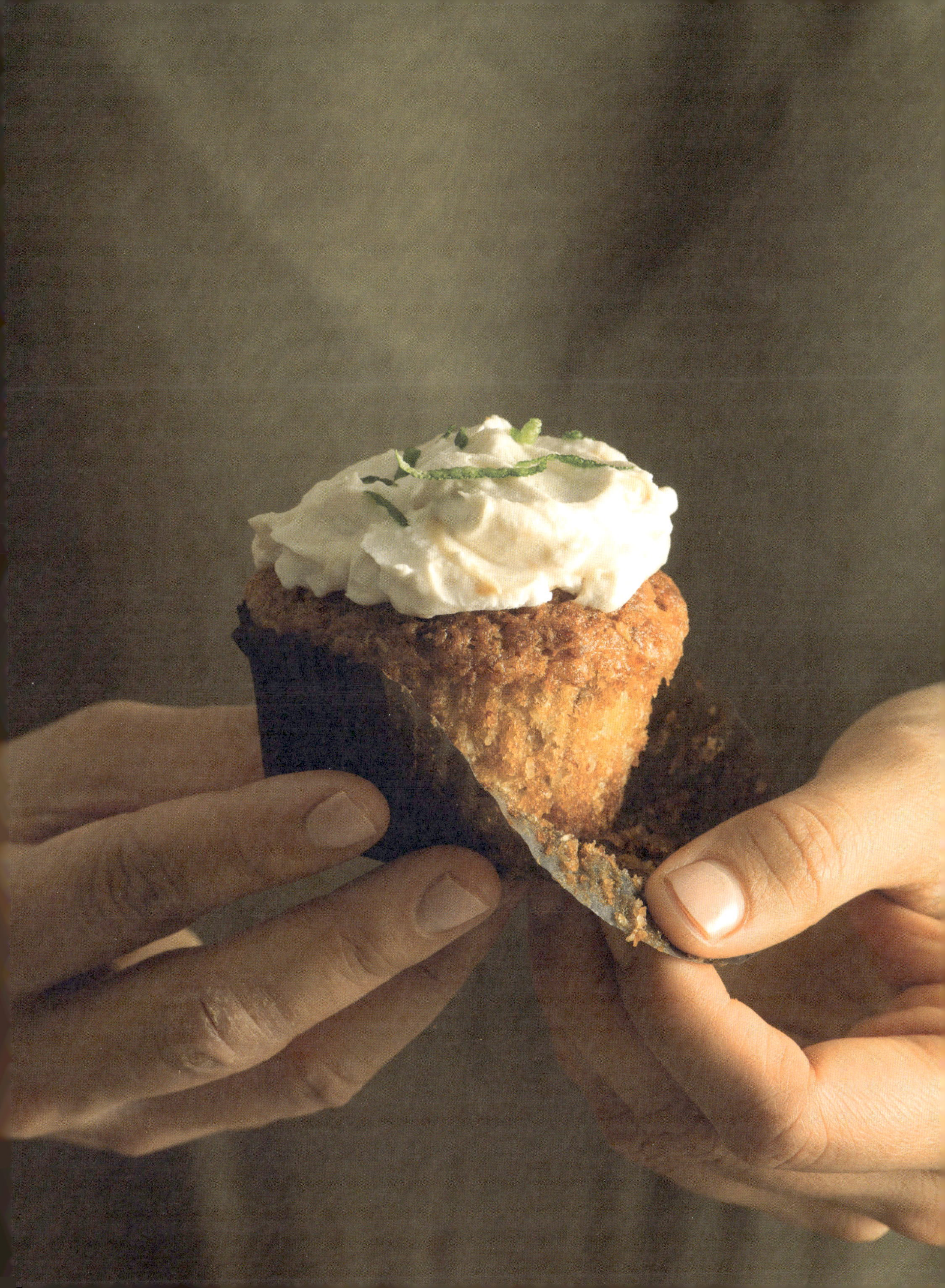

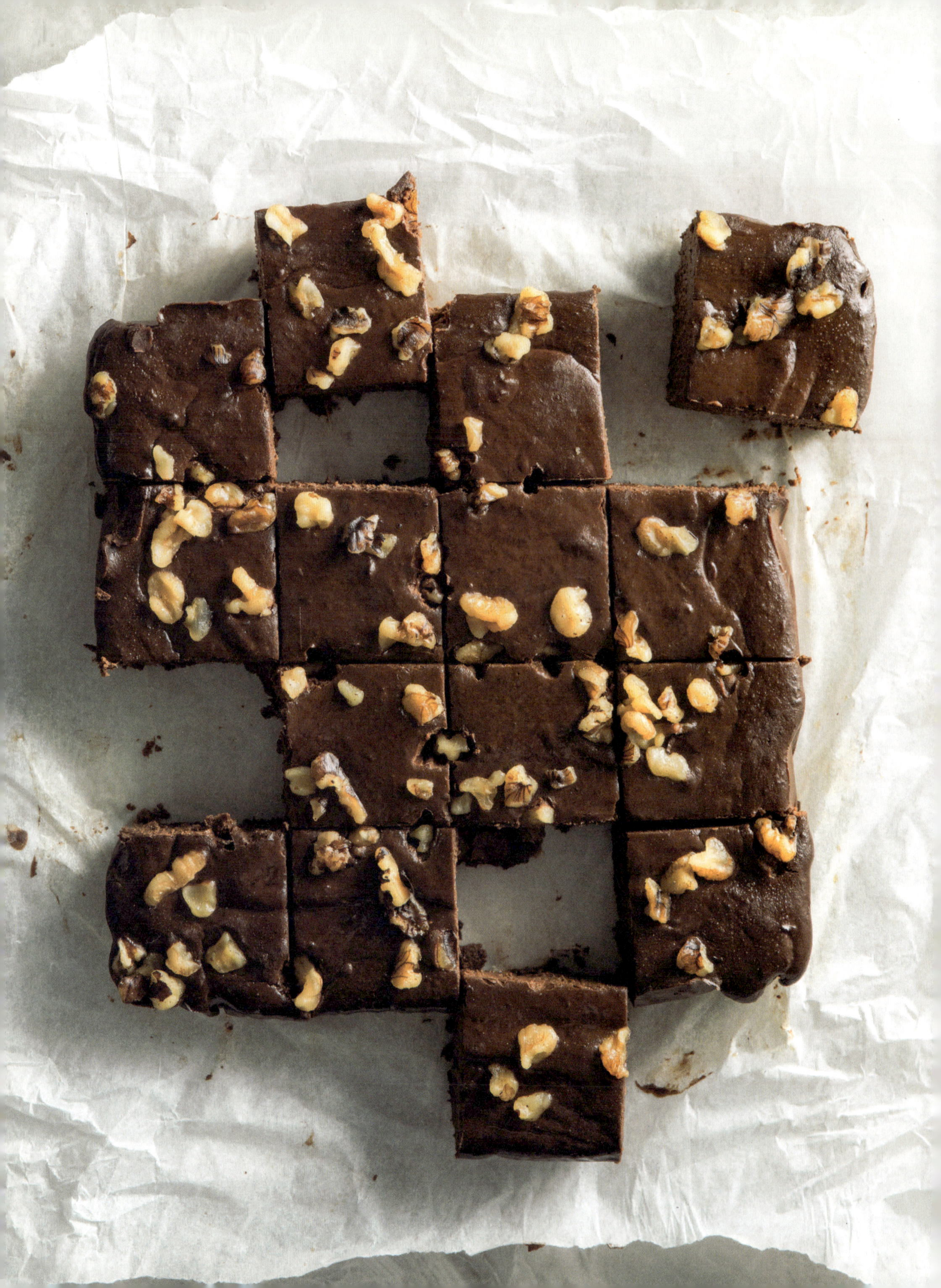

GF | DF use coconut oil

BLACK BEAN CHOCOLATE FUDGE BROWNIE

MAKES ABOUT 16 PIECES
Prep time: 10 minutes
Cook time: 25 minutes

125g butter or coconut oil
½ cup brown sugar or maple syrup
250g good-quality dark (60–75% cocoa) chocolate, chopped
4 free-range eggs
2 x 400g cans black beans or kidney beans, rinsed and drained well
2 teaspoons baking powder
handful of roughly chopped nuts (e.g. walnuts or macadamias), or fresh berries

These brownies were a huge hit from my first Fresh Start cookbook. Their 'secret' ingredient is not so secret any more because so many people have now tried it and been gobsmacked that they contain beans (instead of flour). This makes them extra moist and fudgey, and gluten-free too, not to mention high in fibre and much better for you.

1. Preheat oven to 150°C. Line a 20–22cm square cake or slice tin or baking dish with baking paper.

2. Place butter/coconut oil, sugar/maple syrup and chocolate in a medium pot and gently heat over medium heat, stirring frequently, until chocolate has melted. Allow to cool slightly.

3. Transfer to a blender or food processor and add eggs, beans and baking powder. Blend until smooth and well combined, scraping down the sides with a spatula a few times to make sure everything is incorporated.

4. Pour mixture into prepared tin. Scatter with nuts or berries and bake for 20–25 minutes (20 minutes if you prefer it fudgey, 25 minutes if you prefer it slightly firmer — I go in between!).

5. Refrigerate for about 10 minutes to allow to set slightly. Cut into 16 pieces with a large sharp knife. Eat at room temperature or cold. Keeps in the fridge in an airtight container for up to a week. Store in the freezer.

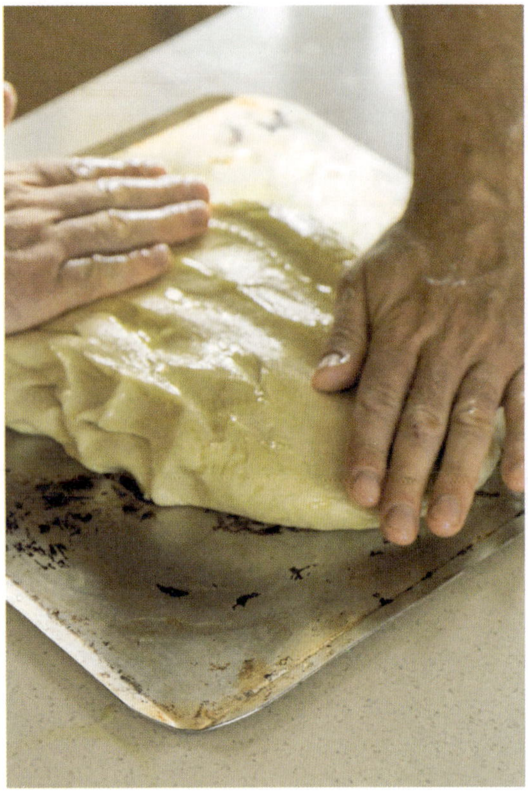
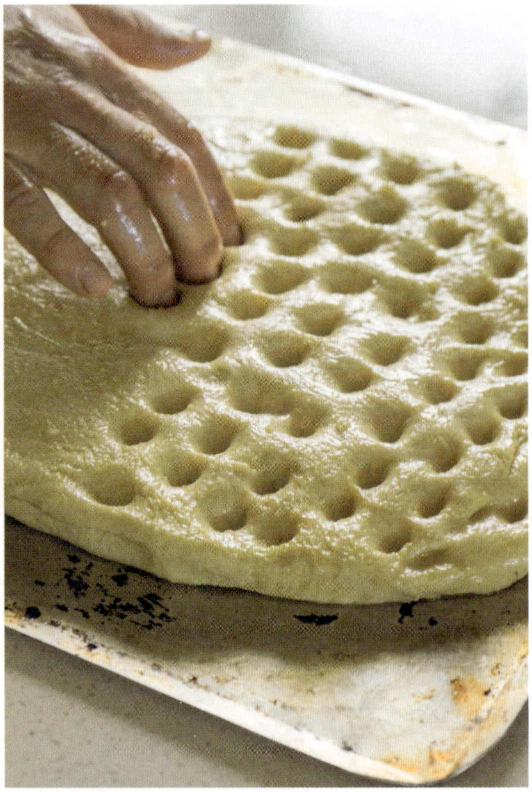
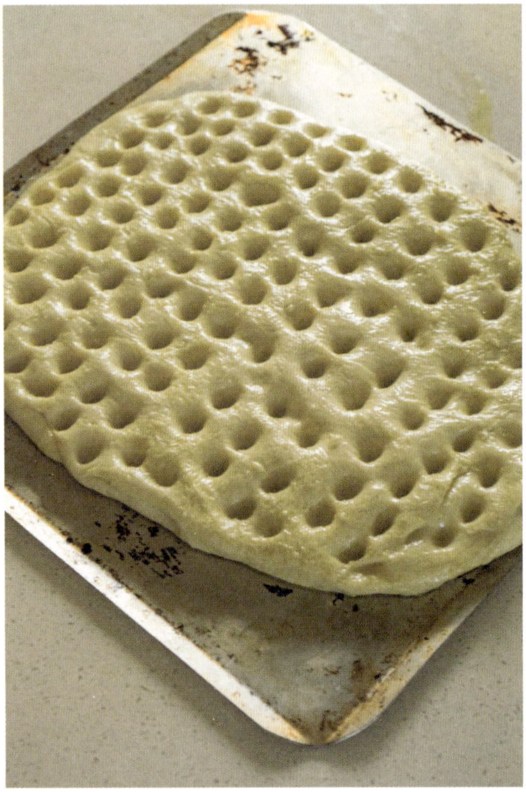
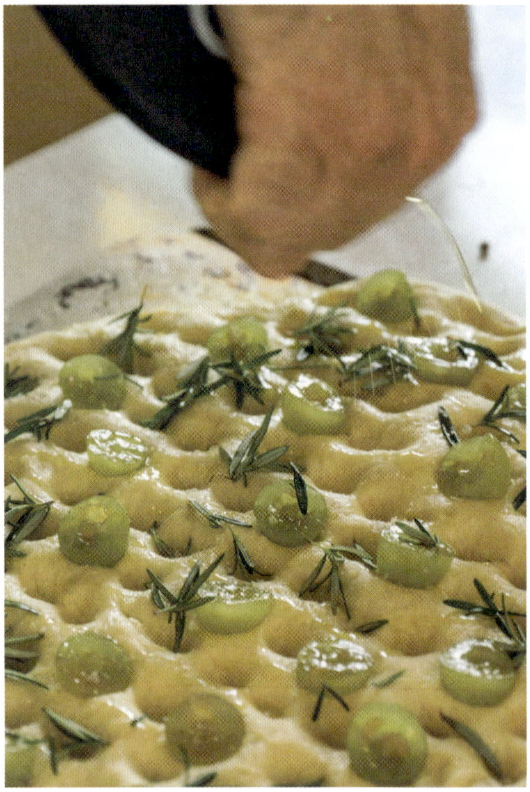

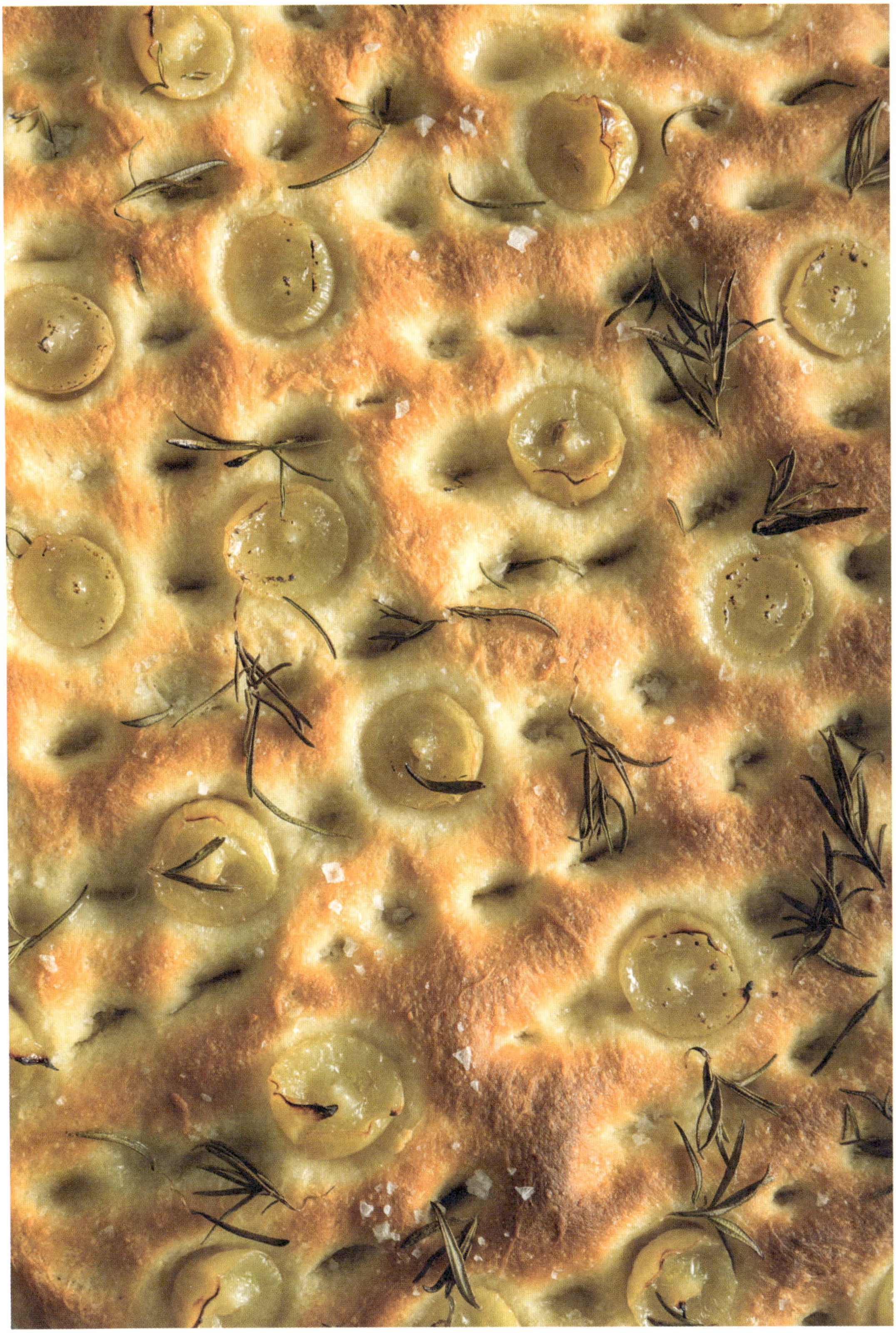

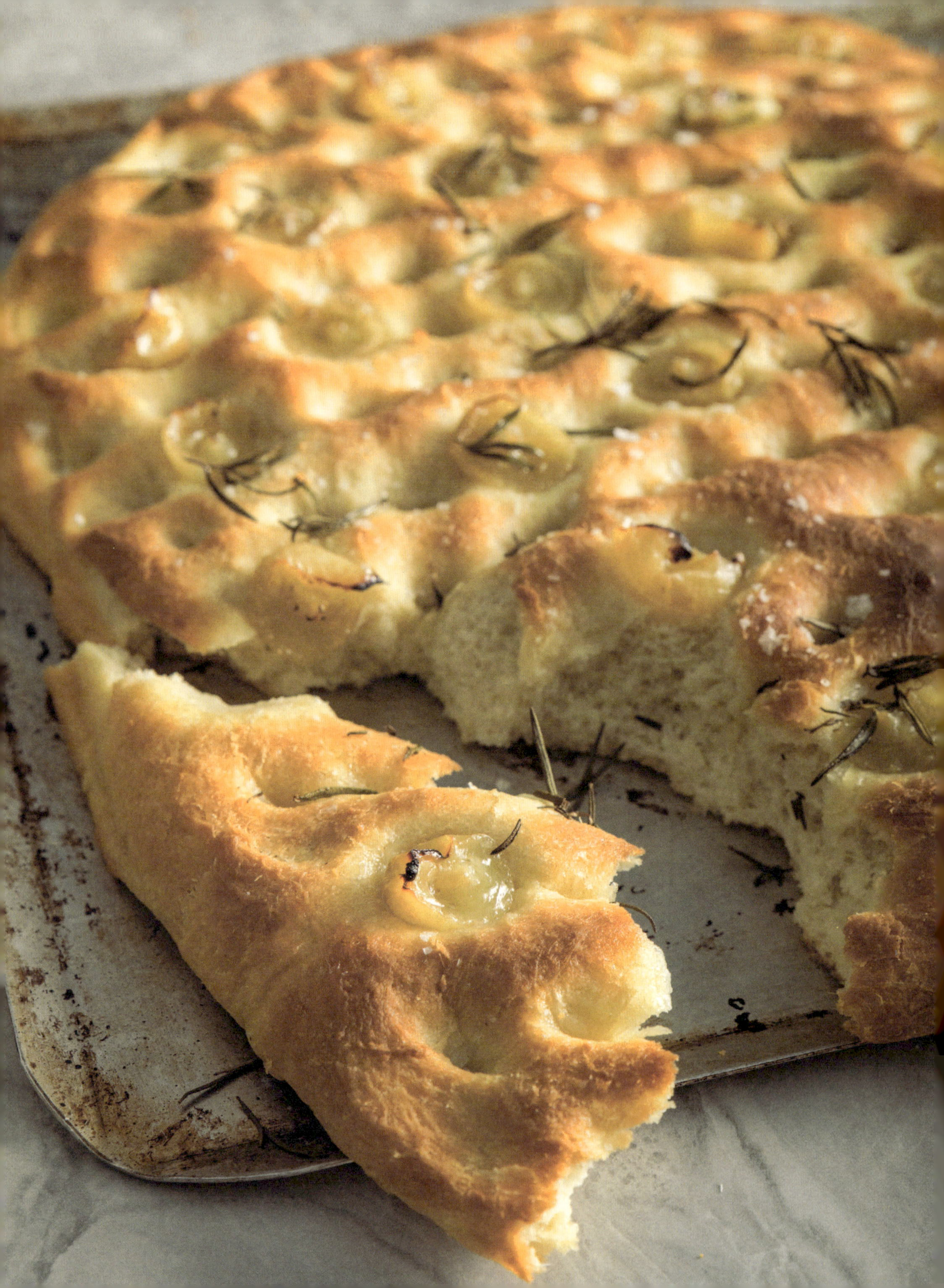

DF | VEGAN

KUMARA FOCACCIA WITH GRAPES & ROSEMARY

SERVES 6–8
Prep time: 25 minutes
(+ 1 hour 45 minutes to rise)
Cook time: 30 minutes

300g kumara (red, orange or gold) or potato, peeled and chopped
250ml warm (not hot) water
1 teaspoon sugar
1 tablespoon active dried yeast
2 teaspoons salt
6 tablespoons extra-virgin olive oil
450g high-grade flour

TOPPING
1 cup grapes, cut in half
leaves from 1–2 sprigs rosemary
1 tablespoon flaky sea salt or rock salt

I reckon everyone needs to experience how satisfying it is to make your own focaccia bread. I feel like an Italian kitchen goddess whenever I make it, squishing my fingertips into the soft dough and dousing it with olive oil! There's nothing quite like it fresh out of the oven, then plonked on the table to pull apart and generously dip into extra-virgin olive oil and balsamic or cut into thick slabs to have with salad or soup.

1. Cook kumara in boiling salted water until soft. Drain and mash well.

2. While kumara is cooking, combine warm water and sugar in a large mixing bowl. Sprinkle yeast on top and stir gently. Set aside for about 10 minutes until frothy.

3. Whisk in mashed kumara, salt, and 3 tablespoons of the olive oil. Sift in flour. Mix until ingredients are just combined.

4. Tip dough out onto a clean, dry surface. Bring together with your hands and knead for 10 minutes until smooth and elastic, adding a little flour as needed. The dough should be soft; if it's really sticky, add a little more flour.

5. Drizzle the inside of the bowl the dough was in with olive oil. Fold edges of the dough underneath to create a smooth, rounded top, then place in the oiled bowl. Drizzle and rub dough with a little more olive oil to prevent a crust forming on top. Cover with a clean tea towel and leave in a warm place for 1 hour until it has risen to be double in size.

6. Drizzle a baking tray with olive oil. Slide dough onto oiled tray. Use your fingertips to make indentations in the dough while gently stretching and flattening it into an oval shape about 1.5cm thick. Drizzle with more olive oil, cover with the tea towel and leave in a warm place for 45 minutes to rise again.

7. Preheat oven to 220°C. Once the dough has risen, press your fingertips into the dough to make more indentations. Dot with grapes and sprinkle with rosemary and sea/rock salt. Drizzle with remaining 3 tablespoons olive oil. Bake for 20 minutes until golden and puffed around the edges. Eat warm, fresh out of the oven.

GF

POLENTA, LEMON & COCONUT SLICE

SERVES 12
Prep time: 15 minutes
Cook time: 30–40 minutes

175g softened unsalted butter
¾ cup caster sugar
3 free-range eggs (at room temperature)
120g fine polenta (cornmeal)
2 cups desiccated coconut
1½ teaspoons baking powder
zest of 2 large or 3 medium lemons
1 teaspoon almond essence (optional)

SYRUP
juice of 2 large or 3 medium lemons
¼ cup caster sugar

I'm a massive lemon lover and also a big fan of flourless cakes and slices that have more texture, moisture and flavour. So this recipe, using polenta instead of flour, is completely up my alley and has become a favourite — it's light, with a crumbly and slightly crusty texture on the outside, and beautifully moist and super lemony from the lemon syrup poured over. I really like it with the hint of almond essence too (which is optional).

1. Preheat oven to 180°C. Line a 21–23cm square baking tin with baking paper.

2. In a large mixing bowl, cream butter and sugar together until light and fluffy (use a wooden spoon or an electric beater).

3. Beat in eggs, one at a time, until well incorporated.

4. Add polenta, coconut, baking powder, lemon zest and almond essence (if using) and gently mix until just combined, keeping the mixture as airy, light and fluffy as possible.

5. Spoon into lined tin and spread out with a knife or back of a spoon. Bake for 30–40 minutes until golden brown and beginning to shrink away from the edges.

6. Meanwhile, make the syrup by boiling lemon juice and sugar together in a small pot for 1–2 minutes until slightly syrupy.

7. Once slice is cooked, prick all over with a skewer or fork. Pour syrup over slice while still warm in the tin, allowing it to seep in. Cut into 12. Enjoy warm, cold or at room temperature.

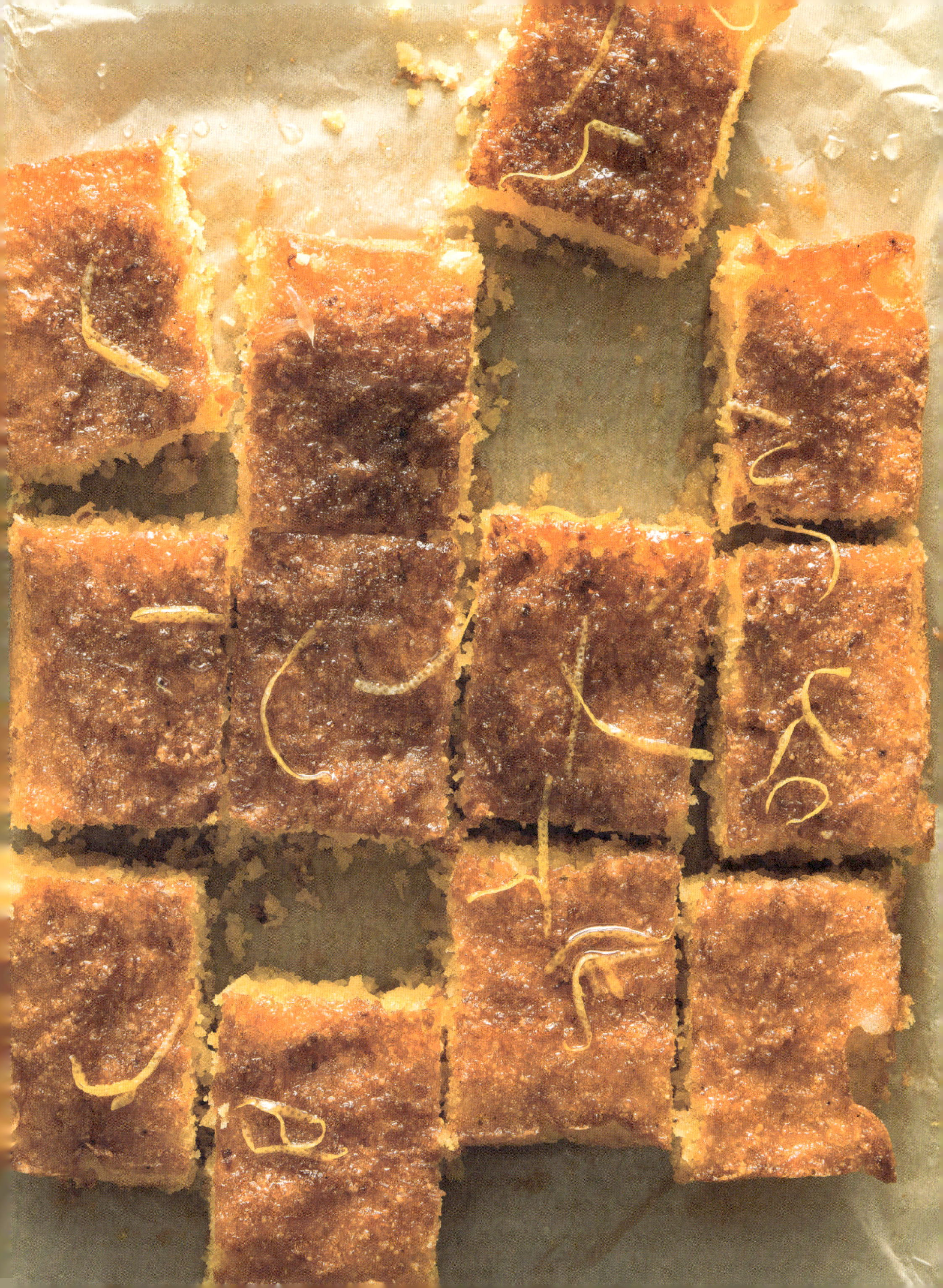

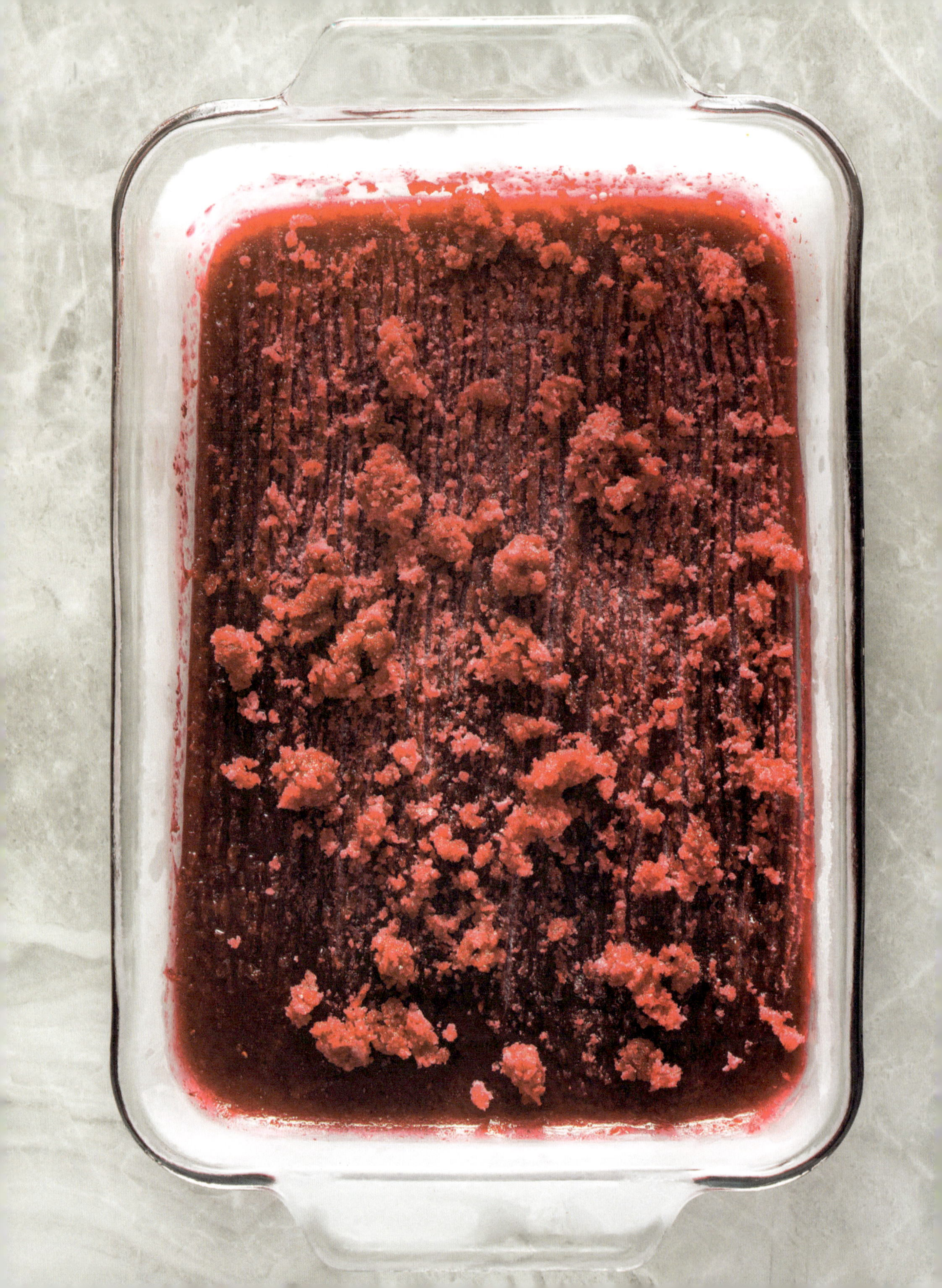

GF | DF | VEGAN

BEETROOT & RASPBERRY GRANITA

SERVES 6
Prep time: 10 minutes (+ 6–8 hours freezing time)
Cook time: 10 minutes

250g beetroot, peeled and chopped
250g raspberries (fresh or frozen and defrosted)
juice of 1 lemon
1¼ cups (300ml) filtered water
125g caster sugar

This makes a stunning, vibrant and refreshing dessert (with a twist) in summer.

1. Place a rectangular dish (ideally metal or Pyrex) in the freezer on a flat surface.

2. Boil beetroot for 10 minutes or until soft, then drain and leave to cool.

3. In a blender, purée beetroot, raspberries, lemon juice and water until smooth. Strain through a sieve into a large bowl, discarding raspberry pips (use the back of a large spoon to help push the juice through the sieve).

4. Measure out 3½ cups beetroot and raspberry juice into a pot (if you don't quite get 3½ cups, make the rest of the volume up with water). Add sugar and stir, on medium heat, until sugar has dissolved.

5. Pour into the chilled dish in the freezer. Stir granita with a fork every 30 minutes, to break up the ice crystals, for the first 2 hours, then keep in the freezer for at least 6–8 hours until frozen solid or ready to serve.

6. Just before serving, scrape up ice crystals with a fork and spoon into chilled serving glasses.

DF | VEGAN use maple syrup

CARROT CAKE BLISS BALLS

MAKES 20
Prep time: 15 minutes

1 cup desiccated coconut + extra to roll balls in
1 cup rolled oats
1½ loosely packed cups grated carrot (about 1 medium carrot)
1 cup chopped dried sweet apricots or dates
finely grated zest of 1 lemon or orange
2–3 teaspoons finely grated fresh ginger
1½ teaspoons ground cinnamon or mixed spice
¼ teaspoon freshly grated nutmeg
4 tablespoons maple syrup or honey
2 tablespoons coconut oil
good pinch of salt
½ cup raisins

These bliss balls have all the delicious flavours of carrot cake and make a great little snack or lunchbox filler.

1. Place all ingredients, except rasins, in a food processor and blitz until well combined and mixture holds together when pressed between your fingers. Add a teaspoon or two of lemon/orange juice if mixture is too dry, and more coconut if it is too wet.
2. Add rasins and pulse a few more times to combine.
3. Roll tablespoons of mixture into balls and roll in extra coconut to coat, if desired. Store in an airtight container in the fridge. They will keep for up to 10 days.

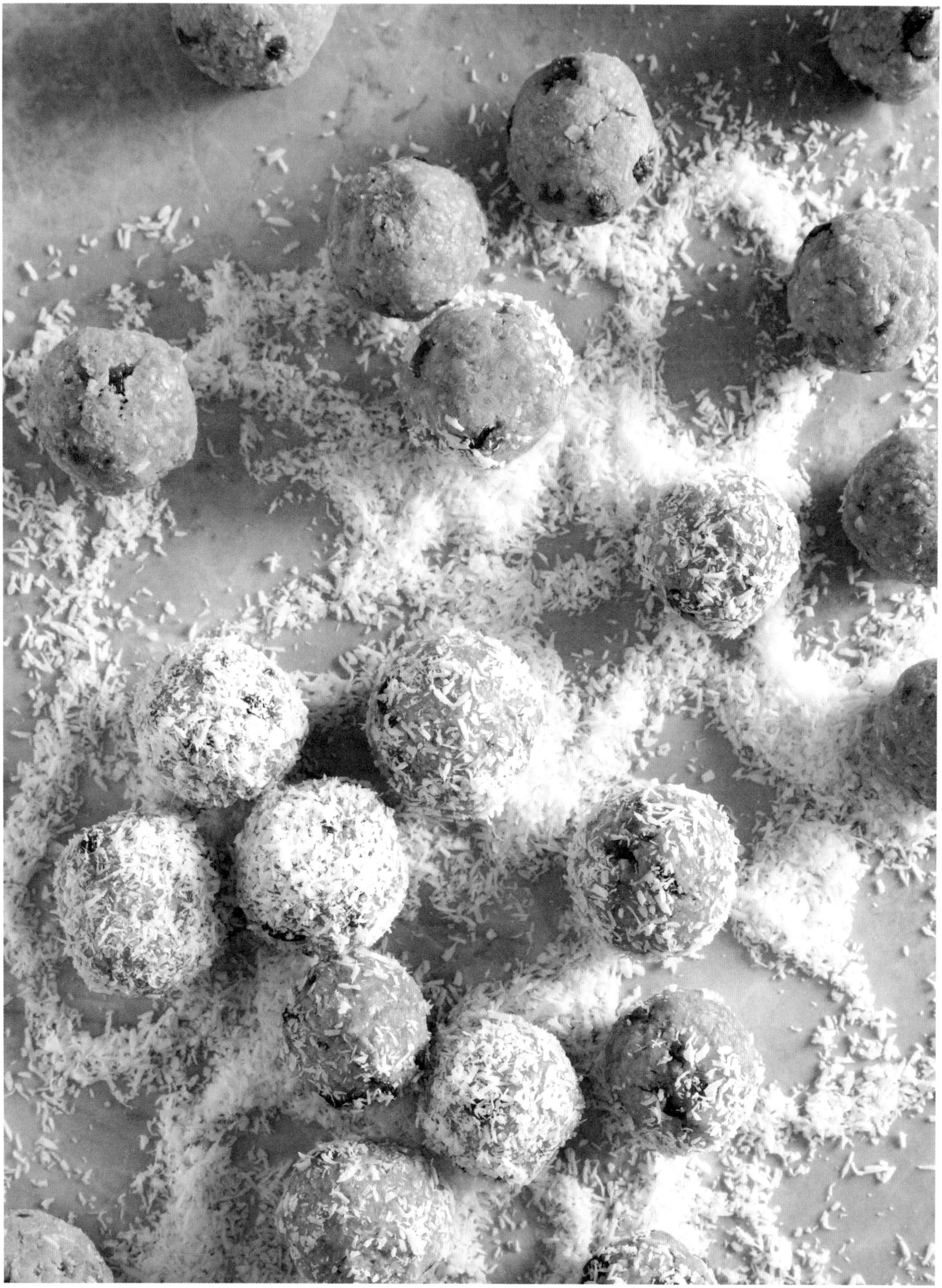

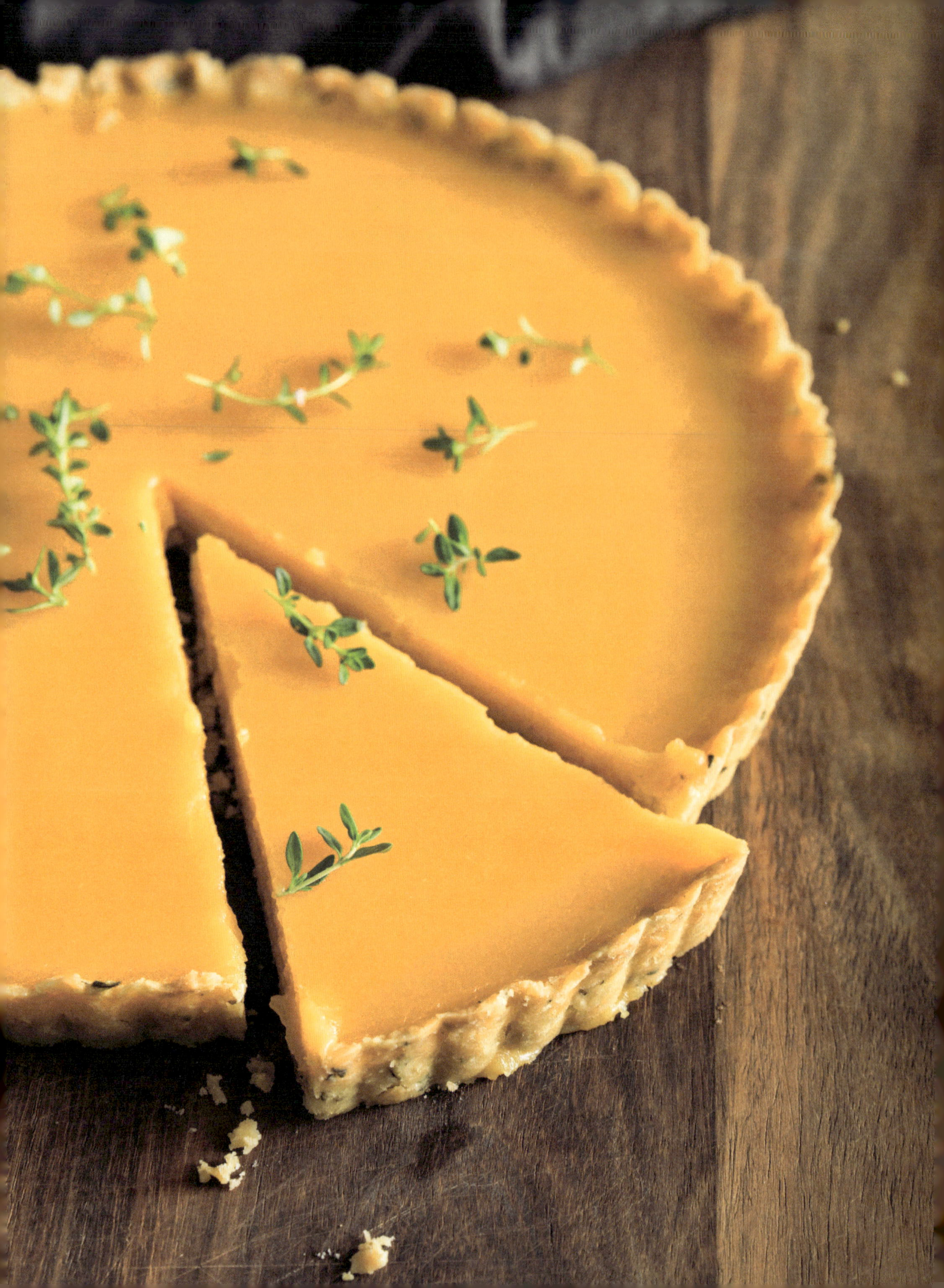

THYME & ROSEMARY CITRUS TART

SERVES 10
Prep time: 30 minutes
Cook time: 30 minutes

THYME AND ROSEMARY BURNT BUTTER PASTRY SHELL
100g butter, cut into cubes
1 tablespoon oil (e.g. grapeseed or canola)
3 tablespoons water
1 tablespoon brown sugar
good pinch of salt
1 tablespoon finely chopped thyme leaves
1 tablespoon finely chopped rosemary leaves
180g plain flour

CITRUS CURD FILLING
3 free-range eggs
4 free-range egg yolks
¾ cup caster sugar
½ cup freshly squeezed lemon or lime juice
½ cup freshly squeezed tangelo, mandarin and/or grapefruit juice
finely grated zest of 2 lemons or limes
150g butter, cut into cubes

This amazing citrus tart is an adaptation of a recipe by David Lebovitz for the best lemon tart I've ever tried. Instead of all lemon, I like to mix the citrus up. Thyme and rosemary go so beautifully with citrus, I've added them in for a fragrant, herbaceous note.

1. Preheat oven to 200°C.

2. Place butter, oil, water, brown sugar, salt and herbs in a medium-sized, ovenproof mixing bowl (e.g. a Pyrex glass bowl). Place in the oven for about 15 minutes or until the butter is bubbling and starting to brown.

3. Carefully remove hot bowl of butter from the oven and place on the bench. Add flour (careful, it may splatter a little) and quickly mix together with a metal or wooden spoon, until the dough comes away from the sides of the bowl.

4. Place dough in a 23–25cm diameter tart tin (with a removable base) and use a spatula to spread the dough out a little. When it's cool enough to touch, use the heel of your hand and fingers to spread and press the dough over the whole base and up the sides of the tart tin. Reserve a small piece of dough to fill in any cracks later.

5. Prick the base all over with a fork, then bake for 12–15 minutes until golden brown. Remove from oven and, if there are any cracks, use bits of the reserved dough to squish and fill in the cracks (you don't have to get too fussy about it though as it'll soon be covered in a beautiful citrus curd). Set aside to cool in the tin.

6. To make the Citrus Curd Filling, whisk eggs, egg yolks, sugar, citrus juices and zest together in a medium-sized pot.

7. Add butter and stir on low to medium heat until butter has melted. Whisk continuously, for about 3–5 minutes, until the mixture thickens and holds its shape when you lift it up with the whisk.

8. Pour the hot curd through a strainer into a bowl, pushing it through with the help of a spatula or back of a large spoon. Place tart shell on an oven tray and pour curd into the cooled tart shell, jiggle it gently to smooth out the top, and pop it back in the oven (on the tray) for about 6 minutes until just set (it will still be slightly wobbly when you take it out). Allow to cool on the bench before placing in the fridge to chill for at least 2 hours before serving. Serve with yoghurt or whipped cream.

THANK YOU

I've always wanted to write a vegetable cookbook and am so happy to have finally done so! I've had a blast creating this book and it has deepened my love for vegetable-based cooking even more.

I'm very thankful to get to work with such great people with amazing minds and energy. A big thank you to Amanda Gaskin and Tim Donaldson for the beautiful design, ideas and being so awesome to work with every time. You guys rock... love working, brainstorming and just hanging out with you both. Thank you Vanessa and Michael Lewis for the gorgeous photography; it has really brought this book and all the recipes in it to life. And it is always a pleasure to work with you both. Thank you Annabel Inglis for being a great friend and always being so keen to help out with shoots and recipe testing (and for the deeeelish Pumpkin and Chocolate Chunk Muffin recipe!).

Thank you Caitlin Rassie for all your work on the book and patiently putting up with me sitting next to you while we meticulously went through every single change.

Thanks to Matt and Ashlee Quérée for stepping in to do the cover shoot during such a chaotic, busy time right in the middle of doing *Dancing with the Stars!* Thanks Aaron Gilmore and Chay Roberts for making me look good — that was a fun shoot! And Victoria Baldwin for stepping in to do some extra food photography.

Thanks to Bella Piper-Jarrett for doing the nutrition analyses, Brian O'Flaherty and Jane Hingston for your editing and proof-reading work, and Kent Bowyer-Sidwell for overseeing this project and making sure that I finally got it off to the printers!

Indefinite thanks go to my awesome husband and partner in crime Carlos, and my mum Julie who has been so helpful with looking after our little boys Bodhi and River when I was stuck for childcare on photo-shoot days!

Last, but not least, a big thank you to all of YOU for your support, love and encouragement.

Big hugs, love and gratitude,   *Nadia* x

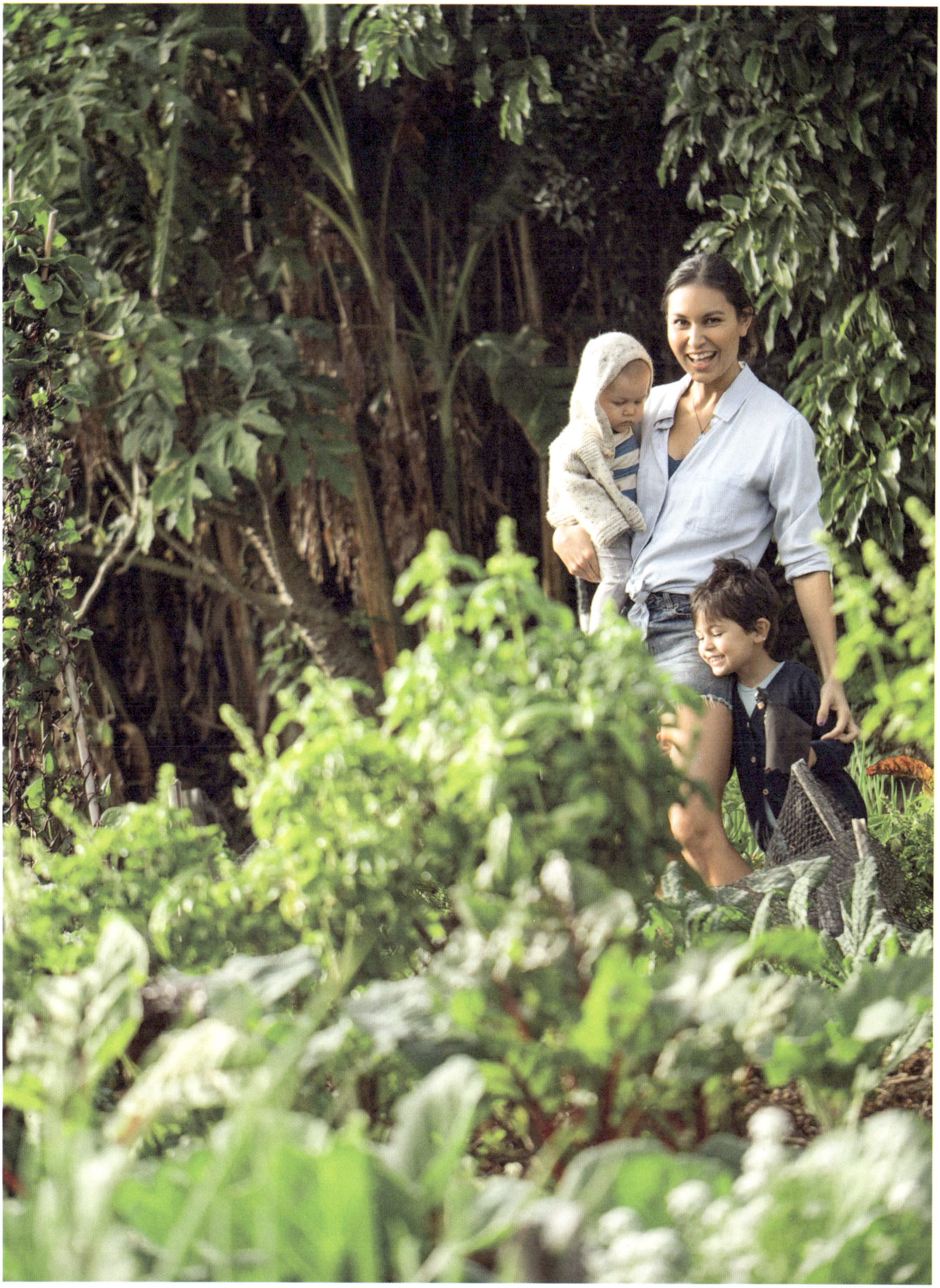

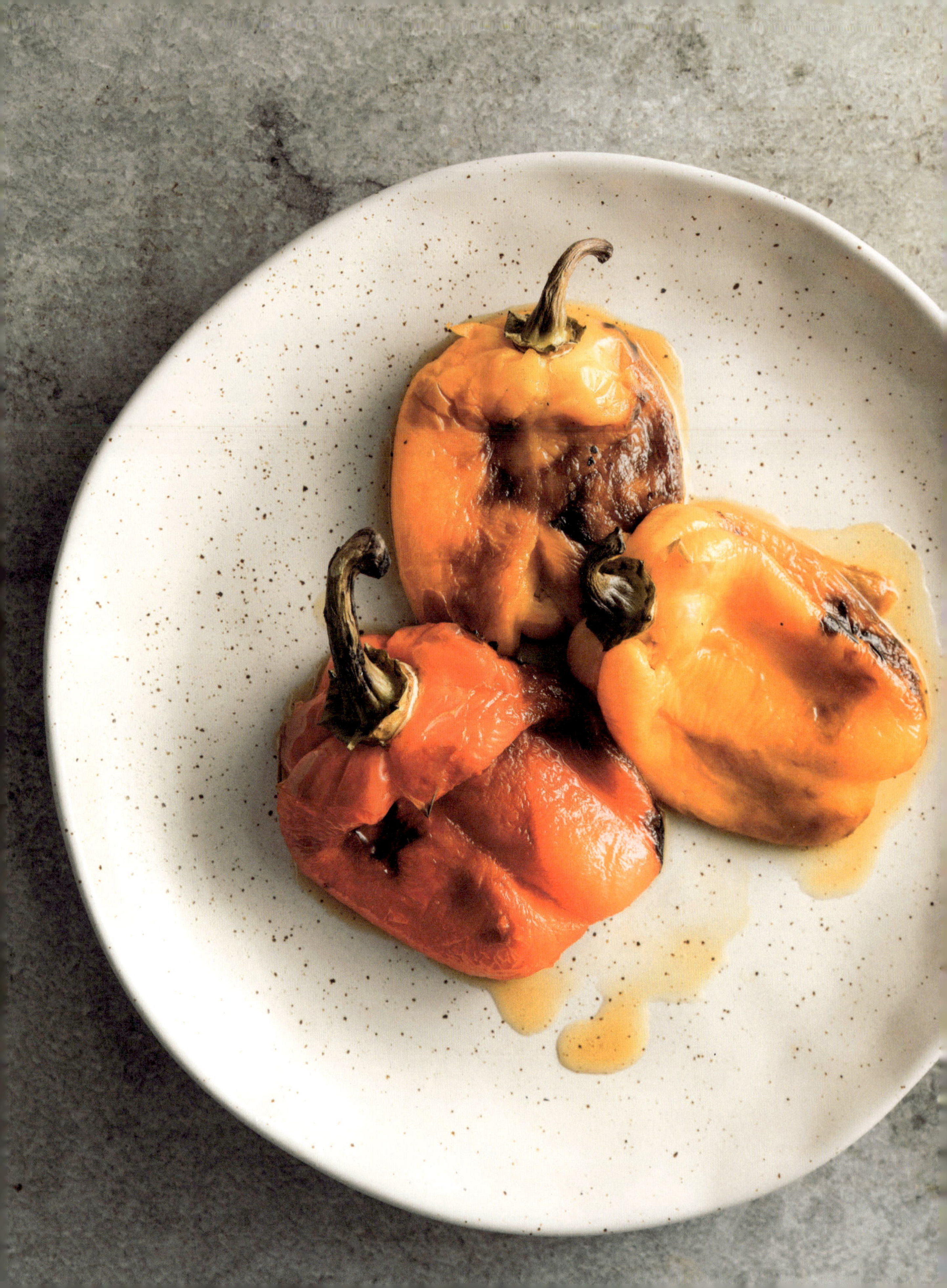

NUTRITION INFORMATION

FEASTS & SHARING

KUMARA, CHICKPEA & MUSHROOM BURGERS
Nutrition per serve
Kj 1991 | Cal 476 | Carbohydrate (g) 52.5 | Protein (g) 18.6 | Fat (g) 19.2 | Sat Fat (g) 6.5 | Sugars (g) 10.4

VEGETABLE GYOZA (DUMPLINGS)
Nutrition per serve
Kj 1524 | Cal 364 | Carbohydrate (g) 55.7 | Protein (g) 10.2 | Fat (g) 10 | Sat Fat (g) 1.6 | Sugars (g) 9.1

BBQ ORZO PASTA SALAD
Nutrition per serve
Kj 1545 | Cal 369 | Carbohydrate (g) 33.7 | Protein (g) 13.9 | Fat (g) 18.4 | Sat Fat (g) 5.8 | Sugars (g) 10.3

TOMATO TOSTADAS WITH LIME MAYO
Nutrition per serve
Kj 1890 | Cal 452 | Carbohydrate (g) 35 | Protein (g) 4.1 | Fat (g) 27.2 | Sat Fat (g) 1.5 | Sugars (g) 5.9

MARINATED VEGGIE KEBABS
Nutrition per serve
Kj 1559 | Cal 373 | Carbohydrate (g) 12 | Protein (g) 5.2 | Fat (g) 28.3 | Sat Fat (g) 10.5 | Sugars (g) 11.7

CUCUMBER, CHUTNEY & HALOUMI CANAPÉS
Nutrition per serve
Kj 636 | Cal 152 | Carbohydrate (g) 5.1 | Protein (g) 8.8 | Fat (g) 10.6 | Sat Fat (g) 6 | Sugars (g) 4.8

MINT CHERMOULA
Nutrition for entire recipe
Kj 2310 | Cal 552 | Carbohydrate (g) 1.9 | Protein (g) 4.6 | Fat (g) 58.4 | Sat Fat (g) 9.7 | Sugars (g) 1.7

CHARRED EGGPLANT, CAPSICUM & MINT
Nutrition per serve
Kj 515 | Cal 123 | Carbohydrate (g) 7.3 | Protein (g) 1.7 | Fat (g) 9 | Sat Fat (g) 1.5 | Sugars (g) 7

BEETROOT & CRÈME FRAICHE DIP
Nutrition for entire recipe
Kj 3039 | Cal 726 | Carbohydrate (g) 36.3 | Protein (g) 10.4 | Fat (g) 58.3 | Sat Fat (g) 32.8 | Sugars (g) 35.6

CORIANDER, LIME & CASHEW PESTO
Nutrition for entire recipe
Kj 3542 | Cal 847 | Carbohydrate (g) 14.6 | Protein (g) 10.7 | Fat (g) 83 | Sat Fat (g) 13.9 | Sugars (g) 4.6

LEMONY, PEA & AVOCADO DIP
Nutrition for entire recipe
Kj 1537 | Cal 367 | Carbohydrate (g) 17.3 | Protein (g) 13.3 | Fat (g) 24 | Sat Fat (g) 3.4 | Sugars (g) 10.2

NACHOS
Nutrition per serve
Kj 3070 | Cal 734 | Carbohydrate (g) 47.6 | Protein (g) 21 | Fat (g) 48.2 | Sat Fat (g) 18.4 | Sugars (g) 11

SPRING BRUSCHETTA
Nutrition per serve
Kj 1611 | Cal 385 | Carbohydrate (g) 18.3 | Protein (g) 6.7 | Fat (g) 31.4 | Sat Fat (g) 4.4 | Sugars (g) 1.5

SUMMER BRUSCHETTA
Nutrition per serve
Kj 1349 | Cal 322 | Carbohydrate (g) 18.4 | Protein (g) 11.1 | Fat (g) 22.4 | Sat Fat (g) 5.8 | Sugars (g) 2.7

AUTUMN BRUSCHETTA
Nutrition per serve
Kj 1317 | Cal 315 | Carbohydrate (g) 24 | Protein (g) 7.6 | Fat (g) 20.5 | Sat Fat (g) 6.3 | Sugars (g) 6.9

WINTER BRUSCHETTA
Nutrition per serve
Kj 1221 | Cal 292 | Carbohydrate (g) 18.4 | Protein (g) 4.9 | Fat (g) 21.8 | Sat Fat (g) 10 | Sugars (g) 2.8

SMALL SALADS & SIDES

SLOW-ROASTED EGGPLANT, CAPSICUM & COURGETTE WITH LEMON, GARLIC & HERB OIL
Nutrition per serve
Kj 1515 | Cal 362 | Carbohydrate (g) 10.2 | Protein (g) 5.6 | Fat (g) 32.5 | Sat Fat (g) 6.7 | Sugars (g) 9.7

TOMATO & RADISH SALAD WITH MINT CHERMOULA
Nutrition per serve
Kj 347 | Cal 83 | Carbohydrate (g) 4.7 | Protein (g) 1.3 | Fat (g) 6.2 | Sat Fat (g) 1 | Sugars (g) 4.6

BRUSSELS SPROUTS, APPLE & ALMOND SLAW
Nutrition per serve
Kj 1155 | Cal 276 | Carbohydrate (g) 19.2 | Protein (g) 7.6 | Fat (g) 17.3 | Sat Fat (g) 1.8 | Sugars (g) 18.1

ROAST SPICED CAULIFLOWER WITH CARAMELISED GARLIC YOGURT
Nutrition per serve
Kj 1270 | Cal 304 | Carbohydrate (g) 7.9 | Protein (g) 6.3 | Fat (g) 26 | Sat Fat (g) 4.4 | Sugars (g) 6.6

GOLDEN PARMESAN PARSNIPS
Nutrition per serve
Kj 1146 | Cal 274 | Carbohydrate (g) 23.5 | Protein (g) 11 | Fat (g) 13.1 | Sat Fat (g) 4.8 | Sugars (g) 13.4

TURKISH SALAD WITH WATERMELON
Nutrition per serve
Kj 1179 | Cal 282 | Carbohydrate (g) 24.4 | Protein (g) 5.8 | Fat (g) 17.6 | Sat Fat (g) 2.1 | Sugars (g) 22.1

PEAR, RADISH, BLUE CHEESE & ROCKET
Nutrition per serve
Kj 300 | Cal 72 | Carbohydrate (g) 5.1 | Protein (g) 2.9 | Fat (g) 4.2 | Sat Fat (g) 2.1 | Sugars (g) 4.4

ESSENTIAL SUMMER SALAD
Nutrition per serve
Kj 750 | Cal 179 | Carbohydrate (g) 3.7 | Protein (g) 2.5 | Fat (g) 16.6 | Sat Fat (g) 2.4 | Sugars (g) 3.7

NUTRITION INFORMATION

ASPARAGUS & STRAWBERRIES WITH BALSAMIC & BASIL
Nutrition per serve
Kj 816 | Cal 195 | Carbohydrate (g) 12.4 | Protein (g) 4.6 | Fat (g) 13.4 | Sat Fat (g) 2 | Sugars (g) 12.2

ASPARAGUS, ORANGE, GOATS CHEESE & DILL
Nutrition per serve
Kj 269 | Cal 64 | Carbohydrate (g) 3.7 | Protein (g) 5 | Fat (g) 2.8 | Sat Fat (g) 1.6 | Sugars (g) 3.7

RED WINE-BRAISED CABBAGE WITH CURRANTS & SPICES
Nutrition per serve
(excludes sour cream and salsa)
Kj 804 | Cal 192 | Carbohydrate (g) 11.3 | Protein (g) 2.2 | Fat (g) 10.1 | Sat Fat (g) 3 | Sugars (g) 10.9

FONDANT POTATOES
Nutrition per serve
Kj 737 | Cal 176 | Carbohydrate (g) 20.3 | Protein (g) 3.3 | Fat (g) 8.5 | Sat Fat (g) 5.3 | Sugars (g) 2.2

ROAST RADISHES
Nutrition per serve
Kj 165 | Cal 39 | Carbohydrate (g) 1.3 | Protein (g) 0.5 | Fat (g) 3.5 | Sat Fat (g) 2.2 | Sugars (g) 1.3

HEARTY SALADS & SOUPS

BALSAMIC ROAST BEETS, LENTILS & HALOUMI
Nutrition per serve
Kj 2000 | Cal 478 | Carbohydrate (g) 41.9 | Protein (g) 23.8 | Fat (g) 21.3 | Sat Fat (g) 8.8 | Sugars (g) 25

CURRIED CAULIFLOWER, CHICKPEAS & MANGO SALAD WITH COCONUT YOGHURT DRESSING
Nutrition per serve
Kj 2059 | Cal 492 | Carbohydrate (g) 32.7 | Protein (g) 12.9 | Fat (g) 32.5 | Sat Fat (g) 7.8 | Sugars (g) 19

CHARRED CORN, FETA & BARLEY SALAD WITH CHIPOTLE LIME DRESSING
Nutrition per serve
Kj 1973 | Cal 472 | Carbohydrate (g) 45.5 | Protein (g) 15.6 | Fat (g) 23 | Sat Fat (g) 7.5 | Sugars (g) 14.5

RAW VEGE PILAV
Nutrition per serve
Kj 862 | Cal 206 | Carbohydrate (g) 12.9 | Protein (g) 5.3 | Fat (g) 14 | Sat Fat (g) 2.1 | Sugars (g) 11.7

JASMIN'S CHRISTMAS SALAD
Nutrition per serve
Kj 1099 | Cal 263 | Carbohydrate (g) 6.8 | Protein (g) 4 | Fat (g) 24 | Sat Fat (g) 2.8 | Sugars (g) 5.2

PEANUT LIME & SESAME DRESSED SLAW
Nutrition per serve
Kj 523 | Cal 125 | Carbohydrate (g) 6.9 | Protein (g) 5.7 | Fat (g) 8.7 | Sat Fat (g) 1.3 | Sugars (g) 5.6

MIDDLE EASTERN QUINOA SALAD WITH HALOUMI & CRISPY PITA
Nutrition per serve
Kj 2380 | Cal 569 | Carbohydrate (g) 36.7 | Protein (g) 19.6 | Fat (g) 37 | Sat Fat (g) 11.2 | Sugars (g) 7.7

ROAST ROOTS & CARAMELISED ONION SOUP WITH LEMON, CHILLI & PARSLEY
Nutrition per serve
Kj 1097 | Cal 262 | Carbohydrate (g) 37.8 | Protein (g) 4.8 | Fat (g) 7.7 | Sat Fat (g) 1.4 | Sugars (g) 28.8

CYPRIOT LENTIL & FREEKEH SALAD WITH HONEY-GLAZED HALOUMI
Nutrition per serve
Kj 3830 | Cal 915 | Carbohydrate (g) 45.6 | Protein (g) 38.9 | Fat (g) 64 | Sat Fat (g) 20.4 | Sugars (g) 14.4

CHUNKY VEGETABLE & BARLEY SOUP WITH GARLIC SOURDOUGH CROÛTONS
Nutrition per serve
Kj 2095 | Cal 501 | Carbohydrate (g) 53.2 | Protein (g) 14.9 | Fat (g) 21.9 | Sat Fat (g) 4.8 | Sugars (g) 19.6

MOROCCAN ROAST CARROTS WITH QUINOA DATES, LIME & CHILLI
Nutrition per serve
Kj 1970 | Cal 471 | Carbohydrate (g) 50 | Protein (g) 11.8 | Fat (g) 22.2 | Sat Fat (g) 3.1 | Sugars (g) 25

HARIRA
Nutrition per serve
Kj 1419 | Cal 339 | Carbohydrate (g) 36.8 | Protein (g) 15.4 | Fat (g) 11.2 | Sat Fat (g) 2.2 | Sugars (g) 14.1

LUNCH & DINNER

MEXICAN STUFFED KUMARAS
Nutrition per serve (excludes sour cream and salsa)
Kj 1927 | Cal 461 | Carbohydrate (g) 45 | Protein (g) 18.9 | Fat (g) 20.1 | Sat Fat (g) 9.1 | Sugars (g) 23.9

CARAMELISED ONION & BEETROOT TART WITH SOFT CASHEW CHEESE
Nutrition per serve
Kj 1457 | Cal 348 | Carbohydrate (g) 28.6 | Protein (g) 6.7 | Fat (g) 22.2 | Sat Fat (g) 7 | Sugars (g) 13.9

CREAMY ASPARAGUS, SPINACH, HERB & GOATS CHEESE TART
Nutrition per serve
Kj 1900 | Cal 454 | Carbohydrate (g) 25.6 | Protein (g) 14.4 | Fat (g) 31.7 | Sat Fat (g) 18.6 | Sugars (g) 3.2

MOROCCAN EGGPLANT BOATS
Nutrition per serve
Kj 1570 | Cal 375 | Carbohydrate (g) 52 | Protein (g) 14.1 | Fat (g) 9.8 | Sat Fat (g) 1.9 | Sugars (g) 23.4

NUTRITION INFORMATION

RUSTIC VEGETABLE PIZZA PIE
Nutrition per serve
Kj 2629 | Cal 628 | Carbohydrate (g) 84.9 | Protein (g) 17.3 | Fat (g) 21.3 | Sat Fat (g) 3.3 | Sugars (g) 20.9

CARAMELISED SHALLOT & THYME TARTE TATIN
Nutrition per serve
Kj 2064 | Cal 493 | Carbohydrate (g) 37.3 | Protein (g) 5 | Fat (g) 35.6 | Sat Fat (g) 18.9 | Sugars (g) 16.6

SELF-CRUSTING SUMMER VEGETABLE QUICHE
Nutrition per serve
Kj 2170 | Cal 519 | Carbohydrate (g) 15.6 | Protein (g) 22 | Fat (g) 40.5 | Sat Fat (g) 20.8 | Sugars (g) 7.8

PUMPKIN, SPINACH AND FETA SELF-CRUSTING QUICHE
Nutrition per serve
Kj 2026 | Cal 484 | Carbohydrate (g) 16.7 | Protein (g) 22.5 | Fat (g) 35.9 | Sat Fat (g) 19.8 | Sugars (g) 7.4

SPINACH, CARAMELISED ONION & FETA FILO PARCELS
Nutrition per serve
Kj 2638 | Cal 630 | Carbohydrate (g) 57 | Protein (g) 18.8 | Fat (g) 35.9 | Sat Fat (g) 18.5 | Sugars (g) 6.5

RATATOUILLE, BUTTERNUT & LENTIL LASAGNE
Nutrition per serve
Kj 3028 | Cal 724 | Carbohydrate (g) 54.3 | Protein (g) 33.5 | Fat (g) 38.7 | Sat Fat (g) 18.4 | Sugars (g) 18.2

CREAMY TOMATO, MUSHROOM, KALE & BLACK BEAN SHEPPARDS PIE
Nutrition per serve
Kj 2755 | Cal 658 | Carbohydrate (g) 41.7 | Protein (g) 26.3 | Fat (g) 40 | Sat Fat (g) 22.1 | Sugars (g) 6.6

PORTOBELLO MUSHROOM & BRIE WELLINGTON
Nutrition per serve
Kj 2148 | Cal 513 | Carbohydrate (g) 14.7 | Protein (g) 15 | Fat (g) 43.6 | Sat Fat (g) 26.6 | Sugars (g) 4.8

SPINACH & RICOTTA DUMPLINGS WITH TOMATO COURGETTE SAUCE
Nutrition per serve
Kj 2196 | Cal 525 | Carbohydrate (g) 23.6 | Protein (g) 30.7 | Fat (g) 33.2 | Sat Fat (g) 14.7 | Sugars (g) 10.5

GNOCCHI
Nutrition per serve
Kj 2221 | Cal 531 | Carbohydrate (g) 48.6 | Protein (g) 24.1 | Fat (g) 25.2 | Sat Fat (g) 8.4 | Sugars (g) 5.5

SLOW-COOKED SMOKY BEANS
Nutrition per serve
Kj 1124 | Cal 269 | Carbohydrate (g) 35.3 | Protein (g) 11.5 | Fat (g) 6.2 | Sat Fat (g) 1 | Sugars (g) 19.4

SOFT CASHEW CHEESE
Nutrition for entire recipe
Kj 4507 | Cal 1077 | Carbohydrate (g) 27.7 | Protein (g) 27.9 | Fat (g) 94.2 | Sat Fat (g) 16 | Sugars (g) 9.3

OLIVE OIL PASTRY
Nutrition for entire recipe
Kj 5892 | Cal 1408 | Carbohydrate (g) 135.1 | Protein (g) 21.7 | Fat (g) 85.6 | Sat Fat (g) 13.7 | Sugars (g) 0.2

DILL TZATZIKI
Nutrition for entire recipe
Kj 774 | Cal 185 | Carbohydrate (g) 8.2 | Protein (g) 9.4 | Fat (g) 12.6 | Sat Fat (g) 7.5 | Sugars (g) 8

PIZZA DOUGH
Nutrition per pizza base
Kj 1816 | Cal 434 | Carbohydrate (g) 73 | Protein (g) 12.7 | Fat (g) 8.7 | Sat Fat (g) 1.1 | Sugars (g) 1.2

MOROCCAN APRICOT & TOMATO CHUTNEY
Nutrition for entire recipe
Kj 2816 | Cal 673 | Carbohydrate (g) 110.2 | Protein (g) 11.2 | Fat (g) 16.6 | Sat Fat (g) 2.5 | Sugars (g) 108.1

CARAMELISED ONIONS
Nutrition for entire recipe
Kj 2581 | Cal 617 | Carbohydrate (g) 48.5 | Protein (g) 7.9 | Fat (g) 41.7 | Sat Fat (g) 6.9 | Sugars (g) 48.3

QUICK EASY & LEFTOVERS

WINTER GREENS WITH A FRIED EGG & PARMESAN
Nutrition per serve
Kj 947 | Cal 226 | Carbohydrate (g) 24.6 | Protein (g) 14.9 | Fat (g) 5.5 | Sat Fat (g) 1.3 | Sugars (g) 8

BOK CHOY & SHIITAKE MUSHROOM MISO NOODLE SOUP
Nutrition per serve
Kj 2014 | Cal 481 | Carbohydrate (g) 65.4 | Protein (g) 17.9 | Fat (g) 14.9 | Sat Fat (g) 2.5 | Sugars (g) 14.1

VEGGIE QUESADILLAS
Nutrition per serve (excludes sour cream and chutney)
Kj 2870 | Cal 686 | Carbohydrate (g) 42 | Protein (g) 25.7 | Fat (g) 41.2 | Sat Fat (g) 15.5 | Sugars (g) 8.3

MUSHROOM & HERB FETTUCCINE WITH CREAMY CASHEW SAUCE
Nutrition per serve
Kj 1697 | Cal 405.6 | Carbohydrate (g) 32.6 | Protein (g) 16.6 | Fat (g) 21.1 | Sat Fat (g) 3.5 | Sugars (g) 4.9

GOURMET MOUSETRAPS
Nutrition per serve
Kj 1033 | Cal 246.9 | Carbohydrate (g) 17.3 | Protein (g) 9.8 | Fat (g) 14.5 | Sat Fat (g) 6.6 | Sugars (g) 3.6

TACOS WITH WALNUT & ALMOND CHILLI & GUACAMOLE
Nutrition per serve
Kj 3153 | Cal 754 | Carbohydrate (g) 29.5 | Protein (g) 16.2 | Fat (g) 61.3 | Sat Fat (g) 7.5 | Sugars (g) 8.6

NUTRITION INFORMATION

BURRITO BOWLS
Nutrition per serve (excludes sour cream and salsa)
Kj 1582 | Cal 378 | Carbohydrate (g) 48.3 | Protein (g) 11 | Fat (g) 13 | Sat Fat (g) 1.9 | Sugars (g) 3.1

LEFTOVER VEG TARTS
Nutrition per serve
Kj 1750 | Cal 418 | Carbohydrate (g) 22.9 | Protein (g) 15 | Fat (g) 28.9 | Sat Fat (g) 18.3 | Sugars (g) 9.7

ANYTHING VEGETABLE FRITTATA
Nutrition per serve
Kj 1589 | Cal 380 | Carbohydrate (g) 9.5 | Protein (g) 23.7 | Fat (g) 26.8 | Sat Fat (g) 14.2 | Sugars (g) 7.1

SAUCY PAD THAI
Nutrition per serve
Kj 2596 | Cal 620 | Carbohydrate (g) 63.9 | Protein (g) 12.5 | Fat (g) 34 | Sat Fat (g) 12.4 | Sugars (g) 13.8

OLIVE TAPENADE
Nutrition for entire recipe
Kj 3426 | Cal 819 | Carbohydrate (g) 5.7 | Protein (g) 3.5 | Fat (g) 86.4 | Sat Fat (g) 13 | Sugars (g) 0.6

JALAPEÑO CHUTNEY
Nutrition for entire recipe
Kj 1271 | Cal 304 | Carbohydrate (g) 35.8 | Protein (g) 4.8 | Fat (g) 14.3 | Sat Fat (g) 2.3 | Sugars (g) 35

TOMATO, JALAPEÑO & CORIANDER SALSA
Nutrition for entire recipe
Kj 1189 | Cal 284 | Carbohydrate (g) 38.1 | Protein (g) 7.8 | Fat (g) 8.3 | Sat Fat (g) 1 | Sugars (g) 37.3

BRUSCHETTA
Nutrition per bruschetta base
Kj 584 | Cal 140 | Carbohydrate (g) 14.5 | Protein (g) 2.9 | Fat (g) 7.5 | Sat Fat (g) 1.2 | Sugars (g) 0.9

AUTUMN HARVEST SAUCE
Nutrition per cup
Kj 756 | Cal 181 | Carbohydrate (g) 15.9 | Protein (g) 3.4 | Fat (g) 10.1 | Sat Fat (g) 1.6 | Sugars (g) 15.4

SPICY & EXOTIC

VEGETABLE LAKSA
Nutrition per serve
Kj 3650 | Cal 872 | Carbohydrate (g) 51.8 | Protein (g) 26.2 | Fat (g) 60.4 | Sat Fat (g) 38.4 | Sugars (g) 14.6

PINEAPPLE FRIED RICE
Nutrition per serve
Kj 3404 | Cal 814 | Carbohydrate (g) 86.3 | Protein (g) 19.1 | Fat (g) 41.8 | Sat Fat (g) 15 | Sugars (g) 23.2

CAULIFLOWER & CHICKPEA KORMA
Nutrition per serve
Kj 2613 | Cal 625 | Carbohydrate (g) 25.8 | Protein (g) 15.5 | Fat (g) 48.8 | Sat Fat (g) 21.4 | Sugars (g) 11.1

VEGETABLE DHAL (LENTIL CURRY)
Nutrition per serve
Kj 1495 | Cal 357 | Carbohydrate (g) 27.8 | Protein (g) 12.3 | Fat (g) 19.8 | Sat Fat (g) 12.1 | Sugars (g) 9.2

QUICK MASALA DOSA
Nutrition per serve (excludes chutney)
Kj 1843 | Cal 440 | Carbohydrate (g) 62.7 | Protein (g) 15.1 | Fat (g) 12 | Sat Fat (g) 2.4 | Sugars (g) 8.4

MASALA POTATOES & CARROTS
Nutrition per serve
Kj 871 | Cal 208 | Carbohydrate (g) 26 | Protein (g) 5.1 | Fat (g) 8 | Sat Fat (g) 1.2 | Sugars (g) 6.7

HARISSA EGGPLANT, TOMATOES & CHICKPEAS
Nutrition per serve
Kj 2190 | Cal 523 | Carbohydrate (g) 53.9 | Protein (g) 14.6 | Fat (g) 25.1 | Sat Fat (g) 7.1 | Sugars (g) 9.2

GARLIC & HERB FLATBREADS
Nutrition per serve
Kj 1476 | Cal 353 | Carbohydrate (g) 48 | Protein (g) 9.1 | Fat (g) 13 | Sat Fat (g) 5.2 | Sugars (g) 2.8

COCONUT CASHEW CREAM
Nutrition for entire recipe
Kj 7283 | Cal 1741 | Carbohydrate (g) 32 | Protein (g) 32.8 | Fat (g) 164.7 | Sat Fat (g) 80.6 | Sugars (g) 13.6

HARISSA
Nutrition for entire recipe
Kj 2204 | Cal 527 | Carbohydrate (g) 13.8 | Protein (g) 3.9 | Fat (g) 50.2 | Sat Fat (g) 8.2 | Sugars (g) 12.4

CASHEW CREAM
Nutrition for entire recipe
Kj 3996 | Cal 955 | Carbohydrate (g) 27.6 | Protein (g) 27.8 | Fat (g) 80.5 | Sat Fat (g) 13.7 | Sugars (g) 9.1

CURRANT & NUT RICE
Nutrition per serve
Kj 711 | Cal 170 | Carbohydrate (g) 29.4 | Protein (g) 3.1 | Fat (g) 4 | Sat Fat (g) 1 | Sugars (g) 4.3

SWEET & BAKING

JALAPEÑO, CHEESE & SPRING ONION CORNBREAD
Nutrition per serve
Kj 1145 | Cal 274 | Carbohydrate (g) 24.5 | Protein (g) 7.8 | Fat (g) 15.7 | Sat Fat (g) 9.2 | Sugars (g) 5.2

AVOCADO CHOCOLATE TRUFFLES
Nutrition per truffle
Kj 396 | Cal 95 | Carbohydrate (g) 4.9 | Protein (g) 1.3 | Fat (g) 7.5 | Sat Fat (g) 3 | Sugars (g) 3.8

CARROT, BEETROOT, APPLE AND BLACKCURRANT COMPÔTE
Nutrition per serve
Kj 542 | Cal 130 | Carbohydrate (g) 26.3 | Protein (g) 1.3 | Fat (g) 0.7 | Sat Fat (g) 0.1 | Sugars (g) 25.6

NUTRITION INFORMATION

SEED & NUT CRUMBLE
Nutrition per serve
Kj 2003 | Cal 479 | Carbohydrate (g) 40.1 | Protein (g) 9 | Fat (g) 30.4 | Sat Fat (g) 9.6 | Sugars (g) 35.3

FLASH-ROASTED RHUBARB & STRAWBERRIES
Nutrition per serve
Kj 269 | Cal 64 | Carbohydrate (g) 13.3 | Protein (g) 0.8 | Fat (g) 0.4 | Sat Fat (g) 0 | Sugars (g) 13.3

RHUBARB, STRAWBS N' CREAM LOADED SHORTBREAD
Nutrition per serve
Kj 3124 | Cal 747 | Carbohydrate (g) 54.3 | Protein (g) 6.5 | Fat (g) 55.5 | Sat Fat (g) 33.9 | Sugars (g) 31.1

THYME & LEMON SHORTBREAD
Nutrition per shortbread
Kj 524 | Cal 125 | Carbohydrate (g) 12.3 | Protein (g) 1.4 | Fat (g) 7.7 | Sat Fat (g) 4.6 | Sugars (g) 4.1

RHUBARB & APPLE PIE
Nutrition per serve
Kj 1749 | Cal 418 | Carbohydrate (g) 61.7 | Protein (g) 5.1 | Fat (g) 16.1 | Sat Fat (g) 8.8 | Sugars (g) 40.2

PARSNIP, PEAR, GINGER & WALNUT CAKE WITH CARAMEL CREAM CHEESE ICING
Nutrition per serve
Kj 2759 | Cal 659 | Carbohydrate (g) 52.7 | Protein (g) 7.6 | Fat (g) 45.4 | Sat Fat (g) 14.3 | Sugars (g) 36.8

PUMPKIN & CINNAMON DONUTS
Nutrition per serve
Kj 1747 | Cal 418 | Carbohydrate (g) 74.2 | Protein (g) 9.4 | Fat (g) 7.9 | Sat Fat (g) 3.9 | Sugars (g) 31.2

SPICED COURGETTE, DATE & APPLE TEA LOAF
Nutrition per serve
Kj 1185 | Cal 283 | Carbohydrate (g) 28.2 | Protein (g) 6.7 | Fat (g) 15 | Sat Fat (g) 5.7 | Sugars (g) 20.4

VEGGIE POPS
Nutrition per ice block
Kj 151 | Cal 36 | Carbohydrate (g) 7.3 | Protein (g) 0.5 | Fat (g) 0.2 | Sat Fat (g) 0 | Sugars (g) 7.2

COURGETTE & CHOC CHIP BUTTERMILK PIKELETS
Nutrition per serve
Kj 1907 | Cal 456 | Carbohydrate (g) 57.7 | Protein (g) 11.2 | Fat (g) 19.2 | Sat Fat (g) 10.8 | Sugars (g) 26

AVOCADO MINT CHOC CHIP ICE CREAM
Nutrition per serve
Kj 2135 | Cal 510 | Carbohydrate (g) 33.3 | Protein (g) 6.6 | Fat (g) 38.5 | Sat Fat (g) 19.1 | Sugars (g) 31.9

ANNABEL'S PUMPKIN & CHOCOLATE CHUNK MUFFINS
Nutrition per muffin
Kj 1179 | Cal 282 | Carbohydrate (g) 36.6 | Protein (g) 4.8 | Fat (g) 12.3 | Sat Fat (g) 7.1 | Sugars (g) 20.4

SWEET POTATO PIE WITH MAPLE-GLAZED NUTS
Nutrition per serve
Kj 2478 | Cal 592 | Carbohydrate (g) 37.3 | Protein (g) 8.1 | Fat (g) 45 | Sat Fat (g) 18.8 | Sugars (g) 25.7

BEETROOT, CHOCOLATE & ORANGE CAKE
Nutrition per serve
Kj 2071 | Cal 495 | Carbohydrate (g) 32.4 | Protein (g) 9.8 | Fat (g) 35 | Sat Fat (g) 20.2 | Sugars (g) 30

CARROT, PINEAPPLE & BANANA CUPCAKES
Nutrition per cupcake
Kj 1228 | Cal 293 | Carbohydrate (g) 32.4 | Protein (g) 3.6 | Fat (g) 16.1 | Sat Fat (g) 4.4 | Sugars (g) 20

BLACK BEAN CHOCOLATE FUDGE BROWNIE
Nutrition per piece
Kj 979 | Cal 234 | Carbohydrate (g) 16.3 | Protein (g) 6.3 | Fat (g) 15.1 | Sat Fat (g) 8.4 | Sugars (g) 9.8

KUMARA FOCACCIA WITH GRAPES & ROSEMARY
Nutrition per serve
Kj 1583 | Cal 378 | Carbohydrate (g) 54.5 | Protein (g) 8.5 | Fat (g) 13 | Sat Fat (g) 2 | Sugars (g) 8.3

POLENTA, LEMON & COCONUT SLICE
Nutrition per serve
Kj 1445 | Cal 345 | Carbohydrate (g) 27.7 | Protein (g) 3.5 | Fat (g) 24 | Sat Fat (g) 17.1 | Sugars (g) 21.4

BEETROOT & RASPBERRY GRANITA
Nutrition per serve
Kj 471 | Cal 113 | Carbohydrate (g) 25 | Protein (g) 1.1 | Fat (g) 0.3 | Sat Fat (g) 0 | Sugars (g) 25

CARROT CAKE BLISS BALLS
Nutrition per ball
Kj 423 | Cal 101 | Carbohydrate (g) 12 | Protein (g) 1.3 | Fat (g) 4.8 | Sat Fat (g) 3.9 | Sugars (g) 9.3

THYME & ROSEMARY CITRUS TART
Nutrition per serve
Kj 1580 | Cal 378 | Carbohydrate (g) 31.6 | Protein (g) 5.2 | Fat (g) 25.6 | Sat Fat (g) 14.1 | Sugars (g) 19.3

INDEX

A
Annabel's pumpkin & chocolate chunk muffins 301
Anything veggie frittata 187
apples
    Brussels sprouts, apple & almond slaw 234
    Carrot, beetroot, apple & blackcurrant compôte 268
    Rhubarb & apple pie 281
    Spiced courgette, date & apple loaf 291
apricots
    Moroccan apricot & tomato chutney 158
    Peanut lime & sesame dressed slaw 104
asparagus 22
    Anything veggie frittata 187
    Asparagus & strawberries with balsamic & basil 246
    Asparagus, orange, goats cheese & dill 249
    BBQ orzo pasta salad 49
    Creamy asparagus, spinach, herb & goats cheese tart 121
aubergine: see eggplant
Autumn bruschetta 76
Autumn harvest sauce 192
avocado
    Avocado chocolate truffles 265
    Avocado mint choc chip ice cream 298
    Charred corn, feta & barley salad with chipotle lime dressing 90
    Cypriot lentil & freekeh salad with honey-glazed haloumi 97
    Essential summer salad 245
    Jasmin's Christmas salad 107
    Lemony pea & avocado dip 62
    Spring bruschetta 74
    Zingy nachos 70

B
baking
    Annabel's pumpkin & chocolate chunk muffins 301
    Beetroot, chocolate & orange cake 307
    Black bean chocolate fudge brownie 311
    Carrot cake bliss balls 320
    Carrot, pineapple & banana cupcakes 308
    Courgette & choc chip buttermilk pikelets 297
    Jalapeño, cheese & spring onion cornbread 262
    Parsnip, pear, ginger & walnut cake with caramel cream cheese icing 282
    Polenta, lemon & coconut slice 316
    Pumpkin & cinnamon donuts 288
    Spiced courgette, date & apple loaf 291
    Thyme & lemon shortbread 278
Balsamic roast beets, lentils & haloumi 84
bananas
    Carrot, pineapple & banana cupcakes 308
    Courgette & choc chip buttermilk pikelets 297
barley
    Charred corn, feta & barley salad with chipotle lime dressing 90
    Chunky vegetable & barley soup with garlic sourdough croutons 98
BBQ orzo pasta salad 49
beans: dried
    Black (or kidney) bean chocolate fudge brownie 311
    Burrito bowls 183
    Creamy tomato, mushroom, kale &

    black bean shepherd's pie 41
    Mexican stuffed kumaras 116
    Ratatouille, butternut & lentil (or black beans) lasagne 138
    Slow-cooked smoky beans 153
    Veggie quesadillas 173
    Zingy nachos 70
beans: green
    Anything veggie frittata 187
    BBQ orzo pasta salad 49
    Chunky vegetable & barley soup with garlic sourdough croutons 98
    Pineapple fried rice 203
    Saucy pad thai 188
    Vegetable dhal (lentil curry) 207
    Vegetarian coconut laksa 200
beetroot 17
    Balsamic roast beets, lentils & haloumi 84
    Beetroot & crème fraîche dip 62
    Beetroot & raspberry granita 319
    Beetroot, chocolate & orange cake 307
    Caramelised onion & beetroot tart with soft cashew cheese 118
    Carrot, beetroot, apple & blackcurrant compôte 268
Black bean chocolate fudge brownie 311
blackcurrants
    Carrot, beetroot, apple & blackcurrant compôte 268
bliss balls 320
blue cheese
    Autumn bruschetta 76
    Pear, radish, blue cheese & rocket 242
bok choy
    Peanut lime & sesame dressed slaw 104
    Bok choy & shiitake mushroom miso noodle soup 170
    Vegetarian coconut laksa 200
bread
    Garlic & herb flatbreads 216
    Jalapeño, cheese & spring onion cornbread 262
    Kumara focaccia with grapes & rosemary 315
brie
    Portobello mushroom & brie Wellington 144
broccoli 23
    Anything veggie frittata 187
    Raw veg pilav 108
    Vegetable dhal (lentil curry) 207
    Vegetarian coconut laksa 200
    Winter greens with a fried egg & parmesan 167
brownie 311
bruschetta
    Autumn bruschetta 76
    Bruschetta bases 191
    Spring bruschetta 74
    Summer bruschetta 74
    Winter bruschetta 77
Brussels sprouts
    Brussels sprouts, apple & almond slaw 234
    Winter greens with a fried egg & parmesan 167
burgers
    Kumara, chickpea & mushroom burgers 40
Burrito bowls 183
butternut: see pumpkin

C
cabbage 29
    Peanut lime & sesame dressed slaw 104

    Pineapple fried rice 203
    Red wine-braised cabbage with currants & spices 250
    Vegetable dhal (lentil curry) 46
    Vegetable gyoza (dumplings) 46
cakes: see baking
camembert
    Portobello mushroom & brie (or camembert) Wellington 144
Candied maple walnuts 282
capsicums (peppers) 16
    BBQ orzo pasta salad 49
    Charred corn, feta & barley salad with chipotle lime dressing 90
    Charred eggplant, capsicum & mint 59
    Marinated veggie kebabs 5
    Moroccan apricot & tomato chutney 158
    Moroccan eggplant boats 122
    Rustic vegetable pizza pie 127
    Saucy pad thai 188
    Self-crusting summer vegetable quiche 133
    Slow-roasted eggplant, capsicum & courgette with lemon, garlic & herb oil 228
    Vegetarian coconut laksa 200
    Zingy nachos 70
Caramel cream cheese icing 282
Caramelised garlic yoghurt 237
Caramelised onion & beetroot tart with soft cashew cheese 118
Caramelised onions 159
Caramelised shallot & thyme tarte tatin 130
carrots
    Peanut lime & sesame dressed slaw 104
    Bok choy & shiitake mushroom miso noodle soup 170
    Carrot cake bliss balls 320
    Carrot, beetroot, apple & blackcurrant compôte 268
    Carrot, pineapple & banana cupcakes 308
    Chunky vegetable & barley soup with garlic sourdough croutons 98
    Creamy tomato, mushroom, kale & black bean shepherd's pie 141
    Harira 103
    Masala potatoes & carrots 211
    Moroccan roast carrots with quinoa, dates, lime & chilli 100
    Pineapple fried rice 203
    Raw veg pilav 108
    Roast roots & caramelised onion soup with lemon, chilli & parsley 94
    Vegetable dhal (lentil curry) 207
    Vegetable gyoza (dumplings) 46
Cashew cream 217
Charred corn, feta & barley salad with chipotle lime dressing 90
Charred eggplant, capsicum & mint 59
cauliflower 28
    Cauliflower & chickpea korma 204
    Curried cauliflower, chickpeas & mango salad with coconut yoghurt dressing 89
    Raw veg pilav 108
    Roast spiced cauliflower with caramelised garlic yoghurt 237
    Vegetable dhal (lentil curry) 207
    Vegetarian coconut laksa 200
cavolo nero
    Jasmin's Christmas salad 107
    Mushroom & herb fettuccine with cashew cream sauce 175
    Winter greens with a fried egg &

parmesan 167
celery
    Chunky vegetable & barley soup with garlic sourdough croutons 98
    Harira 103
Cheese sauce 138
chermoula
    Jalapeño chermoula 57
    Mint chermoula 57
chickpeas
    Cauliflower & chickpea korma 204
    Curried cauliflower, chickpeas & mango salad with coconut yoghurt dressing 89
    Harira 103
    Harissa eggplant, tomatoes & chickpeas 214
    Kumara, chickpea & mushroom burgers 40
Chilli & almond gremolata 237
Chipotle lime dressing 90
chocolate
    Avocado chocolate truffles 265
    Avocado mint choc chip ice cream 298
    Beetroot, chocolate & orange cake 307
    Black bean chocolate fudge brownie 311
    Chocolate ganache 307
    Courgette & choc chip buttermilk pikelets 297
Chunky vegetable & barley soup with garlic sourdough croutons 98
chutney
    Jalapeño chutney 191
    Moroccan apricot & tomato chutney 158
Cinnamon yoghurt cream 302
Ciro's gnocchi 150
Citrus curd filling 323
coconut
    Coconut cashew cream 217
    Coconut yoghurt dressing 89
    Polenta, lemon & coconut slice 316
coleslaw 234
compote 268
Coriander, lime & cashew pesto 63
corn
    Anything veggie frittata 187
    Charred corn, feta & barley salad with chipotle lime dressing 90
    Jalapeño, cheese & spring onion cornbread 262
    Mexican stuffed kumaras 116
    Pineapple fried rice 203
    Veggie quesadillas 173
cornmeal: see polenta
courgettes 18
    BBQ orzo pasta salad 49
    Chunky vegetable & barley soup with garlic sourdough croutons 98
    Courgette & choc chip buttermilk pikelets 297
    Marinated veggie kebabs 54
    Rustic vegetable pizza pie 127
    Self-crusting summer vegetable quiche 133
    Slow-roasted eggplant, capsicum & courgette with lemon, garlic & herb oil 228
    Spiced courgette, date & apple loaf 291
    Tomato courgette sauce 147
    Vegetable dhal (lentil curry) 207
couscous
    Moroccan eggplant boats 122
Creamy asparagus, spinach, herb & goats cheese tart 121
Creamy tomato, mushroom, kale & black bean shepherd's pie 141

croutons 98
crumble 271
cucumber
    Cucumber, chutney & haloumi canapés 56
    Cypriot lentil & freekeh salad with honey-glazed haloumi 97
    Middle Eastern quinoa salad with haloumi & crispy pita 93
    Turkish salad with watermelon 241
    Veggie pops 294
cupcakes 308
Currant & nut rice 219
Curried cauliflower, chickpeas & mango salad with coconut yoghurt dressing 89
curries
    Cauliflower & chickpea korma 204
    Vegetable dhal (lentil curry) 207
Cypriot lentil & freekeh salad with honey-glazed haloumi 97

D
dates
    Moroccan roast carrots with quinoa, dates, lime & chilli 100
    Raw veg pilav 108
    Spiced courgette, date & apple loaf 291
dhal: see lentils
Dill tzatziki 156
Dipping sauce (for gyoza) 46
dips & salsas
    Beetroot & crème fraîche dip 62
    Charred eggplant, capsicum & mint 59
    Lemony pea & avocado dip 62
    Tomato, jalapeño & coriander salsa 190
    Quick salsa 195
donuts 288
dosa 208
dressings
    Caramelised garlic yoghurt 237
    Chipotle lime dressing 90
    Coconut yoghurt dressing 89
    Honey mustard dressing 234
    Jalapeño chermoula 57
    Mint chermoula 57
    Peanut lime dressing 104
dumplings
    Spinach & ricotta dumplings with tomato courgette sauce 147
    Vegetable gyoza (dumplings) 46

E
eggplant 25
    BBQ orzo pasta salad 49
    Charred eggplant, capsicum & mint 59
    Harissa eggplant, tomatoes & chickpeas 214
    Marinated veggie kebabs 54
    Moroccan eggplant boats 122
    Slow-roasted eggplant, capsicum & courgette with lemon, garlic & herb oil 228
Essential summer salad 245

F
fennel 24
Autumn harvest sauce 192
feta
    Anything veggie frittata 187
    Autumn bruschetta 76
    BBQ orzo pasta salad 49
    Charred corn, feta & barley salad with chipotle lime dressing 90
    Creamy asparagus, spinach, herb & goats

cheese (or feta) tart 121
    Mexican stuffed kumaras 116
    Moroccan eggplant boats 122
    Pear, radish, blue cheese (or feta) & rocket 242
    Pumpkin, spinach and feta self-crusting quiche 134
    Self-crusting summer vegetable quiche 133
    Slow-roasted eggplant, capsicum & courgette with lemon, garlic & herb oil 228
    Spinach, caramelised onion & feta filo parcels 137
filo parcels 137
Flash-roasted rhubarb & strawberries 273
flatbreads 216
Flax eggs 291
Fondant potatoes 253
freekeh
    Cypriot lentil & freekeh salad with honey-glazed haloumi 97
frittata
    Anything veggie frittata 187

G
ganache 307
Garlic & herb butter 216
Garlic & herb flatbreads 216
Garlic sourdough croutons 98
Gluten-free olive oil pastry 157
gnocchi 150
goats cheese
    Asparagus, orange, goats cheese & dill 249
    Creamy asparagus, spinach, herb & goats cheese tart 297
    Slow-roasted eggplant, capsicum & courgette with lemon, garlic & herb oil 228
Golden parmesan parsnips 238
Gourmet mousetraps 176
granita 319
gremolata 237
gruyère
    Portobello mushroom & brie (or gruyère) Wellington 144
Guacamole 180
gyoza: see dumplings

H
haloumi
    Balsamic roast beets, lentils & haloumi 84
    Cucumber, chutney & haloumi canapés 56
    Cypriot lentil & freekeh salad with honey-glazed haloumi 97
    Marinated veggie kebabs 54
    Middle Eastern quinoa salad with haloumi & crispy pita 93
Harira 103
Harissa 216
Harissa eggplant, tomatoes & chickpeas 214
Herbed labne 63
herbs 19, 21–23, 26, 27, 30, 31
Honey & thyme roast tomatoes 67
Honey mustard dressing 234

I
ice blocks & ice cream
    Avocado mint choc chip ice cream 298
    Veggie pops 294
icing 282

J
Jalapeño chermoula 57

p. 333

INDEX

Jalapeño chutney 191
Jalapeño, cheese & spring onion cornbread 262
Jasmin's Christmas salad 107

K
kale
    Peanut lime & sesame dressed slaw 104
    Mushroom & herb fettuccine with cashew cream sauce 175
    Winter greens with a fried egg & parmesan 167
kebabs 54
korma 204
kumara
    Anything veggie frittata 187
    Creamy tomato, mushroom, kale & black bean shepherd's pie 141
    Kumara focaccia with grapes & rosemary 315
    Kumara, chickpea & mushroom burgers 40
    Mexican stuffed kumaras 116
    Pumpkin (or kumara) & cinnamon donuts 288
    Roast roots & caramelised onion soup with lemon, chilli & parsley 94
    Sweet potato pie with maple-glazed nuts 302
    Vegetarian coconut laksa 200
    Winter greens with a fried egg & parmesan 167

L
Labne 63
laksa 200
lasagne 138
leeks
    Chunky vegetable & barley soup with garlic sourdough croutons 98
    Pumpkin, spinach and feta self-crusting quiche 134
    Self-crusting summer vegetable quiche 133
Leftover veg tarts 184
Lemony pea & avocado dip 62
lentils
    Balsamic roast beets, lentils & haloumi 84
    Cypriot lentil & freekeh salad with honey-glazed haloumi 97
    Harira 103
    Ratatouille, butternut & lentil lasagne 138
    Vegetable dhal (lentil curry) 207

M
mango
    Curried cauliflower, chickpeas & mango salad with coconut yoghurt dressing 89
Maple yoghurt cream 271
Maple-glazed nuts 302
Marinated veggie kebabs 54
Masala potatoes & carrots 211
Mexican spice mix 195
Mexican stuffed kumaras 116
Middle Eastern quinoa salad with haloumi & crispy pita 93
Mint chermoula 57
miso paste
    Bok choy & shiitake mushroom miso noodle soup 170
Moroccan apricot & tomato chutney 158
Moroccan eggplant boats 122
Moroccan roast carrots with quinoa, dates, lime & chilli 100
Moroccan spice mix 195
mousetraps 176
mozzarella
    Rustic vegetable pizza pie 127
    Summer bruschetta 75
mung bean sprouts
    Peanut lime & sesame dressed slaw 104
    Saucy pad thai 188
    Vegetarian coconut laksa 200
mushrooms 27
    Bok choy & shiitake mushroom miso noodle soup 170
    Creamy tomato, mushroom, kale & black bean shepherd's pie 141
    Gourmet mousetraps 176
    Kumara, chickpea & mushroom burgers 40
    Mushroom & herb fettuccine with cashew cream sauce 175
    Portobello mushroom & brie Wellington 144
    Ratatouille, butternut & lentil lasagne 138
    Rustic vegetable pizza pie 127
    Saucy pad thai 188
    Vegetable gyoza (dumplings) 46
    Winter bruschetta 77

N
nachos
    Zingy nachos 70
noodles
    Bok choy & shiitake mushroom miso noodle soup 170
    Saucy pad thai 188
    Vegetarian coconut laksa 200
nuts
    Sweet potato pie with maple-glazed nuts 302

O
Olive oil pastry 157
Olive tapenade 190
onions
    Caramelised onions 159
    Pink pickled onions 180
    Tomato caramelised onions 127
Orange caramel sauce 288

P
pad thai 188
parmesan
    Creamy tomato, mushroom, kale & black bean shepherd's pie 141
    Golden parmesan parsnips 238
    Ratatouille, butternut & lentil lasagne 138
    Rustic vegetable pizza pie 127
    Spinach & ricotta dumplings with tomato courgette sauce 147
parsnip
    Golden parmesan parsnips 238
    Parsnip, pear, ginger & walnut cake with caramel cream cheese icing 282
    Roast roots & caramelised onion soup with lemon, chilli & parsley 94
pasta
    BBQ orzo pasta salad 49
    Mushroom & herb fettuccine with cashew cream sauce 175
    Ratatouille, butternut & lentil lasagne 138
pastry
    Olive oil pastry 157
    Thyme and rosemary burnt butter pastry shell 323
    Wholemeal herb pastry 121
Peanut lime dressing 104
pears
    Parsnip, pear, ginger & walnut cake with caramel cream cheese icing 282
    Pear, radish, blue cheese & rocket 242
peas 21
    Lemony pea & avocado dip 62
    Pineapple fried rice 203
pesto
    Coriander, lime & cashew pesto 63
pies: see also tarts
    Creamy tomato, mushroom, kale & black bean shepherd's pie 141
    Rhubarb & apple pie 281
    Rustic vegetable pizza pie 127
    Sweet potato pie with maple-glazed nuts 302
pikelets 297
pilav 108
pineapple
    Carrot, pineapple & banana cupcakes 308
    Pineapple fried rice 203
    Veggie pops 294
Pink pickled onions 180
pita, crispy 93
Pizza dough 157
polenta
    Jalapeño, cheese & spring onion cornbread 262
    Polenta, lemon & coconut slice 316
    Thyme & lemon shortbread 278
pomegranate
    Raw veg pilav 108
    Turkish salad with watermelon 241
Portobello mushroom & brie Wellington 144
potatoes
    Anything veggie frittata 187
    Ciro's gnocchi 150
    Creamy tomato, mushroom, kale & black bean shepherd's pie 141
    Fondant potatoes 253
    Masala potatoes & carrots 211
    Winter greens with a fried egg & parmesan 167
pumpkin 26
    Annabel's pumpkin & chocolate chunk muffins 301
    Anything veggie frittata 187
    Autumn bruschetta 76
    Chunky vegetable & barley soup with garlic sourdough croutons 98
    Pumpkin & cinnamon donuts 288
    Pumpkin, spinach and feta self-crusting quiche 134
    Ratatouille, butternut & lentil lasagne 138
    Rustic vegetable pizza pie 127
    Sweet potato (or butternut) pie with maple-glazed nuts 302
    Vegetarian coconut laksa 200

Q
quesadillas 173
quiche
    Pumpkin, spinach and feta self-crusting quiche 134
    Self-crusting summer vegetable quiche 133
Quick masala dosa 208
Quick salsa 195
quinoa
    Middle Eastern quinoa salad with haloumi & crispy pita 93
    Moroccan roast carrots with quinoa, dates, lime & chilli 100

R

radicchio
  Balsamic roast beets, lentils & haloumi 84
radishes
  Middle Eastern quinoa salad with haloumi & crispy pita 93
  Pear, radish, blue cheese & rocket 242
  Roast radishes with lemon 254
  Tomato & radish salad with mint chermoula 233
raspberries
  Beetroot & raspberry granita 319
  Carrot, beetroot, apple & blackcurrant (or raspberry) compôte 268
Ratatouille, butternut & lentil lasagne 138
Raw veg pilav 108
Red wine-braised cabbage with currants & spices 250
rhubarb
  Flash-roasted rhubarb & strawberries 273
  Rhubarb & apple pie 281
  Rhubarb, strawbs 'n' cream loaded shortbread 274
rice
  Burrito bowls 183
  Currant & nut rice 219
  Pineapple fried rice 203
ricotta
  Spinach & ricotta dumplings with tomato courgette sauce 147
Roast radishes with lemon 254
Roast roots & caramelised onion soup with lemon, chilli & parsley 94
Roast spiced cauliflower with caramelised garlic yoghurt 237
rocket
  Pear, radish, blue cheese & rocket 242
Rustic vegetable pizza pie 127

S

salads
  Peanut lime & sesame dressed slaw 104
  Asparagus & strawberries with balsamic & basil 246
  Balsamic roast beets, lentils & haloumi 84
  BBQ orzo pasta salad 49
  Brussels sprouts, apple & almond slaw 234
  Charred corn, feta & barley salad with chipotle lime dressing 90
  Curried cauliflower, chickpeas & mango salad with coconut yoghurt dressing 89
  Cypriot lentil & freekeh salad with honey-glazed haloumi 97
  Essential summer salad 245
  Jasmin's Christmas salad 107
  Middle Eastern quinoa salad with haloumi & crispy pita 93
  Pear, radish, blue cheese & rocket 242
  Tomato & radish salad with mint chermoula 233
  Turkish salad with watermelon 241
salsas: see dips
sauces
  Autumn harvest sauce 192
  Cheese sauce 138
  Gnocchi sauces 150
  Orange caramel sauce 288
  Ratatouille sauce 138
  Tomato basil sauce 150
  Tomato courgette sauce 147
Saucy pad thai 188

Seed & nut crumble 271
Self-crusting summer vegetable quiche 133
shallots
  Caramelised shallot & thyme tarte tatin 130
shortbread 274, 278
silverbeet 30
  Masala potatoes & carrots 211
  Ratatouille, butternut & lentil lasagne 138
Slow-cooked smoky beans 153
Slow-roasted eggplant, capsicum & courgette with lemon, garlic & herb oil 228
snow peas
  Vegetarian coconut laksa 200
Soft cashew cheese 156
soups
Bok choy & shiitake mushroom miso noodle soup 170
  Chunky vegetable & barley soup with garlic sourdough croutons 98
  Harira 103
  Roast roots & caramelised onion soup with lemon, chilli & parsley 94
spice mixes 195
Spiced courgette, date & apple loaf 291
spinach
  Cauliflower & chickpea korma 204
  Charred corn, feta & barley salad with chipotle lime dressing 90
  Creamy asparagus, spinach, herb & goats cheese tart 121
  Creamy tomato, mushroom, kale & black bean shepherd's pie 141
  Curried cauliflower, chickpeas & mango salad with coconut yoghurt dressing 89
  Harissa eggplant, tomatoes & chickpeas 214
  Masala potatoes & carrots 211
  Mushroom & herb fettuccine with cashew cream sauce 175
  Pumpkin, spinach and feta self-crusting quiche 134
  Ratatouille, butternut & lentil lasagne 138
  Spinach & ricotta dumplings with tomato courgette sauce 147
  Spinach, caramelised onion & feta filo parcels 137
  Vegetable dhal (lentil curry) 207
  Veggie pops 294
Spring bruschetta 74
stock 154
strawberries
  Asparagus & strawberries with balsamic & basil 246
  Flash-roasted rhubarb & strawberries 273
Summer bruschetta 74
swedes
  Roast roots & caramelised onion soup with lemon, chilli & parsley 94
  Winter greens with a fried egg & parmesan 167
Sweet cashew cream 217
sweet corn see corn
Sweet labne 63
Sweet potato pie with maple-glazed nuts 302

T

Tacos with walnut & almond chilli & guacamole 180
tapenade 190
tarts: see also pies
  Caramelised onion & beetroot tart with soft cashew cheese 118
  Caramelised shallot & thyme tarte tatin 130
  Creamy asparagus, spinach, herb & goats cheese tart 121
  Leftover veg tarts 184
  Thyme and rosemary citrus tart 323
  Thyme & lemon shortbread 278
  Thyme and rosemary burnt butter pastry shell 323
  Thyme and rosemary citrus tart 323
tofu
  Vegetarian coconut laksa 200
tomatoes
  Autumn harvest sauce 192
  Charred corn, feta & barley salad with chipotle lime dressing 90
  Chunky vegetable & barley soup with garlic sourdough croutons 98
  Cypriot lentil & freekeh salad with honey-glazed haloumi 97
  Essential summer salad 245
  Gourmet mousetraps 176
  Harira 103
  Harissa eggplant, tomatoes & chickpeas 214
  Honey & thyme roast tomatoes 67
  Marinated veggie kebabs 54
  Middle Eastern quinoa salad with haloumi & crispy pita 93
  Moroccan apricot & tomato chutney 158
  Ratatouille, butternut & lentil lasagne 138
  Self-crusting summer vegetable quiche 133
  Summer bruschetta 75
  Tomato & radish salad with mint chermoula 233
  Tomato basil sauce 150
  Tomato caramelised onions 127
  Tomato courgette sauce 147
  Tomato tostadas with lime mayo 52
  Tomato, jalapeño & coriander salsa 190
  Turkish salad with watermelon 241
  Vegetable dhal (lentil curry) 207
tortillas
  Tacos (or tortillas) with walnut & almond chilli & guacamole 180
  Veggie quesadillas 173
truffles 265
Turkish salad with watermelon 241

V

Vegetable dhal (lentil curry) 207
Vegetable gyoza (dumplings) 46
Vegetable stock 154
Vegetarian coconut laksa 200
Veggie pops 294
Veggie quesadillas 173

W

Walnut and almond chilli 180
watermelon
  Turkish salad with watermelon 241
Wholemeal herb pastry 121
Winter bruschetta 77
Winter greens with a fried egg & parmesan 167

Y

yams
  Winter greens with a fried egg & parmesan 167

Z

Zingy nachos 70
zucchini: see courgettes

Text © Nude Food Inc, 2019
Photographs copyright © Vanessa and Michael Lewis 2019, except for pages 105, 143, 151, 166, 168, 169, 177, 186, 189, 202, 230 copyright © Victoria Baldwin and pages 2, 3, 82, 164, 224 copyright © Matt Quéréé 2019. Cover photography copyright © Matt Quéréé 2019.
Book design: Seachange
Published in 2019 by Nude Food Inc,
Auckland, New Zealand

Reprinted 2019, 2020 twice, 2021.

www.nadialim.com

ISBN 978-0-473-48852-9

This book is copyright. Except for the purpose of fair review, no part may be stored or transmitted in any form or by any means, electronic or mechanical, including recording or storage in any information retrieval systems, without permission in writing from the publisher. No reproduction may be made, whether by photocopying or by any other means, unless a licence has been obtained from the publisher or its agent.

No responsibility for loss caused to any individual or organisation acting on or refraining from action as a result of the material in this publication can be accepted by Nude Food Inc or the author.

Prepress and Book Production – Benefitz, New Zealand
Printed in China